Paddlewheelers

Yosemite berthed in Victoria harbour
(Image from Maritime Museum of British Columbia 000410)

PADDLEWHEELERS
of Western Canada and the USA

JOHN MacFARLANE

Copyright © 2021 John MacFarlane

All rights reserved. No part of this publication may be reproduced, distributed, or transmitted in any form or by any means, including photocopying, recording, or other electronic or mechanical methods, without the prior written permission of the publisher, except in the case of brief quotations embodied in critical reviews and certain other noncommercial uses permitted by copyright law. For permission requests, contact the publisher at the email address below.

admin@nauticapedia.ca

ISBN: 978–0–9936954–7–6 (softcover)
ISBN: 978–0–9936954–9–0 (eBook/Kindle)

The information contained in this book is not suitable for any legal purpose. Additional information, such as details of construction or ownership records for these vessels, may be found online in The Nauticapedia at: http://www.nauticapedia.ca/dbase/Query/dbsubmit_Vessel.php

THE NAUTICAPEDIA

The Nauticapedia project was originally started in 1973 to record data about British Columbia vessels. It can be accessed online at www.nauticapedia.ca. Detailed information on all the vessels mentioned in this book can be accessed through the searchable database. Readers with more information to add to these histories can reach the author through the web page.

Editing by Lynn Salmon

Cover and page design and typesetting by Jan Westendorp:
katodesignandphoto.com

Ingram Spark

CONTENTS

When Rivers Were Roads	1
The Sidewheelers and Sternwheelers of Western North America	7
Glossary	383
Abbreviations Used	387
A Guide to Sternwheelers Still Operating or Preserved (in whole or in fragments)	389
Bibliography & Sources	401
Acknowledgements	405
The Author	409
The Nauticapedia	410
Endnotes	411

The *Kaslo* (Image from Maritime Museum of British Columbia 000426)

WHEN RIVERS WERE ROADS

If you speak of paddlewheelers today I will wager that most people will immediately think of the Mississippi River-style boats conjuring images of black smoke belching, a musical whistle sounding, and with salons filled with fancy gamblers—a stereotype rendered familiar from TV and movie screens. Without doubt these vessels were beautiful; no wonder we remember them. They were generally large, flat-bottomed boats with a fascinatingly large paddle arrangement mounted astern.

But the paddlewheeler was not exclusive to the Mississippi River system or the lore of Mark Twain. These unique floating platforms performed an essential service to the opening of the west—both in Canada and the United States. While the majority of these vessels operated in freshwater, some were sea-going. Typically, river and lake boats were propelled by stern paddles while the ocean-going vessels tended to be sidewheelers. The openings in the superstructure through which the power rods passed to the engine were a hazard in following seas so a stern wheel arrangement in rough ocean waters posed a risk of taking on water.

Freighters, passenger vessels, tugs, and specialized vessels such as dredges, have all utilized paddle wheels to enable manoeuverability and operations in shallow waters. A small number naval and military vessels also utilized wheels for propulsion, but this was a rare occurrence on the Pacific coast.

These magnificent vessels passed from existence so quickly that today many people are unaware that hundreds of them traveled on western North American waterways. These essential workhorses, helping to facilitate the construction of railways, roads, and infrastructure, ultimately built a direct path to making themselves obsolete in a relatively short span of time.

Paddlewheelers were usually measured from inside the stem to the inside of the sternpost. However, some authorities record the length at the waterline or length between perpendiculars which can produce different results.

Sternwheelers often had their boilers and engines positioned so that cargo space could be maximized to produce the most efficient revenues.

They also tended to travel faster than sidewheelers, but more bracing was needed at the stern to support the huge weight of the paddlewheel. As many as five rudders were mounted from a bracket outboard of the paddles to manoeuvre these bulky vessels along shallow and tricky navigational routes.

Sidewheeler hulls were considered easier to build than sternwheelers as the designs were often less complex. Sidewheelers that had one engine were difficult to manoeuvre because both sidewheels had to be connected to the same drive shaft. By contrast, sidewheelers with two engines could be maneuvered with a very tight turning radii simply by slowing one or putting it in reverse. Sidewheels were preferred as ferries since the vessel could be docked with no interference to the wheels.

The steam engines of the day could develop more power with a sternwheel than a propeller. A skilled captain could power a vessel ahead and allow the current in a river to drift back when maneuvering. Where a propeller could lose a blade when hitting a rock, the paddlewheel might only lose a few blades which did not disable the vessel. Repairs could then be made by the crew along the shore without having to take the vessel out of the water.

The sidewheel steamer **Beaver** had a long and significant part in the history of the Pacific coast (Image from the Vancouver City Archives Bo_P354)

The first paddlewheeler on the Pacific was the Hudson's Bay Company steamer *Beaver* (which was also the first steam ship on the west coast). Built for the Hudson's Bay Company in 1835 at Blackwall Yard near London England, she sailed from the River Thames to the Pacific Ocean via Cape Horn. At Fort Vancouver (now Vancouver, Washington) her paddlewheels were installed, and she became a working steam vessel. Over her long life she functioned as a fur trading vessel, as a charter to the Royal Navy for coastal surveying, and later, as a tug.

The *Beaver* was as much loved for her service to opening the frontier as for her status as the first steam vessel on the coast. In 1888, when she wrecked on Prospect Point at the entrance to Vancouver Harbour (British Columbia), she was mourned widely, and efforts to commemorate her remain as a brass plaque fitted above the rocks that spelt her ruin. Interestingly, it was another paddlewheeler that tore her from the ledge; the *Yosemite's* wake de-stabilized the wreck, forcing the doomed vessel into deeper water after four years of being abandoned and relentlessly salvaged by souvenir-hunters. The iconic *Beaver* represents, even now, the process of development for modern day British Columbia from Crown Colony to Confederation with Canada.

My own interest in sternwheelers has developed over many years. At first, I was unaware that Canadian waters had any association with river and lake boats. The story of freshwater fleets in western Canada has been largely ignored in favour of the saltwater fleets. Some notable nautical writers shone a light on this subject and thanks to them it ignited an interest in me.

This project started off as a book focussed on the sternwheelers and sidewheelers of western Canada, but nautical heritage is not exceptionally clean and tidy as I discovered. A great many vessels crossed the US-Canada border, either through ownership changes or by their transportation and freight operations, so necessarily the focus of the book was enlarged to cover paddlewheelers on all waters: whether they flow from the west to the Pacific, or north to the Arctic Ocean, or south and around to the US-Mexico border.

The goal of this book project is to create a 'nominal list' or a 'catalogue raisonné' of the paddlewheelers of western Canada and USA and centralize the core information in one handy place for reference. Until now, it has been necessary to consult a wide range of sources to find information on vessels. Often, one source is not enough to satisfy research and reference needs, especially for those not handy to a library or the archives of a maritime museum, potentially creating a bottleneck that stifles inquiry. Therefore, this list, to include as many of the paddlewheelers from Western Canada and the USA as possible, will be handy and useful to researchers, writers, and enthusiasts.

The result is a best effort to collect all the names of all such vessels and, where possible, include a brief overview of their physical and operational history. This does not replace detailed research into individual vessel histories. I have undoubtedly missed some vessels—and any errors are my own.

I employ the term paddlewheeler as a collective to include both sidewheelers and sternwheelers. For the purposes of this publication, they are defined as:
- sidewheeler—a vessel propelled by two paddle wheels, one on each side of the ship.
- sternwheeler—a vessel propelled by one or two paddle wheels mounted at the stern.

The vessels are entered under their first known name. Subsequent names are in parentheses after the first name. The official number of the vessel is entered following the names—sometimes more than one is listed if this number changed over the life of the vessel.

Some vessels are referred to by shortened versions of their official name in articles and books or by nicknames. This is a confusing practice which should be avoided—as sometimes the shortened version duplicates the official name of another vessel or creates a duplication of records. Some vessels changed names more than once—and some vessels adopted names that were never made 'official' with the government registrar of shipping.

The final fate of a vessel was not always known or recorded. Responsible owners usually notified a government authority to provide an account of the demise of the vessel or their fate made for unfortunate headlines if winding up as a wreck. For unknown reasons, some vessels remained in the official list of shipping well beyond the term of their actual existence.

The data contained in this list comes from a myriad of sources. Existing publications and internet references were valuable starting points. The annual US Government publication of *Merchant Vessels of the United States* and the Canadian version *The Canada List of Shipping*, were the most valuable and fruitful sources. When there were differences of opinion between sources, I deferred to these official publications as the authority.

Readers should note that there has often been disagreement among sources on the dimensions, displacement, and other technical specifications of some of the vessels in this list. Sometimes this is due to poor or contradictory contemporary recording of details, but dimensions can also be measured by different methods additionally contributing to the confusion.

Today, only a few relics of this era remain on static display, sadly vulnerable to rot and vandalism. They are the subject of curiosity, admiration and of historical importance and, they remind us of a time when rivers were roads.

THE SIDEWHEELERS AND STERNWHEELERS OF WESTERN NORTH AMERICA

(All are sternwheelers unless otherwise noted as sidewheelers)

A.A. McCully 105725 (US) She was built in 1877 at Oregon City OR USA. 148' x 30' x 4.5' Wood. 498.07gt 363.69nt. Powered by a geared (12" x 24") steam engine. In 187–1884 she was owned by the Peoples Protective Transportation Co. (JW Cochrane), Portland OR USA. She was operated on the Willamette River. In 1885 she was destroyed by fire at Cascades (on the Columbia River).

A.B. Graham[1] (US) She was built in 1898 Puget Sound WA USA. 126'x 26' x ? Wood. Powered by a steam engine. In 1898 she was owned by the Seattle St. Michael and Dawson City Navigation Co. She is reported by Murray Lundberg that it is generally thought that she may not have reached Alaska.

A.C. Freese[2] 106411 (US) (freighter) She was built in 1886 San Francisco CA USA. 119.0' x 27.5' x 4.5' Wood. 205.74gt 175.31nt. Powered by a 200ihp steam engine. In 1886–1910 she was owned by San Francisco CA USA interests. She was in operation on California rivers. She was reported to have gone out of service in 1917.

A.J. Goddard 107517 (Canada) She was built in 1898 at San Francisco CA USA by James H Calvert. In 1898 she was shipped north and assembled at Lake Bennett BC by James H Calvert. In 1897 the frames for the steamers A.J. Goddard and F.H. Killbourne were cut in San Francisco CA, landed at Dyea AK, together with sawmill parts. This was shipped over the Chilkoot Pass by pack train and aerial tramway in 1897–1898 to Bennett Lake BC for assembly. 50.0' x 10.6' x 3.0' composite hull 87.7gt 54.63nt. Powered by two 2nhp horizontal (high pressure 5.5" x 20") steam engines built by Pacific Iron Works, Seattle WA USA. In 1898–1899 she was owned by the Upper Yukon Co. Ltd. In 1899 she was sold to the Canadian Development Co. (Henry A Munn), Victoria BC. In 1901 she was owned by Henry A Munn, Victoria BC. On September 12, 1901, she foundered in a gale at Goddard Point YT near the foot of Lake Laberge YT on with the loss of her crew.

A.R. Helen 126632 (Canada) She was built in 1909 Adams Lake BC Canada by ES Hill. 123.5' x 26.8' x 4.9' Wood. 331gt 209rt. Powered by a 9hp steam engine. In 1909–1917 she was owned by the Adams Lake Lumber Co. Ltd., Chase BC. In 1909–1920 she was used mainly for towing log booms on Adams Lake BC. In 1918–1931 she was owned by the Adams River Lumber Co. Ltd., Chase BC.

Aberdeen 100148 (Canada) She was built in 1892 at Battleford NWT Canada. 58.6' x 42.3' x 3.8' Wood. 26gt. Powered by a steam engine. In 1898–1901 she was owned by John G Oliver, Battleford NWT.

Aberdeen 100675 (Canada) She was built in 1893 at Okanagan Landing BC Canada by EG MacKay. 146.2' x 29.9' x 6.8' Wood. 554.04gt 349.05rt. Powered by a horizontal (16" x 72") 17.3nhp steam engine. In 1893–1916 she was owned by Canadian Pacific Railway Co. Montreal QC. She could carry 250 passengers and had 5 staterooms. In 1893–1907 she was in service between Okanagan Landing to Penticton. In 1907–1914 she was in service as a relief boat on the Okanagan Landing to Penticton route. In 1893 she was on the Okanagan Landing to Penticton run. In 1911 she was severely damaged in a storm. In 1915 she was withdrawn from service and laid up in 1916. Her boiler went to Nelson Shipyard and the engines were sold. In 1919 she was sold to Byron Johnson, dismantled, and beached as a boathouse south of Okanagan Landing BC.

Aberdeen[3] (US) She was built by George Hitchings. Wood. She was powered by a 50hp Wolverine engine. She was built for Grays Harbor river-service but was found to be unsuitable for that role. Ivan Chillman converted her at Hoquiam WA to a twin-screw propeller using her original engine.

Acme[4] 106630 (US) She was built in 1889 at San Francisco CA USA 177.5' x 37.0' x 5.2' Wood. 294gt 275rt. Powered by a 102nhp steam engine. She was reported to have been dismantled in 1911.

Acme 106630 (US) (freighter) She was built in 1889 at San Francisco CA USA. 177.5' x 37.0' x 5.2' Wood. 294gt 275nt. Powered by a 102ihp steam engine. She was employed in the San Francisco Bay area.

Active (US) (sidewheeler) She was built in 1849. She was powered by a steam engine. In 1849 she was employed on the Sacramento River. In 1852–1862 she was owned by the United States Coast Survey. In 1866 she was owned by the California Steam Navigation Co. In 1867 she was owned by the California, Oregon, and Mexico Steamship Co. In 1870 she struck a rock and was wrecked south of Cape Mendocino CA.

Active 001232 (US) 122' x 23' x 5.1' Wood. 259.74gt. She was built in 1865 at Canemah OR USA by JT Appernon. She was powered by a (14" x 54") 13nhp steam engine. In 1865 she was owned by the Willamette Steam Navigation Co. She was sold to the Peoples Transportation Co. In 1871 she was sold to the Oregon Steamship Co. (Ben Holladay). She was reported as having been broken up in Canemah OR.

Active (USS) (see *Gold Hunter*)

Ada 064149 (Canada) (sidewheeler) She was built in 1874 at Burrard Inlet BC Canada by Henry Maloney. She was launched in August 1874. 82.0' x 19.0' x 5.5' Wood. 71gt 56.95rt. Powered by a 75hp steam 2.5' x 36" engine. In 1874–1901 she was owned by James Robinson and Christopher Lee, New Westminster BC. She was reported as having been broken up in 1883 on the Fraser River. She was still listed on the Canada Register of Shipping in 1902.

Ada 105713 (US) She was built in 1875 at Eureka CA USA. 71.0' x 18.0' x 3.5' Wood. 64.01gt 45.13rt. Powered by a 20nhp steam engine.

Ada Belle 203694 (US) (passenger vessel) In 1906 she was built at Mules Head Landing, SD USA. 100.2' x 24.0' x 3.1' Wood. 50gt/rt. Powered by a gasoline engine.

Ada Hancock[5] (US) (freighter) She was built about 1860. Wood. Powered by a steam engine. She was in operation on California rivers. In 1863 her boiler exploded.

Addie 105447 (US) She was built in 1874 at Seattle WA USA. 92.4' x 20.7' x 3.6' Wood. 81.02gt. Powered by a steam engine. This vessel was employed on Lake Washington.

Adelaide 085318 (Canada) She was built in 1882 at New Westminster BC Canada by Henry Maloney. 95.2' x 17.3' x 4.5' Wood. 151gt 96.02rt. Powered by an 80hp steam engine. In 1882 she was owned by Christian Meyers and Alexander Ewen. In 1892 she was reported as having been broken up.

Aetna[6] (US) (freighter) She was built about 1850. Wood. Powered by a steam engine. She was in operation on California rivers. She was reported to have gone out of service about 1868.

Aetna 204893 (US) (freighter) She was built in 1907 at San Francisco CA USA. 81.9' x 24.8' x 4.6' Wood. 130gt 82nt. Powered by a 100ihp steam engine. In 1910 she was employed at San Francisco CA.

Agnes E. Boyd 107351 (US) She was built in 1898 Oakland CA USA. Wood. 31gt 23nt. On May 23, 1908, she was crushed in spring breakup ice at Kobuk River AK USA and became a total loss.

Ahrnklim 207391 (US) (fishboat) She was built in 1910 at Seattle WA USA. 66.0' x 19.5' x 5.2' Wood. 52gt 33nt. Powered by a 50ihp gasoline engine. She was employed on Puget Sound.

Aksala (see *Alaska*)

Alameda 001216 (US) (sidewheeler) (freighter) She was built in 1866 at San Francisco CA USA. 193.0' x 33.8' x 11.3' Wood. 813.14gt 621.85nt. Powered by a 350nhp steam engine. In 1866–1884 she was owned by San Francisco CA USA interests.

Alameda[7] 107257 (US) She was built in 1898 at Lake Bennett BC. 50' x 12' x 2.5' Wood. 32gt 20nt. In 1898 she was owned by John J McKenna and was employed between Lake Bennett and Whitehorse Rapids. She was reported as having been abandoned in 1898.

Alaska (US) She was built in 1867 in the USA. Wood. 4012gt. In 1867 she was owned by the Pacific Mail Steamship Co., San Francisco CA USA. She was employed between New York and Aspinwall, now known as Colón, Panama, and was later used on the San Francisco to Panama City and San Francisco to Hong Kong routes until 1879. On September 23, 1874, under Captain E Van Sice, she was blown ashore in a typhoon at Hong Kong while undergoing repairs on a slipway there. She was salvaged and refloated about 90 days later.

Alaska 106232 (US) (sidewheeler) (passenger vessel) She was built in 1883 at Chester PA USA by John Roach & Sons. 276' x 40' x 13.4' iron 1717gt. Powered by a single cylinder vertical condensing (73" x 144") walking-beam steam engine. In 1883 she was owned by the O.R. & N. Co. In 1884 she worked on the Portland to Ilwaco route. In 1887 she was transferred to Puget Sound on the Victoria BC route. In 1888 she was transferred to the Columbia River. In 1889 she was wrecked off Cape Blanco while enroute from the Columbia River to San Francisco for drydock work.

Alaska 165171 (US) 116621 (Canada) (later *Aksala*) She was built in 1913 at Seattle WA USA by the Nilson & Kelez Shipbuilding Corp. 166.8' x 35' x 5.4' Wood. 1066.67gt 803.31rt. Powered by a 17hp steam engine built by Seattle Machine Works Ltd. In 1913 she was owned by the American Yukon Navigation Co., Chicago IL (in US Registry). In 1927 she was reregistered as *Aksala* (in the Canadian Registry) and subsequently rebuilt to 1067t. In 1927–1961 she was owned by the British Yukon Navigation Co. Ltd., Vancouver BC. In 1951 she was laid up. In 1955 she was beached at Mile 913 Alaska Highway (nr Whitehorse YT) and is still preserved at Whitehorse YT.

Alaska Queen (see *Elizabeth Louise*)

Alaska Union 107405 (US) She was built in 1898 at Nunukik Island, Alaska USA. 110' x 22' x 3.5' Wood. 214gt 114rt. Powered by a steam engine. She had a square bow that in 1898 was said to have caused her stranding at the south fork of the Koyukuk River AK USA.

Alaskan 106232 (US) (sidewheeler) She was built in 1883 Chester PA USA. 276' x 40' x 13.4' iron 1718gt 1259rt Powered by a walking beam (73" x 144") steam engine. In 1883 she was owned by the Oregon Railroad & Navigation Co. In 1884 she was employed on the Portland to Ilwaco route. In 1887 she was transferred to Puget Sound on the Victoria BC route. In 1888 she was transferred to the Columbia River. She was wrecked off Cape Blanco May while enroute to San Francisco for drydock work.

Alaskan 106409 (US) (sidewheeler) She was built in 1886 at Seattle WA USA. 84.5' x 21.6' x 4.9' Wood. 155.07gt 94.54rt. Powered by a steam engine.

Albany 001738 (US) She was built in 1868 at Canemah OR USA. 127' x 27' x 3.5' Wood. 328gt. Powered by two horizontal (16.5" x 50") steam engines. In 1868 she was owned by the Peoples Transportation Co. In 1871 she was owned by the Oregon Steamship Co. (Ben Holladay). In 1876 she was wrecked at Long Tom Bar, on the Columbia River.

Albany (see N.S. Bentley)

Alberta (Canada) She was built in 1883 at Medicine Hat AB Canada. 100' x 20' x 3' Wood. Powered by two 30hp steam engines. On July 12, 1883, she was sponsored by Miss McLellan, a daughter of the Canada Minister of Marine and Fisheries). She was owned by the Coates & Mosher. She was owned by the North Western Coal & Navigation Co. She was beached and broken up in 1886 at Medicine Hat NWT.

Alberta 116950 (Canada) She was built in 1904 at Prince Albert SK Canada. Wood. 315gt. Powered by a 15hp engine. In 1904 she was owned by Rufus Mosher & Fred W Coates. In 1908–1916 she was owned by the Winnipeg Navigation Co. Ltd., Winnipeg MB. In 1916 she was wrecked in a flood at Lockport MB.

Albina 105962 (US) She was built in 1881 at Portland OR USA. 85.0' x 24.0' x 4.8' Wood. 85.26gt. Powered by a steam engine. She was employed on the Columbia River watershed.

Albina No. 2 106244 (US) She was built in 1883 at Portland OR USA. 107.0' x 32.5' x 6.3' Wood. 204.76gt 150.51rt. Powered by a steam engine. She was employed on the Columbia River watershed.

Alcan 195230 (Canada) She was prefabricated in 1942 at Vancouver BC by George F. Askew and assembled on the Peace River at Taylor BC. 65.5' x 18.0' x 4.0' Wood. 51gt. Powered by a 135hp chain driven engine. In 1942–1945 she was owned by the United States Army. She was in service on the Peace River to support the US military construction on the Alaska Highway and for the construction of the Peace River Bridge. After the bridge was finished, she was sold to a mining company. In 1954–1961 she was owned by the Northern Transportation Co. Ltd., Edmonton AB. She was the last sternwheeler to operate on the Peace River. George Duddy notes that "there was a similar vessel also built by George Askew employed on Deas Lake and river for the Watson Lake airport construction but never officially named or registered.

Alert 001233 (US) She was built in 1865 at Oswego NY USA by Louis Paquet. 135' x 25' x 5' Wood. 340.83gt. She was rebuilt in 1871 as the steamer *E.N. Cooke* (8762 [US]) Powered by two horizontal (16.5" x 60" high pressure) steam engines. In 1865 she was owned by the Willamette Steam Navigation Co. She was owned by the Peoples Transportation Co. In 1871 she was owned by the Oregon Steamship Co. (Ben Holladay). She was employed on the Willamette River. She was reported as having been abandoned in 1871. Some sources state that in 1871 she was completely rebuilt and renamed as the *E.N. Cooke* (008762). She was reportedly dismantled in 1875.

Alert[8] (later *Pert*; then *City of Windermere*) 107826 (Canada) (sidewheeler) 49.8' x 10.0' x 2.6' Wood. 6gt 4rt. She was built in 1890 at Golden BC Canada by Fred Wells. In 1890 she was powered with a steam engine and re-built at Golden BC as a side-wheeler by Captain Frank P Armstrong. 50' x 10'. 6gt. She was rebuilt as a screw-driven vessel in 1898. Powered by a steam engine. In 1900 she was re-engined. In 1898 she was sold to Captain Alexander Blakely and renamed as the *Pert*. In 1903 she was sold to Captain EN Russell. In 1910–1919 she was owned by Robert Miller, Golden BC for Upper Columbia River service. In 1903 she was in service on Lake Windermere and the upper Columbia River. In 1908 she was reported as having been abandoned at Lake Windermere BC.

Alert[9] 106768 (US) (workboat) She was built in 1890 at Bandon OR. 81.1' x 18.0' x 4.1' Wood. 65gt 58nt. Powered by an 80ihp steam engine. In 1919 she was owned by Fred Stone, San Francisco CA and was sailed down from Coos Bay OR. In 1918 she was employed in the Coos Bay region. She is thought to have gone out of service before 1924.

Aliex (The) 134104 (Canada) She was built in 1913 at Kamloops BC Canada. 52.2' x 11.5' x 3' Wood. 20gt 13rt. Powered by a 3hp steam engine. In 1913–1931 she was owned by the Northern Construction Co. Ltd., Winnipeg MB.

The sidewheel tug *Alexander* was once reputed to have been the most powerful tug in the world. (Image from Maritime Museum of British Columbia)

Alexander 072671 (Canada) (sidewheeler) She was built in 1875 at Port Essington BC Canada by John McAllister and his brother Angus McAllister 170.0' x 27.2' x 12.5' Wood. 332gt 191rt. Powered by a steam engine. Her machinery was installed in Victoria after being towed there. In 1890 she was rebuilt as a sailing ship. In 1903 she was rebuilt as a barge. In 1875–1880 she was owned by the McAllister Brothers (John and Angus) and used for towing at Cape Flattery. In 1880–1885 she was owned by Robert Dunsmuir and W Diggle, Nanaimo BC. In 1885–1887 she was owned by Robert Dunsmuir, Nanaimo BC. In 1887 she was owned by Joan O Dunsmuir, Victoria BC. In 1890 she was sold to TPW Whitelaw, San Francisco CA and converted to a whaler. In 1895–1898 she was owned by Joan O Dunsmuir, Victoria BC. (She was reported as being "sold to foreign owners (San Francisco) June 30, 1900" by the Registrar of Shipping) In 1902–1905 she was owned by Pacific Towing & Lighterage, Vancouver BC (as a barge). She was nicknamed as 'McAllister's Folly.' As a barge she received the remains from the wreck of the collier *Brotchie* from Brotchie ledge. Later she was used to haul logs from Sooke BC to Victoria BC. On July 11, 1913, she was beached and abandoned in Saanich Arm, British Columbia.

Alexander Griggs 200046 (US) She was built in 1903 at Wenatchee WA USA by George Catterall. 99.7' x 18.9' x 3.7' Wood. 144gt 91rt. Powered by two horizontal (10" x 48" 6.6nhp high pressure) steam engines. In 1903 she was owned by the Columbia & Okanagan Steamboat Co. In 1905 she was wrecked at the Entiat Rapids on the Columbia River WA and was a complete loss. Two months of low water levels on the river caused the low water problem leading to her demise.

Alexandra (Vancouver Island Colonial Register) She was built in 1863 at Victoria, Vancouver Island (Crown Colony) by James W Trahey. 163.8' x 29.6' x 8.5' Wood. 469gt. Powered by a 150hp 21.25" x 72" steam engine. In 1863–1864 she was owned by Captain William Moore, Victoria, Vancouver Island. Moore soon went bankrupt. She was sold to T Pritchard. In 1869 her machinery was removed by the Hudson's Bay Co. and later (in 1874) sold to Captain William Buchanan, Portland, OR USA for the *Ocklahama*. Norman R Hacking[10] states that "It is wrongly listed in Lewis & Dryden as the *Alexandria*." In 1864 she was in service between Victoria and the Fraser River. In 1865 she collided with and sank the *Fidelator* off Clover Point, Victoria BC. In 1869 she was reported as having been broken up.

Alfred J. Beach 107362 (US) She was built in 1898 at Ballard WA USA. 137.9' x 26' x 4.8' Wood. 364.68gt 198.97rt. In 1898 she was owned by the Alaska Mutual Transportation & Mining Co. On June 16, 1898, she left Port Townsend WA under tow by the *Del Norte* and was lost at sea on July 03, 1898, while enroute to St. Michael AK USA.

Alice 001217 (US) (freighter) She was built in 1868 at San Francisco CA. Wood. 74.21gt. Powered by a steam engine. In 1880 she was reported as having been abandoned.

Alice 105098 (US) (freighter) She was built in 1873 at Oregon City, OR USA. 150.5' x 21.0' x 5.2' Wood. 457.16gt 334.22nt. Powered by two 17nhp horizontal high pressure steam engines. In 1873–1884 she was owned by the People's Transportation Co., Portland, OR USA. In 1888 she was reported as having been broken up at Portland OR.

Alice 085673 (US) (sidewheeler) She was built in 1883 at New Westminster BC Canada 50.0' x 10.5' x 3.0' Wood. 54gt 34rt. Powered by a 2.67nhp steam engine. In 1883–1898 she was owned by Captain William F Stewart. She was in service on the North Arm of the Fraser River. In 1889 she was taken out of service. She was reported as having been broken up at the end of her life.

Alice 107253 (US) (passenger) She was built in 1895 at St. Michael AK USA by the Alaska Commercial Co. 160.0' x 33.0' x 8.0' Wood. 400gt 200nt. Powered by a 400ihp steam engine. In 1895 she was owned by the Alaska Commercial Co. She was employed at St. Michael AK USA. She was transferred to the Northern Navigation Co. in 1901. In 1914 she was acquired by the White Pass & Yukon Railway. In 1897–1898 she wintered in a slough 100 miles above the mouth of the Yukon River with the steamers *Thomas Dwyer* and *W.K. Merwin*. She arrived at Dawson City on July 06, 1898, after a one-week delay after stranding on a bar. She was working as late as 1905 on the lower Yukon River and in the Fairbanks AK area. In 1917 she was reported as having been abandoned at St. Mary's AK.

Alice[11] 206095 (US) (passenger/ freight vessel) She was built in 1909 at Seattle WA USA by the Cook & Lake Shipyard. 110.6' x 24.5' x 4.6' Wood. 262.05gt 145nt. Powered by a 100ihp steam engine. Originally, she was owned by the Alaska Commercial Co. She was towed on a barge from Seattle WA to St. Michael AK by the tug *Pioneer*. In 1909 she was owned by the Northern Navigation Co. She was owned by the American Yukon Navigation Co. In 1927 she was owned by the Alaska Railroad. She operated on the Susitna River. In 1953 she was reported as having been laid up and resold to the Roman Catholic Church (Holy Cross Mission).

Alice Garrett[12] 105264 (US) (sidewheeler) (freighter) She was built in 1873 at Stockton CA USA. 150.0' x 38.9' x 6.3' Wood. 485.65gt 430.7rt. Powered by a 90nhp steam engine. She was in operation on California rivers. She was reported to have gone out of service about 1888.

Alice Mattes 122292 (Canada) (passenger/ freight vessel) She was built in 1907 at Prince Albert SK Canada. 72' x 18' x 4' Wood. 121gt 44rt. Powered by a 4hp steam engine. In 1914–1931 she was owned by the Prince Albert Lumber Co. Ltd., Prince Albert SK. In 1950c she was beached at The Pas MB.

Alice Sprague (Canada) (sidewheeler) She was built in 1886 at Selkirk MB Canada by David Kilpatrick. Wood. Powered by a steam engine. In 1886 she was owned by the Sprague Lumber Company. Nathan Kramer[13] states "This steamship carried excursionists from Winnipeg to destinations downstream, including Selkirk and into Lake Winnipeg, when water levels remained sufficient. In 1888, a mid-June advertisement claims the steamer, under the charter of the Winnipeg & Western Transportation Company, was to serve as a passenger and freight express for a round trip of the Saskatchewan River from Winnipeg to Edmonton (Alberta) via the Saskatchewan River, with ports of call along the way to include Prince Albert and Battleford. Whether or not the voyage ever took place remains in doubt. Beyond regular excursion trips, the *Alice Sprague* saw routine use as a freighter, hauling logs and lumber for the Sprague Lumber Company. She was reportedly wrecked, though details surrounding this fate have not been found. In December 1896, she was struck from the Canada Register."

Alida 105028 (US) (passenger vessel) (sidewheeler) She was built in 1870 at Seattle WA USA. 107.0' x 18.5' x 6.6' Wood. 114.46gt. Powered by a 60nhp steam engine. n 1869 she was owned by EA & LM Starr, Olympia WA USA. In 1869 she operated in competition with the *Olympia*. She was moved to San Francisco CA but received a subsidy for not operating in those waters. She ran coastwise to Humboldt Bay and Portland OR with return to Puget Sound. In 1890 she was set on fire while out of service and anchored at Gig Harbor WA by flying burning debris from a nearby serious forest fire.

Alki 106653 (US) (passenger/ freight vessel) She was built in 1889 at Utsalady WA USA. 72.4' x 17.4' x 4' Wood. 378.83gt 48.69nt. Powered by a steam engine. In 1920 she was reported as having been abandoned.

Alki 106062 (US) She was built in 1882 at Seattle WA USA. 65.0' x 17.0' x 3.0' Wood. 45.38gt. Powered by a steam engine employed on Puget Sound.

Alkali 106294 (US) (sidewheeler) (freighter) She was built in 1884 at Alkali OR USA. 61.0' x 15.8' x 3.2' Wood. 24gt 20nt. Powered by a steam engine. She was reported to have been out of service in 1900.

All Nations[14] (US) (passenger/ freight vessel) She was built about 1908. Wood. Powered by a steam engine. She was employed between Fairbanks and Innoko Alaska.

Allice[15] (US) (freighter) She was built in the 1840s. Wood. Powered with a steam engine. She operated on the Sacramento River CA.

Alluvia 130483 (Canada) She was built in 1911 at New Westminster BC. 100' x 23.3' x 5' Wood. 356gt 211rt. Powered by a 9hp steam engine. In 1911–1912 she was owned by S Dawe and Niles P Roman, New Westminster BC. In 1913 she was owned by Alvo von Aldesleben, Vancouver BC. In 1914 she was owned by Robert K Houlgale, Vancouver BC. In 1915 she was rebuilt as a barge. In 1915–1918 she was owned by MR Cliff and ET McLennan, Vancouver BC. In 1919 she was owned by the Coast Steamship Co. Ltd., Vancouver BC. In 1912 she was running daily excursions from Vancouver to the Wigwam Inn on Indian Arm in Burrard Inlet.

Alma 107657 (US) (sidewheeler) She was built in 1901 at Rio Vista CA USA. 42.0' x 15.0' x 2.6' Wood. 11gt 10nt. Powered by a steam engine. In 1910 she was employed in the San Francisco Bay area CA.

Almota[16] 105639 (US) (freighter) She was built in 1876 at Celilo OR USA. 157.0' x 36.0' x 5' Wood. 502.35gt 395.24rt. Powered by two 17nhp horizontal high pressure steam engines. In 1893 she was rebuilt at Texas Ferry. In 1876–1884 she was owned by the Oregon Steam Navigation Co., Portland, OR USA. She spent much of her career employed on the Snake River. In 1901 she was reported as having been out of service.

Alpha (Canada) (sidewheeler) She was built in 1890 at Vancouver BC Canada by the False Creek Shipyard. 82' Wood. Powered by a steam engine. In 1890 she was owned by Captain Richard Gosse, Imperial Steamships Ltd., Vancouver BC. In 1891 she was owned by AW Thompson, New Westminster BC. On September 23, 1891, while owned by AW Thompson, New Westminster BC, she was destroyed by fire in False Creek, Vancouver BC. In the morning, while under the command of Captain McLenean, she entered False Creek under full power while on fire. Her crew jumped overboard to save themselves and the vessel burned in the inlet. As the tide turned, she re-floated and drifted out to sea. Captain McLenean rowed after her and succeeded in getting a line on board, towing her to the beach between the English Bay logging camp and Jericho. She sank and broke in two, with her machinery scattered. She was reported as a re-built vessel from the hull of the *Richmond*, and her machinery, which had been previously destroyed by fire in Victoria in 1887.

Alsop (see H.W. Alsop)

Alta[17] (US) (freighter) She was built in 1866. Wood. Powered by a steam engine. She was in operation on California rivers. She was reported to have ceased operation in 1868.

Alta 105880 (US) (passenger vessel) She was built in 1878 at Fairhaven CA USA by Hans D Bendixsen. 88.6' x 17.9' x 7.2'. Wood. 104.07gt 50.76nt. Powered by an 80nhp steam engine.

Alton[18] 106808 (US) (freighter) She was built in 1891 at Chicago IL USA. 34.6' x 8.0' x 4.0'. Wood. 13.5gt 9.12nt. Powered by a steam engine. In 1891 she was owned by William Eaton & Mr Rosengrant, Chicago IL. Designed for shallow river water work, she was in service, under Captain DC Long, between Bonners Ferry WA to Porthill ID until 1894.

Alton[19] 107584 (US) (tug, later oil tanker). 100.0' x 21.5' x 4.0'. Wood. 106gt 93nt. (She had a flat bottom design). Powered by a 100ihp steam engine. She was owned by James Gillis, San Francisco CA. On May 24, 1904, she was lost at in San Francisco Bay near Point Richmond carrying a cargo of oil bound for Stockton CA. During the voyage she sprang a leak and sank.

Altona[20] 106729 (US) (passenger vessel) She was built in 1890 Portland OR USA. 120.0' x 21.0' x 5.2'. Wood. 201gt 190rt. Powered by two 9.6nhp horizontal high pressure steam engines. In 1890 she was owned by the Oregon City Transportation Co., Portland, OR USA. In 1899 she was reported to have been rebuilt.

Altona (later *Anawanda*) 107453 (US) (passenger vessel) She was built in 1899 at Portland OR USA by David Stephenson 123.4' x 29.7' x 4.8'. Wood.

329gt 242nt. Powered by a 150ihp steam engine. In 1899 she was owned by Captain AB Graham's Yellow Stack Line. Her engines came from the *Altona*. Her frames were constructed at Portland OR USA and assembled at St. Michael AK USA. In 1907 she was moved to Cordova AK USA. In 1907 her registry was transferred to St. Michael Alaska.

Alvarado[21] 001952 (US) She was built in 1870 at San Francisco CA USA. 69.5' x 20.5' x 4.1' Wood. 91.97gt 82.36nt. Powered by a 30nhp steam engine. She was reported to have gone out of operation about 1890.

Alvira 106687 (US) (passenger vessel) She was built in 1889 at San Francisco CA USA. 144.0' x 33.6' x 6.0' Wood. 469gt 443nt. Powered by a 200ihp steam engine. In 1889–1910 she was employed at San Francisco CA.

Alviso[22,23] 107153 (US) (freighter) She was built in 1895 at Sausalito CA USA. 115.0' x 23.0' x 6.0' Wood. 197gt 168nt. Powered by a 75ihp steam engine. She originally worked on the lower Columbia River and then in 1910, was moved to California where she was in operation on California rivers. On December 15, 1920, she was destroyed by fire at Brytes Bend, on the Sacramento River. She is reported by Murray Lundberg to have worked in Alaska/YT in 1898.

Amador[24,25,26] 001953 (US) (sidewheeler) She was built in 1869 at San Francisco CA USA by Patrick Tiernan. 199.0' x 39.0' x 10.6' Wood. 985.57gt 756.94rt. Powered by a 300nhp steam engine. In 1869–1871 she was owned by the California Steam Navigation Company, San Francisco CA USA interests. In 1871 she was owned by the California Pacific Railroad Company. She was in operation on California rivers. She was reported to have been dismantled in 1905.

Amberly[27] (later *White*) (US) (workboat) She was built about 1912 at Flathead Lake MT USA. Wood. Powered by a steam engine. In 1914–1917 she was owned by Gene Hodge, Swan Lake MT.

Amelia[28] 088362 (Canada) (sidewheeler) She was built in 1863 at San Francisco CA USA by Owens. 150.0' x 26.0' x 8.5' Wood. 430.97gt 222.08rt Powered by a walking beam (36" x 72") steam engine built by Joseph

Ketwell, Jersey City NJ USA. In 1863 she was owned by the California Steam Navigation Co., San Francisco CA. In 1884 she was sold to the People's Steam Navigation Company, and she arrived in Victoria on June 3, 1884. In 1890 she was owned by Captain John G Cox, Victoria BC. In 1890 she was owned by Richard S Byrn, Victoria BC. In 1890 she was sold to the Canadian Pacific Navigation Co. Ltd., Victoria BC. In 1863 she was in Sacramento River service. In 1879–1882 she operated as a ferry by the Central Pacific Railroad between Vallejo Junction and South Vallejo in San Francisco Bay. She arrived at Victoria BC on June 3, 1884, in service between Victoria BC and Nanaimo BC in competition with RP Rithet (Canadian Pacific Navigation Co.). On April 27, 1889, while steaming near Chemainus her walking beam broke causing major damage to the engine and the structure of the ship. She was towed to Victoria and sold at auction. She was purchased by the Canadian Pacific Navigation Co. Ltd. to prevent her from being purchased by competitors. She never ran again and was broken up in 1895.

Amelia[29] 001214 (US) (sidewheeler) (ferry) She was built in 1863 at San Francisco CA. 147'. Wood. 385.96gt. Powered by a 200nhp steam engine. In 1863 she was owned and employed as a San Francisco Bay ferry operating between Alviso and San Francisco. In 1869 she converted from coal to oil fuel. In 1871 she was owned by the California Pacific Railroad Co. In 1885 she was sold to non-US interests.

Amelia Po (US) (freighter) Wood. Powered by a steam engine.

Amelia Wheaton (US Army) (passenger/ freight vessel) She was built in 1880 at Fort Coeur d'Alene ID USA by CP Sorensen. Powered by two 4nhp horizontal steam engines. In 1880–1892 she was owned by the United States Army. She was the first steamer to operate on Lake Coeur d'Alene. In 1892 she was laid up. Her engines went to the St. Joseph.

American Eagle[30] (US) (sidewheeler) (freighter) She was built in 1851 at Philadelphia PA. Iron 181gt. Powered by a steam engine. In 1854 she operated on the Sacramento River CA. In 1854–1856, she was owned by the California Steam Navigation Company. In 1854 her boiler exploded. In 1856 she was reported as having been abandoned and secured to a levee in the Sacramento River. In 1859 her topsides were removed, and she was converted to a barge.

American Express (see *Empress of the North*)

American Pride[31] (ex-*Queen of the Mississippi*) (passenger vessel) 1257187 (US) She was built in 2012. 230.6' x 49.2' x 11.8' Steel. In 2012 she was employed on the American River. In 2015 she was renamed and moved west where she was employed on the Columbia and Snake Rivers. In 2015–2021 she was owned by American Cruise Lines.

Anawanda (see *Altona*)

Ancon 001522 (US) (sidewheeler) She was built in 1873 at San Francisco CA USA by Owens. 266' x 49' x 17' Wood. 1540.78gt 1208.05rt (In 1873 she was converted from a coal hulk to a sidewheeler in San Francisco CA.) Powered by a walking beam steam engine. In 1873–1881 she was owned by the Pacific Coast Steamship Co., San Francisco CA USA. In 1881 she was running between San Francisco CA USA and southeastern Alaska. On August 28, 1889, she was wrecked at Loring AK while backing out from the wharf. The procedure was to keep a stern line fixed to the dock so that she would avoid the reef. A wharf hand released the line before the steamer was brought up standing on it and the tide took her onto the rocks punching a hole in the hull. As the tide receded her weight broke her back, and she was a total loss.

Andover (see *Silver Stream*)

Anglian 107512 (Canada) (passenger/ freight vessel) She was built in 1898 at Teslin Lake YT Canada by Captain CE MacDonald. 85' x 20.6' x 4.5' Wood. 161gt 114rt. Powered by a 5.4nhp steam engine built by Vulcan Iron Works, Seattle WA USA. In 1899 she was re-engined. In 1898 she was owned by Captain CE MacDonald, James RP Gaudin and Captain Frank Armstrong. In 1898 she was owned by the F.N. Yorke & Co., Victoria BC. In 1898–1901 she was owned by the Canadian Development Co. Ltd., Victoria BC. In 1901 she was owned by the British Yukon Navigation Co. In 1903 she was retired from Yukon River service. In 1904–1919 she was owned by the British Yukon Navigation Co. Ltd., Vancouver BC. The lumber and machinery was shipped part-way up the Stikine River from Vancouver BC. This was hauled on horse-drawn sledges over the Coast Range mountains to Lake Teslin. Later she was moved to the Whitehorse – Dawson route of the White Pass & Yukon Railroad. In 1931 she was dismantled at Whitehorse YT.

Anita (US) (freighter) She was built in 1894 at McMinnville OR USA. 55' x 15.0' x 3.9' Wood. Powered by two 6nhp horizontal steam engines. In 1894 she was owned by LH Cook. In 1894 she was reported as having been broken up at Salem OR.

Ann[32] 001737 (US) She was built in 1867 at Umatilla OR. 83' Wood. 83gt. Powered by a steam engine.

Anna (later *Pah Loong*) (US) (freighter) She was built in 1859 at San Francisco CA. Wood. 67gt. Powered by a steam engine. In 1859 she was owned by the California Steam Navigation Co. In 1859 she made exploratory voyages up the Sacramento River almost reaching Shasta.

Anna Abernethy[33] (US) (sidewheeler) (freighter) She was built in 1854. Wood. Powered with a steam engine. In 1854 she was in operation on California rivers as a competitor to the California Steam Navigation Co. on the Marysville – San Francisco route. In 1856 she was owned by the California Steam Navigation Co. She was reported as having gone out of service about 1868.

Anna M. Pence 106803 (US) (freighter) She was built in 1890 at Lummi Island WA USA. 89.1' x 18.8' x 6.1' Wood. 139.45gt 89.1nt. In 1890–1895 she was owned by the La Conner Trading & Transportation Co., La Conner WA USA. On June 21, 1895, she was destroyed by fire near Point Lowell WA USA. The hull was salvaged and incorporated into the construction of the T.W. *Lake* in 1896.

Annerly[34] 106963 (US) (freighter) She was built in 1892 at Jennings MT USA. 92.5' x 16.0' x 4.4' Wood. 128.08gt 79.55nt. Powered by a steam engine. In 1892 she was owned by HS DePuy & BW Jones. She was owned by DePuy & Jennings for Upper Kootenay River service based at Fort Benton MT. In 1892 she was reported to have been broken up.

Annie[35] 107266 (US) (freighter) She was built in 1897 at Camas WA. 103' x 18.3' x 5' Wood. 157gt 125nt. Powered by two 4nhp horizontal (high pressure 8" x 36") steam engines. In 1897 she was owned by JG Wickstrom. In 1899 she was reported to have been broken up.

Annie Abernethy (see *Lot Whitcomb*)

Annie Comings 081171 (see *Wm. M. Hoag*) (Some writers refer to this vessel as the Annie "Commings".)

Annie Comings[36] 206116 (US) (freighter, tug) She was built in 1909 at Vancouver WA USA by John G Sound. 151.4' x 32.6' x 5.4' Wood. 464gt 414nt. Powered by a 380ihp steam engine. In 1909 she was employed on the Columbia River. She was owned by the Western Transportation & Towing Co. In 1941 she was reported as having been broken up. (Some writers refer to this vessel as the Annie "Commings.")

Annie Faxon[37] 105718 (US) She was built in 1877 at Celilo OR USA. 165.0' x 36.3' x 5.0' Wood. 708.66gt 564.75nt. Powered by two horizontal (high pressure 17" x 72") steam engines. (Her engines came from the *Yakima*). In 1877 she was owned by the Oregon Steam Navigation Co., Portland, OR USA. In 1887 she was rebuilt at Texas Ferry OR.

Annie Faxon[38] 106558 (US) (ferry) She was built in 1887 at Texas Ferry WA USA. 165.0' x 34.4' x 5.3' Wood. 513.92gt 487.00nt. Powered by a (17" x 72") 19nhp steam engine. In 1877 she was owned by Oregon USA interests. In 1884 she was owned by the Oregon Railroad & Navigation Co., Portland, OR USA. She was employed on the Columbia River above Celilo Falls and on the Snake River to Lewiston ID. On April 14, 1893, she was destroyed by a boiler explosion at Wades Bar on the Snake River with the loss of eight persons. Her hull was used in the construction of the *Lewiston*. The *Lewiston* in turn was destroyed by fire at Lewiston ID in July 1922.

Annie Laurie[39,40] (ex-*Hooligan*, later *Annie Laurie*) (US) (freighter, later an excursion vessel) She was built in 1909 at Klamath Falls OR. 80' Wood. Powered by a steam engine. In 1909 she was employed by the Long Lake Lumber Co. and was employed towing log rafts. In 1914 she was renamed as *Annie Laurie*. In 1932 she was rebuilt by Captain Joe Guthrie, at Klamath Falls OR. In 1914–1932 she was owned by Captain Joe Guthrie, Klamath Falls OR. In 1914–1932 she was employed as an excursion boat on the Upper Lake near Klamath Falls OR.

Annie Stewart 001218 (US) (sidewheeler) She was built in 1864 at San Francisco CA. 155' x 26' x 7' Wood. 316gt 276nt. Powered by two horizontal (high pressure 18" x 72") steam engines. In 1864 she was owned by Gillman, Corbett et al. In 1873 she was owned by the Oregon Steam Navigation Co. In 1881 she was owned by the Oregon Railroad & Navigation Co. She was employed on the Columbia River. In 1881 she was transferred to Puget Sound employed on the Seattle to Tacoma route. She was snagged on the Puyalip River. In 1910 she was reported as having been abandoned.

Annie 106175 (US) She was built in 1883 at Eureka CA USA. 76.6' x 18.2' x 4.4' Wood. 83.47gt 49.06nt. Powered by a steam engine. She was employed at Eureka CA USA.

Anson Northup (see *North Star*)

Antelope[41] 090452 (Canada) (sternwheeler, later sidewheeler) (passenger vessel) She was built in 1887 at Winnipeg MB Canada. 100.5' x 18.1' x 4.5' Wood. 120gt. Powered by an 80hp steam engine. In 1889 she was converted to a sidewheeler. In 1887 she was owned by Sprague Lumber Co. In May 1893 she was destroyed by ice.

Antelope[42,43,44] 001212 (US) (sidewheeler) (ferry) She was built in 1847 at New York USA. 206.6' x 28.0' x 8.8' Wood. 581.05gt 448.26nt. Powered by a 359nhp steam engine. In 1851 she rounded Cape Horn to reach the California coast. In 1851–1854 she was owned by the Independent Line (Captain WE Bushnell). In 1854 she was owned by the California Steam Navigation Company. She brought the first mail from Sacramento to San Francisco for the westbound Pony Express. In 1871 she was taken over by the California Pacific Railroad Co., San Francisco CA. In 1888 she collided with the *Confidence* and sank in the Sacramento River. Captain Bushnell literally inserted his body into the hole in the hull to prevent water from entering before the vessel was beached.

Antelope[45] 106573 (US) She was built in 1888 at Eureka CA USA by Peter Matthews. 95.0' x 23.0' x 5.5' Wood. 155.39gt 82.57nt. Powered by a 566ihp steam engine. In 1888 she was owned by John Vance, Eureka CA. In 1909 she was reported as having been broken up.

Antelope 207031 (US) (ferry) She was built in 1909 at Samoa CA USA. 100.6' x 23.0' x 5.0' Wood. 160gt 101nt. Powered by a steam engine. In 1910 she was owned by Eureka CA USA interests.

Antioch 001215 (US) (sidewheeler) (freighter) She was built in 1865 at Antioch CA. Wood. Powered by a steam engine. In 1876 she was reported as having been abandoned.

Apache[46] 105923 (US) (passenger vessel) She was built in 1880 at Oakland CA by the Southern Pacific Railroad. 203.0' x 42.3' x 8.0' Wood. 773.52gt 620.06nt. Powered by a steam engine. She was in operation on California rivers. She was reported to have been dismantled in 1928.

Arctic[47] 107254 (US) (freighter) She was built in 1889 at St. Michael AK USA. 125.5' x 30.3' x 4.0' Wood. Powered by a steam engine. In 1889–1897 she was owned by the Alaska Commercial Co. In 1897 she was operated by the Alaska Commercial Company employed in Yukon River service. On May 31, 1897, she was crushed in the spring ice at Forty Mile YT. Her machinery went to the *Margaret*.

Arctic Bird[48] 107365 (US) (passenger/ freight vessel) She was built in 1898 at Sausalito CA USA. 50' x 16.5' x 3.5' Wood. 38gt 27nt. Powered by a steam engine. In 1905 she was wrecked at Kobuk River AK USA. In 1910 she was owned by San Francisco CA USA interests.

Arctic Boy[49] 107411 (US) (freighter) She was built in 1898 at St. Michael AK USA. 124' x 25' x 2.6' Wood. 74gt. Powered by a steam engine. In 1898 she was owned by Captain Elbridge Truman "ET" Barnette, Fairbanks AK USA. In 1901 she foundered near St. Michael AK USA.

Arctic Queen (see *Emma Nott*)

Argenta[50] 107825 (Canada) (passenger/ freight vessel) She was built in 1900 at Mirror Lake BC by Harold C Elliott. 92.2' x 20.3' x 4.2' Wood. 206gt 129rt. Powered by a 4nhp steam engine built by DW Swain, Stillwater MN. In 1900 she was owned by the Great Northern Railroad. In 1904 she was owned by Robert Irving, Kaslo BC. In 1910–1914 she was owned by AH MacNeill, Rossland BC. In 1900–1910 she was in K.R.& N. service on Kootenay Lake. She was laid up in 1910 and her machinery and fittings sold to GB Matthews, Riondel BC where she was reported as having been broken up.

Argo (US) Wood. Powered by a steam engine. In 1898 she was lost at sea while enroute to Alaska.

Argo (later *Lieut. Smith*) (US) Wood. Powered by a steam engine. During the winter of 1898–1899 she was owned by the Cleveland-Alaska Gold Mining & Milling Co., Alatna River, Alaska. She was sold to the United States Army in 1899. She was resold in 1905.

Arnold[51] 107353 (US) (passenger/ freight vessel) She was built in 1898 at San Francisco CA USA by Thomas Patrick Henry Whitelaw. 181' x 36.5' x 6.7' Wood. 692gt 402nt. Powered by a steam engine. She was assembled at Dutch Harbor AK for service in the Klondike Gold Rush. She was a sister ship of the *Leon* and *Linda*. In 1898 she was owned by the Alaska Exploration Co. (Liebes & Co., San Francisco CA). In 1901 she was transferred to Northern Navigation Co. In 1914 she was owned by White Pass & Yukon Rail Road. She was not used in 1903 or after 1905. In 1917 she was reported to have been abandoned at St. Michael AK.

Arrowhead Queen[52] (US) (passenger vessel) In 2021 she was owned by LeRoys Boardshops/Lake Arrowhead Queen, Lake Arrowhead, CA where she offers cruises on Lake Arrowhead (east of Los Angeles CA).

Artisan[53] 208820 (US) (passenger vessel) She was built in 1911 at Portland OR by CW Boost. 40.0' x 11.6' x 2.8' Wood. 15gt 8nt. Powered by a 29ihp gasoline engine. In 1911 she was owned by CW Boost. She was employed on the Columbia River. In 1922 she was rebuilt with a propeller.

The paddlewheel from the *Assiniboine* (Image from Alyssa "Aly" Wowchuk, Brandon General Museum)

Assiniboine 103338 (Canada) She was built in the 1894 and broken up at Winnipeg MB in 1900. She was rebuilt as the *Gertie H.* which was destroyed by fire in 1904.

Astoria[54] 001859 (US) (sidewheeler) She was built in 1869 at San Francisco CA USA. Wood. 124.61gt. Powered by a steam engine. She was employed on the Columbia River until about 1885.

Astorian[55] (later *Clara Parker*) 106798 (US) (passenger vessel) She was built in 1890 at Portland OR USA. 142' Wood. 362gt 234nt. Powered by a steam engine. She was employed on the Columbia River. She was reported to have been out of service about 1908.

Astorian 208596 (US) (passenger vessel) She was built in 1911 at Dockton WA USA. 127' Wood. 255gt 173nt. Powered by a steam engine. She was employed on the Columbia River. In 1916 she was employed on the Snake River OR. She was reported to have been out of service about 1923 (wrecked?).

Astotin[56] (USACE) (dredge/ snag boat) She was built in 1913 at Celilo OR. 140' x 28' x 5' Wood. 200gt. Powered by two 13nhp horizontal (high pressure 14" x 60") steam engines. In 1913 she was owned by the United States Army Corps of Engineers. In 1919 she was reported to have gone out of service.

Athabasca 092691 (Canada) (passenger/ freight vessel) She was built in 1888 at Athabasca Landing AB Canada by the Hudson's Bay Co. 146.0' x 28.0' x 4.0' Wood. 167gt 105rt. Powered by a 10hp steam engine. In 1888–1904 she was owned by the Hudson's Bay Co., London UK in service in the Lesser Slave Lake region. In 1888 she was employed from Athabasca Landing to the head of Grand Rapids where goods were trans-shipped by scow, taken to Fort McMurray, and there trans-shipped by the SS *Grahame*. In 1897 she was towing scows to Athabasca Landing. She was laid up and condemned in 1903.

The *Athabasca River* (Image from the Provincial Archives of Alberta)

Athabasca River 130277 (Canada) (passenger/ freight vessel) She was built in 1912 at Athabasca Landing AB Canada by the Hudson's Bay Co. She was designed by Captain JW Mills. 136' x 28' x 3.6' Wood. 341.21gt 230.29rt. Powered by two horizontal (high pressure 12" x 48") 9.6nhp steam engines built by Albion Iron Works, Victoria BC. In 1920 she was laid up and rebuilt as an unpowered barge. In 1912–1919 she was owned by the Hudson's Bay Company, London UK. Her engines came from the Skeena River sternwheeler *Hazelton* (107834). In 1912 she was in service on the upper Athabasca River from Athabasca Landing downstream to the

Grand Rapids and upstream to Mirror Landing. In 1914 she was taken down through the Grand Rapids to Fort McMurray. She was winched up the Vermillion Rapids on the ice in the winter of 1914–1915 and operated out of Peace River Crossing on the Peace River from Fort Vermilion to Hudson's Hope BC. In 1917 at the end of the season she was hauled out at Peace River Crossing and, after her machinery was removed, was not placed in commission for 1918. After 1919 she was used as a warehouse at Peace River Crossing. She is believed to be the vessel that was deliberately burned in 1930.

Athabasca River 150792 (Canada) (passenger/ freight vessel) She was built in 1922 at Fort McMurray AB Canada by George F Askew. 147.5' x 35.6' x 5.9' Wood. 866.16gt 545.68rt. Powered by a 15hp steam engine built by Polson Iron Works, Toronto ON. Her machinery was taken by from the HBC steamer *Port Simpson* which was hauled up at the Grand Trunk Pacific ways at Dodge Cove on Digby Island. While Askew had the hull prefabricated and knocked down in Vancouver, a crew under HBC's John Sutherland and Captain Haight retrieved the machinery. All components had to be dragged down the slope above the Clearwater and hauled along the ice as the railway had, at that point, not reached Waterways. In 1922–1949 she was owned by the Hudson's Bay Company, London UK. In 1922 she was in service between Fort McMurray AB and Fort Fitzgerald NWT and was laid up in 1946 after exhaustive Second World War service. She was reported as having been broken up on February 25, 1949.

Athol 107414 (US) (passenger/ freight vessel) She was built in 1898 at Unalaska AK USA. 47.04' x 12' x 5' Wood. 16gt/rt. Powered by a steam engine. She is reported by Murray Lundberg to have worked in Alaska/ YT in 1898.

Atlantic (later *Leelanaw*) 141524 (US) She was built in 1886 at Newcastle UK. 273.8' x 36.3' x 21.4' Steel. 1923gt 1377nt. Powered by a 1,150ihp steam engine. (She was later converted to a propeller vessel as the *Leelanaw*.) In 1900 she was owned by New York interests.

Aurora 090442 (Canada) She was built in 1885 at Icelandic River (now Riverton) MB Canada. 121.0' x 19.2' x 8.4' Wood. 225gt 141rt. Powered by a steam engine. In 1886, she was owned by a partnership of Jonasson, Frederickson, & Walkey (JF & W) and leased to Clark & Co for use as a fish freezer for the winter season. In 1888 she was owned by the Lake Winnipeg Transportation Lumber and Trading Company. In 1898 she was owned by the Reverend JB Maul, Selkirk, MB. In 1900 she was owned by Crotty & Cross. In 1901 she was owned by William Dewar, Selkirk MB.

Aurora[57] 106369 (US) (passenger vessel) She was built in 1885 at San Francisco CA USA. 145.0' x 30.0' x 7.5' Wood. 406gt 328nt. Powered by a steam engine. She was in operation on California rivers. She was reported as having been abandoned in 1932.

Aurora[58] (US) (freighter) Wood. Powered by a steam engine. She is reported by Murray Lundberg to have worked in Alaska/YT in 1898.

Aurora[59] (US) (freighter) Wood. Powered by a steam engine. She is reported by Murray Lundberg to have worked in Alaska/YT in 1911.

Aurora No. 2[60] 107359 (US) (passenger/ freight vessel) She was built in 1898 at San Francisco CA USA. 63' Wood. 54gt. In 1898 she was owned by Eugene A Mantell, San Francisco CA. She was sold to the Alaska Commercial Co. She was laid up at Bergman, Alaska on the Koyukuk River during the winter of 1898–1899. She was reported to have been broken up in 1899.

Aurum 203357 (US) (tug) She was built in 1904 at Golovin AK USA. 50' x 10.8' x 3.2' Wood. 28gt 16nt. Powered by a 30ihp steam engine. She worked out of Nome AK. In 1917 she was reported to have been broken up at Golovin AK USA.

Australian (later *Barge #1450*) 107525 (Canada) She was built in 1899 at Lake Bennett BC, Canada by the Canadian Development Co. 115.0' x 24.8' x 4.0' Wood. 422.43gt 308.43rt. Powered by two horizontal 10"x54" 6.6nhp steam engines built by James Reese & Sons, Pittsburgh PA USA. In 1899–1901 she was owned by the Canadian Development Co. Ltd., Victoria BC. In 1901–1937 she was owned by the British Yukon Navigation Co. (last used 1904). Her register was closed in 1932. In 1942 she was re-built as a barge by the Public Roads Administration for Alaska Highway construction.

She was transferred back to the White Pass & Yukon Rail Road in 1943. She was employed on the Lake Bennett to Whitehorse run. Later she was taken through Miles Canyon for the Whitehorse to Dawson run.

B.A. Douglass (US) She was built in 1920 at Yankton SD. Wood. Powered by a gasoline engine. In 1920 she was owned by the by Yankton Chamber of Commerce and Captain Joseph Giesler. She replaced the *Josie L.K.* as the ferry at Yankton, SD.

B.C. Express 130883 (Canada) She was built in 1912 at Soda Creek BC Canada by Alex Watson Jr. 121.3' x 27.9' x 4.8' Wood. 449gt 283rt. In 1912–1917 she was owned by the British Columbia Express Co., Ashcroft BC. She was built for service between Fort George BC and Tete Jaune Cache BC but was employed between Soda Creek and Prince George BC after completion of the Grand Trunk Railway. In 1920 she was reported as having been dismantled at South Fort George BC. Her fittings and engines were sold to the Arctic Transportation Co. for a steamer on the Mackenzie River.

B.H. Smith Jr. (see *Bonita*)

B.X. 126516 (Canada) She was built in 1912 at Soda Creek BC Canada by Alex Watson Jr. 121.3' x 27.9' x 4.8' Wood. 449gt 283rt. In 1912–1917 she was owned by the British Columbia Express Co., Ashcroft BC. She was built for service between Fort George BC and Tete Jaune Cache BC but was also employed between Soda Creek and Prince George BC after completion of the Grand Trunk Railway. In 1919 she was damaged below Fort George Canyon, salvaged, and towed to South Fort George BC. Her fittings and engines were sold to the Alberta and Arctic Transportation Co. for a steamer on the Mackenzie River. Although there was lots of talk and even some advertising that she and her sister would be rebuilt, respectively at Fort McMurray and Fort Smith, but no action was taken as the boom fizzled out when it was realized that marketing of the oil would be difficult.

Babine Blondie 193435 (Canada) She was built in 1951 at New Westminster BC, Canada by John Manly Ltd. 8.9m x 3.4m x 1.7m (29.3' x 11' x 5.5') Wood. 9.78gt 6.65rt. Powered by a 165hp diesel engine. In 1951 this tug was owned by Henry Schritt, Burns Lake BC. In 1958–1961 she was owned by the Decker Lake Lumber Co. Ltd., Prince George BC. In 1967 she was owned by Michelle Bay Lumber Ltd., Topley BC. In 1968–2007 she was owned by H. Pearson Lumber Co. Ltd., Burns Lake BC.

Baby[61,62] (US) (passenger/ freight vessel) She was built in 1894 at Eugene OR USA. 30' x 9' x 3' Wood. Powered by two horizontal compound (3.6" x 18") steam engines. In 1894 she was owned by GN Frazer. She was reported as being broken up at Eugene OR in 1895.

Baby Rose 206426 (US) She was built in 1909 at Fort Benton MT USA. 72.0' x 20.2' x 3.1' Wood. 30gt/nt. Powered by a steam engine. In 1909–1910 she was owned by Great Falls MT USA interests.

Baby Ruth 203870 (US) (tug) She was built in 1893 at San Francisco CA USA. 49.3' x 13.0' x 8.0' Wood. 28gt 17nt. Powered by a 30ihp steam engine. In 1893–1910 she was owned by San Francisco CA interests.

Bahia Belle (US) She was built in the USA. Steel. 74' (3 decks) The Bahia Resort Hotel[63] in San Diego CA USA offers complimentary cruises to their guests in this tour vessel on Mission Bay (north San Diego). It travels between the Bahia Resort Hotel and its sister property, the Catamaran Resort Hotel and Spa. After dark it functions as a party boat.

Bailey 107715 (Canada) She was built in 1899 at Lake Bennett BC, Canada, by Louis Paquet. 110.0' x 21.7' x 5.8' Wood. 193gt 132rt. Powered by two horizontal (high pressure 10" x 54" 6.6nhp) steam engines by the Sumner Iron Works, Everett WA USA. In 1899 she was owned by Irwin B Sanborn, Portland, OR USA. She was owned by Algernon Stracey. In 1899 she was owned by the Canadian Development Co. (Henry Maitland Kersey). In 1903–1931 she was owned by the British Yukon Navigation Co., Victoria BC. She worked on Bennett Lake to Whitehorse run. In c1905 she was retired. (Some reports indicate her name was S.S. Bailey). She was moved through Miles Canyon for service between Whitehorse to Dawson run. Her boiler went to the steamer *Gleaner* 1909. In 1931 she was reported as having been broken up and was still listed in the Register of Shipping.

Bailey Gatzert 003488 (US) (passenger/ freight vessel, later a ferry) She was built in 1890 at Ballard WA USA by John Holland (launched in 1892). 177.0' x 32.3' x 8' Wood. 560gt 444nt. Powered by two 32nhp horizontal (high pressure 22" x 84") steam engines. In 1890 she was owned by the Seattle Steam Transportation and Navigation Co., Seattle WA. In 1892 she was owned by Captain UB Scott. In 1892 she was employed on the Columbia River for the White Collar Line. In 1907 she was rebuilt to 194' 878gt. She was reported to have been abandoned in 1926.

Bailey Gatzert[64] 204289 (US) (passenger/ freight vessel, later a barge) She was built in 1907 at Portland OR USA. 194.0' x 32.8' x 8.0' Wood. 878gt 802nt. Powered by 1,300ihp (28" x 96") steam engine. In 1907 she was owned by Dalles, Portland & Astoria Co. She was employed on The Dalles – Portland route. In 1917 she was transferred to Puget Sound as an automobile ferry on the Seattle to Bremerton route. In 1918 she was rebuilt. In 1926 she was converted to a floating marine machine shop. In 1926 she was laid up.

Banjo[65] (US) She was built in the USA. She is a sternwheeler berthed on Lake Union, Seattle WA USA that in 2021 functions as a bed-and-breakfast.

Banner[66,67] (US) (sidewheeler) She was built about 1862. Wood. 175.25gt. Powered by a steam engine. In 1862 she was employed on the Sacramento River. In 1863 she was owned by the California Steam Navigation Company. In December 1864 she was severely damaged by an arsonist. In May 1866 she was repaired and put back into service. In 1868 she was owned by the California Steam Navigation Co. In 1871 she was taken over by the California Pacific Railroad Co., San Francisco CA. She was in operation on California rivers. She was reported to have gone out of service about 1872 with her machinery removed and later broken up.

Banshee[68] (US) (freighter) She was built in 1908 at Coolin ID USA by Cecil H Wheatley. 60' Wood. Powered by a steam engine. In 1908 she was owned by Cecil H Wheatley. She was intended for service on Upper Priest Lake. In 1908 she was reported to have struck a rock on her maiden voyage and foundered in Upper Priest Lake.

Baramba (see *R.P. Rithet*)

Baranoff[69] (later *Rose*) 110234 (US) (sidewheeler) She was built in 1862 at Sitka, Russian Alaska. She was the first steamboat to be built in Alaska.

65.0' x 14.7' x ? Wood. 45.85gt. Powered by a steam engine. In 1871 she was owned by Allen Francis, (United States Consul in Victoria BC). Murray Lundberg reports that in 1872 she was converted to a propeller vessel named as the *Rose*. She was then employed in the Alaskan fur trade until 1873. She carried mail in Puget Sound, before returning to Alaska with the Alaska Oil & Guano Company and worked as a trader with them for many years.

Barge #1450 (see *Australian*)

Barr (see *John C. Barr*)

Barry K. (see *Lewiston*)

Bay Center 003265 (US) She was built in 1883 at Elma WA USA. 51.2' x 14.2' x 2.5' Wood. 42.55gt 31.32rt. Powered by a steam engine. In 1883–1887 she was owned by Port Townsend WA USA interests.

Bay City 003068 (US) (sidewheeler) She was built in 1878 at San Francisco, CA by William Collyer. 247' x 66' x 15' Wood. 1,283 tons Powered by an 860hp 52" x 144" vertical beam steam engine. She was owned by the South Pacific Coast Rail Road and the Southern Pacific Rail Road. She served at the California delta. She was reported to have been broken up in 1929.

Bear[70] (USACE) (snag boat) She was built in 1921 at San Francisco CA USA. 155.5' x 30.0' x 4.5' Wood. 240gt. She was owned by the United States Army Corps of Engineers. She was in employed on the Sacramento River, CA USA. She was reported to have been dismantled in 1926.

Beaver 072668 (UK) (sidewheeler) She was built in 1835 at Blackwall UK by Green, Wigrams & Green. 100.6' x 20' x 8.5' Wood. Powered by two 35nhp steam engines. In 1835–1874 she was owned by the Hudson's Bay Co., London UK. She was launched May 1835 and sailed in brigantine rig for the Pacific under command of Captain David Home, via Cape Horn. She arrived at Fort Vancouver April 10,1836. She generated steam in two boilers for her steam engines May 1836. Additional accommodation was fitted in 1860 and she became a passenger, mail and freight vessel operating between Victoria and New Westminster and Fort Langley. She was chartered to the Royal Navy as a hydrographic survey vessel in from December 1862 to December 1870 when she was returned to her owners. In 1874 she was converted to a towboat and sold to a company under the command of one of the owners, Captain Rudlin. In 1877 she was sold to the B.C. Towing & Transportation Company. In 1880 she was rebuilt. In 1888 she was owned by Henry Saunders, Victoria BC. She was licenced to carry passengers in 1888 and served the logging camps of Burrard Inlet. On July 08, 1888, she was wrecked at the entrance to Vancouver Harbour.

Beaver (Image from Vancouver City Archives)

Beaver[71] 002889 (US) She was built in 1873 at Oregon City OR USA. 125' x 25' x 5' Wood. 291gt. Powered by two horizontal 13nhp (high pressure 14" x 48") steam engines. In 1873 she was owned by the Willamette Transportation Co. In 1875 she was owned by the Willamette Transportation & Locks Co. In 1875–1876 she was employed between Portland and Astoria. In 1876 she was owned by Uriah Nelson for service on the Stikine River for the Cassiar Gold Rush. On May 17, 1898, she hit a rock and was wrecked 60 miles below Glenora. Her engine machinery was salvaged.

Beaver[72] 003649 (US) (passenger vessel) She was built in 1895 at Benicia CA USA. 59.0' x 15.0' x 3.1' Wood. 37gt 29nt. Powered by a 98ihp steam engine.

In 1895 she was owned by Arthur Harper and was employed on the upper Yukon River. In 1898–1910 she was employed at Sitka AK.

Beaver 107096 (Canada) (passenger vessel) She was built in 1898 at Toronto ON Canada by Polson Iron Works Ltd. 140.0' x 28.0' x 5.1' Composite Steel. and Wood. 545gt 344rt. Powered by a 13hp engine one cylinder horizontal direct-acting steam engine built by Albion Iron Works, Victoria BC. In 1898 she was assembled at False Creek, Vancouver BC. In 1906 she was rebuilt to 427t. In 1898 she was owned by the Canadian Pacific Navigation Co. In 1898–1919 she was owned by the Canadian Pacific Navigation Co. Ltd., Victoria BC. In 1919 she was owned by the Minister of Public Works, Ottawa ON. In 1927 she was owned by the Minister of Public Works, Victoria BC. In 1930 she was owned by the Minister of Public Works, Ottawa ON. In 1913 she was on New Westminster to Chilliwack run. In 1919 she was fitted for passengers on the New Westminster to Chilliwack run. In 1919 she was in service as a ferry at Ladner BC. In 1930 her machinery was removed, and the hull was used as a saltery and a bunkhouse for the Cunningham Brothers at Porcher Island in the Skeena River.

Beaver 003763 (US) (passenger/ freight vessel) She was built in 1898 at St. Michael AK USA. 55' Wood. 35gt. Powered by a steam engine. In 1898 she was owned by Arthur Harper. In 1899 she foundered at Nome AK USA.

Beaver[73,74] (ex-*Glenola* 086041) 202837 (US) She was built in 1906 at Portland OR USA. 152.0' x 31.0' x 6.6' Wood. 421gt 367nt. Powered by two 17nhp horizontal (high pressure 16" x 60") steam engines. In 1906 she was owned by the Clatskanie Transportation Company. She was employed on the Portland – Clatskanie run. On Thursday, September 25, 1913, she hit a snag on the river at Clatskanie OR. In 1927 she was taken off her usual route and placed on upper Columbia River service. In 1935 she struck a rock and sank near the Canoe Encampment rapids on the upper Columbia River and abandoned.

Becky Thatcher (later *Spirit of Sacramento*) (US) 87' She was based in Old Town Sacramento, formerly the *Becky Thatcher* based in Cincinnati OH. She traveled under her own power through the Panama Canal to California in 1997. She was owned by Sacramento Yacht Charters LLC providing tours of the Sacramento River delta. The vessel ceased operation when the owner went bankrupt and was laid up. On September 3, 2016, she took on water, capsized and sank near Bethel Island on the Sacramento River delta. She has apparently been broken up prior to 2020.

Bell (see *Iron Belle*)

Bella[75] 003759 (US) (passenger/ freight vessel) She was built in 1896 at St. Michael AK USA by Matthew Turner. 140.0' x 33.0' x 8.0' Wood. 370gt 185nt. Powered by a 400ihp steam engine. She was employed in Yukon River service in 1896 for the Alaska Commercial Company. In 1900 she was employed on the Koyakuk River. In 1901 she was owned by the Northern Navigation Co. in service on the Yukon River. In 1914 she was owned by the White Pass & Yukon Rail Road. In 1917 she was reported as having been employed at St. Michael AK.

Belle[76,77] (later *Swan*) (US) (sidewheeler) She was built in 1853 at San Francisco CA USA. 90' x 16' x 4' Wood. 95.12gt. Powered by a steam engine. In 1853 she was owned by Wells & Williams. In 1854 Captain Gilman made an early exploratory voyage with her on the Sacramento River. In 1854 she was owned by the California Steam Navigation Co. On February 7, 1856, she experienced a boiler explosion and sank at Russian Ford on the Sacramento River with the loss of the captain and 30 others. She was repaired and put back into service as the *Swan* (to disassociate the vessel from the accident). In 1869 she was reported to have been broken up at Portland OR.

Belle[78,79] 002486 (US) She was built in 1865 at Vallejo CA. 93.5' Wood. 89.7gt. Powered by a steam engine. She was in operation on California rivers. On October 18, 1870, while carrying a cargo of coal she was snagged and sank in shallow water.

Belle 003078 (US) She was built in 1878 at San Francisco CA USA. Wood. 50.84gt 45.25nt. Powered by a steam engine. In 1885 she was reported to have been out of service.

Belle of Chelan[80] (US) (passenger/ freight vessel) She was built in 1889 at Lake Chelan WA USA. Wood. Powered by a steam engine. (Most residents on Lake Chelan referred to her as the "Belle" and the owners even painted this shortened form on the side of the vessel.)

Belle of Oregon City[81] (US) (sidewheeler) Rebecca Harrison identifies this vessel built in 1853 at Oregon City, Oregon Territory by the Oregon Iron Works. 90.0' x 16' x ? Iron 54gt. Powered by a steam engine built by the Oregon City Iron Works. In 1853 she was owned by Captain WB Wells and Captain Richard Williams. She was owned by the Oregon Steam Navigation Co., Portland OR. She was employed on the Columbia River on the Portland to Oregon City run. She was reported to have been broken up in 1869 with her engine removed to be used to power a sawmill at Oak Point WT. (Her name was often shortened to *Belle* in popular use. She was the first iron steamboat built on the Pacific coast.)

Bellingham[82] (US) (work boat) She was built in 1898 at Lake Bennett BC Canada by Dignon, Sterzer & Willoch. 35' x 8' x 1.5' Wood. Powered by a steam engine. In 1898 she was owned by Dignon, Sterzer & Willoch. She was in Yukon River service 1898 and shot the Miles Canyon and Whitehorse YT rapids. She was the first vessel to make the voyage from Lake Bennett to Dawson City YT.

Ben Hur 205562 (US) (freighter) She was built in 1906 at Nome AK USA. 76' x 12.8' x 3' Wood. 46gt 29nt. Powered by a 40ihp steam engine. In 1906–1910 she was owned by Nome AK USA interests.

Benicia[83] (US) (freighter) She was built about 1850. Wood. Powered by a steam engine. She was reported to have gone out of service about 1868. She was in operation on California rivers.

Benicia 003185 (US) (freighter) She was built in 1881 Martinez CA USA. 92.0' x 24.0' x 7.0' Wood. 144.77gt 86.98rt. Powered by a steam engine. In 1881–1885 she was owned by San Francisco CA interests.

Bertha 207269 (US) (freighter) She was built in 1910 at Seattle WA. 52.5' x 12.2' x 2.8' Wood. 13gt 8nt. Powered by a 20ihp gasoline engine. She was employed in Puget Sound WA.

Bertha 212991 (US) (ferry) She was built in 1915 at Wallula WA USA. 49.9' x 20.0' x 2.4' Wood. 15gt/rt. Powered by a 15ihp gasoline engine. She was in service on the Columbia River. She was reported to have been out of service about 1925.

Bessie (US) She was a wooden pleasure boat that operated on the Sacramento River. On December 27, 1869, she was moored in shallow water and was left high and dry when the water receded. When the water rose again, she was stuck in the mud, and refused to rise, and then was flooded.

Bessie[84] (US) (freighter) She was built in 1884 at Castle Rock WY USA. 67.0' x 15.0' x 2.7' Wood. Powered by two horizontal (7"x 10" high pressure) steam engines. In 1884 she was owned by Mitchell & Dutton. In 1885 she was reported to have been dismantled at Portland OR.

Big River 221894 (US) (freighter) She was built in 1920 at Mendocino CA USA. 51.5' x 18.0' x 3.8' Wood. 17gt 17nt. Powered by a 15ihp steam engine. In 1922–1924 she was owned by San Francisco CA USA interests.

Bismarck[85] 003561 (US) She was built in 1892 at Woodland WA USA. 104' x 20' x 4.4' Wood. 191.49gt 144.4nt. Powered by a horizontal (high pressure 11" x 36") steam engine. In 1892 she was owned by E Wagner. She was employed on the Lewis and Lake Rivers. In 1898 she was wrecked on the Rogue River.

Bismarck 077279 (US) She was built in 1896 at Pembina ND USA. 120.0' x 21.0' x 4.0' Wood. 93gt 93nt. Powered by a gasoline engine. She was employed at Pembina ND USA.

Black Diamond 002637 (US) 061304 (Canada) (passenger/ freight vessel) She was built in 1864 at Seattle WA USA. 81.8' x 12.0' x 7.0' Wood. 49.68gt. Powered by two steam horizontal (high pressure 8" x 30") 20ihp engines. In 1874 she was owned by Richard Brodrick, Victoria BC.

Black Hills 003039 (US) She was built in 1877 at Pittsburgh PA USA. 150.3' x 23.6' x 7.1' Wood. 339.48gt 233.37nt. Powered by a 125ihp steam engine.

Black Prince[86] 003866 (US) (passenger vessel) She was built in 1901 at Everett WA USA. She was designed by Captain Charles Elwell. 91.6' x 19.6' x 4.6' Wood. 150gt 100nt. Powered by a 90ihp (10" x 48") steam engine. In 1901 she was owned by the Snohomish and Skagit River Navigation Company. She was employed on the Skagit River and Snohomish River. In 1910 she was owned by Puget Sound and Baker River Railroad. In 1922 she was owned by Captain Harry Ramwell (American Tugboat Company). In 1935 she was owned by the Everett Port Commission for the Everett Yacht Club. In 1956 she was reported to have been broken up.

Blackhawk[87] (US) (tug) She was built in the USA. Wood. Powered by a steam engine. In 1850 she was operated on the Sacramento River CA as a towboat by Jacob Kamm.

Blue Sage XXIV 804435 (Canada) (power cruiser yacht) She was built in 1984 at Medicine Hat AB by Yacht Line Industries Ltd. 12.74m x 4.24m x 0.82m Reinforced Plastic 19.63gt/rt. Powered by a 255bhp gasoline engine. In 2011–2013 she was owned by Marion V Doyle, Lethbridge AB.

Bob Irving[88] 003264 (US) She was built in 1883 at Seattle WA USA. 85.6' x 22.6' x 3.6' Wood. 176.03gt 125.3nt. Powered by a steam engine. In 1883–1888 she was owned by Puget Sound WA interests. In 1888 her boiler (from the City of Quincy) exploded at the Ball Rapids, Skagit River WA.

Bob O'Link 150678 (Canada) (tug) She was built in 1908 at New Westminster BC Canada. 100.0' x 27.0' x 6.3' Wood. 315gt 116rt. Powered by a 10nhp engine. (Her engine was removed c1915). In 1908–1931 she was owned by The Minister of Public Works, Ottawa ON. In 1958 she was owned by Nelson Bros. Fisheries Ltd., Vancouver BC.

Bobs 111542 (Canada) (tug) She was built in 1901 at Vancouver BC Canada. 36.0' x 8.0' x 2.0' Wood. 4gt 3rt. Powered by a 1hp engine. In 1901–1918 she was owned by Miss Lucy Fader, Vancouver BC.

Bon Accord[89] 094908 (Canada) (passenger/ freight vessel) She was built in 1890 at Victoria BC. 82.0' x 14.0' x 4.1' Wood. 84gt 57rt. Powered by a 4.8nhp steam engine. In 1896 she was owned by DJ Munn, New Westminster BC.

On September 30, 1898, she was destroyed in a huge fire that destroyed the New Westminster waterfront. She was berthed at the wharf while fire was consuming nearby sheds when the firemen arrived. The *Bon Accord* quickly caught fire along with two other steamers (the *Gladys* and the *Edgar*). The three steamers drifting down the river set each dock and vessel alight as they touched the shore.

Bonanza[90] 002978 (US) (freighter) She was built in 1875 at Portland OR USA. 152.0' x 37.2' x 5.0' Wood. 650.97gt 467.54rt. Powered by two horizontal (16.5" x 50" high pressure) steam engines. In 1875 she was owned by the Oregon Steamship Co. On November 10, 1888, she was wrecked at Wallings OR when she hit a rock while carrying 150 tons of wheat.

Bonanza King (see *Gov. Pingree*)

Boneta[91,92] (US) (passenger vessel) She was built in 1904 at Lake Coeur d'Alene ID by Johnson Boat Works (PW Johnson). 96' x 18' x ? Wood. Powered by a steam engine. In 1906 she was rebuilt to 121'. In 1904 she was owned by the White Star Navigation Co. She collided with the *Idaho* in the St. Joe River, and sank. She was raised and repaired. In 1908 she was owned by the Red Collar Line.

Bonita[93,94] 002960 (US) (passenger vessel) She was built in 1875 at Portland OR USA. 155.0' x 30.0' x 6.2' Wood. 526.52gt 376.94nt. Powered by two 17nhp horizontal (high pressure 16" x 72") steam engines. In 1875 she was owned by the Oregon Steam Navigation Co., Portland OR. She was employed on the Portland – Astoria route. In December 1892 she was wrecked on Fashion Reef.

Bonita[95] (later *Metlako*, then *B.H. Smith Jr.*) 003830 (US) (passenger/ freight vessel) She was built in 1900 at Portland OR USA by Robert Green. 109.0' x 24.4' x 4.8' Wood. 91gt 87rt. Powered by two 5nhp horizontal (high pressure 9" x 48") steam engines. In 1900 she was owned by Bucham & Burns Construction. In 1902 she was renamed as the *Metlako*. In 1909 she was rebuilt at Kelso WA by Robert Green. In 1909 she was owned by Byrnes Construction & Contracting Co. She was employed on the Yamhill River. In 1925 she was renamed as the *B.H. Smith Jr*. In 1931 she was reported to have been abandoned.

The ***Bonnington*** (Image from Maritime Museum of British Columbia 000405)

Bonnington 130555 (Canada) (passenger vessel, later a barge) She was built in 1911 at Nakusp BC by James M Bulger. 202.5' x 39.1' x 7.5' (61.7m x 11.9m x 2.3m) Steel. 1663gt 955rt. Powered by a 98nhp (two cylinder) compound steam engines built by Polson Iron Works Ltd., Toronto ON. In 1911–1937 she was owned by Canadian Pacific Railway Co., Montreal QC in service between Arrowhead to Robson West. In 1931 she was withdrawn from service and laid up at Nakusp BC. In 1942 she was owned by the Government of British Columbia. In 1947 she was owned by FW Sutherland, Arrowhead BC. In 1952–1958 she was owned by James Millar, Beaton BC. In 1961 she was owned by David McInnes (MO), Nakusp BC. The vessel was partially dismantled and rebuilt as a barge. Her funnel and boiler were used in the *Nasookin*. She was abandoned to become partially disintegrated at her mooring in Beaton BC. Her wreck is submerged for most of the year but is visible at low water.

Bonnitoba[96] 122278 (Canada) (passenger/ freight vessel) She was built in 1910 at Winnipeg MB Canada by JL Hyland. 118.6' x 22.3' x 4.0' Wood. 128gt 81rt. Powered by a 4nhp steam engine. In 1913 she was rebuilt in Winnipeg MB. In 1910–1919 she was owned by the Hyland Navigation & Trading Co. Nathan Kramer (The Manitoba Historical Society) stated that she was "built in early 1909 by JL Hyland of the Hyland Navigation & Trading Company, and launched on July 7, 1909, the *Bonnitoba* took excursionists up and down the Red River, delivering them to the privately-owned Hyland Park north of Winnipeg. The ship had a short life, being destroyed by ice near Winnipeg in 1913."

Boston[97] (US) (sidewheeler) (freighter) She was built in 1851 at San Francisco CA. Wood. 71gt. In 1854 she was reported to have been abandoned.

Bradley (see C.H. Bradley)

Brewster Ferry[98] 225768 (US) (sidewheeler) (ferry) She was built in 1926 at Brewster WA USA. 51.6' x 14.0' x 3.6' Wood. 22gt 19nt. Powered by a 40hp gasoline engine. In 1929 she was owned by McPherson Brothers Co., Brewster WA USA. In 1933 she was reported to have been out of service after operating in competition with the Brewster Bridge (Okanagan-Douglas Inter-County Bridge Co.)

Bridgeport[99] 215053 (US) (passenger vessel) She was built in 1917 at Pateros WA USA by Robert Reeves. 121.5' x 28.4' x 6.4' Wood. 438gt. 342nt She was powered by a 600ihp steam engine. In 1929–1935 she was owned by Fred McDermott, Pateros WA USA. She was employed in the Bridgeport, Brewster, and Pateros railhead route on the upper Columbia River handling grain, box shooks, flour, and boxed fruit. In 1941 she was reported as having been abandoned.

Brisk[100] (US) (sidewheeler) She was built in 1869 at Stockton CA by Marcucci. 122' Wood. 132.48gt. Powered by a steam engine. She operated on California rivers. She was reported to have gone out of service about 1885.

Brother Jonathan (later *Commodore*; then *Brother Jonathan*) (US) (sidewheeler) She was built in 1852 at New York NY USA by Perine, Patterson and Stack. 67m x 11m x ? (221' x 36' x ?) Wood. Powered by a steam engine built by Morgan Iron Works. In 1851 she was owned by Edward Mills. She was brought around to the Pacific by Captain CH Baldwin. In 1852 she was owned by Cornelius Vanderbilt. Vanderbilt had the *Brother Jonathan* sailed around Cape Horn and used her on the Pacific coast for his Nicaragua Line. Vanderbilt also had the steamer modified to accommodate more passengers. In 1856 she was owned by Captain John Thomas Wright in northern trade. She operated on the Panama to San Francisco Route from 1852–1856. She worked in British Columbia waters during the Fraser River goldrush in 1858. She arrived in Victoria harbour on April 25, 1858, carrying 450 American miners for the Fraser River goldrush of 1858. She arrived again in May 1858 with 194 passengers. In June 1858 with 900 passengers. In 1861 she was sold to the California Steam Navigation Co. After a refit she was renamed with her original name of *Brother Jonathan* and served northwest ports and San Francisco. She struck a rock off the California coast and was wrecked on July 30, 1865, with a loss of approximately 200 lives. The wreck was found about 1993 by the Deep Sea Research Co. who have been planning to recover artifacts and valuables. In 1997 this project was a subject of controversy in San Francisco CA.

Buena City[101] (US) (freighter) She was built about 1854. Wood. Powered by a steam engine. She was reported to have gone out of service about 1868.

Bullion[102] 002939 (US) She was built in 1874 at San Francisco CA USA by Gates. 116.2' x 30.0' x 5.7'. Wood. 147.46gt 122.45rt. Powered by an 80nhp steam engine. She was reported to have gone out of service about 1888.

Burpee 107157 (Canada) She was built in 1898 at Toronto ON. 45.6' x 9.5' x 2.6' 9gt 6rt. Powered by two horizontal (high pressure 4.5" x 18") 1.4nhp steam engines by Polson Iron Works Ltd., Toronto ON. In 1898–1913 she was owned by Isaac Burpee, Saint John NB. She worked between Dawson and Fortymile 1898–1899. In 1913 she was reported as being "out of existence."

Butte[103] (US) (centerwheel) (freighter) She was built in 1850 at San Francisco CA. Wood. 26gt. Powered by a steam engine. In 1852 she was reported as having been abandoned.

C.J. Brenham[104] 005799 (US) (sidewheeler) (freighter) She was built in 1869 at Noyo River CA. 102.0' x 23.4' x 10.0'. Wood. 133.18gt 69.59nt. Powered by a 200ihp steam engine. She was employed in the vicinity of Astoria OR until about 1895.

C. Minsinger 206353 (US) (tug) She was built in 1909 at Portland OR by Portland Shipbuilding Co. (Charles M Nelson). 122' x 24' x 5.9'. Wood. 179gt

143nt. Powered by two horizontal (high pressure 13.5" x 72") steam engines. In 1909–1935 she was owned by Star Sand Co., Portland OR. In 1940 she was reported to have been abandoned.

C.M. Small[105] 125119 (US) (freighter) She was built in 1872 at Stockton CA USA. 110.7' Wood. 207.89gt 169.73nt. Powered by a 45nhp steam engine. She was reported to have been out of service about 1895.

C.M. Weber[106] 005176 (US) (sidewheeler) (freighter) She was built in 1851 at San Francisco CA. Wood. 144gt. Powered by a steam engine. In 1851 she was employed on the Stockton CA route. In 1854 she was owned by the California Steam Navigation Co. In 1871 she was reported to have been abandoned.

C.R. Lamb[107] 122398 (US) (passenger vessel) She was built in 1907 at Kamloops BC Canada by Captain George B. Ward. 91.3' x 19.9' x 4.0' Wood. 192gt 120rt. Powered by a steam engine. In 1933 she was refurbished. In 1908–1921 she was owned by the Arrow Lakes Lumber Co., Arrowhead BC. In 1926–1929 she was owned by Shuswap Transportation Co., Vancouver BC. In 1932–1949 she was owned by Captain William Louie. In 1920s she ran on the Shuswap Lake. In 1933 she ran excursions to Sorrento to connect with the *Whitesmith* (serving Salmon Arm, Sicamous, Seymour Arm). She carried an orchestra for dancing. In 1939 she was beached and laid up near Kamloops BC. Her Shipping Registry listing was closed in 1949. Her hull could be seen for years afterwards at the foot of 8th Avenue in Kamloops.

C.R.P.A. 216334 (US) She was built in 1918 at Astoria OR. 57.0' x 16.4' x 5' Wood. 30gt 20nt. Powered by a gasoline engine. In 1918–1927 she was owned by the Columbia River Packers Association. In 1927 she was rebuilt as a propeller vessel.

C.R. Smith 131054 (Canada) (passenger/ freight vessel) She was built in 1912 at The Pas MB Canada. 96' x 17.6' x 4.2' Wood. 202gt 127rt. Powered by a 16.5hp engine. In 1912–1919 she was owned by The Finger Lumber Company. In 1931 she was owned by Albert L Mattes, Winnipeg MB. She was reported as having been laid up at The Pas MB.

Cabinet[108] (US) (freighter) She was built in 1866 at Cabinet Rapids WT. 113' x 22' x 4'. Wood. Powered by two 11.5nhp horizontal (high pressure 13" x 48") steam engines. In 1866 she was owned by the Oregon & Montana Transportation Co. (a subsidiary of the Oregon Steam Navigation Co.). In 1870 she was moved through the Heron Rapids to Lake Pend Oreille. In 1876 she was reported as having been dismantled.

Caledonia (Vancouver Island Colonial Register) (sidewheeler) She was built in 1858 at Victoria Vancouver Island (Crown Colony) by James W Trahey. She was powered by a 70hp (20" x 30") oscillating steam engine. In 1858–1859 she was owned by Faulkner, Bell & Co., Victoria, Vancouver Island. Norman R Hacking states that "she is wrongly listed in Lewis & Dryden as the *New Caledonia*." She was launched at the Songhees Village at Victoria Harbour on September 8, 1858, and was based at Victoria, Vancouver Island. She was too small to be profitable. She suffered two boiler explosions. Her boiler exploded November 2, 1859, and the wreck drifted from Plumper Pass to Sucia Island WA where she was salvaged by the *Eliza Anderson*. Her fireman and five others were killed. She was repaired. In November 1865 she was wrecked on the Skeena River.

Caleb Cope[109] (US) (sidewheeler) She was built in 1851 at San Francisco CA USA. Wood. 73gt. Powered by a steam engine. In 1853 she served on the Sacramento River CA. In 1858 she was reported as having been abandoned.

Caledonia 097162 (Canada) (passenger vessel) She was built in 1891 at New Westminster BC Canada by McFee Bros. 100.0' x 25.4' x 4.7' Wood. 237gt 130rt. Powered by two 25hp high pressure steam engines by Albion Iron Works Co. Ltd., Victoria BC. In 1895 she was rebuilt to 132' x 24' x 4.7' 354gt/223rt by being sawn in half and having 30' of new structure spliced-in to the hull. In 1891–1898 she was owned by the Hudson's Bay Co., Victoria BC. She served the Skeena River in 1898. In 1898 she was reported as having been laid up at Port Simpson on the beach, her machinery used in the second *Caledonia*. Eventually the hulk drifted away and broke up.

Caledonia (later *Northwestern*) 107145 (Canada) (passenger/ freight vessel) She was built in 1898 at New Westminster BC Canada by B.C. Iron Works. 142.4' x 30.4' x 4.0' Wood. 569.06gt 358.52rt. Powered by two 17hp high-pressure horizontal steam engines by Albion Iron Works Co. Ltd., Victoria BC. In 1898 she was owned by the Hudson's Bay Co., London UK. In 1907 she was sold to the Caledonia Trading Co. (a Prince Rupert syndicate headed by Major Gibson). She was powered by a steam engine, from a previous *Caledonia* on the Skeena River. In 1903 she was laid up. On August 24, 1908, she was wrecked in the Skeena River BC at Mile Forty-four. Her engines and fittings went to the *Omenica*.

California[110] (US) (sidewheeler) (passenger/ freight vessel) She was built by William H Webb. 203' x 33.5' x 14'. Wood. 1057gt. Powered by a one-cylinder side-lever steam engine built by the Novelty Iron Works, NY. In 1848–1866 she was owned by the Pacific Mail Steamship Company. In 1866–1872 she was owned by California, Oregon & Mexico Steamship Co. In 1872–1874 she was repurchased by the Pacific Mail Steamship Co. In 1874–1874 she was owned by Goodall, Nelson & Perkins. In 1875 she was owned by N Bichard. In 1895 she sank in the Pacific Ocean near Pacasmayo Province, Peru while outbound from Port Haddock WA with a cargo of lumber.

California (US) (sidewheeler) She was built in 1850 in the eastern United States. Wood. 763.50gt. Powered by a steam engine. In 1865 she was owned by Wakeman, Gookin & Dickinson, New York NY. In 1865 she was owned by the California Steam Navigation Co. She operated on the Sacramento River. In 1867 she was owned by the California, Oregon, and Mexico Steamship Co.

California[111] (US) (sidewheeler) She is reported by Murray Lundberg that the mode of her propulsion configuration is not certain and in 1867 to have operated on the Alaska run by the newly formed conglomerate, the North Pacific Transportation Company.

Calliope[112] 005840 (US) (passenger vessel) She was built in 1870 at Corvallis OR USA by SR Smith. 100.0' x 18.5' x 4.0'. Wood. 143.36gt 93.19nt. Powered by two horizontal (high pressure 8" x 30") steam engines. In 1870 she was owned by the Willamette Navigation Co. (Willamette Freighting Co.) In 1887 she was reported as having been broken up at Portland OR.

Camanche[113,114,115] (US) (sidewheeler) (freighter, later a barge) She was built in 1851 in NJ USA. Wood. 148gt. The monitor *Camanche* was shipped out to San Francisco CA from New Jersey in pieces, where she was assembled at Peter Donahue's Union Iron Works. In 1853 she collided with the *J. Bragdon* and sank, with the loss of 10 lives. She was repaired and returned to service. In 1854 she was owned by the California Steam Navigation Co. In 1854–1855 she was owned by the Merchants Line. She operated on the Sacramento River. She was reported as having gone out of service in 1858. Other reports suggest that she was converted to a barge in 1858.

Camano[116] 127303 (US) (passenger vessel) She was built in 1895 at Wenatchee WA by Captain Thomas H. McMillan. 89.6' x 18.5' x 3.9' Wood. 59gt 40nt. Powered by two 4nhp horizontal (high pressure 8" x 36") steam engines. In 1895 she was owned by Captain Thomas H McMillan, Everett WA USA. She was owned by the Columbia & Okanagan Steamboat Co. On May 27, 1904, she was wrecked in the Entiat Rapids. She was later salvaged.

The *Canadian* after having been raised after sinking at Hell's Gate (the tarp covers a hole in the hull) (Image from Maritime Museum of British Columbia 000435)

Canadian 107094 (Canada) (passenger/ freight vessel) She was built in 1898 at Victoria BC Canada by John H Todd. 146.5' x 33.4' x 4.7' Wood. 716.42gt 455.15nt. Powered by a 15hp steam engine by James Reese & Sons, Pittsburgh PA. In 1898–1901 she was owned by the Canadian Development Co. Ltd., Victoria BC. In 1901–1931 she was owned by The British Yukon Navigation Co. Ltd., Vancouver BC. In 1898 she was intended for Wrangel AK service but was diverted to St. Michael AK. In 1918 she sank at

Whitehorse YT. On October 12, 1923, she suffered a fire at Cliff Island BC. She was in Yukon River service. In 1931 her hull was used as riprap in the Yukon River. Her machinery was recovered in 1997.

Canby 127183 (US) (passenger vessel) She was built in 1896 at Portland OR. 78.5' x 14.6' x 5.4' Wood. 59.67gt 49.41nt. She was home ported at Astoria OR. In 1907 she was reported to have been out of service.

Canby 201626 (US) (tug) She was built in 1904 at Keno OR USA. 67.0' x 13.0' x 2.0' Wood. 48gt 30nt. Powered by a steam engine. She was employed in the Coos Bay area.

Canemah (US) (sidewheeler) (freighter) She was built in 1851 at Canemah OT. 135' x 19' x 4' Wood. 88gt. Powered by two 6nhp horizontal (high pressure 10" x 48") steam engines. In 1851 she was owned by Hedges, Bennett et al., Canemah OT. She was in service between Oregon City and Corvallis. In 1853 she experienced a flue explosion. In 1857 she was reported as having been abandoned and in 1858 she was broken up at Canemah OT.

Cannon Ball 127476 (US) (ferry) She was built in 1895 at Rock Haven ND USA. 64.3' x 14.0' x 2.0' Wood. 17gt 17nt. Powered by a gasoline engine. In 1895–1910 she was in service at Pembina ND USA.

Canyon King[117] (US) (tour excursion vessel) She was built in 1972 at Moab UT by Tex McClatchey. Powered by a diesel engine. In 2021 she was owned by Aramark Corp. She was located at Lake Powell and was retired in 2008. Her superstructure was pulled ashore at Page AZ and is now the Canyon King Pizzeria restaurant.

Capt. Weber[118] 126869 (US) (passenger/ freight vessel) She was built in 1892 at San Francisco CA. 174.5' x 36.5' x 8.0' Wood. 612.71gt 501nt. Powered by a 350ihp steam engine. She operated on the California delta rivers. She played a role as the "Cumnerland" in the 1943 Bing Crosby Hollywood film "Dixie". In 1943 she was destroyed by fire at Stockton CA in a conflagration that that included several other old riverboats.

Capital[119,120] (US) (sidewheeler) She was built in 1866 at San Francisco CA USA by John G North. 277' Wood. 1,989.20gt. Powered by a steam engine.

In 1866 she was owned by the California Steam Navigation Co. In 1871 she was taken over by the California Pacific Railroad Co., San Francisco CA. She was reported to have been broken up in 1896.

Capital City (see *Dalton*)

Capital City[121] (later *Port of Stockton*) 208044 (US) (passenger vessel) She was built in 1910 at San Francisco CA USA by Schultze, Robertson & Schultz, Inc. 220.0' x 42.6' x 9.3' Wood. 1142gt 701nt. Powered by a 1242ihp steam engine. In 1910–1929 she was owned by the California Transportation Co., San Francisco CA USA. She was in service on the California delta rivers. She played a part in the 1933 Hollywood movie "Mandalay". In 1942 she was owned by the United States Navy as housing barge YHB-2 at Mare Island Navy Yard, Vallejo, CA. In 1947 she was transferred to the United States War Shipping Administration for disposal. She was purchased by theatrical manager Barney Gould with the intention of converting her to a floating restaurant/nightclub. On March 14, 1952, she was partially sunk during storm in China Basin, San Francisco harbor. She was broken up in situ by the Sherman Crane Service of Oakland, in the fall of 1958.

Capitol[122] 005181 (US) She was built in 1866 at San Francisco CA USA. 377.3' x 47.0' x 10.9' Wood. 1625gt. Powered by a steam engine. On October 19, 1868, the *Capitol* deliberately collided with the *Colusa* near Collinsville CA to eliminate her competition. In 1896 she was reported as having been abandoned.

Capitol[123] 125486 (US) She was built in 1876 at Olympia WT USA. 54.0' x 24.0' x 3.0' Wood. 54.39gt. Powered by a 10nhp steam engine.

Captain Sutter[124] (US) (sidewheeler) (freighter) She was built in 1849 at Yerba Buena CA USA by Domingo Marcucci. Wood. 51gt. In 1849 she was owned by the Aspinwall Steam Transportation Line. In 1853 she served on the Sacramento River CA. In 1854 she was owned by the California Steam Navigation Co. She operated on California rivers. In October 1855 she sank at her berth but was not repaired owing to her poor overall condition. In 1856 she was reported as having been abandoned.

Car Float No. 2 202027 (US) (freighter) She was built in 1905 at Oakland CA. 265.5' x 50.2' x 13.9' Wood. 1374gt 1374nt. Powered by a 600ihp steam engine. In 1905–1913 she was in service on San Francisco Bay.

Cariboo 064140 (Canada) (sidewheeler) (later *Fly*; then *Cariboo Fly*) 130.2' x 22.3' x 6.4' Wood. 199.85gt She was built in 1860 at Victoria, Vancouver Island (Crown Colony) by Captain Archibald Jamieson. In 1861 she was owned by Captain Archibald Jamieson, Victoria Vancouver Island. On her second voyage, in 1861, her boiler exploded killing her master/owner and many others. She was laid up until 1866 when she was sold to the McDougal Bros., Victoria, British Columbia. She was sold to Moody, Nelson & Co. In 1874 she was owned by Hugh Nelson, Victoria BC. In 1875 she was sold to Captain Spratt. In 1888 as a wreck, she was sold to L Goodacre, refloated, and repaired in Victoria BC. In 1892–1894 she was sold to the Royal Canadian Canning Co., Victoria BC. In 1896 she was owned by R Cunningham, Skeena BC. She was rebuilt as the *Cariboo Fly*. In 1866 she was severely damaged in an explosion. In 1875 she was put into service on the northern route. In 1894 she was laid up.

Cariboo Fly (see *Cariboo*)

Caribou 208963 (US) (passenger/ freight vessel) She was built in 1910 at Fairbanks AK USA. 57' x 14.9' x 3.0' Wood. 46gt 28nt. Powered by a 21ihp steam engine. She is reported by Murray Lundberg to have worked in Alaska/YT with home port at Eagle AK.

Carl White (US) (freighter) Wood. Powered by a steam engine. She was reported to have operated on the Yukon River. Murray Lundberg reports that her namesake, Carl White, was active in Alaska mining just prior to the First World War but he has seen no mention of a steamboat being involved.

Carnation No. 1[125] 205698 (US) (freighter) She was built by Ward & Sons. 55.5' x 12.4' x 3.2' Wood. 14gt 9nt. (Designed by Lee & Brinton). Powered by a 50hp gasoline engine built by the Frisco Standard Engine Co. In 1908–1910 she was owned by the Carnation Dairy, Mt. Vernon WA USA. This shallow draft vessel was used to collect fresh milk from dairy farms on the Skagit River and deliver it to the Carnation plant for processing.

Carnation No. 2[126] 205517 (US) (freighter) She was built by Ward & Sons. 55.5' x 12.4' x 3.2'. Wood. 14gt 9nt. (Designed by Lee & Brinton). Powered by a 50hp gasoline engine built by the Frisco Standard Engine Co. In 1908–1910 she was owned by the Carnation Dairy, Mt. Vernon WA USA. This shallow draft vessel was used to collect fresh milk from dairy farms on the Skagit river and deliver it to the Carnation plant for processing.

Carolina (US) (freighter) Wood. Powered by a steam engine. She was built about 1849. In the 1850s she operated on the upper Sacramento River CA.

Caroline[127] 005428 (US) (freighter) She was built in 1868 at Union City CA USA by CM Wylie. 104.0' x 25.0' x 4.3'. Wood. 182.56gt 162.32nt. Powered by a 35nhp steam engine. She operated on California rivers. In 1917 she was reported to have sunk.

Carquinez 005179 (US) (freighter) In 1854 she was built at Martinez CA USA. Wood. 97gt. Powered by a steam engine. In 1881 she was reported as having been abandoned.

Carrie (see *Rainier*)

Carrie Davis 005122 (US) (freighter) She was built in 1867 at Canemah OT. Wood. 29gt. Powered by a steam engine. She was reported as having been abandoned in 1869.

Carrie Ladd[128,129] (US) (passenger vessel, later a barge) She was built in 1858 at Oregon City OR USA by John T Thomas. 126.0' x 24.4' x 4.6'. Wood. 128gt. Powered by two 17nhp horizontal (high pressure 16" x 66") steam engines. In 1858 she was owned by John C Ainsworth and Jacob Kamm, Oregon City OT. She is thought to have been the second sternwheeler constructed in Oregon. She was in service on the Columbia River and the Willamette River. In 1860 she was owned by the Oregon Steam Navigation Co. On June 3, 1862, she hit a rock and sank at Cape Horn on the Columbia River. She was dismantled in 1864 and converted to a barge. Her engines went to the *Nez Perce Chief*.

Carrie Norton[130] 125657 (US) She was built in 1878 at Canemah OR USA by JH Bonsor. 40.5' x 13.4' x 2.6'. Wood. 13gt. She was powered by a steam engine. In 1878 she was owned by W Bonsor and TA Bonsor. In 1880 she was reported to have been out of service.

Casca 103919 (Canada) (passenger/ freight vessel) She was built in 1898 at Esquimalt BC Canada by the Esquimalt Marine Railway Co. 140.0' x 30.5' x 5.0' Wood. 590gt 364rt. Powered by a 480ihp steam reciprocating engine built by Albion Iron Works, Victoria BC. In 1912 she was rebuilt in at Whitehorse YT to 161.0' x 37.0' x ? 1079t. In 1898 she was owned by the Casca Trading & Transportation Co. Ltd. She worked the Stikine River in 1898–1899. In 1899–1901 she was owned by Otto R Bremner. In 1901 she was owned by Bremner & Adair Bros., Dawson YT for Yukon River service in 1901. In 1903 she was owned by the Ironside, Rennie & Campbell Co. In 1904–1931 she was owned by The British Yukon Navigation Co., Vancouver BC. On July 9, 1936, she was wrecked when she hit a rock at Rink Rapids on the Yukon River and beached at Dawson City YT. Her engine was used in the second *Casca*.

Casca 170613 (Canada) (freighter) In 1936 she was built at Whitehorse YT by the White Pass & Yukon Railway. 180.0' x 36.5' x 5.6' Wood. 1300.27gt 1033.32rt. In 1936 she was owned by The British Yukon Navigation Co., Vancouver BC. In 1960 she was transferred to the Canadian Government. In 1958 she was owned by the British Yukon Navigation Co. Ltd., Vancouver BC. During the Second World War she carried equipment and supplies in support of the construction of the Alaska Highway. She was powered by a steam engine from the first *Casca*. She was last used in 1951.

Cascade 005263 (US) (passenger vessel, later a tug) She was built 1864 at Utsalady WT USA. 155' x 27.5' x 5.9' Wood. 538gt 401nt. Powered by two horizontal (high pressure 16" x 72") steam engines. She was later re-engined with two horizontal (high pressure 18.5" x 72" steam engines). In 1864 she was owned by the Washington Territory Transportation Co. (Donohue, Kohl & Ankeny). She was employed on the Columbia River. In 1865 she was taken over by the Oregon Steam Navigation Co. She was owned by the North Pacific Lumber Co. and employed as a tug. She was reported to have been dismantled about 1870 at Portland OT.

Cascade 125720 (US) 077976 (Canada) She was built in 1879 at Seattle WA USA by JFT Mitchell. 129.3' x 26.5' x 4.7' Wood. 288.51gt 312rt. Powered by 150hp 16" x 72" 17nhp steam engines. In 1879 she was re-registered in Canada as the *Cassiar*. 131' x 26.3' x 4.8' 290gt. In 1882 she was rebuilt 462 tons. In 1879 she was owned by WJ Stephens, in Puget Sound service. In 1880 she was owned by Captain Nat H Lane Jr. She was owned by Captain William Moore. In 1884 she was owned by Port Townsend WA USA interests. In 1881 she was in service on the Fraser River. On April 12, 1882, she was wrecked near Hope BC. She was re-built to 462gt. 383rt. Afterwards she was employed on the Yukon River.

Cascade 200816 (US) (passenger vessel) She was built in 1904 at Snohomish WA. 54.9' x 11.4' x 3.2' Wood. 34gt 21nt. Powered by a steam engine. She was employed in Puget Sound.

Cascades[131,132] 127751 (US) (work boat, later a tug) She was built in 1882 at Portland OR. 160' x 28.5' x 5.6' Wood. 451gt 267nt. Powered by two 26.6nhp horizontal (high pressure 20" x 72") steam engines. In 1882 she was owned by the United States Army Corps of Engineers. She was employed as a workboat on the construction of the Cascade Locks and the construction of the South Jetty at the mouth of the Columbia River. She was employed by the North Pacific Lumber Co. towing logs. In 1909 she was owned by the Shaver Transportation Co. (Red Collar fleet). She was rebuilt in 1912.

Cascades of the Columbia[133] 209586 (US) (tug) She was built in 1912 at Portland OR by Charles M Nelson. 160' x 30.8' x 6.5' Wood. 407gt 350nt. Powered by two 26.6nhp horizontal (high pressure 20" x 72") steam engines. In 1912 she was owned by the Shaver Transportation Co. (Red Collar fleet). In 1935 she was employed as an excursion boat and later between Portland and the Bonneville Dam construction. In 1942 she was employed towing in Willamette River shipyards. In 1943 she was destroyed by an explosion and fire while assisting a ship into the Swan Island de-perming station. (She was often referred to by the shortened name "Cascades.")

Cascadilla[134] (US) (freighter) She was built in 1862 at Columbus WT. 106' x 18' x 3.5' Wood. Powered by two 4nhp horizontal (high pressure 8" x 30") steam engines. In 1862 she was owned by Gray, Kummel & Robbins. In 1866 she was reported to have been broken up. Her engines were reported to have gone to a Clarks Fork vessel. (Her name is sometimes spelled as *Kaskadilla*.)

Cassiar 125720 (see *Cascade*)

Caswell 200002 (US) (freighter) She was built in 1903 at Olympia WA USA. 70.6' x 17' x 4' Wood. 95gt 62nt. Powered by a steam engine. In 1903–1909 she was employed on the Copper River AK.

Catharine[135] 222841 (US) (tug) She was built in 1923 at Portland OR USA by WH Gray, Jacob Kemmel and James Robbins. 112' x 25.4' x 3.4' composite hull 95gt 70nt. Powered by two 4nhp (8" x 30") 325ihp steam engines. In 1923–1941 she was owned by the Columbia Contract Co. She was reported to have been used for towing until about 1941.

Cayuse[136] (US) She was built in the Oregon Territory USA. Wood. Powered by a steam engine. In 1865c she was owned by Leonard White. She was employed on the Celilo to Lewiston route.

Cazadero 127756 (US) (sidewheeler) (ferry) She was built in 1903 at Alameda CA USA by the JW Dickie Shipyard. 228.5' x 38.0' x 17.0' Wood. 1682gt 991nt. Powered by a 1600ihp steam engine. In 1903–1910 she was owned by the Northwestern Pacific Railroad. In 1942 she was reported as having been broken up.

Centennial[137] 125529 (US) (freighter) She was built in 1876 at Stockton CA USA by Stephen Davis. 155.5' x 45.3' x 6.3' Wood. 559.5gt 504.66nt. Powered by a 290nhp steam engine. She operated on California rivers. She was reported as having gone out of service about 1895.

Ceres[138] 125537 (US) (sidewheeler) (freighter) She was built in 1876. 130.5' x 30.5' x 3.5' Wood. 201.80gt 160.54nt. Powered by a 160nhp steam engine. She operated on California rivers. She was reported to have gone out of service about 1899.

Champion[139] (British Columbia Colonial Register) (freighter) She was built in 1860 at Seton Lake British Columbia (Crown Colony) 110.0' x 22.0' x ? Wood. Powered by a steam engine. In 1860 she was owned by Taylor & Company. She was in service on Seton Lake. In 1863 she was retired. She was replaced by the *Seaton*.

Champion[140] 125429 (US) She was built in 1875 at Oregon City OR USA. 100.0' x 22.0' x ? Wood. 634.09gt 502.25rt. Powered by a steam engine. In 1875 her installed engine came from the one salvaged from the wreck of the *Shoshone* on the Snake River. In 1875 she was owned by the Willamette River Transportation Co. She was rebuilt to 157' x 35' x 5.6' Wood. 634.09gt 502.25nt. Powered by two 17nhp horizontal (high pressure 16" x 48") steam engines. (Her engines came from the *Shoshone*). In 1891 she was wrecked on Lambert's Bar.

Chance (US) (freighter) She was built in 1849c. Wood. Powered by a steam engine. In the 1850s she was reported to have been in service on the California delta rivers.

Charles Bureau[141] 205193 (US) (passenger vessel) She was built in 1908 at Okanagan WA. 80' x 18' x 2.7' Wood. 99gt 56nt. Powered by 50ihp steam engine. In 1908–1912 she was owned by Captain Charles Bureau. She was in service between Brewster and Riverside. In 1919 she was reported to have been abandoned.

Charles H. Spencer (US) She was built in 1912 at Warm Creek AZ. 92.5' x 25' x ? Wood. Powered by a steam engine. She made a few trips on the Colorado River hauling coal but late in 1912 she was reported as having been employed at Lee's Ferry AZ.

Charles R. Spencer[142] (later *Monarch*) 127574 (US) (freighter) She was built in 1901 at Portland OR USA. 181' x 31' x 6' Wood. 598gt 409nt. Powered by two 26.6nhp horizontal (high pressure 20" x 96") steam engines. In 1901 she was owned by Captain EW Spencer. She was employed on the Portland – The Dalles route. She was owned by the Open River Navigation Co. and in 1911 renamed as the *Monarch*. In 1914 she was reported to have been transferred to California.

Charlotte 103909 (Canada) (passenger/ freight vessel) She was built in 1895 at Quesnelle BC Canada by Alec Watson Jr. 111.4' x 20.6' x 4.6' Wood. 217gt 79rt. Powered by a 10nhp compound steam (11" x 60") engine built by the B.C. Iron Works, Vancouver BC. In 1895 she was owned by the North British Columbia Navigation Co. She was in service between Soda Creek and Quesnel. In 1898–1901 she was owned by John Irving, Victoria BC. In 1910 she was owned by the North British Columbia Navigation Co. Ltd., Vancouver BC. She was launched August 3, 1896. In the winter of 1896, she was at Steamboat Landing, but the lay-up was occupied by the *Victoria*. The *Victoria* was purchased and demolished to make room for the *Charlotte*. On July 15, 1910, she hit a rock in Fort George Canyon and sank. She was brought back to Quesnel and was abandoned there. The boiler was salvaged and used in a sawmill at Quesnel and later abandoned. The boiler was put back into operation in the 1930s in the Cariboo Gold Quartz Mine at Wells, operating until the 1940s.

Charlotte (Image from Vancouver Archives AM54–S4–Bo P265)

Charm[143] (US) (freighter) Wood. Powered by a steam engine. She was reported to have operated on the Cowlitz River for the Lewis River Co.

Chas H. Hamilton 127290 (US) (passenger/ freight vessel) She was built in 1903 at Olympia WA USA by the Moran Bros. & John T Goulett. In 1898 she was assembled at Dutch Harbor AK for service in the Klondike Gold Rush. 190.0' x 38.0' x 5.6' Wood. 595gt 297nt. Powered by two horizontal high pressure (20" x 84") steam engines. In 1903 she was owned by the North American Transportation & Trading Co. In 1911 she was owned by the Northern Navigation Co. In 1914 she was owned by the White Pass & Yukon Rail Road. In 1927 she was reported as having been laid up at St. Michael AK. She was a sister vessel to the *John Cudahy* and the *T.C. Power*.

Chas. R. Spencer 127574 (US) (passenger vessel) In 1901 she was built at Portland OR. 181.0' x 31.0' x 6.0'. Wood. 598gt 409nt. Powered by a steam engine. In 1901–1910 she was owned by Portland OR USA interests.

Cheam 117153 (Canada) (freighter) She was built in 1905 at Harrison Mills BC Canada by Captain Dick Fullbrook. 105.0' x 22.0' x 4.3'. Wood. 285gt 180rt. Powered by a 21nhp steam engine. She was powered by steam engine from the steamer *Courser*. In 1905 she was owned by Captain Dick Fullbrook, Harrison Mills BC. In 1908–1910 she was owned by the Chilliwack Shingle Manufacturers Co. Ltd., Harrison River BC. In 1906 she was wrecked on the Fraser River BC.

Chehalis[144] 005694 (US) She was built in 1867 at Tumwater WT. 90'. Wood. 87.97gt. Powered by two 25ihp horizontal (high pressure 10" x 36") steam engines. She was employed on the Puget Sound. She was reported to have been lost in 1883.

Chelan[145,146] 127647 (US) She was built in 1902 at Wenatchee WA. 125.1' x 20.5' x 4.9'. Wood. 244gt 154nt. Powered by two horizontal (high pressure 10" x 24") steam engines. (Her engines were built in 1895 by DM Swain at Stillwater MN from the *Ruth* 111113). In 1902 she was owned by JD Miller and CS Miller. She was employed between Wenatchee and Riverside. On July 8, 1915, while owned by the Columbia & Okanogan Steamboat Co. she was destroyed by fire at Wenatchee WA when the company's fleet was destroyed by a massive fire.

Cherokee[147] 210046 (US) (freighter) She was built in 1912 at Oakland CA. 179.2' x 40.2' x 7.0'. Wood. 741gt 609nt. Powered by a steam engine. She served the California river delta. She was owned by the Southern Pacific Railroad Co. She was reported to have been abandoned in 1939.

Chester[148] 127201 (US) (passenger vessel) She was built in 1897 at Portland OR by Joseph Supple. 101' x 20.9' x 3.8'. Wood. 130gt 98nt. Powered by two horizontal (high pressure 6" x 24") steam engines. In 1897 she was owned by Joseph Kellogg and Captain Oren. She was employed on the Cowlitz River. In 1917 she was reported to have been abandoned at Kelso WA.

Cheyenne[149,150] (US) (passenger/ freight vessel) (sidewheeler) She was built in 1873 at Grand Forks, Dakota Territory USA by DP Reeves. 120' x 20' x 2' Wood. 136.44gt. Powered by two 13.2hp (high pressure) 13.2hp steam engines built by Coming & Dupree, St. Paul MN USA. Repowered with two horizontal (high pressure) 27.84hp steam engines by Delorme & Co., St. Paul MN USA. In 1873 she was owned by the Red River Transportation Co. In 1874 she was employed on the Red River, (Winnipeg to Lower Fort Garry), for the Kittson Line. In 1878 she was owned by the Winnipeg & Western Transportation Co., Winnipeg MB. In 1881 she was amalgamated with the Hudson's Bay Co., London UK. In 1882 she was owned by Edward Janvier & G Barridger. In 1884 she was owned by Douglas MacArthur. On June 2, 1885, she was stranded and wrecked at Ste. Agathe MB. She was reported as having been broken up at Winnipeg MB.

Chicu San (see *Putah*)

Chila Chula 134040 (Canada) She was built in 1913 at South Fort George BC Canada. 65.5' x 16.4' x 3' Wood. 101gt 64rt. Powered by 2hp steam engine. In 1913–1919 she was owned by the Fort George Trading & Lumber Co. Ltd., Fort George BC. She was powered by steam engines from the Fort Fraser. She was dismantled in 1919.

Chilco (see *Necchacco*)

Chilcotin 126945 (Canada) (passenger/ freight vessel) She was built in 1910 at Soda Creek BC Canada by Donald McPhee. She was launched July 20, 1910. 134.5' x 23.5' x 4.5' Wood. 435gt 273rt. Powered by a 21hp steam engine built by the J. Doty Engineering Co., Toronto ON. In 1910 she was owned by the Fort George Lumber & Navigation Co. She went out of service in 1914. In 1914–1918 she was owned by John K McLennan and Alan J Damson, Winnipeg MB. In 1917 she was sold with the assets of the Fort George Lumber & Navigation Co. In 1919–1931 she was owned by John K McLennan and Alan J Adamson, Winnipeg MB. She worked in competition with the B.X. on the Soda Creek to South Fort George service. In 1920 she was reported broken up but was still in the registry of shipping in 1931.

Chin-Du-Wan[151,152,153] (US) (sidewheeler) (freighter) She was built in 1868 at Stockton CA USA by Stephen Davis. 155' Wood. 181.54gt. Powered by a steam engine. She was owned by the California Transportation Co. In 1871 she was taken over by the California Pacific Railroad Co., San Francisco CA. She carried farm produce on the Sacramento River.

China (US) (sidewheeler) (passenger vessel) She was built in 1889 at Govan Scotland by Fairfield Shipbuilding & Engineering Co. 440.4' x 48.1' x 32.8' Steel. 5,000gt 3186nt. Powered by a 5,500ihp steam engine. In 1889 she was owned by UK interests. She was later registered in Hawaii. In 1915 she was owned by the Atlantic Transport Co. In 1915 she was owned by the China Mail Steamship Co. She was employed in Pacific Mail's pioneering trans-Pacific route between San Francisco and Yokohama, with service also to Shanghai China. In 1923 she was reported to have been laid up and in 1925 she was broken up at Kowloon, Hong Kong.

Chinega 127738 (US) (freighter) She was built in 1903 at San Francisco CA USA. 111.0' x 25.0' x 5.0' Wood. 188gt 167nt. Powered by 125ihp steam engine. In 1903–1910 she was owned by San Francisco CA interests.

Chitina (see *Chittyana*)

Chittyana[154] (later *Chitina*) 203855 (US) 110' x 23' x 1.9' Wood. 187gt 169nt. double decker Built in 1907 at Portland OR by Joe Supple. Her frames and fittings were shipped to Valdez AK where she was assembled at the confluence of the Copper and Tasnuna Rivers. She was launched in July 1907 on the Copper River, Alaska by Captain George Hill. She was employed on the Copper and Chitini Rivers, Alaska. In 1907 she was owned by the Copper River and Northwestern Railway. She was hauled in pieces through Keystone Canyon and over Marshall Pass and floated down the Tasnuna River, in the dead of winter.

Christiana[155] (US) (freighter) She was built in 1860 in California. Wood. Powered by a steam engine. In 1860–1885 she was in operation on the San

Joaquin and Tuolumne Rivers, CA. In 1860 she was owned by the Ling Bros. She was reported to have gone out of service in 1868.

Christine W.[156] (see *Newport Landing Belle*)

Chrysopolis[157,158,159] (later *Oakland*) 019447 (US) (sidewheeler) (US) She was built in 1860 at San Francisco CA by John G North, for $200,000. 245' x 40' x ? Wood. 1086 tons. She was known as the 'Queen of the Sacramento.' 'Chrysopolis' means 'Golden City.' She could carry 1,000 passengers. In 1860 she was owned by the California Steam Navigation Co. She was employed on the Sacramento to San Francisco route, and on the California delta. In 1871 she was taken over by the California Pacific Railroad Co., San Francisco CA. After the silting up of the Sacramento River, the *Chrysopolis* was moved to San Francisco Bay. She was rebuilt and became, in 1875, the ferry, *Oakland* (19447). She served as an Oakland – San Francisco ferry until the completion of the Oakland – San Francisco Bay Bridge. She was reported as having been broken up and burned in 1940.

City of Aberdeen[160] (later *Vashon*) 126766 (US) (passenger vessel) She was built in 1891 at Aberdeen WA USA. 127' x 19.5' x 6' Wood. 244.gt 128.27nt. Powered by a 125ihp steam engine. She was employed as a ferry on the Fauntleroy to Vashon to Harper route. She was converted to a propeller tug, in 1905, renamed as the *Vashon*. 149.0' x 25.0' x 6.8' Wood. 342gt 202nt. In 1911 she was destroyed by fire at Anacortes WA USA.

City of Ainsworth 096998 (Canada) (passenger vessel) She was built in 1892 at Ainsworth BC Canada by Samuel Lovatt. 84.0' x 21.0' x 4.2' Wood. 193gt 122nt. Powered by a 6.6nhp steam engine built by the Charles P. Willard & Co., Chicago IL USA. In 1892 she was owned by Samuel Lovatt, Ainsworth BC. In 1920 she was owned by David Bremner, John Watson & William Jevons. In 1892 she was owned by the Nelson & Lardeau Steam Navigation Co. She was on the Nelson, Kaslo and Lardeau service. She was sold to George T Kane. In 1896 she was owned by John Patterson, Nelson BC. In 1898 she was owned by W Marshall, Kootenay BC. In 1898 she was sold to Braden Bros., Helena MT USA. She was chartered by International Navigation & Trading Co. on the Nelson to Bonners Ferry service. In April 1897 she foundered in Kootenay Lake off Kaslo BC. She was raised and sold.

On November 29, 1898, she capsized off Pilot Bay, BC in a storm with a loss of nine lives. (Her wreck has been designated as a protected heritage site by the Province of British Columbia.)

City of Boston[161] (US) (passenger/ freight vessel) She was built in 1898 at Seattle WA USA by CN Patterson. 121' x 24' x ? Wood. Powered by a steam engine. In 1898 she was owned by the Chace Line.

City of Bradford[162] 127288 (US) (passenger/ freight vessel) She was built in 1898 at St. Michael AK USA. 44.0' x 11.0' x 3.2' Wood. 39gt. Powered by a steam engine.

City of Champagne (see *Henry Bailey*)

City of Chicago 127296 (US) (passenger/ freight vessel) She was built in 1898 at St. Michael AK USA. 85' Wood. 142gt. Powered by a steam engine. Murray Lundberg states that "In June 1898, the British American Line claimed that she, and four other river steamers, would connect at St. Michael with their steamer *Garonne*. On September 18, 1898, she was reported as being seen by a passenger on the *May West*. He is not certain if this was a sternwheeler or a propeller.

City of Corinne[163] (later *General Garfield*) (US) She was built in 1871 at the Bear River UT. (She was prefabricated at Sacramento CA and shipped to Utah by rail for assembly). 130' x 28' Wood. 300gt. Powered by two steam engines built by Girard B. Allen & Co., St. Louis MO. (She had accommodation for 150 persons). In 1871 she was owned by the Corinne Steam Navigation Co., Corinne City UT. After one season of operation, she was considered by her owners to have been a failure. She was sold to H.S. Jacobs & Co. In 1875 she was owned by John Young (the son of Brigham Young), Salt Lake City Utah. It was owned by Thomas Douris who berthed her at the Garfield Beach Resort on Great Salt Lake. Her machinery was removed, and she became a floating hotel, a bather changing room, a boathouse for the Great Salt Lake Rowing Club. In 1904 she was destroyed by fire with the Garfield Beach Resort. Her remains were buried by the roadbed of the Western Pacific Railroad and later by the construction of the Interstate 80 highway.

City of Dawson[164,165] 127256 (US) (freighter) She was built in 1898 at San Francisco CA USA. 114.0' x 26.2' x 5.5' Wood. 230.93gt 206nt. Powered by a 300ihp steam engine. She was employed on California rivers. On March 31, 1901, while alongside at a wharf in San Francisco she was hit by the ferry *Tamalpias*, carried out of control by the rip current. She suffered considerable damage. She was reported to have gone out of operation about 1911. She is reported by Murray Lundberg to have worked in Alaska/YT in 1898.

City of Dixon[166] (US) (passenger/ freight vessel) She was built in 1912. 75' x 16' x ? Wood. Powered by a 65ihp steam engine. In 1912 she was owned by Dixon & Sloan Transportation Co. She was employed carrying passengers and freight between Dixon and Buffalo Ferry on the lower Flathead River. In 1914 she was reported to have been destroyed by fire.

City of Edmonton (Image from the Provincial Archives of Alberta)

City of Edmonton (later *Edmonton Riverboat*) 126448 (Canada) (passenger/ freight vessel) She was built in 1909 at Strathcona AB Canada. 132' x 26.8' x 4' Wood. 301gt 190rt. Powered by a 9nhp steam engine. In 1909–1931 she was owned by the John Walter Ltd., Edmonton AB. She was reported as having been employed at Edmonton AB in 1918 where she was reported to have been abandoned.

City of Ellensburg[167] 126511 (US) She was built in 1888 at Pasco WA USA. 120.2' x 22.9' x 4.5' Wood. 213.68gt 188.92nt. Powered by two 9.6nhp horizontal (high pressure 12" x 36") steam engines. In 1888 she was owned by

Nixon & Post Thomas L Nixon). In 1888–1893 she was the only steamer operating on the upper Columbia River. In 1892 she was owned by MS Donohue & JR Peters. In 1893 she was owned by the Columbia & Okanagan Steamboat Co. In 1893 she was re-engined. In 1896 she was operating on Lake Chelan. In 1899 she was reported to have been laid up and dismantled. Her machinery went to the Selkirk (116844).

City of Eugene[168] 127330 (US) She was built in 1894 at Eugene OR. 130' x 27.5' x 4.5' Wood. 339gt 214nt. Powered by two horizontal (high pressure 11.75" x 60") steam engines. In 1894 she was owned by the Eugene Transportation Co. In 1918 she was reported to be out of service.

City of Frankfort[169] (ex-Traveler) 145181 (US) (passenger vessel) She was built as the Traveler in 1878 at Willamette OR USA. 124.9' x 22.3 x 4.5' Wood. 238.4gt 145.16rt. Powered by two 13nhp horizontal (high pressure 14" x 48") steam engines. In 1878 she was owned by Lewis Love. In 1889 she was rebuilt at Portland OR to 124.9' x 22.3' x 4.5' Wood. 238.4gt 145.16rt. In 1891 she was rebuilt again as the City of Frankfort (126723).

City of Frankfort[170] (later H.C. Grady) 126723 (US) (passenger vessel) She was built in 1891 at Clatskanie OR. 125' x 20' x 7' Wood. 184.87gt 133.47nt. Powered by a 13nhp (14" x 48") steam engine. In 1891 she was owned by FM Leavens, Portland OR. In 1895 she was renamed and re-registered as the H.C. Grady (96316).

City of Klamath[171] (US) (freighter) She was built in 1884 at Klamath Lake OR. Wood. Powered by a steam engine.

City of Moab (later Cliff Dweller; then Vista) (US) She was built in 1905 at Halvorsan Utah. 70' x 20' x ? Wood. Powered originally by a screw and a gasoline engine she was rebuilt as the Cliif Dweller. She was later renamed as the Vista and moved to the Salt Lake, Utah.

City of Paris[172] 127219 (US) (passenger/ freight vessel) She was built in 1898 at Seattle WA USA. 120' x 26' x ? Wood. 300gt 189nt. Powered by a steam engine. In 1898 she was owned by the Missouri-Alaska Gold Co. In 1898 she was owned by the Paris-Alaska Mining Corp. She is thought to have been towed north with the *Lotta Talbot*. In 1899–1901 she was owned by the Alaska Commercial Co. where she was in Yukon River Service for the CPR in 1898. On October 13, 1901, she was destroyed by fire at Bergman AK USA.

City of Prince Albert 122291 (Canada) (passenger vessel) She was built in 1906 at Prince AlberT SK Canada. 96' x 20' x 4.5'. Wood. 89gt 14rt. Powered by a 6nhp engine. In 1906–1914 she was owned by Prince Albert Lumber Co. Ltd. Prince Albert SK. In 1918 she was owned by Mandy Mines. In 1919 she was owned by George R Bancroft, The Pas MB.

City of Providence (US) (passenger/ freight vessel) She was built in 1898 at Seattle WA USA by CN Patterson. 137' x 33' x ? Wood. Powered by a steam engine. In 1898 she was owned by the Chace Line.

City of Quesnel (later *Quesnel*) 126245 (Canada) (passenger vessel) She was built in 1909 at Quesnel BC Canada by John Strand. 70.0' x 16.2' x 3.7'. Wood. 130gt 76rt. Powered by a 3hp steam engine. In 1909 she was rebuilt by Donald McPhee and relaunched September 2, 1909. In 1909–1937 she was owned by Telesphore Marion, Quesnel BC. She was the last steam sternwheeler to serve on the Upper Fraser River. In April 1921 she was wrecked at Fort George Canyon BC.

City of Quincy 125701 (US) (passenger vessel) She was built in 1878 at Willamette OR USA. 109.4' x 22.4' x 4.4'. Wood. 195.4gt. Powered by two 9.6nhp horizontal (12" x 48" high pressure) steam engines. In 1878 she was owned by UB Scott. She was employed on the Lewis River, then moved in 1882 to Puget Sound. In 1900 she was reported to have been broken up on the Snohomish River.

City of St. Boniface 130280 (Canada) (passenger vessel) She was built in 1913 at Winnipeg MB Canada. 100' x 30' x 4'. Wood. 314gt 163rt. Powered by a 13nhp engine. In 1913–1931 she was owned by Lake Winnipeg Shipping Co. Ltd., Winnipeg MB.

City of Salem 125466 (US) (passenger vessel) She was built in 1875 Portland OR USA. 151.0' x 32.9' x 4.6'. Wood. 456.65gt 423.73nt. Powered by two 913nhp horizontal (14" x 48" high pressure) steam engines. She was employed on the Willamette River. In 1875 she was owned by UB Scott et al. In 1895 she was reported to have been broken up at Portland OR.

City of Sault Ste. Marie[173] 012827 (US) (freighter) In 1898 she was built at Hooper Bay AK. (She was fabricated in Seattle but assembled in Alaska). 100' x 18' x ? Wood. Powered by a steam engine. In 1899 she was owned by the North American Transportation & Trading Co. In 1899 she was reported to have been broken up in Dawson City YT.

City of Seattle 126536 (US) (sidewheeler) (ferry) She was built in 1888 at Portland OR USA by John Steffen. 121.5' x 33.2' x 8.6' Wood. 272gt 186nt. Powered by a steam engine. In 1888–1900 she was owned by the Washington State Land and Improvement Co., Seattle WA.

City of Shelton[174] 127066 (US) (passenger vessel) She was built in 1895 at Shelton WA. 99.8' x 20.5' x 6' Wood. 190gt 138nt. Powered by a 300ihp steam engine. She was employed between Olympia and Shelton WA. In 1921 she was reported to have been abandoned.

City of Stanwood[175] 126865 (US) (freighter) She was built in 1892 at Stanwood WA. 101' x 24.3' x 5.3' Wood. 199.87gt 124.8nt. Powered by a 110ihp steam engine. In 1894 she was destroyed by fire.

City of Stockton[176] 125563 (US) (freighter) She was built in 1873 at Stockton CA USA by Stephen Davis. 175.0' x 50.8' x 8.1' Wood. 823.70gt 743.97. Powered by a 450ihp steam engine. She was employed on California rivers. She was reported to have gone out of existence about 1915.

City of Vancouver 206015 (US) (sidewheeler) (ferry) She was built in 1909 at St. Johns OR USA. 142.2' x 34.7' x 8.5' Wood. 400gt 398nt. Powered by a 300ihp steam engine. She was employed on the Columbia River system until about 1915.

City of Windermere (see Alert)

Claire (US) She was built in 1918 at Portland OR USA by Charles M Nelson. 157.3' x 34.3' x 5.6' Wood. 563gt 486nt. Powered by two 17nhp horizontal (16" x 84" high pressure) 450ihp steam engines. In 1918 she was owned by the Willamette Navigation Co. She was owned by the Western Transportation Co. She was employed on the Willamette River. Edward L Affleck states that in 1952 she was dismantled and burned at Portland OR. Rebecca Harrison states that in 1952 she was converted to a floating shop and later, on October 9, 1961, she was destroyed by fire near Hayden Island.

Clan McDonald 126763 (US) (ferry) She was built in 1891 at Aberdeen WA USA. 95.2' x 24.7' x 5.5' Wood. 230.48gt 118.13nt. Powered by a 100nhp steam engine. She was in service carrying freight in Puget Sound. She is reported by Murray Lundberg to have worked in Alaska/YT in 1898.

Clara[177] (US) (freighter, later a ferry) She was built in 1854. Wood. 41gt. Powered by a steam engine. She was employed on California rivers. She was employed briefly as a ferry to Alameda. She was reported to have gone out of operation about 1854, having been sold.

Clara[178] 127249 (US) (passenger/ freight vessel) She was built in 1898 at San Francisco CA by John Cameron. 75.5' x 22.0' x 4.6' Wood. 92gt 81nt. Powered by an 8nhp steam engine. In 1898 she was owned by the California & Northwest Mining Co. In 1898 she was sold to the Alaska Exploration Co. In 1901 or 1903 she was reported to have been broken up at Dawson City YT. Her engines went to the *Monarch*.

Clara Bell[179] 125062 (US) (freighter) She was built in 1871 at Stockton CA USA by Stephen Davis. 80.6' Wood. 98.21gt 85.98rt. Powered by a 40nhp steam engine. She was employed on California rivers. She was reported to have gone out of business about 1885.

Clara Brown[180] 126378 (US) (freighter) She was built in 1886 at Tacoma WA by Hiram Doncaster. 99.8' x 21.1' x 4.1' Wood. 190.93gt 111.86nt. Powered by a steam engine. In 1886 she was owned by Captain Thomas Brown, Seattle WA USA. She served communities in Puget Sound on the Tacoma – Seattle – Everett – Snohomish route. She served communities such as Olympia, Kalmiche, Shelton, Steilacoom, Tacoma, and Seattle. The vessel became famous as the first vessel to reach Seattle with relief supplies after the great Seattle fire in June 1889. On December 4, 1901, she was driven ashore at Al-Ki Point WA by storm winds. In 1930 she was reported as having been abandoned on a beach in West Seattle.

Clara Crow[181] 125061 (US) (freighter) She was built in 1848 at Stockton CA. Wood. Powered by a 50nhp steam engine. She was employed on California rivers. She was reported to have gone out of service about 1885.

Clara Hawes 127532 (US) (freighter) She was built in 1901 at Ballard WA. 45.6' x 14.0' x 3.0' Wood. 44gt 27nt. Powered by a steam engine. She was employed on the Puget Sound.

Clara Monarch[182,183] (US)(freighter) Wood. Powered by a steam engine. Edward L Affleck states that he believes that this vessel was the *Monarch* (107863) but powered by the engines from the *Clara* and popularly known as the *Clara Monarch*. She was abandoned in what is called Clara Monarch Slough across the road from the Walmart in Whitehorse. Her paddlewheel shaft was recovered and is on display at The Wharf downtown.

Clara Parker 125915 (US) (passenger vessel) She was built in 1881 at Astoria OR USA. 107.0' x 24.0' x 5.8' Wood. 257.68gt 194.91nt. Powered by a steam engine. Edward L Affleck states that she was rebuilt in 1889 as the *Astorian* and abandoned in 1908.

Clatsop Chief[184,185] (US) She was built in 1875 at Skipanan OR by SL Willis and GW Siferte. 58.0' x 13.0' x 4.0' Wood. Powered by two horizontal (high pressure 9" x 36") 5nhp steam engines. In 1875 she was owned by Surfits & Cullis. On March 2, 1881, she was wrecked in a collision while with a scow in tow by the propeller steamer *Oregon* near Willow Bar 10 miles from St. Helens. The *Oregon* cut through the scow and struck the *Clatsop Chief*, with both sinking almost immediately. Four members of the crew of the *Clatsop Chief* were killed.

Clatsop Chief[186] 125870 (US) (freighter) She was built in 1881 at Portland OR USA. 74' x 15.2' x 4.4' Wood. 101.85gt 57.21rt. Powered by two horizontal (11" x 36") high pressure) 8.3nhp steam engines. In 1889 she was reported to have been abandoned at Portland OR.

Clear Lake Queen[187] 657650 (US) (excursion boat) She was built in 1983. 64.4'. In 2021 she was based on Clearlake California at Ferndale Resort & Marina in Soda Bay, at Lucerne CA. She carries the Water Color Restaurant & Bar.

Cleona[188] (US) (sidewheeler) (ferry) She was built in 1934 at Hood River OR. 56'. Wood. 10gt. Powered by a gasoline engine. She was reported to have been abandoned.

Cleopatra[189] (US) (sidewheeler) She was built in 1853. Wood. 80gt. Powered by a steam engine. She was employed on California rivers. In 1854 she was owned by the California Steam Navigation Co. She was reported to have gone out of operation about 1862. Her machinery was removed, and she was broken up. Her pilot house was re-used in the *Goodman Castle*.

Cleopatra 127766 (US) (sidewheeler) (workboat) She was built in 1903 at Terminal Island CA. 44.3' x 12.9' x 2.2'. Wood. 50gt 8nt. Powered by a gasoline engine. She was employed in the Los Angeles CA region.

Cleveland[190] 125731 (US) (sidewheeler) (passenger vessel) She was built in 1870 at Portland OR USA. 93.0' x 14.0' x 6.0'. Wood. 47.39gt 23.71rt. Powered by (10" x 36") 6nhp steam engines. In 1870 she was owned by GW Simmonds. In 1884–1888 she was employed on Yaquina Bay.

Cliff Dweller (see City of *Moab*)

Clifford Sifton 107528 (Canada) (later *Hootaliqua*) She was built in 1898 she was built at Lake Bennett BC by John Julian. 120' x 24' x ?. Wood. 291.41gt 183.59rt. Powered by two horizontal (10" x 48" high pressure) 6.6nhp steam engines by Wolff & Zureker, Portland OR USA. In 1900 she was re-engined. In 1904 she was rebuilt, with engines to the *Gleaner*, as a cattle barge on the Yukon River. In 1898–1901 she was owned by the Dominion Steamboat Line Co. Ltd., Victoria BC. In 1903–1905 she was owned by the British Yukon Navigation Co.

Cline (Canada) She was built in 1879 at Golden BC Canada. 31' x 9.3' x 4'. Wood. 20gt. Powered by a one-cylinder (5.5" x 8") steam engine. In 1879 she was owned by JC Hayes for Upper Columbia River service. In 1887 she

was constructed from a square-ended barge used in the railway construction and a boiler from a Manitoba steam plough built at Golden BC. It carried a sawmill from Golden to the south end of Columbia Lake. In 1887 she sank near Spillimacheen BC.

Clifford Sifton entering Miles Canyon (Image from Maritime Museum of British Columbia 000437)

Clinton[191] 005177 (US) She was built in 1854 at San Francisco CA. Wood. 71gt. Powered by a steam engine. She was reported to have been lost in 1877.

Clio 127297 (US) (passenger vessel) She was built in 1898 at St. Michael AK. 64.0' x 15.0' x 4.3' Wood. 34gt 34nt. Powered by a steam engine. She is reported by Murray Lundberg to have worked in Alaska/YT in 1898.

Clive[192] (Canada) She was built in 1879 at Golden BC. Her hull was a scow abandoned by builders on the railway which had been used for setting pilings. It was almost square constructed of 4" wooden planks. She had an upright boiler from a Manitoba steam plough and recycled engines from an old river tug. The sternwheel was constructed from scrap metal from an abandoned sawmill. She worked twice between Golden BC and Columbia Lake. She was reported to have been laid up about 1887.

Cochan[193] 085365 (US) (ex-*Gila*) She was built in 1899 at Yuma Arizona from the Gila. 135' x 31' x ? Wood. 234gt. Powered by a steam engine. In 1899 she was owned by the Colorado Steam Navigation Company. In 1873–1899 she was employed on the Colorado River. In 1909 she was owned by the United States Reclamation Service. The Laguna Dam, above Yuma, ended steam navigation on the lower Colorado River and in the spring of 1910, and she was reported to have been dismantled.

Cocopah[194] 005843 (US) (freighter) She was originally built in 1859 at Gridiron Mexico. She was re-built built in 1867 at Yuma Arizona. 147' x 28' x 1.5' Wood. 231.37gt. Powered by a steam engine. She was the second stern-wheel steamboat of that name running on the Colorado River for the Colorado Steam Navigation Company between 1867 and 1879. In 1881 she was dismantled and repurposed as a boarding house at Port Isabel.

Coeur d'Alene[195] (US) (passenger vessel) She was built in 1884 at Coeur d'Alene ID. 120' x 14' x ? Wood. Powered by a steam engine. She was employed on Lake Coeur d'Alene. She was reported to have been broken up about 1890.

Col. McNaught[196,197] (US) (passenger/ freight vessel) She was built in 1898 at Seattle WA USA by the San Francisco Bridge Co. 168' Wood. Powered by a steam engine. In 1898 she was owned by the Boston & Alaska Transportation Co. In 1898 she was launched without champagne because the manager, Mr. Lockwood, had strict objections to the use of alcoholic beverages. She is reported by Murray Lundberg to have worked in Alaska/ YT in 1898. Robert D Turner states that he believes that she was likely never actually constructed.

Col. Moody (see *Colonel Moody*)

Coldfoot 203173 (US) (freighter) She was built in 1906 at Ballard WA. 54.0' x 11.0' x 2.2' Wood. 12gt 7nt. Powered by a steam engine. In 1906–1910 she was owned by Puget Sound WA USA interests.

Colfax 005121 (US) (sidewheeler) (freighter) She was built in 1865 at Seabeck WT USA. Wood. 83.3gt. Powered by an 85nhp steam engine. She was employed on Puget Sound home ported at Port Angeles WA. She was reported to have been abandoned about 1894.

Colfax (US) She was built in 1902 at Coeur d'Alene ID by PW Johnson. Wood. Powered by a steam engine. In 1902–1904 she was owned by George Reynolds and ED McDonald. In 1904 she was owned by the Coeur d'Alene & St. Joe Transportation Co. In 1902 she was working with the *Spokane* on a passenger and freight route between Coeur d'Alene and St. Joseph.

Colonel Moody (Vancouver Island Colonial Register) (passenger/ freight vessel) She was built in 1859 at Victoria, Vancouver Island (Crown Colony) by James W Trahey. On May 14, 1859, she was launched at Dead Man's Point. 144.9' x 26.7' x 4.0'. Wood. Powered by a (16" x 72") steam engine. In 1859 she was owned by the Victoria Steam Navigation Company. In 1859 she was owned by the British Columbia Navigation Co., Victoria, Vancouver Island. (Her name is also known as the *Col. Moody*.) In 1861 she was working the New Westminster to Yale service. She was reported as having been broken up in 1864.

Colonel Wright[198] (US) (freighter) She was built in 1858 at Deschutes OT by RR Thompson and EF Coe. 110' x 21' x 12.5'. Wood. Powered by a steam engine. She was employed between Cellilo Falls and the Snake River. She was reported to have gone out of service in 1865 and dismantled at Cellilo OT.

Colorado[199] (US) She was built in 1855 at San Francisco CA USA by John G North. She was re-assembled in the Mexican delta estuary of the Colorado River. 120'. Wood. Powered by an 80hp steam engine. She was considered to have been under-powered, over-loaded, and susceptible to grounding on the sandbars in the Colorado River. In 1862 she was reported as having been broken up.

Colorado[200] 125063 (US) (freighter) She was built in 1862 at Yuma Arizona. 145' x 29' x ?. Wood. 178.58gt. She was employed on the Colorado River. She was owned by the Colorado Steam Navigation Co. In 1884 she was reported as having been broken up.

Colorado (US) (sidewheeler) Built in 1863 at New York by William H Webb. Powered by a steam engine by Novelty Iron Works. 314 feet. 3,728gt. She was owned by the Colorado Steam Navigation Co.

Colorado King 992359 (US) (passenger vessel) She was built in 1993. 49' x 18' x 3' 50gt 45nt. In 2020 she was operated by Yuma River Tours at Yuma AZ. She was a double-decker sternwheeler tour boat with an open-air upper deck and an enclosed main deck. There is a small snack bar on board. They offer three-hour, non-stop tours either daytime trips down-river with an optional boxed lunch, or evening sunset dinner cruises with a hot buffet dinner served on board.

Colorado River (US) She was built in wood. Powered by a steam engine. (No further information known.)

Columbia[201] (US) (sidewheeler) She was built at New York, NY by Westervelt and Mackay, New York. 193' Wood. 777gt. Powered by a steam engine built by Novelty Iron Works. She was owned by the Pacific Mail Steamship Company. She was employed on the Portland, Oregon City, Astoria, and Vancouver route. Her engines were removed and placed in the steamer *Fashion*. Her hull was swept away and destroyed by the spring freshet.

Columbia[202] (US) (sidewheeler) She was built in 1850 at Upper Astoria by Thomas Goodwin and George Hewitt. 90.0' x 16.0' x 4' Wood. Powered by a French-built non-condensing (8" x 24") steam engine. In 1850 she was owned by Captain Daniel Frost, General John Adair, and the firm of Leonard & Green. She was employed on the Columbia River. In 1854 she was reported to have been broken up. Her engines were used in the building of the *Fashion*.

Columbia 126880 (Canada) (passenger vessel) She was built in 1891 at Northport WA USA by Joseph Paquet. 152.6' x 28' x 6.3' Wood. 534gt 377.9nt. Powered by a 19nhp (17" x 72") steam engine. In 1891 she was owned by the Columbia and Kootenay Steam Navigation Co. for Arrow Lakes service. In 1894 she was employed on the Revelstoke to Northport service. On August 1, 1894, she was destroyed by fire at Sayward BC (just north of the Canada/US Border). Her engines were salvaged and installed in the *Kokanee*. The

Underwater Archaeology Society of BC has searched for the wreck and published their findings in 2000.

Columbia 202431 (US) (passenger vessel) She was built in 1905 at Wenatchee WA USA. 131.2' x 25.4' x 5.0' Wood. 341gt 215nt. Powered by a 350ihp steam engine. She was reported to have been destroyed by fire in 1915.

Columbia 204678 (US) (tug) She was built in 1907 at Northport WA. 60.8' x 18.9' x 4.0' Wood. 69gt 41nt. Powered by a 75ihp steam engine. In October 1911 she was reported to have been destroyed by a fire near Northport WA.

Columbia Gorge[203,204] 661888 (US) She was built in 1983 at Hood River OR USA by Nichols Boat Works. 119.9' x 32.9' x 5.0' Steel. 92nt. Powered by two Cummins diesel electric engines. In 1983 she was owned by the Cascade Locks Port Authority, Oregon. In 2006 she was owned and operated by American Waterways, Inc. (AWI), Portland OR out of the Cascade Locks on the Columbia River.

Columbia Queen[205] (later *Stehikine*) (US) She was built in 1891 at Birch Flats WA by Burch Bros. 72' x 14' x 4' In 1891 she was owned by Burch Bros. In 1892 she was cut into two pieces, hauled out by wagon, re-assembled, and launched on Lake Chelan WA. In November 1893 she sank, was salvaged, and renamed as the *Stehekine*. In 1905 she was converted to a barge.

Columbian 107091 (Canada) (passenger vessel) She was built in 1898 at Victoria BC Canada by John H Todd. 146.5' x 33.4' x 4.7' Wood. 716gt 455rt. Powered by a 15hp steam engine by James Reese & Sons, Pittsburgh PA USA. In 1898–1901 she was owned by the Canadian Development Co. Ltd., Victoria BC. In 1906 she was owned by the White Pass & Yukon Rail Road, Victoria BC. She was in service on the upper Yukon River for the Canadian Development Company. On September 25, 1906, she was destroyed by an explosion and fire at Five Fingers Rapids (Eagle Rock) on the Yukon River.

Columbus 125869 (US) (ferry) She was built in 1880 at Columbus WA USA. 80.0' x 22.0' x 5.8' Wood. 131.78gt. Powered by a steam engine. She was reported to have gone out of service about 1886.

Colusa[206] (formerly steam barge *Star of the West*) (US) In 1854 she was owned by the California Steam Navigation Company. In 1868 she was owned by McNair & Sherman. She was employed on California rivers. On October 19, 1868, the *Capitol* deliberately collided with the *Colusa* near Collinsville CA in an overt attempt to eliminate competition.

Colusa[207] 005546 (US) She was built in 1868. 129.7'. Wood. 149.67gt. Powered by a steam engine. She was employed on California rivers. She was reported as having been lost in 1868.

Colusa[208] 209203 (US) (sidewheeler) She was built in 1911 at San Francisco CA by Schultz & Robertson. 177.5' x 41.9' x 6.3'. Wood. 795gt 737nt. Powered by a 275ihp steam engine. She was employed on California rivers. On September 15, 1932, she was wrecked near Broderick CA.

Comanche[209] (US) (sidewheeler) She was built in 1851 at Washington CA USA. Wood. 146gt. She was employed on California rivers out of Sacramento CA. She was reported to have been abandoned about 1856.

Comet[210] 005973 (US) (freighter) She was built in 1871 at Seattle WA by Captain Simon Randolph. 65'. Wood. 56.83gt. Powered by a 15ihp steam engine. In 1900 she was reported to have been abandoned.

Commodore Jones[211] (later *Jack Haynes*; then *R.K. Page*) (US) (sidewheeler) (freighter) She was built in 1849. Wood. 31gt. Powered by a steam engine. She was employed on California rivers. In March 1850 she was renamed as the *Jack Haynes*. In February 1851 she was snagged on the Sacramento River. She was rebuilt and renamed as the *R.K. Page*. Lytle says she was renamed as the *Jack Hayes*.

Commodore Stockton (US) (sidewheeler) (freighter) She was built in 1850 at Philadelphia PA by Davis and Burton. 153.7'. Wood. 435gt. Powered by a steam engine. In 1850 she was owned by RF Loper.

Companion 202645 (US) (passenger/ freight vessel) She was built in 1905 at Astoria OR. 45.3' x 12.4' x 4.4'. Wood. 14gt 10nt. Powered by a gasoline engine. In 1929–1935 she was owned by AG Wooten, Anacortes WA. She was rebuilt in 1939.

Confidence[212] (US) (sidewheeler) (freighter) She was probably built in New York c1849. Wood. Powered by a steam engine. In 1849 she was acquired by John Bensley in New York and sailed around to San Francisco CA. In 1854 she was owned by the Union Line. She was employed on the Sacramento River. In 1854 she was owned by the California Steam Navigation Company. She was reported to have gone out of operation about 1872.

Constance 125267 (US) (passenger vessel) She was built in 1874 at San Francisco CA USA. 145.5' x 32.0' x 5.5' Wood. 394.91gt 349.74nt. Powered by a 75ihp steam engine. She was rebuilt (in 1897) to 161.5' x 32.0' x 5.5' 422gt 377nt. She was employed on California rivers. She was reported to have been abandoned about 1918.

Constantine 127240 (US) (tug) She was built in 1897 at Port Blakeley WA USA by Hall Bros. Marine Railway & Shipbuilding Co. (EG Rathbown) 146' x 30' x 5' Wood. 484.1gt 291.8rt. She was powered by a steam engine. In 1897 she was built for Stikine River service. In 1897 she was owned by the Canadian Pacific Railway Co. Montreal QC but never employed (American Registry). In 1898 she was sold to the British American Corporation. Her engines were salvaged from the Ohio River steamer *Mary Morton*. She was being towed to Alaska by the steamer *South Portland* when she broke up on July 04, 1898.

Constitution (US) (freighter) She was built in 1850 in New York. She was funded by Sam Ward (the famous lobbyist) and Rodman Price (later the Governor of New Jersey). She sailed to San Francisco for service in California waters.

Constitution 803552 (Canada) 8971700 (IMO) (passenger vessel) She was built in 1983 at North Vancouver BC Canada by Allied Shipbuilders Ltd. 23.84m x 7.24m x 1.79m Steel. 226.23gt 169.67rt. Powered by 298bhp diesel engine by Gardner Engine Co., Manchester UK. In 2001 she was rebuilt. In 1983–2004 she was owned by the H.F. Management Ltd., Vancouver BC. In 2011–2020 she was owned by Harbour Cruises Ltd., Vancouver BC.

Contra Costa[213] 005180 (US) (sidewheeler) (ferry) She was built in 1857 at San Francisco CA. 332gt. Powered by a steam engine. She was employed in the San Francisco Bay area. In 1882 she was reported as having been abandoned.

Contra Costa 212630 (US) (railcar ferry) She was built in 1914 at Oakland CA USA by the Southern Pacific Shipyard. 414.3' x 67.2' x 18.5' Wood. 4483gt 3276nt. Powered by a diesel engine. In 1926–1927 she was owned by The Southern Pacific Railroad Co., San Francisco CA.

Conveyor 126250 (Canada) (workboat) She was one of four identical steamers designed by Watson for use for GTP railway construction:137.5' x 31.4' x 5.4 Wood. 583gt 379rt. Powered by a 15hp steam engine. In 1909 she was originally owned by the Grand Trunk Pacific Railway, Montreal QC but sometime in 1909 the railway sold her and two of her sisters, the *Distributor* and the *Operator* to its principal contractor Foley, Welch, and Stewart. In 1909 she was in service to the railway construction along the Skeena River. In 1911 she was reported as having been broken up, with her fittings and machinery to the second *Conveyor* at Tete Jaune Cache.

Conveyor 130885 (Canada) (passenger/ freight vessel) She was built in 1912 at Tete Jaune Cache BC Canada by George F Askew from parts prefabricated at a New Westminster shipyard. She and her sister vessel, the *Operator*, were taken to the railhead together with their machinery and dragged to the launching site. She was launched on May 12, 1912. 141.7' x 34.8' x 5.2' Wood. 725gt 456rt. Powered by a 15hp steam engine. She was powered by a steam engine from the first *Conveyor*. In 1912–1919 she was owned by John W Stewart (Foley, Welch, and Stewart), Vancouver BC. In 1931–1937 she was owned by the Pacific Great Eastern Railway Co., Victoria BC. In 1912 she was in service between Tete Jaune Cache and Fort George for construction of the Grand Trunk Pacific Railway. She made some runs between Soda Creek and Fort George. In 1915 she was reported as having been laid up at South Fort George BC and broken up in 1919. In 1931 she was still listed in the Canada Register of Shipping.

Coos 125397 (US) (sidewheeler) (passenger/ freight vessel) She was built in 1874 at Empire City OR USA. 58.0' x 14.0' x 5.0' Wood. 46.53gt. Powered by a steam engine. She was reported to have gone out of service about 1896.

Cora (US) (sidewheeler) (freighter) Wood. Powered by a steam engine. In 1854 she was owned by the California Steam Navigation Co. In 1854 she was operating on the Sacramento River CA. In 1871 she was owned by the California Pacific Railroad Co.

Cora[214,215] 005186 (US) (sidewheeler) (freighter) She was built in 1866 at Stockton CA USA by Stephen Davis. Wood. 298gt. Powered by a steam engine. In 1871 she was taken over by the California Pacific Railroad Co., San Francisco CA. She was employed on California rivers. She was reported to have gone out of operation about 1872.

Cora[216] (US) (freighter) Wood. Powered by a steam engine. She is reported by Murray Lundberg to have worked in Alaska/YT in 1892–1894.

Cormorant[217] (HMS) (sidewheeler) She was built in 1842 at Chatham UK by H.M. Dockyard Chatham. 180' x 35' x 20' Wood. 1054gt. Powered by 300nhp direct-acting Fairbairn steam engine. She was the first steam-powered naval vessel in British Columbia waters. While in the Pacific she was commanded (until paying off at Portsmouth in 1847) by Commander Frederick Beauchamp Paget Seymour RN. She was paid off for disposal in 1853.

Cornelia[218,219] (US) (sidewheeler) She was built in 1853. 165.5' Wood. 382gt. Powered by a steam engine. In 1854 she was owned by the California Steam Navigation Co. In 1871 she was taken over by the California Pacific Railroad Co., San Francisco CA. She was employed on California rivers. In 1872 she was condemned and was reported to have been out of service.

Coronado 126373 (US) (ferry) She was built in 1886 at San Francisco CA USA. 100.0' x 26.0' x 9.2' Wood. 308gt 222nt. Powered by a 75ihp steam engine.

Cortes (see *Saratoga*)

Courser 096997 (Canada) (tug) She was built in 1892 at New Westminster BC Canada by Captain George H Cooper. 125.0' x 14.5' x 3.5' Wood. 161gt

101rt. Powered by a steam engine. In 1892–1896 she was owned by Alexander Peers, New Wevstminster BC. In 1898–1905 she was owned by George H Cooper. In 1898 she was in service to the Glenora Steamship Co. In 1905 she was sold at a Sherriff's auction to Captain Dick Fullbrook. In 1892 she worked on the Fraser River service. Later she moved to the Stikine River in 1898 going as far as Telegraph Creek. Afterwards she towed logs from Harrison Lake to Harrison Mills. She was powered by a steam engine salvaged from the steamer *Colonel Moody*. In 1905 she sank near Cheam BC after striking a stump. In 1905 she was reported as having been broken up with her engines going to the steamer *Cheam*.

Corvallis[220] (US) (dredge/snag boat) She was built in 1877 at Portland OR for the United States Army Corps of engineers. 100.0' x 23.0' x 3.9' Wood. 90gt. Powered by a steam engine. In 1896 she was wrecked at Junction OR.

Corwin[221] (US) (sternwheeler) (freighter) In 1888 she was owned by the Spokane Water Department, Spokane WA USA. In 1893 she was owned by the People's Transportation Co., Salem OR. She was in operation on the Spokane River, but was later transferred to Lake Coeur d'Alene.

Cowlitz (see *Swan*)

Cowlitz 214769 (US) She was built in 1917 at Portland OR by the Portland Shipbuilding Company. 100.2' x 26.6' x 4.8' Wood. 99gt 72nt. Powered by two horizontal 350ihp steam engines. In 1917–1930 she was owned by Milton Smith (Smith Transportation Co.) Rainier WA. She was employed on the Cowlitz River in southwestern Washington. In 1930 she was taken over by the Shaver Transportation Co., Portland OR. In 1930 she was owned by the Columbia River Navigation Company. She was employed between Portland, Hood River, White Salmon, and The Dalles. In September 1931 she foundered and sank on the Columbia River at The Dalles OR.

Craigflower 126233 65.0' x 12.3' x 2.8' Wood. 21gt 12rt. She was built in 1908 at Victoria BC by Captain Roy Troup. Powered by a 2hp steam engine. In 1908 she was owned by Captain Roy Troup, Victoria BC. In 1910–1911 she was owned by James J Slocan, Port Essington BC. She was nicknamed as the 'Cauliflower' and originally operated on the Gorge Waterway in

Victoria from a float in front of the Empress Hotel before being replaced by the passenger steamer *White Swan Flyer*. In 1910 she was moved to the Skeena River but was not a financial success there as she could not handle the strong river currents. She was reported as having been broken up in 1911.

The *Craigflower* on the Skeena River (Image from Maritime Museum of British Columbia 000396)

Crescent[222] (US) (passenger/ Freight vessel) She was built in 1891 at Demersville MT by Peters Bros. 130' x 32' x ? Wood. In 1891 she was owned by HS DePuy and Steve Lanneau, Demersville MT. In 1891 she was employed on the Columbia River. She was active transporting materials and personnel for the construction of the Great Northern Railroad. In 1891 she was wrecked near Demersville Ferry. In 1892 she was laid up. Her machinery was salvaged and used in the *State of Idaho* (US 116557).

Creston 126231 (Canada) (passenger/ freight vessel) In 1908 she was built at Nelson BC. 35.4' x8.9' x 2.7' Wood. 5gt 3rt. Powered by a steam engine. In 1908–1920 she was owned by George W. Hale, Nelson BC. She was reported to have been broken up about 1920.

Creston Ferry (see *West Creston Ferry*)

Cricket 005182 (US) (sidewheeler) (freighter) She was built in 1863 at San Francisco CA USA. 92.0' x 16.0' x 4.0' Wood. 45.92gt 22.96rt. Powered by a 45nhp steam engine. She was based at Wilmington CA. She was reported to have been abandoned about 1885.

Crockett (see *H.J. Corcoran*)

Crombie 134640 (Canada) (freighter) She was built in 1916 at Chase BC Canada. 90.3' x 21.3' x 4.6' Wood. 162gt 101rt. Powered by a 6hp steam engine by Polson Iron Works Ltd., Toronto ON. In 1916–1931 she was owned by Adams River Lumber Co. Ltd., Chase BC. She was powered by engines from the first *Crombie*. She was laid up in 1920.

Cygnet[223] (Canada) (snag boat) She was built about 1910. Wood. Powered by a steam engine. In 1910–1911 she owned by the Canada Department of Public Works, Ottawa ON. In 1910–1911 she was in service as a snag boat on the Skeena River for the Canada Department of Public Works.

Cyrus Walker 005123 (US) (sidewheeler) (tug) She was built in 1864 at San Francisco CA USA. 120.0' x 25.7' x 8.6' Wood. 241.31gt 154.25rt. Powered by a 202nhp steam engine. In 1871 she was brought to Puget Sound from San Francisco CA. She was reported to have been abandoned about 1901.

D 250 (see *P.W.D. 250*)

D.A. Grant[224] (US) This vessel is reported by Murray Lundberg to have worked in Alaska/YT in 1904.

D. Armstrong 157521 (US) (passenger/ freight vessel) She was built in 1898 at St. Michael AK USA. 56.0' x 16.0' x 4.0' Wood. 32gt. Powered by a steam engine. In 1898 she was owned by the St. Marys (Ohio) Mining & Milling Co. In 1900 she was owned by the Alaska Commercial Co. In 1904 she was wrecked in the slough at New Hamilton AK USA.

D.A. Thomas 138420 (Canada) (passenger/ freight vessel) She was built in 1916 at Peace River Crossing AB Canada by George F Askew for the Peace

River Tramway and Navigation Company, a forerunner of DA Thomas, Lord Rhondda's, Peace River Development Co. Ltd. The largest stern wheeler built on the Mackenzie River system she was 161.9' x 37' x 6.3' Wood. 1114gt 798rt. Powered by a 21hp steam engine built by Polson Iron Works Ltd., Toronto ON. In 1916 she was owned by the Peace River Development Co. Ltd.). In 1921–1924 she was owned by the Alberta & Arctic Transportation Co. Ltd.'s original shareholders until they failed, and the HBC assumed control of the company. She was operated by the Hudson's Bay Co., London UK as part of the Alberta & Arctic Transport Co. on the Peace River from Hudson Hope to Fort Dunvegan until 1930. She was taken on a transit of the Vermilion Chutes to the lower Peace River in June 1930. She suffered two serious groundings that took her out of service. Although damaged, she was repaired and made Fort Fitzgerald under her own power. She was used there as a grain storage and was eventually broken up with her machinery being used on other vessels. Her paddle wheel crank was recovered and is now on display at the Peace River Museum.

D.A. Thomas (Image from the Provincial Archives of Alberta)

D.E. Knight[225] 006867 (US) (freighter) She was built in 1875 at Marysville CA USA. 131.5' x 28.4' x 3.3' Wood. 217.22gt 199.29' Powered by a 75ihp steam engine. She was employed on California rivers. She was reported to have been out of service in 1905.

D.P.W. 250 (see P.W.D. 250)

D.R. Campbell[226] 157509 (US) (passenger vessel) She was built in 1898 at Seattle WA USA by the Moran Bros. Shipyard. 176.1' x 35' x 4'. Wood. 718gt 409nt. Powered by two horizontal (20" x 84" high pressure) 700ihp steam engines. In 1898 she was owned by the Seattle-Yukon Transportation Co. In 1898 she was moved to Alaska and employed in Yukon River service. In 1901 she was owned by Northern Navigation Co. In 1914 she was owned by White Pass & Yukon Rail Road. She was sold in 1927. In 1910–1927 she was reported as having been based at St. Michael AK.

D.S. Baker 006984 (US) (passenger/ freight vessel) She was built in 1879 at Celilo OR USA. 165.0' x 36.3' x 5.0'. Wood. 710.13gt 566.22nt. Powered by two horizontal high pressure (17" x 72" 19nhp) steam engines. In 1879 she was owned by the Oregon Steam Navigation Co., OR USA. In 1884 she was owned by Oregon interests. In 1888 she was brought through The Dalles by James Troup. She was brought through the Cascades in 1893 by Michell Martineau. In 1901 she was reported as having been broken up.

Daisy 006970 (US) She was built in 1878 at San Francisco CA USA. 80.0' x 20.5' x 3.4'. Wood. 71.77gt 46.41nt. Powered by a 60ihp steam engine. She was employed on California rivers. She was reported as being out of service in 1890.

Daisy[227,228] 157006 (US) (freighter) She was built in 1880 at Seattle WA USA. 80.5' x 20.3'x 4.0'. Wood. 97.87gt. Powered by a 40ihp steam engine. In 1880–1896 she was owned by the Washington Steamboat Co. On July 17, 1888, she sank in the Sacramento River. In 1896 she sank again alongside the Yesler wharf while carrying a cargo of bricks.

Daisy[229] (US) (freighter) In 1907 she was built at Pend Oreille ID USA. Wood. In 1907 she was in service on the lower Pend Oreille River WA.

Daisy Ainsworth[230] 006771 (US) (passenger/ freight vessel) In 1873 she was built at The Dalles OR USA by JJ Holland. 177' x 28' x 7.8'. Wood. 673gt. Powered by two 26.6nhp (high pressure 20" x 84") steam engines. She was employed on the Cascades-The Dalles route. In 1876 she was wrecked at the Cascades on the Columbia River.

Daisy Andrus 157108 (US) (sidewheeler) (ferry) She was built in 1883 at Portland OR USA. 102.3' x 27.0' x 6.5' Wood. 120.99gt. 60.51rt. Powered by a steam engine. In 1896 she was operating in on the Columbia River.

Daisy Bell[231] (Canada) (passenger/ freight vessel) She was built in 1898. Wood. 8gt. Powered by an 8hp engine. In 1898 she was owned by James Wallwark. She travelled from the North Saskatchewan River to the Great Divide. In 1899 she was registered as being in service on the Athabasca River. The vessel was transported through a mountain pass and relaunched into goldrush service. In 1899 she was reported as having been laid up at laid up Dawson YT.

Dakota[232] (US) (passenger vessel) She was built in 1872 at Breckenridge MN USA. 92' x 23' x ? Wood. In 1881 she was rebuilt at Pembina MB Canada. In 1874–1881 she was owned by the Red River Transportation Co. Wood. She was employed on the Red River from Fargo ND to Fort Garry in Canada. She made her first voyage to Dufferin MB on May 6, 1873. She was operated in 1874 by the Red River Transportation Co. between Fargo ND and Lower Fort Garry. In 1881 she was destroyed by fire at Pembina MB and was rebuilt.

Dalles[233] (US) (sidewheeler) (passenger/ freight vessel) She was built in 1862 at Cascades WT USA. 70' x 18' x 5' Wood. Powered by a (12" x 12") steam engine. In 1862 she was owned by McFarlane & White. She was employed on the Columbia River system. In 1863 (1868?) she was reported to have been broken up.

Dalles City 157315 (US) (freighter) She was built in 1891 at Portland OR USA. 142' x 26.5' x 7' Wood. 402gt 296nt. Powered by two 13nhp horizontal (high pressure 14" x 60") steam engines. In 1891 she was owned by The Dalles, Portland & Astoria Navigation Co. She was employed on a route between Portland and The Dalles. In 1909–1910 she was rebuilt and re-registered as the *Diamond O*. (207330).

Dalles City (later *Diamond O.*) 207330 (US) (passenger vessel) She was built in 1910 at Portland OR USA by Charles M Nelson. 151' x 27.3' x 6.8'. Wood. Powered by two 17nhp horizontal (high pressure 16" x 72") steam engines. In 1912 she foundered at Stevenson WA but was salvaged and put back into service. Her name was changed in 1920 to *Diamond O*. In 1935 she was reported to have gone out of service.

Dalton (US) (passenger/ freight vessel) She was built at San Francisco CA USA by James Robertson. Wood. Powered by a steam engine. She was employed on California rivers. (Note: This vessel is mentioned casually in various sources, but her existence is in some doubt.)

Dalton[234,235,236] (later *Capital City*) 157507 (US) (passenger vessel) She was built in 1898 at Port Blakely WA by Hall Bros. Marine Railway & Shipbuilding Co. 150.2' x 32.0' x 5.0'. Wood. 522.8gt 348.2nt. Powered by two (high pressure 18" x 66") steam engines. In 1898 she was owned by the Canadian Pacific Railway. (She was constructed for Stikine River service but did not work there. In 1897 she was laid up on completion.) In 1901 she was owned by the British Yukon Navigation Co. (White Pass and Yukon Railway). In 1900 she was owned by the S. Wiley Navigation Co. On April 14, 1901, she caught fire while returning to Seattle from the US Naval Base at Bremerton with 400 excursionists aboard. The crew extinguished the fire, and no one was injured. In 1901 she was renamed as *Capital City* in service on the Seattle – Tacoma – Olympia route. On October 29, 1902, she was in transit, with a cargo of canned salmon when she collided with the Canadian vessel *Trader* off Dash Point. The *Capital City* sank but the *Trader* was undamaged. In 1904 she was sold to Olympia-Tacoma Navigation Co. In 1906 she was sold to the Dallas, Portland & Astoria Navigation Co. In 1907 she was transferred to the Columbia River. In 1919 she was reported to have been abandoned and she was broken up after her abandonment.

Dan 207507 (US) (freighter) She was built in 1910 at Seattle WA. 60.0' x 12.4' x 2.3'. Wood. 13gt 8nt. Powered by a 40ihp gasoline engine. In 1910 she was owned by Puget Sound WA USA interests.

Daniel Moore[237] (US) (freighter) She was built in 1852. Wood. 63gt. Powered by a steam engine. In 1853–1868 she was in service on the Sacramento

River CA. In 1854 she was owned by the California Steam Navigation Co. She was reported as having gone out of service about 1868. Lytle reports her name as *Daniel Moor* and that she was abandoned in 1857.

Dashaway[238,239] (US) (freighter) She was built in 1857. 126.2' Wood. 106.15gt. Powered by a steam engine. She was employed on California rivers. She was reported as having gone out of service about 1868. Her hulk was abandoned at Tiburon CA and a fish handling shed was built on it.

Dauntless[240] (later *San Joaquin* (propeller) 157353 (US) (freighter) She was built in 1892 at San Francisco CA. 174.5' x 36.5' x 8.0' Wood. 612gt 501nt. Powered by a 350ihp steam engine. She was employed on California rivers. In 1938 she was rebuilt as a propeller motor vessel, lengthened to 190.5'. She was in service on California rivers. On August 28, 1932, she was destroyed by fire in the conflagration that burned 10 vessels on the Yolo side of the Sacramento River.

David N. Winton 122296 (Canada) (freighter) She was built in 1920 at The Pas, MB. 120' x 25.2' x 4.3' Wood. 289gt 147rt. Powered by a 9hp engine. In 1920–1931 she was owned by Albert L Mattes, The Pas MB. In 1936 she was owned by David D Rosenberry, The Pas MB. She was employed carrying freight on the Saskatchewan River. She was later moved to the Carrot River for log towing. She was crushed in ice in the spring of 1954.

Dawson (Image from Maritime Museum of British Columbia 000399)

Dawson 107836 (Canada) (passenger/ freight vessel) She was built in 1897 at Vancouver BC Canada. 167.0' x 34.0' x 4.5' Wood. 779gt 491rt. Powered by a 19hp steam engine. In 1901 she was rebuilt at Dawson YT Canada. In 1897 she was owned by Canadian Pacific. In 1897 she remained in the original builder's yard in Vancouver BC. In 1899 she was sold. In 1901–1926 she was owned by The British Yukon Navigation Co. Ltd., Vancouver BC. She was rebuilt in Whitehorse YT by WD Hofius & Co. On October 13, 1926, she foundered and was stranded at Rink Rapids, Yukon River, Yukon Territory.

Dayton 006618 (US) (passenger vessel) She was built in 1868 at Canemah OR USA by Joseph Paquet. 116.6' x 20.4' x 4.7' Wood. 203.04gt. Powered by two horizontal 9.6nhp (high pressure 12" x 48") steam engines. (Her engines came from the *Rival*). In 1868 she was owned by the People's Transportation Co., Salem OR. In 1881 she was reported to have been broken up with her engines going to the *Joseph Kellogg*. Lytle states that in 1881 her rig was changed to a scow and that she was removed from the register.

Deapolis 205533 (US) (tug) She was built in 1908 at Bismarck ND USA. 100.9' x 25.9' x 3.8' Wood. 77gt 77nt. Powered by a 38ihp steam engine. In 1910 she was owned by Pembina ND USA interests.

Defender 111597 (Canada) She was built in 1901 at Langley BC Canada. 85.0' x 16.5' x 4.6' Wood. 216gt 137rt. Powered by a 13nhp steam engine. In 1901 she was owned by Henry West, Langley BC. In 1904–1908 she was owned by the Harrison River Mills Timber & Trading Co., Harrison BC. She was in service between New Westminster, Mission City, and Harrison Mills BC. In 1908 she was reported as having been broken up.

Defender (US) (freighter) She was built in the 1850s. Wood. Powered by a steam engine. In 1854 she was in service on the Sacramento River CA.

Defender[241] (US) (passenger/ freight vessel, later a barge). She was built in 1909 at Pend Oreille Lake ID by Richard Tupin. She replaced the *Northern* on the Sandpoint, Hope, and Bayview route. In 1909 she was rebuilt as a barge.

Defiance[242] (US) (freighter) (sidewheeler) She was built about 1849. Wood. Powered by a steam engine. She was in service on San Francisco Bay CA

USA. She was owned by the California Steam Navigation Company. In 1871 she was taken over by the California Pacific Railroad Co., San Francisco CA.

Defiance[243] 006433 (US) (sidewheeler) She was built in 1860 at Sacramento CA. Wood. 44gt. Powered by a steam engine. She was reported as having been abandoned in 1873.

Del Norte 006515 (US) (sidewheeler) (passenger/ freight vessel) She was built in 1864 at San Francisco CA by Henry Owens. 200' x 30' x 9' Wood. Powered by a 225nhp oscillating steam engine. Her twin oscillating steam engines were built by Murray & Hazelhurst, Baltimore MD and were salvaged from the American sidewheeler *Republic*. In 1864 she was owned by the California, Oregon, and Mexico Steamship Co. (Halliday Line). She was employed between San Francisco and Puget Sound, Victoria, and more northerly ports. On October 21, 1866, she went aground in Porlier Pass (Canoe Reef) BC Canada and abandoned. She was not salvaged, and her wreck lies in water of 15m-25m in depth. Her wreck has been extensively documented by the Underwater Archaeology Society of British Columbia.

Del Rio 213572 (US) (passenger/ freight vessel) She was built in 1915 at Wenatchee WA USA. 80.1' x 22.0' x 4.9' Wood. 189gt 177nt. Powered by a steam engine. In 1922 she was reported to have been abandoned.

Delta 202463 (US) (passenger/ freight vessel) She was built in 1905 at St. Michael AK USA by Joseph M Supple & Thomas Achilles. 120.3' x 26.0' x 4.4' Wood. 293gt 237nt. Powered by a 125ihp steam engine. In 1905 she was owned by the Northern Navigation Co. In 1914 she was owned by the White Pass & Yukon Rail Road. She was last used in 1916. In 1936 she was reported as having been employed at St. Michael AK USA.

Delta King[244,245] 225874 (US) (passenger vessel) She was built in 1926 at Stockton CA USA by California Navigation and Improvement Company Shipyard. 285.0' x 58.0' x 11.5' Steel. 1837gt 1318nt. Powered by a 2000ihp steam engine. In 1927–1929 she was owned by California Transportation Co., San Francisco CA. In 1942 she was owned by the United States Army. At a third auction held in September the high bid of $24,000 was submitted by a partnership headed by LG Wingard who planned to tow the boat north to Puget Sound then on to Alaska for use as a fish cannery. In 1952 the partnership sold the boat to Kitimat Constructors who employed it as a dormitory for a major aluminum plant construction project at Kitimat on the north coast of British Columbia. In 1959 John Kessel purchased the *Delta King* for $32,000 with the intention of making it into a hotel, theater, restaurant, and museum.

Delta Queen[246,247,248] 225875 (US) (passenger vessel) She was built in 1926, prefabricated on the River Clyde at the Isherwood Yard in Glasgow, Scotland, and assembled that same year in a small yard in Stockton, California. 250.0' x 58.0' x 11.5' Steel. 1837gt 1318nt. She had 87 staterooms to accommodate 174 passengers. In 1927–1929 she was owned by the California Transportation Co., San Francisco CA USA. In 1927 to the late 1930s she served on the Sacramento River, and the San Francisco to Sacramento route. In 1942 she was owned by the United States Army. In 1947 she was owned by Greene Line Steamers. She was moved from San Francisco to New Orleans for operation on the Mississippi River. In 1958 the Greene Line was purchased by Richard Simonton. In 1970 she was declared to be a national historic monument. In 1973 the Greene Line changed its name to the Delta Queen Steamboat Company, Inc. In 1976 the Coca-Cola Bottling Company, New York NY purchased the Delta Queen Steamboat Company. In 1994 the owners changed the name of the company to American Classic Voyages and this entity subsequently went bankrupt in 2001. In 2002 the vessel was sold to Delaware North Companies. In 2006 she was sold to the Majestic American Line, Seattle WA USA. In 2009 the vessel was berthed in Chattanooga TN and operated as the Delta Queen Hotel. By 2010 she was laid up in a vessel boneyard. In 2011 she was purchased by the Great American Steamboat Company. In 2012 she went back into operation on the Mississippi River. In 2014 she was owned by the Delta Queen Steamboat Company. In 2020 she was laid up at Kimmswick MO. She is a National Historic Landmark and on the National Register of Historic Places. The steamboat is also included in the National Maritime Hall of Fame and was named a National Treasure by the National Trust for Historic Preservation.

Denver No. 2 (US) She was built from parts of the *Denver No. 1*. On May 13, 1880, she was sunk by or crushed by ice opposite Fort Lincoln ND. She was in service at St Joseph and Omaha in ferrying passengers. (She may have been owned by the Hannibal and St Joseph Railroad Co.)

Desert Princess249 978704 (US) (Tour excursion boat) She was built in 1991. 74.2' x 28.0' x 6.0' Steel. She offered cruises on Lake Mead (forty miles east of Las Vegas) Nevada to the Hoover Dam. In 2021 she was operated by Lake Mead Cruises (Aramark) Boulder City NV.

A child's toy version of the *Despatch* (1888) (Image from the Maritime Museum of British Columbia)

Despatch[250] 096986 (Canada) (tug) She was built in 1888 at Revelstoke BC Canada by Robert Sanderson. 54.0' x 10.8' x 4.5' Wood. 37gt 23rt. Powered by a 2.1nhp steam engine by Albion Iron Works, Victoria BC. In 1888 she was owned by J Fred Hume, William Cowan and Robert Sanderson, principals of the Columbia Transportation Co. In 1888 she was owned by the Columbia Transportation Co. In 1888 she was registered at New Westminster BC in service as a snag boat. In 1891–1918 she was owned by the Columbia and Kootenay Steamboat Navigation Co., Nelson BC. She was constructed with a catamaran-style hull. In 1893 she was dismantled, her boiler and engine going to the *Illecillewaet*. (Her name is sometimes also spelled as the *Dispatch*).

Devastation (HMS) (RN) She was built in 1841 at Woolwich UK by H.M. Dockyard Woolwich. 180.0' x 36.0' x ? Wood. 1085gt. Powered by a 400hp steam engine. In 1841–1866 she was a warship of the Royal Navy. She served on the Pacific Station 1862–1864. She undertook anti-whiskey smuggling patrols in April 1863. In this work she arrested the *Langley*, the *Petrel*, and the *Kingfisher*. In 1866 she was reported as having been broken up in the UK.

Dewdrop[251] 157051 (US) (passenger vessel) She was built in 1881 at Portland OR by John W Peterson. 80' x 19.3' x 3.4' Wood. 110gt 81nt. Powered by two horizontal (high pressure 8" x 36") steam engines. In 1881 she was owned by the Lewis & Lake River Transportation Co. In 1887 she was reported to have been broken up.

Diamond O. (see *Dalles City*)

Diamond O. (see *Fannie*)

Diamond O. (see *New Tenino*)

Diana[252] 006620 (US) She was built in 1859 at San Francisco CA. Wood. 78gt. Powered by a steam engine. She was reported to have moved to Canada and on return to the US she was re-registered (006636). This second registration number was later cancelled. She was reported to have been lost about 1874.

Dimond (see *Queen of the Yukon*)

Diogenes[253,254] 913295 (US) Wood. Powered by a steam engine. She is reported by Murray Lundberg to have worked in Alaska/YT in 1904. He states: "(The) *Diogenes* was only mentioned by William R. Hunt who reported that in 1904, she was the scene of a near-riot when men who had paid $200 for first-class tickets from Dawson to Fairbanks arrived to find the *Diogenes* with no staterooms, no bunks, and little food. Trouble was averted when the captain, assisted by Rafael de Nogales, "held a huge party, with lots of liquor and canned delicacies."

Discovery (US)[255] (passenger vessel) She was built in 1955 at Fairbanks AK by Charles M Binkley Jr. 64.7' x 24' x 3.7' Steel. 34gt 28nt. In 1955–2020 she was the smallest of three stern-wheel riverboats operated by the Riverboat Discovery in Fairbanks, on the Chena and Tanana rivers.

Discovery II[256] (ex-*Yutana*) 271285 (US) (passenger vessel) She was built in 1971 at Fairbanks AK by Charles M Binkley Jr & Iver Johnson. (The *Discovery* II was built on the hull of the *Yutana*, a former 1953 freight boat.) 116.0' x 29.0' x 2.5'. Steel. 180gt. Powered by a 6–cylinder diesel 671 engine built by Detroit Diesel. In 1971–2021 she was the second of three *Discovery* sternwheel riverboats operated by the Riverboat Discovery company. She is still in use in 2021 as a tour vessel on the Chena and Tanana Rivers near Fairbanks, Alaska.

Discovery III[257] 913295 (US) (passenger vessel) She was built in 1987 at Whidbey Island WA by Nichols Bros. Shipyard. 156.0' x 34.0' x 3.0'. Steel. 280t. Powered by two 540hp 12V71 diesel engines built by Emerson Diesel. In 1987–2021 she was operated by the Riverboat Discovery company. In 2021 she is still in use as a tour vessel on the Chena and Tanana Rivers near Fairbanks, Alaska.

Dispatch 157278 (US) (passenger vessel) She was built in 1890 at Bandon OR. 92.7' x 18.5' x 5.1'. Wood. 158.25gt 107.09nt. She was employed in the Coos Bay OR area.

Dispatch (later *Jack Wild*) 200081 (US) (passenger vessel) She was built in 1903 at Parkersburg OR USA. 111.5' x 25.2' x 4.5'. Wood. 173gt 167nt. Powered by a steam engine. She was employed on Coos Bay OR.

Distributor 122393 (Canada) (passenger/ freight vessel) She was built in 1908 at Victoria BC Canada by Alex Watson Jr. 136.6' x 30.4' x 5.4'. Wood. 607gt 379rt. Powered by a steam engine built by Polson Iron Works Ltd., Toronto ON. In 1908 she was owned by the Grand Trunk Pacific Railway for railway construction in the Skeena Valley. In 1908 she was chartered by the Hudson's Bay Co. on the Stikine River for several voyages. In 1909 she was sold to Foley, Welch, and Stewart, the contractors for the railway. In 1911 she was reported as having been broken up, near Vancouver, with her machinery and fittings used in the second *Distributor* at Kamloops BC. Her hull was used as a residence in Victoria BC.

Distributor 130619 (Canada) She was built in 1912 at Kamloops BC Canada and launched in April that year by Malcolm MacAskill. 143' x 35' x 5.3'. Wood. 624gt 393rt. Powered by the steam engine from the first *Distributor*.

In 1918 she was rebuilt as a barge, her machinery and fittings shipped to the Mackenzie River for installation in the Distributor III. In 1912 she was owned by the Twohy Brothers, railway contractors. In 1912 she was in service for the Canadian Northern Railway construction in the Thompson River Valley. In 1914 she was owned by John M Mercer, Vancouver BC. In 1928 she was reported as having been abandoned.

Distributor III 150523 (Canada) (passenger/ freight vessel) She was built in 1920 at Fort Smith NT Canada by George F Askew. 151' x 35.3' x 6.1' 876gt 517rt. Powered by a 400hp steam two-cylinder engine. She was powered by a steam engine from the first two Distributors. She was launched in August by Miss Alma Guest. In 1920 she was operated by Lamson and Hubbard in service from Fort Smith to Aklavik NWT. This continued after her ownership was transferred to the Alberta and Arctic Transportation Company which was formed by Lamson and Hubbard and the BC Express Company in 1921. In 1924 her ownership, through Alberta and Arctic Transportation, became that of the Hudson's Bay Company when Lamson and Hubbard sold out. She carried a crew of 32. The high superstructure and flat bottom made it highly susceptible to winds so that navigation on lakes and in the wide sections of the river were often delayed until the weather was calm. Four or five scows carrying freight were often pushed ahead through deep water, but these had to be taken through one at a time in shallow water. It took about 30 days to make the full trip to Aklavik. She was scrapped in 1946 and the paddlewheel was abandoned at Fort Smith NT where the paddlewheel has been preserved in a park.

Dixie II[258] (US) (passenger vessel) Powered by Caterpillar engine and a propeller. She is a 'cosmetic' sternwheeler whose paddles are decorative. She is the largest cruising vessel in South Lake Tahoe based on the Nevada shore since the 1970s. In 2021 she was owned by Zephyr Cove Resort and Lake Tahoe Cruises which are divisions of Aramark, Zephyr Cove NV.

Dixie Belle[259] (ex- *River Queen*) (US) 68gt. She served public cruises on Saguaro Lake (northeast of Phoenix AZ, just north of Mesa and Apache Junction). She was employed on Lake Havasu from the early 1980s through 2011, providing daily service to the community, tourists and for private functions. In 2021 she was owned by Keith Fernung and Aaron Ashbaugh, Lake Havasu AZ.

Dixie Thompson 006694 (US) (passenger vessel/ freighter) She was built in 1870 at Portland OR USA. 155.0' x 28,2' x 6.5' Wood. 443.44gt 296.49nt. Powered by two 21nhp horizontal (high pressure 18" x 84") steam engines. In 1870 she was owned by the Oregon Steam Navigation Co. She was employed on the lower Columbia River out of Astoria. She was owned by the Oregon Railroad & Navigation Co. In 1893 she was reported to have been broken up.

Dixon[260] (US) (tug) She was built in 1913 at Portland OR. 161' x 29.5' x 7.2' Wood. Powered by two 15nhp horizontal (high pressure 15" x 84") steam engines. In 1913 she was owned by the Shaver Transportation Co.

Dogpower[261] (US) (sidewheeler) (freighter) Wood. Powered by a steam engine. She was employed in California rivers.

Dogpower[262] (US) (workboat) She was built in 1911 at the Iditarod River AK. She was a wooden flat-bottom scow design with a small cabin. Powered by two dogs running on treadmills driving a sternwheel. Two extra dogs were kept in reserve for the relief of the working dogs. She was employed on the Iditarod River AK.

Dolphin[263] (US) (sidewheeler) (freighter) She was built in 1850. Wood. Powered by a steam engine. She was employed on California rivers. She was reported to have gone out of operation about 1868.

Don't Bother Me[264] (US) (sidewheeler) (passenger/ freight vessel) She was built in 1873 at Bird Island OR. 74' Wood. Powered by a 4nhp (8" x 24") steam engine. In 1873 she was owned by Edward P Dove. She was reported to have been dismantled in 1880 on Bird Island.

Dora (see *Olive May*)

Dorothy 157505 (US) (passenger/ freight vessel) She was built in 1898 at Seattle WA USA. 75.3' x 26.0' x 3.8' Wood. 126gt 62rt. Powered by a steam engine. In 1912 she was repowered with a gasoline engine. In 1898 she was owned by Koyokuk Mining & Exploration Co. She is reported by Murray Lundberg to have worked in Alaska/YT in 1898. In 1910 she was owned by Tacoma WA USA interests.

Douglas[265] 212684 (US) (passenger/ freight vessel) She was built in 1914 at Wenatchee WA USA. 64.4' x 18.24' x 3.3' Wood. 96gt 88nt. Powered by an 80ihp gasoline engine. In 1920 she was wrecked at the Rock Island Rapids.

Dover[266,267] 006747 (US) (freighter) She was built in 1869 at San Francisco CA USA. Wood. 183.64gt 101.41nt. Powered by an 80nhp steam engine. She was employed on California rivers. In 1869 she was owned by the California Steam Navigation Co. In 1871 she was owned by the California Pacific Railroad Co.

Dover[268,269] 157318 (US) She was built in 1891 at Sacramento CA by the Sacramento Transportation Co. 150' Wood. 244gt 191nt. Powered by a 100ihp steam engine. She was owned by the California Steam Navigation Company. In 1871 she was taken over by the California Pacific Railroad Co., San Francisco CA. She was employed on California rivers. On August 28, 1932, she was destroyed by fire in the conflagration that burned 10 vessels on the Yolo side of the Sacramento River. She was reported as having been broken up in 1935.

Dredger No. 1 157504 (US) (dredge, later a freighter) In 1898 she was built at Portland OR. 100.0' x 26.2' x 6.7' Wood. 282gt 222nt. Powered by a 64ihp steam engine. After her service as a dredge, she was in service carrying freight in Puget Sound.

Driver (HMS) (sidewheeler) She was built in 1840 at Portsmouth UK by H.M. Dockyard (Portsmouth UK). 180' x 36' x 21' (55m x 11m x 6.4m) 1590gt. Powered by two cylinder direct-acting steam engines by Seaward & Capel. In 1840–1851 she served in the Royal Navy. She arrived at Fort Victoria, Vancouver Island on March 10, 1850. On March 11, 1850, she was berthed in Victoria Harbour to witness Richard Blanshard assume the governorship of the newly formed Colony of Vancouver Island, and she issued a seventeen-gun salute. She was wrecked on August 3, 1861, on Mayaguana Island, the most easterly of the Bahama Islands, in the West Indies.

Drone 100209 (Canada) (tug) She was built in 1892 at Vancouver BC. 40.0' x 16.0' x 3.5' Wood. 29gt 18rt. Powered by a 10hp steam engine. In 1896–1901 she was owned by William Braid, Vancouver BC. In 1905–1914 she was owned by British Columbia Iron Works Co. Ltd., Vancouver BC. In 2014 she was owned by William Braid, Vancouver BC.

Duchesnay270 107151 (Canada) (later US) (later *General Jefferson C. Davis*) (passenger/ freight vessel) In 1898 she was built at Vancouver BC by James M Bulger. 120' x 21' x 4'. Wood. 277gt 184rt. Powered by a 9.6nhp steam engine by James Reese & Sons, Pittsburgh PA USA. In 1898 she was owned by the Canadian Pacific Railway Co. Montreal QC. In 1899 she was owned by ET Rathbone. In 1899 she was sold to the United States Army Quartermaster Corps. In 1899 she was transferred to the US Registry. In 1901 she was renamed as the *General Jefferson C. Davis*. In 1922 she was owned by the Alaskan Engineering Commission which in 1923 was reorganized as The Alaska Railroad. In 1923 she was owned by the Alaskan Railroad as a work boat. She was employed at Cook Inlet Alaska, later taken over by the United States Quartermaster Corps. In 1933 she was reported as having been broken up at Nenana AK USA. (General Jefferson C Davis was the first commander of the Department of Alaska from 1867 to 1870 and was not related to the ex-President of the Confederacy).

Duchess (Image from Maritime Museum of British Columbia 000402)

Duchess[271] (Canada) (passenger/ freight vessel) She was built in 1886 at Golden BC Canada by Frank P Armstrong. 60' Wood. 32gt. In 1886 she was owned by Captain Frank P Armstrong for Upper Columbia service. She was powered by a steam engine which was brought from Montreal and had been used in a ferry on the St. Lawrence for 45 years previously. She sank in 1887 after a severe wreck near the Canyon Creek rapids. She sank again three weeks later, which caused her to be dismantled in 1888 with her engines going to the second *Duchess*.

Duchess 090800 (Canada) (passenger/ freight vessel) She was built in 1888 at Golden BC Canada by Alexander Watson. 81.6' x 17.3' x 4.6' Wood. 145.48gt 91.66rt. Powered by two 4.5hp high pressure horizontal steam engines by GA Pontbriand, Sorel QC Canada. In 1888–1902 she was owned by Captain Francis (Frank) P Armstrong, Golden BC. She was built from lumber purchased in a sawmill, designed with cabins and a dining room. The engines came from the dismantled *Duchess*. She was employed on the upper Columbia River and Lake Windermere. In December 1902 she was reported as having been broken up with her engines going to the *Ptarmigan*.

Dude[272] (US) Wood. Powered by a gasoline engine. She was characterized in a 1901 newspaper article as a 'tramp sternwheeler' and was employed in the Stockton CA area.

Duke (The) (see *Putah*)

Dusty Diamon157522 (US) (freighter) She was built in 1898 at St. Michael AK USA. 75.0' x 17.0' x 4.0' Wood. 101gt 86nt. Powered by a steam engine. In 1898 she was owned by the Klondike Promotion Co. She was wrecked in the Upper Tanana River AK USA some time between 1906–1917.

E.D. Baker[273] (US) (passenger vessel) She was built in 1862 at Vancouver WT. 116' x 25' x ? Wood. 131gt. Powered by a steam engine. In 1862 she was owned by the People's Transportation Co., Salem OR. She was employed on the Columbia River. In 1862 she sank near Oswego, raised and her engines were removed and used in the *Reliance* and then later in the *Alice*.

E.G. English (see *S.G. Simpson*)

E.N. Cooke[274] 008762 (US) (passenger vessel) She was built in 1871 at Portland OR USA. 150.0' x 25.0' x 6.0' Wood. 415.95gt 299.28rt. Powered by a steam engine. In 1871–1890 she was owned by Portland OR USA interests. On March 4, 1890, she was wrecked and sunk below the Clackamas Rapids in the Willamette River.

E.W. Purdy[275] (US) She was built in 1888 at Utsalady WA. 97' x 23' x 6.4' Wood. 156.58gt 83.92nt. Powered by a 94ihp steam engine. In 1910 she was reported as having been abandoned.

Eagle[276] (US) She was built in 1902 at Sandpoint ID USA. 92.0' Wood. Powered by a steam engine.

Echo[277] 008142 (US) (passenger vessel) She was built in 1865 at Canemah OT by John Gates. 122.0' Wood. 273gt. Powered by a steam engine. In 1865 she was owned by the Willamette River Steam Navigation Co. In 1866 she was owned by The People's Navigation Co. In 1871 she was owned by the Oregon Steamship Co. She was employed on the Willamette River until about 1870 when she was abandoned and in 1873 she was reported to have been broken up.

Echo 136395 (US) She was built in 1893 at Snohomish WA USA. 70.2' x 10.2' x 2.0' Wood. 36.89gt 30.02nt. Powered by a steam engine. She was home ported at Seattle WA.

Echo 136887 (US) (passenger vessel) She was built in 1901 at Coquille City OR USA by Ellingson. 66.0' x 16.4' x 3.0' Wood. 76gt 53nt. Powered by a steam engine. In 1903 she was employed on the Coquille River OR USA. In 1911 she was reported to have been abandoned.

Eclipse[278] (US) (sidewheeler) She was built in 1854. Wood. 478gt. Powered by a steam engine. In 1854 she was owned by the California Steam Navigation Co. She was in service on the Sacramento River CA. She is reported to have been converted to a barge later in her life. She was reported as having been broken up in 1855 (some sources suggest this occurred in 1861).

Edgar 100682 (Canada) (passenger/ freight vessel) She was built in 1893 at New Westminster BC Canada. 90.0' x 18.0' x 5.0' Wood. 165gt 114rt. Powered by a steam engine. In 1893–1898 she was owned by the Lower Fraser River Navigation Co. On September 30, 1898, a huge fire destroyed New Westminster. She was tied up at the wharf and fire was consuming the sheds on the wharf when the firemen arrived. The *Bon Accord* quickly caught fire along with two other steamers (the *Gladys* and the *Edgar*). The three steamers drifting down the river set each dock and vessel alight as they touched the shore.

Edison 201371 (US) She was built in 1904 at Edison WA USA. 85.0' x 20.5' x 4.1' Wood. 137gt 93nt. Powered by a steam engine. In 1904 she was owned by the American Tugboat Corp. In 1916 she was involved as the base in the gunfire attack on the union members of the International Workers of the World travelling in the steamer *Verona* when they attempted to land at Everett WA—an event known as the Everett Massacre. Gunfire broke out from the dock, and on the *Edison*, resulting in deaths and injuries on both sides. In 1929 at the end of her life, she was moored on Dead Water Slough in the Snohomish River, Puget Sound WA.

Edith R.[279,280] (US) (freighter) She was built in 1883 at Seattle WA USA. 75' x 16' x ? Wood. 109.62gt 57.84nt. Powered by two horizontal (high pressure) steam engines. In 1887 she was owned by Captain Brooks Randolph. She carried railway iron in the White River Valley WA. She was employed on the Snoqualmie River and the White River. In 1905 she was reported as having been abandoned.

Edmonton Queen[281,282] (later *Edmonton Riverboat*) 817706 (Canada) (8888886 IMO) (passenger ferry) She was built in 1993 at Edmonton AB Canada by Scott Steel. Ltd. 51.79m x 12.01m x 2.01m (169.9' x 39.5' x 2.5') Steel. 750.49gt 538rt. Powered by a two 350bhp Cummins NTA855 diesel engines. She was a capacity of 399 passengers. In 1992 she was owned by North Saskatchewan Riverboat Company, Edmonton AB. The Scott Steel interests refused to release the boat, claiming that it was still owed $1.35 million. She remained in Scott Steel's yard during the two years of lawsuits which ended with the North Saskatchewan Riverboat Co. declaring bankruptcy. In 1995 she was owned by Carrington Properties. In 2003–2013 she was owned by Riverboat Inc., Edmonton AB. In 2017–2021 she was owned by 1968868 Alberta Ltd., Edmonton AB.

Edmonton Riverboat (see *Edmonton Queen*)

Edna[283] (US) (freighter) She was built in 1850. Wood. 30gt. Powered by a steam engine. She was employed on California rivers. She was reported to have gone out of service about 1868.

Edward Everett Jr.[284,285] (US) (freighter) She was built in 1849. 56' Wood. 50t. Powered by a steam engine. Her hull was a flat bottom design. She was employed on California rivers. In 1849 she was wrecked when she was snagged in the Sacramento River. Her hull was sold for conversion to a ferry and her engine was sold to gold miners.

Egalite[286] 136243 (US) (tug) She was built in 1891 at Woodland WA USA. 76' x 20' x 4' Wood. 120gt 82nt. Powered by two horizontal (7" x 24" high pressure) steam engines. She was reported to have been dismantled in 1896 at Portland OR.

El Capitan 008230 (US) (sidewheeler) (ferry) She was built in 1868 at San Francisco CA USA. 194.0' x 33.6' x 14.5' Wood. 982.76gt 669.52nt. Powered by a 250ihp steam engine. In 1868–1910 she was owned by San Francisco CA USA interests. In 1927 she was reported to have been abandoned.

El Dorado[287] (US) (sidewheeler) (freighter) She was built in 1849. Wood. 153gt. Powered by a steam engine. In 1850 she was in service on the Sacramento River CA and San Joaquin River. She was converted by Domingo Marcucci from a 3-masted schooner to a sidewheeler at Benicia CA after sailing her out from the east coast. She was reported to have gone out of service about 1868.

Elathine[288] 220306 (US) (ferry) She was built in 1920 at Hover WA. Wood. 56' x 20' x 3.1' Wood. 29gt 21nt. Powered by a 45ihp steam engine. In 1920–1929 she was owned by Frank Knopp, Hover WA USA. In 1931–1941 she was owned by Northwest Ferries Co., Walla Walla WA.

Elbe (US) (freighter) She was built about 1849. Wood. Powered by a steam engine. She was employed on the Sacramento River CA.

Eldorado (see *Philip B. Low*)

Eleanor[289] 214250 (US) (ferry) She was built in 1916 at Burbank WA. 56.3' x 16.0' x 2.7' Wood. 15gt 15nt. Powered by a 16ihp gasoline engine. She was reported to have been abandoned about 1924.

Elenore[290] 136491 (US) (passenger) She was built in 1895 at Portland OR USA. 160' x 34' x 4.5' Wood. 494gt 468nt. Powered by a steam engine.

Eliza (US) She was built in 1824 in the eastern USA. In 1850 she was sailed around Cape Horn to California. In 1854 she was owned by the California Steam Navigation Co. In 1868 she was reported to have been broken up.

Eliza Anderson 007967 (US) (sidewheeler) (passenger vessel) She was built in 1858 at Portland, Oregon Territory USA by Samuel Farnham. She was launched November 27, 1858. 140' x 24.5' x ? Wood. 279gt. Powered by a walking beam steam engine. In 1857 she was owned by the Columbia River Steam Navigation Co. She carried the first large detachment of Royal Engineers from Esquimalt to Sapperton in 1858. She was the first vessel inspected in Victoria after the appointment of a steamship inspector. In 1859 she was sold to John T Wright and the Bradford Bros., Olympia WA USA. In 1859 she was on the Victoria – Olympia run. In 1860 she was involved in an American fugitive slave controversy when an enslaved man escaped from his Washington State owner and made his way on the vessel to Victoria. She had a monopoly in 1866 of the traffic between Victoria and Olympia. In 1870 she was replaced by the *Olympia* and used as a spare boat until 1877. In 1877 she made several trips to Cassiar. At Comox BC she went out of control and rammed the ship *Glory of the Seas*. She was laid up 1877–1882. In 1882 she sank at a wharf in Seattle WA. In 1882 she was raised and overhauled by Captain Tom Wright. She was placed on the New Westminster to Seattle run. In 1884 she was in competition with the *Olympia* on the Victoria run. In 1885 she was seized by Collector Beecher in Port Townsend for carrying illegal Chinese immigrants. She was acquitted of the charges. In 1885c she was sold to Captain JW Tarte, Victoria BC.

She was sold to the Washington Steamboat Co. She was sold to the Puget Sound & Alaska Steamship Co. and laid up in the Snohomish River. In 1897–1898 she was owned by the Northwestern Steamship Co., managed by Captain DB Jackson. In 1897 she was rebuilt at the Moran Shipyard, Seattle WA USA for Alaska service. In 1897 she sailed to Alaska for the Klondike Gold Rush.

Eliza Ladd[291] 135237 (US) (ferry) She was built in 1875 at Portland OR USA. Wood. 118.47gt 94.48nt. Powered by a steam engine. She was employed on the Columbia River. In 1885 she was reported as having been broken up.

Elizabeth J. Irving[292] 080901 (Canada) (passenger/ freight vessel) 167.0' x 33.8' x 8.5' Wood. 848gt 692.99rt. Powered by an 86.07hp steam engine. She was built in 1881 at Victoria BC by Alexander Watson. In 1881 she was owned by the Pioneer Line (John Irving), New Westminster BC. She was launched June 18, 1881. She was powered by a steam engines from the *Royal City*. She was named for the wife of Captain William Irving for service between Victoria and Yale built as a response to the *Western Slope*. She was piloted directly by Captain Irving on her maiden voyage to Yale, arriving after dark using her electric searchlight before an amazed audience on shore. She was a fast vessel making a trip from New Westminster to Victoria in 6 hours. On her second run she caught fire at Hope while landing and had to be cut free from the dock to save the town. She floated to Italian Bar where she was stranded and burned to the waterline. Her life was short—she was launched on June 18, 1881, and was destroyed by fire at Hope BC September 29. 1881.

Elizabeth Louise[293] (later *Alaska Queen*; then *Queen of Seattle*) (US) 138' Steel. She was built in 1975 at Rancho Cordova CA USA. She served in the California delta, at Sacramento CA. and on the Sacramento River. She was owned by Hal Wilmunder. After laying in a scrap yard, the engines were purchased for the *Elizabeth Louise* in 1975. Construction was started in 1975 and finished in 1981. The hull was built in Rancho Cordova, California. In 1984–2003 she was owned by Harold Wilmunder. In 2003, the 78-year-old Wilmunder got a call from police saying it appeared a hatch had been forced open near the boat's bow. Wilmunder went to investigate and was never seen alive again. The boat was barged to Seattle, renovated, and then steamed its way to Ketchikan to begin running tours under the name "*Alaska Queen*." In 2005–2015 she was owned by Alaska Travel Adventures. As the *Alaska Queen* she was offering harbor cruises at Ketchikan AK USA. In 2010–2013 she offered tours on two and a half-hour loops around Lake Union WA. She was advertised for sale at Seattle WA in 2015.

Elk[294] (US) (passenger) She was built in 1857 at Canemah OT by Samuel Farnam. 98' x 18' x 4'. Wood. Powered by two horizontal (10.5'X 48") steam engines. In 1857 she was owned by Chris Sweitzer, FX Mathieu & John Marshall, and George Pease. She was employed on the Yamhill River. In 1861 she was destroyed by a boiler explosion.

Elk[295] (see St. Joseph)

Elk[296] (US) She was built in 1869. 41'. Wood. 24.28gt. Powered by a steam engine. She was employed on California rivers. She was reported to have gone out of service in 1872.

Elk[297] 213314 (US) (tug) She was built in 1915 at Pittsburg CA. 75.0' x 20.5' x 4.4'. Wood. 97gt 65nt. Powered by a 150ihp steam engine. She was employed on California rivers. She was reported to have been dismantled in 1918.

Ella 202300 (US) (passenger/ freight vessel) She was built in 1905 at Seattle WA USA by Henry Bratnober and assembled at Whitehorse YT. 120.3' x 28' x 4.5'. Wood. 419gt 268nt. Powered by a 150ihp steam engine. In 1905 she was owned by the Tanana Trading Co. and employed on the Tanana River. In 1906 she was owned by the North American Transportation & Trading Co. In 1906–1909 she was owned by the Merchants' Yukon Transportation Co. On July 17, 1907, she foundered at Tolovana (on the Tanana River) AK USA.

Ellen[298] 008567 (US) (freighter) She was built in 1869 at Stockton CA USA. 78.5' x 20.2' x 4.5'. Wood. 90.58gt 74.89nt. Powered by 40nhp steam engine. She was employed on California rivers. She was reported to have gone out of service about 1872.

Ellen[299] 135843 (US) She was built in 1885 at Fairhaven CA. 65.5' x 16.0' x 6.3'. Wood. 57.7gt 39nt. In 1910 she was owned by San Francisco CA USA

Interests. Powered by a steam engine. She was employed on California rivers. She was reported to have gone out of service about 1919.

Ellen 213136 (US) (passenger/ freight vessel) She was built in 1915 at Pasco WA. 63' x 14' x 3'. Wood. 55gt 47nt. Powered by two horizontal (8" x 24" high pressure) 4nhp steam engines. In 1915 she was owned by HC Hellpentell. In 1917 she was rebuilt at Portland OR by JD Zinnalt. She was reported to have gone out of service about 1920.

Ellis[300] 136254 (US) (freighter) She was built in 1891 at Ballard WA USA. 129.7' x 27.7' x 7.4'. Wood. 325.08gt 199.28nt. Powered by a 180ihp triple expansion steam engine. In 1891–1893 she was owned by Captain William H Ellis, Seattle WA. She was employed on the Sidney BC – Seattle route. On December 11, 1893, during a weekend layover in Sidney, a new boiler was installed. A fire was lit to test the boiler, and then banked for the night. The vessel caught fire in the middle of the night and this worsened when a barrel of kerosene exploded. The lines to the ship were cut to save the wharf and nearby property. A strong breeze caught the *Ellis* and she drifted. Captain Ellis pursued her in a small steamer and catching up he caused her to be scuttled about one mile from Bremerton WA in shallow water.

Elmore 136491 (US) (passenger vessel) She was built in 1895 at Portland OR USA. 160.0' x 34.0' x 4.5'. Wood. 493gt 467nt. Powered by two Horizontal (16" x 72" high pressure) 125ihp steam engines. In 1895–1910 she was owned by the Oregon Rail Road & Navigation Co., Portland, OR USA. She was employed on the Portland to Oregon City route. In 1917 she was reported to have been abandoned at Oregon City.

Elsie May 136745 (US) She was built in 1899 at Wallula WA. 40' x 22.4' x 3.5'. Wood. 32gt 13nt. In 1907 she was rebuilt and re-registered.

Elsie May 204662 (US) (ferry) She was built in 1907 at Wallula WA. 53.5' x 18.0' x 3.3'. Wood. 26gt 16nt. Powered by a 15ihp gasoline engine. In 1910 she was owned by Puget Sound WA USA interests. She was reported to have gone out of service about 1915.

Elwood[301] 136181 (US) She was built in 1891 at Portland OR USA by Johnston & Oleson. 154' x 30' x 7.5' Wood. 510gt 420rt. Powered by a steam engine. In 1891 she was owned by Elldredge & Abernethy Bros. (She was employed on the Willamette River). On Tuesday August 25, 1891, while carrying passengers and a cargo of 500 sacks of oats, the *Elwood* hit a snag at Ash Island, about 35 miles south of Portland, and sank. In 1893 she was employed between Portland and Albany. In 1894 she was owned by Lewis River Transportation Co. employed on the Lewis River to Lake River service. In 1898 she was owned by William J Stephens, Victoria BC, and she was employed on the Stikine River in 1898 for the Cassiar Central Railway Company and then was laid up at Wrangel AK. In 1903 she was sold to Captain HB MacDonald, Seattle WA for Puget Sound service. On August 16, 1904, while unloading freight at Avon, WA she was destroyed by fire. Her remains were salvaged and she was rebuilt. She was reported to have been abandoned about 1920.

Emerald (US) (tug) She was built in 1869 at San Francisco CA, shipped overland and assembled at Tahoe City, NV. In 1869 she was owned by Ben Holladay for towing logs on Lake Tahoe. In 1881 her boiler was condemned.

Emil[302] (US) Wood. Powered by a steam engine. She is reported by Murray Lundberg to have worked in Alaska/YT in 1902.

Emily M.[303] 136667 (US) (passenger/ freight vessel) She was built in 1898 at Brownsville OR USA. 32.4' x 9.3' x 2.6' Wood. 12gt 9nt. Powered by a steam engine. She was transferred to Alaska in 1900.

Emma[304] 008655 (US) She was built in 1870 at Stockton CA USA by Keeps & Bergen. 85.2' x 22.5' x 4.7' Wood. 87.87gt 76.98nt. Powered by a 25nhp steam engine. She was employed on California rivers. She was reported to have been out of service around 1899.

Emma 107260 (Canada) She was built in 1898 at Lake Bennett BC. 54.0' x 16.0' x 3.0' Wood. 82gt 52rt. Powered by a 3nhp steam engine. In 1898–1910 she was owned by William J Ranta, Lake Bennett BC. She was reportedly wrecked and in 1920 her register was closed.

Emma[305] (freighter) Wood. Powered by a steam engine. She arrived in Dawson YT in 1899 and her engine was removed.

Emma 205288 (US) (tug) She was built in 1902 at Oakland CA USA. 42.0' x 11.0' x 4.2'. Wood. 11gt 7nt. Powered by a 40ihp gasoline engine. In 1910 she was owned by San Francisco CA USA interests.

Emma Hayward[306] 008763 (US) (passenger vessel) She was built in 1871 at Portland OR USA by John Holland. 177.0' x 29.0' x 7.5'. Wood. 613.16 456.07nt. Powered by two horizontal (17" x 84" high pressure) steam engines from the *Webfoot* (026714). In 1871–1882 she was owned by the Oregon Steam Navigation Co. Portland OR USA. She was employed on the Columbia River. In 1882 she was transferred to Puget Sound employed on the Seattle – Tacoma – Olympia route. In 1891 she was transferred back to the Columbia River employed as a tugboat. In 1900 she was reported to have been broken up.

Emma Nott (later *Arctic Queen*) 107236 (Canada) She was built in 1898 at Lake Bennett BC Canada by Robert Joseph Nott. 56.0' x 16.0' x 3.5'. Wood. 73gt 46rt. Powered by a 7nhp engine. In 1898–1901 she was owned by Robert Joseph Nott, Victoria BC. In 1901 she was chartered by the British Yukon Navigation Co. as a mail boat at Dawson YT. In 1903 she was sold to Arthur C Simmonds, Dawson City YT. In 1908 she was reported to have been broken up.

Empire[307] (US) (sidewheeler) (freighter) She was built in 1851 at San Francisco CA USA. Wood. 149gt. Powered by a steam engine. She was employed on California rivers. About 1863 she was reported to have been abandoned.

Empire City[308,309] 008506 (US) (freighter) She was built in 1869 at Stockton CA USA by Stephen Davis. 120.5' x 24.4' x 4.7'. Wood. 187.6gt 158.48rt. Powered by an 80nhp steam engine. She was owned by the California Steam Navigation Company. In 1871 she was taken over by the California Pacific Railroad Co., San Francisco CA. She was employed on California rivers. She was reported to have gone out of service about 1899.

Empress 202834 (US) (sidewheeler) (passenger vessel) She was built in 1906 at Terminal Island CA USA. 77.5' x 18.4' x 2.7' Wood. 39gt 26nt. Powered by a 65ihp gasoline engine. In 1910 she was owned by Los Angeles CA USA interests.

Empress of the North[310] (later *American Empress*) 1140867 (US) 9263538 (IMO) 299.3' x 58.3' x 20' Steel. 296gt 20Int. In 2003 she was owned by the Majestic America Line. In 2013 the *Empress of the North* was acquired by the American Queen Steamboat Company. She was owned by the E.N. Boat Ltd. In 2017–2021 she was owned by Eon Partners LLC, New Albany IN USA. During her years as the *Empress of the North*, the ship ran aground five times. She hit bottom during her launching from the yard when the restraint system failed and some of the boat builders had to jump in the waters of Puget Sound to avoid being run over. She struck a navigation lock in October 2003 at the Ice Harbor Dam on the Snake River and suffered another grounding in November 2003 near The Dalles in the Columbia River. She grounded again in March 2006 near Washougal in the Columbia River. On May 14, 2007, on a clear day, with calm sea she hit a rock off Juneau, AK, and had to be evacuated. The *Empress of the North* did not sink but was heavily damaged. In 2014 she was employed on the Columbia and Snake Rivers for the American Queen Steamboat Company after about six years of lay-up. The *American Empress* is propelled mainly by the stern paddlewheel but has additional Z-drives for higher speed and difficult navigation situations.

Encinal 135972 (US) (sidewheeler) (ferry) She was built in 1888 at San Francisco CA USA. 245.0' x 40.4' x 14.5' Wood. 2,014gt 1,633nt. Powered by a 1,000ihp steam engine. In 1888–1910 she was owned by San Francisco CA USA interests.

Englewood[311] 136716 (US) (passenger/ freight vessel) In 1898 she was built at St. Michael, District of Alaska, USA. 51.0' x 16.0' x 3.6' Wood. 26gt 19nt. Powered by a steam engine.

Enterprise (US) (sidewheeler) (freighter) She was built in 1854 at Sacramento CA. Wood. 94gt. Powered by a steam engine. In 1854–1855 she was owned by the Citizen's Steam Navigation Co. In 1854 she was employed on the Marysville to San Francisco route. Her owners were forced into bankruptcy by the aggressive competition from the California Steam Navigation Co. In 1855 she was owned by the California Steam Navigation Co. In 1863 her machinery and boilers were removed and installed a new vessel being constructed for China interests. In 1864 she was reported to have been sold to foreign interests.

Enterprise (US) In 1855 she was built at Canemah OR USA. 115' x 22' x 3.5' Wood. 194gt. Powered by two horizontal (12" x 48" high pressure) 9.6nhp steam engines. In 1855 she was owned by a syndicate headed by Captain Pease. In 1858 she was the second sternwheeler to work the Fraser River, under the command of Captain Thomas Wright. In 1859 she was transferred to the Chehalis River, WT USA.

Enterprise[312] 008141 (US) She was built in 1863 at Canemah OR by Captain George Pease. 125' x 24' x 4'. Wood. 194gt. Powered by two horizontal (14" x 48" high pressure) 13nhp steam engines. In 1863 she was owned by the People's Transportation Co., Salem OR. She was reported to have been broken up at Canemah about 1875.

Enterprise[313,314,315] 083441 (US) (sidewheeler) (passenger vessel) She was built in 1861 at San Francisco CA USA. 142.5' x 27.7' x 6.9' Wood. 380gt 302nt. Powered by a 75hp walking beam (30" x 72") steam engine. In 1861 she was owned by William Curry and Peter F Doling. In 1861 she was built for service out of Stockton CA but in 1862 she was moved to Victoria for competition with the Hudson's Bay Co. vessel *Eliza Anderson* on the Puget Sound route. In 1862 she was purchased by the Hudson's Bay Co. for the Victoria to New Westminster route. In 1864 she was on the Victoria to Sooke run for the Leechtown Gold Rush. In 1871–1872 she was working between Victoria and New Westminster. In 1883 she was incorporated into the Canadian Pacific Navigation Co. Ltd. In 1878 she was rebuilt to 380t. In 1883 she was owned by the Canadian Pacific Navigation Co. In 1884, for a brief time, she was employed in opposition to the *Amelia* on the Victoria – Nanaimo run. On July 28, 1885, she was in a collision with the R.P. *Rithet* and sank at Cadboro Bay BC with a loss of two passengers.

Enterprise[316] 008434 (US) She was built in 1868 at Stockton CA USA. 136' x 29.8' x 4.7' Wood. 246.06gt. Powered by an 80nhp steam engine. She was reported to have gone out of service about 1895.

Enterprise[317] (US) (sidewheeler) (later *Tatung*) She was built in 1861 at San Francisco CA USA. In 1862 she flew the US flag in Chinese waters under consular documents. In 1866 she was renamed as *Tatung*.

The City of Quesnel has displayed the boilers from the ***Enterprise*** on Front Street beside the Fraser River Walking Bridge (Heritage Corner). (Image courtesy of Elizabeth Hunter, Quesnel & District Museum & Archives)

Enterprise (British Columbia Colonial Register) She was built in 1863 at Fort Alexandria, British Columbia by James W Trahey. 110.0' x 20.0' x ? Wood. Powered by a 60np (12" x 36") steam engine. In 1863 she was owned by Captain Thomas (Tom) Wright and Gustavus Blin Wright. A company was organized in 1863 to operate the steamer *Enterprise* on the Fraser River between Soda Creek and Quesnel. In 1871 she worked up the Nechako-Stuart waterway supplying the Omenica mining camps. She was reported as having been laid up at Trembleur Lake BC.

Enterprise (US) (passenger vessel) She was built in 1870 at Gardiner OR. 140' Wood. 247gt. In 1873 she was reported to have been wrecked.

Enterprise[318] 135642 (US) She was built in 1883 at Astoria OR USA by John McCann. 81.0' x 18.0' x 6.0' Wood. 94.45gt 47.23rt. Powered by a steam engine. In 1883 she was owned by Shavely and Heamble, Astoria OR. She was reported to have been broken up about 1892.

Enterprise 136144 (US) She was built in 1890 at Portland OR. 106' x 27' x 3.3' Wood. 137.41gt 137nt. Powered by two horizontal (10" x 36") 6nhp steam engines. In 1890 she was owned by the Star Sand Co., Portland OR. In 1922 she was rebuilt.

Enterprise 136965 (US) (tug) She was built in 1902 at Portland OR USA. 115.0' x 25.0' x 4.5' Wood. 333gt 309nt. Powered by a steam engine. (Her engines came from the Enterprise 136144). In 1902–1910 she was owned by Portland OR USA interests. She was reported to have been abandoned about 1916.

Enterprise (see North Star)

The sidewheeler tug **Eppleton Hall** (Image from the Library of Congress HAER CAL,38-SANFRA,167-2)

Eppleton Hall 133448 (UK) (US) (sidewheeler) A tug boat built in 1914 in South Shields UK by Hepple & Co. Ltd. 100.5' x 21.1' x 10.8' Steel. 166gt 27nt. Powered by an 80nhp steam engine by Hepple & Co. Ltd. In 1914–1927 she was owned by Lambton, Hetton & Joicey Collieries Ltd. (ET Nisbet, manager). In 1946, she was purchased by France Fenwick, Wear and Tyne Ltd., which operated her in the Wear River until 1964. She was brought to San Francisco through the Panama Canal in 1969–1970. She is on display at the San Francisco Maritime National Historical Park.

Erastus Corning[319] (US) (freighter) She was built in 1850. Wood. 86gt. Powered by a steam engine. She was employed on California rivers. She was reported to have gone out of service around 1868.

Ericsson 007723 (US) (sidewheeler) She was built in 1852 at New York, NY USA by Perine, Patterson & Stack. 260' x 40' x 17' (79.2m x 12.2m x 5.2m) Wood. 1645.68gt. In 1851 the Ericsson-cycle engine was used to power a 2,000-ton ship, the caloric ship *Ericsson*, and ran flawlessly for 73 hours. The caloric engines moved the ship across the water with significantly less fuel consumption than the other steamers of the day. The combination engine produced about 300 horsepower (220 kW). It had a combination of four dual-piston engines; the larger expansion piston/cylinder, at 14 feet (4.3 m) in diameter. Sometime after the trials, the *Ericsson* sank in a storm off New York. On being raised the *Ericsson* was fitted with steam engines. When she was raised, the Ericsson-cycle engine was removed, and a steam engine took its place. In 1852 she was owned by USA interests. She served for five years in the trans-Atlantic route for John Kitching under charter to the Collins Line. In 1861 she was chartered to the United States Navy as a transport for the assault on Port Royal South Carolina USA. In 1861 she was chartered to the North American Steamship Co. for service between New York and Panama. In 1867 her engines were removed, and she was converted to sail. In 1867 she was sold to WW Sherman. In 1884 she was owned by San Francisco CA USA interests. As a sailing vessel the *Ericsson* broke many records around the horn, and still holds the record for the fastest voyage from Shanghai to Victoria, in 28 days. In 1874 she sailed from San Francisco to Liverpool in 103 days. Most of her sail career was spent hauling grain around Cape Horn from San Francisco to Europe until in 1890 she was leased to British interests. In 1892 she was sold to

Boole & Co., San Francisco USA. On November 19, 1892, she while bound for Nanaimo from San Francisco for a cargo of coal she was stranded at Folger Island in Barkley Sound BC. In the Juan de Fuca Strait, a gale drove her onto the Vancouver Island coast into Barkley Sound. The captain went ashore to use the newly installed telegraph line to Victoria at Cape Beale Lighthouse to request assistance. The vessel's bow was on a rock while her stern was awash. The steamer *Alert* offered assistance which the crew declined thinking that the captain had made alternate arrangements. But the captain could not get his message through to Victoria and the departure of the *Alert* left them helpless. Three days later the lightkeeper managed to get a message through to Victoria and the tug *Lorne* picked up the survivors. The ship was destroyed by the waves.

Esmeralda[320] (US) In 1862 she was built at San Francisco CA USA. 93' x 20' x ? Wood. 46gt. Powered by a steam engine. In 1862 she was constructed to tow the barge Victoria up the Sacramento River. In 1864–1865 she was owned by the Union Line. In 1864 she was brought to the mouth of the Colorado River to meet the demand of the mining boom that occurred up river. She moved farther up the Colorado than any previous vessel. In 1865–1866 she was owned by the Pacific & Colorado Steam Navigation Co. In 1866–1867 she was owned by the Arizona Navigation Co. (creditors of the Pacific & Colorado Steam Navigation Co.) In 1866 she navigated as far as Callville UT to service the Mormon warehouse located there. She was seized at Yuma by the sheriff for unpaid debts. In 1868 she was reported to have been broken up. (Some authorities list this vessel as the *Esmerelda*.)

Essington 156817 (Canada) (snag boat, later converted to a boathouse). She was built in 1931 at Prince Rupert BC by Prince Rupert Dry Dock Co. 100.0 x 29.0' x 5.3' Wood. 310.47gt 128.97rt. Powered by a 360ihp horizontal steam engine. In 1931–1960 she was owned by the Minister of Public Works of Canada, Ottawa ON. In 1960–1965 she was owned by The Corporation of the City of New Westminster, New Westminster BC. In 1967 her power machinery was removed, and she was pulled ashore and turned into a Sea Cadet boathouse on Annacis Island. She became a floating restaurant in 1971. Gord Darling (British Columbia Nautical History Facebook Group 17/07/2019) stated "She later became a dry land restaurant just under the Pacific St. end of the Burrard Bridge! The Jib Set sailing school was about to start building on the site and we came down to do things and discovered she had been floated in and pulled up on our lot. The landlord had double leased the property, so instead of damages, etc. gave us use of the water lot in front and we built on pilings. Both were still there when I left the Jib Set sailing school. They were removed shortly afterwards by another developer."

Ethel Ross (see *Scud*)

Etna[321] (US) She was built in 1850 at Sacramento CA. Wood. Powered by a steam engine. In 1852 she was reported to have been abandoned.

Etna[322] 203622 (US) (passenger/ freight vessel) She was built in 1906 at Portland OR. 60.0' x 11.4' x 3.6'. Wood. 41gt 40nt. Powered by two horizontal (high pressure 5" x 32") steam engines. In 1906 she was owned by Horace Campbell, Portland OR. In 1919 she was reported as having been out of service.

Eugene[323,324] (US) (freighter) She was built in 1894 at Portland OR USA. 140' x 28' x 5'. Wood. 413gt 250nt. Powered by two horizontal (12" x 60" high pressure) steam engines. In 1894 she was owned by Willamette River Navigation Co. In 1898 she was owned by Portland & Alaska Trading & Transportation Co. She was employed for service in the Yukon. Edward L Affleck states: "She reached Union Bay BC under her own steam. The steamship *Bristol*, which was supposed to take her in tow at Union Bay did not arrive, and her the master eluded Customs and set off north. Taken in tow by the *Bristol* at Seymour Narrows, her passengers mutinied in Queen Charlotte Sound and transferred to the *Bristol*. The *Eugene* turned back under her own power and reached Port Townsend. She was employed on the Willamette River and was eventually broken up about 1906."

Eureka[325] (US) (freighter) Wood. Powered by a steam engine. She was a trussed-hull shallow draft vessel that was employed on the Sacramento River.

Eva 136459 (US) (passenger vessel) She was built in 1894 at Portland OR USA. 90.4' x 19.4' x 4.6'. Wood. 130.57gt 66nt. Powered by a 50ihp two horizontal steam engines. In 1910 she was employed at Coos Bay OR and the Umpqua River. She is thought to have gone out of service about 1918.

Eva Fay[326] (US) Wood. Powered by a steam engine. She is reported by Murray Lundberg to have worked in Alaska/YT in 1899.

Evelyn (later *Northern Light*; then *Norcom*) 205767 (US) 116613 (Canada) She was built in 1908 at St. Michael AK USA. 122.0' x 28.6' x 4.4' Wood. 352gt 221nt. Powered by a 150ihp steam engine. In 1908 she was owned by the Upper Tanana Trading Company. She was wrecked on the Yukon River and taken to St. Michael's AK for rebuilding and sold to the North American Transportation & Trading Co. In 1913 she was transferred to Canadian Registry. In 1921 she was owned by the Canadian Yukon Navigation Co. Ltd., Dawson YT. In 1914 she was reported as having been laid up at Hootalinqua Island Yukon River and her bones are an interpretive display.

Expansion[327] 136823 (US) (passenger vessel) She was built in 1900. Powered by a steam engine. 123.0' x 26.0' x 3.5' Wood. 78gt/nt. Powered by a steam engine. On March 13, 1910, she was cut down by ice on the upper Missouri River at Bismarck North Dakota USA.

Explorer[328] (US) She was built in 1857 at Philadelphia PA USA and then shipped via the Isthmus of Panama to the delta estuary of the Colorado River where she was re-assembled. 54' x 13' x ? Iron. Powered by a steam engine. As a warship she was armed with a howitzer. In 1857 she was owned by the United States Army. Lieutenant Joseph C Ives used the vessel to explore and map the Colorado River. She was wrecked just below Black Canyon. She was sold to George Johnson who used her to haul firewood up the Gila River. In 1858 her engine was removed. She was employed as a non-powered barge until 1864 when she was stranded and sank.

Explorer 136583 (US) (passenger/ freight vessel) She was built in 1885 at Mare Island CA USA. 50.0' x 12.0' x 2.5' Wood. 15gt Powered by a steam engine. In 1894 she was owned by the Russian Mission. She was owned by the Northern Commercial Co. On May 3, 1906, she foundered at the Russian Mission, Yukon River, AK USA.

Express[329] (US) (freighter) (sidewheeler) She was built in 1851. Wood. 105gt. Powered by a steam engine. She was employed on California rivers. In 1854–1856 she was owned by the California Steam Navigation Co. In 1870 she was owned by a competitor to the California Steam Navigation Co. on the San Francisco – Oakland route. This venture failed and the ship was sold at auction. She was reported to have gone out of service about 1870. Lytle says she was out of service in 1856.

Express[330] (US) She was built in 1854 at Oregon City OT USA. 111' x 20' x 4' 69nt. Powered by two horizontal (11" x 60" high pressure) 8.3nhp steam engines. In 1854 she was owned by AS Murray (MO). She was reported to have been broken up about 1863 with her engines going to the *Mary Moody*.

Express[331] (US) She was built in 1857 at Portland OT. Wood. 69gt. Powered by a steam engine. She was home ported at Astoria OT. In 1859 she was reported to have been abandoned.

Express[332] (US) (freighter) She was built in 1870. 92' Wood. 74gt. Powered by a steam engine. She was employed on California rivers. She was reported to have gone out of service about 1877.

F.B. Jones[333] 121184 (US) (tug and freighter) She was built in 1901 at Portland OR by T Ellingson. 125.0' x 26.0' x 7.0' Wood. 303gt 271nt. Powered by two horizontal (high pressure 14" x 60") 13nhp steam engines. In 1901 she was owned by FB Jones, Portland OR. She was employed on the lower Columbia River. She was owned by the Willamette & Columbia River Transportation Co. She was owned by the Shaver Transportation Co. She was employed on the lower Columbia River. On November 24, 1907, she was involved in a collision with and was sunk by the Standard Oil tanker *Asuncion* near Mount Coffin. In 1937 she was reported to have been abandoned.

F.H. Kilbourne 107516 (Canada) (passenger/ freight vessel) She was built in 1898 at Bennett Lake BC by James H Calvert. 50.0' x 10.6' x 3.0' Wood. 86.7gt 54.63rt. Powered by two horizontal (5.5" x 20" high pressure) 2nhp steam engines by Pacific Iron Works, Seattle WA, USA. In 1898 she was owned by the Upper Yukon Co. Ltd., Bennett BC. In 1899 she was sold to the Canadian Development Co. (HA McMunn), Victoria BC. In 1897 the frames for the steamers *A.J. Goddard* and *F.H. Killbourne* were cut in San Francisco CA, landed at Dyea AK, together with sawmill parts. These were then shipped over the Chilkoot Pass by pack train and aerial tramway in 1897–1898 to Bennett Lake BC for assembly. In 1901 she was wrecked at the north end of Bennett Lake BC.

F.K. Gustin 121071 (US) (passenger/ freight vessel) She was built in 1898 at Seattle WA USA by the Moran Bros. Shipyard. 176.1' x 35.0' x 4.0' Wood. 718.68gt 409.06nt. Powered by two 700ihp 20" steam engines. In 1898 she was owned by the Seattle-Yukon Transportation Co. In 1898 she was owned by the Alaska Exploration Co. (Liebes & Co., San Francisco CA). In 1898 she was in Yukon River service. In 1901 she was owned by Northern Navigation Co. In 1914 she was owned by the White Pass & Yukon Rail Road. In 1917 she was reported to have been abandoned at St. Marys AK. In 1925 she was reported to have been working out of Juneau for American Yukon Navigation Co.

F.M. Smith (see *H.C. Grady*)

F.P. Armstrong 134032 (Canada) (passenger/rreight Vessel) She was built in 1913 at Spillimacheen BC Canada by the F.P. Armstrong Shipyards. 81' x 20' x 4' Wood. 125.91gt 79.32rt. Powered by a horizontal (12" x 72") high pressure 4.3nhp steam engine built by DW Swain, Stillwater MN. In 1913 she was owned by Edward F Burns & Jordan for Upper Columbia River service. In 1913–1931 she was owned by Edward F Burns, Vancouver BC. In 1914 she was used in the Kootenay Central Railway construction. In 1915 she was laid up and abandoned near Fairmont BC.

F.R.M. & D. Co. No. 1 103151 (Canada) (passenger/treight Vessel) She was built in 1894 at Lytton BC Canada. 133.6' x 30' x 6.3' Wood. 715gt 486rt. Powered by a steam engine. In 1894–1898 she was owned by the Fraser River Mining and Dredging Co., Vancouver BC. In 1901–1912 she was owned by Mrs. Rachel McFarlane, Vancouver BC.

F.Y. Batchelor[334] 120331 (US) She was built in 1878 at Pittsburgh PA USA. 178.6' x 31.0' x 4.0' Wood. 313gt. Powered by a steam engine. In 1885 she was based in Bismarck ND. She was employed on the Yellowstone and Missouri Rivers.

Fairhaven 120762 (US) (sidewheeler) (ferry) She was built in 1889 at Tacoma WA USA by John Holland. 130.2' x 26.5' x 6.2' Wood. 319.39gt 240.57rt. Powered by a steam engine. In 1918 she was reported to have been destroyed by fire.

Fairview 103473 (Canada) (passenger/ freight vessel) She was built in 1894 at Okanagan Landing BC Canada. 55.0' x 15.0' x 2.9' Wood. 42gt 26rt. Powered by two (high pressure 6" x 24") 2.4nhp steam engines built by Jencks Machinery Co., Sherbrooke QC. In 1894–1896 she was owned by Mary E Cousens, Vernon BC (registered at Victoria BC). She was owned by WB Cousens for Skaha Lake service between Penticton and Okanagan Falls. She was unsuccessful, too big for the river, and returned to Okanagan Lake service. On July 01, 1896, this sternwheeler had been out with an excursion party at Okanagan Landing BC when she caught fire. By the time the fire was discovered it was impossible to control, and soon the whole vessel was involved. She burned to the water's edge at the Okanagan Landing dock and was later declared as a total loss, and only insured for about half of her value.

Fairy[335] (US) She was the first American steamship to provide regular service among Puget Sound ports arriving in 1853. On October 22, 1857, as she was leaving the Steilacoom wharf for Olympia, her boiler exploded, and she sank. Most of those on board were injured but no one was killed.

Fairy Queen 092773 (Canada) (work boat) She was built in 1888 at New Westminster BC Canada. 65.4' x 10.5' x 4.2' Wood. 25gt 16rt. She was powered by 3.2nhp steam engines. In 1896 she was owned by William West, New Westminster BC. In 1898 she was owned by H Magar, Whonnock BC.

Fannie (later *Diamond O.*) 120685 (US) (passenger/ freight vessel) She was built in 1887 at Portland OR USA. 143' x 28.4' x 6.6' Wood. 316gt 276nt. Powered by two 17nhp horizontal (high pressure 16" x 72") steam engines. She was rebuilt in 1906 and renamed as the *Diamond O*. In 1887 she was owned by the North Pacific Lumber Co. She is reported by Murray Lundberg to have worked in Alaska/YT in 1900. In 1919 she was reported as having been abandoned.

Fannie Patton 009615 (US) (freighter, later a barge) She was built in 1865 at Canemah OR USA by John T Thomas. 132' x 26.5' x 4'. Wood. 297.99gt. Powered by two horizontal (high pressure 17" x 60") steam engines. She was rebuilt 1874 to 151' x 26.5' x 5'. In 1865 she was built for the Peoples Transportation Co. In 1871 she was sold to the Oregon Steamship Co. In 1879 she was owned by the Oregon Steam Navigation Co. In 1880 she was converted to a barge. Her engines went to the steamer Henry Villard in 1881.

Fannie Troup 009616 (US) (passenger/ freight vessel) She was built in 1864 at Portland OR USA. 123.5' x 21.2' x 4.7'. Wood. 229.48gt. Powered by two horizontal (high pressure 12.25" x 48") steam engines. In 1864 she was owned by C Troup et al. In 1874 she sank on the Cowlitz River WA and was abandoned. Her engines went to the steamer Welcome (US 80537).

Fanny Lake 120220 (US) She was built in 1875 at Seattle WA USA. 91.4' x 20.8' x 4.8'. Wood. 163.81gt 118.81nt. Powered by a 60ihp steam engine. In 1893 she was destroyed by fire.

Fargo 206250 (US) (passenger vessel) She was built in 1909 at Georgetown WA. 45.7' x 10.6' x 2.7'. Wood. 9gt 6nt. Powered by a 25ihp gasoline engine.

Fashion[336] (US) (freighter) She was built in 1850 at San Francisco CA. Wood. 87gt. Powered by a steam engine. In 1853–1877 she was in service on the Sacramento River CA. She was reported to have gone out of service about 1877. Lytle says she was out of service in 1856.

Fashion[337] (US) (sidewheeler) She was built in 1853 at Vancouver WT. (She was built from the hull of the James P. Flint). In 1853 she was owned by JO Vanbergen. 80.0' x 12' x 5'. Wood. Powered by two horizontal (high pressure 8" x 24") 4nhp steam engines. (Her engines came from the Columbia). She was employed on the Columbia River and Cowlitz River. In 1856 she ran aground and sank but was later salvaged and put back into service. In 1861 she was reported to have had her engine removed and in 1864 she was reported to have been broken up.

Favorite 009835 (US) (sidewheeler) (tug, later yacht) She was built in 1868 at Utsalady WT USA. 132.0' x 28.2' x 9.8'. Wood. 269.53gt. Powered by a

290nhp steam engine. In 1868 she was owned by Washington interests. In 1876 she was owned by the Puget Sound Mill Co., Seattle WT USA. In 1884 she was owned by Port Gamble WA USA interests. She was in service towing in Puget Sound and later in San Francisco Bay USA as well as carrying freight. She was converted to a yacht after the First World War.

Favourite 111941 (Canada) (freighter) She was built in 1902 at New Westminster BC Canada. 100.0' x 20.6' x 4.2' Wood. 257gt 162rt. Powered by a 9hp steam engine. In 1902–1904 she was owned by G Harvey, New Westminster BC. On January 12, 1909, she was wrecked in ice on the Fraser River BC.

Fawn[338,339] (US) (sidewheeler) (freighter) She was built in 1848. Wood. 90gt. Powered by a steam engine. She was employed on California rivers. In 1850 she experienced a boiler explosion while serving on the Sacramento River.

Fay No. 4[340] 210508 (US) (passenger vessel) She was built in 1912 at North Bend OR USA by Kruse & Banks. 136.2' x 28.4' x 6.2' Wood. 179gt/rt. Powered by a 100hp gasoline engine. In 1912 she was employed on the Columbia River system. In 1913 she was employed on California rivers. She was reported as having been destroyed by fire in 1920.

Feliz (US) She was built about 1850. Wood. Powered by a steam engine. In the 1850s she was employed on the upper Sacramento River CA.

Fenix[341] (later *Franklin*; then *Minnie Holmes*) (US) (sidewheeler) She was built in 1907 at Canemah OR USA. 93.0' x 17.6' x 3' Wood. 49gt. Powered by (12" x 48") 9.6nhp steam engine.

Fenix (see *Shoalwater*)

Ferrell[342,343] (US) (passenger/ freight vessel) She was built about 1906 at Coeur d'Alene ID. 80' Wood. Powered by a steam engine. In 1906 she was owned by William W Ferrell. She was in employed on the St. Joe River and on Lake Coeur d'Alene.

Fidalgo[344] 200817 (US) (freighter) She was built in 1904 at La Conner WA USA. 110.5' x 26.5' x 6.9' Wood. 393gt 235nt. Powered with two horizontal steam engines. Her engines came from the *Northern Light*. She was employed in transporting bales of hay and grain, from Puget Sound to Victoria. In 1923 she was destroyed in a storm at Seattle WA USA. Christopher Cole (In the BC Nautical History Facebook Group 07/11/2015) stated that "In May of 1912 she collided with a scow which was being towed along side of the tug *Sadie*. She was holed and was quickly beached to save her. The *Fidalgo* was described as "an oddly constructed vessel, a shallow flat-bottomed craft with sternwheel. Forward she has an elevator which is used to assist discharging."

Fire King 121776 (Canada) (freighter) She was built in 1906 at Winnipeg MB Canada. 96.0' x 19.0' x 5.0'. Wood. 102gt 69rt. Powered by a 4hp engine. In 1914 she was owned by the Manitoba Sand & Dredging Co. Ltd., Winnipeg MB.

Firefly (US) (passenger/ freight vessel) She was built about 1849 at San Francisco CA. Wood. Powered by a steam engine. In the 1850s she was employed on the upper Sacramento River CA.

Firefly 111593 (Canada) (tug) She was built in 1901 at New Westminster BC. 56.0' x 17.0' x 4.5'. Wood. 46gt 29rt. Powered with a 4nhp steam engine. In 1901–1904 she was owned by the B.C. Mills Timber & Trading Co., New Westminster BC. In 1912 she was owned by TB Duffy & Joseph Save, New Westminster BC. In 1913–1918 she was owned by James HP Draney & Carl All, New Westminster BC. She was employed towing out of Harrison Lake BC.

Flora 103916 (Canada) (passenger/ freight vessel) She was built in 1888 at Bennett Lake BC Canada by the Bennett Lake & Klondike Navigation Co. 79.5' x 16.0' x 4.3. Wood. 100.93gt 68.59rt. Powered by a steam engine. In 1898 she was owned by the Bennett Lake and Klondyke Navigation Co. Ltd., Dawson YT. In 1901 she was owned by the Klondike Corporation Ltd., London UK. The boilers were built by Albion Iron Works Co. Ltd. In 1903 she was reported as having been broken up at Dawson YT and incorporated into a steam dredge on the Fortymile River YT.

Flora[345] 009611 (US) (freighter) She was built in 1865 at San Francisco CA USA. 141.0' x 30.5' x 4.0'. Wood. 224.74gt 173.5nt. Powered by a 90nhp steam engine. She was employed on California rivers to Marysville and had an extra shallow draft of 11 inches. In 1865 she was owned by the California Steam Navigation Company. In 1871 she was taken over by the California Pacific Railroad Co., San Francisco CA. She was reported to have been abandoned in 1885.

Flora[346,347] 120618 (US) She was built in 1885 at Sacramento CA. 141.0' x 30.5' x 4.0' Wood. 185.31gt 94.57nt. In 1865–1910 she was owned by San Francisco CA USA interests. She was employed on California rivers. On August 28, 1932, she was destroyed by fire in the conflagration that burned 10 vessels on the Yolo side of the Sacramento River. She played the part of the steamboat "*Dixie*" in the second version of the movie "Huckleberry Finn." She is reported by Murray Lundberg to have worked in Alaska/YT in 1898–1902.

Flora Temple 009614 (US) (sidewheeler) She was built in 1860 at San Francisco CA. 132.5' Wood. 223.17gt. Powered by a steam engine. She was employed on California rivers. She was reported to have gone out of service about 1881 and abandoned.

Florence 090785 (Canada) (tug) She was built in 1886 at Victoria BC by GG Walker. 64.0' x 18.5' x 4.2' Wood. 59.44gt 40.44rt. Powered by a 5hp horizontal high pressure steam engine by Albion Iron Works, Victoria BC. In 1886–1893 she was owned by Edward B Marvin, Victoria BC. In 1893–1918 she was owned by Henry M Dumbleton, Victoria BC.

Florence[348] 121068 (US) (tug) She was built in 1897. 101.0' x 22.0' x 5.0' Wood 90gt 5int. Powered by a steam engine. In 1898 this vessel had two masts installed by Captain Ivan L Peterson, and she was sailed to Alaska, taking 60 days. In 1898 her keel was removed, and she was rebuilt at St. Michael AK as a sternwheeler tug. On October 10, 1909, this vessel foundered at St. Michael's Canal Alaska USA. She is reported by Murray Lundberg to have worked in Alaska/YT in 1898–1909.

Florence Carlin 121975 (Canada) She was built in 1906 at Knault BC Canada. 97.5' x 20.4' x 4.6' Wood. 143gt 90rt. Powered by a 9nhp steam engine built by Vancouver Engineering Works. In 1906–1920 she was owned by the Columbia River Lumber Co., Golden BC. She served the lumber industry on Shuswap Lake BC. In 1913 she was reported as having been abandoned and later broken up 1919–1920.

Florence Henry[349] 120886 (US) (freighter) She was built in 1891 at Ballard WA USA. 75.2' x 22.8' x 4' Wood. 130.01gt 79.66nt. Powered by a steam engine. She was transferred to Alaska. In 1918 she was reported to have been broken up.

Florence S. 121085 (US) 107857 (Canada) (passenger/ freight vessel later a barge) She was built in 1898 at St. Michael AK by the Moran Bros. Shipyard. 75.0' x 16.0' x 3.6' Steel. 100.2gt 50rt. Powered by a steam engine. She was in US Registry 1898–1900 and again in 1905. In 1898 she was owned by the Seattle-Yukon Transportation Co. On July 16, 1900, as a barge, she foundered and was wrecked at Lewis River AK. After her wreck in 1900 she was converted to a barge. She was transferred in 1900 to Canadian Registry. In 1900 she was owned by Captain Sydney C. Barrington. In 1905 she was sold to Captain Wallace Langley.

Fly (see *Cariboo*)

Flyer 205771 (US) She was built in 1905 at Keewalik AK. 50.0' x 8.6' x 2.2' Wood. 6gt 5nt. Powered by a 15ihp gasoline engine. In 1910 she was owned by Nome AK USA interests.

Flyer[350] (US) (freighter) She was built in 1901 at Chelan ID. 75' x 14' x 6' Wood. In 1906 she was destroyed by fire at Lakeside ID.

Flying[351,352] (US) (freighter) Wood. Powered by a steam engine. She is reported by Murray Lundberg to have worked in Alaska/YT in 1917.

Flying Dutchman[353,354] (British Columbia Colonial Register) (freighter) She was built in 1860 at Victoria, Vancouver Island (Crown Colony) by Peter Holmes. 93.0' x 17.0' x 4.2' Wood. Powered by a 12" x 36" steam engine. She was launched September 26, 1860, by James W Trahey. She made her trial run on January 21, 1861. In 1860 she was owned by Captain William Moore, Victoria Vancouver Island. In 1864 Captain Moore went bankrupt, and an interest was sold in 1864 to Captain Delaware Insley. She was sold to an American company. She was in service in the Stikine area in 1862. In

August 1863 she carried the first output from the Pioneer Mill on Burrard Inlet to New Westminster. In 1862 she was withdrawn from Fraser River service and moved to the Stikine River. In 1865 she was reported to have been broken up.

Forrester (US) (tug) Wood. Powered by a steam engine. She was in service on the Columbia River and Snohomish River.

Fort Bragg[355,356] (later *Gold*) (US) She was built in 1899 at Fort Bragg CA. 155.0' x 35.0' x 6.0' Wood. 317gt 275nt. Powered by an 80ihp steam engine. She was rebuilt in 1921. She was employed on California rivers. On Monday August 19, 1907, she was in collision with the tug *Defiance* at San Francisco. She was reported to have been abandoned in 1940.

Fort McMurray (Image from the Provincial Archives of Alberta)

Fort McMurray 134605 (Canada) (passenger/ freight vessel) She was built in 1915 at Fort McMurray AB Canada. 151.0' x 28.3' x 4.5' Wood. 661gt. Powered by a 9nhp steam engine. In 1915–1921 she was owned by the Hudson's Bay Co., London UK. She was employed on the Mackenzie River. In 1921 she was retired.

Fort Sutter[357,358] (US) (freighter) She was built in 1912 at San Francisco CA USA by James Robertson. 219.2' Wood. 1,139gt. She was employed on California rivers. In 1942 she was taken over by the United States Army.

In 1955 Barney Gould was working on a scheme to convert this vessel to a restaurant in San Francisco CA.

Fort Yale (see *Idahoe*)

Fortune Hunter (see *Helen Bruce*)

Forty-Nine[359] 009525 (US) (passenger/ freight vessel) She was built in 1865 at Marcus WT USA by Leonard White & CW Briggs. 114' x 20' x 5' Wood. 219gt. She was powered by 1854 Baltimore two horizontal (high pressure 12" x 48") 9.6nhp steam engines from the Jennie Clark (on the Willamette River). In 1865 she was constructed by Leonard White and CW Briggs by the Oregon Steam Navigation Co. to work up the Columbia River and Arrow Lakes from Marcus to the Big Bend British Columbia gold mining camps. She was employed between Marcus and La Porte. She was owned by Captain Leonard White for Arrow Lakes service under the Oregon Steam Navigation Co. In 1869 Captain White retired and the Mate, AL Pingston, took command. In 1874 she was laid up and dismantled with her engines going to a vessel on the Snake River. She was owned by Captain AL Pingston between Marcus WT and Downie Creek camp until 1874. In 1874 she was dismantled, and the machinery was hauled out to Wallula WT.

Fran 121148 (US) (tug) She was built in 1900 at East Grand Forks MN USA. 71.7' x 18.8' x 3.2' Wood. 22gt/rt. In 1900–1912 she was owned by Pembina ND USA interests. Powered by a steam engine. On April 10, 1912, she broke her mooring at Grand Forks ND and sank.

Frances[360] 202063 (US) (freighter) She was built in 1905 at San Francisco CA USA. 174.0' x 38.0' x 8.3' Wood. 698.44gt 542nt. She was employed on California rivers. In 1941 she was reported as having been abandoned.

Frank Silva 120566 (US) (freighter) She was built in 1883 at San Francisco CA USA. 99.0' x 28.0' x 5.5' Wood. 200.05gt 181.83nt. Powered by a steam engine.

Franklin (see *Fenix*)

Frayne 206322 (US) (freighter) She was built in 1909 at Washburn ND USA. 120.4' x 20.0' x 4.5' Wood. 90gt/rt. Powered by an 80ihp gasoline engine.

Frederick K. Billings (ferry) She was built in 1881 at Pasco WA USA. 199.0' x 36.9' x 7.2' Wood. 749gt 677rt. Powered by 280ihp two horizontal (high pressure 20" x 96") 26.6nhp steam engines. In 1881 she was owned by the Northern Pacific Railway. She was employed as a railway transfer ferry at Ainsworth WA USA. Her engines went to the *Frederick K. Billings*.

Free Trade[361] (US) (freighter) She was built about 1852 in the USA. Wood. 300gt. She was employed on California rivers. She was reported to have gone out of service about 1868.

Freighter[362] (later *International*) 088481 (Canada) (passenger/ freight vessel, later a barge) She was built about 1858 at Beaver PA USA by McConnel. 113.6' x 25.2' x 4.8' Wood. 107.46gt. Powered by a steam engine. In 1858c she was owned by John P Davis. . In 1860c she was moved overland from the Mississippi River to St. Paul MN USA by Jon P Davis and renamed. In 1860 she was wrecked at Red River MN USA. In 1860 JC & HC Burbank purchased machinery of the stranded freighter and entered a joint arrangement to build and operate a new steamer, the *International*. In 1860 she was owned by JC & HC Burbank.(She was rebuilt to 137' x 26' x 3.8') In 1871 she was transferred to the Red River Transportation Co. (Norman Kittson, Donald Smith, and James Hill). In 1901–1905 she was owned by Northwest Navigation Co. Ltd., Winnipeg MB In 1875 she was down bound, and met the *Manitoba* coming up river and collided. In 1884 she was registered in Winnipeg MB. In 1880 she was sold and dismantled in Grand Forks, North Dakota. Her engine was removed, and she was re-built as a non-powered barge.

Fresno[363] 009613 (US) She was built in 1865 at Stockton CA. Wood. Powered by a steam engine. In 1874 she was reported to have been abandoned.

Frontiersman[364,365] (US) Wood. 32gt. Powered by a steam engine with a chain drive wheel. She is reported by Murray Lundberg to have on been employed on the Hootalinqua and Pelly Rivers Alaska/YT in 1907–1911.

Fruto[366] 121111 (US) She was built in 1899 at Oakland CA USA. 175.0' x 34.0' x 5.6' Wood. 429gt 392nt. Powered by a 325ihp steam engine. She was employed on California rivers. She was reported to have been abandoned in 1925.

Fulton 121086 (US) (passenger/ freight vessel) She was built in 1898 at Oakland CA and assembled at St. Michael AK USA. 65.0' x 16.0' x 4.0' Wood. 66gt 33nt. Powered by a steam engine. She is reported by Murray Lundberg to have worked in Alaska/YT in 1898.

G.K. Wentworth 202772 (US) (passenger/ freight vessel) She was built in 1905 at Portland OR USA by the Portland Shipbuilding Co. 145.0' x 28.5' x 7.0' Wood. 325gt 285nt. Powered by two horizontal (high pressure 16" x 72") 17nhp steam engines. In 1905 she was owned by the Hosford Transportation Co. She was employed on the Columbia and Willamette Rivers. In 1925 she was reported as being abandoned and was broken up in 1934 at Portland OR. Her engines were used in the *Skagit Chief*.

G.M. Dawson 111544 (Canada) She was built in 1901 at Vancouver BC by James M Bulger. 151.4' x 31' x 5.4' Wood. 780gt 472rt. Powered by a steam engine built by William Hamilton Mfg. Co., Peterborough ON. In 1901 she was owned by the Canadian Pacific Railway. In 1901 she was owned by the British Yukon Navigation Co. She was sold out of service as a houseboat at Ikeda Bay, Queen Charlotte Islands. She was reported as having been laid up at Ikeda Bay, QCI BC. She is reported by Murray Lundberg to have worked in Alaska/YT in 1898.

G.M. Walker[367] (later *Woodland*) 086386 (US) (passenger/ freight vessel) She was built in 1897 at Portland OR USA. 84.7' x 20.4' x 4.2' Wood. 154gt 125nt. Powered by two horizontal (10" x 36") 6nhp steam engines. In 1897 she was owned by Alvin & Walker. In 1910 she was owned by Portland OR USA interests. In 1915 she was rebuilt. She operated on the Columbia River.

G.W. Shaver 086041 (US) (passenger/ freight vessel) She was built in 1889 at Portland OR USA. 139.6' x 28.2' x 5.4' Wood. 313gt 276nt. Powered by two horizontal (high pressure 16" x 60" cylinder) steam engines. In 1889 she was owned by the Shaver Transportation Co. (Red Collar fleet), Portland OR. In 1902 she was renamed as the *Glenola*, later in 1905 renamed as the *Beaver*.

Gabriel Winter[368] (later *Secretary*) (US) (sidewheeler) She was built in 1851 at San Francisco CA. Wood. 73gt. Powered by a steam engine. She was employed on California rivers. She was reported to have been lost in 1854 when her boiler exploded.

Galena 096983 (Canada) (freighter) She was built in 1888 at Bonners Ferry WA USA. 79.8' x 16.0' x 5.0' Wood. 73gt 50nt. Powered by a steam engine. (She may have been converted to a propeller in 1898). In 1888 she was owned by the Kootenay Mining & Smelting Co. She was owned by the Kootenay Steam Navigation Co. for Kootenay Lake service. In 1896–1910 she was owned by MT Johnson, Victoria BC. She was employed to haul barges and equipment. In 1898 she was broken up.

Game Cock[369] (US) She was built in 1851. Wood. 24gt. Powered by a steam engine. She was employed on California rivers. She was reported to have gone out of service about 1868. Lytle says she was abandoned in 1853.

Gamecock[370] 008418 (US) (passenger vessel) She was built in 1898 at Portland OR USA by Joseph M Supple. 178.2' x 38' x 7' Wood. 777gt 658nt. Powered by two horizontal (high pressure 18.5" x 84") steam engines. In 1898 she was owned by the Yukon Transportation & Commercial Co., San Francisco CA USA. In 1898 her wreck was purchased by Daniel Kern. In 1899 she was rebuilt as a towboat. In 1899 she was owned by the Willamette & Columbia River Transportation Co. She had originally been built for service in the Klondike Gold Rush. On June 24, 1898, she was wrecked with the *Staghound* while in tow by the *Elihu Thompson* at the Columbia River Bar OR USA. She was reported to have been re-powered and re-built in 1910.

Gamecock[371] 207230 (US) (freighter, later a tug) She was built in 1910 at Portland OR USA by Joseph Supple. 160.1' x 33.6' x 7.8' Wood. 464gt 406nt. Powered by two horizontal (high pressure 18.5" x 84") steam engines from the *Gamecock* (008418). In 1910 she was owned by the Willamette

& Columbia River Transportation Co. Rebecca Harrison identifies this vessel as having been rebuilt and re-engined in the 1920s. In 1938 she was reported as having been dismantled and abandoned.

Garden City 085592 (US) (ferry) She was built in 1879 at San Francisco CA USA. 208.0' x 57.0' x 13.6'. Wood. 1080.7gt 730.42nt. Powered by a 625nhp steam engine.

Gazelle[372] (US) She was built in the 1852. at Canemah OT. 145' Wood. 81gt. Powered by a steam engine. In 1853 she was operating on the Sacramento River CA. In 1854 she was owned by the California Steam Navigation Co. On April 8, 1854, at Canemah OR, her boilers exploded, and she was destroyed. About 60 people had been on board, and twenty people were killed immediately, with the rest injured (of who 4 died later). Her engines went to the *Senorita* and then on to the *Hassalo*.

Gazelle 085474 (US) (passenger/ freight vessel) She was built in 1876 at Portland OR USA by Louis Paquet. 91.8' x 18.0' x 5.0'. Wood. 156.56gt 79.86nt. Powered by a steam engine. In 1876 she was owned by Armstrong, Bryant & Co. She was employed on the Columbia River but in 1884 she was transferred to Puget Sound. In 1884 she was owned by Ferndale WA USA interests. Her engines came from the *Carrie* (005657). In 1885 she was reported as having been destroyed by fire in the Stillaguamish River WA USA.

Gazelle[373] (US) (sidewheeler) Rebecca Harrison identifies this vessel as having been built in 1905. 92.0' Wood. Powered by a gasoline engine. She was reported to have been abandoned in 1929.

Gem[374,375] 010746 (US) (freighter) She was built about 1854. Wood. 235gt. Powered by a steam engine. In 1854 she was owned by the California Steam Navigation Company. In 1871 she was taken over by the California Pacific Railroad Co., San Francisco CA. She was employed on California rivers. She was reported to have gone out of service in 1881. Lytle says she was abandoned in 1878.

Gem 085563 (US) (freighter) She was built in 1878 at Port Townsend WA. 75.7' x 17.0' x 4.4'. Wood. 87.62gt. Powered by a 40nhp steam engine. In 1878 she was owned by Washington State interests. In 1884 she was owned by Skokomish WA USA interests.

Gem[376] 064148 (Canada) (passenger/ freight vessel) She was built in 1874 at Victoria BC Canada by JG Walker. She was launched April 10, 1874. 71.0' x 13.0' x 2.6'. Wood. 60gt 27.06rt. Powered by a 27nhp steam engine. In 1874 she was owned by Charles T Millard & a Mr. Moore, Victoria BC. In 1886 she was owned by James A Clarke (et al.), New Westminster BC. In 1886–1901 she was owned by Charles T Millard, New Westminster BC. She was employed on the Stikine and Fraser Rivers. In 1902 she was reported as having been broken up.

General Custer 085486 (US) She was built in 1870 at Pittsburgh PA USA. 182.0' x 28.0' x 3.8'. Wood. 241.34gt. Powered by a steam engine. In 1870 she was owned by USA interests. In 1884 she was owned by Bismarck Dakota Territory USA interests.

Gen. J.W. Jacobs (USAQMC) (sidewheeler) (freighter) She was built in 1908 at Portland OR USA. 125.5' x 26.6' x 4.3'. Steel. 319gt 232rt. In 1908 she was owned by the US Army Quartermaster Corps. In 1922 she was owned by the Alaskan Engineering Commission. In 1923 she was owned by the Alaska Rail Road. In 1923 she was in service on the lower Yukon River. She was retired in 1933. She was reported as having been broken up at Nenana AK USA.

General Jefferson C. Davis (see *Duchesnay*)

General Jessup[377] (US) (sidewheeler) She was built in 1854 at San Diego CA. She was shipped to the Colorado River estuary in Mexico where Captain George A Johnson re-assembled her. 104' x 17' x 2.9'. Wood. 49gt. Powered by a 70hp steam engine. In 1854–1859 she was owned by George A. Johnson & Co. She carried freight up to Yuma AZ. In 1859, armed with two mountain howitzers, she accompanied the United States Army expedition against the Mojave Tribe. She was retired in 1859 and was broken up.

General Meade 125381 (US) She was built in 1875 at Pittsburgh PA USA. 193.0' x 30.0' x 4.3'. Wood. 171.46gt. Powered by a steam engine. In 1884 she was owned by Bismarck Dakota Territory USA interests.

General Reddington[378] (US) (sidewheeler) Wood. Powered by a steam engine. In 1859 she was owned by Joseph Arcego. On August 11, 1859, she struck the bridge at Sacramento while towing a wooden barge.

General Rosales (US) She was built in July 1878 at Yuma AZ USA. In September 1878 she was moved to Guayamas Mexico.

General Stewart Van Vliet (USAQMDS) (later *Katie Hemrich*; then *Rampart*) 161108 (US) She was built in 1898 at Seattle WA by CN Patterson. In 1898 she was owned by the Seattle-Yukon Gold Dredge Co. In 1900 she was owned by the United States Quarter Master Department. She was owned by the Northern Navigation Co. She was converted to a barge (*Rampart*). She foundered at Nulato AK USA sometime between 1901–1906.

Geo. W. Bates (see *Paloma*)

George Askew 175156 (Canada) (tug) She was prefabricated by George F Askew in Vancouver BC and assembled in 1945 at Waterways AB Canada. 86.8' x 20.8' x 4.2'. Wood. 127gt 82nt. Named in honour of her builder she was the last wooden stern wheeler built on the Mackenzie River system. Chain-driven, she was powered by a 135bhp engine. In 1945–1958 she was owned by the Northern Transportation Co. Ltd., Edmonton AB. After assembly at Waterways, she was taken down the river and over Smith Portage to work on the Bear River.

George E. Starr 085610 (US) (sidewheeler) She was built in 1878 at Seattle WA USA by JFT Mitchell. 148.2' x 28.0' x 8.7'. Wood. 472.66gt 336nt. Powered by a 150nhp steam engine. In 1878 she was in Puget Sound service. In 1897 she was in Alaska service, but was reported to have been abandoned in 1921. (Some authorities list the name as *Geo. E. Starr.*)

George V 122295 (Canada) (passenger/ freight vessel) She was built in 1911 at The Pas MB Canada. 110.0' x 26.7' x 4.0'. Wood. 379gt 239rt. Powered by a 9nhp steam engine. In 1911 she was owned by the City of Prince Albert, Prince Albert SK. In 1914–1919 she was owned by Francis E Simmonds, Saskatoon SK. In 1919 she was crushed in ice at The Pas MB. Her engines were salvaged for the construction of the *David N. Winton*.

George W. Pride (later *Vigilant*; then *Goliah*) 010744 (US) (tug) She was built in 1849 at New York. 154'. Wood. 235.86gt. Powered by a 250nhp steam engine. In 1871 she was owned by Pope & Talbot, San Francisco CA USA. In 1886 she was owned by Spreckles Towboat Co. She was reported to have been the second 'real tug' to have been built in the USA. In 1886 she arrived in San Francisco CA. She was employed on California rivers. She operated as the *Goliah* in Puget Sound in support of the mill at Port Gamble. In 1898 she was burned with the *S.L. Mastick* to recover scrap metal

George Washington[379] (US) (freighter) Wood. Powered by a steam engine. In 1849 she was employed on the Sacramento River CA. On November 5, 1849, she sank at Sacramento CA.

Georgiana[380] (US) (sidewheeler) She was built in 1850. Wood. 30gt. Powered by a steam engine. In the 1850s she was employed on the upper San Joaquin River CA. In 1855 she was destroyed when her boiler exploded.

Georgie Burton[381] 203101 (US) (passenger vessel, later a tug) She was built in 1906 at Vancouver WA USA. 153.5' x 31.5' x 6.5'. Wood. 382gt 342nt. Powered by a 300ihp (16" x 72") steam engine. She was constructed from the remains of the *Albany*. She was rebuilt in 1923 at Portland OR. In 1923 she was owned by the Western Transportation Co. She worked on the Columbia River, retiring in March 1947. She was moored in The Dalles to become a museum, but the 1948 Columbia River floods parted her from her mooring, and she was destroyed when she was overwhelmed by the rising waters.

Georgie Oakes[382,383] (US) (passenger vessel) She was built in 1890 at Coeur d'Alene ID by Sorenson and Johnson. 150.0' x 28' x ?. Wood. Powered by two horizontal (high pressure 16" x 72") 17nhp steam engines. The builders used the house works from the *Coeur d'Alene* in her construction. In 1890 she was owned by the Northern Pacific Railroad. She was owned by the White Star Line. In 1908 she was owned by the Red Collar Line. In her day she was considered by many to be the largest and fastest steamboat on Lake Coeur d'Alene. On July 4, 1927, she was burned as part of public celebrations at Coeur d'Alene ID.

Gerome[384] 086642 (US) (freight/ passenger vessel) She was built in 1902 at Wenatchee WA USA. Wood. Powered by a steam engine. 80.7' x 16.6' x 3.6' Wood. 109gt 74nt. Powered by two horizontal (high pressure 10" x 48") 6nhp steam engine. In 1902 she was owned by the Columbia & Okanagan Steamboat Co., homeported at Wenatchee WA. On September 2, 1905, she foundered in the Homiez Rapids.

Gertrude 064153 (Canada) (freighter) She was built in 1875 at Victoria BC by Alex Watson (Sr.) & Lockhart Smith. 120.0' x 21.0' x 5.0' Wood. 301gt 178rt. Powered by a 56hp 16" x 54" steam engine built by Joseph Spratt, Victoria BC. In 1875 she was owned by Captain William Moore & Mr. Millard, Victoria BC. In 1875–1878 she was in service on the Stikine River, and later the Fraser River in opposition to the *William Irving*. In 1881 she was owned by Edward B Marvin, Victoria BC. In 1881–1883 she was owned by Captain James D, Warren (JO), Victoria BC and John Grant, Victoria BC. In 1883 she was owned by the Canadian Pacific Navigation Co., Victoria BC. In 1887 she was condemned and broken up, with her engines going to the *Lytton*.

Gila (later *Cochan*) 085365 (US) (freighter) She was built in 1873 at San Francisco CA USA and shipped to Port Isabel Mexico where she was assembled by Patrick Henry Tiernan. 135.5' x 31' x ? Wood. 236.47gt. Powered by a steam engine. In 1873 she was owned by the Colorado Steam Navigation Company. In 1899 she was rebuilt as the *Cochan*. In 1873–1899 she was employed on the Colorado River.

Gipsy 085677 (Canada) (tug) She was built in 1884 at New Westminster BC Canada. 48.0' x 12.0' x 3.0' Wood. 50gt 31rt. Powered by a 20nhp steam engine. In 1884 she was owned by David McNair. She was sold to the Royal City Mill, New Westminster BC. In 1895–1909 she was owned by B.C. Mills, Timber and Trading Co., Vancouver BC.

Gipsy Queen 086441 (Canada) (passenger vessel) She was built in 1898 at Cottonwood Island AK USA. 61.8' x 21.6' x 2.6' Wood. 107gt 58rt. Powered by a steam engine. She was a scow working on the Stikine River and then converted to a saltery and icing station at Summit Island at Dry Cove.

Gladys (see *James McNaught*)

Gleaner 107526 (Canada) (passenger/ freight vessel) She was built in 1898 at Lake Bennett BC Canada by Captain John Irving. 113.0' x 24.6' x 5.5' Wood. 241gt 149rt. Powered by a 5nhp steam engine. In 1904 she was re-powered by a steam engine from the *Clifford Sifton*. In 1899–1901 she was owned by the Irving-Spencer Navigation Ltd. In 1901 she was owned by the John Irving Navigation Co. Ltd., Victoria BC. In 1902–1931 she was owned by the British Yukon Navigation Co. Ltd., Vancouver BC. She was laid up in 1917. In 1931 she was still listed in the Canada Registry of Shipping. In 1955c she was scuttled in Nares Lake YT.

Gleaner 204548 (US) (freighter) She was built in 1907 at Stanwood WA USA. 140.0' x 30.0' x 6.7' Wood. 477gt 279nt. Powered by a 180ihp steam engine. In 1907–1910 she was owned by the Skagit River Navigation Co., Mt. Vernon WA USA. On December 9, 1940, while carrying 23 persons on board this vessel she was stranded at the second bend up the Skagit River from the North Fork Bridge (near Bald Island). All were rescued.

Glenola[385,386] (ex-*W.H. Pringle* 081773; ex-*G.W. Shaver*; later *Glenola*, then *Beaver*) 086041 (US) (passenger/ freight vessel) She was built in 1889 at Portland OR USA. 139.6' x 28.2' x 5.4' Wood. 313gt 276nt. Powered by two horizontal (high pressure 16" x 60") steam engines. In 1889 she was owned by the Shaver Transportation Co. (Red Collar fleet). In 1905 she was renamed as *Glenola*. In 1906 she was rebuilt as the *Beaver* (202837).

Glenola (see *G.W. Shaver*)

Glenora 064146 (Canada) (freighter) She was built in 1874 at Victoria BC Canada by Alexander Watson (Sr.) & Lockhart Smith. 102.7' x 20.2' x 4.0' Wood. 193gt 149.32rt. Powered by a 50nhp steam engine. (She was powered by a steam engine from the *Reliance*.) In 1873 she was owned by Nellie Irving, New Westminster BC. In 1874 she was owned by John Irving, New Westminster BC. In 1896–1901 she was owned by Robert Irving, New Westminster BC. On December 07, 1879, she was wrecked at Farr's Bluff BC in the Fraser River.

Glenora[387] 107149 (Canada) 0086413 (US) (tug) She was built in 1898 at Tacoma WA USA by GW Barlow. 126.2' x 28.8' x 5' Wood. 542gt 341nt.

Powered by two horizontal (14" x 72" high pressure) 16nhp steam engines built by the Olympic Iron Works, Tacoma WA USA. In 1898 she was owned by Arthur W Buckland & Tracy W Holland, (Tacoma-Port Orchard Navigation Co.) While intended to be employed in Alaska she was moved to the Yukon River. She was transferred to Canadian Registry 107149. In 1901 she was owned by RP McLennan, Dawson YT. On March 27, 1902, she was destroyed by fire at Dawson YT while laid up in winter quarters. In April 1902 her owner, Joseph Genelle, was arrested by the Northwest Mounted Police for "having procured the burning of the steamer" to defraud the insurers.

Glide[388] 085782 (US) She was built in 1883 at Seattle WA USA. 80.5' x 19.0' x 4.0' Wood. 109.95gt 78.54nt. Powered by a steam engine. In 1884 she was reported to have been operating on the Skagit River.

Globe (US) Wood. Powered by a steam engine. In 1854 she was owned by the California Steam Navigation Co. She was employed as the company office and later as the company storeship.

Gold[389,390] 085816 (US) She was built in 1883 at San Francisco CA USA. 140.0' x 30.0' x 7.0' Wood. 334.75gt 292.45rt. Powered by a steam engine. She was employed on California rivers. On February 11, 1915, she was in collision with the steamer *F.A. Kilburn*. The *Gold*'s forecastle was carried away and some of her planking was torn off. The *F.A. Kilburn* was undamaged and continued to sea. In 1920 the *Gold* was destroyed by fire.

Gold (see Fort Bragg)

Gold Gatherer[391] 086176 (US) She was built in 1890 at Whiskey Bottom ID USA. 66' x 23' x 3' Wood. 40gt 40nt. Powered by a steam engine. In 1904 she was reported to have been out of service.

Gold Hunter[392,393] (US) (later USCSS *Active*) (sidewheeler) She was built in 1849 at New York NY USA by JA Westervelt. 172.5' x 24.5' x 10.25' Wood. 750gt. Powered by two side lever steam engines. In 1850 she was owned by the Pacific Mail Steamship Co. She was owned by United States Coast Survey. In 1853 she was rebuilt and strengthened at Mare Island CA USA. In 1853 she was purchased by the United States Navy from the Pacific Mail Steamship Co. and renamed as USCS *Active*. She was the first steam vessel to transit the Active Pass, Vancouver Island (in 1855). She assisted Captain Richards RN in surveying Semiahmoo Bay in connection with the international boundary dispute. She was a gold ship that arrived at Victoria Vancouver Island in June 1858 with 132 passengers on board. In 1858 she landed US troops on San Juan Island (then part of British Columbia). In 1860 she was owned by the California, Oregon & Mexico Steamship Co. (Holladay Line). In 1862 she was sold to McRuer & Merrill, San Francisco CA. In 1869 she was owned by the North Pacific Transportation Company. On June 5, 1870, while en route from San Francisco to Victoria in a dense fog, she was wrecked at Cape Mendocino. All 1777 passengers on board and her crew were landed safely.

Gold Star 107856 (Canada) 0086440 (US) (passenger/ freight vessel later a barge) She was built in 1898 at St. Michael AK USA. 94.0' x 22.0' x 3.4'. Wood. 168gt 99nt. Powered by a steam engine. In 1902 she was converted to a non-powered barge. In 1898 she was owned by Gold Star Transportation Co. In 1900 she was owned by Thomas C Nixon and William Mogridge. In 1901 she was owned by Thomas Nixon, Dawson YT. In 1909 she was owned by the Klondyke Corp. She was transferred to Canadian Registry 1900–1902. In 1906 she was wrecked at the Tanana River AK USA.

Golden Crown No. 1[394,395] (Canada) (dredge) She was built in 1902 at Vancouver and assembled at Whitehorse YT by William Ogilvie. Wood. 114gt 64nt. Powered by a steam engine. In 1902–1905 she was owned by William Ogilvie, Whitehorse YT. She was constructed in Vancouver BC by the Laurie Engine Company. She was employed as a dredge by the Golden Crown Mining Company on the Stewart River YT where she was later abandoned.

Golden Gate (US) (sidewheeler) She was built in 1851. Wood. Powered by a steam engine. In 1851–1862 she was owned by the Pacific Mail Line. In 1851 she was employed in the San Francisco to Panama City service. On July 27, 1862, she was stranded and destroyed by fire near Manzanillo Mexico.

Golden Hind[396] (US) She was built in 1904 from a St. Michael AK barge, machinery from a hulk and a mine boiler by Wilson and Stackpole. Wood. Powered by a steam engine. In late fall 1904, she left Nome AK carrying 50 passengers. She was frozen-in the ice 10 miles below Fairbanks AK. In

1904 she was wrecked at Fairbanks AK. (Murray Lundgren states that he is unable to confirm these facts recorded by MacBride and Easton.)

Goliah (see *George W. Pride*)

Goliath (see *Samson*)

Goodman Castle[397,398] 010747 (US) She was built in 1857 in the San Francisco Bay area. Wood. 160.13gt. In 1858 she was a competitor to the California Steam Navigation Co. In 1859 she was owned by the California Steam Navigation Company. In 1871 she was taken over by the California Pacific Railroad Co., San Francisco CA. She was employed on California rivers. She was reported to have been abandoned about 1875 and broken up around 1878.

Gov. Newell 085806 (US) (passenger vessel) She was built in 1883 at Portland OR USA. 112.0' x 20.5' x 5.0' Wood. 205.87gt 134.43nt. Powered by two horizontal (high pressure 12" x 48") 9.6nhp steam engines. In 1900 she was reported as having been broken up at Portland OR.

Gov. Pingree (later *Bonanza King*) 107851 (Canada) 086414 (US) (passenger/freight vessel) She was built in 1898 at Dutch Harbor AK USA by Puget Sound Bridge & Dredging Co. She was constructed in Seattle WA USA and assembled at Dutch Harbor AK. In 1898 she was launched and christened without the usual champagne because the manager, a Mr. Lockwood, had strict objections to the use of alcoholic beverages. 140.3' x 31.3' x 5.8' Wood. 466gt 26ont. Powered by a 77nhp steam engine. In 1898 she was owned by the Boston & Alaska Transportation Co. In 1900 she was transferred to Canadian Registry. In 1900–1901 she was owned by the British Yukon Navigation Co. Ltd., Dawson YT. In 1901–1931 she was owned by the British Yukon Navigation Co. Ltd., Vancouver BC. She was converted to a lumber shed at Whitehorse YT in 1917.

Governor Blaisdel (US) She was built in 1864 at Lake Tahoe NV by Captain Augustus W Pray. 42' Wood. Powered by a steam engine built in San Francisco CA and assembled at the building site. In 1877 she broke up in a storm on Lake Tahoe.

Governor Dana[399,400] (US) She was built in 1850 in the eastern United States. Wood. Powered by a steam engine. In 1854 she was owned by the California Steam Navigation Company in service on California rivers. She experienced a boiler explosion. On March 12, 1864, she was in a collision with the Mexican-owned wood barge *Eliza* on the Yolo side of the Sacramento River.

Governor Dana 010745 (US) (sidewheeler) She was built in 1863 at Stockton CA USA. 140.0' x 30.8' x 3.5' Wood. 364.50gt 282.71nt. Powered by a 90nhp steam engine. In 1863 she was owned by the California Steam Navigation Co., San Francisco CA. She was a shallow daft vessel built for the Sacramento-Marysville route. She was reported to have gone out of service after 1885 and abandoned about 1893.

Governor Douglas (Vancouver Island Colonial Register) (passenger/freight vessel) She was built in 1858 at Victoria, Vancouver Island (Crown Colony) by James W Trahey. Miss Agnes Douglas was her sponsor, and she was launched on October 30, 1858. 144.0' x 26.0' x 4.0' Wood. Powered by a steam engine. In 1858 she was owned by Alexander Sinclair Murray and managed by Commodore Irving as the Victoria Steam Navigation Co., Victoria VI. In 1859 he bought out Murray (who went to Australia). She was stuck on the ways at her launch. She made her maiden voyage in January 1859. Alexander Murray (her original owner) went on to make maritime history on the Murray River in Australia.

Governor Fawcett 202523 (US) (tug) She was built in 1905 at Kenmare ND USA. 90.0' x 18.0' x 3.8' Wood. 45gt/nt. Powered by a steam engine.

Governor Grover[401] 085249 (US) She was built in 1873 at Portland OR USA. 140' x 28.6' x 5.5' Wood. 404gt. Powered by two horizontal (high pressure 17" x 60") 19nhp steam engines. In 1873 she was owned by the Willamette River Navigation Co. She was owned by the Willamette Transportation & Locks Co. She was employed on the Willamette River. She was owned by the Oregon Steam Navigation Co. In 1880 she was reported to have been broken up at Portland OR.

Governor Ramsey (see *North Star*)

Governor West 213121 (US) She was built in 1915 at Maryhill WA. 63.2' x 18.1' x 2.9'. Wood. 23gt 23nt. Powered by a 35ihp gasoline engine. She was employed on the Columbia River system. In 1925 she was rebuilt with a propeller.

Grace Barton[402,403] (US) She was built in 1890 at San Francisco CA USA. 100.0' x 26.0' x 6.5'. Wood. 194.84gt 160nt. Powered by a 60ihp steam engine. She was in service on California rivers. In 1905 she was laid up on the mudflats at Sausalito CA. She was used sporadically in the years following. On July 12, 1914, she ran aground on a mud flat while on an excursion from Richmond to Petaluma, CA with 150 people on board. After the ship's boilers and machinery were removed, she was towed to Rio Vista for filming near Wood. Island. In 1916, during filming for the Hollywood silent movie "Jim Bledso", she was destroyed by fire at Rio Vista CA. The simulated fire got out of control, with the unanticipated result that she was destroyed. The fire disaster was filmed by the camera man.

Grace G. 205302 (US) (tug) She was built in 1908 at Seattle WA USA. 50.8' x 12.0' x 2.0'. Wood. 12gt 8nt. Powered by a 30ihp gasoline engine.

Grahame[404] 088478 (Canada) (passenger/ freight vessel) She was built in 1883 at Fort Chipewyan NWT Canada by Captain John W Smith. 135' x 24.4' x 3.5'. Wood. 332gt 220nt. Powered by a steam engine. In 1883–1898 she was owned by the Hudson's Bay Co., London UK. The engines were built in the south and shipped overland to the construction site. In 1883 she was operating from Ft. McMurray to Fort Fitzgerald on the Athabasca and Slave Rivers. In 1885 she went into commercial service Fort McMurray to Lake Athabasca area. In 1895 she was rebuilt by Boyd, Segers & Wylie to 141. In 1899 this vessel carried an official delegation from Canada's Federal government to negotiate Treaty No. 8 with the First Nations. In 1913 she was reported as having been broken.

Grahamona[405,406] (later Northwestern) 210453 (US) She was built in 1912 at Portland OR by Joseph Supple. 149.5' x 30.0' x 4.5'. Wood. 443gt 413nt. Powered by two horizontal (high pressure 13.5" x 72") steam engines. In 1912 she was owned by the Oregon City Transportation Co. In 1912 she was employed on the Willamette River. In 1919 she was employed on the

Columbia and Snake Rivers. In 1920 she was renamed as *Northwestern*. She was owned by the Salem Navigation Co. She was owned by the Alaska Rivers Navigation Co., Juneau AK. In 1939–1949 she was employed on the Kuskokwim River. In 1949 she was in service at the Kuskokwim River AK when she went out of service.

Grand Forks 086332 (US) (passenger vessel) She was built in 1895 at Grand Forks ND USA. 123.0' x 26.5' x 4.1' Wood. 99gt. Powered by a 171ihp steam engine. She was reported as having been wrecked.

Grand Romance[407] 976443 (US) (passenger vessel) She was built in 1991 at Long Beach CA by Bill Barker. In 1991–2021 she was owned by Bill Barker, Long Beach CA. She offered cruises in Rainbow Harbor, Long Beach CA for eighteen years. In 2020 she moved to Vallejo CA.

Great Republic (US) She was built in 1866 at Green Point, Long Island NY by Henry Steer. 380' x 50' x 3.5' Wood. 4750gt. Powered by a vertical beam steam engine. In 1866–1878 she was owned by the Pacific Mail Steamship Co. In 1878–1879 she was owned by PB Cornwall. On April 19, 1879, she was stranded on Sand Island, south of Ilwaco WA. As the crew was being evacuated in the lifeboats the steering oar broke in one of them and caused the boat to capsize with the loss of eleven lives.

Greenwood 103913 (Canada) (passenger/ freight vessel) She was built in 1897 at Okanagan Landing BC Canada. 89' x 17.3' x 3.9' Wood. 142gt 89.77nt. She was powered by a steam engine built by Willamette Iron & Steel., Portland OR, USA. In 1897 she was owned by Andrew L Brownlie and Louis Greenwood. She was employed in Okanagan Lake service. In 1897 she was in Skaha Lake service between Penticton and Okanagan. In 1898–1899 she was owned by the Bank of Montreal, Montreal QC. On February 1, 1899, she was laid up and destroyed by fire at Okanagan Falls BC.

Grenfell (Canada) (passenger/ freight vessel) She was built in 1912 at West Peace River BC Canada by George Magar. Wood. 139gt 81rt. Powered by a 2.7nhp steam engine. In 1912–1914 she was owned by the Peace River Trading & Land Co. She was built for service on the upper Peace River. In September 1915 she was accidentally destroyed about 15 miles above Fort St. John BC.

Gretta A. 200121 (US) (passenger vessel) She was built in 1903 at Freeport CA. 74.0' x 16.8' x 3.8' Wood. 53gt 38nt. Powered by a 40ihp gasoline engine.

Grey Eagle[408] 086300 (US) She was built in 1894 at Newburg OR. 111.0' x 21.0' x 4.7' Wood. 218gt 162nt. Powered by two horizontal (high pressure 10" x 36") 6nhp steam engines. In 1894 she was owned by Fuller, Kemp & Cook. She was employed on the Willamette River. In 1907 she was rebuilt.

Grey Eagle 204691 (US) (passenger vessel) She was built in 1907 at Salem OR USA. 108.6' x 20.5' x 4.8' Wood. 154gt 141nt. Powered by a (10" x 36") 6nhp steam engine. In 1907 she was owned by Salem Towing & Transportation Co. In 1930 she was reported as having been abandoned.

Greyhound[409] 086100 (US) (passenger/ freight vessel, later a float) She was built in 1890 at Portland OR USA. 139' x 18.5' x 6.4' Wood. 197gt 183nt. Powered by two horizontal (high pressure 14.5" x 72") steam engines. In 1890 she was employed on Puget Sound. At the end of her life, she was employed as a float.

Greyhound[410] 220706 (US) She was built in 1920 at Kelso WA. 65.0' x 16.5' x 2.7' Wood. 81gt 62nt. Powered by a 140ihp steam engine. In 1920–1929 she was owned by the Greyhound Transportation Co., Portland OR. She was reported to have gone out of service about 1934.

Guadalupe[411] (US) She was built about 1854. Wood. Powered by a steam engine. In 1854 she was owned by the California Steam Navigation Co. She was in service on California rivers. She was reported to have gone out of service about 1868. (It is unclear whether she was rigged as a paddle-wheeler).

Gulkana[412,413] (US) (ferry, tug) In 1909 she was built at Seattle WA USA by the Moran Bros. 80' Wood. Powered by a steam engine. In 1909–1910 she was employed as a ferry and a tug with a rail car barge on Miles Glacier Lake on the Copper River, District of Alaska USA during construction of the Copper River & Northwestern Railroad.

Gwendoline 100805 (Canada) (passenger/ freight vessel) She was built in 1893 at Hanson's Landing (later called Wasa) BC Canada. 63.5' x 19.0' x 3.2'

Wood. 91gt 57rt. Powered by a steam engine. In 1896 she was rebuilt to 98' x 18'. In 1893–1913 she was owned by the Upper Columbia Navigation & Tramway Co., Golden BC. She was transported to Golden BC for finishing. In 1899 she was wrecked near Kootenai Falls WA, USA after falling from a flatcar on a trestle into a canyon. In 1914 she was owned by the Upper Columbia Navigation and Trading Co., Golden BC in Upper Kootenay service.

Gwendoline (Image from Maritime Museum of British Columbia)

Gypsy[414] 086325 (US) (passenger vessel) She was built 1895 at Portland OR. 101.0' x 24.0' x 3.6' Wood. 213gt 154nt. Powered by two horizontal (high pressure 9" x 48") 5.4nhp steam engines. In 1900 she was reported to have been wrecked at Independence OR.

Gypsy Queen[415,416] (US) She was built in 1897 at Cottonwood Island AK. 61.8' x 21.6' x 2.6' Wood. 107gt 58nt. She is reported by Murray Lundberg to have operated on the Stikine River in 1898.

H.C. Grady[417,418] (later F.M. Smith) 096316 (US) (passenger vessel) She was built in 1895 at Portland OR USA. 125.0' x 26.7' x 6.0' Wood. 295.44gt 244.04nt. Powered by two 13nhp horizontal (high pressure 14" x 48") steam engines. In 1895 she was owned by Joseph Smith, Portland OR. In 1898–1900 she renamed as the F.M. Smith and was employed at San Francisco CA USA.

H.E. Wright[419] 096475 (US) (freighter) She was built in 1899 at Stockton CA USA. 182.1' x 37.6' x 6.5'. Wood. 583gt 536nt. Powered by a 180ihp steam engine. She was in service on California rivers. In 1928 she was reported to have been abandoned.

H.J. Corcoran[420] (later *Crockett*) 096434 (US) She was built in 1898 at Stockton CA USA. 209.5' x 32.0' x 8.5'. Wood. 682gt 569nt. Powered by a 500ihp steam engine. She was in service on California rivers. She ran three times daily to Vallejo, Mare Island and on to San Francisco at the Ferry Building. She also transported passengers for excursions up the Sacramento River. On February 21, 1913, the *H.J. Corcoran* collided with the steamer *Seminole* near Angel Island and both vessels capsized. She was rebuilt in 1914 as the *Crockett*.

H.T. Clay[421] (US) (sidewheeler) She was built in 1850 at San Francisco CA. Her frames were built in New Orleans and shipped to San Francisco where they were assembled in 1850. Wood. 154gt. In 1854 she was owned by the California Steam Navigation Co. She was in service on California rivers. In 1857 she was rebuilt, and her rig was changed to a schooner. She was reported to have gone out of service about 1868.

H.W. Alsop[422] (US) (aka *Alsop*) (passenger/ freight vessel) She was built in 1881 in North Dakota? Wood. Powered by a steam engine. In 1883 she was owned by the Red River Transportation Company.

Hamburg 096468 (US) (passenger/ freight vessel) She was built in 1899 at St. Michael AK USA. 32' x 11' x 7'. Wood. 24gt 12nt. Powered by a steam engine. In 1899 she was wrecked. She is reported by Murray Lundberg to have worked in Alaska/YT in 1899.

Hamlin 107144 (passenger/ freight vessel) She was built in 1898 at Vancouver BC by Thomas J Bulger. 146.2' x 30.8' x 4.5'. Wood. 515gt 453rt. Powered by a 17nhp steam engine. In 1910 she was converted to oil burner. In 1898 she was owned by the Canadian Pacific Railway Co., Montreal QC. In 1898 she was in service on the Stikine River. In 1901 she was owned by the Canadian Pacific Railway Co., Montreal QC. In 1903 she was owned by William McCallum, David Reider and John Banser. In 1904 she was owned by the Thomas J Kickham. In 1910 she was owned by Edward J Coyle, Vancouver BC. In 1911–1914 she was owned by Hamlin Tug Boat Co., Victoria BC. In 1913 she was owned by James H Greer, Vancouver BC. In 1918 she was owned by Defiance Packing Co., Vancouver BC. In 1918 she was reported as having been lost in the Fraser River BC.

Hannah 096428 (US) (passenger/ freight vessel) She was built in 1898 at Unalaska AK USA by Percy Corporation. 222.8' x 42' x 6.2' Wood. 1130gt 588nt. Powered by two 500ihp horizontal (22" x 96" high pressure) steam engines built by Howard Shipyards, Jeffersonville IA. In 1898 she was owned by the Alaska Commercial Company. She was reported to have been laid up at St. Michael AK.

Harbor Belle 096652 (US) (passenger vessel, later a tug) She was built in 1902 in Aberdeen WA USA by Lindstrom Shipbuilding. 98.8' x 20.5' x 4.5' Wood. 179gt 117nt. Powered by a steam engine. She was in service on the Columbia River, Grays Harbor and Snohomish River.

Harbor Queen 207397 (US) She was built in 1910 at Aberdeen WA USA by William HM McWhinney. 86.2' x 20.9' x 4.8' Wood. 126gt 70rt. Powered by a 125ihp steam engine. In 1910 she was owned by James Wilson. In 1916 she was owned by Allman-Hubble. She was employed on the Chehalis River from Montesano to Aberdeen and Hoquiam.

Harriet[423] 095208 (US) She was built in 1869 at Stockton CA USA by Stephen Davis. Wood. 191.43gt 162.67nt. Powered by an 80nhp steam engine. In 1871 she was in service in the upper San Joaquin River CA. She was reported to have gone out of service in 1877.

Harrison[424] (US) (passenger ferry) She was built in 1912 at Lacon ID USA. 150' Wood. (One source[425] claims that she was built in 1909 at Coeur d'Alene ID.) Powered by a steam engine. She carried passengers and freight across the lake from Harrison on the east side to Amwaco on the west side, as a rail connection existed to Spokane. She was reported as having been destroyed by fire in the 1920s.

Hartford (US) She was built in the eastern United States and was sailed around Cape Horn to California in 1849. In 1851 she was damaged by fire and rebuilt. In 1854 she was owned by the California Steam Navigation Co. In 1855 she was reported as having been broken up.

Harvest Moon[426] 096106 (US) (passenger vessel) She was built in 1889 at New Era OR USA. 82.0' x 17.8' x 3.7'. Wood. 68gt 56nt. Powered by two 4.3nhp horizontal (8" x 36") steam engines. In 1889 she was owned by John Welch. In 1897 she was reported to have been broken up at Portland OR.

Harvest Queen[427] 095534 (US) (passenger/ freight vessel) She was built in 1878 at Celilo OR USA. 200.0' x 37.0' x 7.5' Wood. 845.8gt 697.04nt. Powered by two horizontal 26.6nhp (high pressure 20" x 96") steam engines. In 1878 she was owned by the Oregon Steam Navigation Co., Portland OR. In 1881 she was taken through The Dalles, and in 1890 through the Cascades on the Columbia River by Captain James Troup. In 1899 she was reported as having been broken up.

Harvest Queen 096489 (US) (tug) She was rebuilt in 1900 at Stockton CA USA by Peter Carstens. 187.0' x 39.8' x 9.0' Wood. 585gt 511nt. She was powered by two 400nhp horizontal (20" x 96") steam engines. In 1900 she was employed on the lower Columbia River towing from Portland to the Columbia River Bar. In 1925 she was owned by the Oregon-Washington Railway & Navigation Co. In 1926 she was reported as having been abandoned and sunk near Ross Island.

Harvester 210341 (US) (passenger/ freight vessel) She was built in 1912 at Stanwood WA USA. 152' x 36.2' x 6.8 Wood. 638gt 402nt. Powered by a 100ihp steam engine. In 1935–1938 she was owned by the Skagit River Navigation & Trading Co. In 1938 she was badly crushed and sunk by the *President Madison*.

Hassalo[428] (US) (sidewheeler) She was built in 1857 at Cascades WT USA. 135' x 19' x 5' Wood. Powered by 13nhp (14" x 40") steam engines. (Her engines came from the *Gazelle* and the *Senorita*). In 1857 she was owned by Bradford Bros. She was employed on the Columbia River. In 1865 she was reported to have been broken up at The Dalles OR.

Hassalo 095591 (US) (passenger/ freight vessel, later a tug) She was built in 1882 at Salem OR USA. 160' x 30' x 6' Wood. 350.85gt 350.85nt. Powered by two horizontal high pressure (17" x 60" cylinder) steam engines. In 1880 she was owned by the Oregon Railroad & Navigation Co., Portland OR. In 1882 she worked on the Columbia River. In 1888 she was employed at the Cascades. She was transferred to Puget Sound running from Bellingham to Seattle. In 1890 she collided with the *Otter*. In 1892 she worked on the Columbia River as a tug. In 1898 she was reported as having been broken up.

Hassalo[429] 096440 (US) (passenger vessel) She was built in 1899 at Portland OR USA. 181' x 36.8' x 8.4'. Wood. 679gt 428nt. Powered by two horizontal 1200ihp steam engines. In 1899 she was owned by the Oregon Rail Road & Navigation Co., Portland OR. In 1925 she was owned by the Oregon-Washington Railway & Navigation Co. In 1927 she was reported to have been abandoned.

Hattie B. 203008 (US) (freighter) She was built in 1906 at Seattle WA USA. 50.4' x 14.2' x 3.4'. Wood. 59gt 37nt. Powered by a steam engine. In 1906 she was owned by Captain SL Barrington, Seattle WA USA. She was reported to have been broken up at Aberdeen WA. She is reported by Murray Lundberg to have worked in Alaska/YT in 1906.

Hattie Belle 096182 (US) (tug, passenger/ freight vessel) She was built in 1892 at Portland OR USA. 110.0' x 21.0' x 4.5'. Wood. 207gt 129nt. Powered by two 9.6nhp horizontal (high pressure 12" x 48") steam engines. Constructed as a tug she was converted in 1894 to a passenger/ freight vessel. She is reported by Murray Lundberg to have worked in Alaska/YT in 1898. She was reported to have been out of service in 1906.

Hattie Fickett[430] (US) (freighter) She was built in 1872. 151.0' x 43.0' x 5.8'. Wood. 332.55gt. Powered by a 45nhp steam engine. She was in service on California rivers. She was reported to have gone out of service in 1887.

Hattie Young (see *Josie Burrows*)

Hazel B[431] (US) (freighter) Wood. Powered by a steam engine. She is reported by Murray Lundberg to have worked in Alaska/YT in 1918–1930.

Hazelton[432] 107834 (freighter) She was built in 1901 at Victoria BC by Alex Watson Jr. 134.4' x 24.0' x 4.4' Wood. 378gt. Powered by a steam engine built by Albion Iron Works, Victoria BC. In 1901–1902 she was owned by Robert Cunningham, Port Essington BC. In 1902c-1910 she was owned by the Hudson's Bay Co., London UK. She was employed on the Skeena River. "In an incident on May 24, 1904, Captain Bonsor of the *Hazelton* and Captain Wood. of the *Mount Royal*, sternwheelers operating on the Skeena River in British Columbia, drew revolvers in a battle which was the outgrowth of a collision between the two vessels. Passengers interfered in the fracas and prevented any one from being killed and the two captains decided to settle the matter privately." She burned four cords of wood per hour, cut along the way. She made about 13 round trips per summer season. In 1912 she was reported as having been broken up—and the hull was sold to the Prince Rupert Yacht Club as a boathouse and clubhouse. Her machinery went to the HBC steamer *Athabasca River*.

Hecate[433] (HMS) (RN) (sidewheeler) (naval sloop, brigantine rigged) She was built in 1839 at H.M. Dockyard Chatham UK. 165' x 33' x ? Wood. She arrived at Esquimalt from England on December 23, 1860, under Commander Anthony Hoskins RN. All the officers of HMS *Plumper* were transferred to HMS *Hecate* except for Lieutenant Moriarity RN. Captain Richards RN assumed command. Lieutenant Mayne RN became First Lieutenant. Lieutenant Hankin RN of HMS *Hecate* became Second Lieutenant. Mr. Daniel Pender RN was appointed as Master and Senior Surveyor. She ran ashore in a dense fog between Tatoosh Island and the Mainland on August 19, 1861. She was refloated and temporary repairs were made. While she was in San Francisco for repairs, in 1861, her First Lieutenant, Richard Charles Mayne, left the vessel and was relieved by Lieutenant Henry Hand RN. While anchored in James Bay during the winter of 1862 she was frozen fast in the ice at Victoria, Vancouver Island. She sailed for England December 22, 1862, via San Francisco, Australia, and the Cape of Good Hope where she arrived January 04, 1864. She was sold in 1865 and broken up.

Hector,,[434] (US) (sidewheeler) Wood. Powered by a steam engine. She was in operation in 1852 to San Francisco from Bay area ports.

Helen Bruce (later *Fortune Hunter*) 201461 (US) (passenger/ freight vessel) She was built in 1898 at St. Michael AK. She was prefabricated in Chicago by Sepuris. In 1905 she worked the Chena River. 62.0' x 6.0' x 3.0' Wood. 83gt 49nt. Powered by a 28hp steam engine. In 1898 she was owned by the Klondike Promotion Co. She was still afloat in 1910. She is reported by Murray Lundberg to have worked in Alaska/YT in 1898–1905.

Helen Hale[435] 210679 (US) (passenger/ freight vessel) She was built in 1912 at Kennewick WA USA. 100.0' x 15' x 2.9' Wood. 52gt 33nt. She was employed in Puget Sound WA. In 1913 she was destroyed by fire.

Helen Hensley[436,437] 011693 (US) (sidewheeler) (freighter) She was built in 1853 at Stockton CA by Samuel J Hensley. 168.5' Wood. 394.81gt. Powered by a steam engine built in St. Louis and shipped out around Cape Horn. In 1855 she was in service on the Sacramento River CA. In 1854–1856 she was owned by the California Steam Navigation Company. In 1854 she was damaged by a boiler explosion. In 1871 she was taken over by the California Pacific Railroad Co., San Francisco CA. In 1873 she was towed to the back of Wood Island CA, where her engines and boilers were removed. In 1883 she was reported as having been abandoned.

Helen M. Scanlon (later *William H. Ladner*) 126731 (Canada) (tug, later a ferry) She was built in 1909 at Vancouver BC Canada by Wallace Shipyards Ltd. (False Creek), Vancouver BC. 124' x 27.2' x 5' Wood. 285gt 163rt. Powered by a 9.6nhp steam reciprocating engine. In 1914 she was rebuilt to 258t. In 1909–1913 she was owned by the Brooks Scanlon Lumber Co. Ltd., Vancouver BC. In 1914–1919 she was owned by the Government of Canada (Minister of Public Works), Ottawa ON. In 1924–1932 she was owned by the British Columbia Minister of Public Works, Victoria BC. She worked as a tug on Harrison Lake BC. In 1915–1918 she was in service as a ferry between Woodward's Landing and Ladner Landing on the Fraser River. In 1926 she was retired.

Helena 095516 (US) She was built in 1878 at Galena IL USA. Wood. 352.31gt. Powered by a steam engine. In 1884 she was owned by Bismarck, Dakota Territory interests.

Henderson 210030 (US) (tug) She was built in 1912 at Portland OR USA by Charles M Nelson. 159.0' x 31.6' x 7.1' Wood. 430gt. 372nt. Powered by 800ihp two 21nhp horizontal (high pressure 18" x 84") steam engines from the M.F. *Henderson* (393168). In 1945–1956 she was owned by the Shaver Transportation Co. (Red Collar fleet), Portland OR. She was employed on the lower Columbia River. In 1956 she was wrecked when she collided with her tow near Astoria OR.

Henrietta[438] (Vancouver Island Colonial Register) (passenger/ freight vessel) She was built in 1859 at Victoria, Vancouver Island (Crown Colony) by Peter Holmes and designed by James W Trahey. 73.0' x 14.0' x 3.5' Wood. Powered by a 25hp (8" x 26") steam engine. In 1859 she was owned by Captain William (Billy) Moore, Victoria, Vancouver Island. In 1860 she was sold to Captain Charles T Millard, Victoria, Vancouver Island. In 1861 she was re-built and lengthened to 85.0' x 14.0' x 3.5'. She was owned by Captain Henry Devries. In 1866 she was reported as having been broken up with her engines going to the *Chehalis*.

Henrietta (US) (freighter) She was built in 1859 at San Francisco CA. Wood. 46gt. In 1859 she was owned by the California Steam Navigation Co. She was reported to have been abandoned about 1861. In 1863 she was reported to have been out of service with her engine having been sold and exported to China.

Henrietta[439] 095033 (US) (passenger vessel) She was built in 1869 at Sucker Lake OR by Orin Kellogg. 54.0' x 12.0' x 3.0' Wood. 46gt. Powered by a 5.4nhp (9" x 12") steam engine. In 1869 she was owned by the Tualatin River Trading & Navigation Co. and employed at Sucker Lake. In 1879 she was reported to have been broken up at Portland OR USA.

Henry Bailey (later *City of Champagne*) 095974 (US) (passenger/ freight vessel) She was built in 1888 at Tacoma WA USA. 108.6' x 25.4' x 4.7' Wood. 271.2gt 209.59nt. She was powered by a 90ihp steam engine. In 1888 she was owned by the Pacific Navigation Co. In 1888 she worked on the Seattle to Edmonds to Marysville route. In 1898 her machinery were removed and used in the *Skagit Queen*, and she was reported as having been broken up.

Henry Foss[440] (US) (passenger/ freight vessel) She was built in 1898 at Seattle WA USA by the Moran Bros. Shipyard. 192.3' x 32.6' x ? Wood. 819gt. Powered by a steam engine. In 1898 she was owned by the North American Transportation & Trading Co. In 1911 she was owned by the Northern Navigation Co. In 1914 she was owned by the White Pass & Yukon Rail Road. In 1898 she was assembled at Dutch Harbor AK for service in the Klondike Gold Rush. She was the fastest of the North American Transportation & Trading Co. vessels. She was a sister vessel to the T.C. Power and the Chas. H. Hamilton. In 1927 she was reported as having been laid up at St. Michael AK.

Henry Villard (US) (freighter) She was built in 1881 at Sandpoint (Steamboat Landing) ID USA by James Hanahan. Wood. Powered by two 19nhp horizontal high pressure (17" x 60") steam engines. In 1881 she was owned by the Northern Pacific Railroad. She worked with the steamer *Katie Hallett* in the construction of the Northern Pacific Railroad from Thompson Falls to Sandpoint ID. Her engines came from the steamer *Fannie Patton* at Canemah OR USA. She was laid up in the bay at Hope ID for several years and then foundered.

Herald[441] 095524 (US) She was built in 1878 at Stockton CA USA by Stephen Davis. 127.5' x 28.0' x 5.8' Wood. 293.95gt 266.89nt. She was powered by a 400nhp steam engine. She operated on California rivers. She was reported to have gone out of service by 1905. (She was still listed as being registered in the 1910 edition of Merchant Vessels of the United States.)

Herbert 203842 (US) (tug) She was built in 1898 at San Francisco CA USA. 41.5' x 12.5' x 3.8' Wood. 24gt 15nt. Powered by a 25ihp steam engine. She is reported by Murray Lundberg to have worked in Alaska/YT in 1906.

Hercules 096443 (US) (see *Staghound*)

Hercules[442] (US) She was built in 1903 in the USA. 65' Wood. Powered with a naphtha-fueled engine. She was in service on California rivers. She was reported to have been dismantled in 1905.

Hercules 203523 (US) (work boat) She was built in 1906 at Needles CA USA. 44.5' x 9.1' x 2.9' Wood. 10gt. Powered by a 45ihp steam engine. In 1910 she was owned by Los Angeles CA USA interests.

Hercules (US) (work boat) 44.5' x 9.1' x 2.9' Wood. 10gt. Powered by 45ihp steam engine.

Hercules 204856 (US) (freighter) She was built in 1907 at Alameda CA USA. 158.3' x 36.2' x 6.6' Wood. 437gt 347nt. Powered by a 500ihp steam engine.

Herman 096398 (US) (passenger/ freight vessel) She was prefabricated in 1898 at San Francisco CA and assembled at Dutch Harbor AK USA by Thomas Patrick Henry Whitelaw. 155.0' x 36,0' x 6.0' Wood. 456gt 387nt. Powered by a 450hp steam engine. In 1898 she was owned by the Alaska Exploration Co. In 1901 she was owned by the Northern Navigation Co. In 1914 she was owned by the White Pass & Yukon Rail Road. In 1927–1929 she was owned by the American-Yukon Navigation Co., WV USA. In 1927 she was reported as having been laid up at St. Michael AK.

Hooligan (later *Annie Laurie*) (US) (freighter) She was built in 1909 at Klamath Falls OR. 80' Wood. Powered by a steam engine.

Hoosier[443,444] (US) (sidewheeler) (passenger/ freight vessel) She was built in 1851 at Portland OR USA by John T Thomas. 60' x 10' x 3.5' Wood. Powered by a 2.4nhp (6" x 20") steam engine. In 1851 she was owned by AS Murray et al. She was constructed from a ship's long boat. She was powered with a pile driver steam engine. She was the first steamer to work above Willamette Falls. She was employed between Canemah OR and up-river points. In 1853 she sank near Sacramento CA.

Hoosier No. 2 (US) (sidewheeler) (passenger/ freight vessel) She was built in 1855 at Canemah OT. 40' Wood. She was rebuilt in 1857.

Hoosier No. 3 (US) (sidewheeler) (passenger/ freight vessel) She was built in 1857 at Canemah OT. 40' Wood. 27gt. Powered by a steam engine.

Hootalinqua (see *Clifford Sifton*)

Hope[445] 064147 (Canada) (tug) She was built in 1860 at Victoria, Vancouver Island (Crown Colony) by James W Trahey. 95.0' x 17.5' x 4.7' Wood. 167gt 48rt. Powered by a 70hp (13" x 42") steam engine. She was launched September 22, 1860, for service on the Fraser River. In 1860 she was owned by Captain Charles T Millard, Victoria Vancouver Island. In 1867 she was owned by Captain JR Fleming. In 1870 she was rebuilt by Captain Fleming to 105.0' x 17.5' x 4.7' 166gt. 131rt. In 1874–1875 she was owned by John Kriemler, Victoria BC. In 1875 she went into service on the Stikine River. In 1882 she was reported as having been broken up, her engines and boiler removed. The hull was taken to Wrangel AK as a floating boarding house.

Hope[446] 011948 (US) She was built in 1868 at San Francisco CA. Wood. 73gt. Powered by a steam engine. She was rebuilt in 1872 as a barge.

Hope[447] 095167 (US) (freighter) She was built in 1870 at San Francisco CA USA. 86.0' x 26.4' x 4.5' Wood. 74.15gt 63.38rt. She was in service on California rivers. She was reported as having gone out of existence in 1885.

Hudson's Hope (see *Northland Call*)

Hustler[448] 096097 (US) (passenger/ freight vessel) She was built in 1891 at Portland OR USA. 102' x 21' x 7' Wood. 204gt 129nt. Powered by two 9.6nhp (high pressure 12" x 48") steam engines. In 1891 she was owned by the Ham Nickum Co. She was rebuilt in 1908.

Hustler[449] 205178 (US) (tug) She was built in 1908 at Portland OR USA. 104.5' x 23.5' x 4.7' Wood. 96gt 73nt. Powered by a two horizontal (high pressure 12" x 48") 9.6nhp steam engines. Her engines came from the steamer *Hustler* (096097). Repowered with a 175hp motor vessel. In 1908 she was owned by Ham Nickum Co. In 1925 she was owned by Nickum & Kelly Sand & Gravel Co., Portland OR. In 1936 she was reported as having been abandoned.

Hyack 095531 (US) She was built in 1878 at Puget Sound WA USA. Wood. 21.99gt. Powered by a 6nhp steam engine.

Hyak 100637 (Canada) (freighter) She was built in 1892 at Golden BC Canada. 81.0' x 11.2' x 3.9' Wood. 39gt 23rt. Powered by two horizontal high pressure 6" x 24" 2.4nhp steam engines by Jencks Machinery Co., Sherbrooke QC. In 1892–1914 she was owned by the Upper Columbia Navigation & Tramway Co., Golden BC. She was in service on the upper Columbia River service. She was laid up in 1906.

Hydra 009422 (US) (passenger/ freight vessel) She was built in 1876 at St. Helens OR USA by Caples & Forbes. 69.5' x 16.7' x 2.6'. Wood. Powered by a 4.3nhp (8" x 24") steam engine. Rebuilt in 1881 at Albina 76.8' x 16.7' x 2.6'. In 1876 she was owned by Lewis & Lake River Transportation Co. In 1882 she was reported as having been broken up on the Lewis River.

Ida Belle[450] (US) (freighter) Wood. Powered by a steam engine. She is reported by Murray Lundberg to have worked in Alaska/YT in 1899. Her configuration is unknown being 35–40 feet long, 9-10-foot beam. She was probably launched at Lake Bennett, and she was used to bring the original printing plant to Dawson for *The Klondike Nugget*. A poem was written in tribute to the trip (in the Klondike Nugget, Dec. 25, 1900).

Ida May (see W.H. Rideout)

Ida Stockdale 012327 (US) She was built at Pittsburgh PA USA. Wood. 377.39gt. Powered by a steam engine. She was originally owned by USA interests. In 1884 she was owned by Bismarck Dakota Territory USA interests.

Idaho[451] 012298 (US) (sidewheeler) (freighter) She was built in 1860 at Cascades OR USA. 150.8' x 25.5' x 6.9'. Wood. 278.15gt 178.82nt. Powered by a 70nhp (18" x 60") steam engine. She was rebuilt in 1869 at Portland OR to 147.4' x 25' x 6.4'. In 1881 she was moved through the Cascades by James Troup and transferred to employment on Puget Sound. In 1894 she was owned by Northwestern Steamship Co. In 1894 her engines were removed. In 1898 she was sold to Dr. Alexander DeSoto and converted to a floating hospital and mission vessel on the Seattle waterfront. She was reported to have been abandoned about 1909.

Idaho[452,453] (US) (sidewheeler) (passenger vessel) She was built in 1903 at Coeur d'Alene ID by George Ryan. 147' x 23' x ? Wood. Powered by an 800hp steam engine. She was owned by the Red Collar Line. She was laid up in Blackrock Bay and used as an apple sorting and storage facility. In 1915 she was destroyed by fire at Blackrock Bay.

Idahoe (later *Fort Yale*) (Vancouver Island Colonial Register) 110.0' x 22.0' x 4.0' Wood. Powered by a 14" x 54" steam engine. In 1860–1880 she was owned by the Yale Steam Navigation Co., Victoria BC. On April 14, 1861, her boiler exploded near Union Bar on the Fraser River killing her Master and four others. She was renamed as the *Fort Yale*, rebuilt, and re-launched at Victoria Vancouver Island (Crown Colony) on October 15, 1861.

Iditarod[454] (US) (freighter) Wood. Powered by a steam engine. She is reported by Murray Lundberg to have worked in Alaska/YT in 1909.

Idler[455] 209222 (US) (freighter) She was built in 1911 at Fairbanks AK by Fred Noyes. 64.0' x 16.8' x 3.7' Wood. 98gt 6nt. Powered by a 50ihp steam engine. In 1911 she was owned by Fred Noyes, Fairbanks AK.

Illecillewaet 100683 (Canada) (tug) She was built in 1892 at Revelstoke BC Canada by Alexander Watson. 78.0' x 15.0' x 6.0' Wood. 97.92gt 61.69rt. Powered by two horizontal 8" x 24" 4.3nhp steam engines. Her engines came from the *Despatch* (096986). In 1892–1896 she was owned by Columbia & Kootenay Steam Navigation Company. In 1897–1902 she was owned by Canadian Pacific Railway Ltd., Montreal QC. In 1902 she was sold for use as a barge. In 1897 she was in service between Arrowhead and Beaton. In 1898 withdrawn from service when the Castlegar bridge was built. In 1902 she was dismantled and converted to a barge. Her bow was reinforced for ice breaking. She was employed on the Arrow Lakes.

Illinois[456] (US) (passenger/ freight vessel) She was built in 1898 at Puget sound WA USA. 75' x 16' x 4.0' Wood. Powered by a steam engine. In 1898 she was owned by the Galesburg – Alaska Mining & Dredging Co. She is reported by Murray Lundberg to have worked in Alaska/YT in 1898.

Imnaha 100796 (US) (freighter/ passenger vessel) She was built in 1903 at Lewiston ID USA. 124.0' x 25.4' x 4.5' Wood. 330gt 216rt. Powered by a steam engine. She was employed hauling ore from the Eureka mine to Lewiston. In 1904 she was wrecked in the Wild Goose Rapids.

Independence[457] (US) (sidewheeler) (passenger vessel) She was built in 1857 at Monticello WA USA. 100.0' x 18.0' x 4.0' Wood. Powered by a 9.6nhp

(12" x 48") steam engine. In 1857 she was owned by Captain Ankeny. In 1864 she was reported to have been broken up at Portland OR USA.

Independence[458] 100668 (US) She was built in 1890 at St. Michaels AK. 87.0' x 20.0' x 4.0' Wood. 148gt 83nt. Powered by a steam engine. She was reported as being out of service in 1905 at Tanana River AK.

Indiana 100458 (US) (passenger/ freight vessel) She was built in 1889 at Mt. Vernon WA USA. 86.2' x 14.8' x 3.5' Wood. 106.93gt 81.71nt. Powered by a 40ihp steam engine. In 1920 she was reported as having been broken up.

Indianapolis 100667 (US) (passenger/ freight vessel) She was built in 1898 at St. Michael AK USA. 70.0' x 15.8' x 3.2' Wood. 96gt 78nt. Powered by a steam engine. She is reported by Murray Lundberg to have worked in Alaska/YT in 1898.

Indoko Flyer[459] 205667 (US) (freighter) She was built in 1908 at Nome AK. 38.0' x 10.6' x 2.6' Wood. 6gt 5nt. Powered by a 10ihp steam engine. Powered by a steam engine.

Inland Empire (later *Service*) 205882 (US) (passenger vessel) She was built in 1908 at Celilo OR USA. 151.0' x 32.1' x 4.8' Wood. 416gt 375nt. Powered by 600ihp two horizontal (high pressure 16" x 72") steam engines. In 1909–1910 she was owned by Open River Transportation Co. In 1920 she was reported as having been abandoned.

Inlander 126613 (Canada) She was built in 1910 at Victoria BC Canada by Victoria Machinery Depot Co. Ltd. (passenger/ freight vessel) 135.5' x 28.5' x 5.2' Wood. 533gt 340rt. Powered by a 13hp steam engine. In 1910–1937 she was owned by Prince Rupert, Skeena Transportation Co., Prince Rupert BC. She was powered with a steam engines from the *Mount Royal*. She was in Skeena River service and is claimed to have made the last trip on the Skeena River by a sternwheeler. In 1912 she was reported as having been laid up at Port Essington BC. George Duddy reports that "She is likely the vessel from which JK Cornwall obtained the machinery for the new *Northland Echo* that was constructed at Fort McMurray in 1923." (In 1937 she was still listed in the Registry of Shipping.)

International[460,461] 088481 (Canada) (passenger/ freight vessel, later a barge) She was built about 1858 at Beaver PA USA by McConnel. 113.6' x 25.2' x 4.8' Wood. 107.46gt/nt. Powered by two (5.5" x 12"steam engines. (In 1860 JC & HC Burbank bought machinery of the stranded *Freighter* and entered a joint arrangement to build and operate a new steamer, the International.). In 1858c she was owned by John P Davis. In 1860 she was owned by JC & HC Burbank. In 1860c she was moved overland from the Mississippi River to St. Paul MN USA by John P Davis and renamed. In 1860 she was wrecked at Red River MN USA. In 1871 she was transferred to the Red River Transportation Co. (Norman Kittson, Donald Smith, and James Hill). In 1875 she was downbound, and the met the *Manitoba* coming up river and collided. In 1880 she was sold and dismantled in Grand Forks, North Dakota and converted to a non-powered barge. In 1884 she was registered in Winnipeg MB. In 1901–1905 she was owned by Northwest Navigation Co. Ltd., Winnipeg MB.

International 103489 (Canada) (passenger/ freight vessel, later an accommodation vessel) She was built in 1896 at Kaslo BC Canada by James H Calvert. (The Canada List of Shipping indicates that this vessel was built at Rash BC.) 142.0' x 24.9' x 5.6' Wood. 526gt 281rt. Powered by a 17nhp steam engine built by Iowa Iron Works Co. In 1908 she was converted to an accommodation vessel. In 1896–1914 she was owned by International Navigation & Trading Co., Kaslo BC. She was in Kootenay Lake service. In 1908 she was laid up waiting for a new boiler that never arrived. She was sold to Gus Matthew who used the hull as a tourist lodge at Riondel BC. She became a derelict in Galena Bay, Riondel for many years.

International 100059 (US) She was built in 1862 in Georgetown MN USA. 136.0' x 26.0' x 4.0' Wood. 172.17gt. Powered by a steam engine. In 1862 she was owned by USA interests. In 1884 she was owned by Pembina, Dakota Territory USA interests.

International (US) She was built in 1898 at Seattle WA. Wood. Powered by a steam engine. On July 21, 1898, she sank while en route to Alaska for the Klondike Gold Rush.

Interstate (see *Oregona*)

Invincible 208830 (US) (ferry) She was built in 1911 at Wolf Point MT USA. 62.2' x 24.2' x 3.8' Wood. 35gt. Powered by a 25ihp gasoline engine. On March 29, 1929, she was stranded on the Yellowstone River at Winters Landing MT.

Iola[462] 203823 (US) She was built in 1907 at Needles CA USA. 46.8' x 11.0' x 2.6' Wood. 14gt 13nt. Powered by a 56ihp gasoline engine. In 1917 she was owned by the Western Arizona Copper Co.

Ion[463] (US) (sidewheeler) She was built in 1850 at Benicia CA. 30' Wood. Powered by a steam engine. She was in service on California rivers. She was reported to have gone out of service about 1868. She was abandoned about 1854.

Ione 100461 (US) (passenger vessel) She was built in 1889 at Portland OR USA. 130.4' x 24.7' x 5.0' Wood. 273gt 254nt. Powered by two horizontal 13nhp (14" x 72") steam engines built by Willamette Iron and Steel. Works. In 1889 she was owned by WS Buchanan. She was in operation by the West Linn & Canas Mills. Her engines were later salvaged and installed in the *Nespelem*.

Ione 205400 (US) (passenger vessel) She was built in 1908 at Newport WA USA by T Sampson. 129.0' x 26.4' x 5.7' Wood. 431gt 257rt. Powered by two horizontal (high pressure) steam engines built by Willamette Iron and Steel. Works. In 1908 she was owned by Pend Oreille River Navigation Co., Great Falls MT. She was reported to have been laid up in 1910. In 1911 she was rebuilt.

Ione[464] 209156 (US) (passenger vessel) She was built in 1910 at Portland OR USA. 148' x 30.5' x 5.9' Wood. 389gt 339rt. Powered by a 65ihp (14" x 72") steam engine. (Her engine came from a previous *Ione* [100461]).

Iowa[465] (US) (freighter) She was built in 1898 at Lake Bennett (Caribou Crossing) BC Canada. 60' x 18' x ? Wood. Powered by two horizontal (7"x 20" high pressure) 30ihp steam engines. In 1898 she was owned by the Iowa Alaska Mining Co. In 1898 she was in Yukon River service arriving at Dawson City YT where she worked exclusively for the Iowa Alaska Mining

(IAM) Co. Murray Lundberg states that "A group of 38 men and 1 woman from Iowa had freighted 70 tons of supplies and equipment over the White Pass in March, using 15 horses; 1 man and several horses died in the work. They set up a sawmill and built the 65-foot *Iowa* and the smaller *Little Jim*. The *Iowa* was launched June 9, while the *Little Jim* seems to have left earlier (prospectus for the Clear Creek Mining Company 1898). About July 30th, the *Iowa* caught up to the *Little Jim* in the upper reaches of the Koyukuk River, where the current had become too strong for the smaller boat. The group continued in the *Iowa* and staked claims on a creek they named Clear Creek. A new company, the Clear Creek Mining Company, was then formed, and the boats both continued to St. Michael. In late August 1898, the *Little Jim* was sold but the group was unable to find a buyer for the *Iowa*, and she was abandoned."

Irene 100672 (US) (freighter) She was built in 1899 at Seattle WA USA. 84.4' x 16' x 3.8'. Wood. 105gt 66nt. Powered by a 113ihp steam engine. In 1899 she was employed on the Olympia WA to Shelton WA route. In August 1917, this vessel foundered in the Duwamish River WA. In 1929 she was reported as having been broken up.

Iris 012299[466] (US) (sidewheeler) (passenger vessel) She was built in 1863 at The Dalles OR USA by J Biles. 162' x 24' x 7'. Wood. 402gt. Powered by a (16" x 72") steam engine. In 1863 she was owned by the Peoples Transportation Co., Vancouver WA. She served on the Cascades – The Dalles Route. In 1864 she was traded to the Oregon Railroad & Navigation Co. In 1870 she was reported to have been broken up at The Dalles.

Iron Belle (US) (sidewheeler) (freighter) She was built in 1855 at Linn City OT. Wood. 54gt. Powered by a steam engine. Powered by a steam engine. In 1857 she was reported as having been abandoned

Isabel[467] 040386 (Canada) (sidewheeler) (tug, then a barge) She was built in 1866 at Victoria, Vancouver Island (Crown Colony) by James W Trahey. 142.4' x 22.6' x 9.1'. Wood. 233gt 146.56rt. Powered by a 58.8nhp oscillating condensing (42" x 48") steam engine built by Blackwood Gordon, Port Glasgow UK. She was used to tow logs and sailing vessels through First

Narrows into Burrard Inlet. Registered on July 12, 1867, at Victoria, she was the first tugboat built in what would become the Province of British Columbia. In 1893 she was rebuilt to 139.4' (255.36rt). In 1897 her engines were removed and converted to a barge for coal/coke lighterage 194.27gt/rt. In 1866 she was owned by Captain Edward Stamp (Alberni Sawmill). In 1870 she was owned by the Starr brothers on Puget Sound service to Port Townsend. Later she served in Victoria to Nanaimo service and later as a tug. In 1873–1874 she was owned by William Richardson, a merchant in San Francisco CA USA. In 1874 she was owned by Oregon Railway & Navigation Co. In 1875 she was rebuilt to 142.4' x 22.6' x 9.1'. In 1885 she was owned by Peter D Forbes. In 1885 she was owned by Henry J Macdonald, Portland, OR USA. In 1888 she was rebuilt and had new boilers installed. In 1888–1889 she was owned by Robert Dunsmuir for service between Victoria, Nanaimo, and Comox. In 1889 she was owned by Joan O Dunsmuir, Victoria BC. Repowered in 1893 with a 158.92hp steam engine. In 1889–1905 she was owned by the Esquimalt & Nanaimo Railway Co. Ltd., Victoria BC. In 1898 she was still listed in the Canada List of Shipping. In 1901 she was owned by William Richardson, San Francisco CA USA. In 1901–1914 she was owned by the Esquimalt & Nanaimo Railway Co. Ltd., Victoria BC. In 1893 she was still working on the Fraser River. In 1894 she was reported as having been laid up in Esquimalt BC, her machinery removed, and her hull turned into a barge.

Isabel 100321 (US) (passenger vessel) She was built in 1882 at Salem OR USA. 100.6' x 20.7' x 4.6' Wood. 167.68gt 123.22nt. Powered by two horizontal (10" x 36") steam engines. In 1882 she was owned by A. Prescott. In 1890 she was wrecked at Sellwood OR.

Isabella McCormack (later *Isabell*) 122399 (Canada) (passenger/ freight vessel, later a houseboat) She was built in 1908 at Golden BC by Alexander Blakeley. 94.9' x 18.8' x 3.5' Wood. 178gt 11rt. Powered by a 3nhp steam engine built by Albion Iron Works, Victoria BC. In 1908–1921 she was owned by the Columbia River Lumber Co., Golden BC. In 1910–1914 she was laid up on the beach at Athalmer BC and converted to a hotel and houseboat. She appears to have been renamed (possibly informally) as the *Isabell* after conversion to a houseboat.

Isabel McCormack on Windermere Lake in 1909 (Image from Maritime Museum of British Columbia 000427)

Isabelle 100779 (US) (freighter) She was built in 1902 at St. Michael AK USA by ET Barnette. 87.3' x 20.2' x 4.1' Wood. 162gt 76nt. Powered by a 150ihp steam engine from the *Arctic Boy*. In 1902 she was owned by Elbridge Truman Barnette. In 1904 she was owned by the Northern Navigation Co. In 1905 she was employed on the Chena River. In 1907–1908 she was employed between St. Michael and Fairbanks. In 1914 she was owned by the White Pass & Yukon Rail Road. In 1917 she was reported as having been laid up at laid up St. Michael AK USA.

Iskoot 103920 (Canada) (passenger/ freight vessel) She was built in 1898 at Vancouver BC Canada. She was built in 1898 at Vancouver BC Canada. 143' x 30.5' x 5' Wood. 590gt 356rt. Powered by a steam engine built by B.C. Iron Works, Vancouver BC. In 1898 she was owned by the Klondyke Mining & Trading Transport Co. (owned by Sir Charles Tupper, Edgar Dewdney, and others). In June 1898 she was wrecked on delivery (never in actual service), stranded near Alaska.

Islander 225342 (US) (tug) She was built in 1926 at Portland OR USA. 64.6' x 15.2' x 4.0' Wood. 82gt 66rt. Powered by a 100ihp steam engine. In 1929 she was owned by FR Remington, Portland, OR USA. In 1935 she was owned by EB Yoess, Portland OR. (She appears to have gone out of service before 1941).

Isleton[468,469] 100776 (US) (passenger vessel) She was built in 1902 at Wood. Island CA USA. 107.5' x 36.0' x 7.5' Wood. 615gt 534nt. Powered by a 300ihp steam engine. She was in service on California rivers. On July 2, 1909, she was destroyed by fire in the Sacramento River. She was rebuilt by the United States Army as the Army Queen, a motor vessel. In 1942 she was in service with the United States Army.

J. Bragdon[470] (US) (sidewheeler) (freighter, later a barge) She was built in 1852 at San Francisco CA. Wood. 273gt. Powered by a steam engine. In 1854 she was owned by the Merchants Line. She was employed on the Sacramento River. In 1854 she was owned by the California Steam Navigation Co. In 1864 her machinery was removed and installed in the Paul Pry and her hull was converted to a barge. In 1873 she was reported as having been abandoned.

J. Hunter[471] (later Rainbow Hunter) 193303 (Canada) (workboat, later a ferry) She was built in 1950 at Brentwood Bay BC by Clark Bros. Boat Works Ltd. She was designed by HC Hanson, Seattle WA. 27.9' x 9.0' x 3.3' (8.5m x 2.74m x 1.01m) Wood. 4.78gt 3.25rt. Powered by a 20hp gasoline engine. In 1950–1964 she was owned by the British Columbia Cement Co. Ltd., Victoria BC. In 1965–1981 she was owned by the Ocean Cement Ltd., Vancouver BC. In 1982–1984 she was owned by British Columbia Cement Co. Ltd., Mill Bay BC. In 1984–2001 she was owned by Jonathan Vandergoes, Nanaimo BC. In 2001–2010 she was owned by Aquabus Ferry Ltd., Vancouver BC. Vandergoes stated "I owned this boat from 1984, when I bought her from BC Cement, until 2001, when I sold her to Aquabus. She was named the J. Hunter for this period. J Hunter was one of the superintendents at the B.C. Cement factory at Bamberton, and it was named after him on his retirement. When I bought it, it had a 20–30 Easthope engine in it, which I repowered to a 6–cylinder Nissan diesel. She carried workers from Todd Inlet to the new factory at the base of the Malahat. When I had it, I finished the job of putting it through Ship Safety and used it as a school ferry to Protection Island from Nanaimo, as a Sidney Spit ferry, and finally as a Newcastle Island ferry. It was licensed to carry 21 persons, and, had a Beaufort life raft on the roof."

J. Ordway 046155 (US) (freighter) She was built in 1876 at Portland OR USA. 130.7' x 24' x 6'. Wood. 292.07gt 194.74rt. Powered by two 27nhp (14" x 54") steam engine. In 1876 she was owned by Weidler Mills. In 1897 she was reported to have been broken up at Portland OR.

J.A. McClelland[472,473] 013572 (US) (passenger/ freight vessel) She was built in 1861 at San Francisco CA. Wood. 73.31gt. Powered by a steam engine. She was in service on California rivers. On August 25, 1861, while under command of Captain Mills, while in transit from Red Bluff she experienced a boiler explosion three miles from Knight's Landing on the Sacramento River. The pilot was blown 200 feet while 25 others were killed, and many others were wounded. The *Henrietta* came to her immediate aid. The steamer *Gem* carried survivors to the city. This vessel had only been built about eight months previously and was owned by Captain Mills. She was reported to have been abandoned in 1873.

J.A. Munroe 202632 (US) (sidewheeler) (piledriver) She was built in 1905 at Astoria OR USA. 61.5' x 20.0' x 3.8'. Wood. 83gt 57nt. Powered by a steam engine. She was employed in the Columbia River watershed until about 1915.

J.B. Kerr[474] (US) She was built in 1898 at St. Michael AK USA. She was employed on the Lower Yukon River. She is reported by Murray Lundberg to have worked in Alaska/YT in 1898.

J.B. Libby 013464 (US) (sidewheeler) She was built in 1883 at Utsalady WA USA. 111.0' x 18.9' x 6.4'. Wood. 163.19gt. Powered by a 35nhp steam engine. She was based at Port Angeles WA. She was reported to have been lost in 1889.

J.D. Farrell 077280 (US) (passenger/ freight vessel) he was built in 1897 at Jennings MT USA. 130' x 26' x 4.5'. Wood. 359gt 226rt. In 1897 she was owned by the Kootenay River Navigation Co. She was employed on the

Kootenay River in western Montana and southeastern British Columbia from 1898 to 1902. On June 4, 1898, she was wrecked, raised, and put back into service. She was laid up between 1899–1901. In 1901 she was owned by A. Gutherie & Co. for Great Northern Railroad construction to Fernie BC. In 1903 her engines, boiler, fittings went to the *Spokane* (117250).

J.D. McDonald[475] She was built in the late 1890s or early 1900s. 106' Wood. Powered by a steam engine. In 1911 she was employed on the California delta.

J.D. Peters[476] 076787 (US) She was built in 1889 at Stockton CA. 206.5' x 38.0' x 8.1' Wood. 880.7gt 788.07nt. Powered by a 150nhp 600ihp steam engine. She was in service on California rivers. In 1938 she was reported to have been abandoned. Her remains are in a farm field on Mandeville Island. Dikes were closed in around her and she was used to pump out water to reclaim the rich bottom land.

J.L. Grandin 076219 (US) (work boat) She was built in 1878 at Fargo, Dakota Territory. 125.0' x 32.0' x 4.0' Wood. 217.77gt. Powered by a steam engine. In 1878 she was owned by JL Grandin (Bonanza Farms), Pembina Dakota Territory USA. In 1884 she was owned by Pembina Dakota Territory USA interests. In 1897 she sank during a flood at Halstad MN USA.

J.M. Hannaford[477] 077348 (US) (freighter) She was built in 1899 at Potlatch ID USA. 169' x 36.4' x 5.4' Wood. 513gt 456rt. Powered by two horizontal (high pressure 18.5" x 72") steam engines. (Her engines were built at Cincinnati OH in 1859 from the *Arkansas Chief* and later powered the *Shaver*.) In 1899 she was owned by the Clearwater Short Line Railroad (Northern Pacific Railroad) employed on the Snake River. In 1906 she was reported as having been broken up.

J.M. Smith[478] 112309 (Canada) (passenger vessel) She was built in 1905 at Winnipeg MB Canada. 120.0' x 21.0' x 4.0' Wood. 179gt 122rt. Powered by an 8hp steam engine. In 1906–1914 she was owned by the Pioneer Navigation and Sand Company, (a firm owned by the Hall family). In 1914–1917 she was owned by William H Hall, Winnipeg MB for Hall Navigation Company, Winnipeg MB. In 1917 she was owned by Lake Winnipeg

Navigation Company Limited, Winnipeg MB. The Manitoba Historical Society reports that "In April 1920, the vessel sustained heavy ice damage while moored off Hyland Park (then known as Riverside Park) and efforts to salvage and restore it came to naught. According to Captain Fred Hokanson, the vessel (along with the *Bonnitoba*) was sunk just off the park site by 1927 and was later blown up."

J.N. Teal[479,480] 203949 (US) (freighter/ passenger vessel) She was built in 1907 at Portland OR USA. 160.7' x 34.4' x 5.4'. Wood. 513gt 459nt. Powered by 500ihp two horizontal (high pressure 16" x 72") steam engines. In 1907 she was owned by the Open River Navigation Co. In 1925 she was owned by Willamette & Columbia River Towing Co., Portland OR. She was employed between Portland and Big Eddy OR. She was owned by the Willamette and Columbia Towing Co. In 1927 she was reported to have been abandoned and broken up.

J.P. Light 107860 (Canada) 077296 (US) (passenger/ freight vessel) She was built in 1898 at Seattle WA USA by the Moran Bros. Shipyard. 176.1' x 35' x 4'. Wood. 785gt 72rt. Powered by two (20" cylinder) 240ihp steam engines. In 1898 she was owned by Frank Waterhouse & Co. (agents for the British-American Corp.) In 1900 she was owned by Dawson & Whitehorse Navigation Co. In 1901 she was owned by EM Sullivan, Dawson YT. In 1905 she was owned by Tanana Trading Co. In 1906 she was owned by North American Transportation & Trading Co. In 1911 she was owned by Northern Navigation Co. In 1914 she was owned by the White Pass & Yukon Rail Road. In 1927 she was sold and abandoned. In 1898 she was in Yukon River service. She was transferred to Canadian Registry 1900–1905. She was transferred back to US registry 1905–1927. In 1927 she was reported as having been laid up at St. Michael AK.

J.R. McDonald[481] 077346 (US) She was built in 1899 at Stockton CA USA. 104.5' x 25.5' x 5.0'. Wood. 137gt 121nt. Powered by a 150ihp steam engine. She was employed on the San Joaquin River CA. In 1906, on a voyage to Firebaugh, CA she was stranded by low water. The owners had to negotiate with the regulators of the river dam to allow enough water to be released to refloat her.

Jack Hayes (see *Sioc*)

Jack Haynes[482,483] (see *Commodore Jones*)

Jack Wild (see *Dispatch*)

Jack Winton 122293 (Canada) 50.0' x 15.0' x 2.5'. Wood. 18.75gt 11.81rt. She was built in 1907 at Prince Albert SK by Peter Eberhardt. Powered by a 3.2nhp slide valve hoisting steam engine by American Rig & Derrick Co. Ltd., St. Paul MN. In 1907–1919 she was owned by the Prince Albert Lumber Co., Prince Albert SK. In 1919–1920 she was owned by Finger Lumber Co. Ltd., The Pas MB. In 1920–1937 she was owned by Albert L Mattes, Winnipeg MB. In 1937 she was reported to have been broken up.

James Blair[484,485] (US) (freighter) (sidewheeler) She was built about 1857 in the San Francisco Bay area. Wood. 108gt. Powered by a steam engine. In 1858 she was owned by the California Steam Navigation Co. She was a trussed-hull shallow draft vessel that operated on the Sacramento River. On March 10, 1861, she sank after striking a snag in the Feather River in the Sacramento River system.

James Clinton (US) (passenger vessel) She was built in 1856 at Canemah OT USA. 90' x 16' x 4'. Wood. 105gt. Powered by two horizontal (high pressure 9" x 48") 5.4nhp steam engines. In 1856 she was owned by the Cochran, Cassady & Co. In 1858 she was owned by James D Miller. She was owned by the People's Transportation Co. On April 23/24, 1861, she was destroyed by fire at Linn City OR USA.

James D. McCormack 150507 (Canada) (tug) She was built in 1921 at New Westminster BC Canada. 110.5' x 21.4' x 8.3'. Wood. 318gt 145rt. Powered by a 9.6nhp steam engine. In 1921–1939 she was owned by Canadian Western Lumber Co. Ltd., Fraser Mills BC and was retired in 1939. Her hull was abandoned on the shore of the lower Fraser River near Fraser Mills BC.

James Deitrick 077315 (US) (passenger/ freight vessel) She was built in 1898 at Elizabeth NJ USA. 50.0' x 10.0' x 2.3'. Wood. 25gt 18nt. Powered by a steam engine. She was employed in Alaska waters.

James Domville 107154 (Canada) (passenger/ freight vessel) She was built in 1898 at Vancouver BC Canada by Wallace Shipyards Ltd. (False Creek).

121.6' x 25.8' x 4.7' Wood. 486gt 294rt. Powered by a 15rhp reciprocating steam engine built by Polson Iron Works Ltd., Toronto ON. In 1898–1899 she was owned by the Klondike, Yukon & Stewart Pioneers Ltd., London UK (James Domville MP, Managing Director). She was wrecked and destroyed on June 12, 1899. In May 1902, the Dawson Daily News reported that "the Department of Public Works is preparing to remove the wreckage, which has blocked one side of the channel for 3 years, and to cut through the bar that has formed above the wreck"

James H. Hamilton 075761 (US) (ferry) She was built in 1875 at San Francisco CA USA. 219.0' x 32.4' x 9.7' Wood. 730.86gt 592.3nt. Powered by a 290nhp steam engine. She was reported to have been wrecked on the Yukon River in 1899.

James John 204182 (US) (sidewheeler) (ferry) She was built in 1907 at St. Johns OR USA. 90.0' x 28.0' x 6.1' Wood. 114gt 59nt. Powered by a 75ihp steam engine.

James M. Donahue 075761 (US) (sidewheeler) (ferry) She was built in 1875 at San Francisco CA USA by William E Collyer. 219.0' x 32.4' x 9.7' Wood. 730.86gt. 592.3nt. Powered by a 290nhp steam engine. She served on the Sacramento River and San Francisco Bay for the Northwestern Pacific, connecting to that carrier at Sausalito CA. (This was a joint venture between the Southern Pacific and the Atchison, Topeka, and Sante Fe Railways to service the California north coast.)

James McNaught (later *Gladys*) 076323 (US) 085679 (US) (passenger/freight vessel) She was built in 1882 at Seattle WA USA by the Puget Sound Bridge & Dredging Co. 86.9' x 18.4' x 3.6' Wood. 146.02gt 92nt. Powered by a 40nhp steam engine. In 1882 she was owned by Washington State interests. In 1884–1885 she was owned by NR Townsend, La Conner WA USA. In 1885 she was transferred to Canadian Registry. In c1894–c1895 she was owned by RT Power (who was also her Purser). In 1892 she was re-built 101' x 18' x 3.6' 211gt. 94rt. She was transferred to the Fraser River in 1894. On September 30, 1898, burned at New Westminster BC when a huge fire destroyed much of New Westminster. She was tied up at the wharf and fire was consuming the sheds on the wharf when the firemen arrived. The

Gladys quickly caught fire along with two other steamers. The three steamers went drifting down the river and set each dock and vessel alight in turn as they touched the shore.

James P. Flint (later *Fashion*) (US) (sidewheeler) (passenger/ freight vessel) She was built in 1851 at Cascades, OT USA. 80' x 12' x ? Wood. She was employed from the Cascades to The Dalles. In September 1852 she was reported to have been wrecked at Multnomah Falls. In 1853 she was salvaged and rebuilt as the *Fashion* at Vancouver WT, re-engined with the engines from the *Columbia*. In 1861 that engine was removed, and she was broken up.

Jean 237426 (US) (tug) She was built in 1938 at Portland OR USA by Commercial Iron Works. 140.3' x 40.0' x 7.8' Welded steel. 533gt 311nt. She was powered by a 1,200hp steam engine and steered by two independent sternwheels. She was designed by naval architect WD McLaren, Vancouver BC. She was employed on the Columbia and Willamette Rivers towing logs and barges. In 1938–1941 she was owned Western Transportation Co., Portland OR. In 1955 she was laid up and moved to Lewiston ID as a maritime museum and floating community theatre. She was eventually abandoned at Lewiston ID. In 1996 she was owned by Elmer Earl and moved to Astotin WA.

Jennie Clark[486] (US) (sidewheeler) (passenger vessel) She was built in 1855 at Milwaukie, Oregon Territory USA by Jacob Kamm. 115.0' x 18.5' x 4' Wood. 50gt. Powered by two horizontal (high pressure 12" x 48") 9.6nhp steam engines built in Baltimore MD. She was the first sternwheeler built in Oregon for service on the Columbia River between Portland and Oregon City. In 1855 she was owned by JC Ainsworth and Jacob Kamm. In 1862 she was owned by the Oregon Steam Navigation Co. employed as an excursion vessel operating between Fort Clatsop and Portland. In 1863 she was reported to have been broken up. Her engines went to the *Forty-Nine* (009525). In 1865 she was burned to recover metal from her hull construction.

Jennie K[487] (US) Wood. Powered by a steam engine. She is reported by Murray Lundberg to have worked in Alaska/YT in 1899.

Jenny Lind[488] (US) (sidewheeler) She was built in 1850. Wood. 61gt. She was in service on California rivers. Powered by a steam engine. Her boiler exploded in 1852. She was reported to have been abandoned in 1857.

Jennie M. 077320 (US) (passenger/ freight vessel) She was built in 1898 at St. Michael AK USA by Crescent Shipyard. 70.0' x 15.0' x 3' Steel. 49gt 29nt. Powered by a steam engine. In 1899 she was owned by Black Transportation Co. In 1903 she was owned by Hendricks & Belt. She was employed as a barge. She was wrecked by ice at Mt. Romanoff AK USA in 1899.

Jersey 157596 (US) (tug) She was built in 1901 at Stockton CA USA. 54.5' x 15.5' x 3.5' Wood. 41gt 39nt. She was employed on the San Francisco Bay area.

Jessie 077291 (Canada) (passenger/ freight vessel) She was built in 1887 at Okanagan Landing BC. 89' Wood. In 1903 she was reported to have been destroyed by fire.

Jessie[489] 077298 (US) She was built in 1898 at Ballard WA USA. 55.2' x 13.7' x 3.4' Wood. 61gt 21nt. Powered by a steam engine. She is reported by Murray Lundberg to have worked in Alaska/YT in 1898.

Jim Hill (later *Klondike 3*) (US) (snag boat) She was built in 1910 at Flathead Lake MT USA by Eugene Hodge. In 1923 she was rebuilt as *Klondike 3*. She was employed on Flathead Lake. In 1923 she was reported to have been abandoned.

John 3:16 (later *White Horse*) 130742 (Canada) She was built in 1901 at Whitehorse YT Canada. 167' x 34.5' x 4.5' Wood. 987gt 631rt. Powered by a 17nhp steam engine. In 1913 she was owned by The British Yukon Navigation Co. Ltd., Vancouver BC. In 1919 she was owned by Joseph Bethel, Vancouver BC.

John A. Sutter[490] (US) She was built in 1849. Wood. Powered by a steam engine. She was in service on California rivers. Her boiler exploded in 1859.

John Bragdon[491] (US) (sidewheeler) She was built in the eastern United States in 1851. 150'. Wood. 273gt. Powered by a steam engine. She was in service on California rivers. In 1865 she was reported as having been abandoned.

John C. Barr (see *Valley City*)

John Cudahy 077334 (US) (passenger vessel) She was prefabricated in 1898 at Seattle WA and shipped to Dutch Harbor AK USA for assembly by the Moran Bros. (She was built to an Ohio River steamer design.) 192.3' x 32.6' x 5.0'. Wood. 819gt 481nt. In 1898 she was owned by the North American Transportation & Trading Co. (N.A. T. & T. Co.). In 1905–1906 she was employed on the Dawson to Fairbanks route.

John Day Queen[492] (US) (passenger/ freight vessel) She was built in 1895 at Deschutes OR USA by Charlie Clarno. 40.0' x 10' x ?. Wood. Powered by a steam engine. In 1897 she was reported to have been out of service. She was a pleasure craft and substitute ferry that operated during high water along a ten-mile stretch of the river above Clarno Rapids. In the flood of 1899 she was lost, later to be rebuilt by Charlie Clarno in 1905.

John Edward[493] (later *Emerald Queen*) (US) She was built in 1967 in the Puget Sound WA USA. In 1979 she was owned by the Skagit Bay Navigation Co. (Captain Owen (Tony) Tronsdahl, Conway, Skagit County WA, and Captain Ray Hughes). She was employed as an excursion boat on Lake Union WA.

John F. Caples 201352 (US) (sidewheeler) (ferry) She was built in 1904 at Portland OR USA. 100.0' x 30.5' x 7.0'. Wood. 192gt 157nt. In 1927 she was reported as having been abandoned

John Gates 076038 (US) (passenger vessel) She was built in 1878 at Celilo OR USA. 151.0' x 32.0' x 4.8'. Wood. 673.38gt 552.3nt. Powered by two horizontal (high pressure 16" x 54") 17nhp steam engines. In 1878 she was owned by the Oregon Steam Navigation Co. In 1894 she was reported to have been broken up at Riparia WA. The house works went to the hull of the *Lewiston* (141361).

John Hamilton (US)[494] She was built in 1897 at San Francisco CA. Wood. Powered by a steam engine. She sailed from San Francisco to St. Michael for the Klondike Gold Rush.

John H. Couch[495] 013622 (US) (sidewheeler) (passenger vessel) She was built in 1863 at Westport OR USA. 123.0' x 21.0' x 7.0' Wood. 255.24gt 192nt. Powered by a (14.4" x 54") steam engine. In 1863 she was owned by Charles Holman et al. In 1865 she was owned by J Ainsworth. She was employed on the Portland to Astoria route. In 1873 she was reported to have been broken up.

John J. Healy 077238 (US) (passenger vessel) She was built in 1896 at St. Michael AK USA. 175.0' x 36.0' x 5.3' Wood. 450gt 231nt. Powered by a 175ihp steam engine built to a Mississippi River steamer design and was the largest river steamer then in use on the Yukon River. In 1896 she was owned by the North American Transportation & Trading Co. In 1911 she was owned by the Northern Navigation Co. In 1914 she was owned by the White Pass & Yukon Rail Road. She was sold again. In 1927 she was abandoned at St. Michael AK.

John L. Stephens[496] (US) (sidewheeler) Wood. Powered by a steam engine. She is reported by Murray Lundberg to have been a sidewheeler that worked in Alaska/YT. In 1867, she made two trips to Alaska for the newly formed conglomerate, the North Pacific Transportation Company.

John P. Douglas[497] 126079 (Canada) (ferry) She was built in 1908 at Vancouver BC Canada. 83.4' x 20.4' x 5.1' Wood. 237gt 149rt. Powered by a 3nhp steam engine. In 1908–1909 she was owned by Alfred E Yates (MO), Vancouver BC. On January 07, 1909, this mail and passenger ferry was destroyed by fire at Harrison Mills, BC. She was trying to cross the Fraser River when she was hit by pack ice. While freeing themselves the crew found the vessel engulfed in flames made worse by the wind. Only the mail bags were saved by the crew as they hastily abandoned ship. The crew salvaged planks from the burning steamer with which to make their landing from the pack ice. Her engines when salvaged went to the *Vedder River*.

John Reilly 077391 (US) She was built in 1898 at St. Lawrence Island AK. 100.0' x 22.0' x 5' Wood. 220gt 143nt. Powered by a steam engine. On October 13, 1905, she was stranded on Cape Blossom AK USA.

John T. Wright[498] (US) (sidewheeler) She was built in 1860 at Port Ludlow WT. Wood. 369gt. Powered by a steam engine. She flew the US flag while operating in Chinese waters under Consular documents from 1862–1864. She was reported as having been lost in 1864.

John Wildi 200081 (US) (freighter) She was built in 1903 at Parkersburg OR USA. 111.5' x 25.2' x 4.5' 173gt 167nt. Powered by a 150ihp steam engine. She was reported to have been abandoned about 1927.

Joseph Clossett[499] (later *Josie C.*) (US) (She is reported by Murray Lundberg to have worked in Alaska/YT 1898–1903).

Joseph Kellogg[500] 076267 (US) She was built in 1881 at Portland OR. 127.7' x 23.4' x 3.4' Wood. 322gt 272nt. Powered by two 9.6nhp horizontal (high pressure 12" x 48") steam engines. (Her engines were from the *Dayton*). In 1900 she was rebuilt by the Portland Shipbuilding Co. She was owned by the Kellogg Transportation Co. (Joseph Kellogg). She was later owned by the Northwestern Transportation Co. She was employed on the Willamette, Columbia, and Cowlitz rivers.

Joseph Kellogg (later *Madeline*) 077431 (US) (passenger vessel) She was built in 1900 at Portland OR USA by Charles M Nelson. 139.2' x 26.5' x 7.2' Wood. 462gt 342nt. Powered by two horizontal (high pressure 16" x 60" cylinder) steam engines. The hull and house works were from the first *Joseph Kellogg*. In 1900 she was owned by Joseph Kellogg. In 1921 she was rebuilt and renamed as the *Madeline* (72431).

Joseph W. Clossett 107621 (Canada) (passenger vessel) She was built in 1898 at Lake Bennett BC Canada by John F Steffan. 80.0' x 21.0' x 4.5' Wood. 147gt 93rt. Powered by a 3.5nhp steam engine. In 1898 she was owned by William J Rant. She was owned by the Upper Yukon Co. In 1899 she was owned by the Canadian Development Co. In 1901–1931 she was owned by British Yukon Navigation Co., Vancouver BC. She shot the rapids at Miles Canyon on the Yukon River and sank after hitting the shore. She was later salvaged and operated between Dawson City and Whitehorse YT. She was in service Whitehorse to Dawson. She was reported as having been laid up c1905. She was dismantled in Whitehorse YT in 1931.

Josephine[501] 076040 (US) She was built in 1878 at Port Townsend WA USA. 75.9' x 18.5' x 4.3' Wood. 104.4gt 64.53nt. Powered by a steam engine. In 1879 she ascended the Skagit River as far as Minkler's sawmill near Birdsview. During the voyage one of the passengers fell overboard and was drowned. In 1880 she was in regular service on the Skagit River as the portage, a mile above Bacon Creek (and inside today's National Park boundary). She was rebuilt after a boiler explosion in 1883. In 1883 she worked on the Tacoma – Shelton WA USA run. In 1892 she was reported as having been destroyed by fire.

Josie Burrows (later *Hattie Young*) 077098 (US) 103894 (Canada) (passenger vessel) She was built in 1893 at Aberdeen WA USA. 90' x 18.5' x 4.8' Wood. 131.75gt 98.15nt. Powered by a 5.4nhp steam engine. In 1898 she was owned by Captain CS Young, New Westminster BC. In 1898 she worked on the Fraser River, purchased to replace the steamer *Bon Accord* (094908) that was destroyed in the fire at New Westminster of 1898; first as the *Josie Burrows* and then as the *Hattie Young*. On December 08, 1900, while proceeding upriver a fire broke out in the hold beneath the boiler. That extended to a large cargo of hay being carried and the fire spread rapidly. The flames extended over the whole of the boat in a few minutes. Captain George Magar tried to run her ashore, but he had to leave his post before she reached the bank. She burned out and sank in several feet of water opposite Marsh's Landing on the Fraser River.

Josie C. (see *Joseph Clossett*)

Josie McNear[502] 013620 (US) (sidewheeler) (passenger vessel) She was built in 1865 at San Francisco CA USA by Cousins. 108.7' x 23.0' x 6.7' Wood. 159gt 136.72nt. Powered by a 9.6nhp (12" x 48") steam engine. She was owned by Hale Crosby & Winsor. She was employed on California rivers. In 1866 she was transferred to Puget Sound. Later she was owned by Oregon

Steam Navigation Co. and placed on the Portland to Astoria route. She was reported as having gone out of service about 1878 and broken up.

Julia 013621 (US) (see Julia Barclay)

Julia 013570 (US) (sidewheeler) In 1864 she was built at San Francisco CA. 170.0' x 32.0' x 8.8' Wood. 503.20gt 407.31nt. Powered by 200nhp steam engines. In 1864 she was owned by the California Steam Navigation Co.

Julia 013621 (US) (see Julia Barclay)

Julie B. 205169 (US) She was built in 1908 at Ballard WA USA by Cook & Lake Shipyards. 158.7' x 38' x 7' Wood. 835gt 511nt. Powered by two (high pressure 8" x 72") steam engines. She was towed with two barges by the A.G. Lindsay to Alaska. In 1908 she was owned by the Yukon Transportation & Trading Co. Ltd. She was employed between St. Michael and Fairbanks. In 1914 she was owned by the Western Transportation Co. In 1918 she was owned by the White Pass & Yukon Rail Road. She was owned by the Alaska Railroad. In 1942 she was reported as having been laid up at Dawson City YT.

Julia Barclay[503,504,505] (aka Julia) 013621 (US) (passenger/ freight Vessel) She was built in 1858 at Port Blakeley WT USA. Lytle says she was built at Tikalet WT. 146.5' x 25' x 5.7' Wood. 325.43gt. Powered by two 17nhp (horizontal 16" x 72" high pressure) steam engines. She was built to oppose and was eventually defeated by the Beaver in the Fraser River trade. She moved to Puget Sound before being towed to the lower Columbia River to take up new routes. In 1872 she was reported as having been broken up at Portland OR.

Juliette[506] 200592 (US) (freighter) She was built in 1903 at Sausalito CA USA. 170' x 35.0' x 5.6' Wood. 394gt 371nt. Powered by a steam engine. On June 28, 1911, she was rammed by the steamer Thomas L. Wand and sank at the mouth of the Sacramento River. She had been enroute from San Francisco to Crockett for a load of sugar.

Julius 205210 (US) (ferry) She was built in 1909 at Salem OR USA by RO Cummings. 61.4' x 20.1' x 4.9' Wood. 48gt/nt. Powered by a gasoline engine.

In 1909 she was owned by Capital Improvement Co. She was reported as having gone out of service about 1911.

Juno 075802 (US) She was built in 1876 at Coos Bay OR USA. Wood. Powered by a steam engine. She appears to have been out of service before 1884.

Juno (US) (see *Pend Oreille*)

Jupiter 203356 (US) (freighter) She was built in 1906 at Sacramento CA USA. 73.0' x 17.0' x 1.5'. Wood. 14gt 9nt. Powered by a 45ihp gasoline engine. She was employed in California waters.

K.L. Ames 213019 (later *Skookum Chief*) (US) (fishboat) She was built in 1915 at Seattle WA USA. 119' x 29.8' x 5.4'. Wood. 184gt 156nt. Powered by a 275ihp steam engine. She was converted to a diesel engine she was renamed as the *Skookum Chief*.

Kalamazoo (US) (freighter) She was built in 1898. 37.0' x 11.0' x 2.0' Wood. Powered by a steam engine. Murray Lundberg reports that she was powered by the steam engine that was intended to power the sawmill transported north to build her. In 1898 she was owned by the Kalamazoo Mining Co. She was named for the Michigan home town of Captain Stewart Lawrence Campbell, promoter of the Kalamazoo Mining and Prospecting Company, known as "The Kalamazoo Hustlers." The group consisted of Captain Campbell, William A Doyle, Arthur W Rickman, JK Evers, James Doyle, Fred Schied, William Unger, John Ensing, Henry Greendyke, Harry den Bleyker, Fred Longwell, and Arthur Pierson. She was launched May 31, 1898, for trial run, along with a 39' x 10' barge. On June 12, 1898, wrecked at Casey's Rock, in the Thirty Mile River, after she hit a rock while under the command of William Doyle. She finally lodged about 125 feet offshore, in 4 feet of water. Raised two days later and repaired; no holes, "but badly wrenched." They lost an electric plant, winch, and a lot of their medicine and flour in the wreck; back on the river on June 17. They only reached the Indian River, where Campbell stopped to prospect. One of the men, was caught stealing from the boat and crew—he had diverted lumber to put up a building in Dawson. (Gaffin, in the *Yukon News*, September 15, 1995).

Kaleden (Image from Maritime Museum of British Columbia 000424)

Kaleden 130297 (Canada) (freighter) She was built in 1910 at Okanagan Landing BC Canada by James M Bulger. 94' x 18.4' x 4.6' Wood. 180gt 113rt. Powered by a steam engine. In 1910 she was owned by the Canadian Pacific Railway Co., Montreal QC. In 1910 she was Okanagan Lake service as a passenger vessel but was unsuccessful. She then was a powder boat during Kettle Valley Railway construction. In 1917 she was laid up. She was powered by two steam engines from the steamer Victoria. In 1920 she was dismantled.

Kalorama[507] (US) Wood. Powered by a steam engine. In 1874 she was owned by Goodall, Nelson & Perkius. In 1874 she was in service between Los Angeles CA and San Francisco (and way ports).

Kamloops (Canada) (passenger/ freight vessel) She was built in 1872 at Savona BC Canada. 57.0' x 12.5' x 3.0' Wood. 11.79gt. Powered by a 4nhp steam engine. In 1872 she was owned by John Adams.

Kamloops 085680 (Canada) (passenger vessel) She was built in 1885 at Kamloops BC Canada by Alexander Watson. 126.0' x 27.4' x 5.6' Wood. 426gt 268nt. Powered by a steam engine built by Albion Iron Works, Victoria BC. She was powered by a steam engine from the *Myra*. In 1885 she was owned by the Kamloops Steam Navigation Co. (owned by J Mara). In 1896 she was owned by JA Mara, Kamloops BC. She carried freight between Savona and Eagle Pass BC. In 1889 she was reported as having been abandoned

Kanai (US) She was built about 1849. Wood. Powered by a steam engine. She was employed on the Sacramento River CA.

Kangaroo[508] (US) She was built about 1859. Wood. Powered by a steam engine. She was in service on California rivers. She was reported as having gone out of operation in 1868.

Kaslo (Image from Maritime Museum of British Columbia 000426)

Kaslo 107827 (Canada) (freighter) She was built in 1900 at Mirror Lake BC Canada by Harold C Elliott. 173.5' x 27.0' x 7.4'. Wood. 764gt 369rt. Powered by a 32nhp steam engine built by Polson Iron Works Ltd., Toronto ON. In 1900 she was owned by the Great Northern Railroad and chartered to the Kootenay Railway & Navigation Co. She was in Kootenay Lake service. In 1901 she was owned by Robert Irving, Kaslo BC. In 1910 she was owned by AH MacNeill, Rossland BC. In 1910 she sank at the Ainsworth dock after hitting a rock. She was reported as having been broken up at Mirror Lake BC.

Kate and Anna 014376 (US) Wood. Powered by a steam engine. She was built in 1879 at Yaquina Bay OR USA. Wood. 30.7gt 16.49rt. Powered by an 8nhp steam engine. In 1879–1884 she was owned by Portland OR USA interests. (Not listed in the 1885 edition of Merchant Vessels of the United States.)

Kate Connor[509] (US) She was built in 1868 at Jordan River UT by Gammon Hayward. 55' Wood. Powered by a steam engine. (It is uncertain whether she was a sternwheeler or a propeller.)

Kate de Knivet (Also known as the *K. de K.* and *Knyvett de Knyvett*) 085675 (Canada) (sidewheeler) (passenger vessel) She was built in 1884 at New Westminster BC. 52' x 16' x 3.5'. Wood. 61gt 38nt. In c1884 she was operated by Knyvett de Knyvett, as a small ferry at New Westminster BC in service between Brownsville and New Westminster BC. In 1889 she was laid up.

Kate Kearny[510] (US) She was built in 1851 at San Francisco CA. Wood. 112gt. Powered by a steam engine. In 1854–1856 she was owned by the California Steam Navigation Co. She was in service on California rivers. In 1856 she was reported to have been out of service. She was reported as having been abandoned in 1859.

Katie Hallett (US) (passenger/ freight vessel) She was built in 1882 at Clark Fork ID USA. 135' x 22' x ? Wood. Powered by two horizontal (high pressure 13nhp 14" x 60") steam engines built by the Willamette Iron Works, Portland, OR USA. She was employed on Pend Oreille Lake. Her engines came from the steamer *McMinnville*. She worked in company with the steamer *Henry Villard* during the construction of the Northern Pacific Railroad from Thompson Falls to Sandpoint ID. After completion of the railroad in 1885 she was laid up at Clark Point ID. Her engines and fittings went to the steamer *Kootenai* (144436).

Katie Hemrich (see *General Stewart Van Vliet*)

Katie Ladd (US) (sidewheeler) (passenger/ freight vessel) She was built in 1871 at Portland OR USA. 90.0' Wood. 110gt. Powered by a steam engine. In 1878 she was reported to have gone out of service.

Kavatka[511] (US) Wood. Powered by a steam engine. (She is reported by Murray Lundberg to have worked in Alaska/YT 1907. In September 1907, she was reported by Captain John Smith of the *Will H. Isom* to be at Koyukuk Station on the Yukon River (YA: MSS 104, 80/72).)

Kehani (later *Ottawa*) 161034 (US) (passenger/ freight vessel) She was built in 1892 at Portland OR USA. 90.0' x 17.0' x 6.0' Wood. 118.42gt 85.41nt. Powered by two 6.6nhp horizontal (high pressure 10" x 48") steam engines. In 1892 she was owned by Ham, Nickum & Co. She was rebuilt in 1905 and renamed as *Ottawa*.

Kennebec[512] (US) She was built in 1850. Wood. 44gt. Powered by a steam engine. In 1853 she was employed on the Sacramento River CA. In 1868 she was reported as having gone out of existence.

Keno 116618 (Canada) In 1922 she was built at Whitehorse YT Canada. 130.5' x 29.2' x 4.8' Wood. 553gt 349rt. Powered by a 9ihp steam engine. She was rebuilt in 1937 at Whitehorse YT to 140.6' x 30.4' x 4.9' 613gt 416rt. In 1922–1940 she was owned by The British Yukon Navigation Co. Ltd., Vancouver BC. In 1933 her Master, Captain John D. Murray died while in command on the Stewart River YT. During the Second World War she carried United States Army troops that were constructing the Alaska Highway between Teslin and Watson Lake. She was the last of the small sternwheelers to operate on the Yukon River. In 1960 she was transferred to the Canadian Government.On August 26, 1960, she made her last trip, under Captain FS Blakely. In 1960 she was beached and is still preserved at Dawson City YT.

Kevlin (US) She was built in 1989. She was reported[513] as a private dual sternwheel house boat on Lake Union WA. In 2011 she was owned by Kevin and Linda Bagley, Seattle WA USA. In 2020 she was listed for sale.

Key West/New Iberia (US) 200' X 33' X 5.4' Wood. Powered by a steam engine. In 1871 she was owned by John Todd and Nicholas Bruson, Columbia County OH and Sanford S Coulson, William S Evans, and David SH Gilmore of Pittsburgh PA (companies associated with American Fur Company and Coulson Line). She was employed on the Upper Missouri River and Yellowstone River. She travelled 460 miles to the mouth of the Powder River. On May 6, 1873, Captain Marsh took her into mouth of the

Yellowstone River, up to the mouth of the Powder River and back to the Missouri River. This was an exploratory trip by the United States Army in preparation for Colonel George A Custer's ill-fated expedition.

Keystone[514] (US) Wood. Powered by a steam engine. She is reported by Murray Lundberg to have worked in Alaska/YT c1900. MacBride reports that she was a shallow draft boat operated on the Iditarod River. She was probably a sternwheeler.

Kieukik[515] (US) Wood. Powered by a steam engine. She is reported by Murray Lundberg to have worked in Alaska/YT 1897. She was probably a sternwheeler. Pierre Berton reports that "in the fall of 1897, the "rickety steamboat" was "commandeered" at Dawson by Thomas McGee. He was one of thousands of people desperate to get out of the Klondike before winter; "so often did the machinery break down on the shuddering little craft that after a week the fifteen freezing passengers aboard the vessel found that they had moved only thirty-five miles. The boat, its hull ripped open, was abandoned . . ." (Pierre Berton).

King Edward 150502 (Canada) (later P.W.D. No. 305) (dredge, later a barge) She was built in 1901 at New Westminster BC Canada. She was rebuilt to 127.6' x 33' x 7'. Wood. 543gt 543rt. Powered by a 17nhp engine. In 1901–1958 she was owned by The Minister of Public Works, Ottawa ON. In 1961 she was owned by Tide Bay Dredging Co. Ltd., New Westminster BC. In 1922 she worked on the Sumas Lake reclamation project.

Kiyus (US) (passenger/ freight vessel) She was built in 1863 at Celilo OR USA. 140' x 18' x 6'. Wood. Powered by two 17nhp (16" x 72") horizontal high pressure steam engines. In 1863–1866 she was owned by the Peoples Transportation Co. She was employed between Celilo Oregon to Lewiston ID. In 1866 she was reported as having been wrecked at Kyle WT.

Klahowya[516] 126946 (Canada) (passenger/ freight vessel) She was built in 1910 at Golden BC Canada by George Rury. 92' x 19' x 3.5'. Wood. 175.41gt 110.51rt. Powered by two 3nhp (high pressure 7" x 42") horizontal steam engines built by Albion Iron Works, Victoria BC. She was powered by two

1896 steam engines from the *Isabella McCormack*. In 1914 she was rebuilt as a barge. In 1910–1915 she was owned by the Columbia River Lumber Co. for upper Columbia River service. In 1915 she was laid up.

Klondike wrecked in 1936 below Thirty Mile (Image from Maritime Museum of British Columbia 000439)

Klondike 116627 (Canada) (passenger/ freight vessel) She was built in 1929 at Vancouver BC by the British Yukon Navigation Co. Ltd. 210.25' x 42.1' x 6.35' Wood. 1284.7gt 1040.85rt. Powered by a 70.15nhp steam engine built by Gillette and Eaton Inc., Lake City MN. In 1929 she was rebuilt at Whitehorse YT. In 1929–1936 she was owned by the British Yukon Navigation Co. Ltd., Vancouver BC. On June 12, 1936, she was wrecked while grounding on a rock bluff at Hootalinqua YT (on the Yukon River) and in 1937 her machinery was removed for use in the *Klondike* (II).

Klondike[517] 156744 (passenger/ freight vessel) She was built in 1937 at Whitehorse YT Canada. 210' x 41.9' x 5.8' Wood. 1363gt 1020rt. Powered by a 522hp steam engine. In 1945 extra staterooms were added and a bar and lounge was added in 1953. In 1937–1960 she was owned by The British Yukon Navigation Co. Ltd., Vancouver BC in service between Whitehorse and Dawson City YT. In 1960 she was transferred to the Canadian Government. She was powered by a 522hp steam engine from the *Klondike* (I), and the boiler from the *Yukoner*). In 1955 she was taken out of operation and beached and was the last commercial sternwheeler on the Yukon River. She was later she was owned by Minister of the Environment (Canadian Parks Service) Ottawa ON, preserved at Whitehorse YT as a National Historic Park.

Klondike[518] (US) (passenger/ freight vessel) She was built in 1900 at Flathead Lake MT by Eugene Hodge. Wood. Powered by a steam engine. In 1900 she was owned by Eugene Hodge. She was employed between Polson and Somers. In 1909 she was reported to have been laid up.

Klondike No. 2[519] (US) (passenger/ freight vessel) She was built in 1909 at Flathead Lake MT by Eugene Hodge. 120' x 25' x ? Wood. In 1909 she was owned by the Hodge Navigation Co. Later she was owned by HA Palmer and George Williams, employed between Somers and Polson. In 1924 she sank at Polson, was raised, and dismantled. Her engine went to the Silver City.

Klondike No. 3[520] (US) (workboat) She was built in 1923 at Flathead Lake MT. Wood. Powered by a steam engine from the *Jim Hill*. In 1923 she was owned by Eugene Hodge.

Klondike Spirit[521] 832858 (Canada) (passenger vessel) She was built in 2006 at Eagle AK USA by Eagle Boat Co. 25.91m x 5.49m x 1.22m Steel. 118gt 35rt. Powered by two 168kw diesel engines. In 2012–2013 she was owned by Klondyke Spirit Tours Inc., Newmarket ON. In 2017–2021 she was owned by Klondike Spirit Tours Inc., Dawson City YT.

Klondyke 161114 (US) She was built in 1898 at Seattle WA USA by the Moran Bros. Shipyard. In 1898 she was assembled at Dutch Harbor AK for service in the Klondike Gold Rush. 120.8' x 27.5' x 5.8' Wood. 406gt 242nt. Powered by a 190ihp steam engine. In 1898 she was owned by the North American Transportation & Trading Co. In 1911 she was owned by the Northern Navigation Co. In 1914 she was owned by the White Pass & Yukon Rail Road. She was the fastest of the North American Transportation & Trading

Co. vessels. In 1936 she was reported as having been laid up at St. Michael AK. (She was reported to have been converted to a barge.)

Kluahne 126942 (Canada) (passenger/ freight vessel) She was built in 1909 at Victoria BC Canada. 55' x 13.3' x 2.5' Wood. 19gt 7rt. Powered by a steam engine. In 1909–1931 she was owned by Isaac Taylor & William S Drury (JO), Whitehorse YT.

Knight No. 2[522] 014434 (US) She was built in 1885 at Marysville CA. 137.0' x 32.8' x 4.5' Wood. 247.88gt 146.71nt. Powered by a steam engine. She was in service on California rivers. In 1905 she was reported as having gone out of operation.

Kokanee (Image from Maritime Museum of British Columbia 000422)

Kokanee 103303 (Canada) (passenger vessel) She was built in 1896 at Nelson BC Canada by Thomas J Bulger. 143.0' x 25.0' x 6.0' Wood. 348gt 165rt. Powered by a one-cylinder 19nhp steam engine. In 1896 she was owned by Columbia & Kootenay Steam Navigation Co. In 1897 she was owned by the Canadian Pacific Railway Co., Montreal QC. She was laid up in 1923 when she was purchased by Lieutenant-Commander Richard T Deane RCNVR and moored in front of Deanshaven, his property near Riondel, as a tourist lodge. She had a reputation as the fastest of the Canadian Columbia River steamers. In 1930 she was abandoned and sank at Riondel BC. The wreck has been documented by the Underwater Archaeology Society of British Columbia.

Kootenai (Image from Maritime Museum of British Columbia 000440)

Kootenai 014436 (US) (passenger/ freight vessel) She was built in 1885 at Little Dalles WA by Paquet & Smith. 139.0' x 22' x 5' Wood. 370.88gt 268.52nt. Powered by two horizontal (high pressure 14" x 60") 13nhp steam engines. Her engines were built by the Willamette Iron Works from the *McMinnville* 090960 and the *Katie Hallett*. In 1885 she was owned by Henderson McCartney. On her first voyage she was employed carrying supplies to Farwell for the Canadian Pacific Railway construction. On September 4, 1885, she ran onto rocks at Little Dalles. After repair, and brief operation, she was laid up. In 1890 she was owned by the Columbia Kootenay Steam Navigation Co. On December 3, 1895, the *Kootenai* ran onto a rock near Bannock Point and Wigwam, BC on Upper Arrow Lake. Although the steamer was floated off, the vessel was not considered worth repairing.

The *Kootenai* was towed to Nakusp, BC and dismantled. The steamer's machinery and fittings were used in building the sternwheeler *Trail*.

Kootenai[523] (US) She was built in 1887 at Coeur d'Alene ID USA. 110.0' x 30.0' x 8.0' Wood. Powered by a 480ihp steam engine built by the Willamette Iron Works. In 1887 she was owned by DC Corbin. In 1898 she was reported as having been broken up.

Kootenay (Image from Maritime Museum of British Columbia 000425)

Kootenay 103164 (Canada) (passenger vessel) She was built in 1897 at Nakusp BC Canada by James M Bulger. 183.5' x 32.6' x 6.2' Wood. 1117gt 732rt. Powered by a 21nhp steam engine. She was powered by steam engine from the *William Irving*. She had four rudders with steam powered steering. She replaced the *Kootenai* (1885) taken over with the Columbia & Kootenay Navigation Co. In 1897 she was owned by Canadian Pacific Railway Ltd., Montreal QC. She was in Arrow Lakes service. In 1919 she was withdrawn from service and rebuilt as a houseboat. In 1920 she was owned by Captain Sanderson, Nakusp BC.

Kootenay Star (Canada) She was built in 2013 at Kaslo BC by Dave May (who also designed her). 48' x 12' x ?' Powered by a diesel engine that also powered the hydraulic system. In 2013–2021 she was a power yacht owned by Dave May, Kaslo BC.

Kotzebue 161106 (US) (passenger/ freight vessel) She was built in 1898 at Sausalito CA USA interests. 47.0' x 15.5' x 3.5'. Wood. 39gt 28nt. Powered by a steam engine.

Koyokuk 161204 (US) (tug) 54.6' x 17.7' x 1.9'. Wood. 14gt 9nt. She was built in 1902 at Seattle WA USA. She was powered by a gasoline engine. She was employed in Puget Sound Service.

Koyukuk 161202 (US) (passenger/ freight vessel) She was built in 1902 at Portland OR USA by Joseph M Supple. 120.5' x 24.5' x 4.3'. Wood. 286gt 199nt. Powered by a 100ihp steam engine. In 1902 she was owned by the Northern Commercial Co. In 1904–1906 she was employed on the Tanana River. On May 20, 1906, she was reported as having been stranded and later broken up at Little Delta AK USA. Her engines went to the new Koyukuk.

Koyukuk 203496 (US) In 1906 she was built in St. Michael AK USA. 120.9' x 24.4' x 4.1'. Wood. 260gt 149nt. Powered by as 100ihp steam engine. In 1906 she was owned by the Northern Navigation Co. In 1906–1909 she was employed on the St. Michael, Koyukuk River and Fairbanks routes. On May 12, 1911, she foundered on the Upper Tanana River AK USA. Her engines went to the M.L. *Washburn* (209341).

Koyukuk No. 2[524] (US) Wood. Powered by a steam engine. She is reported by Murray Lundberg to have worked in Alaska/YT 1906–1911.

Kuskanook (Image from a private postcard collection.)

Kuskanook 121758 (Canada) (passenger vessel) She was built in 1906 at Nelson BC Canada. 194' x 31' x 7' Wood. 1008gt 547nt. Powered by a 32.8nhp steam engine built by Polson Iron Works Ltd., Toronto ON. In 1906 she was owned by the Canadian Pacific Railway Ltd., Montreal QC. In 1906 she was in service between Nelson and Kootenay Landing. In 1914 she was in service between Nelson and Kaslo. In 1930 she took her last run. In 1931 she was dismantled. In 1931 she was sold to AD Pochin and converted to a floating hotel at Nelson BC. She was towed to Kokanee Landing where she was abandoned and sank in 1936.

La Center[525] 209642 (US) (passenger/ freight vessel) She was built in 1912 at La Center WA USA by Pete Moe and the Uriah Brothers. 65' Wood. 67gt 64nt. She was originally powered with a gasoline engine and carried only freight. Later the *La Center* was converted to steam and a second deck was added for passengers. In 1925 she was moved from Puget Sound service to Oregon. She was in service on the East Fork of the Lewis River until 1931. In 1931 she was reported as having been abandoned

La France 107866 (Canada) (passenger/ freight vessel) She was built in 1902 at Lake Laberge YT Canada by the Klondyke Co. 99.8' x 19.4' x 3.4' Wood. 169gt. Powered by a 4hp steam engine. In 1902 she was owned by the Klondyke Corp. In 1903 she was owned by the White Pass & Yukon Rail Road. In 1904 she was owned by RW Claderhead, Dawson YT. In 1908 she was owned by Side Streams Navigation Co. In 1911 she was wrecked and destroyed by fire at Lake Laberge YT.

Labouchere[526,527] (bark-rigged sidewheeler) (passenger vessel) She was built in 1858 at Blackwall UK by Green, Wigrams & Green. 202' x 28' x 15' Wood. 507.25gt 319rt. The hold was 15' deep. She was built of teak and Baltic oak. Powered by a 181hp steam engine built by Penn & Co. In 1858–1866 she was owned by the Hudson's Bay Co., London UK. She was brought out to Victoria by Captain John F Trivett arriving January 31, 1859. She was the first ocean steamer to arrive at Queensborough (New Westminster) on July 16, 1859. She was seized by First Nations people, during a dispute over the price of sea otter skin, while under command of Captain Swanson 150 miles north of the Stikine River. Swanson was able to peaceably regain control of the vessel. She was not a profit center for her owners. In 1866 she was extensively altered in San Francisco CA. In 1866 she had the contract to transport mail for the Colonial Government between Victoria and San Francisco. On April 01, 1866, she struck a reef and was lost (with two lives) near Point Reyes in dense fog while enroute from San Francisco to Victoria under Captain Mouat. (This was only her second voyage on this route).

Ladner-Woodward Ferry #3 154322 (Canada) (Ferry, passenger/car) She was built in 1926 at New Westminster BC Canada. 137.4' x 40.4' x 5.2' Wood. 389gt 250rt. Powered by a 13hp engine. In 1926–1936 she was owned by The Minister of Public Works, Victoria BC. In 1926 she took over service from the *Beaver*.

Lady Dufferin 085315 (Canada) (sidewheeler) (passenger vessel) She was built in 1878 at Tranquille BC by Neil Morrison. 87' x 30.4' x 5.4' Wood. 59gt. 52.38rt. Powered by two 20hp wood-burning horizontal (high pressure 8" x 24") steam engines built by Joseph Spratt, Victoria BC. She was a Wood. burner. She was launched by Wilhelmina Campbell (daughter of cattle rancher Louis Campbell). In 1878 she was owned by William Fortune, Tranquille BC. In 1901 she was owned by Joseph A. Russel, Vancouver BC. She was in service on the Thompson River, Shuswap Lake and Kamloops Lake (Savonna's Ferry, Eagle Pass and Spallumcheen). In 1886 she was damaged by fire in the burning of the Tranquille Mill but later repaired. She was laid up in 1888. In or sometime prior to 1897 she was reported as having been broken up at Tranquille BC.

Lady Lou 200801 (US) (work boat) She was built in 1904 at Terminal Island CA USA. 55.5' x 11.0' x 2.7' Wood. 14gt 11nt. Powered by a 18ihp gasoline engine.

Lady of the Lake (British Columbia Colonial Register) (passenger/ freight vessel) She was built in 1860 at Anderson Lake, British Columbia. 72.0' x 15.0' x 4.0' Wood. Powered by a 14hp (6" x 24") steam engine. In 1860 she was owned by Chapman, Co. She was in service on Anderson Lake.

Lady Washington[528] (US) She was built in 1849. Wood. Powered by a steam engine. She was shipped to the California delta on a sailing ship where she was reassembled. She was employed up the American River. She was snagged and sank on the return trip. She went out of service about 1868.

Lady Washington 019419 (US) (freighter) She was rebuilt in 1874 at Portland OR (presumably from the earlier Lady Washington). 140' x 25' x 3.5' Wood. 347gt. Powered by 6.6nhp (10" x 15") steam engine. She was the first light draft river steamer in the northwest. She had a non-traditional scow-like hull. In 1874 she was owned by UB Scott. She was employed on the Willamette River. In 1881 she was dismantled at Portland OR.

Lafleur 122298 (Canada) She was built at The Pas MB Canada. 63.6' x 14' x 3.4' Wood. 54gt 39rt. In 1922 she was rebuilt in Prince Albert SK Canada. Powered by a 2hp engine. In 1931–1936 she was owned by Barney Anderson and Sidney B Coffey, The Pas MB.

Lagunitas[529] 141853 (US) (ferry) She was built in 1903 at Oakland CA USA by W.A. Boole & Son. 250.0' x 36.5' x 10.7' Wood. 767gt. Powered by a 400ihp steam engine built by the Risdon Iron Works. She was employed carrying rail cars of the North Shore Railroad Co.

Lark 015224 (US) (sidewheeler) She was built at San Francisco CA USA. Wood. 140gt. Powered by a steam engine. She was reported to have been abandoned in 1878.

Lark 015223 (US) She was built in 1865 at Stockton CA. Wood. 25gt. Powered by a steam engine. Her home port was Sacramento CA. In 1869 she was reported to have been lost.

Lark[530] (US) (freighter) Wood. Powered by a steam engine. She was owned by the California Steam Navigation Company. In 1871 she was taken over by the California Pacific Railroad Co., San Francisco CA. In 1876 she was reported as having been broken up.

Lark 111951 (Canada) She was built in 1904 at New Westminster BC. 76' x 13' x 2.8' Wood. 58gt 37rt. Powered with a 7nhp steam engine. In 1904 she was owned by the Truro Condensed Milk Co. Ltd. In 1910 she was owned by Peter Burrill Ltd., Vancouver BC. In 1911 she was withdrawn from service.

Larkin 140037 (US) (sidewheeler) Her place and year of construction are not known. 72.5' x 13.3' x 2.7' Wood. 23.92gt. Powered by a 30ihp steam engine. She was home-ported at San Francisco CA. In 1870 she was owned by the California Steam Navigation Co. In 1871 she was owned by the California Pacific Railroad Co. In 1876 she was reported to have been broken up.

Latona[531] (US) She was built in 1859. Wood. Powered by a steam engine. She was a trussed-hull shallow draft vessel that was employed on the Sacramento River. She was touted in 1859[532] as being the largest river boat built in California to that date. In 1868 she was reported as having gone out of operation. In 1892 she was reported as having been broken up.

Latona[533] 140344 (US) (passenger/ freight vessel) She was built in 1878 at La Center WA USA by William Mulins. 90.0' x 18.4' x 3.8'. Wood. 128.91gt 73.59rt. Powered by two (11.25" x 36" high pressure) horizontal steam engines. In 1878 she was owned by Lewis & Lake River Transportation Co., Astoria, OR USA.

Laura (US) (freighter) She was built about 1849. Wood. Powered by a steam engine. She was employed on the Sacramento River CA.

Laura Ellen 015225 (US) (sidewheeler) (freighter) She was built in 1862 at Sacramento CA USA. 66.1' x 4.5' x 5.8'. Wood. 26.21gt. Powered by a 30nhp steam engine. In 1869 she was reported to have been lost.

Lavelle Young 141529 (US) (dredge, later a passenger/ freight vessel) She was built in 1898 at Portland OR USA by Joseph Paquette. 140.0' x 32.0' x 6.9' Wood. 506gt. 396nt. Powered by a steam engine. In 1898 she was owned by the Columbia River Pilot's Association. In 1898 she was employed as a dredge on the Columbia River. In 1900 she was owned by Captain Charles W Adams, Thomas Bruce and George Crummy. In 1903 she was owned by the Northern Navigation Co. In 1914 she was owned by the White Pass & Yukon Rail Road. In 1920 she was sold to Thomas A. McGowan and converted to a barge. She contributed to the founding of Fairbanks AK. She was reported as having been laid up at McGrath AK and then remnants moved to Pioneer Park at Fairbanks AK.

Lawrence[534] (US) She was built in 1849. Wood. 36.5gt. Powered by a steam engine. She was one of the first steamboats operating above Sacramento on the Sacramento River. In 1868 she was reported as having gone out of service.

Leader[535] 140718 (US) (passenger vessel) She was built in 1884 at Stockton CA. 144.0' x 32.0' x 6.5' Wood. 236gt 156nt. Powered by a 550ihp steam engine. She was employed in the rivers of the California delta. She showed up as the *Claremore Queen* in John Ford's Hollywood film starring Will Rogers in "Steamboat Round the Bend." She was dismantled in 1938.

Leah 141556 (US) (passenger/ freight vessel) She was built in 1898 at St. Michael AK USA. 138.7' x 31.0' x 6.3' Wood. 477.89gt 295nt. Powered by a steam engine. In 1898 she was owned by the Alaska Commercial Co. In 1901 she was owned by the Northern Navigation Co. On September 19, 1906, she foundered at Quail Island AK on the Yukon River.

Leelamaw (see *Atlantic*)

Lena[536] (US) She was built in 1884 at Sauvies Island OR USA. 59.0' x 10.9' x 2.5' Wood. Powered by a (5" x 6") steam engine. In 1895 she was owned by Thomas & Co. In 1895 she was reported to have been broken up.

Lena C. Gray 140032 (US) (passenger/ freight Vessel) She was built in 1874 at Seattle WA USA. 75' Wood. 155.34gt. Powered by steam engine.

Leon 141533 (US) (passenger/ freight vessel) She was built in 1898 at San Francisco CA USA by Thomas Patrick Henry Whitelaw. She was towed partially completed to Dutch Harbor by the *Linda* and the *Sintram*. She was assembled at Dutch Harbor AK for service in the Klondike Gold Rush. 181.0' x 30.5' x 6.7' Wood. 638gt. 402nt. Powered by a steam engine. In 1898 she was owned by the Alaska Exploration Co. (Liebes & Co., San Francisco CA). In 1899 she was owned by the Alaska Commercial Co. In 1901 she was owned by the Northern Navigation Co. In 1901 she was employed on the Koyukuk River. In 1914 she was owned by the White Pass & Yukon Rail Road. In 1943 she was reported as having been laid up at St. Michael AK.

Leona[537] (ex-*McMinnville* 092959) 141710 (US) (passenger/ freight vessel) She was built in 1901 Portland OR USA. 105.0' x 21.0' x 4.0' Wood. 145gt

136nt. Powered by two horizontal (high pressure 7.5" x 30") steam engines. In 1901 she was owned by the Oregon City Transportation Co. (O.C.T. Co.) (Yellow Stack Line). In 1912 she was destroyed by fire on the Lewis River.

Leota 141541 (US) (passenger/ freight vessel) She was built in 1898 at Alameda CA. 50.5' x 16.0' x 3.5' Wood. 36gt 24nt. She was powered by a steam engine. On May 25, 1920, this sternwheeler (with 36 persons on board) was stranded near Fairbanks AK. In 1920 she was reported as having been broken up at Fairbanks AK USA.

Lewis and Clark[538] (US) 40' Steel. Powered by two Cummins diesel engines. In 1990 she was owned by North Dakota interests. In 2006–2021 she was owned by Missouri Riverboat Inc., Bismarck ND USA. She was operated privately for several years, it is currently owned and operated by the Fort Abraham Lincoln Foundation. The Fort Abraham Lincoln Foundation supports heritage tourism.

Lewiston (later Ann) 001737 (US) (passenger/ freight vessel) She was built in 1867 at Umatilla, Yakima Co. Washington Territory USA by A. Clifford. 83.0' x 14.0' x 6.0' Wood. 83.22gt. Powered by two 4nhp horizontal steam engines. In 1867–1869 she was owned by Long Tom Transportation Co., OR USA. In 1869 she was owned by Willamette Steamboat Co., OR USA. In 1869 she was owned by Tualatin River Navigation & Manufacturing Co., OR USA. In April 1869 she foundered at Eulery's Bar on the Willamette River OR USA. In 1871 she reported as having been abandoned.

Lewiston[539] 141361 (US) (passenger/ freight vessel) She was built in 1894 at Riparia WA. 165.0' x 34.4' x 5.3' Wood. 513gt 487nt. Powered by two horizontal (high pressure 17" x 72") 19nhp steam engines. In 1894 she was owned by the Oregon Railroad & Navigation Co. She was employed on the Snake River. In 1905 she was rebuilt at Riparia WA.

Lewiston 202007 (US) (passenger/ freight vessel) She was built in 1905 at Riparia WA USA. 165.5' x 34.8' x 6.0' Wood. 548gt 518nt. Powered by two horizontal (high pressure 18" x 84") 21nhp steam engines. In 1905 she was owned by the Oregon Railroad & Navigation Co. In 1922 she was reported to have been destroyed by fire at Lewiston ID.

Lewiston (later *Barry K.*) 223498 (US) (passenger/ freight vessel later a tug). She was built in 1903 at Portland OR by Supple & Martin. 160.2' x 35.8' x 5.9'. Wood. 581gt 442nt. Powered by two horizontal high pressure (17" x 72") 21nhp steam engines. In 1903 she was owned by the Union Pacific Railroad. In 1923 she was owned by the Oregon-Washington Rail Road & Navigation Co. (Union Pacific Rail Road). In 1940–1942 she was owned by the Alaskan Railroad. In 1940–1942 she was in service on the Yukon River as the *Barry K.* employed on the Yukon River. During the winter of 1948 she was damaged by ice. In 1950 she was reported as having been broken up.

Liard River[540] 138625 (Canada) (tug) She was built in 1919 at Fort Smith NWT probably by Captain JW Mills (her first master). 82.0' x 16.8' x 3.0'. Wood. 113gt. Powered by a 3.25ihp steam engine fueled by cordwood. In 1919–1922 she was owned by the Hudson's Bay Co., London UK. George Duddy states: "She was designed and constructed with a bowstring truss hull support structure like that employed by Mills in constructing the Slave River in 1912." In 1919 she is said to have been employed on the Fort Liard/Fort Nelson run and on Great Slave Lake for the Fort Simpson fishery. She was hauled out at Fort Simpson. She was wrecked in 1922 about 35 miles below Fort Nelson. Some of her equipment (probably her boilers and steam engines) was salvaged by the second *Liard River* (a propeller vessel with a tunnel type hull).

Liberty 200083 (US) (passenger vessel) She was built in 1903 at Bandon OR USA. 90.7' x 20.8' x 4.6'. Wood. 174gt 120nt. Powered by a steam engine. In 1918 she was reported to have been abandoned.

Lightning 107156 (Canada) (freighter) She was built in 1898 at Vancouver BC by the B.C. Iron Works. 140' x 30' x 5.5'. Wood. 556.91gt 350.86nt Powered by a steam engine built by B.C. Iron Works, Vancouver BC. In 1898 she was owned by the Stacey Hiebert Yukon Syndicate, London UK. She was owned by the British America Corp. In 1900 she was owned by the Dawson & White Horse Navigation Co. In 1902 she was owned by Edward M Sullivan. In 1903 she was owned by the Coal Creek Coal Co. In 1904 she was owned by Donald W Davis. In 1904 she was owned by James A. Williams and Thomas W O'Brien (JO), Dawson YT. In 1907 she was owned by Andrew S Grant, Dawson YT. In 1907 she was owned by the Sour Dough

Coal Co. In 1909–1914 she was sold to the Northern Light Power & Coal Co., Dawson YT. In 1917 she was owned by the White Pass & Yukon Rail Road. In 1898 she was registered at Vancouver BC. In 1907 she was registered in Dawson YT. She was in Yukon River service to 1916. In 1918 she was reported as having been broken up at Dawson City YT.

Lillooet (Vancouver Island Colonial Register) (passenger vessel) She was built in 1863 at Victoria, Vancouver Island by James W Trahey. 130.0' x 28.0' x 5.0' Wood. Powered by a 115hp (17" x 60") steam engine. In 1863 she was owned by the Port Douglas Steam Navigation Co. (owned by Captain JR Fleming). She was launched on September 12, 1863. In 1863 she was in New Westminster to Yale service on the Fraser River. In 1874 she was reported as having been broken up at Victoria BC.

Lily 140478 (US) (tug) She was built in 1881 at Seattle WA USA. 92.5' x 16.4' x 3.7 Wood. 134.23gt 86.8. Powered by a 65ihp steam engine. In 1930 she was reported as having been abandoned

Lily[541] (Canada) She was built in 1877 by Yarrow & Co., Glasgow and assembled at Grand Rapids NWT Canada. 100' x 24' x ?. She was constructed with a wood and steel composite hull. 130.42rt. Powered by two 31.8ihp horizontal non-condensing engines built by Yarrow & Co. In 1877 she was employed on the Upper Saskatchewan River. She was rebuilt 1880–1881 at Prince Albert SK. In 1877–1883 she was owned by the Hudson's Bay Company. In 1883 she was owned by the Winnipeg & Western Transportation Co. In August 1879 she was damaged, repaired and laid up for the winter at Edmonton. On a voyage to transfer her to the South Saskatchewan she departed Prince Albert for Medicine Hat in July 1883. She left Medicine Hat August 29, 1883. She hit a rock and sank in shallow water at Drowning Ford (about 40 miles down river from Medicine Hat NWT). She was not salvaged.

Lilly C.[542] (US) (tug) (aka Lully C) She was built in 1898 or 1899 at Lake Bennett BC. Wood. Powered by a steam engine. She is reported by Murray Lundberg to have worked in Alaska/YT 1896–1900. She was employed on Lake Bennett and later in 1899 she was run through Miles Canyon. In May 1900, Captain Grant and crew arrived at Fort Selkirk to get her ready to use for towing between Dawson and Fort Selkirk. In 1900, she left Dawson to work as a lighter at Nome, towing barges with freight from larger ships to shore. Edward L Affleck lists her as the Lully C.

Linda[543] (US) (sidewheeler) (freighter) She was built in 1849 at Benicia CA. Wood. 52gt. Powered by a steam engine. She was one of the first steamboats operating above Sacramento on the Sacramento River. Lytle reported her abandoned in 1853 but McMullin reported that in 1868 she had gone out of service.

Linda 141561 (US) (passenger/ freight vessel) She was built in 1898 at San Francisco CA USA by Thomas Patrick Henry Whitelaw. She was assembled at Dutch Harbor AK for service in the Klondike Gold Rush. 181.0' x 36.5' x 6.7'. Wood. 602gt 386nt. Powered by a 700ihp steam engine. In 1898 she was owned by the Alaska Exploration Co. (Liebes & Co., San Francisco CA). In 1901 she was owned by the Northern Navigation Co. In 1914 she was owned by the White Pass & Yukon Rail Road. In 1917 she was reported as having been laid up at St. Michael AK.

Linderman 107519 (Canada) (freighter) She was built in 1898 at Lake Lindeman BC Canada by James H Calvert (Carroll Johnson & Co.) 40'. Wood. 53gt 43rt. Powered by a steam engine built by the Vulcan Iron Works, Seattle WA USA. In 1898 she was owned by John Irving. In 1899 she was owned by the Northern Lakes, Rivers Navigation Co. Ltd., Victoria BC. In 1899 she was wrecked near Whitehorse YT on the Yukon River.

Linnie 015621 (US) (passenger/ freight vessel later a barge) She was built in 1869 at Utsalady WT USA. 75'. Wood. 152.77gt. Powered by a 48ihp steam engine. She was later converted to a non-powered barge.

Lionel R. Webster 201330 (US) (sidewheeler) (ferry) She was built in 1904 at Portland OR USA. 139.0' x 32.7' x 8.3'. Wood. 343gt 26int. Powered by a 200ihp steam engine. She was reported to have been laid up after 1915.

Little Annie[544] 140220 (US) (passenger vessel) She was built in 1877 at Coquille River OR USA by William E Rackliffe. 69.5' x 16.4' x 4.2'. Wood. 85.56gt 72.73nt. Powered by a 40ihp steam engine. She was employed in the Columbia River watershed. In 1890 she was reported to have been wrecked.

Little Delta 208038 (US) (passenger/ freight vessel) She was built in 1905 at Fairbanks AK USA. 66.7' x 16.7' x 3.2'. Wood. 71gt 44nt. Powered by a steam engine. In 1905 she was owned by Cy B Atwell. She was employed on the Iditarod River. She was reported as having been laid up at Iditerod AK USA

Little Jim[545,546] (US) She was built in 1898 at Carcross YT Canada. 35' x 10' x ? Wood. Powered by a steam engine. She was owned by the Iowa Alaska Mining (IAM) Co. at Koyukuk River, Alaska during the winter of 1898–1899. Murray Lundberg states "A group of 38 men and 1 woman from Iowa had freighted 70 tons of supplies and equipment over the White Pass in March, using 15 horses; 1 man and several horses died in the work. They set up a sawmill and built the 65-foot Iowa and the smaller Little Jim. The Iowa was launched June 9th, while the Little Jim seems to have left earlier (from the prospectus for the Clear Creek Mining Company 1898). About July 30th, the Iowa caught up to the Little Jim in the upper reaches of the Koyukuk River, where the current had become too strong for the smaller boat. The group continued in the Iowa and staked claims on a creek they named Clear Creek. A new company, the Clear Creek Mining Company, was then formed, and the boats both continued to St. Michael. In late August 1898, the Little Jim was sold but the group was unable to find a buyer for the Iowa, and she was abandoned."

Little Klondike Queen[547] (later *The Neo-Watin*) 193259 (Canada) (passenger vessel) She was built in 1964 at Edmonton AB Canada by Canada Iron Foundries Ltd. 14.48m x 3.96m x 1.01m Steel. 22.65gt 18.65rt. Powered by an 80bhp diesel engine. In 1967–1979 she was owned by Leslie R Solymos, Waskesiu SK. In 2001 she was owned by Leslie R Solymos, Waskesiu Lake SK. In 2004–2015 she was owned by Neo-Watin Marine Services Ltd., Waskesiu Lake SK. In 2017–2021 she was owned by Neo-Watin Marine Services Ltd., Prince Albert SK. She originally was employed between Laurier Park and Big Island on the North Saskatchewan River. She is located (in 2021) on Waskesiu Lake SK, in Prince Albert National Park.

She once offered public excursion tours there but is now considered as a derelict vessel.

Little Maud (later *Weston*) 140734 (US) She was built in 1882 at Sioux City Iowa USA. 110.0' x 30.0' x 4.5' Wood. 89gt/nt. Powered by a steam engine. On September 7, 1909, she foundered at Bismarck North Dakota USA.

Little Sitka[548] (later *Rainbow*) (Imperial Russian Register) (US) (sidewheeler) 37' William Leidesdorff purchased her from the Russian American Co. She was re-assembled on Yerba Buena Island. In 1847 she was the first steamboat to sail on the Sacramento River CA to Sutter's Fort. Its engines removed she was converted to a sailing vessel and renamed as the *Rainbow*. She sank in San Francisco Bay before the end of 1848.

Little Snug[549] 208263 (US) (sidewheeler) (passenger/ freight vessel) She was built in 1910 at Fairbanks AK USA. 59.2' x 13.4' x 3.7' Wood. 50gt 31nt. Powered by a 20ihp steam engine. In 1910–1911 she was owned by Amos J Tucker. She is reported by Murray Lundberg to have worked in Alaska/YT 1910.

Lively 205364 (US) (tug) She was built in 1907 at Vallejo CA USA. 57.3' x 12.0' x 4.3' Wood. 18gt 8rt. Powered by 100ihp gasoline engine.

Lizzie 015227 (US) (sidewheeler) She was built in 1867 at San Francisco CA USA. 90.0' 17.5' x 4.6' Wood. 124.62gt 90.86rt. Powered by a 50nhp steam engine.

Lizzie B.[550] (US) Wood. Powered by a steam engine. She is reported by Murray Lundberg to have worked in Alaska/YT in 1898.

Lizzie Linn[551] 140676 (US) (sidewheeler) (ferry) She was built in 1883 at Wallula WA USA. 54.5' x 15.5' x 5.5' Wood. 23.17gt/nt. Powered by a steam engine. In 1887 she was rebuilt. In March 1892 she was destroyed by fire at Arlington OR. This was apparently an arson intended to eliminate her as opposition to the vessel *Alkali*.

Lizzie Warden[552] (US) (ferry) Wood. Powered by a steam engine. She was a ferry operating at Yankton ND to Green Island NE on the Missouri River.

Logger 224389 (US) (tug) She was built in 1924 at St. Helens OR USA. 155.7' x 35.0' x 6.6'. Wood. 447gt 322nt. Powered by a 750ihp steam engine. Her engines came from the *Olympian*. In 1929 she was owned by Smith Transportation Co., Rainier, OR USA. She was employed towing log rafts. In 1930 she was owned by the Shaver Transportation Co. In 1938 she was reported as having sunk at her berth and she was abandoned.

Lola Lee Collins[553] (US) She was built in 1898 at Seattle WA USA. Wood. Powered by a steam engine. In 1899 she was owned by Dave Cohn and SM Hirsch. She was reported to have operated on the lower Yukon River AK in 1898–1904.

Loma 206763 (US) (freighter) She was built in 1909 at Everett WA USA. 67.7' x 19.6' x 4.3'. Wood. 45gt 28nt. Powered by a 30ihp steam engine.

Lorelei (see *Shamrock*)

Lorelei 141427 (US) (tug) She was built in 1895 at Lewiston ID USA. 50.5' x 11.0' x 3.5'. Wood. 9gt 7nt. Powered by a gasoline engine. In 1898 she was reported to have been broken up.

Lorenda[554] 141568 (US) (passenger/ freight vessel) She was built in 1898 at St. Michael AK USA. 50.0' x 17.0' x 5'. Wood. 49gt. Powered by a steam engine.

Los Angeles[555] 141569 (US) (passenger/ freight vessel) She was built in 1898 at St. Michael AK USA. 48.0' x 16.0' x 4.0'. Wood. 29gt. Powered by a steam engine.

Los Angeles 015843 (US) (freighter) She was built in 1869 at Wilmington CA USA. 99.0' x 18.4' x 5.3'. Wood. 102.02gt 63.75nt. Powered by a 100hp steam engine.

Lot Whitcomb[556] (later *Annie Abernethy*) (US) (sidewheeler) (passenger vessel, later tug) She was built in 1850 at Milwaukie OT USA. 160' x 24' x 5.6'. Wood 600gt. Powered by a 140hp steam engine built in New Orleans LA. In 1850 she was owned by SS White, Berryman Jennings, and Lot Whitcomb. In 1850 she was employed on the Willamette and Columbia

Rivers. In 1854 she was owned by the California Steam Navigation Co. and moved to San Francisco CA. In 1854 she was employed on the Marysville – San Francisco route. In 1857 she was on the San Francisco – Petaluma run. She was renamed as the *Annie Abernethy*.

Lotta Talbot 141551 (US) (passenger/ freight vessel) She was built in 1898 at Seattle WA USA. 145.7' x 24.8' x 4.2' Wood. In 1898 she was owned by the Pacific Cold Storage Co. She was owned by the Alaska Meat Co. She was owned by Waechter Bros. On May 22, 1906, she was reported to have been destroyed by ice at Fairbanks AK USA.

Louise[557] 015222 (US) (sidewheeler) She was built in 1864 at San Francisco CA USA. Wood. 369gt. Powered by a steam engine. In 1879 she was reported to have been abandoned.

Louise 140620 (US) (passenger/ freight vessel) She was built in 1883 at Seabeck WA USA. 91.6' x 22' x 4.2' Wood. 167.65gt. 129.77rt. Powered by a 66ihp steam engine. In 1883–1884 she was owned by Port Townsend WA USA interests. In 1898–1899 she was owned by the Klondike Mining Trading & Transportation Co. She was in Yukon River service. On July 12, 1899, she was destroyed by fire while at her mooring in Victoria Harbour BC. The fire started in the engine room of the *Nahleen*, but the city's fire department having no equipment to fight such a fire could only stand and watch the vessels burn.

Louise[558] 141572 (US) (passenger/ freight vessel) She was built in 1898 at Unalaska AK USA by Howard Shipyards & Dock Co. 165.0' x 36.5' x 5.0' Wood. 717gt 384nt. Powered by an 800ihp steam engine. In 1898 she was owned by the Alaska Commercial Co. In 1907 she was owned by the British Yukon Navigation Co. In 1920 she was reported as having been laid up at St. Michael AK.

Loyal Ellsworth[559] (US) (passenger vessel) She was built in 1864. Wood. Powered by a steam engine. In 1864 she was owned by the Farmers Packet Line.

Lucia Mason 140603 (US) (passenger vessel, later a tug) She was built in 1882 at St. Helens OR USA by JH Peterson. 108.5' x 20.0' x 4.2' Wood.

177.73gt. 140.1nt. Powered by two 8.3nhp horizontal (high pressure 11" x 48") steam engine. In 1882 she was owned by the Farmers Transportation Co. In 1891 she was wrecked on the Lewis River.

Luckiamute Chief[560] (US) She was built in 1878 at Salem OR USA. 60.0' x 14.6' x 3.6' Wood. 69gt. Powered by a (7" x 10") steam engine. In 1878 she was owned by A. Prescott, Salem OR. In 1879 she was reported as having been broken up at Salem OR.

Luella[561] 141540 (US) (freighter) She was built in 1898 at Stockton CA USA. 90.0' x 17.0' x 3.0' Wood. 115gt 88nt. Powered by a steam engine. In 1890 she was owned by the Alaska Commercial Co. On October 20, 1920, this sternwheeler (with 21 persons on board) foundered at Little Salmon, on the Yukon River YT.

Ludine[562] (later *Rose*) (US) She was built in 1983 at Astoria OR by John Hendrickson. 65' Steel. Powered by a diesel engine. In 1985 she was owned by Oregon Steam Navigation Company, Portland OR. She was moved to Portland and renamed as the *Rose*. She has been employed mostly on the Willamette River. In 2004 she was owned by Willamette Sternwheel Navigation, Portland OR. In 2010 she was moved to Oregon City.

Lulu Stewart[563] (US) (passenger/ freight vessel) She was built in 1898 at Puget Sound WA USA. 130' x 25' x ? Wood. Powered by a steam engine. In 1898 she was owned by the Klondike-Chicago Transportation & Trading Co. She is reported by Murray Lundberg to have worked in Alaska/YT.

Lurline[564] 140341 (US) (passenger vessel) She was built in 1878 at Willamette OR USA by Jacob Kamm. 157.7' x 30.7' x 6.6' Wood. 481.42gt 338.38nt. Powered by a steam engine. In 1878 she was owned by Vancouver Transportation Co. (Jacob Kamm), Willamette OR. She was employed in opposition to Oregon Railroad & Navigation Co. vessels on the Portland to Astoria route. In 1889–1892 she was chartered to Oregon Railroad & Navigation Co. employed on Portland to Cascades route. In 1892–1906 Jacob Kamm again employed her managed by the Harkins Transportation Co. on the Portland to Astoria route. She was involved in a collision at Rainier OR, sank, was raised, repaired, and put back in service. She was rebuilt in 1917 as the *Lurline* (215058).

Lurline[565] 215058 (US) (passenger vessel) Wood. Powered by a 700ihp steam engine. She was built in 1917 at Portland OR by Charles M Nelson. 152.0' x 30.7' x 6.1' Wood. 406gt 318nt. Powered by two horizontal (high pressure 18" x 72") 19nhp steam engines. In 1917 she was owned by Harkins Transportation Co. In 1929–1931 she was owned by the Harkins Transportation Co., Portland OR. In 1931 she was reported to have been dismantled at Portland OR. Her house works went to the L.P. Hosford.

Columbia and Lytton laid up at Revelstoke BC (Image from Maritime Museum of British Columbia 000438)

Lytton 094905 (Canada) (passenger/ freight vessel) She was built in 1890 at Revelstoke BC Canada by Alexander Watson. 131.0' x 25.5' x 4.8' Wood. 452gt 285rt. Powered by two 10nhp steam engines from the *Gertrude*. In 1890–1896 she was owned by the Columbia & Kootenay Steam Navigation Company, Nelson BC. In 1890 she was in service between Revelstoke and Little Dalles WA. In 1897–1904 she was owned by the Canadian Pacific Railway, Montreal QC. In 1903 she was beached at Robson BC. In 1904 she as dismantled at Nakusp BC. An entry in the British Columbia Provincial Archives database states "created in 1890 in response to the increasing traffic on the Columbia and Kootenay waterways, the Columbia & Kootenay Steam Navigation Company was well-situated to take advantage of the mining boom in the region. The company was founded by the partners JF Hume, W Cowan, and Captain R Sanderson who had built the SS *Despatch* for use on the Columbia River and Arrow Lakes run, and joined by Captain J Irving, JA Mara, and FS Barnard. The first ship built by the Columbia & Kootenay Steam Navigation was the *Lytton* for the run on the Columbia River from Revelstoke, BC to Northport, Washington. The company soon expanded to the Kootenay Lake and River south to Bonners Ferry, Idaho, with the construction of the SS *Nelson* in 1891. The SS *Spokane* was purchased in 1893, lengthened and put to work on Kootenay Lake. The Columbia & Kootenay Steam Navigation Co. continued to enlarge its fleet; the SS *Kootenai* and SS *Nakusp* were used on the Columbia River-Arrow Lakes, and the SS *Kokanee* for Kootenay Lake. In February of 1897, the Canadian Pacific Railway Company purchased the Columbia & Kootenay Steam Navigation for $200,000, thus eliminating a strong rival and positioning themselves to take over the growing shipping trade in southeastern British Columbia."

M.F. Henderson[566] 093168 (US) (passenger vessel) She was built in 1901 at Portland OR USA. 158.7' x 31.0' x 7.5'. Wood. 534gt 315nt. Powered by two 21nhp horizontal (high pressure 18" x 84") steam engines. In 1901 she was owned by the Shaver Transportation Co. In 1911 she was reported to have been wrecked at Bugby OR. Her engines were later installed in the *Henderson* (210030).

M.L. Washburn 209341 (US) (passenger/ freight vessel) She was built in 1911 at St. Michael AK. 120.3' x 26.0' x 4.1'. Wood. 284gt 179nt. Powered by a 170ihp steam engine (from the *Koyukuk*). In 1911 she was owned by the Northern Navigation Co. In 1914 she was owned by the White Pass & Yukon Rail Road. On October 20, 1920, she struck a rock, foundered, and sank near the Little Salmon River YT.

M.S. Latham[567] 17931 (US) (sidewheeler) She was built in 1860 at San Francisco CA. Wood. 166gt. Powered by a steam engine. In 1887 she was reported to have been abandoned,

Mable 092839 (US) (aka *Mabel*) (passenger/ freight vessel) She was built in 1898 at Huntingdon OR USA. 70.4' x 13.7' x 3.9'. Wood. 59gt 49rt.

Powered by two horizontal (high pressure 6" x 24") 2.4nhp steam engines. (Sometimes referred to as the *Mabel*. In 1898 she was owned by Seven Devils Transportation Co. In 1899 she was reported to have been dismantled at Huntingdon OR.

M.L. Washburn after her wreck near the Little Salmon River YT
(Image from Maritime Museum of British Columbia 000394)

Mabel C. 092984 (US) (freighter) She was built in 1898 at St. Michael AK USA. 54.0' x 12.7' x 5.9' composite hull 74gt 37nt. Powered by a steam engine.

Mackenzie River[568] 130279 (Canada) (passenger vessel, later a barge and an accommodation vessel) She was built in 1908 at Fort Smith AB Canada by JW Mills (for the Hudson's Bay Co.) 126.0' x 26.0' x 5.0' She had a composite hull constructed as a wooden hull with a steel frame). 412.92gt. Powered by a 9.5ihp steam engine. She was initially a cord-wood burner but was converted to burn crude oil from Norman Wells. In 1939 she was the first sternwheeler to ever transit through the Mackenzie Delta bringing vital supplies to Tuktoyaktuk on the Arctic coast. She was rebuilt to 125' 115 ton as a cargo barge that could carry 40 passengers. She was owned by the Hudson's Bay Co., London UK. About 1947 she was damaged by ice and repaired and became a houseboat for commercial fishermen at Yellowknife NWT. In 1951–1965 she was a barge owned by McInnes Products Corporation Ltd., Edmonton AB. In 1965 she was owned by

George McInnes, Edmonton AB. In 1967 she was owned by Maud McInnes (widow), Edmonton AB. She carried 100 tons of cargo. She was in service between Fort Smith and the Mackenzie Delta in 1908–1923. She pushed barges ahead—and had to shuttle them one at a time through open water or fast currents. She was mothballed by the HBC in 1923 but re-entered service during 1929/1930. The Second World War was the last significant use of paddlewheelers on this river. She was involved during the Canol Oil Project along the Mackenzie River transporting supplies for United States Army to Norman Wells. In 1976 she was reported as having been broken up.

Mackenzie River (Image from the Provincial Archives of Alberta)

Madeline[569] 072431 (US) (passenger vessel) (formerly the *Joseph Kellogg* 076267 [US]) She was built in 1900 at Portland OR USA. 139.0' x 26.5' x 7.2' Wood. 408gt 336nt. In 1921 she was owned by the Harkins Transportation Co. and renamed as Madeline. She was reported as having been abandoned in 1929.

Maggie (Canada) (sidewheeler) (tug, later a barge) She was built in 1873 at Burrard Inlet BC. 71.5' x 16.0' x 4.5' Wood. 71gt 49rt. Powered by a 20nhp steam engine. She was converted to a barge at Winnipeg MB 1878. In 1873 she was owned by Jeremiah Rogers. She was owned by James Bell. She was owned by FT Rollin.

Maggie Lauder (later Union) (British Columbia Colonial Register) (passenger/ freight vessel) She was built in 1861 at Victoria, British Columbia (Crown Colony) by James W Trahey. 66.0' x 17.5' x 3' Wood. Powered by a steam engine. In 1861 she was owned by the Yale Steam Navigation Co., Victoria BC. The company went into liquidation. She was re-launched as the Union owned by Gustavus Wright and Uriah Nelson & Co. She was launched on May 7, 1861. She could carry 4 passengers and 20 tons of freight. In 1864–1865 she worked on the Skeena River and was chartered by the Collins Overland Telegraph.

Major Tompkins (US) (sidewheeler) (passenger/ freight vessel) She was built in 1847 at Philadelphia PA USA. Powered with a steam engine. She was in service on California rivers. She was operating on the Olympia to Victoria run. On February 10, 1855, she was wrecked on Macauley Point at the entrance to Victoria Harbour. The crew jumped ashore as the ship broke up in the surf. The wreck was sold at auction to Robert Laing and then to the Muirs at Sooke for use in constructing a steam sawmill. The bell of the ship hung at the old Craigflower Schoolhouse in Craigflower BC.

Manaskua[570] (US) (freighter) Wood. Powered by a steam engine. In 1915 she was employed in Alaskan waters. A newspaper article reported that while attempting to deliver cargo that she was forced away by ice in Cook Inlet AK in November 1915. She does not appear to have been registered.

Manitoba[571,572] (Canada) (passenger/ freight vessel) She was built in 1874 at Moorehead MB designed and built by James Douglas. 165' x 31' x 4'. Wood. 194.6rt. Powered by two horizontal non-condensing steam engines built by North Star Iron Works, Minneapolis MN. In 1874–1876 she was owned by the Merchants International Steamboat Line, Winnipeg MB. In 1876–1879 she was owned by the Red River Transportation Company, Winnipeg MB. On June 4, 1876, she was rammed and sunk by the rival vessel, the *International*, near Winnipeg. She was salvaged and put back into operation. In 1879–1885 she was owned by the Winnipeg & Western Transportation Co., Winnipeg MB. In 1880 she was employed on the Assiniboine River. In 1882 she was moved to Saskatchewan. In 1883 she sailed to Cumberland House, Edmonton, Prince Albert, Battleford, and Fort Pitt. In 1884–1885 she was laid up at the mouth of the Sturgeon (Shell) River. In 1885 she was intended for use as a troop transport for the army forces in the Riel Rebellion, but when river ice broke up at Sturgeon River NWT (nr Winnipeg) she filled with water and was a total wreck. Her boiler was salvaged for use in a succession of sawmills. The engine was reported to have been scrapped in the 1940s.

Manook[573] (US) (freighter) Steel. Powered by a steam engine. In 1899 she was owned by the Empire Transportation Co. She is reported by Murray Lundberg to have worked in Alaska/YT in 1899.

Mansion Belle (see *Putah*)

Manzanilla 091373 (US) (aka *Manzanillo*) (freighter) She was built in 1881 at Portland OR USA by Charles Bureau. 110.0' x 22.0' x 4.0' Wood. 217.23gt 129.87nt. Powered by two horizontal (high pressure 12" x 60") 9.6nhp steam engines. In 1881 she was owned by Charles Bureau, Portland OR. In 1884–1886 she was owned by the Shaver Transportation Co. In 1893 she was reported to have been broken up at Portland OR.

Marathon[574] (Canada) Wood. Powered by a steam engine. She is reported by Murray Lundberg to have worked in Alaska/YT in 1909. MacBride reported that she passed Tanana in 1909 while en route to Iditarod.

Marcella (see *Marzelle*)

Mare Island[575] 090428 (US) (sidewheeler) (ferry) She was built in 1870 at San Francisco CA USA. 124.0' x 28.2' x 7.6' Wood. 337.51gt 295.96nt. Powered by a 125nhp steam engine. She was employed as a ferry between San Francisco and Vallejo. She steamed to Alaska under her own power in 1897. Her sidewheels were not powerful enough or suitable for shallow river waters. In 1897 she was employed on the Yukon River in Alaska.

Margaret[576] 092890 (US) (passenger vessel) She was built in 1897 at St. Michael AK USA. 140.0' x 33.0' x 7.0' Wood. 520gt 200nt. Powered by a 250ihp steam engine (from the *Arctic*). In 1897 she was owned by the Alaska Commercial Co. She was employed on the St. Michael – Dawson City route. In 1905 she was employed on the Tanana River. She was reported to have been abandoned on the beach at St. Michael AK.

Margey 091779 (US) (passenger vessel) She was built in 1885 at East Portland OR USA. 104.0' x 30.2' x 5'. Wood. 118gt 98rt. Powered by two horizontal (high pressure 8" x 48") 4.3nhp steam engines. In 1885 she was owned by Callahan & O'Neil. In 1885 she was employed on the Columbia River system. In 1890 she was employed on the Puget Sound WA.

Maria[577,578] (US) (Canada) (sidewheeler) She was built about 1857 at San Francisco CA USA. 127' x 24' x 3.6'. Wood. 69gt. Powered by two horizontal (high pressure 12.5" x 48") steam engines. In 1858 she was owned by Captain Will Lubbock. She was a trussed-hull shallow draft vessel that operated on the Sacramento River. In 1859 she was owned by the Victoria Steam Navigation Co. In 1861 she was in service between Harrison Mills to Port Douglas. In 1862 she was owned by the Independent Line for lower Columbia River service Portland to Cascades. In 1864 she was reported to have retired and having been broken up at Portland OR.

Maria 091960 (US) (tug) She was built in 1887 at Portland OR USA. 115.0' x 24.0' x 5.9'. Wood. 202gt 184nt. Powered by two horizontal (15" x 50") 15nhp steam engines. In 1887 she was owned by FB Jones. In 1923 she was reported to have been abandoned.

Maria Wilkins 090423 (US) (passenger/ freight vessel) She was built in 1872 at Portland OR. 76.5' x 17.5' x 4.8'. Wood. 97gt. Powered by two horizontal (high pressure 8" x 48") steam engines. In 1872 she was owned by FM Warren. In 1882 she was reported to have been broken up at Portland OR.

Marion (US) She was built about 1849. Wood. Powered by a steam engine. In 1850–1854 she operated on the San Joaquin River CA. In 1854 she was employed on the Sacramento River CA.

Marion 094801 (Canada) (passenger/ freight vessel) She was built in 1888 at Golden BC Canada by Alexander Watson. 61.0' x 10.0' x 3.0'. Wood. 14.78gt 9.33rt. Powered by two 2.1hp horizontal (high pressure 5.5" x 8") 2.1nhp steam engines built by Polson Iron Works Ltd., Toronto ON. In 1888 she was owned by FP Armstrong, Golden BC. She was employed between Revelstoke and Sproat's Landing in opposition to the *Despatch*. In 1890 she was sold to Captain Robert Sanderson. She was employed in low water service to Arrowhead, Beaton, Robson. In 1896–1898 she was owned by JB Armstrong, Golden BC. She was moved to Kootenay Lake, Duncan River and Kootenay Flats. In 1901 she was owned by FP Armstrong, Golden BC. She was in Upper Columbia River service. She was transferred in 1889. She was transferred in 1897 to Kootenay Lake service. In 1901 she was laid up and her engines removed and used for boring wooden pipes at St. Leon in 1907. In 1910 her hull sank at Kaslo BC during a gale.

Mariposa (US) (sidewheeler) (freighter) She was built in 1850 at San Francisco CA. Wood. 60gt. Powered by a steam engine. In 1850 she was employed on the San Joaquin River CA. On November 1, 1851, she collided with the *West Point*. She was towed to shallow water, sank, and was later refloated. She was reported to have gone out of service in 1868 but Lytle reports that she was abandoned in 1852.

Marjorie[579] (US) Wood., Powered by a steam engine. She is reported by Murray Lundberg to have worked in Alaska/YT 1899–1904.

Mark Twain Riverboat[580] (US) She was built in 1955 at Long beach CA at Todd Shipyard. (She is not a true vessel but one with a sternwheel operated on a marine monorail in Frontier Land at Disneyland, at Anaheim CA). She was designed by Long Beach CA naval architect DM Callis. She is a 5/8th scale replica of an original vessel. She has been in service since her maiden voyage in 1955.

Marquette[581] (Canada) (freighter) She was built in 1879 at Moorhead NWT Canada, designed by John S Irish. 130' x 28' x 1.5' Wood. 266.47rt. Powered by two 29.4hp horizontal non-condensing steam engines built by Coming & Dupree of St. Paul, Minneapolis MN. In 1878–1880 she was owned by the Peter McArthur, Winnipeg MB. In 1879 she was employed on the Assiniboine River to Fort Ellice and Fort Pelly. In 1880–1881 she was owned by Peter McArthur, Winnipeg MB, and Walter J Pratt (JO), Winnipeg MB. In 1881 she was owned by Peter McArthur, Winnipeg MB, and WH Lyon (Winnipeg & Western Transportation Co) (JO), Winnipeg MB. In 1881–1882 she was owned by Peter McArthur, Winnipeg

MB. In 1882 she was owned by the North West Navigation Co. Ltd., Winnipeg MB. In 1883 she was moved to Lake Winnipeg and Red River for fishing operations at Selkirk MB. In August 1894 she sank in the Red River.

Marquis[582] 088488 (Canada) (passenger/ freight vessel) She was built in 1882 at Grand Rapids NWT Canada by a Mr. Gregory. 201.0' x 33.5' x 5.3' Wood. 753.76gt 474.87rt. Powered by two horizontal high pressure steam engines by Iowa Iron Works, Dubuque, IA. In 1882 she was owned by the Winnipeg and Western Transportation Co., Winnipeg MB. In 1882 she was towed by the *Princess* to Grand Rapids. In 1882 she sailed across Lake Winnipeg after her machinery was installed and was employed from Grand Rapids to Prince Albert. In 1885 she was chartered to the Canadian Government, employed as General Middleton's flagship and troop transport in the Riel Rebellion. In 1886 she carried freight and lumber to Battleford. She struck a rock at the foot of Thorburn's Rapids. Two salvage attempts failed, and she was reported as having been abandoned. In 1887–1901 she was owned by the Winnipeg and Western Transportation Co. Ltd., Winnipeg MB. In 1888–1890 she was beached at Cumberland House and later taken to Prince Albert but was again beached and abandoned. Her salon was used variously as a dance hall, some wood salvaged from her was used for house construction, some fretwork was used in Saskatchewan. Her anchor went to The Pas Museum, her bell, and part of the flue is preserved in the Prince Albert City Museum. She was destroyed by fire c1909.

Marquis of Dufferin 107444 (Canada) (passenger/ freight vessel) She was built in 1898 at Vancouver BC Canada. Wood. 629gt. Powered by a steam engine. In 1898 she was owned by the British America Corp. On July 1st, 1898, this sternwheeler was being towed to her destination on the Yukon River from Vancouver by the passenger steamer *Progreso* (Captain Gilboy). The tow was difficult, and heavy seas caused the towline to repeatedly tighten and then go slack putting a great strain on it. In the evening distress rockets were launched by the *Marquis of Dufferin* which had started to break up. A lifeboat was sent from the *Progreso* to rescue the ten-man crew of the *Marquis of Dufferin* which was then abandoned. Several days later she was sighted twelve miles northeast of Cape Beale by the steamer *Tartar*. She had rolled over and was standing on end with her bow submerged. Her final wreck site is not known.

Marten (British Columbia Colonial Register) (passenger/ freight vessel) In 1866 she was built at Savona (Shuswap Lake) British Columbia (Crown Colony) by AG Pemberton & James McIntosh. 125.0' x 25.0' x 5' Wood. 375gt 282.51rt. Powered by a 40.25hp steam engine. In 1866 she was owned by the Hudson's Bay Company, London UK. In 1874 she was owned by Mara & Wilson, Kamloops BC. In 1866 she was built on the Whitfield Chase farm at Kamloops Lake from locally whipsawn lumber. She was the first on the Thompson system for the Big Bend Gold Rush. She had a black hull, white superstructure, and gold lettering. She was launched in May and towed to Savona for the fitting of the engines. She was employed between Savona's Ferry and Seymour Arm on Shuswap Lake. In 1877 she was wrecked on a rock at Kamloops Lake BC. Her engines went to the *Peerless* (1881). Her hull was abandoned on the beach.

Martha Clow 092859 (US) (passenger/ freight vessel) She was built in 1898 at Stockton CA USA. 65.0' x 17.0' x 3.0' Wood. 52gt 46nt. Powered by a steam engine. In 1908 the boiler from the *Minneapolis* was installed. In 1910 a new engine was installed. In 1908 she was lengthened to 81'. She is reported by Murray Lundberg to have worked in Alaska/YT 1898–1910.

Martha Jane[583] (US) (freighter) She was built about 1850. Wood. Powered by a steam engine. She was in service on California rivers. She was reported as having gone out of operation in 1868.

Martin White[584] (US) (sidewheeler) (freighter) She was built in 1854 at Philadelphia PA. Wood. 189gt. Powered by a steam engine. She was in service on California rivers. In 1862 she was sold to Far Eastern interests but continued to fly the US flag under Consular documents. She was reported to have gone out of operation in 1877.

Mary[585] (US) (sidewheeler) She was built in 1854 at Cascades WT. 80.0' x 16.0' x 5' Wood. Powered by a (14" x 30") 13nhp steam engine. In 1854 she was owned by Bradford & Co. She was employed between the Cascades and Lewiston ID. In 1858 she was reported as having been dismantled at The Dalles OT.

Mary Ann 017438 (US) (freighter) She was built in 1852 at Philadelphia PA USA. 88.3' x 19.8' x 9.8' Wood. 88.82gt. Powered by a 40nhp steam engine.

Mary B. Williams[586] (later *Victory*) 091017 (US) (freighter) She was built in 1877 at Stockton CA USA by Bissett & Delaney. 98.6' x 23.5' x 4.1' Wood. 137.98gt 118nt. Powered by a 110ihp steam engine. She was employed on California rivers. She was reported as having gone out of operation in 1917.

Mary Bell[587] 090141 (US) (sidewheeler) (passenger vessel, later a float) She was built in 1865 at Cascades WT by Leslie Farnworth. 102.5' x 18.0' x 5.0' Wood. 138.25gt. Powered by a 13nhp (14" x 30") steam engine. In 1865 she was owned by Robert C Smith. She was employed on the Cowlitz and lower Columbia Rivers. In 1873 she was converted to a float.

Mary Ellen[588] (US) (freighter) She was built about 1862. Wood. Powered by a steam engine. She was in service on California rivers. She was reported as having gone out of service in 1868.

Mary Ellen Galvin[589] (US) She was built in 1898 in Seattle WA USA. Wood. Powered by a steam engine. She was designed and owned by Pat Galvin. The vessel was considered by her owner to have been a failure. She is reported by Murray Lundberg to have worked in Alaska/YT in 1898.

Mary Emma[590] 017439 (US) She was built in 1866 at Stockton CA. Wood. 47gt. Powered by a steam engine. In 1875 she was reported to have been abandoned.

Mary F. Graff 107838 (Canada) 092856 (US) 177.6' x 35.7' x 6.0' Wood. 864gt 544rt. two 20" steam engines. She was built in 1898 in Seattle WA USA by the Moran Bros. Shipyard. In 1898 she was owned by the Seattle-Yukon Transportation Co., Seattle WA USA. In 1898 she was owned by the Alaska Exploration Co. (the Liebes & Co., San Francisco CA) for Yukon River service. In 1900 she was owned by the Canadian Development Co. In 1900 she was transferred to Canadian Registry. In 1901 she was owned by The British Yukon Navigation Co. Ltd., Victoria BC. In 1901–1931 she was owned by the White Pass & Yukon Rail Road. In 1928 she was reported as having been abandoned in Dawson City YT. In 1931 she was still listed in the Canada Register of Shipping.

Mary Garratt[591] 091085 (US) She was built in 1878 at Stockton CA USA by Marcucci. 172.0' x 45.0' x 8.2' Wood. 810.28gt 728.14nt. Powered by a

605ihp steam engine. She was employed on California rivers. In 1915 she was reported as having gone out of service.

Mary H. (later *Hazel & Helen* 206178) (US) (sidewheeler) (freighter) She was built in 1909 at Astoria OR. 35'. Wood. 10gt 6nt. Powered with a steam engine. She was later repowered with a gasoline engine. In 1911 she was renamed as *Hazel & Helen*. (She may have been converted to a propeller about 1911.)

Mary Moody[592] (US) She was built in 1866 at Idelwilde Bay ID. 108' x 20' x 4.9'. Wood. Powered by two horizontal (high pressure 11" x 60") steam engines from the *Express*. (Fritz Timmen claimed the engines came from the *Colonel Wright*). In 1866 she was operating from Haines Landing on Lake Pend Oreille ID USA where she was used for carrying passengers and pack mules to the gold mines of Montana as part of a combined land and water route controlled by the Oregon Steam Navigation Company and its subsidiary the Oregon and Montana Transportation Company. She was laid up at Lake Pend Oreille and in 1876 she was reported to have been broken up.

Mary Woodruff[593] 17065 (US) (sidewheeler) She was built in 1863 at Port Madison WT. She was reported to have been abandoned about 1875.

Marysville[594] (US) (freighter) She was built in 1851 at San Francisco CA USA. Wood. 51gt. Powered by a steam engine. In 1853 she was employed on the Sacramento River CA. She was owned by the California Steam Navigation Co. In 1868 she was reported as having gone out of service but Lytle states that she was abandoned about 1855.

Marzelle[595] (British Columbia Colonial Register) (freighter) In 1860 she was built at Lillooet Lake British Columbia. 60.0' x 13.0' x 2.5'. Wood. Powered by two 18nhp 7" x 22" steam engines. In 1860 she was owned by Goulding & Co. She was launched June 12, 1860. She was in Lillooet Lake Service. In 1864 she was retired. Norman R Hacking states that "she is wrongly listed in Lewis & Dryden as the *Marcella*. It should be the *Marzelle*.

Mascot 092253 (US) (passenger/ freight vessel) She was built in 1890 at Portland OR USA. 132.0' x 24.0' x 5.0'. Wood. 267.35gt 199.46nt. Powered by two horizontal (high pressure 13" x 60") steam engines. In 1890 she was owned by the Lewis & Lake River Co. In 1890 she was employed on the Lewis River. In 1908 she was rebuilt as the *Mascot* (204927) by Jacob Kamm.

Mascot[596] 204937 (US) (passenger vessel) She was built in 1908 at Portland OR USA by Jacob Kamm. 140.5' x 26.8' x 6.8' Wood. 299gt 258nt. Powered by two horizontal (high pressure 13" x 60") steam engines from the *Mascot* (092253). In 1908 she was owned by the Lewis & Lake River Co. In 1911 she was reported to have been destroyed by fire in the Lewis River.

Mascotte (US) In 1898 she was built in Puget Sound WA. 130.0' x 25.0' x ? Wood. In 1898 she was owned by the Klondike-Chicago Transportation & Trading Co. She is reported by Murray Lundberg to have worked in Alaska/YT in 1898.

Mata C. Hover[597] 203118 (US) (passenger vessel) She was built in 1906 at Hover WA. 61' x 11' x 2.9' Wood. 14gt 10nt. Powered by a gasoline engine. She was home ported at Tacoma WA. In 1910 she was reported as being out of service.

Matanauska (US) (tug) She was built in 1915 at Seattle WA USA. 66' Wood. Powered by a gasoline engine. In 1915 she was owned by the Alaska Engineering Commission. In 1923 she was owned by the Alaskan Rail Road. In 1951 she was owned by the Civil Aeronautics Administration.

Mathloma (USACE) (snag boat) In 1896 she was built in Portland OR USA. 134' x 33' x 4' Wood. 270gt. Powered by two horizontal (high pressure 16" x 60") 17nhp steam engines. In 1906 she was rebuilt at Portland OR. 160' x 34.6' x 5.6' Wood. 177gt. In 1896–1927 she was owned by the United States Army Corps of Engineers. In 1906 she was rebuilt as a snag boat 160' 177gt. In 1927 she was reported as being laid up and out of service.

Matthew McKinley[598] (US) In 2008 she was owned by Sacramento Yacht Charters LLC, Sacramento CA. In 2012 she was owned by Gary Stone, Oakland CA. In 2012 she was moved to Suisun City CA. In 2017 she was owned by Scott Locker, Suisun City CA. In 2020 she was berthed at a marina on the Threemile Slough, where the Sacramento and San Joaquin Rivers merge, sixty miles east of San Francisco Bay.

Maude 064136 (Canada) (sidewheeler) (freighter, later a barge) She was built in 1872 at San Juan Island BC Canada (later a part of Washington State) by Burr & Smith. 113.5' x 21.2' x 9.0' Wood. 214gt 156rt. Powered by a 13hp compound two-cylinder steam engine by Albion Iron Works, Victoria BC. In 1872 she was owned by East Coast Mail Line (J Spratt), Victoria BC. In 1874 she was owned by Joseph Spratt, Victoria BC. Her engines were removed in 1884 and she was converted to a barge. She was re-engined in 1885. In 1898 she was converted to a side-wheeler and rebuilt again. In 1883–1901 she was sold to the Canadian Pacific Navigation Company. In 1901 she was owned by the Canadian Pacific Navigation Co. Ltd., Victoria BC. In 1903–1914 she was owned by the British Columbia Salvage Company, Victoria BC. Her original machinery came from the steam barge *Transport* built in Puget Sound. In 1883 she began a passenger and freight service between Victoria and Burrard Inlet. In 1884 she was in service on the Victoria – Alberni run. In 1903 she was converted to a salvage vessel. In 1914 she was dismantled in Victoria Harbour, her hull used as a barge. She was reported as having been broken up in 1914.

Maunsell White[599] (US) (sidewheeler) She was built in 1850 at San Francisco CA. Wood. 36gt. Powered by a steam engine. She was in service on California rivers. She was reported as having been abandoned about 1852.

May[600] (Canada) (launch) She was built c1898 at Lake Bennett BC Canada. Wood. Powered by a steam engine. In 1898 she was employed on Lake Bennett BC.

May D. 092853 (US) (passenger vessel) She was built in 1898 at San Francisco CA USA. 61.5' x 16.5' x 4.4' Wood. 66gt 48nt. Powered by a steam engine. In 1898 she was owned by the Alaska Exploration Co. In 1901 she was owned by the Northern Navigation Co. In c1902 she was owned by HM Bolander.

May Queen 091920 (US) (passenger/ freight vessel) She was built in 1886 at Seattle WA USA. 74.3' x 14.8' x 3.8' Wood. 86.37gt 47.99nt. Powered by a 38nhp steam engine. In 1886–1890 she was owned by Captain George Gove, Port Townsend WA USA.

May West 107869 (Canada) 0092896 (US) (later *Scout*; then RNWMP *Vidette*) (passenger vessel, later police vessel) She was built in 1898 at Seattle and she was finished at St. Michael AK USA by Payson C Richardson. 96.0' x 18.0' x 3.5' Wood. 134gt. Powered by a 5nhp steam engine from the *Florence Henry* built by Gillette & Eaton. In 1898 she was owned by Payson C Richardson. On August 08, 1899, she was wrecked in a storm at Cape Nome. She was salvaged and repaired. In 1901 she was owned by George B Wilson. In 1902–1909 she was purchased by the Royal North West Mounted Police, at a cost of $3,000, for service as a patrol and supply vessel on the Yukon River between Dawson and Whitehorse. In 1909 she was owned by the Merchants Yukon Transportation Co. and renamed as the *Vidette*. In 1911 she was rebuilt to 119.0' x 17.5' x 3.4' Wood. 254gt 16ort. In 1911 she was owned by Side Streams Navigation Co. Ltd., Dawson YT. In 1916–1917 she was owned by the White Pass & Yukon Railroad. In 1897–1902 she was registered in the USA, and then in Canada (1902–1917). On October 9, 1917, she foundered 14 miles above Lower Laberge YT while being towed by the *Canadian*.

May West (US) (passenger/ freight vessel) She was built in 1897 at Seattle WA USA. 100' Wood. Powered by a steam engine. She was the first sternwheeler to reach Dawson, on the Yukon River, in 1898 for the gold rush. She was constructed at Seattle WA and shipped to St. Michael AK with engines from the Skagit River steamer *Florence Henry* aboard the schooners *Bering Sea* and *Fischer Brothers* and assembled by PC Richards. She could carry 30 passengers and 50 tons of freight.

Mazatlan (US) (freighter) She was built about 1849. Wood. Powered by a steam engine. She was employed on the Sacramento River CA.

McConnell 107152 (Canada) (sidewheeler) (passenger/ freight vessel) She was built in 1898 at Vancouver BC Canada by James M Bulger. 142' x 30' x 5' Wood. 727gt 445rt. She was powered by a steam engine built by Albion Iron Works, Victoria BC. In 1898 she was owned by the Canadian Pacific Railway. In 1901 she was owned by the British Yukon Navigation Company and towed to Skagway AK. She collided with the steamer *Hamlin* in Stikine Canyon and was heavily damaged. In 1901 she was reported as having been broken up at Skagway AK with her machinery sent to the steamer *Whitehorse* and her hull possibly rebuilt as a barge.

McMinnville[601] 090960 (US) She was built in 1877 at Canemah OR. 132.0' x 28.0' x 5.0' Wood. 417gt. Powered by two horizontal (high pressure 14" x 60") 13nhp steam engines. In 1877 she was owned by the Peoples Protective Transportation Co. In 1881 she was reported to have been broken up at Salem OR. Her engines went to the *Katie Hallett*.

McMinnville[602] (later *Leona* 141710) 092959 (US) (passenger vessel) She was built in 1899 at Portland OR by Joseph Supple. 90.0' x 21.0' x 4.0' Wood. 137gt 104nt. Powered by two horizontal (high pressure 7" x 28") 3.3nhp steam engines. In 1901 she was rebuilt as the *Leona* (141710). In 1901 she was owned by the Oregon City Transportation Co. (O.C.T. Co.) (Yellow Stack Line). In 1912 she was destroyed by fire on the Lewis River.

Medea[603] (US) (freighter) She was built in 1853 at Corte Madera CA. Wood. 25gt. Powered by a steam engine. She was in service on California rivers. She was reported as having gone out of service and abandoned in 1858.

Meadowlark[604] (US) Wood. Powered by a steam engine. In 1889 she was a flat-bottomed wooden pleasure boat with no superstructure, built and owned by Augustus Bidwell, Oroville CA.

Melrose 205918 (US) (sidewheeler) (ferry) She was built in 1908 at Oakland CA USA. 273.0' x 43.0' x 17.9' Wood. 2662gt 1677nt. Powered by a 1,340ihp steam engine.

Mercer 201059 (US) In 1904 she was built at Seattle WA USA. 64.6' x 18.0' x 3.6' Steel. 84gt 53nt. Powered by a steam engine. She was employed in Puget Sound. She was owned by JL Anderson.

Mermaid 088367 (Canada) (tug) She was built in 1884 at Victoria BC Canada by HB Bolton. 94.0' x 18.0' x 4.6' Wood. 129gt 87rt. She was powered by a 18hp compound two-cylinder steam engine by McKelvie. In 1893 she was owned by the Northern Shipping Co. Ltd., Victoria BC. In 1895–1901 she was owned by the New Vancouver Coal Mining and Land Co. Ltd., Nanaimo BC. In 1902 she was owned by BA Wardle, Nanaimo BC. In 1905–1912 she was owned by Thomas Morgan & Co., Vancouver BC. In 1902 she struck a rock at Newcastle Island. On March 25, 1904, she struck a rock in Jervis Inlet and sank near Moorsam Bluff.

Mermaid (see *Saanich*)

Merrimac (US) (freighter) She was built in the 1849c. Wood. Powered by a steam engine. In 1849 she was employed on the San Joaquin River CA.

Messenger (US) (freighter) She was built in 1872 at Empire City OR USA by Captain M Lane. 91' Wood. 136gt. Powered by a steam engine. In 1876 she was destroyed by fire at Coos Bay OR USA.

Messenger 090954 (US) (passenger/ freight vessel) She was built in 1876 at Olympia WA USA. 90.3' x 29.7' x 4.8' Wood. 121.95gt. Powered by a 50nhp steam engine.

Messenger 092388 (US) She was built in 1891 at Portland OR. 100' x 16' x 3' Wood. 126gt 95nt. Powered by two horizontal (high pressure 7.25" x 24") steam engines. In 1891 she was owned by Frederick Lewis. In 1896 she was reported to have been destroyed by fire at St. Helens OR.

Messenger[605] (US) (bucket dredge) She was prefabricated in 1898 at Seattle WA and assembled at Hooper Bay AK. She was employed in Alaskan waters in 1898.

Metaline[606] 092664 (US) (see *Pend Oreille*)

Metlako (see *Bonita*)

Midnight Sun[607] (Canada) (passenger/ freight vessel) She was built in 1904 at Athabasca Landing by Captain GH Wood. 100' Wood. Powered by a steam engine. In 1904–1908c she was owned by the Northern Transportation Company. Depending on water levels she was also employed on the Lesser Slave River sometimes as far as Lesser Slave Lake. George Duddy notes that: "there is no evidence that she was ever properly registered. She was employed mainly on the upper Slave River between Mirror Landing and the Great Upper Rapids.

Midnight Sun[608,] (US) She was built in 1912 at Whitehorse YT. 45' x 9' x 1.3' Wood. Powered by a slow speed Doak engine. She was hauled on sleds to

Lake Laberge for service on the Porcupine and Crow Rivers to supply the United States Boundary Survey crews.

Midnight Sun (Image from the Provincial Archives of Alberta)

Midnight Sun (see *Northland Sun*)

Mike Anderson (later *Cora Blake*; then *Bried*) (US) Wood. Powered by a steam engine. She was destroyed by fire on Lake Whatcom (near Geneva WA).

Millicoma 206650 (US) (passenger vessel) She was built in 1909 at Marshfield OR USA by Frank Lowe. 55.0' x 11.0' x 2.4'. Wood. 14gt 12nt. Powered by a 30ihp gasoline engine. In 1909–1915 she was in service at Coos Bay OR.

Milton S. Latham 017931 (US) (passenger/ freight vessel) She was built in 1860 at San Francisco CA USA. 150' x 30.0' x 5.0'. Wood. 263.51gt 230.37nt. Powered by a 90nhp steam engine.

Milwaukee 091524 (US) She was built in 1880 at Portland OR. 50.0' x 18.0' x 2.0'. Wood. 37.2gt 29.7rt. Powered by a steam engine. In 1880–1885 she was employed on the Columbia River.

Milwaukee 092865 (US) She was built in 1898 at Ballard WA USA. 135.5' x 30.5' x 5.3' Wood. 396.33gt 219nt. She was towed with the *C.H. Bradley* by the *Del Norte* to Alaska. In 1898 she was owned by the Milwaukee-Alaska Gold Dredge Mining Co. In 1899 she was owned by the British-American Steamship Co. In 1900 she was owned by the Seattle-Yukon Transportation Co.

Miner[609,610] (US) (sidewheeler) She was built in 1850 at San Francisco CA. Wood. 75gt. Powered by a steam engine. She was in service on California rivers. On October 9, 1851, she was destroyed by fire at New York of the Pacific.

Minneapolis 092864 (US) (passenger/ freight vessel) She was built in 1898 at Tacoma WA USA. 108.6' x 21.8' x 4.9' Wood. 235.9gt 157.56nt. Powered by a 76ihp steam engine from the *Otter*. In 1898 she was owned by the Minnesota-Alaska Development Co. In 1905 she was employed on the Tanana River. In 1909 she was owned by the Alaska Transportation Co. In 1912 she was owned by the Western Transportation Co. In 1918 she was owned by the White Pass & Yukon Rail Road. She was owned by the Dominion Commercial Company. She was owned by the Northern Navigation Co. She was owned by the Alaska-Yukon Navigation Co. She was owned by the Alaska Rail Road.

Minneapolis 092864 (US) (passenger/ freight vessel) She was built in 1898 at Tacoma WA USA by Thomas C Reed. 108.6' x 21.8' x 4.9' Wood. 235.9gt 157.56rt. Powered by a 76ihp steam engine. In 1898 she was owned by the Minnesota-Alaska Development Co. In 1909 she was owned by the Alaska Transportation Co. In 1912 she was owned by the Western Transportation Co. In 1918 she was owned by the White Pass & Yukon Rail Road. She was owned by the Dominion Commercial Company. She was owned by the Northern Navigation Co. She was owned by the Alaska-Yukon Navigation Co. She was owned by the Alaska Rail Road. In 1905 she was in service on the Tanana River AK USA.

Minnehaha[611] 009084 (US) (passenger vessel) She was built in 1866 at Oswego Lake OR USA by JC Trulinger. 104' x 16' x 3' Wood. 45nt. Powered by a (12" x 12") steam engine from the *Skedaddle*. She was employed on

Oswego Lake. In 1876 she was reported as having been broken up at Portland OR.

Minnehaha 093341 (US) (passenger vessel) She was built in 1894 at Canton SD USA. 40.0' x 9.9' x 5.0' Wood. 8gt. Powered by a steam engine. In 1910 she was owned by Sioux City IA USA interests. (She was likely operating in the Missouri River watershed.)

Minnesota (later City of Winnipeg) (Canada) Wood. She was built in 1875 in the USA? In 1875 she was owned by the Merchants International Steamboat Line, Winnipeg MB. In 1875 she was owned by the Red River Transportation Company. In 1876 she was in service on the Red River in Manitoba and Minnesota. In 1876 she was in service on the Red River in Manitoba and Minnesota. In 1881 she was owned by the Winnipeg & Western Transportation Co. and later that year she was wrecked at Long Point, Lake Winnipeg MB.

Minnesota[612] (US) In 1898 she was built in Puget Sound WA USA. 110' x 21' x ? Wood. Powered by a steam engine. In 1898 she was owned by the Minnesota-Alaska Development Co. She is reported by Murray Lundberg to have worked in Alaska/YT in 1898. Edward L Affleck states that he found no record of her clearing customs out of Port Townsend WA.

Minnie[613] 204480 (US) (freighter) She was built in 1907 at Portland OR. 46.8' x 8.7' x 1.7' Wood. 11gt 10nt. Powered by a steam engine. She was employed on the Columbia River watershed. In 1910 she was reported as having been out of service.

Minnie Holmes (see Fenix)

Minnow[614] (Canada?) (passenger/ freight vessel) She was built in 1884 at SK Canada. Wood. Powered by a steam engine. In 1884 she was owned by the North Western Coal & Navigation Company. In 1887 she was owned by the Lamoreux Brothers. In 1898–1900 she was owned by Percy C Cunliffe. In 1885 she participated in the movement of troops during the Riel Rebellion. She was 'armoured' with barn boards from Gabriel Dumont's farm by General George Middleton and travelled with the steamer *Northcote*. In 1900 she was reported as having been employed on the North Saskatchewan River.

Mint[615] (US) (sidewheeler) She was built in 1849 at New York. Iron 36gt. Powered by a steam engine. She was in service on California rivers. She was reported as having gone out of service in 1852.

Minto 107453 (Canada) (passenger/ freight vessel) She was built in 1898 at Nakusp BC Canada by Thomas J Bulger. 161.7' x 30.1' x 5.1'. Wood. 829gt 522rt. Powered by a 17hp steam engine by Bertram Iron Works, Toronto ON. In 1898–1954 she was owned by the Canadian Pacific Railway, Montreal QC. In 1954 she made her last voyage from Robson to Arrowhead. Mark MacKenzie (in the British Columbia Nautical History Facebook Group 27/02/2019) states that "When the *Minto* was retired, the town of Nakusp petitioned the CPR to let them buy her for a buck. The CPR agreed and Nakusp promptly sold the machinery to a Nelson BC scrap dealer for $500. A man named John Nelson bought her then and towed her up the lake to his property and tried to preserve her as a private museum. He had a lot of heart, but few resources and when he passed away his son was unable to raise interest in preserving her. In the face of the flooding of the valley she was towed out and burned. She refused to sink. Like her sister the *Moyie*, she was a composite ship built for use on the Yukon River with steel sides, frames, and a Douglas fir planked bottom with 18 watertight compartments. After being rammed repeatedly by the tug she eventually slipped under. The Underwater Archaeology Society of BC has tried to find her with side-scan sonar searches, but she remains hidden to this day."

Minto 111591 (Canada) (passenger/ freight vessel) She was built in 1900 at Harrison River BC Canada. 60.0' x 9.2' x 2.4'. Wood. 36gt 23rt. Powered by a 2nhp engine. In 1900–1910 she was owned by RC Menton, Harrison River BC. She was in service as a ferry from Harrison Mills to Harrison Lake and Chilliwack Landing BC. In 1909 she was laid up.

Miss Liberty[616] (US) (passenger vessel) She was built in 1994. 64' Steel. She was refurbished in 2006. In 2006–2020 she offered tours of Big Bear Lake, based out of Pine Knot Marina located about 100 miles east of Los Angeles. She was a Skipperliner 1500 LX with a carrying capacity of 125 passengers.

Minto (Image from Maritime Museum of British Columbia 000421)

Missoula[617] (US) (passenger vessel) She was built in 1866 at Thompson Rapids MT USA. 93' Wood. Powered by a (10" x 48") 6.6nhp steam engine. In 1866 she was owned by the Oregon & Montana Transportation Co. She was employed between Thompson Falls and the mouth of the Jocko River. In 1870 she was moved to Lake Pend Oreille. She was laid up. In 1876 she was reported as having been broken up.

Missouri[618] (US) (freighter) She was built in 1850 at San Francisco CA. Wood. 27gt. Powered by a steam engine. She was in service on California rivers. She was reported as having gone out of service in 1852.

Mocking Bird 092854 (US) (passenger/ freight vessel) She was built in 1898 at Tacoma WA USA. 73.5' x 16.9' x 4.4' Wood. 82.47gt 29.01nt. Powered by a steam engine. She is reported by Murray Lundberg to have worked in Alaska/YT in 1898.

Modoc[619] 091263 (US) (passenger vessel) She was built in 1868 at Oakland CA USA. 204.0' x 42.3' x 8.0' Wood. 929gt 779nt. Powered by a 566nhp steam engine. In 1880–1884 she was owned by the Southern Pacific Railroad, San Francisco CA. She was employed on California rivers. She was reported as having been abandoned in 1928.

Modoc[620] 092103 (US) (freighter) She was built in 1889 at Portland OR. 142.0' x 30.1' x 4.4' Wood. 372gt 338nt. Powered by two horizontal (high pressure 14" x 60") 13nhp steam engines. In 1889 she was owned by the Oregon Railroad & Navigation Co. In 1898 she was rebuilt at Portland OR.

Modoc[621] 092898 (US) (passenger vessel) She was built in 1898 at Portland OR USA. 155.0' x 35.3' x 4.8' Wood. 394gt 350nt. Powered by a (14" x 60") 13nhp steam engine. In 1898 she was owned by the Oregon Railroad & Navigation Co. She was employed on the Columbia River. In 1916 she was moved to Puget Sound and rebuilt at Bellingham WA with a propeller.

Mohave (US) (freighter) She was built in 1864 at the Estuary of the Colorado River Mexico. 135' x 28' x ? Wood. 193gt. Powered by a gasoline engine. She was in service on the Colorado River. In 1875 she was reported as having been broken up.

Mojave 090931 (US) (freighter) She was built in 1875 at Port Isabel Mexico. 149.5' x 31.5' x ? Wood. 188gt. Powered by a steam engine. In 1875–1876 she was owned by the Colorado Steam Navigation Co. for service on the Colorado River. She was retired in 1900 and abandoned (some reports say broken up).

Mollie 090742 (US) (freighter) She was built in 1874 at Elk City, OR USA. 54.0' x 11.0' x 5.0' Wood. 37.86gt/rt. Powered by a steam engine.

Monarch[622] (US) She was built in 1875. 109.0' Wood. 195.47gt. Powered by a steam engine. She was in service on California rivers. In 1911 she was reported as having gone out of service.

Monarch 127574 (see *Charles R. Spencer*)

Monarch 092855 (US) She was built in 1898 at Ballard WA USA by Thomas C Reed. 150' x 35' x ? Wood. 463gt. In 1898 she was owned by the Columbia Navigation Co. In 1901 she was owned by the Yukon Independent Transportation Co. In 1902 she was owned by Edward Sondheim & DW Dobbins. In 1907 she was owned by Albert Reber Heilig. In 1913 she was owned by the Northern Navigation Co. In 1914 she was owned by the

White Pass & Yukon Rail Road. She was sold again. She traveled to St. Michael's AK and Dawson YT in 1898 for the Klondike Gold Rush. In 1927 she was reported as having been laid up at St. Michael AK USA.

Monarch 107863 (Canada) (see also *Clara Monarch*) (freighter) She was built in 1898 at San Francisco CA USA by Matthew Turner. 120.3' x 32.2' X 5.4' Wood. 285gt 179rt. Powered with a steam engine. Repowered with engines from the *Clara* (127249) installed in 1900. In 1898–1901 she was owned by Fernand de Journal, Dawson YT. In 1902 she was owned by Domenic Burns, Dawson YT. In 1903–1904 she was owned by George S Wilkins, Dawson YT. She was employed on the Yukon River. In 1904 she foundered at Whitehorse YT.

Monarch 092855 (US) (freighter) She was built in 1898 at Ballard WA USA by TA Reed. 149.6' x 30.3' x 5.0' Wood. 463.10gt 269.50nt. Powered by a 280ihp steam engine. She was towed to St. Michael AK from Seattle WA by the *Rival*. In 1898 she was owned by the Columbia Navigation Co. In June 1905 she was stranded below Eagle on the Yukon River. She was reported to have been abandoned at St. Michael AK.

Mono[623] 107102 (Canada) (passenger/ freight vessel) She was built in 1898 on the Stikine River BC Canada by Frank P Armstrong & AF Henderson. 120.0' x 23.0' x 4.5' Wood. 278gt 154rt. Powered by a steam engine. In 1898–1902 she was owned and operated by Teslin Transportation Co. Ltd., Victoria BC. In 1901 she was sold in Wrangel AK. On August 23, 1902, she was destroyed by fire at Dawson City YT while laid up in winter quarters. In April 1902 her owner, Joseph Genelle, was arrested by the Northwest Mounted Police for "having procured the burning of the steamer" to defraud the insurers.

Montana (see *Willamette*)

Monte Cristo 107824 (Canada) 092382 (US) (freighter) She was built in 1891 at Ballard WA USA. 90.2' x 24.1' x 3.0' Wood. 188gt 126rt. Powered by a steam engine by the Moran Bros., Seattle WA USA. In 1899 she was rebuilt to 109' x 20'. In 1898 she was transferred to the Canadian Registry (107824). In 1901–1910 she was owned by Robert Cunningham, Port Essington

BC. In 1901 she operated on the Skeena River. She was chartered by the Government of Canada for the construction of the Yukon Telegraph line. In 1903 she was reported as having been laid up, and she disintegrated on the beach at Port Essington, her engines salvaged as scrap.

Montesano[624] 091400 (US) (passenger vessel) She was built in 1882 at Astoria OR USA by John H Johnston. 79.0' x 17.0' x 4.0' Wood. 87.91gt 41.49nt. Powered by two horizontal (high pressure 12" x 48") 9.6nhp steam engines. In 1882 she was owned by Shoalwater Bay Transportation Co. In 1889 she was moved to Grays Harbor. In 1906 she was reported to have been broken up at Aberdeen WA.

Moose[625] (US) (passenger vessel) She was built in 1859 at Canemah OT USA. 75.0' x 16' x 4' Wood. Powered by a (12" x 48") 9.6nhp steam engine. In 1859 she was owned by Smith, Moore, Marshall Co. In 1861 she was reported to have been wrecked at Peoria OR.

Moulton[626] 017440 (US) (freighter) She was built in 1867 at Stockton CA USA by Cousins. 150.5' Wood. 192.76gt. Powered by a steam engine. She was in service on California rivers. She was reported to have gone out of service in 1878.

Mount Eden[627] 050210 (US) (sidewheeler) She was built in 1863 at Eden CA. Wood. 72gt. In 1866 she was rebuilt and converted to a barge.

Mount Eden[628] 090826 (US) She was built in 1875 at Stockton CA USA by C Small. 89.5' x 24.0' x 4.4' Wood. 73.66gt 62.76nt. Powered by a 25nhp steam engine. She was employed on California rivers. She was reported to have gone out of service in 1910.

Mount Royal[629,630] 111778 (Canada) (freighter) She was built in 1902 at Victoria BC Canada by Victoria Machinery Depot Co. Ltd. 138' x 28' x 2' Wood. 471.03gt 295rt. Powered by two (14" x 60" stroke) steam engines. In 1902–1907 she was owned by the Hudson's Bay Co., London UK. She was registered at Victoria BC. She was employed on the Skeena River and Stikine River in opposition to the *Hazelton*. "On May 24, 1904, Captain Bonsor of the *Hazelton* and Captain Wood of the *Mount Royal*, sternwheelers operating on the Skeena River in British Columbia, drew revolvers in a battle which was the outgrowth of a collision between the two vessels. Passengers interfered and prevented any one from being killed and the two captains decided to settle the matter privately." On July 6, 1907, she was caught in a cross current which drove her against Ringbolt Island, in the Kitselas Canyon where she struck a rock (on the Skeena River) and broke in two and capsized. Six lives were lost (passengers, and some furs were saved). Her engines went to the *Inlander*.

Mount Royal (Image from Maritime Museum of British Columbia 000443)

Mountain Belle 092700 (Canada) (passenger vessel) She was built in 1886 at Winnipeg MB Canada. 20.0' x 4.7' x 1.5'. Wood. 1gt 1rt. Powered by a steam engine(?) In 1898 she was owned by John J Ryan, Banff AB NWT.

Mountain Belle 092780 (Canada) (work boat) She was built in 1888 at Carleton Place ON Canada. 30.2' x 6.1' x 3.0' Wood. 5gt 3rt. Powered by a 5hp engine. In 1896–1919 she was owned by Thomas R Lane, Vancouver BC.

Mountain Buck[631] (US) (sidewheeler) (passenger vessel) She was built in 1857 at Portland OT USA. 133' Wood. Powered by a (12" x 48") steam engine. In 1857 she was owned by Ruckle & Olmstead. She was absorbed into the Union Transportation Co. and then into the Oregon Railroad & Navigation Co. She was employed on the Portland to Cascades route. In 1864 she was reported as being dismantled and burned in 1865.

Mountain Gem[632] 201045 (US) (freighter/ passenger vessel) She was built in 1904 at Lewiston ID USA by HC Banghman. 150.0' x 26.6' x 5.0' Wood. 469gt 282nt. Powered by a 600ihp steam engine. In 1904 she was owned by the Lewiston Navigation Co. In 1906 she was operated by the Open River Navigation Co. In 1924 she was reported as having been abandoned.

Mountain Queen 090979 (US) (passenger vessel) She was built in 1877 at The Dalles OR USA. 196.0' x 32.0' x 7.5' Wood. 718.63gt 510.62rt. Powered by two horizontal (20" x 84") 26.6nhp steam engines. Her engines came from the Daisy Ainsworth. In 1877 she was owned by the Oregon Steam Navigation Co. She was employed on the Snake River. In 1889 she was rebuilt as the sidewheeler *Sehome* (116301) employed on Puget Sound.

Moyie (Image from John MacFarlane collection)

Moyie 107454 (Canada) (passenger/ freight Vessel) She was built in 1898 at Toronto ON Canada by the Bertram Iron Works and assembled at Nelson BC. On October 22, 1898, she was sponsored by Mrs. J Troup, wife of Captain J Troup. 161.7' x 30.1' x 5.1' Wood. 835gt 526rt. Powered by 17nhp steam engine. In 1898–1957 she was owned by the Canadian Pacific Railway Co., Montreal QC. In 1958 she was owned by the Corporation of the City of Kaslo, BC. In 1957 she made her last voyage and then retired. In 1957 she was towed to Kaslo BC and beached. In 1989 she was restored as a community museum vessel. Mark MacKenzie (British Columbia Nautical History Facebook Group 27/02/2019) states: "When the Village of Kaslo tried to get the CPR to sell them the *Moyie* for a buck a couple of years after the *Minto*'s retirement debacle, the CPR demanded proof that they were serious this time—they did not want to leave that scrap money on the table. A man named Noel Bacchus rowed around the communities and homesteads of upper Kootenay Lake collecting money for the Kootenay Lake Historical Society to save the *Moyie* and they then petitioned the Provincial Government to match the funds. When the CPR saw they had done this they transferred over the *Moyie*. Formerly interned Nikkei shipwright Tomio Baba, who had stayed on in Kaslo post-war (and built our house among other things) built a cradle out of old Kaslo & Slocan Railway bridge timbers and they winched her out of the water in early 1958. In the late 1980s local shipwright Dick Smith built a steel cradle to match Parks Canada engineering specs and the *Moyie* remains to this day."

Moyie 325590 (Canada) (passenger vessel) She was built in 1965 at Vancouver BC by Allied Shipbuilders Ltd. Designed by Philip F Spaulding. 75' x 23' x 6' (22.86m x 7.01m x 1.83m). Steel. 121.75gt 81.6rt. Powered by a 180bhp diesel engine. In 1965–2021 as a passenger vessel, she was owned by Heritage Park Society, Calgary AB.

MS Dixie II (see *Dixie II*)

Mudhen[633] (US) (passenger/ freight vessel) She was built in 1878 at Coquille River OR USA. 32'. Wood. Powered by a steam engine. She was reported to have been out of service in 1892.

Mud Hen 207625 (US) (tug) She was built in 1910 at Marietta WA USA. 34.9' x 11.8' x 4.0'. Wood. 13gt 9nt. Powered by a 7ihp gasoline engine.

Multnomah[634] (US) (sidewheeler) (passenger vessel) She was built in 1851 in the eastern USA and shipped to Oregon on the bark *Success*. (She was assembled at Oregon City, the first instance of prefabricated shipbuilding in the Oregon Territory). 108' x 18' x 1.' Iron and Wood. Powered by two horizontal (high pressure 10" x 48") 6.6nhp steam engines. In 1851 she was employed between Oregon City and Corvallis OR. In 1852 she was employed on the Portland – Astoria route. She was owned by the Oregon Railroad & Navigation Co. In 1864 her engines were removed, and her hull was abandoned at Portland OR.

Multnomah 091765 (US) (passenger Vessel) She was built in 1885 at East Portland OR USA. 143.0' x 28.0' x 5.3'. Wood. 312gt 278nt. Powered by 384ihp two horizontal (high pressure 16" x 72") 17nhp steam engines. In 1885 she was owned by the Multnomah Steamboat Co. on charter to the Oregon Railroad & Navigation Co. She was employed on the Columbia and Willamette Rivers. In 1889 she was owned by Puget Sound WA interests. In 1907 she was converted from wood fuel to oil. In 1911 she was reported as being wrecked.

Multnomah 210854 (US) (freighter) She was built in 1912 at St. Helens OR USA by St. Helens Shipbuilding Co. 205.5' x 40.5' x 13.8' Wood. 969gt 583nt. Powered by an 88nhp triple expansion steam engine built by United Engine Works Co., Alameda CA. In 1926–1929 she was owned by Charles R. McCormick Lumber Co., San Francisco CA USA. She was in service carrying freight in Puget Sound. On June 16, 1929, she lost her deck load of lumber. Calling for assistance, the US Coast Guard then escorted her safely across the Columbia River Bar. After the incident she was condemned as unseaworthy having suffered damage in the incident.

Mumford 017706 (US) (freighter) She was built in 1865 at Port Ludlow WT USA. 110.0' x 19.0' x 4.8' Wood. 69gt. Powered by a steam engine. In 1865 she was constructed by the Russian-American Telegraph Co. In 1866 she was owned by the Western Union Extension Telegraph Co. (Collins Overland Telegraph Co.). She was reputed to have been in service on the Skeena River carrying construction material up to Kitselas Canyon "2 or 3 times". In 1868 she was transferred to San Francisco CA USA. In 1870 she was reported as having been sold to foreign interests.

Munroe (US) This name is probably a contracted short form name or nickname of another vessel—related to two other sternwheelers, the *J.A. Munroe*, or the *William F. Munroe*.

Muskrat[635] (Canada) (snag boat) She was built in 1892 at Golden BC. 84' Wood. 380gt 265rt. She was employed on the Columbia River.

Myra (see *Pacific Slope*)

Myrtle 206743 (US) (passenger vessel) She was built in 1909 at Myrtle Point OR USA by Nels Nelson. 57.4' x 13.8' x 2.9' Wood. 36gt 29rt. Powered by a 20ihp steam engine. She was reported to have been rebuilt about 1922 as a freighter. In 1922 she was owned by the Myrtle Point Transportation Co.

Myrtle[636] (US) She was built in 1922 at Prosper OR. 60' Wood. 36gt. In 1940 she was reported as having been abandoned.

N.R. Lang[637] 130884 (US) (passenger vessel/ freighter) She was built in 1900 at Portland OR USA from the hull of the *Salem* (115778). 152.0' x 30.7' x 6.2' Wood. 528gt 381nt. Powered by a steam engine. In 1900 she was owned by the Willamette Pulp & Paper Co. In 1925–1935 she was owned by the Western Transportation Co., Portland OR. She was in service on the lower Columbia River. In January 1930 she was frozen in ice while carrying a cargo of paper and sank near Vancouver WA. She was raised a month later, lashed between two barges and towed to Portland to be repaired. She was moved to San Francisco Bay. In 1940 she was reported as having been dismantled.

N.S. Bentley[638] (later *Albany*) 130364 (US) She was built in 1886 at East Portland OR. 151.0' x 32.0' x 4.5' Wood. 432gt 401nt. Powered by two horizontal (high pressure 16" x 60") 17nhp steam engines. In 1886 she was owned by Oregon Development Co. In 1896 she was rebuilt as the *Albany* (US 107218) at Portland OR USA. 151.0' x 32' x 4.5' Wood. 431gt 401nt. The *Albany*'s engines came from the N.S. Bentley (130364 [US]). The *Albany* was rebuilt in 1906 and renamed and re-registered. Her engines went on to the *Georgie Burton* (203101 ([US]).

Nahleen 107104 (Canada) She was built in 1898 at Vancouver BC. 146.5' x 33.4' x 4.7' Wood. 599gt 356rt. Powered by a steam engine. In 1898 she was owned by the Klondyke Mining, Trading & Transportation Co. Ltd., Victoria BC. She served one season on the Stikine River. On July 12, 1899, she burned while at her mooring in Victoria Harbour BC. The fire started in the engine room of the *Nahleen*, with the fire spreading to the *Louise*, but the fire department having no equipment to fight such a fire could only stand and watch the vessels burn. She had been scheduled to travel to the Yukon the next morning.

Nahlin 209802 (US) (freighter) She was built in 1912 at Wrangell Alaska. 85.5' x 14' x 4' Wood. 107gt 6nt. Powered by a steam engine?

Nakusp[639] 103302 (Canada) (passenger/ freight vessel) She was built in 1895 at Nakusp BC Canada by Thomas J Bulger. 171.0' x 34.0' x 6.3' Wood. 1083gt 831rt. Powered by two 26nhp horizontal (high pressure 20" x 72") steam engines built by the Iowa Iron Works Co., Dubuque IA. The machinery installed in her originally came from the *Columbia* which had burned on August 2, 1895, on the Columbia River. In 1895–1896 she was owned by Columbia & Kootenay Steamship Navigation Company. In 1897 she was owned by the Canadian Pacific Railway, Montreal QC. In the summer of 1896, the *Nakusp* ran aground on Kootenay Bar and remained there for a couple of months. On December 23, 1897, she was destroyed by fire while at her berth at Arrowhead BC.

Nancy Belle[640] (US) Wood. Powered by a steam engine. She is reported by Murray Lundberg to have worked in Alaska/YT.

Nanaimo 094803 (Canada) (freighter) She was built in 1882 at Nanaimo BC Canada by John McLeod. 56.0' x 20.0' x 32.0' Wood. 70.79gt 44.61rt. Powered by two 2.9hp horizontal steam engines by Bannerman & Powers, Ottawa ON. In 1888–1895 she was owned by Peter Taylor, Nanaimo BC. In 1895 she was owned by Thomas E Atkins, Vancouver BC. In 1895 she was owned by The British Columbia Iron Works Co. Ltd., Vancouver BC. In 1895 she was owned by James Hartney, Vancouver BC. In 1895–1897 she was owned by The British Columbia Iron Works Co. Ltd., Vancouver BC. In 1897–1901 she was owned by William R Taylor, Vancouver BC.

Naomi 130717 (US) (passenger/ freight vessel) She was built in 1896 at Wallula WA. 43.0' x 11' x 3.3' Wood. 19gt 7nt. In 1899 she was reported to have gone out of service.

Napa City[641] 130562 (US) She was built in 1891 at Benicia CA USA. 106.0' x 26.8' x 6.0' Wood. 178.87gt 162.92rt. Powered by a 120ihp steam engine. She was in service on California rivers. She was reported to have been abandoned in 1931.

Nasbena 222522 (US) She was built in 1922 at Fairbanks AK USA. In 1922 she was owned by Clarence D O'Flanagan. 65' Wood. 73gt. Powered by a steam engine.

Nasookin (Image from Vancouver City Archives AM170_CVA 372-09)

Nasookin[642] 133885 (Canada) (passenger/ freight vessel) She was built in 1913 at Port Arthur ON by the Western Drydock & Shipbuilding Co. In 1913 she was built in sections and was assembled at Nelson BC. 200.2' x 40.0' x 8.0' Steel. 1869gt 1035.24rt. Powered by two compound two-cylinder 101nhp steam engines in tandem built by the North West Dry Dock and Shipbuilding Co. Ltd. In 1913–1932 she was owned by Canadian Pacific. In 1913–1947 she operated on Kootenay Lake BC. In 1920 she was used as a car ferry. In 1930 she was withdrawn from service. In 1932–1945 she was owned by the British Columbia Minister of Public Works, Victoria BC. for use as a ferry. In 1947 she was owned by The Navy League of Canada, Toronto ON as a sea cadet training vessel. In 1950–1976 she was owned by

Earle M Cutler, Taber AB. In 1948 she ran aground and was reported to have been dismantled at Nelson about 1950. In 1967 she was still listed in the List of Shipping as being owned by Earle Cutler of Taber AB. In 1976 it was reported that the wheelhouse was used as a curio shop on Highway 3A about 5 miles east of Nelson BC and later as a dwelling.

Nasutlin[643] (US) (passenger/ freight vessel) In 1898 she was owned by the Empire Transportation Co. employed on the Yukon River.

Nasutlin 133885 (Canada) (passenger/ freight vessel) She was built in 1912 at Whitehorse YT Canada. 141.3' x 27.3' x 4.2'. Wood. 570gt 393rt. Powered by a 200hp steam engine. She was rebuilt at Whitehorse YT in 1938. In 1912 she was owned by The British Yukon Navigation Co. Ltd., Vancouver BC. In 1938 she was owned by The British Yukon Navigation Co. Ltd., Vancouver BC. In 1951–1958 she was owned by The British Yukon Navigation Co. Ltd., Vancouver BC. She was trapped in the ice in the fall of 1919 and on May 24, 1920, she sank in Yukon River above Mayo YT after being damaged by ice and was abandoned. She was later rebuilt and foundered at Dawson City YT in 1952.

Native (Image from the John MacFarlane collection.)

Native[644] 805718 (Canada) (passenger vessel) In 1985 she was built at Richmond BC Canada by Thorvald B Larsen. 21.34m x 6.71m x 1.43m Steel. 108.43gt 81.43rt. Powered by two 125bhp diesel engines. In 1985–1991 she was owned by Thorvald B Larsen, Richmond BC. In 1992–2021 she was owned by Fraser Connection Cruises Ltd., New Westminster BC. She was employed providing tourist excursions on the Fraser River between Fort Langley and Steveston BC. In 2021 she was reported as having been laid up.

Navajo[645,646] 206685 (US) (passenger vessel) She was built in 1909. 219.8' x 42.0' x 8.9' Wood. 968gt 506rt. Powered by a 1,340ihp steam engine. In 1909 she was owned by the Southern Pacific Railway. She operated on the Sacramento River. She was reported to have been abandoned in 1938. Dikes were closed in around her and she was used to pump out water to reclaim the rich bottom land. Her remains are in a farm field on Mandeville Island.

Nechacco (later *Chilco*) 126512 (Canada) She was built in 1909 at Quesnel BC by Donald McPhee. 80.0' x 16.4' x 3.0' Wood. 128gt 75rt. Powered by a 12hp steam engine built by the J. Doty Engineering Co., Toronto ON. In 1909–1910 she was owned by the Fort George Lumber & Navigation Co., Vancouver BC. In 1911–1912 she was owned by John K McLennan, Winnipeg MB & Alan J Adamson, Vancouver BC. In May 1911 she was wrecked at Cottonwood Canyon in the Fraser River BC.

Nellie 130079 (US) (passenger/ freight vessel) She was built in 1876 at Seattle WA USA. 82.2' x 19.3' x 4.9' Wood. 100.22gt 55.03rt. Powered by 40ihp steam engine.

Nellie[647] 130149 (US) (passenger vessel) She was built in 1879 at Salem OR. 50.0' x 12.2' x 3.0' Wood. 47gt. Powered by a (7" x 10") steam engine. In 1879 she was owned by Smith & Harris. In 1881 she was rebuilt to 75.5' x 12.2' x 3'. In 1882 she was reported to have been broken up at Salem OR.

Nellie[648] 130819 (US) (tug) She was built in 1899 at Portland OR. 115' Wood. 180gt 59nt. Powered by two horizontal (high pressure 16" x 48") steam engines. In 1899 she was owned by JF Boone. In 1908 she was reported to have been broken up at Portland OR. She is reported by Murray Lundberg to have been employed on the Stikine River 1878–1888. She was out of service some time after 1907.

Nelson 096987 (Canada) (passenger vessel) She was built in 1891 at Revelstoke BC Canada by David Stephenson. 134.0' x 27.0' x 6.0' Wood. 496gt 312rt. She was powered by a two 13nhp steam engines from the Skuzzy (II). In 1891–1896 she was owned by Columbia & Kootenay Steamship Navigation Company, Nelson BC. In 1897–1913 she was owned by Canadian Pacific Railway Co., Montreal QC. In 1913 she was withdrawn from service and her machinery sold. In July 1914, her hull was burned as a feature attraction during the Chako Mika Fireworks Carnival at Nelson BC.

Nenana 223315 (US) (tug) She was built in 1922 at Nenana AK USA. 39.7' x 9.9' x 2.8' Wood. 8gt 5nt. Powered by a 46hp steam engine. In 1922–1935 she was owned by John H Bailey, Seward AK USA.

Nenana[649] (US) She was built in 1933 she was built at Nenana Alaska USA by Berg Shipbuilding Co. 210' x 42.0' x 3.6' Wood. Powered by two horizontal compound (17.28" x 72") 600ihp steam engines. In 1933 she was owned by the Alaskan Rail Road. In 1954 she was leased to the Yutana Barge Line. In 1956 she was owned by the Greater Fairbanks Opportunities Inc., Fairbanks AK. She was the last steamboat in regular service on the Lower Yukon River in 1954. She was retired in 1955. In 1965 she was put on display in Pioneer Park, Fairbanks AK. The Fairbanks North Star Borough Parks and Recreation Department is committed to preservation of the vessel. In 1989 she was designated as a National Historic Landmark.

Neo-Watin (The)[650] (ex-*Little Klondike Queen*) 193259 (Canada) She was built in 1964 at Edmonton AB by Canada Iron Foundries Ltd. 14.48m x 3.96m x 1.01m Steel. 22.65gt 18.65nt. Powered by a D-4 Caterpillar diesel engine. This vessel was originally built as a 40-passenger excursion vessel at Edmonton AB. She was underpowered for the strong river current and put up for sale. Owner Jodi Balon stated "*Neo-Watin* is Cree for "no wind." My dad, Dave Balon, bought the *Neo-Watin* in 1974 after finishing a 14-year star career in the National Hockey League (celebrated by two Stanley Cup victories with the Montreal Canadiens ice hockey team in 1966 and 1967). He moved the vessel to Waskesiu Lake in Prince Albert National Park,

Saskatchewan. I took over operations in 1995 and ran the vessel until the dam was removed in 2002 by Parks Canada and the lake became unnavigable. I spent the next 12 years writing new business plans while being my parent's sole care giver until they both had passed in 2014. The vessel is now an abandoned wreck at the Waskesiu Marina's dry dock."

The *Neo-Watin* conducting tours on Waskesiu Lake (Prince Albert National Park) SK (Image from the Jodi Balon collection)

Neponset No. 2[651,652] 130324 (US) (freighter) She was built in 1884 at San Francisco CA USA. 125.1' x 27.5' x 4.8'. Wood. 224gt 155nt. Powered by a 200ihp steam engine. She was the last of the trading vessels operated on the Sacramento River that called at ranches and farms to buy directly from producers. She foundered in Georgiana Slough, in the Sacramento River.

Neptune 130161 (US) She was built in 1879 at Seattle WA USA. 42.2' x 13.4' x 2.5'. Wood. 33.13gt Powered by a 10nhp steam engine. She was in service in Puget Sound.

Nespelem (later *Robert Young*) 215759 (US) (tug, later a barge) She was built in 1917 at Wenatchee WA USA by Charles S Miller. 130.5' x 26.1' x 5.2'. Wood. 349gt 292nt. Powered by a 185ihp steam engine by Willamette Iron and Steel. Works. In 1918–1935 she was employed on the Columbia and Willamette Rivers. In 1917–1920 she was owned by the Miller Navigation Co., Wenatchee WA USA. In 1920 she was renamed as the *Robert Young*. In 1920–1935 she was owned by the Western Transportation Co., Portland OR. In 1920 she was employed on the lower Columbia River. In 1918–1935 she was employed on the Columbia and Willamette Rivers. In 1937 she was reported to have been wrecked, salvaged, and converted to a floating machine shop.

Nestor[653] 130998 (US) (tug) She was built in 1902 at Catlin OR USA. 82.4' x 19.6' x 5.0'. Wood. 97gt 31rt. Powered by a 150ihp two horizontal (high pressure 12" x 48") 9.6nhp steam engines. In 1902 she was owned by CP Stayton. In 1925 she was owned by the Smith Transportation Co., Rainier OR. She was employed towing log rafts. In 1923 she was owned by the Columbia and Cowlitz River Transportation Co. In 1925 she was rebuilt at Rainier OR. In 1929 she was reported to have been abandoned near Rainier OR.

Nevada[654,655] (US) (sidewheeler) She was built in 1861 at San Francisco CA USA. Wood. 757gt. Powered by a steam engine. She was in service on California rivers. On July 2, 1862, this vessel was racing the *New World* when she hit a snag in Steamboat Slough. She sank by the Cache Slough near Sacramento. Her hull became caught in the sand and as the water levels rose and fell she became a total loss.

New England (US) (sidewheeler) She was built in 1849 at Benicia CA. 50'. Wood. 28gt. Powered by a steam engine. She was in service on California rivers. She was reported to have gone out of service around 1852.

New Era 206248 (US) She was built in 1909 at Stanwood WA USA. 53.2' x 11.7' x 2.7'. Wood. 14gt 9nt. Powered by a 36ihp gasoline engine.

New Liberty Belle (US) (passenger vessel) She was associated with the Water Valley Resort Residential Community, Windsor CO USA. (In 2021 she may be out of existence.)

New Orleans[656] (US) She was built about 1850. Wood. Powered by a steam engine. She was in service on California rivers. She was reported to have gone out of service about 1868.

New Racket 130228 (US) (sidewheeler) She was built in 1882 at San Francisco CA USA. 42' x 11' x 3' Wood. 14.29gt Powered by a steam engine. In 1896 she was re-fitted for service. In 1882 she was transported to St. Michael AK. She was used by the mining promoter Edward Scheiffelin to prospect for a year along the Yukon and Tanana Rivers. In 1883 she was sold to Arthur Harper, Captain A Mayhue and Leroy McQuesten (free traders and Alaska Commercial Co. agents) ran her on the Stewart and Yukon Rivers. In 1893 she was owned by the Alaska Commercial Co. She was hauled out of the water in a slough near Pelly YT. In 1896 she was destroyed by rising ice near Pelly YT (Yukon River).

New Tenino[657] 130067 (US) (formerly *Tenino* [024491]) (Name later changed to *Diamond O.* (207330) (passenger vessel) She was built in 1876 at Celilo OR USA. 142.5' x 28.4' x 6.6' Wood. 316gt 276nt. Powered by two horizontal (high pressure 17" x 72") steam engines. Her engines came from the *Tenino* (024491). In 1876 she was owned by Oregon Steam Navigation Co. In 1879 she was reported to have been dismantled at Celilo OR. In 1887 she was rebuilt at Portland OR as the *Diamond O.* (207330). She was employed on the Columbia River system.

New Volunteer[658] 130926 (US) (passenger vessel, later a houseboat) She was built in 1901 at Newport WA USA. 72.0' x 16.0' x 3.8' Wood. 105gt 73nt. Powered by a steam engine. In 1901 she was owned by JW Cusick. In 1905 she was reported to have been out of service. She was employed as a landing stage and office for the Pend Oreille Navigation Co. At Newport OR. In 1908 she was converted to a houseboat by HWD Roy.

New Western Queen 130773 (US) (sidewheeler) (ferry) She was built in 1898 at The Dalles OR USA. 75.5' x 38.0' x 8.0' Wood. 99gt 74rt. Powered by a 65ihp steam engine. She was in service on California rivers. She was reported to have been broken up in 1904.

New World[659,660] (US) (sidewheeler) (passenger vessel) She was built in 1849 at New York USA. 225'x 27' x 9' Wood. 531gt. Powered by a walking beam (46" x 121") steam engine. In 1854–1855 she was owned by the Peoples Line and was employed in Long Island Sound NY. She was sailed around to California. She was employed on the Sacramento River. In 1855 she was owned by the California Steam Navigation Company. In 1850 she offered the first continuous service between San Francisco and Sacramento. On May 3, 1851, her boiler exploded near Sacramento CA, resulting in 3 dead and 15 injured. In 1864 she was owned by the Oregon Steam Navigation Co. and employed on the Columbia River. On January 5, 1876, she collided with the sloop *Salinas* while carrying a cargo of bran, which being buoyant prevented her from disappearing underwater. She was reported as broken up in 1879.

New York 201292 (US) She was built in 1904 at Nome AK USA. 34.0' x 10.0' x 3.3' Wood. 8gt 5rt. Powered by a steam engine. She is reported by Murray Lundberg to have worked in Alaska/YT.

Newport 203874 (US) (passenger vessel) She was built in 1907 at Newport WA USA. 91.6' x 18.2' x 4.2' Wood. 129gt 81nt. Powered by a 95ihp steam engine. In 1907–1910 she was owned by the Pend Oreille River Navigation Co. In 1910 she was reported to have been laid up.

Newport 130118 (US) (sidewheeler) (ferry) She was built in 1877 at San Francisco CA USA. 268.0' x 42.5' x 18.8' Wood. 2197gt 1758nt. Powered by a 1,200ihp steam engine.

Newport Belle[661] (US) She was built in 1993 at Bandon Oregon by Joe Bolduc. 97' x 24' x 2.9' Steel. Powered by a diesel engine. This is a sternwheeler berthed in Newport OR USA that operates as a bed and breakfast.

Newport Landing Belle (later *Christine W.*)[662] (US) (passenger vessel) 68' x 15' x 3.3' Steel. Powered by a 76hp Cummins diesel air-cooled engine. She is still afloat and offers charter cruises on Lake Union and Lake Washington, out of Fisherman's Terminal, Seattle WA.

Newton (US) She was built in 1901. 75' Wood. 77gt. Powered by a steam engine. She was in service on California rivers. She was reported to have been broken up in 1904.

Newtown No. 2[663] 202506 (US) (freighter) She was built in 1905 at Benicia CA USA. 131.5' x 30.5' x 5.2' Wood. 217.18gt 185nt. Powered by a 180ihp steam engine. She was in service on California rivers. She was reported to have been abandoned in 1926.

Nez Perce Chief[664] 018399 (US) (sidewheeler) (passenger vessel, later a barge) She was built in 1863 at Celilo OR USA. 126' Wood. 327gt. Powered by two horizontal (high pressure 16" x 66") 17nhp steam engines. (Her engines came from the *Carrie Ladd*). In 1863 she was owned by the Oregon Steam Navigation Co., Astoria OR. She was employed on the Columbia River and later, on the Snake River up to Lewiston ID. In 1871 she was converted to a barge. In 1874 she was reported to have been broken up.

Niagara 107158 (Canada) (work boat) She was built in 1898 at Vancouver BC Canada by John F Walker. 39' x 8.6' x 2.6' Wood. 62.5gt 39.4rt. Powered by two 2nhp upright (high pressure 6" x 6") steam engines built by the Lake City Engineering Co., Erie PA USA. In 1898 she was owned by John F Walker, Vancouver BC. In 1899 she was reported as having been broken up at Dawson City YT.

Nina Tilden[665] 018645 (US) (freighter) She was built in 1864 at San Francisco CA USA. 98.0' Wood. 107.4gt. In 1864–1865 she was owned by the Philadelphia Silver & Copper Mining Co. (AF Tilden, mgr.). In 1865–1866 she was owned by the Pacific & Colorado Steam Navigation Co. In 1866–1867 she was owned by the Arizona Navigation Co. (creditors of the Pacific & Colorado Steam Navigation Co.) She was in service on the Colorado River. In September 1874 she was wrecked.

Ninsongis 103377 (Canada) (freighter) She was built in 1894 at Simcoe ON Canada. 45.0' x 11.0' x 5.5' Wood. 7gt 5rt. Powered by a 3hp engine. In 1921–1931 she was owned by The Rat Portage Lumber Co. Ltd., St. Boniface MB.

Nipawin 138029 (Canada) (freighter) She was built in 1918 at The Pas MB Canada. 86.6' x 20.0' x 4.1' Wood. 185gt 128rt. Powered by 3hp engine. In 1918–1935 she was owned by the Ross Navigation Co. Ltd., The Pas MB. In 1935 she was reported as having been laid up at The Pas MB.

Nizina[666] (US) (freighter) She was built in 1909 at Seattle WA USA by the Moran Bros. She was assembled at Copper River, District of Alaska. 110' Wood. Powered by a steam engine. In 1909–1910 she was employed on the Copper River in the District of Alaska USA carrying both freight and passengers during construction of the Copper River and Northwestern Railroad in Alaska.

No Wonder (later *Wonder*) 130458 (US) (tug) She was built in 1877 at Portland OR USA by George Washington "Old Man" Weidler. 131.0' x 24.0' x 6.0' Wood. 319.9gt 225.62rt. Powered by two 16nhp horizontal (16" x 48") steam engines. In 1889 she was rebuilt at Portland OR USA as the *Wonder*. 135.3' x 27.8' x 5.6' Wood. 269gt 235nt. In 1877 she was owned by Willamette Steam Mills & Lumber Co. In 1884 she was owned by Weidler Mills. Portland OR USA. In 1889 she was owned by Willamette Steam Mills Co. In 1897 she was owned by the Shaver Transportation Co. (Red Collar fleet), Portland OR. She worked in the log towing service and was the first log towing vessel on the Willamette River. In 1933 she was reported to have been abandoned.

Nora 103915 (Canada) (passenger/ freight vessel) She was built in 1898 at Lake Bennett BC Canada by William Jenkin Stephens. 79.5' x 16' x 4.3' Wood. 100.93gt 64nt. Powered by a steam engine by Albion Iron Works, Victoria BC . In 1903 her engine was removed, and she was converted to a floating landing dock. In 1898 she was owned by Bennett Lake & Klondyke Navigation (B.L. & K.N.) Co. Ltd., Victoria BC. In 1900–1901 she was sold to the Klondyke Corporation Ltd. In 1903 she was owned by Harold B Robertson, Dawson YT. In 1898 she was registered at Victoria BC. In 1898 she was in Yukon River service. In 1903 she was reported as having been broken up at Dawson City YT.

Norcom (see *Evelyn*)

Norma 130787 (US) (passenger vessel) She was built in 1891 at Bridgeport ID USA by Jacob Kamm. 160.0' x 32.6' x 5.6' Wood. 488gt 452nt. Powered by two horizontal (high pressure 16" x 84") 17nhp steam engines. In 1891 she was owned by Miller, Kamm & Kerr. In 1895 she was employed on the Lewiston – Riparia route on the Snake River. In 1915 she was reported to have been abandoned at Portland OR.

North Pacific 018685 (US) (sidewheeler) (passenger/ freight vessel) She was built in 1871 at San Francisco CA USA. 166.8' x 29.0' x 10.3' Wood. 488.73gt 345nt. Powered by a 175nhp steam engine. In 1903 she ran on rocks off Marrowstone Point WA and sank.

North Pacific entering Vancouver Harbour
(Image from Vancouver Archives CVA 371–2215)

North Star (ex-*Governor Ramsey*; then *Anson Northup*; then *Pioneer*) (US register) (UK register) In 1858/1859 she was built on the Mississippi River by Captain Anson Northup, dismantled, and moved overland and re-assembled on the Red River. 90.0' x 24.0' x ? Wood. 75gt. Powered by a steam engine. In 1859 she was refitted at Netley Creek. In 1862 she was rebuilt in Georgetown MN USA. In 1858–1859 she was owned by Anson Northup. In 1859–1861 she was owned by JC & HC Burbank (J.C. Burbank & Co.), St. Paul, Minnesota USA. In 1861 she was purchased by the Hudson's Bay Co., London UK. She travelled from St. Paul MN to Fort Garry on June 10 to claim the $3000 prize offered by a group of American merchants for the first voyage up the Red River to Manitoba. In 1862 she was crushed by winter ice at Cook's Creek (off the Red River). In 1862 she carried gold prospectors but was abandoned at Fort Abercrombie because of Sioux unrest. In 1869, after the Riel Rebellion, she carried the Metis leader Louis Riel to Lower Fort Garry. In 1870 she carried Father Richot to negotiate with the Metis. Her boiler, which was transferred to the *White Horse Plains*, and was reused in the *Chief Commissioner*.

North Star 130739 (US) (passenger vessel) She was built in 1897 at Jennings MT USA by Louis Paquet. 130' x 26' x 4'. Wood. 379.88gt 265nt. Powered by two horizontal (high pressure 14" x 48") 13nhp steam engines. (Her engines were from the City of Salem [125466]). In 1897 she was owned by the International Transport in upper Kootenay service by Upper Kootenay Transportation Co. (American flag). In April 1898 she was wrecked. In 1898 she was laid up at Jennings MT when the Southern B.C. Railway was completed. In 1901 she was chartered by the A. Guthrie & Co. (the Great Northern Railroad contractor). In 1902 she was transferred to the Upper Columbia Tramway & Navigation Co. She was laid up in 1902 when her owner proved unwilling to pay the duty on the vessel after she was imported into Canada and in 1903 she was seized by Canada Customs.

North Star[667] (US) (freighter) She was built in 1897 at St. Michael AK. 75'. Wood. 28gt. Powered by a steam engine. In 1897 she was owned by Galesbury-Alaska Mining Co. She was reported to have been abandoned along the Koyukuk River.

North Star 130770 (US) (passenger/ freight vessel) In 1898 she was built at San Francisco CA USA. 46'. Wood. 28gt. Powered by a steam engine. She was reported as having been abandoned.

North Star[668,669] 200312 (US) (later Enterprise) 130967 (US) She was built in 1902 at Wenatchee WA. 84.5' x 17.1' x 3.6'. Wood. 129gt 92nt. Powered by two horizontal (8" x 36" high pressure) steam engines. In 1902 she was owned by O'Connor, Evans, and Ingram. On September 3, 1902, she was wrecked in the Entiat Rapids. She was salvaged by IJ Bailey. In 1903 she was sold to HS DePuy and Will Lake and renamed as the Enterprise (130967). She was employed in shallow draft service between Brewster and Riverside on the Okanagan River. In 1906 she was owned by the Columbia & Okanagan Steamboat Co. In 1908 she was moved through the Spokane Rapids to Kettle Falls. On July 12, 1915, she foundered at Brewster WA USA.

North Star[670] 204761 (US) (passenger vessel) In 1907 she was built at Wenatchee WA USA by Alex Watson Jr. 99.7' x 21.4' x 4.1'. Wood. 198gt 125nt. Powered by 130ihp two horizontal (high pressure 9" x 42") 5.4nhp steam engines. In 1907 she was owned by the Columbia & Okanagan Steamboat

Co. On July 8, 1915, while owned by the Columbia & Okanogan Steamboat Co. she was destroyed by fire at Wenatchee WA when the company's fleet was destroyed by a massive fire.

North West 130459 (US) (passenger vessel) She was built in 1889 at West Kelso OR USA by Joseph Kellogg. 134.7' x 27.5' x 4.8' Wood. 324gt 30int. Powered by two horizontal (12.5" x 54") 9.6nhp steam engines. In 1889 she was owned by Joseph Kellogg's Transportation Co. She was employed on the Portland – Toledo WA route. In 1907 she was owned by the North Coast Land Co. freighting supplies to the Bulkley Valley. In 1907 she was wrecked on the Skeena River.

Northcote and Minnow (Image from the Provincial Archives of Alberta)

Northcote[671,672] 078028 (Canada) (passenger/ freight vessel) She was built in 1877 at Grand Rapids MB Canada by Captain J Reeves and shipwrights from St. Paul MN. 150.0' x 28.5' x 4.5' Wood. 461.34gt 290.65rt. Powered by two horizontal (high-pressure) steam engines built by C Dumont, Cincinnati OH. (She used the engines from the *Saskatchewan* which was wrecked in August 1873). In 1880 her accommodation was rebuilt to hold 50 passengers. In 1877–1882 she was owned by the Hudson's Bay Co., London UK. In 1882 she was owned by the Winnipeg &Western Transportation Co., Winnipeg MB after being hauled above Grand Rapids. In 1898 she was owned by The Winnipeg and Western Transportation Co. Ltd., Winnipeg MB. She sailed down the Red River to The Pas, Fort a la Corne and Carleton House on the Saskatchewan River. In 1882 she sailed across Lake Winnipeg to Grand Rapids. She was hauled above the rapids and then sold. In 1883 she hit a rock and was repaired at Fort Pitt. In 1884 she sank at Medicine Hat, was refloated, and berthed for the winter. In 1885 she was employed as a troop ship at Batoche during the Riel Rebellion. In 1888 she was reported as having been out of service at Cumberland House MB. In 1899 she was declared as a hazard to children and was burned by the Cumberland House residents.

Northern[673] (US) (freighter) Wood. Powered by a steam engine. She is reported by Murray Lundberg to have worked in Alaska/YT in 1898.

Northern Light[674] 013789 (US) (passenger/ freight vessel) She was built in 1895 at San Francisco CA and assembled at St. Michael AK USA. 40' x 10' x 2.5'. Wood. 18gt 10nt. Powered by a steam engine. She foundered at the Koyukuk River AK and was reported to have been abandoned.

Northern Light 130778 (US) She was built in 1898 at Seattle WA USA. 119.8' x 22.9' x 4.1'. Wood. 265gt 147nt. Powered by a steam engine. Although she was built for the Klondike Gold Rush service on the Yukon River, she spent her career in Puget Sound. In 1920 she was reported as having been abandoned. Her engines were removed and installed in the sternwheeler *Fidalgo*.

Northern Light 212575 (US) (freighter) She was built in 1914 at Tanana AK. 410.0' x 11.0' x 2.3'. Wood. 12gt 13nt. Powered by a 35ihp steam engine.

Northern Light (see *Northland Light*)

Northern Light (see *Evelyn*)

Northern Pacific 130153 (US) She was built in 1879 at Mound City IL USA. Wood. 328.82gt. Powered by a steam engine. In 1879 she was owned by USA interests. In 1884 she was owned by Bismarck Dakota USA interests.

Northern Pacific No. 2 130195 (US) She was built in 1881 at Mound City IL USA. Wood. 253.94gt. Powered by a steam engine. In 1881 she was owned by USA interests. In 1884 she was owned by Bismarck Dakota USA interests.

Northerner (US) (sidewheeler) She was built in 1847 at New York USA by William H Brown. 203.6' Wood. Powered by a steam engine built by the Novelty Iron Works. In 1847–1850 she was owned by the Spofford & Tileston Company. In 1850 she was owned by a Mr. Howard as part of the Empire City Line. In 1850–1860 she was owned by the Pacific Mail Steamship Co. On October 10, 1858, while travelling southbound from Olympia to San Francisco, the Northerner was hit broadside by the steam tug Resolute in Dana's Straits. On January 8, 1860, she hit a rock near Centreville Beach south of Humboldt CA and was wrecked. Thirty-eight passengers and crew died.

The ***Northland Call*** with a boiler being winched aboard.
(Image from the Provincial Archives of Alberta)

Northland Call (later Northland Star) 134312 (Canada) (freighter, later a barge) She was built in 1912 at Athabasca Landing AB Canada (reportedly previously unregistered when built). 95.3' x 18.0' x 2.4' Wood. 103gt 55rt. Powered by a 3nhp steam engine. In 1911–1914 she was owned by the Northern Transportation Co., Athabasca Landing AB. George Duddy states that "After 1914, when the E.D. & B.C. Railway from Edmonton reached Mirror Landing, she was disassembled, and her machinery was sent to Peace River Alberta for use in the construction of a new vessel of the same name."

Northland Call[675] (later *Hudson's Hope*) 138024 (Canada) (passenger/ freight vessel) She was built in 1915 at Peace River Crossing AB Canada by Captain George Magar. 99.5' x 18.0' x 4.0'. Wood. 192gt 111rt. Powered by a 3.5nhp steam engine. Her engines, boiler and fittings came from the first *Northland Call*. In 1920 she was re-built and re-engined to 100' x 18' x ? 192gt. In 1915 she was owned by the Peace River Navigation Co., Peace River Crossing AB. In 1919–1920 she was owned by the Peace River Development Corp. In 1920 she was rebuilt but her new engines were too heavy for her framework. In 1921–1924 she was owned by the Alberta and Arctic Navigation Co. Ltd. She was in service on the Peace River. The re-building was not successful, and after removal of her machinery she was reported as later having been abandoned. In October 1924 she was burned "to tidy up the waterfront". In 1931 she was still listed in the Canada Registry of Shipping. George Duddy notes: "The name of this vessel does not seem to have ever been officially changed from *Northland Call*. So whatever name she displayed as *Hudson Hope* or *Hudson's Hope* is speculative as they were not official names."

Northland Echo 134311 (Canada) (freighter) She was built in 1912 at Athabasca Landing AB Canada. 120.0' x 24.0' x 3.5'. Wood. 147gt 79rt. Powered by a 5hp steam engine. In 1912–1923 she was owned by the Northern Transportation Co. Ltd., Athabasca Landing AB. In 1914 she was one of the two remaining vessels that J.K. Cornwall reportedly took down from Athabasca Landing through the upper rapids of the Athabasca River after the railway construction reached Lesser Slave Lake. She was successively employed on the lower Athabasca River until 1922 when she was hauled onto the riverbank at Waterways AB to serve as a bunkhouse for construction workers for a replacement vessel of the same name. George Duddy notes that "Northern Transportation Company sternwheelers were not registered prior to 1914 when the feet was registered as a batch. It is difficult to follow her history as there appears to have been a confusion of names used between the vessel in the fleet and reporting of vessel dimensions in newspaper articles that vary considerably."

Northland Echo[676] 138812 (Canada) (passenger/ freight vessel) She was built in 1923 at Waterways AB Canada by the Northern Boat Building Co.

Ltd. 137.6' x 24.3' x 5.4' Wood. 532.11gt 335.23rt. Powered by a 5ihp horizontal non-condensing steam engine built by the Vulcan Iron Works (her boilers were fired by cordwood). In 1923–1928 she was owned by the Athabasca Shipping Company (JK Cornwall), Edmonton AB. In 1928–1947 she was owned by the Hudson's Bay Co., London UK. She was employed on the Athabasca and Upper Slave Rivers between McMurray and Fitzgerald. In 1945 she was reported as having been laid up and in 1946 as having been broken up.

Northland Echo (Image from Alberta Provincial Archives)

Northland Light (ex-Northern Light) 122607 (Canada) (sidewheeler) (freighter) She was built in 1907 at Athabasca Landing AB. 122.0' x 22.0' x 4.5' Wood. 148gt 94rt. Powered by a 5ihp steam engine. In 1909–1914 she was owned by Northern Transportation Co Ltd., Athabasca Landing AB and was employed on Lesser Slave Lake. (She was registered in Kenora ON). She was converted to a propeller in 1913. George Duddy states, "She was originally named as the *Northern Light* but years after when the owners went to register her, they apparently found that there was at least one other vessel with that name, so her registered name became the *Northland Light*. She was employed primarily crossing Lesser Slave Lake before the new railway put her and her competitors out of business. The registrations and dimensions of the *Northland Sun* and *Northland Light* may have been mixed up."

Northland Star (ex-*Northland Call*) 134313 (Canada) (freighter, later a barge) She was built in 1909 at Athabasca Landing AB Canada by Captain C.D. Barber. (She was reported to have been unregistered when built and later renamed as the *Northland Star* for registration purposes. 67.0' x 12.5' x 2.0' Wood. 19gt 12rt. Powered by a steam engine. In 1918 she was rebuilt as a barge. In 1909–1914c she was owned by The Northern Transportation Co. Ltd., Athabasca Landing AB. In 1914, when the railroad construction reached Lesser Slave Lake and railways made water transportation redundant, she was taken through the Grand Rapids of the Athabasca River by JK Cornwall to Fort McMurray. She was employed on the Athabasca-Slave Rivers from Fort McMurray to Fort Fitzgerald. George Duddy notes that the "Northern Transportation Company sternwheelers were not registered prior to 1914 when the fleet was registered as a batch. It is difficult to follow their histories as there appears to have confusion of names used between the vessel in the fleet and reporting of vessel dimensions in newspaper articles that vary considerably."

Northland Star (Image from the Provincial Archives of Alberta)

Northland Sun 122608 (Canada) (freighter) She was built in 1907 at Athabasca Landing AB Canada by Captain Charles Barber. 122.0' x 22.0' x 4.5' Wood. 148gt 94rt. Powered by a 5nhp steam engine. In 1907 she was owned by Charles Barber. In 1913–1931 she was owned by The Northern Transportation Company Ltd., Athabasca Landing AB. She was employed on the Athabasca River from Athabasca Landing to Mirror Landing. In 1915 she was reported as having been abandoned. Her machinery was reported being removed at Sawridge on Lesser Slave in September 1917. In 1931 she was still listed in the Canada Register of Shipping. George Duddy notes that the "Northern Transportation Company sternwheelers were not registered prior to 1914 when the fleet was registered as a batch. It is difficult to follow their histories as there appears to have confusion of names used between the vessel in the fleet and reporting of vessel dimensions in newspaper articles that vary considerably."

Northland Sun (Image from the Provincial Archives of Alberta)

North-West[677,678] 078005 (Canada) (passenger/ freight vessel) She was built in 1881 at Moorhead MN USA by John Irish. 200' x 33' x 4.5' Wood. 425gt 325rt. Powered by two horizontal non-condensing steam engines built by Pioneer Iron Works, La Crosse WI. In 1881 she was owned by Peter McArthur. In 1881 she was owned by the North Western Transportation Co. Ltd., Winnipeg MB. In 1883 she was damaged at Victoria Rapids, repaired at Grand Rapids, and beached as Cumberland House. In 1884–1899 she was owned by The Winnipeg and Western Transportation Co. Ltd., Winnipeg MB. In 1885 she served carrying forces during the Riel Rebellion. In 1886–1898 she was employed between Grand Rapids and Prince Albert and Edmonton. In 1899 she was wrecked at Edmonton NWT during a flood. Her boilers were salvaged and used to power a sawmill at Victoria Settlement near Smoky Lake AB.

Northwest[679] 122366 (Canada) 0122366 (US) (passenger/ freight vessel) She was built in 1889 at Portland OR USA by Kellogg Transportation Co. 135' x 28' x ? Wood. 638.14gt 387.63rt. Powered by two horizontal (high pressure 12.5" x 54") steam 9.6nhp engines. In 1889 she was owned by the Joseph Kellogg Transportation Co. In 1907 she was owned by the North Coast Land Co., WA USA. In 1907 she was owned by the British Columbia Transportation & Commercial Co. Ltd., Vancouver BC. She was reported to have been constructed in West Kelso WA USA. In 1907 she was registered in Vancouver BC. She was employed by the North Coast Land Co. for transporting material to Telkwa where they were developing. On September 13, 1907, she was wrecked on the Skeena River.

Northwest 130101 (US) (passenger vessel) She was built in 1877 at Columbus WA by Small Bros. 124' x 24' x 4.5' Wood. 356.18gt 274.62rt. Powered by two horizontal (high pressure 14" x48") 13nhp steam engines. In 1885 she was reported as being broken up at Celilo OR.

Northwestern (see *Caledonia*)

Northwestern (see *Grahamona*)

Nowitka 130604 (Canada) (freighter) She was built in 1911 at Golden BC Canada by Esquimalt Marine Railway Co. 80.5' x 19' x 3.5' Wood. 113gt 62rt. Powered by a 4nhp steam engine. In 1911 she was owned by Captain FP Armstrong. In 1911–1937 she was owned by the Columbia River Lumber Co. for Upper Columbia River service. She was powered by a steam engine originally built in 1840 and used in the *Duchess* (I), *Duchess* (II) and the *Ptarmigan*. Her pilot house was from the *North Star*. She was laid up in 1920. In 1931 she was still listed in the Canada Registry of Shipping.

Nugget[680] (US) (freighter) In 1898 she was built at St. Michael AK. Wood. 5gt. Powered by a steam engine. She is reported by Murray Lundberg to have worked in Alaska/YT in 1898.

Nunivak 200528 (USCGS) (sidewheeler) (passenger/ freight vessel) She was built in 1898 at San Francisco CA USA by Union Iron Works (Bethlehem Steel. Company). 180' x 37' x 7' Steel. 681gt 429nt. Powered by a steam engine. In 1898 she was owned by the United States Coast & Geodetic Survey. She was employed on the Yukon River. In 1900 she was owned by the United States Revenue Cutter Service. In 1905 she was owned by the American Transportation & Trading Co. On May 07, 1909, she was wrecked at Tenana River AK.

O. & C.R.R. Ferry No. 1 (sidewheeler) (ferry) She was built in 1870 at Portland OR. 180' Wood. 658gt. In 1880 she was reported to have been out of service.

O. & C. R. R. Ferry No. 2 (later *Vallejo*) 155011 (US) (sidewheeler) (ferry) She was built in 1879 at East Portland OR USA. 123.2' x 31.5' x 9.9' Wood. 414gt 255nt. Powered by a 445ihp steam engine. In 1898 she was moved to California waters.

O.K.[681] 019150 (US) (sidewheeler) She was built in 1862 at San Lorenzo CA. Wood. 78.35gt. Powered by a steam engine. In 1862–1864 she was employed in the California river delta system, on the San Joaquin River. In 1862–1864 she was owned by the Mokelumne River Steam Navigation Company. She was reported to have been lost in 1867.

Oakes (US) (freighter) She was built in 1892 at Flathead Lake MT by Mike Birne. 75' Wood. In 1892 she was owned by the Columbia Falls Improvement Co. In 1892 she was wrecked on the North Fork of the Flathead River attempting to carry coal from the North Fork mine.

Oakland 019149 (US) (ferry) She was built in 1859 at San Francisco CA USA. Wood. 308gt. Powered by a steam engine. She was abandoned about 1874.

Oakland 019447 (US) (sidewheeler) (ferry) She was built in 1875 as the *Chrysopolis* at Oakland CA USA by Patrick H Tiernan 265.0' x 41.5' x 16.0' Wood. 1672.24gt 1108.45nt. Powered by a 200nhp steam engine. She was rebuilt and became, in 1875, the ferry, *Oakland* (19447). She served as an Oakland – San Francisco ferry until the completion of the Oakland · San Francisco Bay Bridge. She was reported as having been broken up and burned in 1940.

Occident[682] 019448 (US) (passenger vessel) She was built in 1875 at Portland OR. 154' x 35.8' x 5' Wood. 587gt 430nt. Powered by two horizontal (high pressure 16" x 66") steam engines. In 1875 she was owned by the Willamette River Transportation Co. In 1891 she was reported to have been broken up at Portland OR.

Ocean Wave 155207 (US) (sidewheeler) (ferry) (passenger) She was built in 1891 at Portland OR USA by Jacob Kamm. 180.0' x 29.0' x 9.0' Wood. 724gt 507nt. Powered by a 500ihp (18" x 84") 21.6nhp steam engine. In 1891 she was employed on the Portland to Ilwaco route. In 1898 she was employed on Puget Sound – Vancouver route. In 1899 she was transferred to California. In 1920s she was converted to a floating restaurant.

Ocklahoma[683] 019471 (US) (freighter) She was built in 1876 at Portland OR USA by the Buchanan Bros. 162.0' x 31.5' x 8.0' Wood. 581.62gt 394.19rt. Powered by (21" x 72") steam engine. (Her engines came from the *Alexandria*). In 1876 she was owned by the Willamette Transportation & Locks Co. employed towing on the Columbia and Willamette Rivers. She was owned by the Oregon Steam Navigation Co. In 1886 she was crushed by the unballasted bark *Alliance* when she capsized. She was rebuilt in 1897.

Ocklahama[684,685] 155310 (US) (tug) She was built in 1897 at Portland OR USA from the earlier *Ocklahoma*. 161.1' x 33.5' x 8.3' Wood. 676gt 565rt. Powered by steam engines from the first *Ocklahama*. In 1897–1916 she was owned by the Port of Portland, Portland OR. On August 23, 1913, while in tow of the *Ocklahama* the German bark *Thielbek* collided with the *Thode Fagelund*. In 1916–1930 she was owned by the Western Transportation Co. In 1930 she was reported to have been abandoned.

Odd Fellow (US) She was built about 1850. Wood. Powered by a steam engine. She was employed on the Sacramento River CA.

Ogilvie 107148 (Canada) (passenger/ freight vessel) She was built in 1898 at Vancouver BC by James M Bulgar. 146.8' x 30' x 4.6' Wood. 741gt 453rt. Powered by a steam engine. In 1898 she was owned by the Canadian Pacific Railway, Montreal QC. In 1901 she was owned by the British Yukon Navigation Company. In 1901 she was reported as having been broken up at Skagway AK (and she may possibly have been rebuilt as a barge?).

Ogilvie[686] (US) (freighter) Wood. Powered by a steam engine. She is reported by Murray Lundberg to have worked in Alaska/YT in 1898–1901.

Ohio (see *Lady Washington*)

Oil City 155318 (US) She was built in 1898 at Seattle WA USA by the Moran Bros. Shipyard. 176.1' x 35.4' x 5.9'. Wood. 718.68gt 409.06nt Powered by two horizontal high pressure, (20" x 84"), steam engines by the Moran Bros., Seattle WA USA. In 1898 she was owned by Standard Oil Co. of California. In 1904 she was owned by Charles W Adams. In 1905 she was owned by Charles W Adams, Mersereau Clark and the Dominion Commercial Co. In 1908 she was owned by the Northern Navigation Co. She was owned by the Alaska-Yukon Navigation Co. In 1914 she was owned by the White Pass & Yukon Rail Road. She worked with the fuel barge *Petrolia* on the Yukon River distributing kerosene and candles and towing five general cargo barges. She was used by the White Pass & Yukon RR as an office and warehouse at Holy Cross AK and abandoned in 1943.

Okanagan (Image from Maritime Museum of British Columbia 000408)

Okanagan 090787 (Canada) (passenger/ freight vessel) She was built in 1887 at Enderby BC Canada by Gray & Drumbledon. 33' x 9' x ? Wood. 15gt. Powered by a steam engine. In 1888 she was rebuilt to 53' and installed with new machinery. In 1887 she was owed by the Columbia Milling Co. (J Nichols). In 1891 she was sold to the Lequime Brothers as a log tow boat. In 1894 she was sold for general service to Captain Angus Campbell. She was transferred in 1895 to Kootenay Lake service. She was employed in Shuswap River service, but her draught was too deep. She was reported as having been damaged, and the hull salvaged in 1888 and taken to the head of Okanagan Lake. In 1888 she was employed as a tugboat until 1913.

Okanagan 123378 (Canada) She was built in 1907 at Okanagan Landing BC Canada by James M Bulger. 193.2' x 32.3' x 8' Wood. 1078gt 679rt. Powered by a 32nhp steam engine. In 1907–1938 she was owned by Canadian Pacific Railway Co., Montreal QC. In 1934 she was laid up. In 1938 she was sold as a hulk to GRC Kerr at Kelowna BC and dismantled.

Okanogan[687,688] 204319 (US) (passenger vessel/ freighter) She was built in 1907 at Wenatchee WA USA by Alex Watson Jr. 136.5' x 34.0' x 6.0' Wood. 432gt 255nt. Powered by two 13nhp horizontal (14" x 72") steam 350ihp engines. In 1907 she was owned by the Columbia & Okanagan Steamboat Co. In 1912 she was based at Chelan Falls WA on the Columbia River. On July 8, 1915, while owned by the Columbia & Okanogan Steamboat Co. she was destroyed by fire at Wenatchee WA when the company's fleet was destroyed by a massive fire. (The name of this vessel is also reported as being spelled as *Okanagan*).

Okanagon[689] 019153 (US) She was built in 1861 at Deschutes OR. 118' x 24' x 5' Wood. 278gt. Powered by two 13nhp horizontal (high pressure 14" x 60") steam engines. In 1861 she was owned by Thompson & Co. She was employed on the Celilo to Wallula route. Later she was employed on the Astoria run. In 1876 she was reported to have been broken up at Portland OR USA.

Old Settler 019493 (US) (freighter) She was built in 1878 at Puget Sound WA USA. 39.5' x 10.0' x 2.6' Wood. 11.38gt. Powered by a 6nhp steam engine.

Olive 107623 (Canada) (freighter) She was built in 1899 at Nicomen BC Canada. 72.4' x 12.5' x 3.5' Wood. 71gt 45rt. Powered by a 4nhp steam engine. In 1899–1901 she was owned by Thomas M Wymonde, Vancouver BC. In 1902 she was owned by Captain Burr & C Merrick, Vancouver BC. In 1904 she was owned by John Leckie & TFE Kinnell, Vancouver BC. In 1906 she was owned by Fraser River Oil & Gas, Vancouver BC. In 1910–1916 she was owned by Canadian Fish Products Ltd., London UK.

Olive May (later *Dora*) 107514 (Canada) (passenger/ freight vessel) She was built in 1898 at Lake Bennett BC Canada by Albert S Kerry. 60' x 16.7' x 5' Wood. 85.26gt 53.72nt. Powered by two horizontal high pressure (6.5" x 40") steam engines by Washington Ironworks, Seattle WA USA. In 1898 she was owned by Albert S Kerry, Lake Linderman BC. In 1899 she was owned by the Bennett Lake, Klondyke Navigation Co. Ltd. She was sold in 1900 to the Klondyke Corporation, London UK. In 1902–1904 she was sold to Nathaniel B Raymond. In 1904 she was owned by L Roy. She was on the Taku City service. In 1899 she struck a rock and sank. She was salvaged. It was on this vessel that an incident is said to have occurred that inspired the poem written by Robert Service—"The Cremation of Sam McGee"—on the fictional steamer *Alice May*. In 1908 she was reported as having been broken up.

Olivia (US) She was built about 1850. Wood. Powered by a steam engine. She was employed on the Sacramento River CA.

Olympia[690] (later *Princess Louise*); (sidewheeler) (US); 072682 (Canada) She was built in 1869 at New York NY USA by John Roach and Sons. 180.0' x 3020' x 13.0' Wood. 931.76gt 544.01rt. Powered by a 350hp compound walking beam two-cylinder steam engine built by John Roach & Son, New York. In 1882 new boilers were installed by Victoria Iron Works. In 1885 she was rebuilt as a non-powered barge. In 1869 she was owned by Finch & Wright, Seattle WA employed in river service. In 1878–1883 she was owned by the Hudson's Bay Company for New Westminster to Victoria service. In 1883–1896 she was owned by the Canadian Pacific Navigation Co. Ltd., Victoria BC. In 1901–1907 she was owned by the Canadian Pacific Railway, Montreal QC. In 1907–1917 she was owned by the Vancouver Dredging & Salvage Co. (Clarence Marpole), Vancouver BC as a barge. In 1917–1921 she was owned by the Whalen Pulp & Paper Mills, Port Alice BC. In 1884 she was registered at Victoria BC. She was briefly involved in carrying ore to Tacoma WA. In 1919 she sank at Port Alice BC.

Olympian[691] 155089 (US) (sidewheeler) (ferry) She was built in 1883 at Wilmington CA by Harlan & Hollingworth. 261.5' x 40.0' x 12.5' Iron 1419.6gt 1083.2nt. Powered by 452nhp (70" x 144") steam engine. In 1884 she was owned by the Oregon Railway & Navigation Co. She was employed on the Victoria BC – Tacoma WA route. Later she was transferred to the Columbia River. Later she served on charter in Alaska. In 1906 she sank in the Pacific during a storm on her repositioning voyage from San Francisco CA to the eastern US via Cape Horn.

Olympian (see *Telegraph*)

Omenica 126248 (Canada) (passenger/ freight vessel) She was built in 1909 at Victoria BC by Alex Watson Jr. 137.5' x 31.4' x 5.1' Wood. 168gt. Powered by two horizontal (6" x 72" high pressure) 17nhp steam engines by Albion Iron Works, Victoria BC. In 1909–1915 she was owned by John William Stewart, Vancouver BC (Foley, Welch & Stewart contractors to GTP). In 1915 she was owned by the Alaskan Engineering Commission. In 1923–1930 she was owned by the Alaskan Rail Road. Her engines came from the *Caledonia* (107145). On November 8, 1909, she was wrecked in the Skeena River when she was ascending with supplies for Duncan Ross' construction camp at Hazelton BC. She had been lining over a particularly bad section of rapids when the cable parted, and the bow swung out into the main current, and she was driven on the rocks at full speed. The cargo was salvaged, and the passengers put ashore and walked the 15 miles to Hazelton. The steamer *Distributor* gave aid, and she was left for the winter. She was later used on the Susitna River and on Cook Inlet during construction of the US Government Rail Road. In 1930 she was laid up.

Omilak Chief 205772 (US) She was built in 1906 at Chinik AK USA. 70.0' x 15.0' x 2.2' Wood. 65gt 57nt. Powered by 60ihp gasoline engine. She was employed in Alaskan waters.

Oneatta 019357 (US) (sidewheeler) She was built in 1872 at Pioneer City OR USA. 82' x 14' x 2'. Wood. 118.15gt 76.54rt. Powered by a (13" x 36") steam engine. In 1872 she was owned by George Kellogg. In 1881 she was rebuilt to 89.5' x 15.3' x 4.7' as a sternwheeler. In 1881 she was owned by Frederick Congdon. In 1882 she was employed on Humboldt Bay.

Oneonta[692] 019151 (US) (sidewheeler) (passenger vessel, later a barge) She was built in 1863 at Cascades OR by Samuel Forman. 182' x 28.5' 8.5'. Wood. 497gt. Powered by a (18" x 72") 21nhp steam engine. She had distinctive design with two funnels side-by-side. In 1863 she was owned by the Oregon Steam Navigation Co. employed in service between the Cascades and The Dalles. In 1870 she was owned by John C Ainsworth. She was transferred to the Portland route. In 1877 she was converted to a barge until she was reported as abandoned in 1880.

Onisbo[693,694] 155384 (US) (passenger vessel) She was built in 1900 at Wood. Island CA USA. 178.1' x 36.6' x 6.5'. Wood. 632gt 605rt. Powered by a 250ihp steam engine. She was in service on California rivers. On June 18, 1903, she collided with the British ship *Castle Rock* laying at anchor off Benicia CA. She was run onto the mudflats in serious condition. She was reported to have been abandoned about 1923.

Onward 040392 (Canada) (passenger/ freight vessel, later a barge) She was built in 1865 at Victoria, British Columbia by James W Trahey. 120.5' x 21.3' x 7.4'. Wood. 283gt 220rt. Powered by a 90hp 14" x 54" steam engine. In 1876 she was rebuilt as a barge. In 1865 she was owned by Captain William Irving, New Westminster BC. In 1865 she was owned by the Pioneer Line. In 1865 she was chartered to the Cowlitz Coal Mining Co. to carry supplies from Victoria to the miners at Cowlitz in the Queen Charlotte Islands. She was registered on March 02, 1871. In 1873–1896 she was owned by William Irving, New Westminster BC. She had 21 staterooms. She was in Fraser River service in 1865. In 1876 she was reported as having been broken up with her engines going to the *Reliance*.

Onward[695] 019154 (US) She was built in 1858 at Canemah OT. 120' x 26' x 4'. Wood. 120gt. Powered by two 17nhp (high pressure) 16" x 60") steam engines. In 1858 she was owned by A. Jameson. In 1864 she was owned by the People's Transportation Co. In 1865 she was reported as having been dismantled at Canemah OR.

Onward[696] 019274 (US) She was built in 1867 at Tualatin River Landing OT by CF Kent and John Colman. 98' x 18.3' x 4.6'. Wood. 155gt 81nt. Powered by two (10.25" x 48") horizontal steam engines. In 1867 she was owned by Joseph Kellogg. In 1875 she was employed on the Umpqua River. In 1878 she was reported to have been abandoned.

Onward at Emery Bar (Image from Maritime Museum of British Columbia 000442)

Onward[697] 019480 (US) She was built in 1877 at San Francisco CA USA by George D Damon. Wood. 388.8gt 337.3rt. Powered by a 262nhp steam engine. She was employed on California rivers. She went out of service about 1909.

Operator 126501 (Canada) (passenger/ freight vessel) She was built in 1909 at Victoria BC Canada. She is sometimes reported to have been built by GA MacNicholl, but this seems unlikely as he was only the GTP Purchasing

Agent. 137.5' x 31.4' x 5.4'. Wood. 583gt 37rt. She was powered by a steam engine. In 1909–1911 she was owned by the Canadian Pacific Railway, Montreal QC. She was in service in railway construction up the Skeena River. She could carry 200 passengers and 200 tons of cargo. She pushed a loaded barge also carrying 100 tons of cargo. In 1911 she was reported as having been broken up and her machinery used for installation in new vessels. The machinery was later shipped to Tete Jaune Cache and her machinery eventually ended up being sold for use in sawmills.

Operator 130886 (Canada) (passenger/ freight vessel) She was prefabricated at New Westminster BC and assembled in 1912 at Tete Jaune Cache BC Canada by George F Askew. 141.7' x 34.8' x 5.2'. Wood. 698gt 439rt. Powered by a 15ihp steam engine. In 1912–1918 she was owned by John W Stewart, Vancouver BC. In 1919–1937 she was owned by the Pacific Great Eastern Railway Co., Victoria BC. Her machinery originated in the *Operator* (I). She was used for the construction of the Grand Trunk Pacific Railway. In 1915 she was laid up at Prince George BC. In 1931 she was still listed in the Canada Registry of Shipping.

Ora 103914 (Canada) (passenger/ freight vessel later a barge) She was built in 1898 at Lake Bennett BC. 79.5' x 16.0' x 4.3'. Wood. 101gt 64rt. Powered by a steam engine. The boilers were built by the Albion Iron Works Co. Ltd. In 1902 she was converted to a non-powered barge. In 1898 she was owned by Lake Bennett & Klondyke Navigation (LB & KN) Co. Ltd., Victoria BC. In 1900–1901 she was owned by the Klondyke Corp. In 1902 she was incorporated into a gold dredge on the lower reaches of the Forty Mile River. In 1909–1910 she was owned by Edward J Smythe, Victoria BC.

Oregon[698] (US) (sidewheeler) (passenger vessel) She was built in 1852 at Fairfield OT. 120' x 22' x 5'. Wood. Powered by a 13nhp (14" x 48") steam engine. In 1852 she was owned by B Simpson et al. In 1854 she was wrecked in the Kaiser Rapids.

Oregon[699] 155347 (US) (sidewheeler) (ferry) In 1899 she was built at Arlington OR USA. 48.4' x 25.5' x 3.5'. Wood. 39gt 21rt. Powered by a steam engine. She was employed on the Columbia River. In 1918 she was reported as having gone out of service.

Oregon Pony (US) Wood. Powered by a steam engine. In 1864 she carried passengers and freight past the rapids at The Dalles on the Columbia River.

Oregona[700] (later *Interstate*) 200949 (US) (sidewheeler) (passenger vessel) She was built in 1904 at Portland OR USA. 131.5' x 26.7' x 5.0' Wood. 370gt 281rt. Powered by 500ihp two horizontal (high pressure 9" x 48") steam engines. In 1904–1910 she was employed on the Columbia River. In 1924 she was rebuilt at Vancouver WA as the *Interstate* (223545). She was operated by the Greyhound Transportation Co. In 1936 she was reported to have been abandoned.

Oregonian[701] 019219 (US) (sidewheeler) She was built in 1866 at Wiliiamsburg NY. Wood. 1,914gt. Powered by a steam engine. She was home ported at Portland OR. In 1875 she was reported to have been sold to foreign interests.

Orient[702] (US) (freighter, later a barge) She was built in 1851 at San Francisco CA USA by Ralph Butler. Wood. 47gt. Powered by a steam engine. In 1854 she was owned by the California Steam Navigation Co. She was employed on California rivers. She was reported to have gone out of service about 1858 after she sank in the Old River and her machinery was removed and she was converted into a barge.

Orient 019449 (US) (passenger) She was built in 1875 at Portland OR USA. 154.4' x 35.8' x 5.0' Wood. 586.95gt 429.76nt. Powered by two 17nhp horizontal (high pressure 16" x 72") steam engines. In 1875 she was owned by the Willamette River Transportation Co. In 1892 she was owned by Captain Callahan. In 1893 she allided with the Morrison Street Drawbridge. In 1894 she sank in the Cowlitz Rive. She was destroyed by a fire.

Oriflamme (US) (sidewheeler) She was built in 1864 at New York NY USA. Powered by a steam engine. In 1864 she was a gunboat for the United States Navy, but never commissioned. She came to the US northwest in 1866. She was sold into the China trade. She was owned by Benjamin Holladay, San Francisco CA USA who used this ship for private parties, some of which lasted all the way from San Francisco to Alaska. She is reported by Murray Lundberg to have worked in Alaska/YT.

Oriole[703] 201749 (US) (passenger vessel) In 1905 she was built at Sacramento CA USA. 81.5' x 17.8' x 3.9'. Wood. 68.1gt 59nt. Powered by a 75ihp steam engine. She was in service on California rivers. She was destroyed by fire in 1921.

Orizaba 019148 (US) (sidewheeler) She was built in 1854 at New York NY USA by Jacob A. Westervelt and Co. Wood. 1244.08gt 894.18rt. Powered by a 500nhp steam engine. In 1854 she was owned by the New York-New Orleans-Vera Cruz line of Morgan and Harris. In 1865 she was owned by the Pacific Mail Steamship Co. In 1865 she was sold to the California Steam Navigation Company. In 1867 she was owned by the California, Oregon, and Mexico Steamship Co. In 1884–1887 she was owned by San Francisco CA USA interests. She was a gold ship which arrived at Victoria in July 1858 with 786 passengers on board. She made two voyages from New York to San Juan de Nicaragua in April and May 1856 but was sent to San Francisco (arriving October 30, 1856) for service on the San Francisco – Panama run. In 1865 she served on the San Francisco-Portland-Victoria run. She continued service on the Pacific coast until broken up in 1887.

Oro 019497 (US) She was built in 1878 at San Francisco CA USA. 39.0' x 9.8' x 2.6'. Wood. 6.1gt. She was powered with a 7nhp steam engine.

Oro[704] 155285 (US) (passenger/ freight vessel) She was built in 1896 at Wenatchee WA USA. 83.7' x 18.9' x 4.4'. Wood. 103.42gt 42.57nt. Powered by a steam engine. In 1896 she was owned by the Columbia & Okanagan Steamboat Co., Wenatchee WA USA. In 1898 she was reported to have been out of service.

Orondo Ferry[705] 225272 (US) (sidewheeler) (ferry) She was built in 1925 at Orondo WA. 51.4' x 14.0' x 3.2'. Wood. 21gt 19nt. Powered by an 80ihp gasoline engine. In 1931 she was owned by Fred Boyd, Orondo WA.

Oroville[706] (sidewheeler) She was built in 1856 at Marysville CA. Wood. 49gt. Powered by a steam engine. She was home ported at San Francisco CA. In 1867 she was reported to have been lost.

Ottawa (see *Kehani*)

Ottawa 202283 (US) (tug) She was built in 1905 at Portland OR USA. 89.0' x 18.0' x 5.0' Wood. 77gt 72nt. Powered by two horizontal (high pressure 10.5" x 48") steam engines. The fittings from the *Kehani* (161034) were used in her construction. In 1905 she was owned by the Oregon Round Lumber Co. She was in service on the Columbia River. In 1902 she was reported as having been abandoned at Portland OR.

Otter 019407 (US) (passenger/ freight vessel, later tug) She was built in 1874 at Portland OR USA. 87.3' x 17.9' x 6.3' Wood. 123gt 92nt. Powered by a steam engine. In 1874 she was owned by Fred Congdon, Portland, OR USA. In 1874 she was owned by the Oregon Steam Navigation Co. (on completion). In 1877 she was owned by Starr Brothers for the Tacoma – Olympia route. In 1888 she was owned by T Cook & R Brown, Tacoma WA USA as a trading boat on Puget Sound WA USA. In 1874 she was transferred to Puget Sound for towing barges for the Renton Coal Co. In 1890 she was severely damaged in a collision with the *Hassalo* off Des Moines. In 1897 she was in service on the Stikine River. Her engines were transferred to the *Minneapolis* in 1898. In 1897 she was reported as having been broken up at the Puyallip River WA USA.

Owen Tronsdahl (US) (passenger vessel) She was built in 1966 at Conway WA USA by Howard Boling. 65' x 18' x ? Wood. Powered by a 180hp diesel engine by Gray Marine. In 1966 she was owned by Owen Tronsdahl, Conway WA.

Owyhee[707] 019152 (US) She was built in 1864 at Celilo OT by JW Gates. 123.5' x 24.2' x 4.6' Wood. 313.46gt. Powered by two 16nhp horizontal (high pressure 16" x 48") steam engines. In 1864 she was owned by the Oregon Steam Navigation Co. In 1876 she was reported as having been broken up at Celilo OR. Her engines went to the *Welcome* (080537).

P.W.D. 250 (later D.P.W. 250; then D 250) (Canada) (dredge) She was built in 1946 at Edmonton AB Canada. 100.1' x 24.6' x 5.7' Steel. 209gt 121rt. Powered by a 135hp engine. In 1953 she was rebuilt at Waterways AB. In 1946–1979 she was owned by The Minister of Public Works, Ottawa ON. In 2001–2003 she was owned by the Minister of Public Works and Government Services, Ottawa ON. When the vessel was retired the federal government deposited the vessel in the collection of the Fort McMurray Heritage Shipyard where it has been restored and put on display.

P.W.D. No. 305 (see King Edward)

P.W.D. 250 / D.P.W. 250 dredge hauled out (Image from the Dwight LaRiviere collection)

P.W.D. Red River 150799 (Canada) She was built in 1922 at Selkirk MB Canada. 116.8' x 31.6' x 6.1' Wood. 404gt 208rt. Powered by a 13nhp steam engine. In 1922–1945 she was owned by The Minister of Public Works, Ottawa ON. She was employed in Manitoba waters.

P.W.D. Red River II 175565 (Canada) (dredge) She was built in 1947 at Selkirk MB Canada by Dominion Bridge Co. Ltd. 106.0' x 33.8' x 6.6' Steel. 253.19gt 210.97rt. Powered by two 180bhp diesel engines by Caterpillar Tractor Co., Peoria IL USA. In 1947–1961 she was owned by The Minister of Public Works, Ottawa ON. She was employed in Manitoba waters. In 1966 she was reported to have been broken up.

Pacific (US) (sidewheeler) Powered by a steam engine. She was originally owned by the Pacific Mail Steamship Co. In 1860 she was owned by the California Steam Navigation Co. In 1867 she was owned by the California, Oregon, and Mexico Steamship Co. During the Cassiar Gold Rush many miners arrived in Victoria seeking transportation to San Francisco and there the vessel took on an overload—132 passengers added to the 35 added in Puget Sound. It is thought that an additional unrecorded twenty passengers were also carried. Thinking he had seen the Lighthouse light at Tatoosh Island, the mate of the *Orpheus* ordered a course correction. The captain heaved-to while they considered the situation. Realizing that there was a steamer headed toward them they blew their whistle in warning. The *Pacific* struck the sailing ship *Orpheus* causing considerable damage and did not stop to stand by the injured vessel.

Pacific Slope (later *Myra*) 083444 (Canada) (passenger/ freight vessel) She was built in 1882 at Victoria BC by JG Walker. 92.0' x 22.7' x 3.3' Wood. 81gt 71.88rt. Powered by a 26.97hp steam engine. In 1881 she was owned by Captain William Moore, Victoria BC. In 1882 she was sold to Andrew Onderdonk. In 1895–1901 she was owned by John Trutch, Yale BC. She was launched March 1882. In 1884 she was reported as having been broken up, her fittings and engine to the Kamloops.

Paddlewheel Princess 322531 (Canada) (passenger/ freight vessel, later a ferry) She was built in 1966 at Selkirk MB Canada by Selkirk Machine Works Ltd. 21.6m x 7.8m x 1.4m (71.0') Steel. 216gt 174rt. Powered by a 226bhp diesel engine by Scripps Motor Co., Detroit MI USA. In 1974–2013 she was owned by Paddlewheel Riverboats Ltd., Selkirk MB. In 2013–2017 she was owned by Red One Investment Ltd., Winnipeg MB. In 2013 she was laid up in a slough at Selkirk MB. On May 11, 2017, she was set afire and destroyed by arsonists.

Paddlewheel Queen 322527 (Canada) (passenger/ freight vessel) She was built in 1965 at Selkirk MB Canada by Selkirk Machine Works Ltd. 89.8' x 31.5' x 4.6' Steel. 288.52gt 226.19rt. Powered by two 145bbhp diesel engines by General Motors Corporation, Detroit MI USA. In 1968 she was rebuilt by Selkirk MB. 34.7m x 9.6m x 1.4m Steel. 446.22gt 408.17rt. In 1965–1966 she was owned by Red River Construction Co. Ltd., Winnipeg MB. In 1966–1968 she was owned by Red River Excursions Ltd., Winnipeg MB. In 1968–2017 she was owned by Paddlewheel Riverboats Ltd., Selkirk MB. In 2018–2020 she was owned by Breezy North Construction Inc., Selkirk MB.

Pah Loong (see *Anna*)

Paloma (later *Geo. W. Bates*) 150941 (US) (passenger vessel) She was built in 1902 at Portland OR USA. 107.5' x 21.4' x 4.7' Wood. 137gt 115nt. Powered by two horizontal (high pressure 11" x 36") steam engines. In 1902–1909 she was owned by the Columbia Digger Co., Portland OR. In 1909 she was rebuilt at St. Johns OR by Thomas Thompson. 107.5' x 21.4' x 4.7.' In 1919 she was renamed as the *Geo. W. Bates*. In 1935 she was reported as having been abandoned.

Panama[708] 214696 (US) (ferry) She was built in 1914 at White Salmon WA by AJ Shipler. 52.0' x 20.8' x 2.7' Wood. 15gt 14nt. Powered by a gasoline engine. In 1914 she was owned by Dean & Shipler, Portland OR. In 1922 she was transferred to Mexican registry.

Parthenius[709] (US) (sidewheeler) She was built in 1869 at San Francisco CA by John G North. 154' Wood. 294gt. Powered by a steam engine. She was employed on California rivers. She went out of service about 1881.

Pasco-Burbank Ferry 214397 (US) (ferry) She was built in 1916 at Pasco WA. 57.7' x 22.0' x 3.2' Wood. 37gt. Powered by a gasoline engine. In 1922 she was reported to have been abandoned.

Pastime[710] 150866 (US) (workboat) She was built in 1900 at Coquille WA USA. 45' x 9.5' 1.8' Wood. 11gt 5nt. Powered by a gasoline engine. In 1901 she was reported to have been out of service.

Paul Pry[711,712] 020107(US) (sidewheeler) She was built about 1856 at San Francisco CA by Patrick H. Tiernan. Wood. 229gt. Powered by a steam engine. In 1854 she was owned by the California Steam Navigation Co. In 1871 she was taken over by the California Pacific Railroad Co., San Francisco CA. She was in service on California rivers. She went out of service in 1877 and was reported to have been abandoned.

Paul Waters (aka *Paul Walters*) (US) (passenger/ freight vessel) She was built in 1898 at Puget Sound WA USA. 130' x 25' x ? Wood. Powered by a steam engine. In 1898 she was owned by the Klondike-Chicago Transportation

& Trading Co. She is reported by Murray Lundberg to have worked in Alaska/YT 1898.

Pauline[713,714] 116611 (Canada) (freighter) She was built in 1907 at Whitehorse YT Canada by Nathaniel B Raymond. 86.0' x 16.0' x ? Wood. 145gt 91.46rt. Powered by s steam engine. In 1907 she was owned by the Stewart River Navigation Co. In 1909 she was owned by the Side Streams Navigation Co. In 1910 she was owned by Nathaniel B Jones and John S Raymond, Whitehorse YT. In 1915 she was crushed in the ice at Dawson City YT. She was wrecked in May 1917 by ice at Sunnydale BC.

Paystreak 126279 (Canada) She was built in 1909 at New Westminster BC Canada. 126.5' x 26.4' x 4.9' Wood. 282gt 210rt. She was powered by a steam engine. In 1920 she was rebuilt as a barge. In 1909–1910 she was owned by the Royal City Navigation Co., New Westminster BC. In 1920–1931 she was owned by the Millerd Packing Co. Ltd., Vancouver BC. She was in service in construction of the Canadian Northern Pacific Railway on the Fraser River.

Peace River (Image from the Provincial Archives of Alberta)

Peace River 121777 (Canada) (freighter) She was built in 1906 at Fort Vermillion AB Canada by Alex Watson Jr. 110.0' x 24.0' x 4.5' Wood. 282.02gt 183.98rt. Powered by two horizontal (high pressure 10" x 48")

6.7nhp steam engines. In 1906–1916 she was owned by the Hudson's Bay Company, London UK. She was employed on the Peace River. She could carry 40 tons of freight and 25 passengers as well as shepherding a barge. She was reported as having been abandoned in 1916 at Fort Vermillion AB.

Pearl[715,716] (US) (sidewheeler) (freighter) She was built in 1854 at San Francisco CA. Wood. 78gt Steam engine. On January 27, 1855, her boiler exploded at the mouth of the American River, near Sacramento CA killing 54 people. She was salvaged.

Pearl[717] 150341 (US) 094803 (Canada) (passenger vessel, then a work boat) In 1884 she was built at Seattle WA USA. 62.4' x 14.4' x 3.4'. Wood. 75gt 53nt. Powered by a 30hp steam engine. In 1884 she was owned by USA interests. While serving on the Sacramento River she experienced a boiler explosion. In 1887 she was brought to the Fraser River by Charles Mallory, New Westminster BC. On November 10, 1887, she was snagged at the mouth of the Fraser River and wrecked. In 1895 she was owned by John H Low, Vancouver BC. In 1901 she was owned by WR Taylor, Vancouver BC. In 1905–1937 she was owned by John H Low, Vancouver BC.

Pearl (US) (tug) She was built in 1897 at Portland OR USA. 45' Wood. Powered by a steam engine. She was employed on the Columbia River.

Pedler[718] 205068 (US) (freighter) She was built in 1908 at Marshfield OR USA by S Gilroy. 124' Wood. 407gt 350nt. Powered by a steam engine. In 1908 she was in service at Coos Bay OR. In 1910 she was moved to California waters.

Peep[719] (US) (freighter) Wood. Powered by a steam engine. She is reported by Murray Lundberg to have worked in Alaska/YT in 1909.

Peerless 085314 (Canada) She was built in 1881 at Kamloops BC Canada by Alexander Watson. 133.0' x 24.4' x 5.0'. Wood. 307gt 256.03rt. Powered by two high pressure steam 16" x 54" engines by Joseph Spratt, Victoria BC. In 1885 she was re-built by Captain Troup. In 1881 she was owned by Mara, Willson, Barnard and Menanteau & Co., Kamloops BC. In 1896–1898 she was owned by Mara & Wilson, Kamloops BC. In 1901–1910 she was owned by John A Mars (MO), Kamloops BC. After the completion of the Canadian Pacific Railway, she was employed carrying coal on the North Thompson River. Some of the machinery from the *Marten* was used in her engine room. In 1907 she was retired in Kamloops and was destroyed by fire.

Peerless (Image from Maritime Museum of British Columbia 000430)

Pelly[720] (US) Wood. Powered by a steam engine. She is reported by Murray Lundberg to have worked in Alaska/YT c1890. She is thought to have been the first boat to travel upstream from Dawson; getting as far as Selkirk, and wintering in the Steamboat Slough no date given, but apparently pre-1892, when the *Artic* was at Fort Selkirk (MacBride). She operated on the lower river during the Nome gold rush.

Pend Oreille[721] (later *Metaline*) (US) (sidewheeler) (passenger vessel) She was built in 1884 at Pend Oreille Lake ID. 108.0' x 17.8' x 4.9' Wood. 218gt

159nt. Powered by two horizontal (high pressure 10" x 24") 6.6nhp 222ihp steam engines. Her engines came from the St. Joseph/Elk. In 1884 she was owned by JN Boyd. In 1894–1895 she served on the Pend Oreille River. In 1894 Boyd sold a half interest in the vessel to Captain James D Miller. In 1895 Captain Miller purchased sole ownership of the vessel. She was rebuilt at Newport OR and renamed as the Metaline (92664). In 1895 she was reported to have been wrecked during an attempt to line her up through Albeni Falls. Her engines went to the Ruth (111113).

Pend Oreille[722] (later Juno) (US) (passenger vessel) She was built in 1900 at Sandpoint ID USA by Captain FM Lucas. 127' x 22' x ? Wood. Powered by a steam engine. In 1900 she was owned by the Sand Point Lumber Co. In 1902 she was owned by the Humbird Lumber Co. In 1902 she was renamed as the Juno—an enlarged refitted version of the steamer Pend Oreille as a tugboat.

Pentona[723] (US) (sidewheeler) (work boat) She was built in 1853 at Portland OR. 81' Wood. Powered by a steam engine.

Pert (Image from Maritime Museum of British Columbia 000431)

Pert (see *Alert*)

Pert[724] (US) (sidewheeler) Wood. 48gt. Powered by a steam engine. She was home ported at San Francisco CA. In 1864 she was reported to have been abandoned.

Pet[725] 020108 (US) (sidewheeler) She was built in 1866 at Sacramento CA USA. 70.0' x 15.8' x 4.3'. Wood. 35.72gt. Powered by a 25nhp steam engine. She was a trussed-hull shallow draft vessel that was employed on the Sacramento River. In 1870 she was owned by McNair & Brewer. On March 10, 1870, this vessel, while enroute from Rio Vista to Sacramento CA, was snagged and sank near Steamboat Slough on the Sacramento River.

Petaluma[726] 020105 (US) (sidewheeler) (passenger/ freight vessel) She was built in 1857 at San Francisco CA USA. Wood. 365.34gt 281.15nt. Powered by a 150nhp steam engine. She was in service on California rivers. She went out of service about 1900 and was reported to have been abandoned.

Petaluma (see *Resolute*)

Petaluma[727] 212915 (US) (passenger/ freight vessel) She was built in 1914 at Benicia CA by James Robertson. 148.4' x 32.3' x 7.5'. Wood. 448gt 339nt. Powered by a steam engine. She was employed on California rivers.

Peytona (US) (sidewheeler) She was built about 1858 at San Francisco CA by Patrick H. Tiernan. Wood. 101gt. Powered by a steam engine. She was in service on California rivers. She went out of service about 1864 and was abandoned.

Pheasant[728] 111952 (Canada) (freighter) She was built in 1904 at New Westminster BC Canada. 112' x 17.2' x 5.2'. Wood. 251gt 158rt. Powered by a steam engine. In 1904–1906 she was owned by J Alexander Cunningham, New Westminster BC. In 1906 she took a contract to remove rocks from river locales known as the "Beaver Dam" and the Hornet's Nest" on the Skeena River. In 1906 she was wrecked at Beaver Dam Rapids near Skeena Crossing Bridge on the Skeena River BC. On June 10, 1917, it is stated that she was stranded in Prince Rupert Harbour BC. Norman V Bennett (1997) states that she was wrecked at Redrock Canyon near the site of the Skeena Crossing Bridge and was a total loss.

Philip B. Low (later *Eldorado*) 150776 (US) 107852 (Canada) She was built in 1898 at Seattle WA by the San Francisco Bridge Co. 140.3' x 31.3' x 5.8' Wood. 466.03gt 260.48nt. Powered by two horizontal (16" x 72" high pressure) steam 17nhp engines. In 1898 she was towed north by the *Lauredo*. In 1898 she was owned by Boston & Alaska Transportation Co. In 1901 she was owned by Captain Ernest C Miller, Dawson City BC. In 1899 transferred to Canadian Registry by Yukon Flyer Line. In 1898 she was launched without champagne because the company manager, a Mr. Lockwood, had strict objections to the use of alcoholic beverages. She was employed by the Yukon Flyer Line in Yukon River service. She was known as the "Fill Up Below" because she had sunk several times. In 1901 she was owned by EC Miller. In 1903 she was reported as having been broken up.

Phoebe Ann[729] 346322 (passenger vessel) She was built in 1971 at Surrey BC Canada by the Nahanni Manufacturing Ltd. 18.59m x 4.57m x 1.16m Steel. 29.89gt 22.92rt. Powered by two 150bhp diesel engines. In 1971–1999 she was owned by Shuswap Lake Ferry Service Ltd., Sicamous BC. In 2001–2021 she was owned by Narrows Village Investments Ltd., Banff AB. She was employed with a barge from Sicamous up Seymour Arm of Shuswap Lake. The barge that carried cars and became the ferry from Sicamous to Seymour Arm as well as the mail carrier. Initially, the boat operated as a sternwheeler, but in 1976, the sternwheeler portion was disabled, and two Olympic drive propellers were added, providing more power and speed. When the road was extended to Seymour Arm, the *Phoebe Ann* continued doing tours on the lake and delivering freight, capable of holding up to 100 tonnes.

Phoenix 150441 (US) (freighter) She was built in 1888 at Fairhaven CA USA. 85.0' x 19.0' x 7.0' Wood. 73gt 36nt. Powered by a steam engine.

Phoenix (US) She was built in 1924 for passenger service to and from Catalina Island as well as for the "glass bottom boat" excursions at the island. She was a "cosmetic sidewheeler" as she was driven by propellers. She is thought to have sunk.

Piedmont 150313 (US) (sidewheeler) (ferry) 257.1' x 39.5' x 15.6' Wood. 1854.36gt 1169.83nt. Powered by a 257ihp steam engine. She ran between Oakland and San Francisco from 1883 to 1940 for the Southern Pacific Railroad's ferry service. In 1884, the tug *Wizzard* and the *Piedmont* collided. In 1898, the *Piedmont* and the *Garden City* collided in the fog. In 1920, the *Edward T. Jeffrey* collided with the *Piedmont* while approaching Oakland CA. The *Piedmont* took a final, ceremonial voyage on January 14, 1939. She was briefly put into service for the Key System carrying passengers to the exhibition on Treasure Island in 1939 and 1940.

Pike (see *Rip*)

Pilgrim 150778 (US) She was built in 1898 at Seattle WA by the Moran Bros. Shipyard. 176.1' x 35.4' x 5.9' Wood. 718.68gr 409.06rt. Powered by two 26.6nhp horizontal high pressure (20" x 84") steam engines by the Moran Bros., Seattle WA USA. In 1898 she built for the Blue Star Navigation Co. In 1898 she was purchased at a sheriff's auction by Frank Waterhouse & Co. agents for the British-American Corp. In 1900 she was owned by the Columbia River Navigation Co. In 1901 she was owned by the Northern Navigation Co. She was owned by the Alaska-Yukon Navigation Co. In 1914 she was owned by the White Pass & Yukon Rail Road. She was towed to Alaska but lost her tug and was forced to reach St. Michael AK under her own power. In 1898 she was in Yukon River service. In 1917 she was reported as having been laid up at St. Michael AK USA.

Pilot[730] (US) She was built in 1865. Wood. 145gt. Powered by a steam engine. She was in service on California rivers. She went out of service about 1885. (It is unclear if she was a paddle-wheeler or a propeller).

Pinafore[731] (US) (freighter) Wood. Powered by a steam engine. She is reported by Murray Lundberg to have worked in Alaska/YT in 1898. In June 1898, she was advertised as connecting at St. Michael with the Ladue Yukon Transportation Company steamer *Grace Dollar*, and offering "the same elegance of equipment, the same capability in the service, and the same thoughtful attendance to the wants of the company's guests" as the coastal ships (Yukon Archives, PAM 1898-22).

Pioneer (see North Star)

Pioneer (US) (sidewheeler) (freighter) She was built in 1849. 80' Wood. She was in service on California rivers. Powered by a steam engine. In 1849 she was snagged.

Pioneer[732] 020042 (US) (sidewheeler) (freighter) She was built in 1862 at Milwaukie OR. 98.1' x 13.2' x 3' Steel. Powered by a 9.6nhp (12" x 48") steam engine. In 1866 she was owned by Columbia Transportation Co. In 1866 she was transferred to Yaquina Bay OR. In 1873 she was reported to have been broken up.

Pioneer 020109 (US) (freighter) She was built in 1867 at San Francisco CA. 100.5' Wood. 137.27gt. Powered by a steam engine. She was in service on California rivers. She went out of service about 1877 and was reported to have been abandoned about 1884.

Pioneer 020422 (US) She was built in 1869 at Soquel CA USA. 41.0' x 16.5' x 5.2' Wood. 22.11gt. Powered by a 30nhp steam engine.

Pioneer[733] (US) Wood. Powered by a steam engine. In 1872 she sank in the Sacramento River CA.

Pluck (see White Swan)

Plumas[734,735] (US) (sidewheeler) (freighter) She was built in 1853 at San Francisco CA by Littleton & Co. 51' Wood. 51gt. Powered with a steam engine. In 1854 she was owned by the California Steam Navigation Co. In 1854 she was employed on the Sacramento River in California. On July 11, 1854, she was snagged and sank on the Sacramento River. Her machinery was salvaged but the hull was abandoned.

Plymouth 223789 (US) (ferry) She was built in 1924 at Pasco WA USA. 55.0' x 20' x 3.4' Wood. 30gt 20nt. Powered by a 40ihp steam engine. In 1928 she was reported to have been abandoned.

Poco Tiempo[736] 020106 (US) (sidewheeler) Wood. 34gt. Powered by a steam engine. In 1889 she was reported to have been abandoned.

Pointer[737] (US) (sidewheeler) (freighter) Wood. Powered by a steam engine. She is reported by Murray Lundberg to have worked in Alaska/YT. In 1898, she made a trip up the Stikine River to Telegraph Creek, but grounded trying to turn around; though saved, she never made another Stikine run (Lawrence, p.116).

Politkofsky[738] (Imperial Russian Register) 020304 (US) (sidewheeler) (tug) She was built in 1863 at Sitka, Russian America. 129.5' x 21.3' x 8.9'. Wood. 255.44gt 174.89rt. Powered by a 352ihp low pressure steam engine supplied by a copper boiler. In 1863 she was owned by the Russian American Co., Sitka, Alaskan Territory, Russia. In 1866 she was a gunboat of the Imperial Russian Navy. She was admitted to the US under Treaty dated June 20, 1867, with the sale of Alaska to the Government of the United States. In 1868 under new American owners, she sailed for San Francisco for overhaul, stopping at Victoria for temporary repairs. There her copper boiler was removed and replaced by an iron one. It is documented that the owners sold the copper boiler for $4,400 which more than covered the price the buyers had paid for her. In 1869 she was taken to Puget Sound where she worked for several owners until 1896 as a mail and passenger boat, tugboat, and freighter. Her final thirteen years was spent in service towing logs at Port Blakely WA. In 1896 she was retired her engines and cannons were taken off and her hull was cut down to a barge and then she was beached for a year. In 1897 she was hastily resurrected for use as a coal barge. As documented in Pierre Berton's book "Klondike—The Last Great Gold Rush" she traveled north to St Michael Alaska as part of convoy of five vessels overloaded with passengers and supplies. She and the mothballed sternwheeler *W.K. Meryn* and the yacht *Bryant* were towed by the powerful steam tug *Richard Holyoke*. The fifth member of the convoy was the ancient side-wheeler *Eliza Anderson*, which carried the bulk of the expedition passengers. As the *Eliza Anderson*'s coal bunkers were totally inadequate for the trip, it was intended that she would be replenished from *Politkofsky* enroute. Unfortunately, the *Eliza Anderson* became separated from the other vessels and was subsequently abandoned near Dutch Harbor. All the other vessels safely reached St. Michaels. The *Politkofsky* was left at St Michaels as her final home. She was employed there as a lighter, but she was eventually abandoned as a hulk, which could be viewed for many years in St Michaels Harbour in front of the old Russian Fort. One of her Russian guns and her whistle (which was used to signal the opening of the Seattle Alaska-Yukon-Pacific Exposition of 1909 and the Century 21 Exposition of 1962) is in the collection of the Seattle Museum of History and industry. Another gun is in the collection of the Washington State Historical Museum, Tacoma WA USA.

Pomona 150782 (US) (passenger vessel, later a tug) She was built in 1898 at Portland OR USA. 133.5' x 28.4' x 6.1' Wood. 365gt 295nt. Powered by two 9.6nhp horizontal (high pressure 12" x 48") steam engines. In 1898 she was owned by Oregon City Transportation Co. (O.C.T. Co.) (Yellow Stack Line). She was employed on the Columbia, Cowlitz, and Willamette Rivers. In 1926 she was rebuilt. In 1926 she was owned by Knappton Towboat Co., Astoria, OR USA.

Pomona[739] 226079 (US) (tug) She was rebuilt in 1926 at Portland OR USA. 120.3' x 28.7' x 4.7' Wood. 216gt 183nt. Powered by two horizontal 9.6nhp (12" x 48") steam engines. Her engines came from the first *Pomona*. In 1926–1936 she was owned by Cowlitz Towing Co., Portland OR. In 1940 she was reported to have been converted to a floating storehouse before being broken up.

Popcum 100687 (Canada) She was built in 1894 at Popcum BC. 50.0' x 12.0' x 3.5' Wood. 13gt 8rt. Powered by a steam engine. In 1896–1936 she was owned by W Knight, Popcum BC.

Port of Stockton (see *Capital City*)

Port Simpson[740] 122390 (UK) (freighter) She was built in 1908 at Victoria BC by Alex Watson Jr. 136.6' x 30.4' x 5.4' Wood. 607gt 379rt. Powered by a steam engine. In 1908–1919 she was owned by the Hudson's Bay Co., London UK. She was reportedly sold in 1915 to MM Stephens, Prince Rupert BC. She was built to replace the *Mount Royal*. She was idle since the suspension of HBC Skeena River service in 1912. In 1922 she was reported as having been broken up and the hull lay on the beach at Digby Island for many years. Her engine went to a Mackenzie River steamer.

Port Suisun[741] 150300 (US) She was built in 1883 at Seattle WA USA. 40.0' x 12.3' x 2.8' Wood. 28.82gt 14.42rt. Powered by a steam engine.

Portland[742,743] (US) (sidewheeler) (passenger vessel) She was built in 1853 at Multnomah Falls OT USA. 90.0' x 15.5' x 6' Wood. Powered by a (8" x 36") steam engine. In 1857 she was owned by Alexander S Murray and John Torrence. She was employed on the Willamette River. In 1857 she was wrecked at Multnomah Falls OT.

Portland 203363 (US) She was built in 1897 at Portland OR USA. 329.33gt 195.25nt. Wood. Powered by a 120nhp steam engine. She was employed in the Columbia River system.

Portland 218331 (US) (tug) She was built in 1919 at Portland OR USA by Portland Shipbuilding Co. 185.2' x 40.8' x 8.1' Wood. 801gt 683nt. Powered by two 1,500ihp horizontal (high pressure 36" x 108") steam engines. In 1919–1929 she was owned by the Portland Port Authority, Portland, OR USA. In 1947 she was rebuilt.

Portland 253590 (US) (tug) She was built in 1947 at Portland OR USA by Northwest Marine Iron Works. 186.1' x 42.1' x 9.4' Wood. 928gt 723nt. Powered by two 1,500ihp horizontal (high pressure 36" x 108") steam engines. In 1947–1981 she was owned by the Port of Portland operated by the Shaver Transportation Co. She is reputed to have been the last steam-powered, sternwheel tugboat to be built in the United States. In 1991 she was turned over to the Oregon Maritime Center & Museum which in 2004 became the Oregon Maritime Museum at Portland OR. In 2021 she is still afloat and on public display.

Portland No. 1[744] 020309 (US) (sidewheeler) (ferry) She was built in 1865 at Westport OR. 101' Wood. 107gt. Powered by a steam engine. She was employed on the Columbia River. In 1874 she was reported to have gone out of service.

Portus B. Weare 150646 (US) She was built in 1892 at Fort Get There, Alaska USA. 175' x 28' x 4.6' Wood. 400gt 200nt. Powered by a 230ihp steam engine. In 1892 she was owned by the North American Transportation & Trading Co. In 1901–1911 she was owned by the Northern Navigation

Co. She was employed on the Tanana River. In 1914 she was owned by the White Pass & Yukon Rail Road. In 1922–1924 she was owned by Alex John Noble, North Vancouver BC. Her framework was built at Captain JJ Holland's yard in Ballard WA USA. This, and the machinery, was carried by the steam schooner *Alice Blanchard*. She was assembled near St. Michael's AK USA. In 1896 she was the second largest steamer in service on the Yukon River (after the *John J. Healy*). In 1894 she was in service St. Michael Alaska to Forty-Mile River. In 1927 she was reported as having been laid up at St. Michael AK USA.

Potlach 150793 (US) (passenger/ freight vessel) She was built in 1898 at Unalaska AK USA. 35.0' x 10.0' x 1.5' Wood. 18gt 9nt. Powered by a stream engine.

Potrero[745] 150855 (US) (freighter) She was built in 1900 at Alameda CA USA. 145.0' x 35.0' x 8.0' Wood. 531gt 452nt. Powered by a 300ihp steam engine. She was in service on California rivers.

Powell[746] (US) Wood. Powered by a steam engine. She was reported by Murray Lundberg to have worked in Alaska/YT in 1898. In June 1898, she was advertised as connecting at St. Michael with the Ladue Yukon Transportation Company steamer *Morgan City*, and offering "the same elegance of equipment, the same capability in the service, and the same thoughtful attendance to the wants of the company's guests" as the coastal ships.

Power City[747] (US) (work boat) She was built in 1910 at American Falls ID USA. 65.0' Wood. Powered by a steam engine. In 1915 she was reported to have been out of service.

Powers 206621 (US) (passenger/ freight vessel) She was built in 1909 at North Bend OR USA by Kruse & Banks. 89.7' x 25.2' x 5.8' Wood. 212gt 150nt. Powered by a 150ihp steam engine. In 1926 she was reported to have been abandoned.

Prairie Princess II[748] (US) (passenger vessel) She was built in 1983. 42' x 13.8' x 3.2' 15gt 12nt. She was based in Colorado as a tour excursion boat.

Pride of Newport (see *Reuben E. Lee*)

Pride of the River[749] 150146 (US) She was built in 1878 at San Francisco CA USA by George D Damon. 175.0' x 39.0' x 8.0' Wood. 619.15gt 553nt. Powered by a 650ihp steam engine. She was employed on California rivers.

Prince Alfred (British Columbia Colonial Register) (sidewheeler) (passenger vessel) She was built in 1862 at Seton Lake British Columbia (Crown Colony). Wood. Powered by a steam engine. In 1862 she was owned by Rosenfeld & Bermingham. In 1862 she was reported in Seton Lake service. She was reported to have been wrecked at San Francisco CA USA

Prince of Wales (Vancouver Island Colonial Register) (passenger/ freight vessel) She was built in 1862 at Victoria, Vancouver Island (Crown Colony). By Henry Sweden. 115.0' x 20.0' x ? Wood. Powered by a 90hp (14" x 54") steam engine. In 1863 she was owned by Goulding & Co. In 1863 she was in service on Lillooet Lake BC. In 1867 she was reported as having been broken up and her engines were later fitted into the upper Fraser River steamer *Victoria*.

Princess 020104 (US) (ferry) (sidewheeler) She was built in 1858 at San Francisco CA USA. Wood. 163gt. Powered by a steam engine. In 1880 she was reported as having been abandoned.

Princess Louise (Image from Maritime Museum of British Columbia 000434)

Princess (Canada) (sidewheeler) (passenger/ freight vessel) She was built in 1881 at Winnipeg MB. 153' x 24' x 8'. Wood. Powered by a steam engine. In 1881 she was owned by (William Robinson) the North Western Navigation Company. In 1881 she was in freight service on the Saskatchewan River. In 1883 she was rebuilt. In 1904 she was rebuilt at the North West Transportation Shipyard, Winnipeg MB as a freighter and fitted with a screw. In 1883 she was connecting at Grand Rapids with the *North West, Northcote,* and the *Marquis.* She had two funnels with golden beavers painted on the wheel guards. She could carry 600 passengers. In 1883 she was in service from Fort Garry to Grand Rapids across Lake Winnipeg. In 1895 she was abandoned at Swampy Island (lake Winnipeg) MB and towed to Selkirk MB in 1900.

Princess Louise (see Olympia)

Promontory[750] (US) She was built in UT USA. Wood. Powered by a steam engine. (No further information known.)

Pronto 203020 (US) (tug) She was built in 1906 at Portland OR USA. 100.0' x 19.0' x 6.0'. Wood. 94gt 72nt. Powered by two 19.6nhp (high pressure 12" x 60") steam engines. In 1906 she was owned by FB Jones. In 1925 she was employed by the Port of Portland Commission, Portland OR. In 1935 she was reported as having been out of operation.

Prospector 107865 (Canada) She was built in 1901 at Whitehorse YT Canada. 110.9' x 22.2' x 4.5'. Wood. 263gt 165rt. Powered with a 10hp steam engine. In 1901 she was owned by the Stewart River Navigation Co., Whitehorse YT. In 1901 she was owned by Emil Stanf and HE Riley, Dawson YT. In 1902 she was owned by M McConnell. In 1904–1910 she was owned by RP McLellan, Dawson YT. In 1911–1912 she was owned by the White Pass & Yukon Rail Road. In 1912 she was reported as having been broken up at McIntyre Creek YT.

Ptarmigan[751] 111950 (Canada) (passenger/ freight vessel) She was built in 1903 at Golden BC Canada by Frank P Armstrong. 110' x 20.5' x 4'. Wood. 246.45gt 155rt. Powered by two horizontal (high pressure 8" x 30") 4.26nhp steam engines. In 1903–1910 she was owned by the Upper Columbia Navigation & Tramway Co., Golden BC. In 1910 she was owned by the

Columbia River Lumber Company, later becoming the Upper Columbia Transportation Co. Her engines came from the steamer *Duchess*. In 1907 she hit a snag near Redrock. In 1907 she had a fire that destroyed her upper works. She was repaired and was employed one more year. In 1909 she was reported as having been broken up.

Pup 201964 (US) (tug) She was built in 1905 at Ballard WA by Chindern. 54.0' x 15.6' x 3.4' Wood. 33gt 21rt. Powered by a steam engine. She is reported by Murray Lundberg to have worked in Alaska/YT in 1905.

Puritan[752,753] (US) 176' Wood. Powered by a steam engine. She is reported by Murray Lundberg to have possibly worked in Alaska/YT in 1898. There is no sternwheeler by this name listed in contemporary editions of the Merchant Vessels of the United States.

Putah[754] (later *Chicu San*; then *Mansion Belle*; then *Spirit of Sacramento*; then *The Duke*). 267869 (US) (snag boat, later a yacht then a tour excursion boat) She was built in 1942 at Berkeley CA by the Berkeley Steel Construction Co. In 1946 she was owned by the United States Army Corps of Engineers. In 1955 she was owned by Fifth Corp., Los Angeles CA USA. In 1946 she was in service as a snag boat on the Sacramento River and Delta. In 1954, as the *Chicu San*, she was employed in the John Wayne, Lauren Bacall movie "Blood Alley" After the movie, she was renamed as the *Mansion Belle* as an excursion boat. In 1955c she was owned by Frank Parisi, Sacramento CA USA. In 1959 she was employed in Oregon as tour boat participating in the Oregon State Centennial celebrations. In 1961 she was moved back to Sacramento. In 1964 she moved to Marina del Rey also doing cruises. In 1965 she was owned by Bob Morris. In 1966 she moved to Long Beach offering harbor cruises. In 1991 she was owned by Channel Star Excursions, Sacramento CA. On February 3, 1996, she burned nearly to the waterline. In 1997 the wreck was purchased by William Barker. Restoration efforts failed and she was reported as having been abandoned. She sank at her mooring. In 2012 she was hauled out of the water on to dry land next to the Garden Highway in North Sacramento. (Several of the names attributed to this vessel may have been informal changes that were not registered with federal government authority.)

Quartzite (see *Texas*)

Queen 100688 (Canada) In 1894 she was built at Kamloops BC Canada. 70.0' x 12.8' x 3.6'. Wood. 77gt 48rt. Powered by a steam engine. The boiler from the *Lady Dufferin* was used in her construction. She was rebuilt as a barge after exploding in 1894. In 1894 she was owned by Malcolm Martin for the Kamloops Coal Co. (JE Saucier). In 1894 she was wrecked in explosion at Heffley Riffle on the North Thompson River with the loss of two crew members (Louis Broulette the cook and the fireman, Joseph Rachon). In 1896–1898 she was owned by A. Lamontane Saucier, Kamloops BC. In 1901–1910 she was owned by Mrs. Antoinette L Saucier, Kamloops BC. The Kamloops Coal Co. hoped to develop coal deposits 50 miles north of Kamloops on the North Thompson River.

Queen 203245 (US) (passenger vessel) She was built in 1906 at Portland OR USA. 38.0' x 13.0' x 2.8'. Wood. 14gt/nt. Powered by a 12ihp gasoline engine.

Queen City (US) She was built in 1854 at San Francisco CA USA. Wood. 379gt. Powered by a steam engine. In 1854–1855 she was owned by the Citizens Steam Navigation Co. Her owners were driven into bankruptcy by the aggressive actions of the California Steam Navigation Co. She was employed on the Sacramento River Delta, CA. In 1855 she was owned by the California Steam Navigation Co. In 1861 she was reported as having been abandoned.

Queen of New Orleans (later *Royal City Star*) (US) 820950 (Canada) She was built in 1993 built at Lockport LA USA by Halter Marine Inc. 66.48m x 18.29m x 3.66m Steel. 4165gt 1249rt. Powered by twin screw 1600hp diesel engines. The ship was brought from New Orleans, on the *Swan*, a heavy lift ship and off-loaded at Royal Roads (near Victoria) where she underwent some conversion and overhaul work. She was moved to New Westminster and began casino operations on October 6, 1999, as the Royal City Star Casino. In 1999 she was owned by Gateway Casinos & Entertainment Inc., Burnaby BC. The *Royal City Star* closed the doors to the casino on December 9, 2007. The casino operation moved ashore, and the vessel remained tied up on the Fraser River waterfront for several years. She disappeared from the New Westminster waterfront without fanfare. She was purchased by Art Belliveau of Campbell River BC who apparently originally intended that she function as an accommodation vessel for the 2010 Winter Olympic Games. This use did not pan out and on December 3, 2009, she was towed to Campbell River. As of 2021 the *Royal City Star* is berthed at the closed Elk Falls Pulp Mill just north of Campbell River.

Queen of Seattle (see *Elizabeth Louise*)

Queen of the Mississippi (see *American Pride*)

Queen of the West[755] (US) (overnight cruise boat) She was built in 1995. 230'. Steel. 2,115gt. Powered by a hydraulic propulsion system—a revolutionary propulsion that uses environmentally safe biodegradable hydraulic oil. In 1995–2021 she was owned by American West Steamboat Company. She operates on the Columbia, Willamette, and Snake Rivers, out of Portland OR USA.

Queen of the Yukon[756] (later *Dimond*) 020618 (US) (freighter, later a ferry) She was built in 1898 at San Francisco CA USA. 120.0' x 25.6' x 5.0' Wood. 225gt 212nt. Powered by a 175ihp steam engine. In 1901 she was owned by the Dimond line. She was employed between Oakland and San Francisco.

Queen Mary[757,758] (Canada) (passenger vessel) She was built c1928 in Saskatchewan Canada. Wood. In 1928–1952 this passenger vessel was operated as a tour boat on Wascana Lake in Regina SK. She was operated by the Owens Family, who charged 10 cents (later 15 cents) each to take 30 passengers on a half hour tour of the lake.

Quesnel (see *City of Quesnel*)

Quick 107861 (Canada) (passenger/ freight vessel) She was built in 1900 at Dawson City YT Canada by Edward J Smythe. 60.0' x 11.0' x 3.0' Steel. 67gt 61rt. Powered by a 55hp steam engine. In 1900 she was owned by Robert C. Smith, Dawson YT. In 1901 she was owned by Emil Stanf and HE Ridley, Dawson YT. In 1905 she was owned by Tom Smith. In 1907–1910 she was owned by Captain AF Daugherty and George Waltenberg, Whitehorse YT.

Quickstep 020617 (US) She was built in 1898 at Seattle WA USA. 123.8' x 24.8' x 4.4' Wood. 343gt 244rt. Powered by a 300ihp steam engine. In 1898 she was owned by the Alaska-Yukon Transportation Co. In 1905 she was owned by the Kuskokwim Commercial Co. In 1918 she was owned by Captain Wallace Langley. She was reported as having been abandoned.

R.C. Young[759] 110966 (US) (passenger vessel) She was built in 1892 at Corvallis OR by Young & Dove. 83' x 16' x 4' Wood. 108gt 85nt. Powered by two horizontal (high pressure 10.5" x 36") steam engine built by the Salem Iron Works. (Her machinery was installed at Salem OR.) In 1892 she was owned by Young & Dove with R.C. Young. She was employed on the Columbia River. On July 22, 1892, she was destroyed by fire at Dove's Landing (above Salem). She had been laid up by low water levels but was preparing to resume service towing logs. The fire burned her lines and the burning hull drifted in the current.

R.K. Page 760,761 (formerly the *Jack Haynes*) (US) (freighter) She was rebuilt from the wrecked *Jack Haynes* in 1852 at San Francisco CA USA. Wood. 69gt Powered by a steam engine. She was employed on the river at Sacramento CA. On February 22, 1853, while enroute Sacramento-Marysville she was racing with the *Governor Dana*. The engineer was adding pitch, tar, and oil to the firebox of her boiler (to increase heat for extra speed) when she exploded near Nicholas CA. The captain, one of the owners, the pilot and the ship's clerk were all killed in the incident. The force of the explosion blew the dome of the boiler 800 yards resulting in 24 persons were killed, and a large number were injured. She sank in six feet of water; the deck was partially covered but it was possible to remove the engines. In 1855 she was reported as having been abandoned

R.P. Rithet[762] (later *Baramba*) 085316 (Canada) (passenger/ freight vessel later converted to a barge) She was built in 1882 at Victoria BC Canada by Alexander Watson. 177.0' x 33.6' x 8.5' Steel. 817gt 686.16rt. Powered by two 90hp compound (20" x 60") steam engines. In 1882–1892 she was owned by Commodore John Irving's Pioneer Line, New Westminster BC. In 1883–1896 she was absorbed into the Canadian Pacific Navigation Co. On July 28, 1885, she collided with the *Enterprise* near Victoria BC. About

1928 she was beached at Sturt Bay, Texada Island BC. In 1901 she was taken over by the Canadian Pacific Navigation Co. Ltd., Victoria BC. In 1909–1914 she was owned by the Terminal Steam Navigation Company. In 1917 she was owned by the Pacific Lime Co., Vancouver BC and converted as a barge 1012gt. In 1918–1922 she was owned by the Kingsley Navigation Company, Vancouver BC. In 1922 she was owned by J Wray, Blubber Bay BC. In 1923–1931 she was owned by Captain George Smith, Blubber Bay BC. In 1931 she was still listed in the Canada List of Shipping. An 1882 newspaper report states "Perfect in lines and model, she is finished and found in every respect in first-class style. The carving in the saloons is elaborate and ornate, while the upholstering, gilding and general finish are simply gorgeous. The staterooms are spacious and convenient provided with luxurious spring beds and fittings. In short, in the perfection of her lines the completeness of her appointments and the elegance of her design and finish the R.P. Rithet is truly a floating palace. She is provided with the patent hydraulic steering gear and is brilliantly lighted throughout with 'electricity' having two powerful headlights placed in huge reflectors. These lights with dazzling brilliance as the noble steamer came into our harbour on Saturday night, the New Westminster Militia band also were on board, playing a lively air. The wharves were literally crowded with people who went down to welcome Captain Irving and congratulate him upon this his last great triumph in marine architecture." In 1928 she was reported as having been laid up at Sturt Bay, Texada Island BC.

R.P. Rithet (Image from Maritime Museum of British Columbia 000409)

R.R. Thompson[763] 110367 (US) (freighter) She was built in 1878 at Willamette OR USA by John Holland. 215.0' x 38.0' x 9.0' Wood. 1158.04gt 912.06nt. Powered by two horizontal (high pressure 11.25" x 36") steam engines. In 1878 she was owned by the Oregon Steam Navigation Co. In 1878–1882 she was employed between the Cascades and The Dalles. In 1882 she was transferred to the Portland and Astoria route. In 1904 she was reported to have been broken up.

Rainbow (US) She was built in the late 1840s. Wood. Powered by a steam engine. In the late 1840s she was in service on the Sacramento River CA.

Rainbow 209564 (US) (passenger vessel) She was built in 1912 at Marshfield OR USA by Frank Lowe. 64.4' x 18.0' x 3.8' Wood. 75gt 58nt. Powered by a 100ihp steam engine. In 1912 she was owned by the Coos River Transportation Co., Coos Bay OR USA. In 1923 she was reported as having been abandoned or broken up.

Rainbow Hunter (see J. Hunter)

Rainier[764] (later *Carrie*) 005687 (US) (passenger vessel) She was built in 1867 at Rainier, OT USA by JJ Holland. 82.4' x 18.5' x 3.5' Wood. 110gt 80nt. Powered by a (8.25" x 36") steam engine. In 1867 she was owned by the Cowlitz Steam Navigation Co. In 1868 she was rebuilt and renamed as the *Carrie*. She was employed on the Portland – Monticello route in opposition to the Oregon Railroad & Navigation Co. steamers. In 1876 she was reported as having been abandoned and later broken up at Portland OR.

Rambler[765] (US) (sidewheeler) She was built in 1859 at San Francisco CA USA. Wood. 128gt. Powered by a steam engine. She was in service on California rivers. In 1863 she was reported to have been abandoned.

Ramona[766] 110964 (US) She was built in 1892 at Portland OR. 100' x 18' x 5' Wood. 177gt 144nt. Powered by two horizontal (high pressure 11.25" x 36") steam engines. In 1892 she was owned by the Oregon City Transportation Co. (O.C.T. Co.) (Yellow Stack Line). In 1896 she was rebuilt.

Ramona[767] 111130 (US) 107253 (Canada) (passenger/ freight vessel) She was rebuilt in 1896 at Portland OR USA. 118.2' x 25' x 4.4' Wood. 251gt 209nt. Powered by a steam engine. In 1896 she was owned by Oregon City Transportation Co. (Yellow Stack Line) for the Willamette River trade but transferred to Alaska the same year. In 1898 she was owned by The Lower Fraser River Navigation Co., New Westminster BC. The hull was sold to the Western Steamboat Company and rebuilt. The hull was sold to the Western Steamboat Company and rebuilt. In 1898 this sternwheeler was sent from her service at Wrangel AK to the mouth of the Stikine River. Later she was sent to the Fraser River. On April 17, 1901, her boiler exploded at Henry West's Landing near Langley BC killing four persons including Engineer Richard Powers, Mrs. Bailey, a First Nations man known as 'Alec' and Mrs. Hector Morrison. Six others were injured. The hull was sold to the Western Steamboat Company, and she was later rebuilt. In October 1903 she allided with the Mission Railway Bridge. She was repaired and put back in service. On April 22, 1908, she sank at Wharton's Landing near Harrison River.

Ramona 111474 (US) (ferry) She was built in 1902 at San Francisco CA USA by the J.W. Dickie Shipyard, Alameda CA. 118.0' x 29.0' x 12.2' Wood. 575gt 362nt. Powered by a 700ihp steam engine. In 1902 she was owned by Pacific Coast Co., San Diego CA USA. In 1911 she was wrecked off Spanish Island.

Rampart 116615 (Canada) (passenger/ freight vessel). She was built in 1908 at Dawson City YT Canada by Alphonse Geoffrey. 42.8' x 9' x 1.7' Wood. Powered by a steam engine. In 1908–1931 she was owned by Daniel Cadzow, Rampart House YT. In 1914 she was wrecked.

Rampart (see *General Stewart Van Vliet*)

Ranger[768] (US) She was built in 1853. Wood. 30gt. Powered by a steam engine. She was in service on California rivers. In 1854 she was destroyed by a boiler explosion.

Ranger[769] 021603 (US) She was built in 1866 at Portland OT by James N Fisher. 113.0' x 20.0' x 4' Wood. 199gt. Powered by a 13nhp (14" x 24") steam engine. She was employed on the Cowlitz River. In 1869 she was destroyed by fire at Sauvies Island OR.

Rattler 110627 (US) (ferry) She was built in 1884 at Ainsworth WA USA. 76.0' x 19.6' x 4.0' Wood. 52.08gt 40.56nt. Powered by a steam engine. In 1904 she was reported to have been out of service.

Reaper (see *Zealandian*)

Rebecca C 110598 (US) (freighter) She was built in 1883 at South Beach OR USA. 60.8' 16.0' x 3.0' Wood. 15.65gt 10.21nt. Powered by a steam engine.

Red Bluff[770,771] (US) She was built about 1868 by Patrick Tiernan. Wood. 243.66gt. Powered by a steam engine. In 1868 she was owned by the California Steam Navigation Company. In 1871 she was taken over by the California Pacific Railroad Co., San Francisco CA. She was employed on California rivers. She was reported to have foundered in 1880.

Red Bluff[772] (US) She was built in 1884. 150.6' Wood. 246.17gt. Powered by a steam engine. She was in service on California rivers. She went out of service about 1890.

Red Bluff[773,774] 110067 (US) She was built in 1894 at Sacramento CA USA by the Sacramento Transportation Co. 150.5' x 33.0' x 3.2' Wood. 246gt 185rt. Powered by a 160ihp steam engine. She was in service on California rivers. On August 28, 1932, she was destroyed by fire in the conflagration that burned 10 vessels on the Yolo side of the Sacramento River.

Red Jacket[775,776] (later *Kate Hayes*) (US) (freighter) She was built about 1850. Wood. Powered by a steam engine. She was in service on California rivers. She was renamed as the *Kate Hayes*. She went out of operation about 1862. She was converted to a passenger and freight depot and gradually fell into disrepair and was abandoned.

Red Rider[777] (US) She was built at Seattle WA. Wood. Powered by a gasoline engine. She is reported by Murray Lundberg to have worked in Alaska/YT.

Red Star 090787 (Canada) (passenger/ freight vessel) She was built in 1887 at Victoria BC by George Dumbleton. 33.0' x 9.0' x 3.0' wood. 14.81gt 10.08nt. Powered by two horizontal high pressure steam engines built by Charles Willard, Chicago IL USA. In 1888 she was rebuilt to 53' and installed with new machinery. In 1887–1889 she was owned by George Lawes, and George Rashdell, Spallumcheen BC. In 1889 she was owned by Joseph D Pemberton, Victoria BC. In 1889 she was owned by RP Rithet, Victoria BC. In 1891 she was owed by the Columbia Milling Co. (John Nicholls and Clement Renouff, both of Victoria BC). In 1894 she was sold for general service to Captain Angus Campbell. In 1898–1913 she was owned by MP Reid, Kaslo BC. She was used in Shuswap River service, but her draught was too deep. She was reported as having been salvaged in 1888 and taken to the head of Okanagan Lake. In 1888 she was used as a towboat until 1895. She was transferred in 1895 to Kootenay Lake service.

Red Star[778] 094805 (Canada) (ferry) She was built in 1888 at Enderby BC Canada by John Hamill. 57.0' x 14.0' x 3.0' Wood. 36gt 23rt. Powered by two 1.7hp horizontal high pressure steam engines built by Charles P Millard & Co., Chicago IL USA. In 1888–1889 she was owned by Robert P Rithet, Victoria BC. In 1889–1898 she was owned by the R.P. Rithet Co., Victoria BC. She worked on the Spallumcheen River to c1904. She was reported as having been broken up in 1905.

Redding[779] (US) She was built about 1850. Wood. Powered by a steam engine. She was in service on California rivers. She went out of service about 1868.

Redlands 111178 (US) She was built in 1898 at San Francisco CA. 50.0' x 12.0' x 3.6' Wood. 14gt 9rt. Powered by a steam engine. She is reported by Murray Lundberg to have worked in Alaska/YT in 1898.

Reform[780] 021646 (US) She was built in 1866 at San Francisco CA. Wood. 181gt. Powered by a steam engine. In 1884 she was reported to have been abandoned.

Reform[781] (US) She was built in 1877 at San Francisco CA by John G North. Wood. 181gt. Powered by a steam engine. She was employed on California rivers. She went out of operation about 1885.

Reform[782] 203596 (US) (passenger vessel) She was built in 1898 at Wood Island CA USA. 178.0' x 40.0' x 6.0' Wood. 627gt 560rt. Powered by a 375ihp steam engine. She was in service on California rivers. She was reported to have been abandoned in 1938. Her remains are in a farm field on Mandeville Island. Dikes were closed in around her and she was used to pump out the remaining water to reclaim the rich bottom land.

Refrigerator No. 3 (US) (freighter) Wood. Powered by a steam engine. (No further information known.)

Regulator[783] 110935 (US) (passenger/ freight vessel) She was built in 1891 at Portland OR. 152.0' x 28' x 6.5' Wood. 434gt 335nt. Powered by two horizontal (high pressure 14" x 24") steam engines. She was rebuilt in 1899 at Portland OR USA. 157.0' x 34.4' x 7.7' Wood. 508gt 308nt. Repowered by two17nhp horizontal (16" x 72") steam engines. In 1899 she was owned by the Dalles, Portland & Astoria Navigation Co. In 1906 she was destroyed by fire while on the ways at St. Johns OR.

Reindeer (see *Sioc*)

Reindeer 107099 (Canada) (passenger/ freight vessel) She was built in She was built in 1898 at Victoria BC Canada by Thomas H. Trahey. 121.3' x 22' x 4.4' Wood. 357.84gt 224.8rt. Powered by two 9.6nhp horizontal (high pressure 12" x 60") steam engines built by the Polson Iron Works Ltd., Toronto ON. In 1898 she was owned by The Yukon Hootalinqua Navigation Co. Ltd., Victoria BC. In 1899 she was owned by the British America Corp. She travelled to St. Michael AK under her own power, accompanied by the *Garonne*. In 1898–1899 she wintered on the Dahl River. She wintered 1899–1900 above Five Finger Rapids. On April 26, 1900, she was destroyed by fire at Five Finger Rapids YT.

Reliance[784] 021600 (US) (passenger vessel) In 1865 she was built at Canemah OT by Allison Lambert. 141.0' x 23.8' x 4.7' Wood. 316.27gt. Powered by two 17nhp (high pressure 16" x 72") steam engines. In 1865 she was owned by the People's Transportation Co. In 1871 she was reported to have been broken up at Canemah OR.

Reliance[785] (Vancouver Island Colonial Register) (freighter) She was built in 1862 at Victoria, Vancouver Island (Crown Colony) by Captain William Irving. She was launched October 8, 1862. 126.0' x 26.0' x 4.5' Wood. Powered by a 110hp (16" x 54") steam engine. She was built for the New Westminster to Yale run. In 1862–1881 she was owned by Captain William Irving, New Westminster BC. On December 09, 1881, she struck a snag downstream from Hope BC and sank in shallow water off Wildcat Point (near Chilliwack). The *William Irving* took off the freight, the vessel was salvaged and taken to New Westminster BC for repairs. In 1881 she was reported as having been broken up.

Reliance[786] 072669 (Canada) (passenger vessel) She was built in 1876 at Victoria BC Canada by Alexander Watson. She was launched on March 7, 1876. 122.0' x 35' x 4.5' Wood. 314gt 121.06rt. Powered by a 120hp steam engine built by Joseph Spratt, Victoria BC. She was rebuilt to 314gt. 216rt. In 1876 she was owned by John Irving, New Westminster BC. In 1883 she was absorbed into the Canadian Pacific Navigation Co. In 1881 she was snagged in the Fraser River were she regularly operated. In 1892 she was reported as having been broken up.

Reliance 204486 (US) She was built in 1907 at St. Michael Alaska USA by St. Johns Shipbuilding Co. 120.0' x 25.6' x 4.6' Wood. 291gt 171rt. Powered by a steam engine. In 1907 she was owned by the Northern Navigation Co. In 1914 she was owned by the White Pass & Yukon Rail Road. In 1926 she was owned by the Alaska Rail Road. On October 6, 1917, she was wrecked at Minto on the Tanana River.

Relief[787] (US) (passenger vessel) She was built in 1858 at Oregon City OT. 110' x 24' x 3.5' Wood. 97gt. Powered by two 9.6nhp (high pressure 12" x 48") steam engines. In 1858 she was owned by the Cassidy & Co. In 1865 she was reported to have been broken up at Canemah OT.

Relief[788] 021644 (US) (sidewheeler) She was built in 1864 at Stockton CA. 99' Wood. 145gt. Powered by a steam engine. She was in service on California rivers. She went out of operation about 1895. She was reported to have been abandoned about 1906.

Relief 203513 (US) (passenger vessel) She was built in 1906 at Blalock OR USA. 117.5' x 22.5' x 4.7' Wood. 214gt 209nt. Powered by two 6.6nhp (10" x 36") steam engines. In 1906 she was owned by the Open River Navigation Co. In 1910 she was owned by Portland OR USA interests. She was owned by the Lewis River Transportation Co. In 1917 she was rebuilt at Portland OR by William Lemon. 229gt 198nt. Powered by a 150ihp steam engine. In 1931 she was reported to have been abandoned.

Relief 214263 (US) (passenger/ freight vessel) She was built in 1916 at Coquille OR by Ellingson. 64.0' x 15.6' x 3.0' Wood. 44gt 37nt. Powered by a 60ihp steam engine. She was home ported at Marshfield OR. In 1927 she was reported to have been out of service.

Rescue[789] 021601 (US) (passenger/ freight vessel, later a barge) She was built in 1864 at Monticello WT USA by Fred Congdon. 95' x 21' x 3' Wood. 126.14gt 95nt. Powered by a (10" x 48") steam engine. In 1864 she was owned by Cliff Olsen. In 1865 she was owned by Captain JC Ainsworth. She was employed on the Portland to Monticello route. She was employed on the Cowlitz River. In 1871 she was owned by Joseph Kellogg. In 1876 she was reported as having been laid up and in 1878 she was reported as having been re-rigged as a barge at Portland OR USA.

Research 202298 (US) She was built in 1898 at Liverpool UK. 60.2' x 14.0' x 4.3' Wood. 45gt 21nt. Powered by a steam engine. She is reported by Murray Lundberg to have worked in Alaska/YT 1898–1911. She was shipped to St. Michael AK on the steamer Garonne. In 1911 she foundered at Nixon-Tacotna Fork, AK.

Resolute[790] 110006 (US) (tug) She was built in 1870 at Portland OR USA by Fred Congdon. 57.0' x 12.8' x 3.8' Wood. 50.9gt. Powered by a 6.6nhp (10" x 36") steam engine. In 1870 she was owned by Hamill & Lewis. In 1872 she was destroyed at Portland OR by an explosion.

Resolute[791] (later *Petaluma*) 110635 (US) She was built in 1883 at Benicia CA USA by the Turner Yard. 134.2' x 29.0' x 5.5' Wood. 264gt. Powered by a 250hp steam engine. In 1884–1911 she was owned by the Petaluma

Transportation Company. In 1911 she was owned by the Petaluma & Santa Rosa Rail Road In 1911 she was renamed as the *Petaluma*. She was in service on California rivers. On March 24, 1914, during the night, she caught fire and was cast adrift to save the wharf. Her engine was salvaged and used in the rebuilt *Petaluma*.

Restless 110291 (US) (passenger vessel) She was built in 1876 at Gardner OR USA. 70.9' x 16.6' x 3.1' Wood. 101.02gt 85.87nt. Powered by a 40nhp steam engine. She was employed at Coos Bay OR. In 1895 she was reported to have been out of service.

Retta (US) (excursion vessel, later a freighter) She was built in 1900 at Yuma AZ by Captain Frank Friant. 36' x 6' x ? Wood. She was an open decked boat carrying a scalloped canvas canopy in Colorado River service. In 1900 she was owned by Captain Frank Friant. In 1901 she was owned by Captain Alphonso B. Smith. She carried rails to Picacho for the California King's narrow-gauge railroad. In February 1905 she was reported to have sunk.

Reuben E. Lee[792,793] (later *Pride of Newport*) (US) She was built at Long Beach CA by Todd Shipyard. The *Reuben E. Lee* was not really a boat, but rather a building on a barge. The faux stern-wheeler had no engine, and the paddle wheel was merely a show prop. Her funnels emitted fake smoke, a small motor rotated the paddle wheel, and her made-up name was a tribute to her sister restaurant "Reuben's," part of the Far West chain of high-end restaurants. Constructed by the Reuben's Steakhouse restaurant chain, the *Reuben E. Lee* opened as a dining establishment in 1964 at 151 East Coast Highway. She was then transferred to the Newport Harbor Nautical Museum and rechristened as *The Pride of Newport*. When the Nautical Museum was transferred to the Fun Zone, the *Reuben E. Lee* was left vacant. In 2007, with no one willing to buy the boat and no new tenants in sight, the boat was sold for scrap. She was a Newport Beach landmark for 40 years before being dismantled in 2013.

Revelstoke 111777 (Canada) (passenger/ freight vessel) She was built in 1901 at Nakusp BC Canada. 126.9' x 22.7' x 4.3' Wood. 308.55gt 178.59rt. Powered by two horizontal (high pressure 12" x 60") 9.6nhp team engines built by the Polson Iron Works Ltd., Toronto ON. In 1901 she was owned by the Columbia River Steamship Co. and employed in Arrow Lakes service. In 1910 she was owned by the Revelstoke Navigation Co., Revelstoke BC. She replaced the steamer *Lytton* on the Columbia River run above Revelstoke Narrows doing excursion and relief voyages on the Upper Arrow Lake and the Columbia River. On April 15, 1915, she was destroyed by fire when the town of Comaplix BC was consumed by fire. Her boiler can be seen at low water on the northeast arm of Upper Arrow Lake on the Columbia River.

Richmond 090810 (Canada) (tug) She was built in 1887 at New Westminster BC Canada. 76.0' x 15' x ? Wood. 103gt. Powered by a steam engine. In 1887–1888 she was owned by Captain F. Stewart and Duncan Rowan. On November 27, 1888, she was destroyed by fire at False Creek in Vancouver BC while carrying a cargo of produce from New Westminster BC. The vessel was a total loss but there are reports that the machinery was used in the *Alpha*. There are two end of life scenarios—in one the hull was either placed in a breakwater at Vancouver BC or alternatively she was incorporated into the *Alpha*.

Riffle 111946 (Canada) (passenger vessel) She was built in 1902 at Kamloops BC Canada by George Brown and Theodore Brookfield. 45.0' x 11.6' x 3.5' Wood. 37gt 23nt. Powered by a 2nhp engine. She was eventually converted with a screw propeller, and she served until 1938. In 1902 she was owned by George Brown, Kamloops BC employed as an excursion vessel. In 1910–1937 she was owned by the Lamb & Watson Lumber Co. Ltd., Arrowhead BC.

Rip[794] (later *Pike*) (US) (freighter) She was built in 1852 at San Francisco CA by the Walton Boatyard. 153' Wood. 109gt. Powered by a steam engine. In 1854 she was owned by the California Steam Navigation Co. She was employed on California rivers. She went out of operation about 1856, abandoned and was later broken up.

Ripple (Canada) (passenger/ freight vessel) She was built in 1885 at Selkirk MB Canada. Wood. 7gt 4rt. Powered by a steam engine. In 1891 she was rebuilt at Winnipeg MB to 9gt/6nt. In December 1899 she was reported as having been broken up.

Rival[795] 021602 (US) She was built in 1860 at Oregon City OT. 110.9' x 23.7' x 4.7' Wood. 211gt. Powered by two 9.6nhp horizontal (high pressure 12" x 48") steam engines. In 1860 she was owned by Pease & Dement. In 1864 she was owned by the People's Transportation Co. In 1868 she was reported to have been broken up at Portland OR.

Robert C. Hammond 133979 (Canada) (passenger/ freight vessel) She was built in 1914 at Fort George BC Canada. 101.0' x 21.6' x 4.2' Wood. 250gt 158nt. Powered by a 5hp steam engine. In 1914–1916 she was owned by the Fort George Lake & River Transportation Co. Ltd., Fort George BC. In 1915 she was laid up and in 1916 she was reported as having been abandoned. She was still in the Canada List of Shipping in 1919.

Robert Dunsmuir 085320 (Canada) (sidewheeler) (passenger vessel) She was built in 1885 at Vancouver BC by Henry Maloney. 105.0' x 17.5' x 6.7' Wood. 232gt 146rt. Powered by a 65nhp steam (2.5" x 36") engine. In 1885 she was owned by the Mainland & Nanaimo Steam Navigation Co. (William Rogers and A.C. Fraser). In 1888 she was rebuilt with an 18nhp engine and twin-screw propellers. In 1895 she was owned by William Rogers, New Westminster BC. In 1896 the company was taken over by Dunsmuir coal interests. She was employed as a collier for the Esquimalt & Nanaimo Railway Co. In 1898–1905 she was owned by William Rogers, New Westminster BC. In 1910 she was owned by Monarch Towing & Trading Co., New Westminster BC. In 1915–1919 she was owned by the Ocean Falls Co. Ltd., Vancouver BC. She inaugurated the first regular passenger service between Vancouver and Nanaimo. In 1885 she was used in BC coast mail, passenger, and freight service. She was known as 'Dirty Bob' carrying coal from Nanaimo. In 1913 she was reported as having been laid up, and in 1917 as having been broken up.

Robert Kerr 111180 (US) She was built in 1898 at Seattle WA USA by the Moran Bros. Shipyard. 176.1' x 35.4' x 5.9' Wood. 718.68gt 409.06rt. Powered by two 26.6nhp horizontal high pressure (20" x 84") steam engines. In 1898 she was owned by Frank Waterhouse & Co. agents for the British-American Steamship Corp. She was sold to the Pacific Cold Storage Co. for hauling meat between St. Michael AK and Dawson YT. In 1924 she was owned by the Waechter Bros. In 1898 she was employed on Yukon River service.

Robert's Island 110432 (US) She was built in 1880 at Stockton CA USA. 79.5' x 20.2' x 4.4'. Wood. 82.72gt 63.17nt. Powered by a 20nhp steam engine. She was employed in California waters.

Robert Young (see *Nespelem*)

Rock Island No. 1[796] 111177 (US) (passenger/ freight vessel) She was built in 1898 at Seattle WA USA by the San Francisco Bridge Co. 134' x 32.2' x 5.9'. Wood. 533.69gt 336.23nt. In 1898 she was owned by the Boston & Alaska Transportation Co. She was towed north by the *New England*. In 1899 she was owned by the Seattle Yukon Transportation Co. In 1901 she was employed on the Koyukuk River. On May 16, 1906, she was crushed by spring ice at Chena AK.

Rock Island No. 2[797] 111187 (US) (passenger/ freight vessel, later a barge) She was built in 1898 at Seattle WA USA by the San Francisco Bridge Co. 106.3' x 30.2' x 5.2'. Wood. 333.39gt 171.19nt. Powered by a steam engine. In 1898 she was owned by Rock Island Alaska Mining Co. In 1899 she was owned by the Seattle-Yukon Transportation Co. In 1899 her engines were sold, and she was converted to a barge. She was owned by the Yukon Mill Co. In 1901 she was owned by the Northern Transportation Co. In 1914 she was owned by the White Pass & Yukon Rail Road. In 1918 she was crushed in ice at Nenana AK USA.

Rogue River[798,799] 111381 (US) (tug) She was built in 1901 at Portland OR. 66.0' x 16.4' x 3.6'. Wood. 80gt 50nt. Powered by a 2.4nhp (6" x 30") steam engine. In 1901 she was owned by the Rogue River Transportation Co. She was employed in towing at Portland OR. On November 16, 1902, she was wrecked at Boiler Rapids, on the Rogue River OR.

Roosevelt[800] 221647 (US) (sidewheeler) (ferry) She was built in 1921 at North Bend OR by Kruse & Banks. 95.8' x 29.2' x 9.2'. Wood. 197gt 134nt. Powered by a 108ihp steam engine. In 1921-1933 she was owned by the State of Oregon (Oregon State Highway Commission), Salem OR. She was reported to have gone out of service in 1939.

Rose (see *Baranoff*)

Rossland (Image from Maritime Museum of British Columbia 000419)

Rossland 107442 (Canada) (passenger/ freight vessel) She was built in 1898 at New Westminster BC Canada. 144.0' x 30.0' x 5.0' Wood. 553gt. Powered by a team engine. In 1898–1904 she was owned by Rothesay Shipping Co. Ltd., Vancouver BC. She was in service on the Lower Fraser River. In 1905 she was reported as having been broken up.

Rothesay (Image from Vancouver Archives LP 303)

Rothesay 107442 (Canada) (passenger/ freight vessel) She was built in 1898 at New Westminster BC Canada. 144.0' x 30.0' x 5.0' Wood. 553gt. Powered by a steam engine. In 1898–1904 she was owned by the Rothesay Shipping Co. Ltd., Vancouver BC. She was in service on the Lower Fraser River. She was intended for use on the Stikine River but never voyaged north. In 1905 she was reported as having been broken up.

Rough[801,802] 204626 (US) (passenger/ freight vessel) She was built in 1907 at Ainsworth WA. 52.8' x 9.0' x 2.0' Wood. 17gt 10nt. Powered by a steam engine. She was employed in a feeder service on the upper Columbia River wheat trade. In 1908 she was reported to have been out of operation.

Rough Rider 111410 (US) She was built in 1902 at Ballard WA USA. 60.3' x 10.0' x 2.2' Wood. 11gt 7nt. Powered by a 60ihp gasoline engine. She is reported by Murray Lundberg to have worked in Alaska/YT in 1902–1905.

Rowena Lyle[803] 221619 (US) (sidewheeler) (passenger vessel) She was built in 1921 at Rowena WA USA. 48.5' x 22.7' x 4.8' Wood. 14gt 9nt. Powered by a 15ihp gasoline engine. She was employed on the Columbia River watershed. She was reported to have gone out of service in 1928.

Royal City 064155 (Canada) (passenger/ freight vessel, later a barge) She was built in 1875 at Victoria BC Canada by Collings & Cook. 128.1' x 26' x 5' Wood. 555gt 322.16rt. Powered by a 280hp steam (20" x 60") engine. In 1881 she was converted to a barge 322rt. In 1875 she was owned by Otis Parsons, Victoria BC. She serviced Sumas Landing BC. In 1882 she was wrecked at Fraser River BC. She lay for some time, bottom up, near the Sand Heads Lightship.

Royal City Star (see *Queen of New Orleans*)

Rush (US) (sidewheeler) She was built in 1889 at Hood River OR. 40' Wood. 12gt. In 1895 she was reported to have been out of service.

Rustler[804] 085678 She was built in 1882 at New Westminster BC Canada. 80.0' x 16.0' x 3.0' Wood. 39gt 25rt. In 1882–1896 she was owned by George W Gilley, New Westminster BC.

Rustler 097193 (Canada) (work boat) She was built in 1891 at Newcastle NB Canada. 97.4' x 20.6' x 4.6' Wood. 102gt 64rt. Powered by a steam engine. In 1901 she was owned by Joseph A. Russel, Vancouver BC.

Rustler[805] 110525 (US) (sidewheeler) (tug) She was built in 1882 at Portland OR USA. 78.0' x 18.5' x 4.8' Wood. 89.77gt 58.12nt. Powered by two horizontal (10.25" x 48") steam engines. In 1882 she was owned by Ham, Taylor & Co., Portland, OR USA. She was based at Portland OR for Columbia River service. In 1892 she was destroyed by fire at Goble WA.

Rustler[806] 111114 (US) (passenger vessel) She was built in 1896 at Jennings MT USA. 124' x 22' x 4' Wood. 258.09gt 196.14nt. Powered by two horizontal 317hp (high pressure 10" x 72") steam engine. In 1896 she was owned by Upper Columbia Navigation & Tramway Co. under control of their American subsidiary the International Transportation Co. She was built for passengers and ore freighting on the upper Kootenay River. On July 12, 1896, while under command of Captain HS DuPuy, she was wrecked in the canyon near Jennings MT USA.

Ruth[807] 111103 (US) (tug) She was built in 1895 at Portland OR USA. 156.4' x 34.0' x 4.6' Wood. 416gt 372rt. Powered by two 13nhp horizontal (high pressure 14" x 54") steam engines. Her engines came from the *Metaline* (092664). In 1895 she was owned by the Oregon Railroad & Navigation Co., Portland OR.

Ruth 111113 (US) (passenger freight vessel) She was built in 1896 at Libby MT USA by Louis Paquet. 131' x 22' x 4.5' Wood. 315.02gt 275.23 nt. Powered by two horizontal (10" x 74" high pressure) steam engines. In 1896 she was owned by the International Transportation Co. She was owned by the Upper Columbia Tramway & Navigation Co. She was employed on the Jennings MT to Fort Steele BC route. In 1895 she was owned by DM Swain, Stillwater MN. She collided with the *Gwendoline* in 1897 but both vessels were later repaired. In 1902 her engines went to the *Chelan* at Wenatchee WA.

Ruth 111155 (US) (passenger/ freight vessel) She was built in 1893 at San Francisco CA USA. 40.6' x 10.0' x 2.9' Wood. 14gt 10nt. Powered by a steam engine. She was employed at Coos Bay OR. In 1907 she was reported to have been out of service.

Ruth 107518 (Canada) She was built in 1898 at Lake Bennett BC Canada by James H, Calvert. 50' x 15' x 3' Wood. 51.88gt 32.7rt. Powered by two 1.6hp horizontal (high pressure 5" x 20") steam engines by the Vulcan Iron Works, Seattle WA USA. In 1898 she was owned by John Irving. In 1899 she was sold to the Northern Lakes & Rivers Navigation Co. Ltd., Victoria BC. She was employed on Taku service in 1899. In 1900–1901 she was owned by the Atlin Transportation Co. Ltd., Victoria BC. In 1901 she was destroyed by fire on Atlin Lake BC.

Ruth[808] 205786 (US) (passenger vessel) She was built in 1908 at Newport WA USA by John Sound. 115.6' x 22.9' x 4.8' Wood. 274.12gt 172.70nt. Powered by a 500ihp steam engine. In 1908 she was owned by the Metaline Navigation Co. In 1909 she was sold in a bankruptcy sale to Martin Woldson. In 1910 she was reported as having been laid up.

S.B. Matthews 116660 (US) (freighter) She was built in 1895 at San Francisco CA USA. 101.0' x 30.0' x 5.5' Wood. 200gt 104nt. Powered by a 75ihp steam engine. She was laid up on the Koyukuk River AK.

S.B. Wheeler[809] (US) She was built in 1849 in the eastern United States. 110' Wood. 120gt. She was employed on the San Joaquin River to San Francisco to Stockton route. She was reportedly carried as cargo aboard a sailing freighter and shipped to California. She was destroyed by fire in 1854.

S.G. Reed[810] 115620 (US) She was built in 1878 at Willamette OR. 175' x 33.6' x 7.3' Wood. 800gt 607nt. Powered by two 21nhp (18" x 84" high pressure) steam engines. In 1878 she was owned by the Oregon Steam Navigation Co. She was employed on the Portland to Cascades route, later moving to the Portland – Astoria route. In 1894 she was reported as having been broken up.

S.G. Simpson (later E.G. English) (204649 (US) She was built in 1907 at Tacoma WA USA by Crawford & Reid. 115.4' x 26.3' x 6.1' Wood. 267gt 168nt. Powered by a 350ihp steam engine. In 1907 she was owned by the Shelton

Transportation Co., Tacoma WA USA. In 1929–1945 she was owned by Tom Moore Boom Co., Seattle WA USA. She started service on the Olympia to Shelton run. She retired from towing log rafts from the mouth of the Skagit River to Camano Island. She was reported to have sunk in c1946.

S.L. Mastick[811] 023803 (US) (Canada) (sidewheeler) (tug) She was built in 1869 at Port Discovery WT USA. 118' x 24' x 12' Wood. 213gt 106.5nt. Powered by 300nhp steam engine. In 1869 she was owned by S.L. Mastic & Co. sawmill, Port Discovery WA USA. In 1891–1898 she was owned by Ross & McLaren Milling Co., Victoria BC. In 1898 she was burned with the *Goliah* to recover metal scrap. Her wheel house was saved for use in the tug *Augusta*.

S.M. Whipple[812] 023223 (US) (sidewheeler) She was built in 1866 at San Francisco CA. Wood. 325gt. She was reported to have been abandoned about 1885.

S.T. Church[813] 115514 (US) (passenger) She was built in 1876 at Portland OR USA. 154.0' x 36.0' x 5.4' Wood. 555.99gt 293.27nt. Powered by two horizontal 19nhp (17" x 72") steam engines. In 1876 she was owned by the Farmer's Transportation Co. In 1884 she was reported to have been broken up at Portland OR.

S.W. Whipple[814] (US) She was built in 1877 at Stockton CA by Cousins. 173' Wood. 292.01gt. Powered by a steam engine. She was owned by the California Transportation Co. She was employed on California rivers. In 1873 she carried farm produce on the Sacramento River. On November 11, 1875, she sank at Suisun Bay CA.

S.W. Kootenay 322489 (Canada) (ferry) She was built in 1964 at Cranbrook BC Canada by Russel W Anderson. 14.63m x 4.27m x 0.98m Wood. 49.07gt/rt. Powered by a 147bhp diesel engine built by the General Motors Corporation, Detroit MI USA. In 1964–2008 she was owned by Walter A. Anderson, Cranbrook BC. (Her register closed in 2008.)

Saanich (later *Mermaid*) 088364 (Canada) (freighter) She was built in 1884 at Victoria BC by William B Bolton. 82.0' x 17.0' x 4.1' Wood. 65.92gt

34.98nt. Powered by two high pressure steam engines built by the Albion Iron Works, Victoria BC. In 1884 she was owned by Alexander Grant, Vancouver BC, and the Northern Shipping Co. Ltd. In 1896–1904 she was owned by MD McLennan, Victoria BC. In 1887 she was reported as broken up. In 1904 the Registrar of Shipping reported that he had not heard of the vessel for more than 20 years and that "the owner could not be found."

Sacramento[815] (US) (sidewheeler) She was built in 1849. 60' Wood. Powered by a steam engine. She was employed on the Sacramento River CA. She went out of service about 1868.

Sacramento[816,817] 023221 (US) (sidewheeler) (ferry) She was built in 1861 at San Francisco CA by Patrick H Tiernan. 171.5' Wood. 540.8gt. She was employed on the Sacramento River. In 1872 she was reported to have been laid up.

Sacramento[818] (US) She was built in 1869. 75' Wood. 60.22gt. Powered by a steam engine. She was in service on California rivers. She was reported to have out of operation about 1877.

Sacramento[819] (US) She was built in 1914 by Schultz & Robertson. 178' Wood. 760gt. Powered by a steam engine. She was in service on California rivers. On August 28, 1932, she was destroyed by fire in the conflagration that destroyed 10 vessels on the Yolo side of the Sacramento River.

Sagadahock (US) (freighter) She was built in c1849. Wood. Powered by a steam engine. She was employed on the Sacramento River CA.

Sagamore[820] (US) (sidewheeler) She was built in 1850. Wood. 66gt. Powered by a steam engine. On November 1, 1851, she was destroyed when her boiler exploded while departing the wharf with 50 persons killed or injured. In 1850–1851 she served in the California delta and the San Joaquin River.

Saga (Burma Registry) She was built in 1917 at Esquimalt BC Canada by B.C. Marine Railway Co., Esquimalt BC. 132' x 31' x 4.7' Steel. 419gt. Powered by a 300ihp steam reciprocating engine. In 1917 she was owned by the Burmah Oil Company.

Saginaw[821] (USS) (sidewheeler) She was built in 1860 at San Francisco CA USA by the Mare Island Navy Yard. 155' x 26' x 4.5' Powered by two inclined oscillating steam engines, both with bores 39 inches in diameter and 48 inches stroke (Union Iron Works, San Francisco). In 1860 she was owned by the United States Navy. She was built as the USS *Tocey* but was renamed on commissioning. "The ship intending to touch at Ocean Island enroute home to rescue any shipwrecked sailors who might be stranded there. On October 29, as she neared this rarely visited island, the *Saginaw* struck an outlying reef and grounded the surf battered the ship to pieces, but the crew was able to get ashore with some of the ship' stores. On November 18th, a party of five men, headed by Lieutenant John G Talbot, the executive officer, set out for Honolulu in a small boat to get relief for their stranded shipmates. As they neared Kauai, 31 days and some 1,500 miles later, their boat was upset by breakers. Only Coxswain William Halford survived to obtain help for the marooned men of the *Saginaw*."

Saidie[822] 116831 (US) (sidewheeler) (tug, passenger/ freight vessel) She was built in 1898 at San Francisco CA USA by the Union Iron Works. 150.0' x 30.0' x 8.0' Steel. 328gt 197nt. Powered by a steam engine. In 1898–1900 she was owned by the Alaska Commercial Company, San Francisco CA. In 1900 she was rebuilt and given a second deck for passenger accommodation for the St. Michael – Cape Nome – Kotzebue run. There are two versions of her demise. "On September 04, 1904, this vessel was either beached in sudden gale near York City Alaska (35miles NW of Teller) while the crew was hunting ducks ashore or she hit an uncharted reef in calm weather because of navigational error of the Second Mate. The vessel settled in 6 feet of water. The tug *Meteor* and steamer *Rosencrans* tried without success to pull the vessel off, and it was later crushed by ice and became a total loss."

St. Claire[823] (US) (sidewheeler) (passenger vessel) She was built in 1859 at Rays Landing OR. 80.0' x 16.0' x 4' Powered by (10" x 12") steam engine. In 1865 she was reported as having been broken up at Canemah OT.

St. Helena[824] 117146 (US) (passenger vessel) She was built in 1902 at San Francisco CA USA. 135.0' x 30.5' x 6.8' Wood. 344gt 263nt. Powered by a 450ihp steam engine. She was employed in the California rivers. In 1918 she was snagged and sank in 18 feet of water in the Napa River CA. After being raised by Captain TPH Whitelaw, she was towed to Vallejo CA for repair.

St. James 116857 (US) (passenger/ freight vessel) She was built in 1898 at St. Michael AK USA. Wood. 63gt. Powered by a steam engine. In 1899 she foundered at Anvik AK USA.

St. Joe[825] (see St. Joseph)

St. Johns[826] 209839 (US) (sidewheeler) (ferry) She was built in 1912 at Portland OR by Portland Shipbuilding Co. 125.4' x 37' x 8.2' Wood. 379gt 338nt. Powered by a 225ihp engine. In 1912 she was owned by Multnomah County OR. In 1923 she was reported to have been abandoned.

St. Joseph 107215 (Canada) (sidewheeler) (mission boat) She was built in 1893 at Fort Chipewyan NWT Canada. 59.0' x 9.5' x 4.0' Wood. 27gt 16rt. Powered by a 1.66nhp steam engine. In 1893–1901 she was owned by the Roman Catholic Church (The Right Reverend Emile Grouard, Fort Smith, Athabasca District NWT). In 1892 she was used between Fort McMurray Alberta and Fort Fitzgerald NWT until about the beginning of World War One. Some sources say it was built at Fort Chipewyan, but others say she was built at Athabasca Landing from lumber cut in the Church's sawmill there to provide an alternative to high freight rates charged by the Hudson's Bay Company. She was an Oblate Order mission ship, on the Athabasca, Peace, and upper Slave Rivers.

St. Joseph 116863 (US) (passenger/ freight vessel) She was built in 1898 at St. Michael AK USA. 96.0' x 22.5' x 4.5' Wood. 96gt/rt. Powered by a steam engine. In 1898 she was owned by the Holy Cross Mission, Holy Cross AK for Father Tosi.

St. Joseph[827] (aka St. Joe) (later Elk) 008851 (US) (passenger vessel) She was built in 1869 at Tomales CA USA. Wood. 24.28gt. Powered by a 25ihp steam engine. Originally a propeller she was originally powered by steam engines from the *Amelia Wheaton*. In 1893 she was converted to a sternwheeler, rebuilt with new machinery at Coeur d'Alene ID. 100' x 20' x ?

Wood. She was in operation on Lake Coeur d'Alene. In 1900 she was broken up and her machinery, fittings and superstructure were shipped to Lake Pend Oreille to be installed on the sternwheeler *Pend Oreille*.

St. Joseph[828] (US) (tug) 80' x 16' x ? Wood. She was built in 1900 at Lake Pend Oreille ID by PW Johnson. In 1900 she was owned by the St. Joe Booming Co. for operations on Lake Pend Oreille ID. In 1943 she was scuttled in Lake Pend Oreille.

St. Michael 115674 (US) (passenger/ freight vessel) She was built in 1879 at San Francisco CA USA. 67' Wood. 28gt 20nt. Powered by a steam engine. In 1879 she was owned by the Western Fur & Trading Co. She was owned by the Alaska Commercial Co. In 1883 she was stranded on St, Michael Bar. In 1884 she was owned by the Mission at Holy Cross AK (Father Tosi). In 1897 she was owned by Elbridge Truman Barnette (et al) as a harbour boat employed at St. Michael. In 1920 she was laid up at St. Michael AK USA.

St. Michael 116816 (US) (freighter, then accommodation vessel) Built at 1898 at Seattle WA USA by the Moran Bros. Shipyard. 176.1' x 35.4' x 5.9' Wood. 718gt 409nt. Powered by two horizontal (high pressure 20" x 84") steam engines built by the Moran Bros. In 1898 she was owned by the Empire Transportation Co. (William Cramp & International Navigation Co.) In 1901 she was owned by the Northern Transportation Co. In 1914 she was owned by the White Pass & Yukon Rail Road. In 1898 she was employed on Yukon River service. In 1906 she was employed as an accommodation vessel. In 1913 she was laid up at Andreaofsky Slough. In 1943 she was reported as having been laid up at St. Marys AK USA.

St. Paul[829] 203615 (US) (passenger vessel) She was built in 1906 at Trinidad WA USA. 116.4' x 22.4' x 4.9' Wood. 208gt 131nt. Powered by two 6.6nhp horizontal (10" x 48") steam engines. In 1915 she was destroyed by fire at Wenatchee WA.

St. Vallier[830] 116883 (US) She was built in 1899 at Needles CA USA. 74.3' x 17.1' x 3.4' Steel. 92gt 53rt. Powered by a steam engine. In 1899–1900 she was owned by the Santa Ana Mining Co. In 1901 she was owned by the Mexico-Colorado Navigation Co., Nogales AZ USA. She was in Colorado River service. In March 1909 she sank.

Salem No. 2[831] 115136 (US) (sidewheeler) (ferry) She was built in 1876 at Salem OR. 50' Wood. Powered by a steam engine. In 1882 she was reported to have been out of service.

Salem No. 3[832,833] 115768 (US) (later *N.R. Lang*) (sidewheeler) (ferry) She was built in 1881 at Salem OR. 149.9' x 29.5' x 4.4' Wood. 351.68gt 236.0ont. Powered by two 13nhp (high pressure 14" x 48") steam engines. In 1881 she was owned by George W Graham. In 1900 she was rebuilt and renamed as the *N.R. Lang*.

Salvador 115135 (US) She was built in 1862 at Wilmington DE USA. 222.5' x 32.0' x 21.4' Wood. 1065.64gt. Powered by a steam engine. She was employed at San Francisco CA.

Samson[834,835] (later *Goliath*) 117160 (Canada) (snag boat) She was built in 1884 at Victoria BC Canada by WB Bolen. Wood. Powered by a steam engine built by the Albion Iron Works, Victoria BC. In 1906 she was rebuilt and registered 100' x 28' x ? 312t. In 1884 she was in service on the Fraser River. In 1898 she was a snag boat on Stikine River service. Eric Anderson states that "Though she was the smallest of them all, the first *Samson* had a long and colourful career, including helping the riverside communities when the 1884 freshet raised the river's height by over a foot and almost flooded the Fraser Valley. The first *Samson* was built almost entirely of wood, and when the wood began to rot, the government requested that a new snag boat be built to replace her. In 1905, the *Samson* was sold to the Gilley Bros, where she was reconstructed and renamed as *Goliath*. She worked at the Gilley Quarry on the Pitt River until 1909." In 1909 she was removed from the registry.

Samson 134304 (Canada) (fishboat) She was built in 1914 at Coquitlam BC Canada. 115.6' x 30' x 6.7' Wood. 436gt 227rt. Powered by a 13nhp engine. In 1931–1937 she was owned by H. Bell-Irving & Co. Ltd., Vancouver BC.

Samson 208262 (US) (passenger/ freight vessel) She was built in 1910 at Fairbanks AK USA by Brumbaugh, Hamilton & Kellogg. 85.0' Wood. 272gt. Powered by a steam engine. In 1910 she was owned by Leonard Joseph Heacock. Jn 1917 she was wrecked on the Upper Tanana River AK USA.

Samson II 116925 (Canada) (passenger vessel) She was built in 1905 at Victoria BC Canada by Turpel Marine Railway Co. 115.5' x 30.2' x 5.3' Wood. 425gt 248rt. Powered by a 13nhp steam engine built by the Victoria Machinery Depot Ltd., Victoria BC. In 1905–1913 she was owned by William A. Turpel, Victoria BC. In 1913 she was broken up. Many components of her engines, as well as the crank and paddlewheel shaft, were reused in the *Samson III*, *Samson IV*, and *Samson V*.

Samson III (Canada) (snag boat) She was built in 1914 at Port Coquitlam BC Canada. Wood. Powered by a steam engine. In 1914 she was owned by the Minister of Public Works, Ottawa ON.

Samson IV (later *N.B.F. No. 4*; then *K.5*; then *Langara Lodge*) 152686 (Canada) (snag boat, later a barge) She was built in 1924 at New Westminster BC Canada by Edward Mercer. 113.1' x 30.3' x 6.8' (35.17m x 9.24m x 2.07m) Wood. 400gt 217rt. Powered by a 13hp steam engine built by Victoria Machinery Depot Ltd., Victoria BC. Later her engine was removed. In 1937 she was rebuilt as a non-powered barge 115' 575gt 552rt. In 1924–1927 she was owned by the Minister of Public Works, Ottawa ON. In 1928–1937 she was owned by H. Bell-Irving & Co. Ltd., Vancouver BC. In 1937 she was retired. In 1958–1972 she was owned by the Nelson Bros. Fisheries Ltd., Vancouver BC. In 1973–1985 she was owned by the British Columbia Packers Ltd., Richmond BC. In 1986–2019 she was owned by Langara Fishing Lodge Ltd., Richmond BC. Peter Bader (British Columbia Nautical History Facebook Group 18/08/2019) stated that "She used to be the mother ship for the Nelson Bros fleet of gillnetters. It had a net loft, a store, and a machine shop. In the stern it had a lift so that the fishboats could be repaired."

Samson V 170681 (Canada) (snag boat) She was built in 1937 at New Westminster BC Canada by Star Shipyards (Mercers) Ltd. In 1937 she was built for $48,850 Her hull was built of pre-framed creosoted timber, sheathed for icebreaking. In 1937 she was christened by Margaret Reid, daughter of Tom Reid MP. 115.0' x 31.0' x 6.6' (35.05m x 9.45m x 2.01m) Wood. 421gt 250rt. Powered by 13hp high pressure steam engines built by Victoria Machinery Depot Ltd., Victoria BC. She had a 'one gunbarrel' boiler built in 1905 at Victoria Machinery Depot all from the

Samson IV. In 1937 she was owned by the Minister of the Department of Public Works. In c1940 her coal grates were converted to oil burners. In 1954 she was gutted by fire. In 1955 her Certificate of Registration was cancelled. In 1960 she was re-registered. In 1960 her superstructure was rebuilt, fire tube boiler from Vancouver Iron Works installed and returned to service at New Westminster BC by Star Shipyards (Mercer's) Ltd. In 1980 she was retired by the Canada Department of Public Works. In 1980 she was turned over to The Corporation of the City of New Westminster and the Hyack Festival Association. She burned and sank at her berth in New Westminster. Mark MacKenzie (British Columbia Nautical History Facebook Group 21/02/2017) stated "The way I heard it the night watchman was drinking below by the light of a kerosene lantern which broke setting the creosote hull timbers on fire. You can still see charred parts of her hull when you are down inside. All the decking to the engine room and the top chord of the keelsons were replaced in the rebuild." In 1983 she was opened to the public as a floating maritime museum. In 2021 she was berthed in the Fraser River at New Westminster and was open to the public.

Samson V (Image from Vancouver City Archives CV_ 447-7930.1)

Samuel Soule[836,837] (US) (sidewheeler) (freighter) She was built in 1855 at San Francisco CA. Wood. 87gt. In 1856 she was in service on the Sacramento River CA USA. In 1854–1856 she was owned by the California Steam Navigation Company. She was reported to have gone out of operation between 1862–1868.

San Antonio 023218 (US) (sidewheeler) (freighter, later a barge) She was built in 1858 at San Antonio CA. Wood. 577gt. Powered by a steam engine. She was owned by the California Steam Navigation Co. She was converted into a barge. In 1868 she was reported to have been abandoned.

San Blasina (US) (freighter) She was built about 1850. Wood. Powered by a steam engine. She was employed on the Sacramento River CA.

San Joaquin (see *Dauntless*)

San Joaquin[858] (US) (sidewheeler) She was built in 1850 at San Francisco CA. Wood. Powered by a steam engine. She was reported to have been abandoned in 1854.

San Joaquin No. 1[839,840] (US) (freighter) She was built in 1860. Wood. 77.6gt. Powered by a steam engine. She was in service on California rivers.

San Joaquin No. 2[841,842] 115417 (US) She was built in 1875 at Broderick CA. 145.0' x 32.5' x 4.8'. Wood. 242.77gt 133.62nt. Powered by a 90nhp steam engine. In 1874 she was owned by the Sacramento Transportation Co. She was owned by the United States Army Corps of Engineers. She was in service on California rivers. On August 28, 1932, she was destroyed by fire in the conflagration that burned 10 vessels on the Yolo side of the Sacramento River.

San Joaquin No. 3[843,844] 115545 (US) (passenger vessel) She was built in 1877 at Broderick CA. 145.0' x 32.2' x 3.7'. Wood. 180.49gt 138.72nt. Powered by an 80nhp steam engine. In 1877 she was owned by the Sacramento Transportation Co. She was in service on California rivers. On September 25, 1910, she was destroyed by fire at Sacramento CA.

San Joaquin No. 4[845,846] 116068 (US) She was built in 1885 at Broderick CA USA by the Sacramento Transportation Co. Powered by a steam engine. Wood. 365gt. She was employed on California rivers. On September 30, 1932, she was destroyed by fire at Broderick CA.

San Jose[847] 116850 (US) (freighter) She was built in 1898 at Benicia CA USA. 101.0' x 28.0' x 5.5'. Wood. 192gt 165rt. Powered by a 125ihp steam engine. She was in service on California rivers. On August 28, 1932, she was destroyed by fire in the conflagration that burned 10 vessels on the Yolo side of the Sacramento River.

San Lorenzo[848] 115263 (US) She was built in 1874 at San Francisco CA USA by Dickie Brothers. 89.0' x 34.0' x 4.0'. Wood. 97.93gt 83.05gt. Powered by a 40nhp steam engine. In 1874–1885 she was owned by San Francisco CA USA interests. She was employed on California rivers. She was reported to have gone out of operation about 1885.

San Pablo 117008 (US) (passenger vessel) She was built in 1900 at San Francisco CA USA. 226.1' x 30.2' x 17.6'. Wood. 1584gt 906rt. Powered by a 1820ihp steam engine. In 1900–1910 she was owned by San Francisco CA USA interests.

Santa Barbara[849] (US) (yacht, recreational duck hunting boat) She was built in 1913 at Santa Barbara CA by Dr. BR Clow. Wood. Powered by a 6hp gasoline engine. In 1913 she was owned by Dr. BR Clow, Santa Barbara CA.

Santa Clara[850] (US) She was built in 1851. Wood. Powered by a steam engine. She was employed on California rivers. She was destroyed by fire in 1851. (It is unclear whether she was a paddle wheeler or a propeller).

Santa Rosa 115979 (US) She was built in 1884 at Chester PA USA. 326.5' x 40.9' x 20.7'. Steel. 2416.78gt 1335.69nt Powered by a 2,000hp steam engine. In 1884 she was owned by USA interests. In 1910 she was owned by San Francisco CA USA interests.

San Rafael 115556 (US) (sidewheeler) (ferry) She was built in 1877 at San Francisco CA USA. Wood. 692.43gt 401.79nt. Powered by a 750nhp steam engine. She was employed at San Francisco CA.

Sarah[851] (US) She was built in the eastern United States in 1850. Wood. Powered by a steam engine. She was in service on California rivers. She was reported to have gone out of service about 1868. (It is unclear whether she was a paddle wheeler or a propeller).

Sarah 116856 (US) She was prefabricated in 1898 at Seattle WA by the Percy Corp. and shipped north and assembled at Unalaska AK USA from the molds of the river steamer *Bluff City*. 222.8' x 42.0' x 6.2' Wood. 1130gt 588rt. Powered by two horizontal compound steam 1,000ihp steam engines built by the Howard Shipyard, Jeffersonville IN. In 1898 she was owned by the Alaska Commercial Company. In 1901 she was owned by the Northern Navigation Co. In 1902 she was damaged by fire. In 1904 she was employed between St. Michael and Dawson. In 1914 she was owned by the White Pass & Yukon Rail Road. She was sold after 1918. She was in Yukon River service for the Klondike Gold Rush. She boasted electric lights and could accommodate 150 first-class passengers. In 1927 she was reported as having been laid up at St. Michael AK. In 1944 she was destroyed by fire at St. Michael AK.

Sarah Dixon[852] 116470 (US) (passenger/ freight vessel) She was built in 1892 at Portland OR USA by Johnson & Olson. 140.0' x 26.0' x 6.5' Wood. Powered by a steam engine. In 1892–1906 she was owned by People's Freighting Company, Portland, OR USA interests. in 1906 she was completely rebuilt and re-registered as *Sarah Dixon*.

Sarah Dixon 203009 (US) (passenger/ freight vessel) She was built in 1906 at Portland OR USA by Portland Shipbuilding Co. (from the hull of a vessel by the same name).161.0' x 29.5' x 7.2' Wood. 368gt 334rt. Powered by a steam engine. In 1906–1926 she was owned by the Shaver Transportation Co. (Red Collar fleet), Portland OR USA. Originally built in 1892 as a passenger freight vessel, in 1906 she was completely rebuilt and re-registered as the *Sarah Dixon*. In 1906–1926 she towed on the Columbia River and lower Willamette River in Oregon. In 1926 she was destroyed by fire while being reconstructed in a shipyard.

Sarah Hoyt[853] (later *Senorita*) (US) (sidewheeler) (passenger vessel) She was built in 1855 at Oregon City OT. (She was created from the hull of the *Gazelle*). 145' x 23' x 5' Wood. Powered by two 13nhp horizontal (high pressure 14" x 72") steam engines. In 1855 she was renamed as the *Senorita*. In

1857 she was re-engined. She was employed on the Astoria to Portland to Cascades route. In 1859 she was reported as having been broken up.

Sarak[854] (Burma Register) She was built in 1917 at Esquimalt BC Canada by the B.C. Marine Railway Co., Esquimalt BC. 132' x 31' x 4.7' Steel. 419gt. Powered by a 300ihp steam reciprocating engine. In 1917 she was owned by the Burmah Oil Company.

Saranac (USS) (sidewheeler) She was built in 1850 at Portsmouth NH USA at the US Navy Yard (Portsmouth NH). 215.5' x 37.6' x 17.25' (65.68m x 11.51m x 5.28m) 1463gt 1484nt. In 1850 she was a warship of the United States Navy. Wikipedia states that "Recommissioned on 5 November 1853, the steamer sailed for the Mediterranean where she was employed until returning to Philadelphia on 26 June 1856. She was decommissioned there on 1 July for repair of her machinery and installation of new boilers. After re-commissioning on September 17, 1857, she got underway to begin the long voyage south round Cape Horn and back up the Pacific Ocean coast of the Americas for duty along the west coast of the United States." She served in the United States Navy North Pacific Squadron in 1871–1873. She operated in that region until she was wrecked on June 18, 1875, on the submerged Ripple Rock in Seymour Narrows near Campbell River, British Columbia and was under the command of Captain WW Queen USN while enroute from San Francisco CA to Alaska while on a mission to collect natural curiosities for the Philadelphia Centennial Exposition. Her bow was immediately run onto the Vancouver Island shore and made fast with a hawser to a tree, but within an hour she had sunk completely from sight. Lieutenant Commander Sanders, with a pilot and thirteen men, made their way on foot to Victoria.

Saratoga (later *Cortes*) (US) (sidewheeler) She was built in 1852 at New York NY by Westervelt and Mackay. 220' Wood. 1,117gt. She was powered by two double walking-beam steam engines by Morgan Iron Works. She was owned by Davis, Brooks and Company.

Saskatchewan[855] 088495 (Canada) (freighter, later a barge) She was built in 1882 she was built in Winnipeg MB Canada. (Apparently some of the framework of the *Marquis* was used in her construction). 146.4' x 24.5' x 7.2'

Wood. 219gt. Powered by a steam engine. In 1882 she was owned by Peter McArthur. In 1905–1914 she was owned by The Northwest Navigation Co. Ltd., Winnipeg MB. She was owned by the Hudson's Bay Company (HBC), London UK. The HBC employed her in freighting from High Portage on Cedar Lake to Prince Albert. The HBC Archive reports her as having been abandoned in 1910. In 1921–1931 she was owned by the Manitoba Transport Co. Ltd., Winnipeg MB.

Satellite[856] (US) She was built about 1860. Wood. Powered by a steam engine. She was in service on California rivers. She was reported to have gone out of service about 1868. (It is unclear if she was a paddle wheeler or a propeller).

Satellite 115380 (US) (freighter) She was built in 1871 at Coos Bay OR USA. Wood. 164.55gt. Powered by a steam engine. She was owned by Empire City OR USA interests. She was reported to have gone out of service about 1885.

Sausalito 115586 (US) She was built in 1877 at San Francisco CA USA. Wood. 692.43gt 401.78nt. Powered by a 750nhp steam engine. She was reported to have been out of service before 1884.

Sausalito 116635 (US) She was built in 1894 at San Francisco CA USA by the J.W. Dickie Shipyard, Alameda CA. 236.0' x 38.0' x 15.0' Wood. 1766gt 1372nt. Powered by a 1,200nhp steam engine. In 1894 she was owned by the North Shore Rail Road Co., San Francisco CA.

Sayak 203844 (US) She was built in 1899 at San Francisco CA USA. 98.0' x 28.4' x 3.1' Wood. 209gt 132nt. Powered by a 60ihp steam engine. She is reported by Murray Lundberg to have worked in Alaska/YT in 1900.

Scenic Belle (see *Yukon Belle*)

Scenic Queen (see *Yukon Queen*)

Schley (US) She was built in 1899 in Idaho USA. Wood. Powered by a steam engine. Her machinery came from the laid up *General Sherman*.

Schwatka 116812 (US) (passenger vessel) She was built in 1897 at Port Blakeley WA USA by the Hall Bros. Marine Railway & Shipbuilding Co. 146.0' x 30.0' x 5.0' Wood. 484gt 291nt. Powered by two horizontal (16" x 72" high pressure) 17nhp 400ihp steam engines by the Willamette Iron & Steel, Portland, OR USA. In 1897 she was owned by the Canadian Pacific Railway. In 1904 she was sold to Charles Thebo for the Yukon River trade. In 1905–1907 she was owned by the Northern Navigation Co. and was employed on the Lower Yukon and Tanana Rivers. In 1914 she was owned by the White Pass & Yukon Rail Road. She was sold to the Alaska Rail Road. In 1916 she was laid up near Dawson City Yukon.

Scona (see *Strathcona*)

Scotia 107829 (Canada) (passenger/ freight vessel) She was built in 898 at Atlin Lake YT Canada. 80.0' x 19.0' x 3.5' Wood. 214gt 134rt. Powered by a 4hp steam engine. In 1901 she was rebuilt to 214gt. In 1899–1902 she was owned by the John Irving Navigation Co. Ltd., Victoria BC. In 1902–1949 she was owned by the British Yukon Navigation Co. Ltd., Vancouver BC. She was in service at Atlin Lake BC. She was rated for 70 tons of freight and berths for 12 passengers. She was reported as having been abandoned in 1918, reported beached on March 23, 1949, and destroyed by fire in 1967 at Atlin Lake BC.

Scout (see *May West*)

Scowlitz 126080 (Canada) (tug) She was built in 1908 at Harrison River BC Canada. 92.0' x 22.8' x 4.9' Wood. 178gt 112rt. Powered by a 17hp steam engine. In 1908–1925 she was owned by The Rat Portage Lumber Co. Ltd., St. Boniface MB. In 1926–1930 she was owned by Thurston-Flavelle Lumber Co., Port Moody BC. In 1931–1932 she was owned by The Rat Portage Lumber Co. Ltd., Vancouver BC. She was in service on Harrison Lake BC. In 1926 she was retired.

Scud (later *Ethel Ross*) 103898 (Canada) She was built in 1897 at Kamloops BC by Captain George B Ward. 84.0' x 14.0' x 4.0' Wood. 82gt 52rt. Powered by a 15hp engine by B.C. Iron Works, Vancouver BC. She was repowered with a screw engine. In 1897 she was owned by Captain George B. Ward. In 1898 she was owned by Amelia C Ward, Kamloops BC. In 1901–1939 she was owned by Claude R Doxat, Ashcroft BC. In 1897 she was built for passenger freight and excursion service in the Thompson River district. She started out as an excursion vessel but later moved into towing logs for the Kamloops Sawmill. In 1912 she was reported as having been broken up. In 1931 she was still reported in the Canada Registry of Shipping.

Sea Bird[857] (US) (sidewheeler) (passenger vessel) She was built about 1850. 225' x ? x ? Wood. 450gt. Powered by a 110bhp steam engine. She was built in the eastern USA. She took 240 days to make the voyage out to the Pacific coast around Cape Horn, calling at 13 ports on the way in 1851. She was in service on California rivers. In 1858 she travelled as far as Murderer's Bar on the Fraser River, (the first vessel to do so). She arrived at Port Townsend WT on March 18, 1858. She carried passengers on the Fraser River and ran onto a bar a few miles below Hope on what is now known as Sea Bird Bar and was stuck there for four months. After her removal she burned to the waters edge while enroute to Victoria on September 07, 1858.

Sea Gull[858] 116889 (US) (freighter) She was built in 1899 at San Francisco CA USA. 84.5' x 18.5' x 4.5' Wood. 44gt 28nt. Powered by a 70ihp steam engine. She was in service on California rivers. She is reported to have been broken up in 1912.

Searchlight[859] (US) (passenger/ freight vessel) She was built in 1902 at Needles CA USA by FL Hawley. 91' x 18' x ? Wood. 98t. Powered with a 100hp steam engine. In 1902 she was owned by the Colorado River Transportation Co. She was the last steamer employed on the lower Colorado River below the Grand Canyon. She was employed between Needles to Quartette Landing. In October 1916 she was lost.

Seaton (British Columbia Colonial Register) (sidewheeler) (passenger vessel) She was built in 1863 at Seaton Lake, British Columbia. 100.0' x 22.0' x 5.0' Wood. Powered by a 60hp (12" x 36") steam engine. In 1863 she was owned by Taylor & Co. In 1863 she was in Seaton Lake Service. She was retired in 1866.

Seattle 116817 (US) She was built in 1898 at Seattle WA USA by the Moran Bros. Shipyard. 176.1' x 35' x 4' Wood. 718.68gt 409.06nt. Powered by two horizontal (20" x 84" high pressure) 26.6nhp steam engines built by the Moran Bros. She was shipped to Dutch Harbor in sections and re-assembled there. In 1898 she was owned by the Empire Transportation Co. (William Cramp & International Navigation Co.) In 1898 she was owned by the Seattle-Yukon Transportation Co. In 1901 she was owned by the Northern Navigation Co. In 1918 she was owned by the White Pass & Yukon Rail Road. In 1900 she was converted to a barge. In 1898 she was in Yukon River service. In 1917 she was reported as having been laid up at St. Michael AK USA.

Seattle No. 2 116854 (US) (passenger vessel) She was built in 1898 at St. Michael AK USA by the Moran Bros. Shipyard. 151.0' x 34.9' x 6.2' Wood. 548gt 326nt. Powered by a 450ihp steam engine. In 1898 she was owned by the Seattle-Yukon Transportation Co. In 1901 she was owned by the Northern Navigation Co. In 1914 she was owned by the White Pass & Yukon Rail Road. She was sold to the Alaska Rail Road. In 1898 she was built at Seattle WA, transported to St. Michael, and re-assembled there. She was in service on the upper Yukon River. In 1943 she was reported as having been near Dawson YT.

Seattle No. 3 116854 (US) She was built in 1898 at Seattle WA USA by the Moran Bros. Shipyard. In 1898 she was built at Seattle WA, transported to St. Michael Alaska, and re-assembled there. 151.0' x 34.9' x 6.2' Wood. 548gt 326rt. 450ihp steam engine. In 1898 she was owned by the Seattle-Yukon Transportation Co. In 1901 she was owned by the Northern Navigation Co. In 1914 she was owned by the White Pass & Yukon Rail Road. She was sold to the Alaska Rail Road. She was in service on the upper Yukon River. In 1943 she was reported as having been abandoned near Dawson YT.

Secretary[860] (ex-*Gabriel Winter*) (US) She was built in 1851 at San Francisco CA. Wood. 73gt. Powered by a steam engine. She was employed on California rivers. She was reported to have been lost in 1854 when her boiler exploded.

Sehome (ex-*Mountain Queen*) 116301 (US) (sidewheeler) (passenger vessel) She was built in 1889 at Portland OR USA. (She was rebuilt from the *Mountain Queen*). 192.4' x 32.2' x 10.5'. Wood. 692.46gt 615.21nt. Powered by a 700nhp steam engine. She was in operation on the Columbia River based in Portland OR.

Seizer[861] (US) (snag boat) She was built in 1881. 157'. Wood. Powered by a steam engine. She was in service on California rivers. She was reported to have been broken up in 1921.

Selkirk 115121 (US) (passenger/ freight vessel) She was built in 1871 at McCauleyville MN USA. 108'. Wood. 119.08gt. In 1871 she was owned by James Hill, Griegs & Company. In 1872 she was owned by the Red River Transportation Co. In 1884 she was owned by Pembina Dakota Territory USA interests. She was employed on the Red River to Fort Garry to compete with the *International* and the *Pioneer* of the Kittson Trading Company and HBC alliance. In 1884 she was wrecked at Grand Forks, Dakota Territory USA.

Selkirk 103299 (Canada) (passenger vessel) She was built in 1895 at Kamloops BC Canada by Alexander Watson. 62.0' x 11.2' x 3.6'. Wood. 58gt 37rt. Powered by a steam engine. She was repowered with a gasoline engine. In 1895–1901 she was owned by Harold E Forster, Kamloops BC, for Knips Lake service. She was transferred in 1899 to Golden BC for Harold E Forster. In 1910 she was owned by Harold E Forester, Kamloops BC. In 1916 she was owned by Captain EN Russell. She worked on the North Thompson River. In 1898 she capsized and was salvaged. In 1898 she was partially dismantled and shipped by rail to Golden for Kootenay service.

Selkirk[862] 116884 (US) (passenger vessel) She was built in 1899 at Wenatchee WA. 110.8' x 24.5' x 5.5'. Wood. 233gt 172nt. Powered by two 13nhp horizontal (high pressure 14" x 72") steam engines. The engines came from the *City of Ellensburg*. In 1899 she was owned by the Columbia & Okanagan Steamboat Co. On May 15, 1906, this vessel was stranded in the Rock Island Rapids.

Selkirk 107835 (Canada) (freighter) She was built in 1901 at Whitehorse YT Canada by WD Hofius. 167.0' x 34.0' x 4.5' Wood. 777gt 490rt. Powered by a 17hp steam engine. In 1901–1920 she was owned by The British Yukon Navigation Co. Ltd., Victoria BC. She was wrecked in 1920 on Yukon River.

Selma 217327 (US) (passenger/ freight vessel) She was built in 1918 at Ruby AK USA. 48' Wood. 27gt. Powered by a steam engine. In 1918 she was owned by Ed Simon.

Seminole[863,864] 208767 (US) (passenger vessel) She was built in 1911 at Oakland CA USA by the Southern Pacific Railway. 220' Wood. 1,102.48gt 88nt. Powered by a 1,340ihp steam engine. She operated on the Sacramento River. On February 21, 1913, the *H.J. Corcoran* collided with the steamer *Seminole* near Angel Island and both vessels "turned turtle", rolling over.

Senator[865,866,867] (US) (sidewheeler) (passenger/ freight vessel) She was built in in 1848 in New York USA. 226' x 30' x 9.5' Wood. 750gt. Powered by a steam engine. She was originally employed on the New England coast. (The *Senator* sailed around Cape Horn and reached Sacramento on November 5. 1849.) She undertook the first successful steam navigation of the Sacramento River. She was employed on the Sacramento River, making three round trips a week, and carried three hundred passengers and three hundred tons of freight per trip. Charging thirty dollars for a one-way trip and thirty dollars a ton for freight. The *Senator* made a monthly profit of sixty thousand dollars (a fortune in those days). In 1854 she was owned by the Peoples Line. In 1854 she was owned by the California Steam Navigation Co. In 1867 she was owned by the California, Oregon, and Mexico Steamship Co. In 1882 she was retired after thirty-three years service her engines were removed, and she ended her days as a coal hulk in New Zealand.

Senator[868] 023148 (US) She was built in 1864 at Milwaukie OR by John Thomas. 132.0' x 24.5' x 4.5' Wood. 297.99gt. Powered by two 13nhp horizontal (high pressure 14" x 60") steam engines. The engines came from the *Surprise*. In 1864 she was owned by the Peoples Transportation Co. She was employed on the Willamette River. In 1875 her boiler exploded at Portland OR.

Senator Jansen 126272 (Canada) (passenger/ freight vessel) She was built in 1909 at New Westminster BC Canada by Alexander Watson. 112.0' x 24.0' x 3.0' Wood. 229.98gt 93.29rt. Powered by a 9hp steam engine. In 1909–1919 she was owned by the Fraser River Lumber Co., Fraser Mills BC. In 1919–1937 she was owned by the Canadian Western Lumber Co. Ltd., Fraser Mills BC. In 1921 she was reported to have been broken up.

Senator Wm. B. Allison[869] (US) 50' x 14' x 2.2' Wood. 10gt 10nt. Powered by a steam engine. She is reported by Murray Lundberg to have worked in Alaska/YT 1898.

Senorita (see *Sarah Hoyt*)

Sentinel[870] 205050 (US) She was built in 1903 at Oakland CA USA. 90.1' x 19.0' x 4.5' Wood. 99gt 91rt. Powered by a 150ihp steam engine. She was in service on California rivers. She was reported to have foundered in 1919.

Service (see *Inland Empire*)

Shamrock (later *Lorelei*) 107940 (Canada) 141598 (US) (passenger vessel) She was built in 1896 at Portland OR USA. 49.6' x 10.0' x 3.1' Wood. 32gt 20nt. Powered by a 1nhp steam engine. In 1898 she was rebuilt at Skagway AK USA. She was later converted to a gas engine. In 1900 she was owned by George Finlay. In 1901 she was owned by EG Tennant, Atlin BC. In 1904 she was owned by John Leech, Dawson YT. In 1915 she was owned by the Klondike Airways. In 1938 she was laid up.

Shasta[871,872] (US) (sidewheeler) She was built in 1853 at San Francisco CA USA by Littleton & Co. 110' x ? x 1.5' Wood. 120gt. Powered by a steam engine. In 1854 she was owned by the California Steam Navigation Co. She was employed on California rivers. In 1854 she was reported as having been laid up and abandoned in 1856.

Shaver 205179 (US) She was built in 1908 at Portland OR. 155.0' x 30.8' x 6.7' Wood. 368gt 305nt. Powered by 725ihp two horizontal (high pressure 18.5" x 72") steam engine. Her engines came from the Mississippi River vessel *Arkansas Chief*, which were originally employed in the *J.M Hannaford* that had been manufactured in Cincinnati OH in 1859. In 1908–1926 she was owned by the Shaver Transportation Co. (Red Collar fleet), Portland OR. In 1926 she was converted to become the first twin screw tunnel-stern Atlas Imperial diesel powered towboat in the United States.

Shillong (Burma Register) She was built in 1917 at Esquimalt BC Canada by the B.C. Marine Railway Co., Esquimalt BC. 132' x 31' x 4.7' Steel. 419gt. Powered by a 300ihp steam reciprocating engine. In 1917 she was owned by the Burmah Oil Company.

Shoalwater[873] (later *Fenix*) (US) (sidewheeler) (passenger vessel) In 1852 she was built at Canemah OT USA. 93' x 17.6' x 3' Wood. Powered by a (12" x 48") steam engine. In 1852 she was renamed as the *Fenix*. In 1855 she was owned by Judge McCarver. In 1858 she was reported to have been broken up at Salem OR USA.

Shoo Fly 023975 (US) She was built in 1870 at Canemah OT USA by Joseph Paquet. 126' x 23' x 4.5' Wood. 317gt. Powered by two 13nhp horizontal (high pressure 14" x 48") steam engines. In 1870 she was owned by the Peoples Transportation Co., Vancouver WT. In 1878 she was reported as having been broken up.

Shoo Fly 023979 (US) She was built in 1881 at Coupeville WA USA. 60.0' x 11.0' x 4.0' Wood. 54.63gt 27.32nt. Powered by a steam engine. She was employed on Puget Sound WA.

Shoshone[874] 023961 (US) She was built in 1866 at Boise ID USA. 136' x 27' x 4.5' Wood. 299.73gt. Powered by two 16nhp horizontal (high pressure 16" x 48") steam engines. In 1866–1872 she was owned by the Oregon Steam Navigation Co. In 1870 she was transferred down the Snake River to work the Celilo Rapids and the Cascades. In 1872 she was owned by the Willamette River Transportation Co. In 1874 she was wrecked after hitting a rock in the Willamette River near Salem OR.

Shoshone[875,876] 209110 (US) (passenger vessel) She was built in 1908 at Coeur d'Alene ID USA. 53.6' x 9.9' x 3.0' Wood. 11gt 7nt. Powered by a 72ihp steam engine. In 1908 she was employed on the St. Joe River. In 1912 she was transferred to the Columbia River.

Show Boat[877] (US) She was built in 1908 at Coeur d'Alene ID. Powered by a 1200hp John Deere diesel engine. "The hull was originally a barge from the Sacramento River delta that was converted into a replica of a Mississippi river boat including the requisite sponsons 4 rudders and a paddlewheel, driven via jackshafts and chain drive just like the originals. She did have a bow thruster fitted which was essential for close quarters maneuvering and docking in the busy channels of Los Angeles Harbour." In 1908 she was owned by the Carscallen Bros.

Shubrick[878] (USLHC) (sidewheeler) (patrol vessel) She was built in 1858c. 140' Wood. Powered by a steam engine. In 1865, the US Lighthouse tender Shubrick, then operating under the Revenue Cutter Service, became the service's first vessel to be deployed to Alaska. In 1862–1865 she was operating as part of the United States Lighthouse Service. She was transferred to the United States Revenue Cutter Service (RCS). The RCS was charged with ending pelagic seal hunting and protecting the seal herds and rookeries in the Pribilof Islands. In 1861 she was transferred from the US Lighthouse Service to the US Revenue Service. She spent the Civil War as the guard ship to San Francisco. The US Revenue Cutter Shubrick was nearly captured by Confederate States agents during the US Civil War at Victoria around 1863. Letters of Marque were issued to the southern sympathizers in Victoria by the Confederate States President, Jefferson Davis, and they planned to capture the Shubrick in Victoria and start raiding US gold ships and burning mills along the US west coast. The Confederate agents had convinced most of the crew of the Shubrick to take over the vessel when in Victoria, but northern spies had got wind of the plot and what were thought to be passengers on the Shubrick going to Victoria turned out to be a replacement crew. When the Shubrick crossed the border in the Strait of Juan de Fuca the new crew took control of the Shubrick, and the old crew was discharged in Victoria. In 1865 she was supporting the Western Union expedition to erect a telegraph cable from North America to St. Petersburg Russia.

Shubrick (USRC) (see Shubrick [USLHC])

Shusana 211609 (US) She was built in 1913 at Fairbanks AK USA. 79.8' x 20.9' x 3.9' Wood. 49gt. Powered by a 100ihp steam engine. In 1914 she was owned by Alaska Rivers Navigation Co. She was owned by the Alaska Rivers Navigation Co. On May 11, 1920, this sternwheeler (with a crew of 11) was stranded on the Tanana River near Nenana AK. In 1920 she was reported as having been broken up at Nenana AK USA.

Sibilla[879] (US) (freighter) Wood. Powered by a steam engine. She is reported by Murray Lundberg to have worked in Alaska/YT in 1916.

Sierra Nevada (see *Texas*)

Sicamous 134276 (Canada) (freighter) She was built in 1914 at Okanagan Landing BC Canada. 200.5' x 40.0' x 8.0' Steel. 1787gt 994rt. Powered by a 101nhp steam engine. In 1914–1945 she was owned by Canadian Pacific Railway Ltd., Montreal QC. In 1914 she was in service from Okanagan Landing to Penticton. In 1930 she was converted to a cargo vessel. In 1935 she made her last voyage. In 1949 she was owned by the City of Penticton as a museum. In 1985 she was operating as a restaurant. She was employed on Okanagan Lake service between Penticton, Kelowna, and Vernon. She was most important in transporting fruit from the agricultural communities along the lake to the rail head for transportation to the world. She is currently beached as part of a heritage shipyard operated by the Penticton Museum and Archives in Penticton, British Columbia where she functions as a museum, an events facility and banquet hall.

Silver City[880] (US) (freighter) She was built in 1936 at Polson MT USA by Eugene Hodge. 100' Wood. Edward L Affleck reported that in 1943 she sank at Big Fork MT and was salvaged in 1946.

Silver Queen (see *Sternwheeler*)

Silver Stream (later *Andover*) 126331 (Canada) (passenger vessel) She was built in 1907 at Kamloops BC Canada by G & Elmer & Arthur B Ward. 91.3' x 19.9' x 4' Wood. 177gt 111rt. Powered by an 8nhp steam engine. In

1907–1910 she was owned by G Ward, Elmer Ward and Arthur B Ward, Kamloops BC. In 1911–1931 she was owned by Arrow Lakes Lumber Co. Ltd., Arrowhead BC. She was employed a passenger service to Sicamous 1907–1915 and 1918–1921 on Shuswap Lake.

Sima (Burma Register) She was built in 1917 at Esquimalt BC Canada by the B.C. Marine Railway Co., Esquimalt BC. 132' x 31' x 4.7' Steel. 419gt. Powered by a 300ihp steam reciprocating engine. In 1917 she was owned by the Burmah Oil Company.

Sind (Burma Register) She was built in 1917 at Esquimalt BC Canada by B.C. Marine Railway Co., Esquimalt BC. 132' x 31' x 4.7' Steel. 419gt. Powered by a 300ihp steam reciprocating engine. In 1917 she was owned by the Burmah Oil Company.

Sioc[881] (later *Jack Hayes*; then *Reindeer*) (US) She was built about 1850. Wood. Powered by a steam engine. In 1853 she was owned by Colonel JB Huie, Petaluma CA. In 1853 she was in service between Petaluma CA and New Town CA.

Sitka[882] (later *Rainbow*) (US) (sidewheeler) She was built in 1847. 37' Wood. 40gt. Powered by a steam engine. She was in service on California rivers. In 1848 she was rebuilt as the schooner *Rainbow*.

Skagit Belle 241154 (US) (freighter) She was built in 1941 at Everett WA USA. 164.5' x 40.3' x 6.7' Wood. 555gt 513nt. Powered by a 500hp high pressure steam engine. In 1941–1947 she was owned by the Skagit River Navigation Co., Seattle WA USA. She was requisitioned for war service. She was returned to the Skagit River Navigation Co. until 1947. In May 1965 she sank while alongside in Seattle Harbor when pumps were unable to keep up with a serious leak in the hull. The wreckage was cleared away in 1973. It has been claimed that she was the last commercial stern-wheel steamboat employed on Puget Sound.

Skagit Chief (later *Tourist*) 116159 (US) 203932 (US) (passenger/ freight vessel) She was built in 1887 at Tacoma WA USA. 137.5' x 26.3' x 5.5' Wood. 345gt 241.17nt. Powered by a steam engine. She was repowered with a diesel engine. In 1907 she was rebuilt by the Carlson Brothers at Port Blakely WA to 156.8' x 27.9' x 7.6' 467gt 294rt and renamed as the *Tourist*. She was in service for the US Navy Yard route of the Puget Sound Navigation Co. In 1929 she was owned by the Puget Sound Freight Lines. In May 1888 she was sent up from the Puget Sound to Wrangel AK and worked the Stikine River. She was sold to satisfy creditor's demands and returned to service on the Puget Sound for the rest of her career.

Skagit Chief[883] 233755 (US) (passenger/ freight vessel) She was built in 1935 at Seattle WA USA by Lake Union Dry Dock & Machine Works. 165.0' x 40.1' x 6.4'. Wood. 502gt 469nt. Powered by a 400hp steam engine. Her engines came from the *G.K. Wentworth*. In 1935–1954 she was owned by the Skagit River Navigation & Trading Co. (owned by Mrs. Anna Grimison, sister of Captain Harry McDonald) Seattle WA. In 1956 she was sold to the Portland Harbour Marina, Portland OR. She was fitted with spuds to help her manoeuvre over sand bars. She was employed on the Seattle-Stanwood-Mount Vernon-La Conner WA run. On October 29, 1956, she foundered about 12 miles west of Grays Harbor WA USA. She broke loose from the tug *Martha Foss* while being towed to Portland Oregon to be converted into a floating restaurant.

Skagit Queen 116866 (US) (passenger vessel) She was built in 1898 at West Seattle WA USA. 125.5' x 25.7' x 4.6'. Wood. 327gt 196nt. Powered by a steam engine. Her engines and house works came from the *City of Champagne*. In 1898 she was owned by the Skagit River Navigation & Trading Co. In 1930 she was reported as having been broken up.

Skedaddle[884] (US) (passenger/ freight vessel, later a barge) She was built in 1862 at Portland OT USA by George Pease. 160' x 14' x 3'. Wood. Powered by a (7" x 12") steam engine. She was owned by the People's Transportation Co. In 1869 she was reported as having been broken up at Portland OT.

Skeena 126212 (Canada) (passenger vessel, later an accommodation barge) She was built in 1908 at Vancouver BC Canada by Donald McPhee. 121.2' x 26.8' x 5.6'. Wood. 515gt 310nt. Powered by two 8hp horizontal steam engines built by Albion Iron Works, Victoria BC. In 1929 she was rebuilt as a dormitory barge and then as a fuel barge 169.17 gt/rt. In 1908–1910 she was owned by John W Stewart for service in railway construction on the Grand Trunk Pacific Railway. In 1914 she was sold to Captain Charles E Seymour (North Arm Steamship Co.) for Fraser River service. In 1919–1931 she was owned by the Mainland Navigation Co. Ltd., New Westminster BC. In 1936 she was owned by Wilfred G Dolmage, Vancouver BC. In 1936–1937 she was owned by Harbour Towing Co. Ltd., Vancouver BC. In 1912 she was running daily trips from Vancouver BC to Wigwam Inn on Indian Arm in Burrard Inlet. She served as a bunkhouse vessel and then as an oil barge.

Skeena at the Wigwam Inn (Image from Vancouver Archives AM54–S4–LGN 546)

Skookum 200803 (US) She was built in 1904 at Aberdeen WA USA by William HM McWhinney. 112.0' x 26.8' x 5.6' Wood. 302gt 173nt. Powered by a 400ihp steam engine. In 1904 she was owned by Burrows & Stockwell. She was originally employed towing logs on Grays Harbor. In 1910 she was owned by Port Townsend WA USA interest. She was later employed on the Columbia River for Milton Smith. She was reported as having been broken up in 1945.

Skookum Chief (see K.L. Ames)

Skuzzy[885] 085317 (Canada) (passenger/ freight vessel) She was built in 1882 at Spuzzum BC Canada by William Dalton. She was launched on May 4, 1882, christened by Sarah Onderdonk. 127.0' x 24.2' x 4.5' Wood. 319gt 254.37rt. Powered by a 60nhp steam engine built by Joseph Spratt, Victoria BC. In 1882 she was owned by John Trutch, William Van Horne, and Andrew Onderdonk. She was built to compete with the *Peerless*. She was underpowered for navigation on that stretch of the river. She managed to pass through Hell's Gate (the only steamer ever to have done so). In 1885 she was reported as having been broken up. Her machinery was removed and taken to Savona and installed in the second *Skuzzy* on the Thompson River.

Skuzzy[886] 090801 (Canada) (freighter) She was built in 1885 at Savonna BC Canada. 133.3' x 28' x 6.5' Wood. 472gt 297rt. Powered by a steam engine. In 1885 she was owned by John Trutch, Victoria BC. In 1886–1896 she was owned by John Mara, Kamloops BC. She carried some of the machinery from the first *Skuzzy*. In 1885 she carried track for construction of the Canadian Pacific Railway and as accommodation and mess hall for workers. Mara used her for towing logs occasionally. In 1887 she was reported as having been abandoned on the beach at Kamloops. Her engine went to the *Nelson* in 1889.

Skwala[887] 126334 (Canada) (freighter) She was built in 1909 at Vancouver BC Canada. 92.7' x 19.2' x 5.0' Wood. 165gt 103rt. Powered by a 13nhp steam engine. In 1909–1919 she was owned by Rat Portage Lumber Co. Ltd., St. Boniface MB. In 1912 she was reported as having been abandoned.

Slackwater 319316 (Canada) (power cruiser yacht) She was built in 1962 at Kamloops BC Canada by George A. Slack. 32.2' x 12.0' x 1.7' Wood. 17.48gt/rt. Powered by an 80bhp gasoline engine built by International Harvester Co. of Canada Ltd., Hamilton ON. In 1962–1977 she was owned by George A. Slack, Kamloops BC.

Slave River 130276 (Canada) (passenger/ freight vessel) She was built in 1912 at Athabasca Landing AB by Captain J.W. Mills. 109.0' x 22.3' x 5.0' Wood. 318gt 205rt. Powered by a 5nhp steam engine. In 1912–1914 she was owned by the Hudson's Bay Company, London UK. She served on the Lesser Slave River and Lesser Slave Lake. In 1919 she was owned by the Lamson & Hubbard Canadian Co. Ltd., Edmonton AB. She was run through the Grand Rapids of the Athabasca to Fort McMurray. In 1921 she was transferred to the new Alberta and Arctic Transportation Company when Lamson & Hubbard amalgamated with the BX Company. She was rebuilt during which process her unusual bow string truss hull supports were replaced by more conventional hog posts and rods. She was reported as having been broken up c1925 at which point the Hudson's Bay Company had assumed ownership of the Alberta and Arctic Transportation Co.

Slocan at New Denver BC (Image from Maritime Museum of British Columbia 000417)

Slocan 103168 (Canada) (passenger vessel, later a barge) She was built in 1897 at Roseberry BC. 155.7' x 25.2' x 6.5' Wood. 578gt 364rt. Powered by a 17nhp steam engine built by the B.C. Iron Works, Vancouver BC. In 1905 she was rebuilt at Roseberry BC. In 1905 she was re-registered as the *Slocan* (121680) 155.7' x 27.5' x 6.7' 604gt 337rt. In 1897–1928 she was owned by Canadian Pacific Railway Co., Montreal QC. In 1928 she was sold as a logging camp warehouse on Slocan Lake. She was reported as having been broken up.

Slocan 121680 (see *Slocan* 103168) (freighter) She was built in 1905 at Roseberry BC Canada by James M Bulger. 157.7' x 27.5' x 6.7' Wood. 605gt

338rt. Powered by a 17nhp steam engine. In 1905–1919 she was owned by the Canadian Pacific Railway, Montreal QC. In 1928 her hull was purchased by Lingle & Johnson for use as a warehouse at Trout Creek Landing BC until it was destroyed by fire in 1931.

Snake River 216046 (US) (ferry) She was built in 1918 at Ainsworth WA USA by JA Groener. 52.4' x 18.1' x 2.1' Wood. 13gt 10nt. Powered by a 32hp gasoline engine. In 1918 she was owned by JA Groener, Paterson WA. In 1929 she was owned by Gordon Holmes, Paterson WA. In 1935 she was owned by the Paterson Ferry, Paterson WA USA. In 1941 she was reported as having been abandoned and broken up.

Sockeye 116425 (Canada) (sidewheeler) (fishboat) She was built in 1900 in Vancouver BC. 29.5' x 8.0' x 2.6' Wood. 3gt 2rt. Powered by a 1nhp engine. In 1910–1919 she was owned by Anton Klavanes, Vancouver BC.

Solano[888,889] 023224 (US) (sidewheeler) She was built in 1866 at Oakland CA by the Middlemas shipyard. 109.5' Wood. 146.88gt. Powered by a steam engine. She was owned by the California Steam Navigation Company. In 1871 she was taken over by the California Pacific Railroad Co., San Francisco CA. She was employed on California rivers. She was reported to have been abandoned in 1873.

Solano 115694 (US) (ferry) She was built in 1879 at San Francisco CA USA. 407.0' x 65.5' x 17.4' Wood. 3549.31gt 3057.13rt. Powered by a 2,000nhp steam engine. In 1879–1910 she was owned by San Francisco CA USA interests. She was in service on California rivers.

Sonoma[890] 115298 (US) She was built in 1874 at San Francisco CA USA. 136.0' x 29.0' x 6.5' Wood. 305gt 250nt. Powered by a 60ihp steam engine. She was in service on California rivers. She was reported to have been abandoned in 1915.

Sophie[891] (US) (sidewheeler) She was built in 1851 at San Francisco CA. Wood. 148gt. Powered by a steam engine. She was in service on California rivers. In 1854 she was owned by the California Steam Navigation Co. She was reported to have been abandoned in 1859.

Sophie McClean/Sophie McLean[892] (US) (sidewheeler) She was built in 1859 at San Francisco CA. Wood. 242gt. Powered by a steam engine. In 1859 she was owned by the California Steam Navigation Company. She originally was employed on the San Francisco – San Jose route. She was employed on the Sacramento River, CA. On November 26, 1864, her boiler exploded at the Suisun CA wharf resulting in 13 dead. (Her name has been spelled variously by different authorities as Sophie McLane (Lytle), Sophie McClean and Sophie McLean (McMullin).

Sovereign 116813 (US) (passenger/ freight vessel) She was built in 1898 at Ballard WA USA by Thomas C Reed. 125.6' x 26.5' x 4.7' Wood. 326.4gt 188.7nt. Powered by a steam engine. In 1898 she was owned by the Columbia River Navigation Co. In 1898 she was towed to St. Michael by *the Lakme*. She was employed between St. Michael and Dawson 1898–1904. She was reported to have been wrecked on the beach at Nome AK.

Spallumcheen 085313 (Canada) (sidewheeler) (passenger/ freight vessel) She was built in 1878 at Kamloops BC Canada by Alexander Watson. 83.25' x 26.3' x 5.0' Wood. 256gt 50.54rt. Powered by a 12nhp steam threshing machine engine built by the Hoadley Lawrence & Co., Manchester UK. In 1878 she was owned by the Kamloops Steam Navigation Co., Kamloops BC. In 1896 she was owned by Mara & Wilson, Kamloops BC. She was launched on July 2, 1874. She was known as the "Noisy Peggy." She ran between Savona's Ferry and Eagle Pass. She worked in the Enderby area but was made obsolete by the railway. In 1894 she was reported as having been broken up after breaking her mooring and becoming wrecked.

Speilei[893] 212809 (US) (tug) She was built in 1914 at St. Helens OR USA by James H Price. 76.3' x 24,0' x 4.0' Wood. 75gt 55nt. Powered by 40ihp steam engine. In 1914–1940 she was owned by Lewis River Boom & Logging Co., Ridgefield WA. In 1940 she was reported as having been abandoned.

Spieler 207602 (US) She was built in 1906 at Ridgefield WA USA. 60.8' x 22.2' x 3.6' Wood. 36gt/nt. Powered by a steam engine. In 1915 she was reported to have been out of service.

Spirit of Sacramento (see *Becky Thatcher*)

Spirit of Sacramento (see *Putah*)

Spokane 115577 (US) (freighter) She was built in 1877 at Celilo OR USA. 150.0' x 32.0' x 4.0' Wood. 673.38gt 531.68rt. Powered by two 13nhp horizontal (high pressure 14" x 48") steam engines. Her engines came from the *Colonel Wright*. In 1888 she was rebuilt to 150' x 32' x 4.8'. Powered by (18" x 84") steam engines. In 1899 she was rebuilt again.

Spokane 116411 (US) (passenger vessel) In 1891 she was built at Eaton ID. 126' Wood. 217.52gt 162.31nt. Powered by a 240nhp engine. In 1895 she was reported to have been destroyed by fire.

Spokane 0116557 (US) 100684 (Canada) (passenger/ freight vessel, later a float) She was built in 1894 at Bonners Ferry WA by GR Gray. 103.8' x 24.4' x 5.3' Wood. 115.19gt 110.74nt. Powered by 9.6nhp horizontal (high pressure 12" x 48") steam engines built by the Willamette Iron Works, Portland OR. In 1893 she was rebuilt and lengthened to 125.8' x 24.8' x 5.3' 399.77gt 251.66rt. In 1891 she was owned by Burns & Chapman. In 1893–1896 she was owned by the Columbia, Kootenay Steam Transportation Co. In 1893 she was transferred to Canadian Registry. In 1893 she was owned by the Columbia and Kootenay Steam Navigation Co. In 1891 she was in service on Great Northern Railway from Bonners Ferry to Jennings MT. On July 04, 1891, she snagged at Moyie Landing but was salvaged. She was used as a landing stage at Kaslo BC after the Kaslo wharf washed out in a flood in 1894. On March 25, 1895, she burned to the waterline at Kaslo BC and was declared a total loss. Her engines were salvaged.

Spokane 116876 (US) (passenger vessel) She was built in 1899 at Riparia WA USA. 160.4' x 38.6' x 6.3' Wood. 561gt 421nt. Powered by a 700ihp steam engine. In 1888 she was owned by the Oregon Railroad & Navigation Co. In 1899 she was rebuilt 160.4' x 38.6' x 6.3' 676gt. 408nt. Powered by two horizontal (high pressure 18" x 84") steam engines. In 1922 she was destroyed by fire at Lewiston ID.

Spokane 117250 (US) She was built in 1903 at Newport ID USA. 132.0' x 26.0' x 5.0' Wood. 367gt 231nt. Powered by a 240ihp steam engine. (Her engines came from the *J.D. Farrell*) In 1899 she was rebuilt. In 1903–1910 she was owned by the Pend Oreille River Navigation Co., Great Falls MT.

In 1908 she was rebuilt. In 1909 she was owned by the Panhandle Lumber Co. In 1922 she was reported to have been abandoned.

Spray 023147 (US) She was built in 1862 at Deschutes OT USA. 116' x 22.9' x 5' Wood. 122gt. Powered by two horizontal (high pressure 14" x 48") steam engines. In 1862 she was owned by a consortium of HW Corbett, W Gates, DS Baker, AF Ankeny, and Captain Harry Baughman. She was employed on the upper Columbia and Snake Rivers. In 1863 she was owned by the Oregon Railroad and Navigation Co. In 1867 she was reported to have been laid up. In 1869 she was broken up at Celilo OR USA. Her engines went to the *Orient* (19449).

St. Charles (Canada) (mission boat) She was built in 1903 at Dunvegan AB Canada. 67' x 12' x ? Wood. 28.79gt 19.5rt. Powered by a steam engine. In 1903 she was owned by Bishop Emile Grouard, Vicar Apostolic and Bishop of Athabasca. She was a Roman Catholic Church mission boat in Peace River service as far as Hudson's Hope BC. In 1911 she was sold to Lawrence & Ford. She was the first steamship on the upper Peace River. In 1915 she was grounded during freeze-up. On April 29, 1915, The Peace River Record reported that she was "grounded on a bar in the river during freeze up, was thrown high and dry on the bank when the ice went out and is undamaged." She was dismantled in 1916–1917.

Staghound (later *Hercules*) 116823 (US) 096443 (US) (passenger/ freight vessel) She was built in 1898 at Portland OR USA. 178.2' x 38' x 7.9' Wood. 772gt 658nt. Powered by two horizontal high pressure (18.5" x 84") steam engines. In 1899 she was rebuilt by Dan Kern at Portland OR and repowered with two horizontal high pressure (18.5" x 34") 700ihp steam engines. In 1898 she was owned by the Yukon Transportation & Commercial Co., San Francisco CA USA. In 1898 she snapped her hog chains, and her wreck was purchased by Daniel Kern and rebuilt as the *Hercules*. In 1899 she was owned by the Hosford Transportation Co. In 1925 she was operated by Shaver Transportation Co. (Not worked after 1935). She had been built for service in the Klondike Gold Rush. On June 24, 1898, she was wrecked with the *Gamecock* while in tow by the *Elihu Thompson* at the Columbia River Bar OR USA when she had snapped her hog chains. She was salvaged and rebuilt as the *Hercules* (096443) for service on the Columbia River.

Star[894] (US) She was built in 1850 in the eastern USA. Wood. 22gt. Powered by a steam engine. She was employed on California rivers. She was reported to have been abandoned about 1852.

Star 203048 (US) (passenger vessel) She was built in 1906 at Seattle WA USA. 39.7' x 10.0' x 2.9'. Wood. 8gt 5rt. Powered by a gasoline engine. She was employed on Puget Sound WA.

Stark Street Ferry 115747 (US) (sidewheeler) (ferry) She was built in 1881 at Portland OR USA. 138.0' x 17.0' x 5.0'. Wood. 231.33gt. Powered by a steam engine. In 1897 she was reported to have been out of service.

Stark Street Ferry No. 7 116022 (US) (sidewheeler) (ferry) She was built in 1884 at Portland OR USA. 130.0' x 41.3' x 6.3'. Wood. 299.36gt/nt. Powered by a steam engine. In 1897 she was reported to have been out of service.

Starkey[895] (US) (passenger/ freight vessel) She was built in 1898 at St. Michael AK USA by the Moran Bros. Shipyard. 60' x 16' x ?. Wood. Powered by a steam engine. In 1898 she was owned by the Seattle-Yukon Transportation Co. She is reported by Murray Lundberg to have worked in Alaska/YT in 1898.

State of Idaho[896] (later *Alberta*) 116557 (US) 103296 (Canada) She was built in 1893 at Bonners Ferry WA. 141' x 23.3' x 6.3; Wood. 341.04gt 272.74ynt. Powered by two horizontal (high pressure 12" x 72") steam engines. Her engines were built in 1888 for the steamer *Crescent* on Flathead Lake ID. She worked from Bonners Ferry to Kaslo and Nelson. In 1893 she was owned by Bonners Ferry & Kaslo Transportation Co. In 1894 she was renamed as the *Alberta* and owned by Alberta & B.C. Exploration Co. and registered in Canada (103296). In 1895–1901 she was owned by The International Trading, Calgary NWT. In 1904 she was owned by International Navigation Co., Kaslo BC. Following a grounding in 1893 at Ainsworth BC she was sold for salvage and rebuilt at Kaslo BC. She was laid up in 1902. She grounded in 1905 at the dock in Kaslo. She was laid up at Mirror Lake. Her hull was sold to Gus Matthew at Riondel, and her machinery was sold to the Columbia & Okanagan Steamboat Co. for the American steamer *Columbia*. In 1895 she worked on the Bonners Ferry to Kaslo and Nelson run. After the steamer *Kaslo* appeared, she was relegated to the role of a relief steamer. She sank at the dock in Kaslo 1895, was raised and dismantled on the ways with her machinery going to the *Columbia* (202431). Her hull became a houseboat at Galena Bay where as a derelict she was destroyed by fire in 1920.

State of Montana[897] (US) (passenger vessel) She was built in 1891 at Polson MT USA. 150' x 26' x ? Wood. Powered by a steam engine. In 1891 she was owned by James Kerr. In 1892 she was stranded at Foys Bend MT.

State of Washington 116272 (US) In 1889 she was built at Tacoma WA USA by John J Holland. 170.4' x 31.3' x 7.0' Wood. 605gt 449rt. Powered by a 504ihp steam engine. From 1889 to 1902 the vessel was in employed on the Seattle – Bellingham route. From 1902 to 1907, the vessel was a standby boat on the Tacoma – Seattle run. In 1913, the vessel was transferred to the Columbia River. On June 24, 1920, this sternwheeler's boiler exploded with the loss of a fireman and injuries to six of the crew at Astoria OR. The explosion occurred off Tongue Point while she was towing an oil barge en route to Portland. She sank quickly by the stern.

Stehikine (see *Columbia Queen*)

Stella[898] (US) (freighter) Wood. Powered by a steam engine. In 1860 she was employed on the Sacramento River.

Sternwheeler (later *Silver Queen*) 170758 (Canada) (tug) She was built in 1934 at Waterways AB Canada by George F Askew. (Designed by George F Askew). 84.0' x 15.4' x 4.0' Wood. 46gt 31rt. Powered by a 100nhp engine. In 1934–1945 she was owned by Northern Transportation Co., Edmonton AB. George Duddy reports that "She ran from Fort Norman up the Bear River to Bear River Rapids going over the portage between Fort Fitzgerald and Fort Smith. In 1934 there was a ship building boom at both Waterways and Fort Smith to provide vessels to support the mining boom on Great Bear. Some of the vessels were built by Askew but many by his competitor from Edmonton. All this mining activity preceded the "Manhattan Project." The radium ore was rich material and there were other ores."

Sternwheeler No. 1 (India Register) (freighter). She was built in 1916 at Esquimalt BC Canada by Yarrows Ltd. This vessel was shipped in pieces to India where it was assembled and put into service.

Sternwheeler No. 2 (India Register) (freighter). She was built in 1917 at Esquimalt BC Canada by Yarrows Ltd. This vessel was shipped in pieces to India where it was assembled and put into service.

Stikine Chief[899] 107147 (Canada) (passenger/ freight vessel) She was built in 1898 at Vancouver BC Canada by Colin J McAlpine. 150' x 32.3' x 5.4' Wood. 846.91gt 577.02rt. Powered by two 19nhp horizontal (high pressure 17" x 72") steam engines built by the William Hamilton Mfg. Co., Peterborough ON. In 1898 she was owned by Stikine Navigation Co. Ltd. She was built for service on the Stikine River and worked there briefly. On November 29, 1898, she was wrecked on delivery while under tow north to St. Michael AK by the British tramp steamer *Fastnet*. She was never used in service off Yakutat AK.

Stockton[900] (US) She was built about 1853. Wood. Powered by a steam engine. She was in service on California rivers. She ceased operation about 1868.

Storm King[901] (US) (sidewheeler) (passenger/car ferry) She was built on Lake Crescent WA. 112' x 31.5' x ? Wood. (She was designed by Treiber). Powered by a 40hp Fairbanks-Morse gasoline engine. She had a capacity of 21 automobiles and 150 passengers and was employed on Clallam County Crescent Lake service.

Stranger 227888 (US) (tug) She was built in 1928 at Portland OR USA. 129.8' x 28.4' x 4.5' Wood. 358gt 312nt. In 1928–1929 she was owned by GM Walker, Portland, OR USA. In 1931–1935 she was owned by the Salem Navigation Co., Portland OR. In 1939 she was reported to have been dismantled at Salem OR USA.

Strathcona[902] 107146 (Canada) (passenger/ freight vessel) She was built in 1898 at Vancouver BC, designed and built by J Macfarlane (B.C. Iron

Works). 142.4' x 30.4' x 4.0' Wood. 596.28gt 375.66rt. Powered by two horizontal (high pressure) steam engines built by B.C. Iron Works. She was rebuilt in 1898. In 1898–1901 she was owned by the Hudson's Bay Company, London UK. In 1901–1902 she was owned by Charles Spratt, Victoria BC. In 1902c she was sold to SJV Spratt and then to the Sidney & Nanaimo Transportation Co. In 1910 she was owned by William A Rannie et al., Vancouver BC. She was a sister ship of the *Caledonia* (III). She served on the Stikine River. This steamer helped start the Sidney and Nanaimo ferry route on June 24, 1902. This service was called the Sidney and Nanaimo Transportation Company. The *Strathcona* had worked for three months of that year before she blew a cylinder on August 19, 1902. The ship was unable to be repaired, so she was retired from the Sidney & Nanaimo Transportation Co. immediately and replaced. Afterwards she worked on Howe Sound. On November 17, 1909, she was wrecked at Page's Landing (Fraser River) BC by striking a snag. In 1910 she was raised with pontoons and floated to New Westminster BC where her hull was reported to have been abandoned. (The Canada Register of Shipping says that she was reported as having been broken up.)

Strathcona (later *Scona*) 126450 (Canada) She was built in 1910 at Strathcona AB Canada. 120' x 22' x 4' Wood. 114gt 72rt. Powered by a 4nhp engine. In 1904–1913 she was owned by John Walter, Strathcona AB. In 1916–1918 she was owned by John Walter, Edmonton AB. In 1919–1931 she was owned by John Walter Ltd., Edmonton AB. She was reported as having been abandoned at Edmonton AB.

Success 023717 (US) She was built in 1868 at Canemah OR USA by John Thomas. 131' x 24.5' x 4' Wood. 344gt. Powered by two horizontal (high pressure 16" x 48") steam engines. In 1868 she was owned by Captain EW Baughman (Canemah Transportation Co.). In 1869 she was owned by the People's Transportation Co. In 1877 she was reported to have been broken up at Oregon City.

Sunbury 096992 (Canada) (tug) She was built in 1891 at New Westminster BC Canada. 60.0' x 12.6' x 4.8' Wood. 38gt 26rt. Powered by a 3nhp engine. In 1895–1896 she was owned by MD McLennan, New Westminster BC. In

1901 she was owned by JD Foreman (MO), Vancouver BC. In 1905–1912 she was owned by AT Ingram & Peter McLaggan, Vancouver BC. In 1913–1947 she was owned by The Silica Sand & Gravel Co. Ltd., Vancouver BC.

Sunflower 116848 (US) (passenger/ freight vessel) She was built in 1898 at St. Michael AK USA. 60.0' x 11.5' x 2.7' Wood. 57gt 36nt. Powered by a steam engine. In 1898–1900 she was employed on Alaska inland waters.

Sunol[903] 116371 (US) She was built in 1890 at San Francisco CA USA. 135.0' x 27.5' x 7.0' Wood. 294gt 246rt. Powered by a 120ihp steam engine. In 1916 she was owned by W.P. Fuller & Co. In 1916 she was owned by the California Salt Co. In 1916 she was rebuilt to 161' at the Robertson Schultze Shipyard.

Sunset[904] 206414 (US) She was built in 1909 at Prosper OR USA by Carl Herman. 40.2' x 9.2' x 3.6' Wood. 13gt 8nt. Powered by a 15ihp gasoline engine. In 1909 she was owned by the Drane Line (Frederick Elmore). She was employed at Coos Bay OR. On November 2, 1924, she sank on the Coquille River at Bandon OR with the loss of Clarence H. Hurley. She was salvaged and put back into service. In 1929 she was reported to have been abandoned.

Surprise (US) She was built in 1855 at San Francisco CA USA. In 1855 she was owned by the California Steam Navigation Co. In 1861 she was sold to China interests, and she was transferred there to carry freight on the Yangtze River. She originally ran in opposition to the California Steam Navigation Co. In She was destroyed by fire at Shanghai China.

Surprise[905] (US) (sidewheeler) She was built in 1855 at Williamsburgh NY by Lawrence Foulkes. 181.1' x 27.9' x 9.6' Wood. 458gt. Powered by a steam engine. She was in service on California rivers. In 1854 she was owned by AN Brown. In 1858 she was owned by the California Steam Navigation Co. (Captain Thomas Huntington). She worked only one season as the first steamer on the Fraser River—the first to travel to Hope. On June 7, 1858, she was a merchant vessel which made her first trip up the Fraser River beyond Fort Langley to Fort Hope, British Columbia. Her capacity was

400 but she often carried 500 at a time on her 15 round trips on the river. The fare from Victoria to Hope at that time was $25. She was destroyed by fire in 1868.

Surprise (US) She was built in 1857 at Canemah OT USA by Cocran, Cassidy & Gibson. 130' Wood. 120gt. Powered by two horizontal (high pressure 14" x 60") steam engines. Her engines came from the *Senator*. In 1864 she was reported as having been laid up and later broken up.

Surrey 094909 (Canada) (passenger vessel) She was built in 1890 at New Westminster BC Canada by NS Terhune. 100.0' x 22.0' x 6.0' Wood. 263.26gt 181.66rt. Powered by a steam engine. In 1899 she was rebuilt. In 1890–1905 she was owned by the Corporation of the City of New Westminster BC. In 1905–1910 she was owned by DC Irwin and JG Scott, Vancouver BC. She was the second ferry in service on the Fraser River at New Westminster BC from Brownsville to New Westminster BC. She was made obsolete by the opening of the first bridge across the river built in 1904. In 1909 she was reported as having been broken up.

Susana/Susannah[906] (US) Wood. Powered by a steam engine. She is reported by Murray Lundberg to have worked in Alaska/YT in 1913.

Susie 116855 (US) In 1898 she was built at Jeffersonville IA USA by Howard Shipyards & Dock Co. She was shipped in sections by the builders from the molds of the river steamer *Bluff City* to Unalaska Alaska where they were re-assembled. 222.8' x 42' x 6.2' Wood. 1130gt 388nt. Powered by a 1000ihp steam engine by CT Dumont, Cincinnati OH USA. In 1898 she was owned by the Alaska Commercial Company. In 1901 she was owned by the Northern Navigation Co. In 1914 she was owned by the White Pass & Yukon Rail Road. She was sold to the Alaska Rail Road. She was in Yukon River service for the Klondike Gold Rush. Her engines were originally built in 1865 for the sidewheeler *Phil Sheridan* and later powered the Lake Minnetonka sidewheeler *Belle of Minnetonka*. She was equipped with electric lights and could accommodate 150 first-class passengers. She was reported as having been abandoned in 1943 and was destroyed by fire in 1944 at St. Michael AK.

Suwannee[907,908] (USS) (sidewheeler) (gunboat) She was built in 1864 at Chester PA USA by Reaney, Son & Archbold. Powered by a 58" bore, 8 ft 9 in stroke inclined direct-acting steam engine, surface condensing with 4 boilers. She was a double-ended iron sidewheel steamer. On July 09, 1868, she was wrecked in Shadwell Passage (QCI) BC after striking a rock on a voyage to Alaska. HMS *Sparrowhawk* came to her aid and removed the crew to Victoria. The *New World* salvaged her armament and some machinery and carried them to San Francisco CA.

Swallow 023222(US) She was built in 1860 at San Francisco CA by Patrick H Tiernan. Wood. 141gt. Powered by a steam engine. Her engines and machinery came from the *Willamette*. In 1860 she was owned by the California Steam Navigation Co. She was reported to have been abandoned in 1868.

Swallow[909] 023775 (US) (passenger vessel) She was built in 1867 at Portland OR USA by Thomas Bulger. 45' x 11' x 3.33'. Wood. Powered by a (5" x 10") steam engine. In 1867 she was owned by Vallard & Underwood. In 1877 she was reported as having been broken up on the Cowlitz River.

Swan (see *Belle*)

Swan[910] (US) She was built in 1856 at San Francisco CA. Wood. 91gt. Powered by a steam engine. She was home ported at Sacramento CA. She was reported to have been abandoned in 1865.

Swan (formerly *Wenat*; later *Cowlitz*) 080026 (US) (passenger vessel) She was built in 1857 at Tualatin River OR USA by Captain George Pease and S Smith. 76' x 17.6' x 3.6'. Wood. 87.79gt 41nt. Powered by a steam (8.25" x 36") engine. In 1857 she was owned by Captain George Pease. She was sold on the ways to Huntingdon & Holman for Cowlitz River service. She was renamed as *Cowlitz* and was employed on the Cowlitz River. In 1866 she was moved to employment on the Lewis River and then on the Oregon City route.

Swinomish (later *W.T. Preston*) (US) (freighter, then a snag boat, later a house boat) She was built in 1903 at Winslow WA USA. 161.9' x 31.5' x 5.5'

Wood. 313gt. In 1948 she was converted to a houseboat in Seattle WA. In 1915–1929 she was owned by the US Army Corps of Engineers. In 1929 she was rebuilt again. She was owned by the American Tow Boat Co. She was retired in 1948. In 1915 she was built as a snag boat. In 1939 some parts of this vessel were incorporated into a second *W.T. Preston*. In 1929 she was based in Seattle WA and employed in Puget Sound. She was on display as a museum vessel at Anacortes WA USA. As the *Swinomish* she worked on Puget Sound carrying freight, passengers and doing some towing. In 1956 she was burned as a public spectacle at the Seattle Seafair.

Sybil 107523 (Canada) (freighter, later a barge) She was built in 1898 at Victoria BC Canada by James C Stratford. 101.0' x 28.8' x 4.3' Wood. 621.87gt 364.22rt. Powered by two 17nhp horizontal (high pressure 16" x 72") steam engines built by the B.C. Iron Works, Vancouver BC. In 1901 she was rebuilt 167' x 29' 653gt 411.7rt. In 1904 she was rebuilt as a non-powered barge. In 1898 she was owned by the British American Steamship Co. In 1898–1901 she was owned by Alfred S Reed, Victoria BC. In 1900 she was owned by the Canadian Development Co. In 1901–1914 she was owned by the British Yukon Navigation Co., Vancouver BC. In 1899 she was towed north for the Klondike Gold Rush. In 1899 she was the first to arrive in Dawson City YT. In 1900 she carried the Governor General of Canada, Lord & Lady Minto, on their tour from Whitehorse to Dawson City YT. In 1902 she worked on the Yukon River. Her engines went to the steamer *Bonanza King* in 1904 and she was converted to a barge.

T.C. Power 145790 (US) (passenger/ freight vessel) She was built in 1898 at Seattle WA USA by the Moran Bros. Shipyard. 192.3' x 32.6' x 5.0' Wood. 819.64gt 481nt. In 1898 she was assembled at Dutch Harbor AK for service in the Klondike Gold Rush. Powered by a steam engine. In 1898–1911 she was owned by the North American Transportation & Trading Co. In 1911 she was owned by the Northern Navigation Co. In 1914 she was owned by the White Pass & Yukon Rail Road. She was sold again. She was a sister vessel to the *John Cudahy* and the *Charles H. Hamilton*. She was sent with the *Charles H. Hamilton* in the Fall of 1903 to carry food for Fairbanks and the Tanana Valley. She was employed mainly between St. Michael AK and Dawson City YT. In 1927 she was reported as having been laid up at St. Michael AK USA.

T.C. Reed 145744 (US) (passenger vessel) She was built in 1897 at Aberdeen WA USA. 116.2' x 20.8' x 6.0' Wood. 237gt 149nt. Powered by a 229ihp steam engine. She was employed on passenger and freight service on the Chehalis River and at Grays Harbor with the eastern terminus at Montesano.

T.C. Reed 216193 (US) (freighter) She was built in 1918 at Seattle WA USA by Ballard Marine Railway Co. Inc. 109.1' x 28.3' x 4.7' Wood. 277gt 209nt. Powered by a 150ihp steam engine. In 1928 she was owned by the American Tug Boat Co., Everett WA. In 1949 she was reported as having been abandoned.

T.C. Walker[911] (US) She was built about 1868. Wood. 256gt. Powered by a steam engine. She was owned by the California Steam Navigation Company. In 1871 she was taken over by the California Pacific Railroad Co., San Francisco CA. She was in service on California rivers. She operated until about 1881.

T.C. Walker[912] 145403 (US) (passenger vessel) She was built in 1885 at Stockton CA USA by Stephen Davis. 200.0' x 38.0' x 9.1' Wood. 786.90gt 702.19nt. Powered by a 380ihp 285nhp steam engine. In 1929 she was owned by the California Navigation & Improvement Co., Stockton CA. In 1935 she was owned by the California Transportation Co., San Francisco CA. She was employed on California rivers. She was reported to have been abandoned in 1938.

T.J. Nestor 145792 (US) (passenger/ freight vessel) She was built in 1898 at St. Michael AK USA. 72.0' x 14.0' x 4.0' Wood. 95gt 73nt. Powered by a steam engine. She was employed in Alaskan waters.

T.J. Potter 145489 (US) (sidewheeler) (ferry) She was built in 1888 at Portland OR USA. 230.0' x 35.1' x 10.6' Wood. 659gt 589.6nt. Powered by a 1,700ihp steam (32" x 96") engine. In 1901 she was rebuilt to 233.7' x 35.6' x 11.4' 826gt 676nt. In 1888 she was owned by the Oregon Railway & Navigation Co., Portland OR. She was employed on the Portland to Astoria route. She was transferred to Puget Sound and was employed on the Seattle to Olympia route. In 1921 she was reported to have been abandoned.

Tacoma 145382 (US) (sidewheeler) (train ferry, later a barge) She was built in 1884 at Portland OR USA. 334' x 42' x 11.2'. Wood. 1362gt 1311nt. Powered by (36" x 108") steam engine. In 1884 she was owned by the Northern Pacific Railway. She was used to ferry trains across the Columbia River from Kalama to Goble.

Tacoma 145773 (US) (sidewheeler) She was built in 1898 at Seattle WA USA by the Moran Bros. Shipyard. 176.1' x 35.4' x 5.9'. Wood. 718.68gt 409.06nt. Powered by two 26.6nhp horizontal high pressure (22" x 84") steam engines. In 1898 she was owned by the Empire Transportation Co. (William Cramp & International Navigation Co.) In 1901 she was owned by the Northern Pacific Steamship Co. (subsidiary of Northern Pacific Railroad). In 1904 she was owned by the Northwestern Steamship Co. In 1914 she was owned by the White Pass & Yukon Rail Road. In 1898 she was in Yukon River service. In 1904 she was on the Nome AK run. She was originally registered in the UK but during the Spanish-American War an act of Congress permitted her to be placed under US Registry. In 1927 she was reported as having been laid up at Andreaofsky Slough AK USA.

Tahoe Queen (US) (passenger vessel) She was built in 1983. She is in service on Lake Tahoe, based on the California shore. In 2021 she was owned by the Aramark Corp.

Tahoma 145842 (US) (passenger vessel) She was built in 1900 at Portland OR USA. 118' x 27' x 6'. Wood. 261gt 154nt. Powered by two 9.6nhp horizontal (high pressure 12" x 48") steam engines. In 1900 she was owned by CO Hill. She was employed on the Columbia River. In 1910 she was rebuilt.

Tahoma 207185 (US) (tug, later a barge) She was built in 1910 at Portland OR USA. 118.0' x 26.0' x 5.6'. Wood. 192gt 146nt. Powered by two 9.6nhp horizontal (12" x 48") steam engines. Her engines came from an earlier *Tahoma* (145842). In 1916 she was transferred to Puget Sound. She was later converted to a barge. In 1928 she was reported as having been abandoned.

Talco 145964 (US) (freighter) She was built in 1903 at Ballard WA USA. 60.3' x 10.7' x 2.9'. Wood. 14gt 8nt. Powered by a gasoline engine. She was employed on Puget Sound.

Tamalpais (later YHB-21) 145873 (US) (ferry, later a housing barge) She was built in 1901 at San Francisco CA USA. 224.0' x 36.0' x 16.0'. Steel. 1631gt 1013rt. Powered by a 1,800ihp steam engine. She served with the United States Navy during the Second World War as the housing barge YHB-21 at Mare Island CA.

Tana 210820 (US) (tug) She was built in 1905 at Seattle WA USA. 106.0' x 25.4' x 4.2'. Wood. 234gt 175rt. Powered by a gasoline engine. In 1905 she was owned by the Langley Transportation Co. and employed on the Tanana River. In 1906 she was converted to a steam engine. In 1933 she was owned by the Alaska Rivers Navigation Co. on the Kuskokwim River.

Tanana[913,914] 059482 (US) (tug, later a barge) She was built in 1898 at Elizabeth NJ USA. 100.3' x 35.2' x 5.4'. Steel. 383gt 355nt. Powered by a steam engine. (In 1900 she was rebuilt as a barge). In 1898 she was owned by the Empire Transportation Co. In 1899 she was operated by the Empire Transportation Company, Dawson YT. She is reported by Murray Lundberg to have worked in Alaska/YT in 1898–1900.

The *Tanana* (Image from Library of Congress LC-H261– 6164 P&P LC-DIG-hec-06761)

Tanana 201297 (US) She was built in 1904 at Portland OR by Joseph M Supple and shipped to Alaska and assembled at St. Michael AK USA. 149.6' x 30.4' x 5.9' Wood. 495gt 225nt. Powered by a 550ihp steam engine. In 1904 she was owned by the Northern Navigation Co. In 1914 she was owned by the White Pass & Yukon Rail Road. She worked the tributaries of the Yukon River. In 1915 she sank at Thirtymile River. She was salvaged and repaired. In 1921 she sank at Minto (on the Tanana River).

Tanana Chief 145795 (US) (passenger/ freight vessel) She was built in 1898 at Unalaska AK USA. 59.2' x 12.9' x 3.9' Wood. 72gt 36nt. Powered by a steam engine. In 1898 she was owned by Hendricks & Bell. She was laid up at Chena AK USA. In 1906 she was wrecked at Kautishua River AK USA.

Tatung (see *Enterprise*)

Teaser (later *Teazer*) 145002 (US) She was built in 1874 at The Dalles OR USA. She was retired in 1878. In 1879 she sank, was raised, and then in 1880 she was converted to a schooner (as the *Teazer*) owned by Seattle WA interests. She was rebuilt to 69.0' x 12.0' x 8.0' Wood. 33.27gt. In 1889–1893 she was owned by Puget Sound interests.

Teddy H[915] 208037 (US) (passenger/ freight vessel) She was built in 1910 at Fairbanks AK USA. 743' x 20.8' x 4.3' Wood. 153gt 96rt. Powered by a 40ihp steam engine. In 1910 she was owned by Leonard Joseph Heacock. In 1921 she was owned by Sam Dubin. She sank in a slough above Nenana on the Tanana River AK USA.

Tee Pee 134258 (Canada) In 1913 she was built at Athabasca AB Canada. 42.0' x 7.5' x 3.0' Wood. 7gt 4rt. In 1919 she was owned by Mrs. Mabel M Patterson, Athabasca AB.

Tehema[916] (US) (sidewheeler) She was built in 1850 at San Francisco CA. Wood. 83gt. Powered by a steam engine. She was employed on the San Joaquin River CA until about 1883 when she was reported to have been abandoned.

Telegraph[917] (later *Olympian*) 200012 (US) (passenger vessel) She was built in 1903 at Everett WA USA by the Portland Shipbuilding Co. 153.7' x 25.7' x

8.0' Wood. 386gt 243rt. Powered by two horizontal (24" x 72") steam engines. In 1903 she was owned by UB Scott. She was employed in the Seattle to Everett route. In 1912 the *Alameda* allided with the *Telegraph* at the Coleman Dock and she sank. She was raised, rebuilt and in 1913 she was renamed as the *Olympian*. She was employed on the Columbia River between Portland and The Dalles. In 1921 she was laid up and in 1924 she was reported as having been abandoned.

Telegraph 212094 (US) (passenger/ freight vessel) She was built in 1914 at Prosper OR USA by Carl Herman. 103.0' x 16.2' x 3.2' Wood. 96gt 63nt. Powered by a 250ihp steam engine. In 1916 she was rebuilt to 115'. In 1929 she was owned by the Myrtle Point Transportation Co., Bandon, OR USA. In 1935 she was owned by John W Exon, Portland, OR USA. In 1940 she was reported as having been abandoned.

Telephone 094910 (Canada) She was built in 1890 at New Westminster BC Canada. 70.0' x 14.0' x 4.0' Wood. 81gt 51rt. In 1890 she was owned by Lower Fraser River Transportation Co. (Captain Richard Baker, Joseph B Oliver, Captain Holman, and D Hennessey), New Westminster BC. In 1895 she was owned by Captain William Watts for the Fraser River to Harrison River route. In 1895–1898 she was owned by DJ Munn, New Westminster BC. She was built for the Lower Fraser River service. In 1900 she was towing fish boats and scows. On September 24, 1900, she was destroyed by fire in Vancouver Harbour.

Telephone 145400 (US) She was built in 1885 at Portland OR USA. 172' x 28.3' x 7.2' Wood. 386gt 334nt. Powered by two 32nhp horizontal (high pressure 22" x 96") steam engines. In 1885 she was owned by UB Scott. On November 20, 1887, she was destroyed by fire and had to be beached north of Astoria OR with the loss of a crew member.

Telephone 145477 (US) She was built in 1888 at Portland OR USA. 200.9' x 28.3' x 6.8' Wood. 500.13gt 443.24nt. Powered by a (25" x 96") steam engine. In 1903 she was rebuilt. She was chartered to the Dalles, Portland & Astoria Line for service between Portland and The Dalles. In 1909 she was transferred to San Francisco CA. In 1918 she was reported to have been broken up.

Telephone 200263 (US) She was built in 1903 at Portland OR USA. 201.5' x 31.5' x 8.0' Wood. 794gt 539rt. Powered by a steam engine. In 1907 she was chartered to the Regulator Line and in service between Portland Oregon and The Dalles on the Columbia River. She was in operation until about 1918.

Tenino[918] 024491 (US) She was built in 1861 at Des Chutes OR. Wood. Powered by a steam engine. In 1873 she was reported to have been abandoned.

Tenino (later *New Tenino*) 124491 (US) (passenger vessel) She was built in 1861 at Deschutes OT USA by RR Thompson. 135' x 25' x 5.5' Wood. 329gt. Powered by two 19nhp 17" x 72") steam engines. In 1869 she was rebuilt. In 1861 she was owned by the Oregon Steam Navigation Co. In 1875 she was rebuilt as the *New Tenino* (130067).

Tennessee (US) (sidewheeler) (passenger/ freight vessel) She was built in 1848 by William H Webb. 211.9' x 35.6' x ? Powered by a steam engine. In 1848 she was owned by the New York and Savannah Steamship Navigation Co. In 1849 she was owned by the Pacific Mail Steamship Company. In 1850–1852 she was employed between San Francisco and Panama City. On March 6, 1853, when she went aground in dense fog near San Francisco and broke up. She was on the Pacific Mail's Panama – San Francisco route when she ran aground at Tennessee Cove in Marin County in 1853.

Tetlin 208036 (US) (passenger/ freight vessel) She was built in 1908 at Fairbanks, District of Alaska, USA. 60.5' x 12.7' x 3.7' Wood. 65gt 41nt. Powered by a 32ihp steam engine. In 1911 she was wrecked at Tanana River AK USA.

Texas (later *Quartzite*; then *Sierra Nevada*) (US) (sidewheeler) Wood. In 1851 she was built at New York NY USA by William Collyer. Powered by a steam engine. She was a gold ship which arrived in Victoria in June 1858 with 900 passengers on board, again in July 1858 with 900 passengers on board. She "operated from New York to Chagres from February until October 1852 by the Empire City Line and originally advertised for this line as the *Quartz Rock*. She made a trial trip as the *Sierra Nevada* on February 7, 1852.

She was eventually purchased by Cornelius Vanderbilt and sent to San Francisco, where she arrived March 23, 1853. She remained employed on the San Francisco – San Juan del Sur service until March 1857. In 1860 she was purchased by the Pacific Mail Line and placed in coastal service. In February 1861, she was purchased by Holladay and Brenham and was wrecked on a reef south of Monterey on October 17, 1869."[919]

The Dalles (see Undine)

The Duke (see Putah)

Thistle[920] (US) She is reported by Murray Lundberg to have worked in Alaska/YT in 1897.

Thistle 107867 (Canada) (passenger/ freight vessel) She was built in 1902 at Dawson City YT by Donald McPhee. 102.0' x 19.8' x 3.9' Wood. 224.75gt 152.83rt. Powered by two 6.6nhp horizontal (high pressure 10" x 48") steam engines built by the United Engineering Works, San Francisco CA. Her engines came from the steamer Gold Star. In 1902 she was owned by RW Calderwood. In 1903 she was owned by the Klondyke Corp. In 1904–1919 she was owned by the British Yukon Navigation Co. Ltd., Vancouver BC. In 1919 she was acquired by Taylor & Drury Co., Whitehorse YT. She was towed to Whitehorse by the steamer La France to have fittings installed, then back to Dawson for installation of engines. On August 30, 1928, she was stranded at Lake Laberge YT. She was still listed in the Canada List of Shipping in 1931.

Thlinket 145849 (US) She was built in 1893 at San Francisco CA USA. 86.0' x 21.0' x 4.5' Wood. 94gt 59nt. Powered by a steam engine. She worked in the fishing industry. She is reported by Murray Lundberg to have worked in Alaska/YT in 1893–1904.

Thomas Dwyer 145407 (US) She was built in 1885 at San Francisco CA USA. 87.0' x 16.0' x 4.0' Wood. 73.25gt 63.44rt. Powered by a steam engine. In 1895 she was owned by the Sacramento Transportation Co., Sacramento CA USA. In 1897 she was owned by the Yukon Exploration Co. In 1897 she was dismantled and shipped to Alaska on a schooner. In 1897–1898 she wintered in a slough 100 miles above the mouth of the Yukon River with the steamers *Alice* and *W.K. Merwin*. Edward L Affleck states that she did not complete her voyage to Dawson City YT.

Thomas Flyer [921] (US) 60' Wood. Powered by a steam engine with two wheels side-by-side. She had one enclosed deck. She is reported by Murray Lundberg to have worked in Alaska/YT in 1912 on the Iditarod River.

Thomas Hunt [922] (US) (sidewheeler) She was built in the eastern USA in 1851. Wood. 370gt. Powered by a steam engine. In 1854 she was owned by the California Steam Navigation Co. In 1854–1855 she was employed on the Sacramento River CA. She was destroyed by fire in 1855. One source suggests that she was transferred to the Columbia River and then on to China coastal service.

Thomas L. Nixon 145494 (US) (train ferry, later passenger ferry) She was built in 1888 at Pasco WT USA. 159.6' x 36.1' x 5.8' Wood. 515.53gt 477.48nt. Powered by two 19nhp horizontal (high pressure 17" x 60") steam engines. In 1888 she ferried trains across the Columbia River at Pasco WT. In 1891 she was a transfer vessel for the Great Northern Railway while the train bridge at Wenatchee was being constructed. In 1893 she was owned by Columbia & Okanagan Steamboat Co. In 1901 she was reported as having been broken up. Her machinery went to the *W.H. Pringle*.

Thompson 103298 (Canada) (passenger vessel) She was built in 1895 at Knault Siding BC Canada. 94.3' x 16.6' x 4.6' Wood. 150gt 94nt. Powered by a steam engine. In 1895–1896 she was owned by Joe Genelle, Knault Siding BC. In 1901–1917 she was owned by the Columbia River Lumber Co., Golden BC. She was built as an excursion vessel but became a log towing tug. She was in Shuswap Lake service. In 1905 she was retired.

Thoroughfare 024855 (US) She was built in 1871 at San Francisco CA USA. 248.0' x 38.0' x 12.0' Wood. 1012.27gt 667.5nt. Powered by a 400nhp steam engine.

Three Sisters 145423 (US) (passenger vessel) She was built in 1886 at East Portland OR USA. 120.7' x 30.2' x 4.4' Wood. 320.79gt 296.29nt. Powered by two 9.6nhp horizontal (12" x 48") steam engines. In 1886 she was owned by the Oregon Development Co. In 1896 she was reported to have been broken up at Corvallis OR.

Tiburon 145377 (US) (ferry) She was built in 1884 at San Francisco CA USA. 220.0' x 34.6' x 13.5' Wood. 1257.14gt 883.42nt. Powered by a 750ihp steam engine.

Tiger[923] 145091 (US) She was built in 1875 at San Francisco CA by Dickie Brothers. 100.0' x 25.0' x 5.1' Wood. 85.37gt 43.03nt. Powered by a 150nhp steam engine. She was employed on California rivers. She was reported to have been broken up in 1916.

Timely Gull (The)[924] (US) She was built at Great Salt Lake UT. 45' Wood. She was powered by a horse-powered treadmill and sidewheels. In 1854 she was owned by Brigham Young, Salt Lake UT. In 1858 she was wrecked in a storm on Great Salt Lake UT.

Tobin 138815 (Canada) In 1923 she was built at The Pas, MB Canada. 62.5' x 15.0' x 3.4' Wood. 50gt 32rt. In 1923–1936 she was owned by The Ross Navigation Co. Ltd., The Pas MB.

Toledo 145186 (US) (passenger vessel) She was built in 1878 at Willamette OR USA. 109.0' x 22.0' x 4.0' Wood. 202.43gt 142.56nt. Powered by two 6.6nhp (high pressure 10" x 48") steam engines. She was rebuilt at Portland OR in 1885 to 128' 226gt 207nt. In 1878 she was owned by Joseph Kellogg. She was employed on the Cowlitz River.

Tolo 201341 (US) She was built in 1904 at Seattle WA USA. 71.0' x 16.0' x 4.5' Wood. 35gt 22nt. Powered by a steam engine.

Tongue Point 214854 (US) (dredge) She was built in 1911 at Portland OR USA. 64.9' x 30.0' x 4.0' Wood. 87gt/nt. Powered by a 35hp gasoline engine. She was assembled at Rapids Landing on the Middle Copper River. In 1929 she was owned by Columbia Rock & Sand Co., Astoria OR. She was employed on the Columbia River system. In 1931 she was reported as having been abandoned.

Tonsina (US) (passenger/ freight vessel) She was built in 1909 at Cordova Alaska by the Moran Bros. Shipyard. 120' x 28' x ? Wood. Powered by two 300ihp horizontal (high pressure 11" x 60") steam engines. In 1907 she worked briefly in Alaska but spent the balance of her time in Puget Sound.

Topsy 145413 (US) (passenger vessel) She was built in 1885 at Corvallis OR USA. 59.0' x 12.0' x 2.2'. Wood. 30gt 28nt. Powered by a (6.75" x 24") steam engine. In 1885 she was owned by Kemp Bros. & Wheeler. In 1893 she was reported as having been broken up at Portland OR USA.

Torpedo[925] (US) She was built at Lake Coeur d'Alene ID by CP Sorenson. Wood. Powered by a steam engine. She was owned by CP Sorenson. She was in service on Lake Coeur d'Alene. In 1891 she was transferred to the Pend Oreille River.

Tosi[926] (US) About 1949 she was owned by the Roman Catholic Church (Holy Cross Mission) as a mission boat. She was employed on the Yukon River.

Tourist 203932 (US) She was built in 1907 at Port Blakeley WA USA. 156.8' x 27.9' x 7.6'. Wood. 467rt 294nt. She is reported by Murray Lundberg to have worked in Alaska/YT in 1907.

Trail (Image from Maritime Museum of British Columbia 000414)

Trail 103306 (Canada) (tug) She was built in 1896 at Nakusp BC Canada by Thomas J Bulger. 165.0' x 31.0' x 4.9' Wood. 633gt 418rt. Powered by a steam engine. In 1896 she was owned by the Columbia & Kootenay Steam Navigation Company. In 1897–1901 she was owned by the Canadian Pacific Railway, Montreal QC. She was designed for barge handling. In 1900 she was withdrawn from service. On June 02, 1902, she was burned out while alongside her wharf at Robson West BC on the Columbia River.

Transfer (Image from Vancouver Archives AM54-S4-B0_P439)

Transfer 100794 (Canada) 122.0' x 24.5' x 5.6' Wood. 264gt 98rt. Powered by a 18hp two-cylinder (12" x 60") compound steam engine. In 1893–1901 she was owned by Canadian Pacific Navigation Company, Victoria BC. In 1903 she was transferred to Canadian Pacific Navigation Co. Ltd., Victoria BC. . In 1893–1895 she serviced Chilliwack Landing on the Fraser River. In 1910 she was reported as having been broken up. In 1909–1913 she was owned by Robert Jardine, New Westminster BC for use as a cannery power plant at Redonda Bay. In 1931 she was still listed in the Canada List of Shipping. In 1917–1938 she was owned by the Redonda Canning & Cold Storage Co. Ltd., Vancouver BC. In c1945 her boilers went to the Redonda Bay Cannery & Reduction Plant.

Transfer 204759 (US) (ferry) She was built in 1907 at Allegany OR USA. 27.5' x 8.4' x 1.6' Wood. 8gt 6nt. Powered by a 4ihp gasoline engine. In 1921 she was reported to have been out of service.

Transfer 205735 (US) (ferry) She was built in 1908 at Marshfield OR USA. 60.0' x 26.0' x 4.8' Wood. 38gt 24nt. Powered by a 40ihp gasoline engine. In 1908–1910 she was owned by Coos Bay OR USA interests.

Transit 145079 (US) (ferry) She was built in 1875 at San Francisco CA. 313.5' x 40.5' x 15.7' Wood. 1566.81gt 1079.77nt. Powered by a 500ihp steam engine. In 1875–1910 she was owned by San Francisco CA USA interests.

Transit 205735 (US) (ferry) She was built in 1908 at Marshfield OR USA. 60.0' x 26.0' x 4.8' Wood. 38gt 24rt. Powered by a 40ihp gasoline engine. In 1908–1910 she was owned by Coos Bay OR USA interests.

Transit Mills (Image from Vancouver Archives collection)

Transit Mills 094891 (Canada) (sidewheeler) 72.0' x 20.0' x 3.0' Wood. 103gt 63rt She was built in 1888 at New Westminster BC Canada. In 1888–1896 she was owned by Joseph L Leeson, Vancouver BC. in the Spring 1891 she was destroyed by fire.

Traveler[927] (later City of Frankfort) 145181 (US) (passenger vessel) She was built as the Traveler in 1878 at Willamette OR USA. 124.0' x 22.0' x 4.0' Wood. 238.4gt 145.16rt. Powered by two 13nhp horizontal (high pressure 14" x 48") steam engines. In 1878 she was owned by Lewis Love. In 1889 she was rebuilt as the City of Frankfort (145181). In 1891 she was rebuilt again as another City of Frankfort (126723).

Triumph (US) (freighter) Wood. 66.97rt. Powered by a steam engine. She was employed on the Nooksack River, WA. was destroyed by fire near the town of Marietta, WA, in Whatcom County.

Try 100201 (Canada) She was built in 1891 at Vancouver BC. 61.0' x 15.0' x 3.0' Wood. 42gt 26rt. Powered by a 10hp steam engine. In 1896–1898 she was owned by JM Stewart, Vancouver BC. In 1901–1919 she was owned by E Burns, Vancouver BC.

Tulare[928,929,930] 024671 (US) She was built in 1867 at Stockton CA USA by Stephen Davis. 111.8' Wood. 162.02gt. Powered by a 50nhp steam engine. She was owned by the California Steam Navigation Company. In 1871 she was taken over by the California Pacific Railroad Co., San Francisco CA. She was employed on California rivers. She ceased operation about 1885. Her engines went to the Merrin.

Tuolumne City[931,932] (US) (freighter) She was built in 1868 at Stockton CA USA by Stephen Davis. 90' Wood. Powered by a steam engine. She was owned by the California Steam Navigation Company. In 1871 she was taken over by the California Pacific Railroad Co., San Francisco CA. She was employed on California rivers. She ceased operation about 1885.

Tutshi[933,934] 138695 (Canada) (passenger vessel) She was built in 1917 at Carcross YT Canada by Cousins Bros. 167.0' x 35.3' x 6.4' Wood. 1040.51gt 746.31rt. Powered by two 17nhp horizontal (high pressure 16" x 84") steam engines built by the Dubuque Iron Works, Dubuque IA. Repowered in 1927 with two 46.9nhp horizontal compound oil burning steam engines built by the Drydock Engine Works, Detroit MI USA. In 1917–1955 she was owned by The British Yukon Navigation Co. Ltd., Vancouver BC in service on Lake Tagish. She was on the Carcross to Grahame Inlet on the Atlin run. Later she was on a tourist route between Carcross to Ben-My-Cree. In 1954 she was removed from service and beached in 1955 at Carcross YT as a museum display. The vessel was destroyed by fire in 1990. Her name was pronounced as "Too Shy".

Twin Cities 205912 (US) (passenger vessel) She was built in 1908 at Celilo OR USA. 151.0' x 32.1' x 4.8' Wood. 418gt 375nt. Powered by two17nhp horizontal (16" x 72") steam engines. In 1908 she was owned by Open River Transportation Co. In 1925 she was owned by the Willamette & Columbia River Towing Co., Portland, OR USA. In 1931 she was reported as having been abandoned.

Tyconda 145889 (US) (passenger/ freight vessel) She was built in 1901 at Tacoma WA USA. 104.3' x 21.9' x 4.3' Wood. 186gt 117rt. Powered by a 130ihp steam engine. In 1901 she was owned by the Loney Brothers, Tacoma WA USA. In 1910 she was owned by Tacoma WA USA interests. She worked on Puget Sound until May 1915 when she was transferred to Wrangel AK USA for Stikine River service. She turned out to be underpowered for the Stikine River. She was transferred to Anchorage AK for Susitna River service. On September 08, 1915, she was destroyed by fire at Anchorage AK.

Tyrrell[935] 107159 (Canada) (passenger/ freight vessel) She was built in 1897 at Toronto ON Canada by the Polson Iron Works Ltd. (In 1897 she was assembled at False Creek Vancouver BC.) 142.0' x 30.2' x 4.8' composite hull. 678gt 408rt. Powered by a 17nhp steam engine built by the Polson Iron Works Ltd., Toronto ON. In 1897 she was owned by the Canadian Pacific Railway Co., Montreal QC. In 1898 she was owned by the British American Corporation Ltd. In 1900 she was owned by the Dawson & Whitehorse Navigation Co. In 1901 she was owned by Edward M Sullivan, Dawson YT. In 1904 she was owned by John Macauley Carson. In 1905 she was owned by DW Davis, Yukon Territory. In 1910–1919 she was owned by the British Yukon Navigation Company. In 1918 she was reported as having been near Dawson City Yukon. In 1931 she was still listed in the Canada List of Shipping.

Umatilla (see *Venture*)

Umatilla 207024 (US) (passenger vessel) She was built in 1908 at Plymouth WA USA. 58.5' x 20.5' x 2.2'. Wood. 14gt 9nt. Powered by a 45ihp gasoline engine. In 1908–1910 she was owned by Seattle WA USA interests. In 1927 she was reported to have been abandoned.

Umatilla (USACE) (dredge, later a tug) (see *Umatilla*)

Umatilla[936] 227556 (US) (dredge, later a tug) She was built in 1928 at Celilo OR USA by Portland Shipbuilding Co. 159.7' x 34.2' x 5.6'. Wood. 551gt 532rt. Powered by two 750inp horizontal (16" x 74") steam engines. In 1928 she was owned by the United States Army Corps of Engineers. In 1929 she was owned by the Willamette & Columbia River Towing Co. Portland OR USA. She was owned by the Shaver Transportation. She was alternately reported to have been wrecked in 1941 or broken up at Portland OR in 1942.

Uncle Sam[937] (US) (sidewheeler) (freighter) She was built in 1852 at the Colorado River estuary, Mexico, by Domingo Marcucci. 65' x 16' x ?. Wood. 40gt. Powered by a 20hp steam locomotive engine. She was carried on board the schooner *Capacity* from San Francisco CA USA. In 1852 she was the first steamer on the Colorado River carrying freight from San Francisco. In May 1853 she sank at Fort Yuma AZ USA. The wreck broke loose, and she drifted down river and disappeared.

Uncle Sam 208344 (US) (freighter) She was built in 1911 at Corvallis OR USA by RJ Galbraith. 81.0' x 18.0' x 3.3'. Wood. 82gt 76nt. Powered by a 70ihp steam engine. In 1911 she was owned by RJ Galbraith, Portland OR. In 1915 she was reported as having been out of operation.

Underwriter[938] (US) (sidewheeler) (freighter) She was built in the eastern USA in 1854. Wood. 433gt. Powered by a steam engine. She was in service on California rivers. She was reported to have been destroyed by fire in 1857.

Undine 025266 (US) (passenger vessel) She was built in 1888 at Portland OR USA by JH Steffen. 150.0' x 27.0' x 6.6'. Wood. 327gt 280nt. Powered by two horizontal (high pressure 16.25" x 60") steam engines. In 1917 she was rebuilt at Portland OR by Charles M Nelson. In 1888 she was owned by Jacob H Kamm, Portland OR. She was employed between Portland and Astoria. In 1917 she was owned by the Harkins Transportation Co. In 1921 she was rebuilt.

Undine (US) (freighter) She was built in 1901 at Green River UT USA. 60.0' x 10.0' x 1.0' Wood. Powered with a 20hp steam engine (coal fired boiler). She was a flat-bottomed design. In 1901–1902 she was owned by Captain Frank H Summeril. In 1901 she was employed on the Colorado River to Moab (later history shows that she was the only steamer to reach Moab). In May 1902 she was reported to have capsized and been wrecked.

Undine (later *The Dalles*) 221499 (US) 221400 (US) (passenger/ freight vessel, later tug) She was built in 1921 at Portland OR USA. 170' x 28.5' x 7.3' Wood. 516gt 485nt. 260ihp (16.25" x 60") steam engine. In 1921–1929 she was owned by the Harkins Transportation Co., Portland, OR USA. In 1939 she was owned by Lew Russel, Portland, OR USA. In 1940 she was reported as having been broken up at Portland OR USA.

Unio (later *Union*) 025165 (US) (sidewheeler) (passenger vessel) She was built in 1861 at Canemah OR USA. 96' x 16' x 4' Wood. 112gt. Powered by two 5.4nhp horizontal (9" x 48" high pressure) steam engines. In 1861 she was owned by JD Miller. In 1865 she was owned by the Willamette Steam Navigation Co. In 1866 she was owned by the Peoples Transportation Co. She was reported as having been broken up in 1869. Her engines were transferred to the Umpqua River steamer *Swan*.

Union (see *Maggie Lauder*)

Union (see *Unio*)

Union (Canada) (tug) She was built in 1974 at Burrard Inlet BC Canada. 54.0' x 13.0' x 4.0' Wood. 39gt 25.98rt. She was known as the "Sudden Jerk", powered by a threshing machine engine. In 1874 she was owned by JC Hughes, Vancouver BC. She was owned by Captain George Odin. She was sold to Moodyville Mill. She had no superstructure. She was employed on Burrard Inlet. On July 29, 1878, she burned on the north arm of the Fraser River BC.

Union[939] (US) (sidewheeler) She was built in 1850. Iron 87gt. Powered by a steam engine. In 1849 she was operating on the Sacramento River. In 1851 she was operating on the San Joaquin River CA. She was reported to have been abandoned in 1856.

Union Driver 204148 (US) (piledriver) She was built in 1907 at Porter WA USA. 60.9' x 21.0' x 3.9' Wood. 59gt 38nt. Powered by a steam engine.

Unit (US) She was built in 1846. Wood. Powered by a steam engine. She was owned by William Mckee. In 1846 she was employed between San Francisco and San Joaquin City CA.

Urilda[940,941] (US) (sidewheeler) She was built in 1850 in the eastern USA. Wood. 140gt. Powered by a steam engine. In 1854 she was owned by the Merchants Line. In 1854 she was owned by the California Steam Navigation Co. She was employed on the Sacramento River. She was reported as having been converted to a barge about 1860.

Vallejo (see O. & C. R.R. Ferry No. 2)

Valley City (later *John C. Barr*) 107853 (Canada) 077326 (US) She was built in 1892 at Toledo OH USA. 144.6' x 28.2' x 4.8' Wood. 547gt 316nt. Powered by a 200hp direct-acting steam engine. In 1898 she was owned by the North American Transportation & Trading Co. In 1901 she was owned by John Steinhoff, Dawson YT. In 1911 she was owned by the Northern Navigation Co. In 1914 she was owned by the White Pass & Yukon Rail Road. She was sold again. In 1892 she was employed on Lake Michigan and the Maumee River routes. In 1898, six days after her purchase she was dismantled and packed on five flat cars and a box car and shipped to Seattle WA. She was placed on board the steamer *Portland* and shipped to St. Michal AK for re-assembly by the Craig Shipbuilding Co. She had ten watertight compartments and boasted electric lighting. In 1899 she was transferred to Canadian Registry and in 1902 she was transferred back to US Registry. In 1917 she was converted to a stationary power plant for the marine ways at St. Michael AK. In 1927 she was abandoned at St. Michael AK.

Valley Queen 161824 (US) (passenger/ freight vessel) She was built in 1898 at Independence OR USA. 85.6' x 18' x 3.2' Wood. 92gt 73rt. Powered by two

7.5" x 30" high pressure steam engines. In 1898 she was owned by Alice Skinner. In 1899 she was reported as having been broken up at Portland OR USA.

Vancouver (US) (sidewheeler) (passenger vessel) She was built in 1857 at Milwaukie OT USA. 84' x 13.2' x 3.9' Wood. Rebuilt in 1870. Powered by a two 4.3nhp 8" x 48" horizontal high pressure steam engines. In 1857 she was owned by Captain Turnbull and WH Troup. She was employed on the Fort Vancouver route, based at Vancouver WA. In 1870 she was laid up and replaced by the sternwheeler *Vancouver*.

Vancouver 025835 (US) (passenger vessel) She was built in 1870 at Vancouver WA USA. 95' x 20' x 4' Wood. 130gt 78rt. Powered by a two horizontal (12" x 48") steam engines 9.6nhp. In 1870 she was owned by the Vancouver Steamboat Co., Portland, OR USA. In 1870 she replaced the earlier *Vancouver* (sidewheeler) on the Columbia River. In 1873–1885 she was owned by the Willamette River Transportation Co., Portland, OR USA. In 1885 she was laid up. In 1887 she was rebuilt to 115' x 24' x 5.9' 203gt 185rt re-registered and re-named as the *Maria* (091960).

Vancouver 161717 (US) (ferry) She was built in 1893 at Portland OR USA. 108.0' x 32.0' x 7.0' Wood. 211gt 157nt. Powered by a steam engine. In 1893–1910 she was owned by Portland OR USA interests.

General Stewart Van Vliet (see *Rampart*)

Vaquero[942] 025710 (US) (sidewheeler) She was built in 1865. 100' Wood. 105.92gt. Powered by a steam engine. She was in service on California rivers. She was reported to have been abandoned about 1881.

Varuna[943] 025877 (US) She was built in 1873 at San Francisco CA USA. 141.0' x 32.0' x 3.0' Wood. 216.10gt 130.59nt. Powered by an 80nhp steam engine. She was employed on the Sacramento River CA until about 1895.

Varuna[944] 161765 (US) She was built in 1895 at Sacramento CA. 143' Wood. 230.36gt 123.29nt. Powered by a steam engine. In 1895 she was owned by the Sacramento Transportation Co. She was employed on California rivers. She ceased operation in 1907.

Vashon (see City of Aberdeen)

Vedder 126273 (Canada) (freighter) She was built in 1909 at New Westminster BC. 75.0' x 16.0' x 3.3'. Wood. 103gt 60.64rt. Powered by a 3nhp steam engine. In 1910–1913 she was owned by Alfred E Yates (MO), New Westminster BC. On June 13, 1914, she was destroyed by fire 20 miles from Wrangell AK.

Veloz (US) (freighter) She was built about 1849. Wood. Powered by a steam engine. She served on the Sacramento River CA.

Venture[945,946] (later Umatilla) (US) (passenger vessel) She was built in 1858 at Cascades WT USA by Thompson & Co. 110' x 22' x 4.6'. Wood. 91gt. Powered by two 13nhp (high pressure 14" x 48") steam engines. She had a flat-bottomed hull, a 'shovelnose' bow and short 18-inch paddle blades. She was built as the Venture but documented as the Umatilla after being wrecked on her first trip. She was employed at the Cascades and The Dalles. In July 1858 as the Umatilla, she was the first sternwheeler to operate on the Fraser River and reaching Yale. Later in the year she was transferred to the Sacramento River.

Veto[947] 025962 (US) (ferry) (sidewheeler) She was built in 1879 at Portland OR. 85.0' x 22.0' x 6.0'. Wood. 74.55gt 38.85nt. Powered by a steam engine. In 1887 she was reported to have been destroyed by fire.

Veto No. 2[948] 025977 (US) (ferry) (sidewheeler) She was built in 1880 at Portland OR. 90.0' x 23.9' x 6.0'. Wood. 116.62gt. Powered by a steam engine. In 1892 she was reported to have been out of service.

Victor[949,950] (US) She was built in 1859 in the San Francisco Bay area. Wood. Powered by a steam engine. In 1859 she was in service between Sacramento and Marysville in competition with the California Steam Navigation Co. In 1860 she was owned by the California Steam Navigation Co. In March

1868, she was snagged and sank at Pike's Cutoff on the Sacramento River. In 1871 she was owned by the California Pacific Railroad Co.

Victor[951] 025712 (US) She was built in 1862 at San Francisco CA. Wood. 127gt. Powered by a steam engine. In 1873 she was reported to have been abandoned.

Victor Constant[952,953] (US) (sidewheeler) She was built in 1850. Wood. 57gt. Powered by a steam engine. She was in service on California rivers. She ceased operation about 1852.

Victoria[954] 085312 (Canada) (passenger/ freight vessel) She was built in 1868 at Quesnelle British Columbia (Crown Colony) by James W Trahey. 116.0' x 23.0' x 4.5' Wood. 364gt. Powered by a 90hp (14" x 54") steam engine. In 1868 she was owned by Gustavus B Wright, New Westminster BC. In 1868 she was owned by Edgar Marvin. In 1879 she was purchased by Captain John Irving, New Westminster BC. In 1896 she was owned by Robert McLeese, Soda Creek BC. She was powered with engines from the Lillooet Lake steamer *Prince of Wales*. In 1886 she was reported as having been laid up at Steamboat Landing BC occupying the only winter lay-up there. She was purchased by the Northern British Columbia Navigation Co. who dismantled her to make space for the newer *Charlotte*.

Victoria 107530 (Canada) (freighter) She was built in 1898 at Trout Lake City BC Canada. 75.0' x 15.0' x 3.7' Wood. 107gt 67rt. Powered by a steam engine. In 1898–1901 she was owned by Captain Nils Pierson Roman, Trout Lake City BC. In 1901–1903 she was owned by the Canadian Pacific Railway, Montreal QC. On June 06, 1902, she hit a rock (later named *Victoria Rock*) in Trincomali Channel on a passage from Ladysmith with a cargo of coal while under command of Captain Laurence Casey. She was lost on April 09, 1903, at Ta-Chu-Shan in the Gulf of Pechili on a voyage from Port Blakeley to Taku China via Mororan with a cargo of timber.

Victoria[955] 116811 (Canada) (passenger/ freight vessel) She was built in 1898 at Seattle WA USA by the Moran Bros. Shipyard. 176.1' x 35.0' x 4.0' Wood. 718gt 409nt. Powered by two horizontal (22" x 84" high pressure) 26.6nhp steam engines built by the Moran Bros. In 1898 she was owned by the Empire Transportation Co. (William Cramp & International Navigation

Co.) In 1901 she was owned by the Northern Pacific Steamship Co. (subsidiary of Northern Pacific Railroad). In 1904 she was owned by the Northwestern Steamship Co. In 1914 she was owned by the White Pass & Yukon Rail Road. In 1898 she was in Yukon River service. In 1904 she was employed on the Nome AK run. In 1927 she was reported as having been laid up at St. Marys AK USA.

Victoria 161820 (US) (tug) She was built in 1897 at St. Michael AK USA by Matthew Turner. 75.0' x 20.5' x 5.0' Wood. 55gt 30nt. Powered by a steam engine. In 1897 she was owned by the Alaska Commercial Co. In 1901 she was owned by the Northern Navigation Co. In 1906 she was owned by George A. Fredericks. She was employed as a pilot boat on the Yukon Flats to guide steamers between Fort Yukon and Circle City. She was reported as having been laid up and later abandoned at St. Michael AK USA.

Victoria[956] 206524 (US) (passenger vessel) She was built in 1909 at Independence OH USA by Cyrus Purvine. 63.0' x 15.0' x 2.6' Wood. 42gt 37nt. Powered by a 40ihp steam engine. In 1909–1910 she was owned by WH Parrish, Oregon USA. In 1913 she was reported to have been laid up

Victorian[957] 107520 (Canada) (passenger/ freight vessel) She was built in 1898 at Lake Bennett BC Canada by James H Calvert. 56' x 16' x 3' Wood. 53gt 33rt. Powered by a steam engine. In 1898 she was owned by John Irving. In 1899 she was owned by the Northern Lakes & Navigation Co. In 1899 she was reported as having been broken up at Bennett Lake BC.

Victorian 103917 (Canada) (passenger vessel) She was built in 1898 at Victoria BC Canada by John H. Todd. 146.5' x 33.4' x 4.7' Wood. 716gt 455rt. Powered by a 15nhp steam engine. In 1898–1901 she was owned by the Canadian Development Co. Ltd., Victoria BC. In 1901–1919 she was owned by the British Yukon Navigation Co. In 1898 she hit a rock on the BC coast but was refloated by the crew, traveling to St. Michael AK for repairs. She traveled up the Yukon River to Fort Yukon where she was frozen-in. In 1899 she was reported as having been broken up on Lake Bennett BC. In 1931 she was still listed in the Canada List of Shipping.

Victory (see *Mary B. Williams*)

Vidette (RNWMP) (see *May West*)

Vigilant (see *George W. Pride*)

Viola (Canada) (yacht) She was built at Lake Bennett BC Canada. 30' Wood. 3.7gt 2.69nt. Powered by a 0.5nhp steam engine. She is reported by Murray Lundberg to have worked in Alaska/YT in 1898. Edward L Affleck describes her as a 'prospecting yacht.' MacBride states that "she was the smallest steamer to travel through the Whitehorse Rapids, (under Captain EJ Smythe)."

Viola 203823 (US) (freighter) She was built in 1907 at Needles CA USA. 46.8' x 11.0' x 2.6'. Wood. 14gt 13nt. Powered by a 56ihp gasoline engine. In 1910 she was owned by Los Angeles CA USA interests.

Virago[958] (HMS) (sidewheeler) (torpedo boat destroyer) She was built in 1842 at Chatham UK by H.M. Dockyard (Chatham). Designed by Sir William Symonds. Powered by a 300nhp two cylinder direct-acting steam engine built by Boulton & Watt. She was on the Pacific Station August 09, 1851. She served on the Pacific Station 1897–1903. She had three commanders: William Houston Stewart, James Charles Prevost 1852, and Edmond Marshall 1854. She was one of the vessels which tried to capture Petropavlovsk (Asiatic Russia) between August 31 and September 04, 1854, during the Crimean War. She arrived back in Esquimalt on October 03, 1854. She left Esquimalt October 22, 1854, for San Francisco, Mexico, and Valparaiso. She was paid off at Plymouth UK August 09, 1855. She was reported as having been broken up at Chatham Dockyard in 1876.

Visalia[959,960] 025711 (US) (freighter) She was built about 1860 at San Francisco CA by Patrick H Tiernan. Wood. 135.88gt. Powered by a steam engine. She was in service on California rivers. On May 25, 1864, she was snagged and sank at Hayes Bend, three miles above Nicholas on the Sacramento River. She was reported to have been abandoned about 1868. (It is unclear whether this vessel was a sternwheeler or a propeller.)

Vivian 107251 (Canada) (freighter) She was built in 1898 at Lake Bennett BC Canada by James H Calvert. 50' x 15' x 3'. Wood. 51gt 32rt. Powered by a steam engine. In 1898–1899 she was owned by John Irving. In 1899 she was sold to the Northern Lakes & Rivers Navigation Co. Ltd. In 1899 she was wrecked near Dawson City YT.

Volunteer[961] 161832 (US) (passenger vessel) She was built in 1900 at Footner WA USA. 51.0' x 12.6' x 3.0' Wood. 40gt 25nt. Powered by a steam engine. In 1900–1901 she was owned by Portland OR US interests. In 1914 she was reported as having been laid up at Portland OR USA.

Vulcan 161698 (US) (tug) She was built in 1892 at Portland OR USA. 144.0' x 26.0' x 7.0' Wood. 328gt 220nt. In 1892 she was owned by FB Jones, Portland, OR USA. In 1910 she was owned by Portland OR USA interests. In 1914 she was reported as having been laid up at Portland OR USA.

W.H. Bancroft 208384 (US) (fishboat) She was built in 1911 at Winslow WA USA by Hall Bros. Marine Railway & Shipbuilding Co. 112.0' x 26.5' x 5.6' Wood. 179gt 103nt. In 1911 she was owned by the Northwestern Fisheries Co. She was towed to Alaska by the tug *Richard Holyoake* and employed on the Copper River.

W.H. Evans 081599 (US) (passenger/ freight vessel) She was built in 1898 at Ballard WA USA. 182.5' x 36.0' x 6.2' Wood. 729gt 408nt. Powered by a steam engine. In 1898 she was owned by the Lewis-Klondike Exploration Co., Baltimore MD. She was towed to St. Michael AK. In June 1899 she grounded in the Yukon River. In 1900 she was owned by the Alaska Commercial Co., broken up and her engines employed in a Yukon River saw mill.

W.H. Pringle 081773 (US) (passenger vessel) She was built in 1901 at Pasco WA USA. 166.8' x 30.9' x 5.4' Wood. 575gt 507nt. Her engines came from the *Thomas L. Nixon* 145494 (US). Powered by two horizontal (high pressure 16" x 60") steam engines. In 1889 she was owned by the Shaver Transportation Co. (Red Collar fleet). In 1905 she was renamed as the *Glenola*. She was wrecked and rebuilt as the *Glenola* 086041 (US). In 1906 she was rebuilt as the *Beaver* (202837).

W.H. Rideout (later *Rideout*; then *Ida May*) 107855 (Canada) 111182 (US) (passenger vessel) She was built in 1898 at Stockton CA USA by the California Navigation & Improvement Co. 150.0' x 32.0' x 4.0' Wood. 278gt

267rt. Powered by a steam engine. In 1898 she was owned by California Yukon Trading Co. and chartered by the Gold Star Transportation Co. In 1899 she was employed between Whitehorse and Dawson. In 1902 she was renamed as *Ida May*. In 1901–1910 she was owned by AJ Smilie, Dawson YT. In 1902 she was registered in Canada as *Rideout*. In 1914–1917 she was owned by the White Pass & Yukon Rail Road. She was re-registered in Canada in 1900–1905, and re-registered in the USA in 1905. In 1906–1910 she was employed between St. Michael and Fairbanks. In 1917 she was reported as having been laid up at St. Michael AK.

W.H. Seward[962] (US) She was built in 1898. Wood. Powered by a steam engine. In 1898 she was owned by the Alaska Commercial Co. She is reported by Murray Lundberg to have worked in Alaska/YT in 1898.

W.K. McKenzie[963] 107854 (Canada) She was built in 1883 at Seattle WA. Wood. Powered by a steam engine. It is not certain that she was a sternwheeler. She is reported by Murray Lundberg to have worked in Alaska/YT in 1899. She was reported to have been taken out of service in 1900.

W.K. Merwin 0080959 (US) (passenger/ freight vessel) She was built in 1883 at Seattle WA USA. 108.0' x 22.5' x 4.2' Wood. 229.08gt 166.04nt. Powered by a steam engine. In 1883 she was owned by Captain WK Merwin, Seattle WA. In 1897 she was sold to the Washington Steamboat Co. She was sold to the Northwestern Steamship Co. She was owned by the Alaska Commercial Co. In 1894–1896 she was laid up with the *Eliza Anderson*. On January 19, 1896, she collided with the half-open draw span of the railway bridge at Mount Vernon WA USA. All her upperworks to the funnel were demolished and the skipper was slightly injured. In 1897–1898 she wintered in a slough 100 miles above the mouth of the Yukon River with the steamers *Thomas Dwyer* and *Alice*. She formerly carried farm produce on the Skagit River WA and was intended to be used for a trip up the Yukon River in 1899. On August 9, 1900, she was wrecked at St. Michaels AK USA.

W.R. Todd 203141 (US) (passenger vessel) She was built in 1906 at Ainsworth WA USA. 111.6' x 20.8' x 3.8' Wood. 172gt 108nt. Powered by two

6.6nhp (10" x 48") 150ihp steam engines. In 1906 she was owned by the P.R.T. Co. In 1912 she was wrecked and broken up at Kennewick WA.

W.S. Mason 081529 (US) (sidewheeler) (ferry) She was built in 1894 at Portland OR USA. 1220' x 32.4' x 7.4' Wood. 322.70gt 252.00nt. Powered by a 59nhp steam engine. In 1894–1896 she was owned by Portland OR USA interests.

W.J. Stratton[964] 0081623 (US) (passenger/ freight vessel) She was built in 1898 at Seattle WA USA by James Casey. 75.0' x 16.0' x 3.1' Steel. 200.2gt 51nt. Powered by a steam engine. In 1898 she was owned by Stratton, Otis & Casey, Seattle WA USA. In 1898 she was owned by Alec McDonald. On October 24, 1899, she foundered and sank in the Yukon River 35 miles north of Selkirk.

W.T. Preston (see *Swinomish*)

W.T. Preston[965] (USACE) (snag boat) She was built in 1939 at Seattle WA USA by Lake Union Dry Dock & Machine Works. 163.0' x ? x ? Steel. In 1939–1980 she was owned by the United States Army Corps of Engineers. She was constructed using some of the gear from the *W.T. Preston*. She was placed on the National Register for Historic Places in 1979. She was retired in 1983 and became a museum exhibit owned by the City of Anacortes WA. She was designated a National Historic Landmark in 1989, serving as an important reminder of Puget Sound maritime and riverine history.

Wallace Langley (later *General Otis*) 235010 (US) She was built in 1936 at Seattle WA by Johnson Shipbuilding Co. (She was assembled at McGrath for Kuskokwim River service.) 109.1' x 29.1' x 4.5' Wood. 200gt 182nt. In 1936 she was owned by the United States Army Quartermaster Corps.

Wallamet[966] (US) (sidewheeler) (passenger vessel) She was built in 1853 at Canemah OR USA by John T Thomas. 150' x 23' x 5.0' Wood. 272gt. Powered by two 13nhp (high-pressure 14" x 60") steam engines. She was designed by Captain John McCrosky. In 1853 she was owned by Captain John McCrosky and was employed on the Willamette and Columbia Rivers in Oregon.

She was lined over the Willamette Falls and was employed at Astoria as a replacement for the *Lot Whitcomb* which had transferred to California. In 1854 she was towed south to San Francisco by the steamer *Peytonia* and became part of the Defiance Line operating on the Sacramento and San Joaquin Rivers in California. She was laid up in 1857 and broken up in 1860. Her engines were removed and placed in the small steamer *Swallow*.

Wallamet (Image from Library of Congress LC-USZ62-17463)

Wallowa (US) (dredge) She was built in 1904 at Riparia WA USA. 125' x 25.6' x 5' Wood. 175gt. Powered by two 13nhp (high pressure 14" x 60") steam engines. In 1904 she was owned by the United States Army Corps of Engineers. She was employed on the Columbia River. In 1914 she was reported as having been broken up at Celilo OR USA.

Wallulah[967] (US) She was built in 1914 at Corvallis OR USA by August W Fischer. 81' x 18' x 3.3' Wood. 98gt 95nt. Powered by a gasoline engine. In 1914 she was owned by August W Fischer. She was employed on the Columbia River. In 1919 she was reported as having been abandoned.

Walsh[968] 081601 (US) (freighter, later a ferry) She was built in 1898 at Port Blakely WA by EG Rathbown. 150.2' x 32.0' x 5.0' Wood. 522.8gt 348.2nt. Powered by a steam engine. She was constructed for service on the Stikine River but was not employed there. In 1897 she was laid up at Lulu Island BC. In 1902 she was owned by United States interests in service as the Seattle-Bremerton ferry. In 1902 she was sold. In July 1903 she was destroyed by fire at Bremerton WA.

Wanista 205245 (US) (ferry) She was built in 1908 at Ainsworth WA USA by SA Ash. 57.9' x 24.2' x 3.0'. Wood. 34gt 29rt. Powered by a 20ihp gasoline engine. In 1908 she was owned by SA Ash. She was employed on the Columbia River.

Wanista 214711 (US) (ferry) She was built in 1917 at Kennewick WA USA. 56' x 20' x 4'. Wood. 53gt 42nt. Powered by a steam engine. She was employed on the Columbia River. In 1927 she was reported as having been abandoned.

Wasco (US) (sidewheeler) (passenger vessel) She was built in 1855 at Cascades WT USA. Wood. Powered by a steam engine. She was employed on the Columbia River.

Wasco 081168 (US) She was built in 1887 at Hood River OR USA. 135' x 22' x 6.8'. Wood. 250.12gt 214.59nt. Powered by a steam engine. In 1900 she was serving Tacoma, Seattle, Anacortes, and Bellingham in Puget Sound. In 1924 she was reported as having been abandoned.

Washburn 081805 (US) She was built in 1908 at Bismarck ND USA. 98.7' x 24.8' x 3.1'. Wood. 57gt/nt. Powered by a steam engine. She was employed at Pembina ND.

Washington[969] (US) Wood. Powered by a steam engine. She originally was employed on the Sacramento River. In 1851 she was transferred on the bark *Success* to Oregon to replace the *Hoosier*. She was in employed on the Yamhill River. Later she was employed between Portland and Oregon City. In 1853 she was transferred to the Umpqua River.

Washington[970] 026799 (US) She was built in 1866. 99.7'. Wood. 148.58gt. Powered by a steam engine. She was in service on California rivers. She was reported to have ceased operation about 1877. She was reported to have been lost in 1880.

Washington[971] 080815 (US) (passenger vessel/ freighter) She was built in 1881 at Vancouver WT USA. 141.0' x 24.0' x 5.9'. Wood. 292.28gt 193.08nt. Powered by two 15nhp (high pressure 15" x 60") steam engines. In 1881 she was owned by the Peoples Transportation Co., Vancouver WT. She was employed on the Columbia River. In 1882 she was transferred to Puget Sound. In 1884 she was reported to have been operating on the Skagit River. In 1885 she was owned by the Washington Steamboat Co. In 1900 she was reported to have been abandoned.

Washoe[972,973] 026797 (US) (sidewheeler) She was built at San Francisco CA USA by Owens. Wood. 580gt. Powered by a steam engine. She was employed on the Sacramento River CA. On September 5, 1864, her boiler exploded at Rio Vista CA with 103 lives lost, 11 others were unaccounted for and presumed drowned. Another 80 persons were injured, and 3 died later.

Wauna 203573 (US) (tug) She was built in 1906 at Portland OR USA. 118.0' x 24.0' x 5.2'. Wood. 149gt 134nt. Powered by two 9.6nhp horizontal (12" x 48") steam engines. In 1906 she was owned by the Shaver Transportation Co. She was originally employed as a tug towing on the Lake River. Late in her life she towed oil barges on the Willamette River. In 1937 she was reported as having been abandoned.

Web Foot 026714 (US) (sidewheeler) (passenger vessel) She was built in 1863 at Celilo OT USA. 150'. Wood. 504gt. Powered by a steam engine. In 1863 she was owned by the Oregon Steam Navigation Co. She was employed on the Columbia River. In 1871 she was reported to have been broken up at Celilo OR USA.

Web Foot No. 2 090100 (US) (passenger vessel) She was built in 1866 at Portland OT USA by Thomas Bulger. 50' x 11' x 3'. Wood. 31.6gt. Powered by a steam engine. She was employed on the Columbia River.

Weithpec[974] 201066 (US) (sidewheeler) (passenger vessel) She was built in 1904 at Fairhaven CA USA. 100.9' x 20.3' x 4.2'. Wood. 150gt 132nt. Powered by a 90ihp steam engine. She was in service on California rivers. On December 15, 1920, she was destroyed by fire at Brytes Bend on the Sacramento River.

Welcome 080537 (US) (passenger vessel) She was built in 1874 at Portland OR USA. 127' x 27' x 5.7' Wood. 327gt 251nt. Powered by a steam engine. Her engine came from the *Owyhee*. She was employed on the Columbia River. In 1881 she was transferred to Puget Sound. In 1900 she was reported to have been broken up.

Welcome 081707 (US) (passenger vessel) She was built in 1900 at Coquille OR USA. 56' Wood. 30gt 21nt. She was employed on the Columbia River. In 1907 she was wrecked.

Wenat[975] 080026 (US) (passenger vessel) She was built in 1868 at Portland OR USA by Silus E Smith. 77.0' x 18.0' x 4.0' Wood. 87gt. Powered by two horizontal (8.25" x 36") steam engines. She was employed on the Columbia River. In 1878 she was transferred to Puget Sound.

Wenatchee 081671 (US) (passenger vessel) She was built in 1899 at Wenatchee WA USA. 79.3' x 14.0' x 3.0' Wood. 77gt 48nt. Powered by two 6.6nhp (high pressure 10" x 36") steam engines. In 1899 she was owned by IJ Bailey and JJ O'Connor. She was employed on the Columbia River. On January 10, 1901, she was destroyed by fire at Wenatchee WA.

Weown 203994 (US) (tug) She was built in 1907 at St. Johns OR USA. 154' x 31.5' x 6.5' Wood. 372gt 319nt. Powered by two 17nhp horizontal (16" x 72") steam engines. In 1907 she was owned by Oregon & Cowlitz Towing Co. She was owned by the Hosford Transportation Co. She was owned by the Shaver Transportation Co. (Red Collar fleet), Portland OR. She was in service on the Columbia River. In 1938 she was reported as having been abandoned.

Weona[976] (US) (tug) She was built in 1898 at St. Michael AK. 40.4' x 9.6' x 3.8' Wood. 27gt 19nt. Powered by a steam engine.

West Creston Ferry[977] (Canada) (sidewheeler) Wood. She was built in 1937. In 1937–1950 she was owned by the British Columbia Ministry of Transportation on the Kootenay River west of Creston BC. In 1937 to 1950 this ferry operated on the Kootenay River west of Creston BC. In 1950 it was replaced by a vessel of a similar design.

West Creston Ferry[978] (Canada) (sidewheeler) She was built in 1950 in the Okanagan region of BC. In 1950–1973 she was owned by the British Columbia Ministry of Transportation on the Kootenay River west of Creston BC. This ferry was made obsolete by the construction of a bridge in 1973.

West Point[979,980] (US) (freighter) She was built in the eastern USA. Wood. Powered by a steam engine. She was in service on California rivers. On October 28, 1850, she collided with the *Mariposa* and sank on the Sacramento River. She was later salvaged.

West Seattle 203946 (US) She was built in 1907 at Tacoma WA USA 145.0' x 48.7' x 10.8' Wood. 773gt 487nt. Powered by a 450hp steam engine. . In 1907–1913 she was owned by the Port of Seattle, Seattle WA USA. In 1919 she was owned by King County, Seattle WA. In 1951 she was converted to a barge for storing fish nets. In 1907–1913 she was owned by the Port of Seattle, Seattle WA USA. In 1919 she was owned by King County, Seattle WA.

Western Queen 080407 (US) (passenger/ freight vessel) She was built in 1872 at Pittsburgh PA USA. Wood. 475gt. Powered by a steam engine.

Western Queen 080724 (US) (sidewheeler) (ferry) She was built in 1879 at Portland OR USA. 72' Wood. 95gt 75nt.

Western Slope 072685 (Canada) (passenger/ freight vessel, later a barge) She was built and launched on May 8, 1879, at Victoria BC Canada by Alexander Watson. 156.0' x 26.5' x 8.5' Wood. 831gt 725.71rt. Powered by an 86.32hp (20" x 60") steam engine. In 1879–1881 she was owned by Charles Hayward. In 1881 she was owned by Captain John William Moore, Victoria BC. In 1879 she was in Stikine River service under command of her owner. In 1880–1882 she was in Fraser River service. In 1883 she was owned by Charles Hayward and William P Hayward, Victoria BC. In 1883 she was owned by William B Kyle, Victoria BC. In 1883 she was owned by the Canadian Pacific Navigation Co. Ltd. (Captain John Irving), Victoria BC. In 1888 she was owned by William Rogers, New Westminster BC. In 1883 she was owned by the Canadian Pacific Navigation Co. Ltd. (Captain John Irving), Victoria BC. In 1891 her engines were removed, and she was converted to a barge. In 1895 she was reported as having been broken up.

Western Star 081603 (US) (passenger vessel) She was built in 1898 at Seattle WA USA by the Moran Bros. Shipyard. 176.1' x 35' x 4' Wood. 72gt. Powered by two horizontal (22" x 84") 26.6nhp steam engines built by the Moran Bros. In 1898 she was owned by the Blue Star Navigation Co. In 1898 she was wrecked at Shelikoff Strait AK on her way to the Yukon River for the Klondike Gold Rush.

Weston (see Little Maud)

Westport 080676 (US) (passenger/ freight vessel) She was built in 1878 at Westport OR USA. 118.0' x 22.0' x 5.0' Wood. 204gt 154nt. Powered by a (10" x 16") steam engine. She was employed on the Columbia River. In 1886 she was destroyed by fire at Westport OR.

White (see Amberly)

White Horse (Image from Vancouver Archives Bo P327)

White Horse (later *Whitehorse*; then *White Horse*) 107837 (Canada) (Passenger/ freight vessel) She was built in 1901 at Whitehorse YT Canada by WD Hofius. 171.0' x 36.3' x 5.6'. Wood. 1120gt 764rt. Powered by a 51nhp steam engine. In 1930 she was rebuilt at Whitehorse YT. In 1901–1960 she was owned by The British Yukon Navigation Co. Ltd., Vancouver BC on Yukon River service (Whitehorse – Dawson.) In 1960 she was transferred to the Canadian Government. She was known locally as "The Old Grey Mare". She was in Yukon River service. In 1955 she was retired and beached beside the *Casca* at Dawson City YT. She was destroyed (by arson) in 1974 at Dawson City YT.

Whitehorse (see *White Horse*)

White Seal 202409 (US) (passenger vessel) She was built in 1905 at Fairbanks AK USA by George P Sproul. 96.8'. Wood. 193gt 116nt. Powered by a steam engine. In 1905 she was owned by George P Sproul, George Coleman and Bert Smith, Fairbanks AK. In 1905 she was owned by the Tanana Mines Rail Road, Eagle AK USA. In 1915 she was owned by the White Pass & Yukon Rail Road. In 1926 she was owned by the Alaska Rail Road. She was sold again. She was reported as having been abandoned

White Swan (later *Pluck*) (US) (sidewheeler) Wood. Powered by a steam engine. She had been in service on the Mississippi River when in 1878 she was disassembled, shipped to the Red River and re-assembled. In 1886 she was reported as having been broken up at Grand Forks, Dakota Territory USA. In c1880 she was owned by Bonanza Farms. In 1882 she was owned by the Red River Transportation Co.

Wide West 080650 (US) (freighter) She was built in 1877 at Portland OR USA by John Holland. 218.0' x 39.0' x 8.0'. Wood. 1200.8gt 928.75nt. Powered by two horizontal (high pressure 28" x 96") steam engines. She was employed on the Columbia River on service between Portland to Cascades and Portland to Astoria. In 1887 she was reported to have been broken up with her engines going to the *TJ Potter*.

Wilbur Crimmin 107864 (Canada) 0081606 (US) (passenger/ freight vessel) She was built in 1898 at Coupeville WA USA by Howard Bently Lovejoy. 80.7' x 19.0' x 3.9'. Wood. 168.76gt 105.97nt. Powered by a steam engine.

She was towed north by the *Del Norte*. In 1898–1899 she was owned by owned by John D Crimmin, Jr, Peavey, Alaska US. In 1901 she was transferred to US Registry. In 1900–1904 she was owned by AJ Engvick and Wallace Langley, Dawson YT. In 1904 she was owned by Captain Wallace Langley, Dawson YT. In 1904 she was owned by USA interests. In 1905 she was employed on the Tanana River. In 1906 she was owned by Charles W Adams, the Dominion Commercial Co., and Mersereau & Clark. In 1908 she was owned by the Northern Navigation Co. In 1914 she was owned by White Pass & Yukon Rail Road In 1923 she was owned by the Waechter Bros. She was registered in the USA (1898–1900 & 1906–1935). In 1898–1899 she was in operation on the Koyukuk River. In 1935 she was reported as having been laid up at Seward AK.

Wild Cat 081370 (US) (work boat) She was built in 1892 at Alameda CA USA. 90.0' x 22.5' x 4.6'. Wood. 121.37gt 104.96nt. Powered by a 120nhp steam engine. She was owned by the California Pacific Steam Whaling Co. She was wrecked in Prince William Sound AK c1895/1896.

Wilder[981] (US) Wood. Powered by a steam engine. She was employed on the Yukon River. She was owned by the Russian-American Telegraph Co. She is reported by Murray Lundberg to have worked in Alaska/YT in 1866–1867, the first sternwheeler to ascend the Yukon River.

Wilhelmina 204869 (US) (freighter) She was built in 1907 at Lewiston ID USA. 59' x 13' x ? Wood. 13gt 8nt. She was powered by a gasoline engine. She was employed on the Columbia River. In 1910 she was reported to have been laid up.

Will H. Isom 081758 (tug) She was built in 1901 at Ballard WA USA by Andrew Axton & Son Co. 183.8' x 36.5' x 5.6'. Wood. 983gt 619nt. Powered by two horizontal compound (24" x 104") 880ihp steam engines. In 1901 she was owned by the North American Transportation & Trading Co. She sailed to Alaska under her own steam power. In 1910 she was owned by St. Michael Alaska USA interests. In 1911 she was owned by the Northern Navigation Co. In 1914 she was owned by the White Pass & Yukon Rail Road. She was sold again. In 1927 she was reported as having been laid up at St. Michael AK.

Willamette[982] (US) (sidewheeler) (passenger vessel) She was built in 1853 at Canemah OR USA. 150' x 22' x 5' Wood. Powered by two horizontal (14" x 60" high pressure) steam engine. She was employed on the Columbia River. In 1853 she was owned by J McCrosby et al. In 1854 she was transferred to San Francisco where she was in service on California rivers. In 1854 she was in competition on the Sacramento River with the California Steam Navigation Co. In 1855 she was owned by the California Steam Navigation Co. In 1855 she was laid up and abandoned. She was broken up and her machinery used in the *Swallow*.

Willamette (later *Montana*) 080808 (US) (freighter, collier) She was built in 1881 at Chester PA USA. Steel. 2561.24gt 1695.36nt. Powered by a steam engine. In 1881 she was owned by the Oregon Improvement Co. In 1901 she was owned by the Pacific Coast Steamship Co. On March 15, 1901, while enroute to Ladysmith in a dense fog to Oyster Bay this collier, owned by the Pacific Coast Steamship Co., struck Village Point, Denman Island in Baynes Sound. Part of her cargo was removed, and she was salvaged and repaired. The hull was winched out of the water and a repair crew from Moran Bros, Seattle WA replaced plates in situ, and she was refloated and put back in service.

Willamette Chief 080701 (US) (passenger vessel) She was built in 1878 at Willamette OR USA. 163' x 35.8' x 5.4' Wood. 693gt 524nt. Her engines came from the *Willamette Chief* (088405). She was employed on the Columbia River. In 1894 she was destroyed by fire at Portland OR.

Willamette Chief 088405 (US) (passenger vessel) She was built in 1874 at Portland OR USA. 163' x 31.0' x 6.0' Wood. 586gt. Powered by two 26nhp (high pressure 20" x 60") steam engines. In 1878 she was rebuilt. She was employed on the Columbia River.

Willamette Queen[983,984,985] 959851 (US) (passenger vessel) She was built in 1990 at Newport OR. 64' x 24' x 6' Steel. 62gt 50nt. In January 2019 she was damaged when she ran aground near Salem OR. She operates on the Willamette River. In 2021 she is based in Salem OR USA and is designed for dinner cruising on the Willamette River based in Salem towards Independence or Keizer, depending on water levels.

Willamette Squaw 080519 (US) (passenger vessel) She was built in 1875 at Willamette OR USA. 75' x 14' x ? Wood. 332gt. Powered by a steam engine. She was employed on the Columbia River. In 1880 she was reported to have been laid up.

William D. Evans[986] (US) She was built in 1986 at Mission Bay CA. In 1986–2021 she was owned by the Bahia Resort Hotel. She offered cruises on Mission Bay (north San Diego).

William H. Ladner (see *Helen M. Scanlon*)

William Ogilvie (Canada) (passenger/ freight vessel) She was built in 1899 at Lake Bennett BC Canada by JB Colvin. 63.0' x 14.4' x 4.5' Wood. 82gt 56rt. Powered by a 5nhp steam engine. In 1899–1901 she was owned by Teslin Yukon Steam Navigation Co. In 1911–1913 she was owned by Harry E Brown, Atlin BC. In 1913–1937 she was owned by Inland Trading Co., Victoria BC. In 1937 she was reported as having been laid up at Taku City BC.

William Irving 080900 (Canada) (passenger/ freight vessel) She was built in 1880 at Burrard Inlet BC by Alexander Watson. 166.3' x 34.3' x 4.5' Wood. 737gt 591.04rt. Powered by a 74.4nhp steam engine. In 1880–1883 she was owned by John Irving's Pioneer Line, New Westminster BC. In 1883–1894 she was owned by the Canadian Pacific Navigation Co. In 1891 she was rebuilt and re-engined. In 1894 she struck a rock and was wrecked near Farr's Bluff on the Fraser River. Her machinery was salvaged later.

William Robinson[987] (US) (sidewheeler) (freighter) She was built about 1850. Wood. Powered by a steam engine. She was in service on California rivers. She was reported to have gone out of operation about 1868.

William Tabor 026896 (US) (freighter) (She was built in the eastern United States). 223,0' x 35.0' x 13.0' Wood. 974.27gt. Powered by a 1500nhp steam engine. She was owned by John T. Wright Jr. who brought her around to the Pacific coast from the East coast. She was employed at San Francisco CA USA.

Willie 103309 (Canada) 008074 (US) (passenger/ freight vessel) She was built in 1883 at Shelton WA USA. 65.6' x 15.5' x 4.5' Wood. 82.6gt 55.94rt. (Powered by 3.3nhp horizontal steam engines). In 1896 she was rebuilt at Olympia WA USA to 80.0' x 20.2' x 3.0'. In 1883–1884 she was owned by Captain WH Ellis, Seattle WA. In 1884 she was operated by the Wiley Navigation Co. in Samish River service. In 1886 she was owned by Captain Ed Gustafson. In 1895 she went on Fraser River service. In 1896 she was employed on the Olympia – Shelton route. In 1901 she was owned by George A Huff, Alberni BC. In 1910 she was owned by William C Brown, Vancouver BC.

Willie Irving (a local nickname for the vessel *William Irving*)

Willie Irving 103918 (Canada) (passenger/ freight vessel) She was built in 1898 at Lake Bennett BC Canada by Captain John Irving. 80' x 20.2' x 3' Wood. 102gt 64rt. Powered by a steam engine. In 1898 she was owned by John Irving. In 1898 she was owned by Ed McConnell. Captain Edward M Barrington, and CH Hamilton. In 1899 she was owned by a consortium consisting of CH Hamilton, N Cowan, DH Dwyer, CF Griffith, and N Allen. In 1898 she was in Yukon River service. In 1899 she was wrecked by ice at Dawson YT.

Wilson 080671 (US) She was built in 1878 at San Francisco CA USA. 31.0' x 8.0' x 3.0' Wood. 6.53gt. Powered by a 10nhp steam engine.

Wilson G. Hunt[988] 072676 (Canada) 026713 (US) (sidewheeler) 186.0' x 26.0' x 8.0' In 1854–1855 she was owned by the Union Line. She operated on the Sacramento River.

Wilson G. Hunt[989,990] 072676 (Canada) 0026713 (US) (sidewheeler) (passenger vessel) She was built in New York NY. 185.5' x 26.0' x 8.0' Wood. 459gt 350nt. Powered by two (36" x 108") steam engines. In 1854 she was in service on California rivers by the California Steam Navigation Co. She was employed on the Columbia River. In 1858 she was transferred to British Columbia for service between Victoria VI to New Westminster BC later expanding to Olympia WT. In 1860 she was transferred to the Oregon Steam Navigation Co. in Oregon service. In 1862 she was in service on the Columbia River between Portland and the Cascades. In 1877 she was owned by John Irving in service between Victoria and New Westminster. In 1881 she was owned by Joseph Spratt in service on the east coast of Vancouver Island. In 1883 she was owned by the Canadian Pacific Navigation Co. She was laid up soon after. She was reported to have been broken up in 1890.

Winema[991] (US) (passenger vessel) She was built in 1905 at Klamath Falls OR USA. 110' x 22.5' x 2' Wood. 125gt. Powered by a steam engine. She was employed on Upper Klamath Lake OR. In 1905 she was owned by the Klamath Lake Navigation Company, Klamath Falls OR. In 1907 she foundered and sank. She was raised and put back into service. In 1919 she was reported as having been abandoned and was destroyed by fire in 1925.

Winfield Scott (US) (sidewheeler) She was built in 1850 at New York by Westervelt & Mackay. 225' x 34.6' x ? Wood. 1,291gt. Powered by two side-lever steam engines built by Morgan Iron Works. She arrived at San Francisco in April 1852 and operated to Panama City until April 1853 for the Independent Line. In 1850 she was owned by Davis, Brooks & Co. In 1852 she served the New York & San Francisco Steamship Company. She was then purchased by the Pacific Mail Steamship Company in July 1853. On December 2, 1853, she was wrecked on Middle Anacapa Island CA in thick fog while bound for Panama City. All 450 passengers and crew survived, but the ship was lost. The wreck is in the Channel Islands National Park and Marine Sanctuary. The *Winfield Scott* wreck site is listed on the National Register of Historic Places.

Winnitoba[992,993] (Canada) (sidewheeler) (passenger/ freight vessel) She was built in 1909 at St. Boniface MB by JL Hyland. 187.5' x 44.0' x 9.0' Wood. 883gt. In 1909–1912 she was owned by Hyland Navigation & Trading Co. She was carrying passengers to and from Hyland Park (or other riverside destinations, such as Selkirk MB), the ship carried cargo and pulled barges along the Red and Assiniboine rivers, and could handle the open waters of Lake Winnipeg. On September 29, 1912, she burned at the docks of the Hyland Navigation and Trading Company at Winnipeg MB.

Wm. F. Munroe 081009 (US) (passenger vessel) She was built in 1883 at Seattle WA USA. 105.3' x 17.5' x 5.5' Wood. 181.49gt 99.81rt. Powered by a steam engine. She was employed on Puget Sound WA.

Wm. M. Hoag[994,995] (later *Annie Comings*) 081171 (US) (passenger vessel) She was built in 1889 at East Portland OR USA. 150' Wood. 452gt 431nt. Powered by two 17nhp (16" x 60") steam engines. In 1903 she was rebuilt. In 1889 she was owned by the Oregon Pacific Railroad. She was employed on the Columbia River. In 1907 she was wrecked at St. Johns OR and rebuilt in 1909 as the *Annie Comings* (206116) at Vancouver WA.

Wonder[996,997] (later *No Wonder* 130458) 080648 (US) She was built in 1877 at Portland OR USA by George Washington "Old Man" Weidler. 131.0' x 24.0' x 6.0' Wood. 319.9gt 225.62rt. Powered by two 16nhp horizontal (16" x 48" cylinder) steam engines. In 1889 she was rebuilt at Portland OR USA as the *No Wonder*. 135.3' x 27.8' x 5.6' Wood. 269gt 235nt. In 1877 she was owned by the Willamette Steam Mills & Lumber Co. In 1884 she was owned by Weidler Mills. Portland OR USA. In 1889 she was owned by the Willamette Steam Mills Co. In 1897 she was owned by the Shaver Transportation Co. (Red Collar fleet), Portland OR. She worked in the log towing service and was the first log towing vessel on the Willamette River. In 1933 she was reported to have been abandoned.

Woodland (see *G.M. Walker*)

Woodland[998] (USACE) (tug) She was built in 1915 at Portland OR USA. 97' x 24' x 4.6' Wood. 91gt. Powered by two 6.6nhp (high pressure 10" x 36") steam engines. In 1915 she was owned by the United States Army Corps of Engineers. She was employed on the Columbia River. She was reported as having been employed as a tug on the Cowlitz and Lewis Rivers. In 1929 she was reported as having been abandoned.

Woodside 072680 (Canada) She was built in 1878 at Sooke BC by Samuel Sea. 70.0' x 15.2' x 6.5' Wood. 50.27gt 32.87nt. Powered by a 20hp steam engine by John Dougall, Victoria BC. In 1878 she was owned by John Muir, Michael Muir, and Robert Muir (brothers), Sooke BC. In 1888 she was owned and was employed by Captain Trenchard in service towing between Sooke and Victoria. In 1878 this tug was in Victoria-Sooke service. On March 12, 1888, while under the command of Captain Colin Cluness she was bound from Victoria for Barkley Sound with three passengers (Mrs. Wrede and two children) and six crew members with general cargo when she lost her rudder and went aground near Pachena Point. All were saved, but the vessel was abandoned. During the night, the vessel drifted ashore and became a total loss. The survivors were paddled in a canoe to Victoria by the First Nations people of Nitinat.

Wyvern[999] (US) (freighter) She was built in 1896 at Dartmouth UK. Wood. 8gt. Powered by a steam engine. She was shipped to Alaska and served on the Snake River. In July 1900 she was wrecked on the Snake River AK.

Yakima[1000] 027551 (US) (passenger vessel) She was built in 1864 at Celilo OR USA. 150' x 29' x 0.5' Wood. 455gt 393nt. Powered by two 19nhp horizontal (17" x 72") steam engines. In 1864 she was owned by the Oregon Steam Navigation Co. She was employed on the Columbia River. In 1876 she was wrecked and reported to have been abandoned in 1877.

Yakima 027601 (US) (freighter) She was built in 1874 at Port Gamble WT USA. 117.0' x 26.0' x 6.0' Wood. 173.54gt. Powered by a steam engine.

Yakima[1001] 020552 (US) (passenger vessel) She was built in 1906 at Ainsworth WA USA by Louis Paquet. 137' x 28.8' x 4.9' Wood. 393gt. Powered by two 13nhp (high pressure 14" x 76") steam engines. In 1906 she was owned by C.S. Miller & Co. She was employed above Wenatchee WA. In 1924 she was reported as having been abandoned.

Yamhill[1002] (US) She was built in 1851 at Canemah OT USA. Wood. Powered by a steam engine. She was reported to have been out of service after 1852.

Yamhill[1003,1004] (US) (sidewheeler) (passenger vessel) She was built in 1860 at Canemah OR USA. 76' x 15' x 2.5' Wood. 72gt. Powered by a 4.3nhp (8" x 12") steam engine. She was owned by the People's Transportation Co. She was employed on the Tualatin River to Hillsboro OR. She had a hinged funnel which, when dropped over, allowed her to pass under low-built bridges over the river.

York Barrington[1005] (US) (freighter) She was owned by Captain Syd Barrington in operation on Lake Laberge, YT. She is reported by Murray Lundberg to have worked in Alaska/YT in 1911. She does not appear to have been listed in the annual editions of the Merchant Vessels of the United States so she may not have been officially registered.

Yosemite (Image from Vancouver Archives AM1576-S6-12-F47-2011-010.1711)

Yosemite[1006] 027550 (US) 083455 (Canada) (sidewheeler) She was built in 1862 at San Francisco CA. 282.3' x 34.9' x 13.2'. Wood. 631gt. Powered by a steam engine. In 1862 she was owned by the California Steam Navigation Co. She was in service on California rivers. In 1864 she collided with and sank the power schooner *Commodore* on the Sacramento River 3 miles south of Freeport CA. On October 12, 1865, her boiler exploded at Rio Vista killing or injuring about 100 passengers. She was salvaged and put back into operation. She sank in Port Orchard Narrows, Rich Pass, Puget Sound on October 12, 1865.

Yosemite[1007] (US) (sidewheeler) Wood. Powered by a steam engine. In 1871 she was taken over by the California Pacific Railroad Co., San Francisco CA.

Yosemite 202806 (US) (passenger vessel) She was built in 1906 at Fairhaven CA USA. 193.0' x 40.0' x 15.3'. Wood. 827gt 525nt. Powered by a steam engine. In 1906 she was owned by Puget Sound Excursion Company, Seattle WA USA. In 1907 she was owned by CD Hillman, Seattle WA USA. In 1910 she was owned by San Francisco CA USA interests. The University of Washington Library states "On July 9, 1909, at Port Orchard Narrows she ran full-speed onto the beach in broad daylight. It was suspected that she was intentionally wrecked for insurance money. The ship had recently been sold to real estate promoter CD Hillman, the namesake for the Hillman City District in south Seattle, who was later sent to prison."

Youkon 027578 (US) (passenger/ freight vessel) She was built in 1869 at San Francisco CA USA by John W Gates. 49' Wood. 20.21gt. Powered by a steam engine. In 1869 she was owned by Parrot & Co. In 1870 she was owned by the Alaska Commercial Co. In 1884 she was owned by San Francisco CA USA interests. In 1880 she was crushed in ice at Fort Yukon AK USA.

Young America[1008] (US) (sidewheeler) She was built in 1854 at San Francisco CA. Wood. 67gt. Powered by a steam engine. She was in service on California rivers. In 1855 she was sold to foreign (non-US) owners.

Young America (US) (sidewheeler) (freighter) She was built in 1856 at San Francisco CA. Wood. 179gt. Powered by a steam engine. She was reported to have been lost in 1865.

Yuba[1009,1010] (US) (freighter) She was built about 1849. She was in service on California rivers. In February 1851 she was snagged in the Sacramento River, sank and was a total loss.

Yuba[1011] (US Army) (sidewheeler) (snag boat) 166.0' x 37.8' x 5.6' 410gt. She was built in 1925 at Alameda CA USA. Powered by a steam engine. In 1925–1929 she was owned by the United States Army Corps of Engineers, Washington DC. In 1929 she was based in San Francisco CA employed at Sacramento CA.

Yuba City Belle[1012] (US) (freighter) She was built in 1875 at Yuba City CA USA by Orr. 74' Wood. 31.9gt. Powered by a steam engine. She was employed on California rivers. She was reported to have ceased operation about 1885.

Yukon[1013] 027670[1014] (US) (passenger/ freight vessel) She was built in 1895 at Rufus OR USA. 48' x 24' x 3' Wood. 33gt 17rt. She was employed on the Columbia River. In 1904 she was laid up.

Yukon[1015] 276623 (US) She was built in 1883 at St. Michael, Department of Alaska, USA. 70.0' x 18.5' x 3.5'Wood. 20.66gt 10.33nt. Powered by a steam engine. In 1883 she was owned by the Alaska Commercial Co. In 1898 she was employed up river from St. Michael. She was crushed in the ice at Koyukuk River AK USA.

Yukon 165172 (US) She was built in 1913 at Seattle WA USA by Nilson & Kelez Shipbuilding Corp. 164.8' x 35.3' x 5.9' Wood. 642gt 303nt. Powered by a 400ihp steam engine. In 1913 she was owned by the White Pass & Yukon Rail Road. In 1929–1941 she was owned by the American Yukon Navigation Co., Seattle WA USA. Her hull was built at Seattle WA and her superstructure was constructed at Whitehorse YT (by the White Pass Rail Road). In 1945 she was no longer listed in Merchant Vessels of the United States. In 1947 she was damaged by ice at Tanana AK. In 1948 she was destroyed by fire at Tanana AK.

Yukon Belle (later *Scenic Belle*) 320073 (Canada) (passenger vessel) She was built in 1964 at Victoria BC Canada by McKay-Cormack Ltd. 34.9' x 12.1' x 2.6' (13.08m x 3.69m x 0.79m) Wood. 18.97gt 14.64rt. Powered by a 60hp engine built by the Newage (Manchester) Ltd., Manchester UK. Repowered with a 75bhp diesel engine. In 1964–1967 she was owned by Yukon Queen Tours Ltd., Victoria BC. In 1967–1983 she was owned by Harbour Ferries Ltd., Vancouver BC. In 1984–1990 she was owned by HF Management Ltd., Vancouver BC. In 1991–2010 she was owned by Jonathan Van der Goes, Nanaimo BC.

Yukon Queen (later *Scenic Queen*) 320069 (Canada) (passenger vessel) She was built in 1964 at Victoria BC Canada by McKay-Cormack Ltd. 34.9' x 12.1' x 2.6' (13.08m x 3.69m x 0.79m) Wood. 18.97 gt 14.64rt. Powered by a 60hp engine built by the Newage (Manchester) Ltd., Manchester UK. Repowered with a 75bhp diesel engine. In 1964–1969 she was owned by the Yukon Queen Tours Ltd., Victoria BC. In 1970–1983 she was owned by Harbour Ferries Ltd., Vancouver BC. In 1984–1991 she was owned by HF Management Ltd., Vancouver BC. In 1992–2001 she was owned by Jonathan Van der Goes, Nanaimo BC. In 2003–2021 she was owned by Front Street Java Ltd., Clearwater BC.

Yukoner 107098 (Canada) (passenger/ freight vessel) In 1898 she was built at St. Michael AK USA by Alexander Watson. She was re-assembled in in sections at St. Michael AK (US Registry.) 170.8' x 32.0' x 5.7' Wood. 781gt 492nt. Powered by a 17hp steam engine. In 1898 she was owned by the Canadian Pacific Navigation Co. Ltd., Victoria BC. In 1898 she was owned by the North British American Trading & Transportation Co. In 1899 she was owned by the Trading & Exploration Co. In 1898 she was transferred to Canadian Registry for the Canadian Development Company. In 1901–1957 she was owned by British Yukon Navigation Co. Ltd., Vancouver BC. She was beached in 1905 at Whitehorse YT and in 1937 the boilers were removed for use in the *Klondike* (II). In 1957 she was sold for firewood.

Zack Johnson (US) (freighter) She was built about 1849. Wood. Powered by a steam engine. In 1849 she was in service on the Sacramento River CA.

Zealandian (later *Reaper*; then *Zealandian*) 107830 (Canada) She was built in 1900 at Lake Bennett BC by Alexander Watson. 102' x 23' x 5' Wood. 179.82gt 141.18rt. Powered by two 6.6hp horizontal (high pressure 10" x 48") steam engines built by the Sumner Iron Works, Everett WA USA. In 1900–1901 she was owned by the Canadian Development Co. Ltd. Victoria BC. In 1901–1931 she was owned by the British Yukon Navigation Co., Vancouver BC. She was employed on the Whitehorse – Dawson route. In 1905 she was retired. She was reported as having been broken up in 1931.

Zephyr 028074 (US) (passenger vessel later a tug) She was built in 1871 at Seattle WA USA by JFT Mitchell & MM Robbins. 100.0' x 20.3' x 4.8' Wood. 161.54gt 109.75nt. Powered by an 80nhp steam engine. In 1871 she was owned by Seattle WA USA interests employed on Puget Sound. In 1879 she was owned by Captain WK Ballard, Seattle WA. In 1887 she was owned by the Tacoma Mill Co., Tacoma WA USA and converted to a tug towing log rafts. In 1907 she was reported as having been broken up.

Zinfandel[1016,1017,1018] 028115 (US) She was built in 1889 at San Francisco CA USA. 125.0' x 29.5' x 7.0' Wood. 329.15gt 270.36rt Powered by a 90nhp 230ihp steam engine. In 1889–1910 she was owned by San Francisco CA USA interests. She was in service on California rivers. On September 5, 1922, she foundered at Miner Slough, on the Sacramento River CA USA. She was rebuilt as a barge. On May 26, 1929, she capsized by the wind while carrying a cargo of sugar in San Pablo Bay while enroute from the Crockett Refinery to San Francisco. She was righted and towed to San Francisco for repairs.

Zodiak No. 1[1019] (US) (passenger/ freight vessel) She was built in 1898 at Puget Sound WA by James Casey. 45' x 12' x ? Wood. Powered by a steam engine. In 1898 she was owned by James Casey, Seattle WA USA. She was employed on Puget Sound WA.

Zodiak No. 2 (US) (passenger/ freight vessel) She was built in 1898 at Puget Sound WA by James Casey. 45' x 12' x ? Wood. Powered by a steam engine. In 1898 she was owned by James Casey, Seattle WA USA. She was employed on Puget Sound WA.

The Lytton during road construction between Hobson and Greenwood BC.
Note the team of horses being coaxed up the gangway.
(Image from Maritime Museum of British Columbia 000441)

GLOSSARY

Abandoned describes a vessel that is deliberately neglected by its owner. Often these vessels are run onto a beach or grounded in shallow water with no intent to salvage them.

(to) Alide/(an) Allision occurs when a vessel strikes a stationary object, such as a bridge, float, buoy, or another vessel that is berthed or moored and not under command.

Anchored means a vessel or structure temporarily held fast be a temporary weight that can be retrieved to allow a vessel to move.

Berthed describes a vessel secured alongside a float, a wharf, or pier.

Broken Up describes the careful demolition of a vessel so that equipment or metals can be salvaged for recycling.

Collide/Collision is when two vessels strike each other.

Compound Engine[1020] An engine where the steam is expended in two stages—the first in the high-pressure cylinder and the second in the low-pressure cylinder.

Derelict a vessel abandoned at sea, or on the shore, by its guardian or owner.

Dismantled describes a vessel that was broken up. The terms are interchangeable but broken up is more commonly used.

Docked describes a vessel in a drydock or graving dock.

Flotsam are those parts of the wreckage of a ship or its cargo found floating on the sea because of shipwreck.

Founder is when a vessel is overcome by forces of nature so that it is unable to remain afloat.

Gross Tonnage is a ship's total internal volume expressed in "register tons", each of which is equal to 100 cubic feet (2.83 m^3). Gross register tonnage uses the total permanently enclosed capacity of the vessel as its basis for volume. Typically, this is used for dockage fees, canal transit fees, and similar purposes where it is appropriate to charge based on the size of the entire vessel.

Grounding describes a vessel touching bottom or being stuck on the bottom.

Horizontal Engine[1021] An engine where the cylinder is near horizontal. Sternwheelers and sidewheelers required a high-pressure cylinder. (Low pressure was employed in screw driven vessels.)

ihp[1022] **(Indicated Horsepower)** is an engine rating calculated by the area of the piston x psi x the number of feet travelled by the piston per minute divided by 33,000.

Joint Owner (JO) a person who owns part of the shares in a vessel.

Laid Up describes a vessel that is still potentially operational but that has no current employment.

Licence Number is the alphanumeric number issued to vessels by Transport Canada or by a US Government authority.

Managing Owner (MO) is the partner owner who is designated to act on behalf of the overall interests in a vessel.

Moored describes a vessel secured to a buoy or independent float, but not secured to a wharf or pier or anchor.

Net Tonnage is denoted by the volume of the ship's revenue-earning spaces in "register tons", units of volume equal to 100 cubic feet (2.83 m^3)

Registered Tonnage is a ship's cargo volume capacity expressed in "register tons", one of which equals to a volume of 100 cubic feet (2.83 m³). It is calculated by subtracting non-revenue-earning spaces (i.e., spaces not available for carrying cargo, for example engine rooms, fuel tanks and crew quarters, from the ship's gross register tonnage. Net tonnage is thus used in situations where a vessel's earning capacity is important, rather than its mere size.)

Registration Number is the unique identification number assigned by the Canada Register of Shipping or the United States Government to vessels.

Retired describes a vessel that is no longer in use in its primary role but is still afloat but unused. This term can also be interchanged with "laid up."

Scrapped describes a vessel that is demolished, sometimes by totally destructive means such as burning. If a vessel is taken apart for recycling parts or metals "broken up" is a more appropriate term.

Scuttle means to deliberately cause a vessel to sink.

Sidewheeler is a vessel propelled by blades mounted on either side of the hull of a vessel.

Spud is a term for pointed temporary pilings used by dredgers to temporarily anchors themselves to carry out operations. They can be raised again when it is time to re-position the vessel.

Sternwheeler is a vessel propelled by blades mounted on the stern of a vessel.

Stranding describes when a vessel is grounded securely and cannot move under its own power.

Triple Expansion Engine is a steam engine where steam is expanded three times before being recovered or exhausted.

Vertical direct-acting engine[1023] is an engine where the pistons, supported on columns, are above the crankshaft.

Waterlogged[1024] William Falconer states: "the state of a ship when, by receiving a great quantity of water into her hold, by leaking, &c., she has become heavy and inactive upon the sea, so as to yield without resistance to the efforts of every wave rushing over her decks. As, in this dangerous situation, the center of gravity is no longer fixed, but fluctuating from place to place, the stability of the ship is utterly lost. She is therefore almost totally deprived of the use of her sails, which would operate to overset her, or press the head under water. Hence there is no resource for the crew, except to free her by the pumps, or to abandon her by the boats as soon as possible."

Wreck is a vessel, or part of a vessel, that is sunk, partially sunk, adrift, stranded, or grounded, including on the shore; or, equipment, stores, cargo, or any other thing that is or was on board a vessel and that is sunk, partially sunk, adrift, stranded, or grounded, including on the shore.

ABBREVIATIONS USED

AB	Alberta	**NJ**	New Jersey
AK	Alaska	**nt**	net tons
AZ	Arizona	**NT**	North West Territory
BC	British Columbia	**NV**	Nevada
bhp	brake horsepower	**NWT**	North West Territories
CA	California	**NY**	New York
CPR	Canadian Pacific Railway	**OH**	Ohio
		ON	Ontario
gt	gross tons	**OR**	Oregon
HBC	Hudson's Bay Company	**OT**	Oregon Territory
HI	Hawaii	**PA**	Pennsylvania
HMCS	Her/His Majesty's Canadian Ship	**QC**	Québec
		rt	registered tons
HMS	Her/His Majesty's Ship	**SC**	South Carolina
IA	Iowa	**SD**	South Dakota
ID	Idaho	**shp**	shaft horse power
ihp	indicated horsepower	**SK**	Saskatchewan
IL	Illinois	**US**	United States
IN	Indiana	**USA**	United States of America
KY	Kentucky		
LA	Louisiana	**USACE**	United States Army Corps of Engineers
MB	Manitoba		
ME	Maine	**USAQMC**	United States Army Quartermaster Corps
MI	Michigan		
MN	Minnesota	**USCG**	United States Coast Guard
MO	Missouri		
MT	Montana	**USN**	United States Navy
NB	New Brunswick		
NC	North Carolina	**USRC**	United States Revenue Cutter
ND	North Dakota		
nhp	nominal horsepower		

(continued on following page . . .)

USS	United States Ship (a ship of the United States Navy)	**WA**	Washington State
		WT	Washington Territory
		WV	West Virginia
UT	Utah	**WY**	Wyoming
VA	Virginia	**YT**	Yukon Territory
VI	Vancouver Island		

A GUIDE TO STERNWHEELERS STILL OPERATING OR PRESERVED (in whole or in fragments)

ALASKA

Fairbanks AK

The *Discovery II*[1025] In 1971–2021 she was the second of three Discovery sternwheel riverboats operated by the Riverboat Discovery company. She is still in use in 2021 as a standby tour vessel on the Chena and Tanana rivers near Fairbanks, Alaska.

The *Discovery III*[1026] In 1987–2021 she was operated by the Riverboat Discovery company. In 2021 she is still in use as a tour vessel on the Chena and Tanana rivers near Fairbanks, Alaska.

The *Nenana* was put on display in Pioneer Park, Fairbanks AK. The Fairbanks North Star Borough Parks and Recreation Department is committed to the preservation of the vessel.

The pilot house of the *Lavelle Young* is on public display near the *Nenana*.

The University of Alaska Museum of the North has the steering wheel from the *Alice*; a handsome nameboard with brass letters for the *Alice*; the steering wheel and nameboard of the *General Jeff Davis*; and a fine model of the *Yukon*.

St. Michael AK

The remains of several sternwheelers and other vessel are located on the waterfront and in the vicinity.

ALBERTA

Calgary AB

The *Moyie* is a half-scale replica of the original sternwheeler Moyie. It is owned and operated

Edmonton AB

The *Edmonton Riverboat*[1027] (She is a riverboat operating on the North Saskatchewan River since 1995.

Fort McMurray AB

When the P.W.D. 250 (dredge) was retired the federal government deposited the vessel in the collection of the Fort McMurray Heritage Shipyard where it has been restored and put on display. (She does not have her sternwheel in place.

Medicine Hat AB

The Esplanade Museum's[1028] collection includes a model of the *City of Medicine Hat* sternwheeler, launched in 1907 and wrecked at Saskatoon in 1908. A kedge anchor was recovered from the wreck site in 2006 and for a time was displayed at River Landing in Saskatoon—is presently located at Saskatoon's Meewasin Valley Centre. The Esplanade also has on display in the Medicine Hat Gallery the case of a commercial music box that was removed from the *City of Medicine Hat* before the journey on which it sank. Also on display in the Medicine Hat Gallery is a mostly complete engine room telegraph that was salvaged from the South Saskatchewan River which they speculate came off the *Baroness*, which was reputedly broken up at Medicine Hat. There is a plaque that commemorates riverboats on the South Saskatchewan River on Medicine Hat's riverbank, just below the Public Library.

Peace River AB

The wheel shaft of the D.A. *Thomas* (recovered and installed at the Peace River Museum) is on public display.

ARIZONA

Lake Havasu AZ

The **Dixie Belle**[1029] served public cruises on Saguaro Lake (northeast of Phoenix, just north of Mesa and Apache Junction).

Page AZ

The superstructure of the *Canyon King* was pulled ashore at Page AZ and is now the Canyon King Pizzeria restaurant.

Yuma AZ

The *Colorado King1030* is a double-decker sternwheeler tour boat with an open-air upper deck and an enclosed main deck. There is a small snack bar on board. They offer three-hour, non-stop tours either daytime trips downriver with an optional boxed lunch, or evening sunset dinner cruises with a hot buffet dinner served on board.

BRITISH COLUMBIA

Campbell River BC

The *Royal City Star* (ex-*Queen of New Orleans*) is laid up near Campbell River and can be easily seen from the water.

Fort Langley BC

There is an interesting monument to the *Beaver* on the grounds of Fort Langley National Historic Site.

Kamloops BC

The *Wanda Sue* is a former excursion boat) is now a private yacht on a stiff-legged mooring at a private residence on the Thompson River and is visible from the road.

Kamloops Lake BC

The *Kootenay Star* is a private power yacht that sometimes (with luck) can be viewed when under way.

Kaslo BC

The sternwheeler *Moyie* is prominently dry berthed on the waterfront. It has been designated as a National Historic Site. The collection there includes a model of the Great Northern Railway's 1901 sternwheeler *Kaslo*.

Kelowna BC

The *Spirit of Kelowna* is an active excursion vessel with cosmetic sidewheels but is a twin-screw vessel.

Nakusp BC

A fragment of the *Minto* is on public display in a city park. The boiler of the *Revelstoke* can be seen when the Columbia River water levels subside in late summer.

Nelson BC

The superstructure of the *Nasookin* has been pulled ashore and turned into a private residence. This can be easily viewed from the roadside (but private property should be respected).

The *Touchstones Museum* has a collection of original photographs of interior water sternwheelers. They also have a model collection which is on public display from time to time.

New Westminster BC

The *Samson* V[1031] was the last steam-powered sternwheeler to operate in Canada. She is an ex-government snag boat, is afloat as a heritage vessel on the waterfront. She is maintained and operated by the City of New Westminster. She is usually accessible to the public over the spring and summer period.

There is an haute relief carving of the *Yukoner* on a wooden panel at the Royal Columbian Hospital.

The *Native*[1032] is a commercial excursion and charter vessel that operated in 2020 between Fort Langley and Steveston on the Fraser River. At the time of publication her operating future was uncertain, but it is hoped that she will remain in service.

Penticton BC

The *Sicamous*[1033] is dry-berthed and easily publicly accessible and functions as a museum. She is preserved on the shore of Okanagan Lake, in Penticton BC. It open as a museum and heritage site and is cared for by a non-profit organization called the SS Sicamous Marine Heritage Society.

The Penticton Museum Archives has a model of the *Aberdeen* on display. In the collection there is a child-sized kapok life jacket, a circular life preserver of unknown origin, another marked SS *Naramata*, a large cleat from a dock, and a huge crescent wrench that was used on the *Sicamous*.

Quesnel BC

The Quesnel & District Museum & Archives[1034] has a model of the *Beaver* and the BX (both models built by Jim Williams who was a shipwright in the North Kootenay and Cariboo Districts). They have the wooden name plate from the *Nechako*, and a kerosene lamp base on a swivel whose provenance is from one of the sternwheelers, but the ship is not identified. They have a ship's clock that belonged to Captain AD Foster from his father's Nova Scotian vessel, used on sternwheelers in the upper Fraser—the *Charlotte*, the *Chilcotin* and the *Quesnel*, and a tablespoon said to have been used on the BX. They also have a large collection of archival photographs depicting sternwheelers.

Saanich BC

The bell of the *Major Tompkins* On March 8 [1855], the bell from the wrecked steamboat Major Tompkins was hung at the end of the school and used to call the children to classes. This bell is still in use, in the belfry of the new Craigflower School. [*This refers to the 2nd Craigflower School which was built after the original was closed in 1912.*]

Shuswap Lake BC

The *Phoebe Ann* is laid up but still in existence on the shore.

Sicamous BC

The Sicamous Museum[1035] holds a collection of images of sternwheelers that operated in that area.

Vancouver BC

The Vancouver Maritime Museum contains a variety of artifacts from the *Beaver*, including a galley bell, sheathing, anchor, davit, rudder, and wheel. There is fine model of the *Beaver* in their collection. They hold several images of paddlewheelers in the archive collection. They hold a collection of artifacts related to the *Beaver*.

There is a monument dedicated by the National Historic Sites and Monuments Board of Canada commemorating the *Beaver* in Stanley Park.

The *Constitution*[1036] is an excursion and event boat operated in Vancouver Harbour by Fairweather Cruises based in Vancouver BC.

Victoria BC

The Maritime Museum of British Columbia has a child's toy model of the *Despatch* and a model of the Beaver in the collection.

Yale BC

The Teague House B & B has a half-hull model of a sternwheeler (exact name uncertain) on display inside that would normally be available for viewing by guests of the B&B.

CALIFORNIA

Anaheim CA

The *Mark Twain Riverboat* is an attraction within Frontierland at Disneyland Anaheim. The vessel is afloat but travels along a hidden I-beam guide rail throughout the ride. The paddle wheels propel the vessel forward.

Big Bear Lake CA

The *Miss Liberty* has a seating capacity of 125 she features 1 1/2 hour-long narrated tours. She offered tours of Big Bear Lake, based out of Pine Knot Marina located about 100 miles east of Los Angeles.

Lake Arrowhead CA

The *Arrowhead Queen*[1037] is located at the San Bernardino National Forest. The excursion tour lasts about an hour and takes you around the perimeter of Lake Arrowhead.

Lake Tahoe CA

The M.S. *Dixie II* excursion cruises depart directly from Zephyr Cove Resort & Marina. She is the largest cruising vessel in South Lake Tahoe.

The *Tahoe Queen* is in service on Lake Tahoe, based on the California shore. In 2021 she was owned by the Aramark Corp.

Long Beach CA

The *Grand Romance*[1038] is located at Long Beach Harbor. She offers excursion and event cruises in the harbor.

Lucerne CA

The *Clear Lake Queen* is based on Clearlake California at Ferndale Resort & Marina in Soda Bay. It carries the Water Color Restaurant & Bar.

Mission Bay CA

The *Bahia Belle*[1039] operates seasonally, the *Bahia Belle* is a turn-of-the-century, Mississippi-style sternwheeler boat that cruises Mission Bay between the Bahia Resort Hotel and its sister property, the Catamaran Resort Hotel and Spa. Complimentary for hotel guests, this Mission Bay boat cruise is a scenic way to see the area.

The *William D. Evans* is based at the Bahia Resort Hotel, San Diego,

Oxnard CA

The *Scarlett Belle*[1040] is based at Channel Islands Harbor. It is an event boat, operating by arranging a previous appointment. She is located at the Marine Emporium Landing on the west side of Channel Islands Harbor.

Sacramento CA

The *Spirit of Sacramento* is dry berthed on private property next to the Garden Highway in North Sacramento.

The Center for Sacramento History has a boiler fragment from the *Washoe*; the pilot wheel from the *Capital City*; a model of the *Capital City*; technical drawings for the *Capital City*; and a collection of photographs.

San Francisco

The *Eppleton Hall* and the *Eureka* afloat in the collection of the San Francisco Maritime National Historical Park. On their pier, they have an 18' paddlewheel from the *Petaluma* on display and a model of the *Red Bluff*. They also have also a collection of plans, photographs, and printed material on paddlewheel ferries. They state that they have the largest maritime collection on the West Coast of America.

Threemile Slough Marina CA

In 2020 the *Matthew McKinley* was berthed at a marina on the Threemile Slough, where the Sacramento and San Joaquin Rivers merge, sixty miles east of San Francisco Bay.

IDAHO

Coeur d'Alene ID

The Museum of North Idaho[1041] has a magnificent model of the *Georgie Oakes* on display. It was built in 1998 by Robert Brune. The original signal bells and steering wheel from the steamboat *Flyer* are exhibited along with photos and artifacts from other steamboats which cruised Lake Coeur d'Alene.

MANITOBA

Brandon MB

The paddle wheel of the *Assiniboine* is on display on the grounds of Brandon Tourism/Riverbank Discovery Centre. There is a publicly accessible outside interpretive panel on display with the theme "The Prairie Navy."

Rural Municipality of Richot MB[1042]

The boiler from the *Cheyenne* is on public display on the bank of the Red River, in the village of Ste. Agathe MB.

The Pas MB

The Sam Waller Museum holds the anchor of the *Marquis*; a life preserver from the *David N. Winton*; and half a ship's wheel and parts from the *Prince Albert*.

Winnipeg MB

The Manitoba Museum[1043] has a fine little model of the *International* which is part of a mini diorama of Winnipeg in 1870. The diorama was completed in 1974. have the ship's wheel that was used on the *Nipawin* and *Tobin*.

MONTANA

Helena MT

The Montana Historical Society[1044] has a partial steering wheel, and the light from the steamboat *Rosebud* (ca. 1877). They also have the bell from the *Yellowstone* (1876–1879). They also have a model of the steamboat *Chippewa*; and a small cannon that was used on Missouri River steamboats to Fort Benton (they do not know for certain which boat it came from).

NEVADA

Lake Mead NV

The *Desert Princess*[1045] offers cruises on Lake Mead (forty miles east of Las Vegas) Nevada to the Hoover Dam. In 2021 she was operated by Lake Mead Cruises (Aramark) Boulder City NV.

Laughlin NV

The *Fiesta Queen* and *Celebration* are excursion boats with a propeller that carry simulated paddle wheels.

NORTH DAKOTA

Bismarck ND

The *Lewis and Clark*[1046] is an excursion boat operating on the Missouri River from May through to September.

NORTHWEST TERRITORY

Yellowknife NT

The Prince of Wales Northern Heritage Centre has a small sign that is from the *Distributor*.

OREGON

Astoria OR

The *American Empress*[1047] is the largest overnight riverboat west of the Mississippi River, the American Empress cruises the Columbia and Snake Rivers.

The *Queen of the West* is a cruise ship offering tour packages on the Columbia and Snake Rivers.

The *Rose* cruises up the Willamette River out of the Jon Storm Dock in Oregon City each weekend. She is a replica of a 19th century paddle-wheeler. The boat takes guests on a tour of the Willamette River and Willamette Falls from its port in Oregon City, just south of Portland, all year except December, when it is docked in Portland.

The Columbia River Maritime Museum has a model of the *Harvest Queen* sternwheeler.

Canemah OR

A monument commemorates the April 8, 1854, explosion at Canemah OR, of the *Gazelle*. In this boiler explosion disaster 24 person were killed.

Cascade Locks Marine Park OR

The *Columbia Gorge*[1048] is owned by American Waterways Inc. It operates in the Cascade Locks, on the Columbia River Oregon from May – October and at Portland OR from November – April.

The Friends of Cascade Locks Historical Museum photographs of paddle-wheelers, four models/replicas of the *Mary*, *Harvest Queen*, the *Tahoma* and the *Hassalo*; a small journal kept by a US Army Corps officer, and an oral history of the *Mary* written by a Mr Attwell.

Hood River OR

Hood River Co. Museum has the stern wheel of the *Henderson* on public display.

Newport OR

The *Willamette Queen*[1049] is a twin sternwheeler that sails along the Willamette River towards Independence or Keizer, depending on water levels.

Portland OR

The *Portland*[1050] is owned and operated by the Portland Maritime Museum. She is moored at the Willamette River in downtown Portland's Waterfront Park. They bill her as "the last operating sternwheel steam tug in the United States."

SASKATCHEWAN

Prince Albert SK

The Prince Albert City Museum holds the bell, and part of the flue of the *Marquis*.

Saskatoon SK

The *Prairie Lily*[1051] is a tour boat but is a propeller vessel with simulated wheels. The excursions explore the Meewasin Valley for an hour on the South Saskatchewan River.

The Western Development Museum[1052] has several artifacts in their collection (some on display). These include: a bronze deadlight recovered from the *Qu'Appelle*; the steam whistle from the *David N. Winton*; the ship's steering wheel from the *David N. Winton*; an anchor from the *Qu'Appelle*; an anchor recovered from the *City of Medicine Hat*; and a steering wheel from the *Alice Mattes*.

WASHINGTON STATE

Anacortes WA

The snag boat *W.T. Preston*[1053] is preserved and dry berthed at the Snag Boat Heritage Center. No admission is charged, and she is operated by the City of Anacortes. She is one of only two snag boats remaining in the contiguous United States. The *W.T. Preston* was placed on the National Register for Historic Places in 1979.

Seattle WA

The *Banjo* is a sternwheeler (houseboat?) berthed on Lake Union, Seattle WA USA that in 2021 functions as a bed-and-breakfast. It does not appear to have a website.

The *Christine W.*[1054] offers charter cruises on Lake Union and Lake Washington, out of Fisherman's Terminal, Seattle WA.

The *KevLin*[1055] is a dual sternwheel houseboat vessel built in 1989 and based on Lake Union (Seattle WA). In 2020 she is/was also a charter excursion vessel.

The Seattle Museum of History and Industry (MOHAI) has a model of the *Beaver* along with its ship's bell, nine wood fragments, two canes and three gavels made from the wood of the steamer. We also have at least two drawings of the *Beaver*. They also have a model of the sternwheeler, the *Puget Sound*. They have a ship's bell and a cane carved by a deckhand from the *Swinomish*, which was later called the *W.T. Preston*. One of the Russian guns from the *Politofsky* and her whistle (which was used to signal the opening of the Seattle Alaska-Yukon Exposition of 1909 and the Century 21 Exposition of 1962) is in the collection.

Tacoma WA

One of the guns from the *Politofsky* is in the collection of the Washington State Historical Museum in Tacoma WA.

YUKON

Dawson City Yukon

The *Klondike Spirit*[1056] She was owned by Klondike Spirit Tours Inc., Dawson City. She carries up to 50 passengers on board and can accommodate them all in the dining area. They offer cruises from mid-May until the beginning of September.

The *Keno*[1057] is a dry berthed National Historic Site located on Front Street in Dawson City, 541 kilometers north of Whitehorse on the Klondike Highway.

The *Mary F. Graff, Victorian, Tyrrell, Julia B., Seattle No. 3, Schwatka,* and *Lightning*—are all collapsed wooden vessel remains with boilers and hardware enduring along the Yukon River near Dawson. Soon nature will reclaim the site and their metal fittings will become archaeological assets.

Whitehorse Yukon

The *Klondike*[1058] is a dry berthed National Historic Site, managed by Parks Canada. The vessel has been meticulously restored and refurnished and is available for public viewing.

BIBLIOGRAPHY & SOURCES

Affleck, Edward L. A Century of Paddlewheelers in the Pacific Northwest, the Yukon and Alaska. Vancouver, BC: Alexander Nicolls Press, 2000.)

Athabasca Historical Society. Athabasca Landing: An Illustrated History. Athabasca Historical Society. Athabasca, AB, 1986.

Barris, Ted. Fire Canoe: Prairie Steamboat Days Revisited. Toronto, ON: Dundurn, (2015).

Bennett, Norman V. Pioneer Legacy: Chronicles of the Lower Skeena River. Terrace, BC: Dr. REM Lee Hospital Foundation, 1997.

Boudreau, Jack. Sternwheelers & Canyon Cats: Whitewater Freighting on the Upper Fraser. Madeira Park, BC: Caitlin Press, 2006.

Bush, Warren Oliver, and Jacques Marc. Historic Shipwrecks of the Southern Gulf Islands of British Columbia. Victoria, BC: Friesen Press, 2020.

Byrd, Robert. Lake Chelan in the 1890s: Steamboats, Prospectors & Sightseers. Wenatchee, WA: Byrd-Song Publishing, 1992 rev.

Cohen, Stan. Yukon River Steamboats: A pictorial history. Missoula, MT: Pictorial Histories Publishing Co., 1982.

College, JJ, and Ben Warlow. Ships of the Royal Navy: the complete record of all fighting ships of the Royal Navy from the 15th Century to the present. Philadelphia & Oxford: Casemate, 2010.

Delgado, James P. To California by Sea: A Maritime History of the California Gold Rush. Columbia, SC: University of South Carolina Press, 1990.

Delgado, James P. The Beaver: First Steamship on the West Coast. Victoria, BC: Horsdahl & Schubart, 1993.

Downs, Art. Paddlewheels on the Frontier, Volume One. Surrey, BC: Foremost Publishing Co. Ltd., 1967.

Downs, Art. *Paddlewheels on the Frontier Volume Two*. Surrey, BC: Foremost Publishing Co. Ltd., 1971.

Gibbs, Jim, and Joe Williamson. *Maritime Memories of Puget Sound in Photographs and Text*. Atglen, PA: Schiffler Publishing Co., 1987.

Gullick, Bill. *Steamboats on Northwest Rivers*. Caldwell, ID: Caxton Press, 2004.

Hacking, Norman. "Steamboating on the Fraser in the 'Sixties." *British Columbia Historical Quarterly*, Vol. X Jan 1946. Victoria, BC: British Columbia Historical Association, pages 1–42.

Hacking, Norman. "Steamboat Days on the Upper Columbia and Upper Kootenay." *British Columbia Historical Quarterly*, Vol. XVI Jan-Apr 1952, Victoria, BC: British Columbia Historical Association, pages 1–52.

Harrison, Rebecca. *Aboard the Portland: A History of the Northwest Steamers*. 2016.

Harvey, RG. *Carving the Western Path by River, Rail, and Road Through Central and Northern BC*. Surrey, BC: Heritage House Publishing Co. Ltd., 1999.

Hult, Ruby El. *Steamboats in the Timber*. Cladwell, ID: The Caxton Printers Ltd., 1953.

Kane, Adam L. *The Western River Steamboat*. College Station, TX: Texas A & M University Press. 2004.

Large, Dr. RG. *The Skeena: River of Destiny*. Surrey, BC: Heritage House, 1996.

Lingenfelter, Richard E. *Steamboats on the Colorado River*. Tucson, AZ: University of Arizona Press 1978.

List of Ships (Ships on Register in Canada and Fishing Vessels). Published annually up to 2003 by Transport Canada, Ottawa, ON.

Lytle, William M and Forrest R Holdcamper (revised and edited by C Bradford Mitchell with the assistance of Kenneth R Hall). *Merchant Vessels of the United States 1790–1868*. Staten Island, NY: The Steamship Historical Society of America Inc., 1975.

MacBride, William. (William MacBride Fonds), Yukon Archives.

MacMullen, Jerry. *Paddlewheel Days in California*. Stanford, CA: Stanford University Press, 1944.

McCarthy, Martha. *Economic History Theme Study Steamboats on the Rivers and Lakes of Manitoba 1859–96*. Winnipeg, MB: Historic Resources Branch (https://www.gov.mb.ca/chc/hrb/internal_reports/pdfs/Steamboats_Rivers_Lakes_Manitoba.pdf (website viewed 12/02/2021).

McFadden, Molly. "Steamboating on the Red." MHS *Transactions*, Series 3, 1950–51 season (http://www.mhs.mb.ca/docs/transactions/3/steamboating.shtml (website viewed 12/02/2021).

Mills, John M. *Canadian Coastal and Inland Steam Vessels 1809–1930*. Providence, RI: The Steamboat Historical Society of America Inc., 1979.

Mills, Randall V. *Sternwheelers Up Columbia: A Century of Steamboating in the Oregon Country*. Palo Alto, CA: Pacific Books, 1947.

Morrow, Trelle A. *Sternwheelers on the Upper Fraser*. Prince George, BC: College of New Caledonia Press, 2008.

Newell, Gordon, and Joe Williamson. *Pacific Steamboats*. New York: Bonanza Books, 1958.

Peel, Bruce. *Steamboats on The Saskatchewan*. Saskatoon, SK: The Western Producer, 1972.

Pollack, John, Edward L Affleck, and Wendy Boulianne (Eds). *Historic Shipwrecks of the West Kootenay District British Columbia*. Vancouver, BC: Underwater Archaeological Society of British Columbia, 2000.

Potter, Tracy. *Steamboats in Dakota Territory: Transforming the Northern Plains*. Charleston, SC: History Press, 2017.

Sheret, Robin E. *Smoke Ash and Steam: Steam Engines Used on the West Coast How They Worked*. Victoria, BC: Western Isles Cruise & Dive Co. Ltd., 1996.

Timmen, Fritz. *Blow For The Landing: A Hundred Years of Steam Navigation on the Waters of the West*. Caldwell, ID: The Caxton Printers Ltd., 1963.

Tolton, Gordon E. *Prairie Warships: River Navigation in the Northwest Rebellion.* Surrey, BC: Heritage House, 2007.

Turner, Robert D. *Sternwheelers and Steam Tugs: an illustrated history of the Canadian Pacific Railway's British Columbia Lake and River Service.* Victoria, BC: Sono Nis Press, 1984.

Turner, Robert D. *The Klondike Gold Rush Steamers: a History of Yukon River Steam Navigation.* Winlaw, BC: Sono Nis Press, 2015.

Merchant Vessels of the United States. (published annually by the United States Government)

Van Alfen, Pater G. "Sail and Steam: Great Salt Lake's Boats and Boatbuilders, 1847–1901." in *Utah Historical Quarterly,* Volume 63, No. 3, 1995 (Utah State Historical Society), pages 6–33, https://issuu.com/utah10/docs/uhq_volume63_1995_number3 (website viewed February 5, 2021).

Wright, EW (ed.). *Lewis and Dryden's Marine History of the Pacific Northwest.* Seattle, WA: Superior Publishing Co., 1967.

ACKNOWLEDGEMENTS

Thanks to the many persons who assisted me in my research and inquiries during the life of this project:

Without the forbearance, encouragement and support of my wife, Catherine MacFarlane, I could not have completed this project. For this I am incredibly grateful, because otherwise these projects would not have been possible.

My long-time nautical research colleague, Lynn Salmon, was vitally helpful with her reviews of my text and feedback from a reader perspective. Our professional association over the last thirty years has been useful beyond measure. Her review of my text made it more accurate and readable—I am forever indebted.

Another research associate, George Duddy, checked Canadian entries, found new vessels to add to the list, and provided encouragement at the times my energy lagged. His research on western Canada's freshwater fleet is breaking new ground with his discoveries. Our collaboration now extends over ten years.

Particularly helpful in my research was Murray Lundberg, a marine historian whose research specializes in vessels of Alaska and the Yukon and who interprets their histories. He generously shared research and checked my own for accuracy. It is a rare treat to collaborate with such a fine fellow—whom I hope to meet in person some day.

Many others contributed information and images:

Robert G Allan (Naval Architect, Robert Allan Ltd. [Vancouver BC])

Jodi Balon, (Sternwheeler Captain, Neo-Watin Marine Services Ltd., [Prince Albert SK])

Gina Bardi [Reference Librarian, San Francisco Maritime National Historical Park Research Center])

Daryl Betenia (Director, Collections, Glenbow Museum [Calgary AB])

Dick Blust, Jr. (Sweetwater County Historical Museum [Green River, WY])

Jennifer Bottomly-O'looney (Senior Curator, Montana Historical Society [Helena MT])

Ian Buxton, Visiting Professor in the School of Marine Science & Technology at Newcastle University UK Hannah Chipman (Sicamous Museum [Sicamous BC])

Brittany Churchwell (Friends of Cascade Locks Historical Museum [Cascade Locks, OR])

Chad Edwards (Collections Manager, Fort McMurray Heritage Society [Ft. McMurray AB])

Kristin Halunen (Director of Collections Resources / Registrar, MOHAI [Seattle WA])

Christopher James Cole (Marine Historian, Photographer [Sooke BC])

George Duddy (Marine Historian, Civil Engineer, and author [White Rock BC])

Mark Garner (Nautical Historian specializing in the Beaver [Toronto ON])

Gordon Goldsborough (Manitoba Historical Society [Winnipeg MB])

Steven Greif (Research Volunteer, Coos History Museum [Coos Bay OR])

Captain Steve Hawchuk (Sternwheel Master Mariner and historian [Winnipeg MB])

Lauren Hope (Programing and Visitor Services Supervisor [Regina SK])

Rick Howie (Biologist, Historian, Heritage Interpreter, Photographer [Kamloops BC])

Elizabeth Hunter (Museum & Heritage Manager, Quesnel & District Museum & Archives [Quesnel BC])

Julie Jackson (Collections Manager, Western Development Museum (Saskatoon SK)

Ken Johnson, (President of Hallmark Heritage Society, [Victoria BC])

Sharain Jones (Museum Director, Sam Waller Museum [The Pas MB])

Sue Kemmis (Curator, Boundary County Museum [Bonners Ferry])

Frank Korvemaker (Archivist / Construction Historian, Provincial Archives Saskatchewan)

Nathan Kramer (Marine Historian, Manitoba Historical Society [Winnipeg MB])

Angela J Linn (Senior Collections Manager, University of Alaska Museum of the North [Fairbanks AK])

Murray Lundberg (Marine Historian, Alaska & Yukon heritage interpreter [Whitehorse YT])

Adam Lyon (Library Associate, Museum of History, and Industry [Seattle WA])

Catherine MacFarlane (Educator, heritage interpreter, and social innovator [Qualicum Beach BC])

Duncan MacLeod (Curator, Vancouver Maritime Museum [Vancouver BC Canada])

Scott Marsden Curator, Prince of Wales Northern Heritage Centre [Yellowknife NT])

Tim McShane (Museum Assistant, Esplanade Museum [Medicine Hat AB])

Sean Pól MacÚisdin (Sternwheeler Researcher, [Esquimalt BC])

Duncan MacLeod (Curator, Vancouver Maritime Museum [Vancouver BC])

Sean Mathan Mor (Nautical History Researcher)

Jeffrey Olafson (Assistant Archivist, Maritime Museum of British Columbia [Victoria BC])

Dennis Oomen (Manager/Curator Penticton Museum [Penticton BC])

Nicholas Piontek (Archivist, Center for Sacramento History [Sacramento CA])

Tom Pope (Proprietor of Mulberry Books [Parksville and Qualicum Beach BC])

Jim Proehl (Museum Volunteer, Bandon Historical Society Museum [Bandon, OR])

Judy Robertson (Writer, film maker, cultural affairs specialist [Vancouver BC])

Bruce Rohn (Author, Arrow Lakes Historical Society)

Jack Russell (Sternwheeler owner, master and builder, and marine historian [Seattle WA])

Lynn Salmon (Marine Historian, best selling marine author, writer, researcher [Courtenay BC])

Paige Sanders (Newport Belle Riverboat [Newport OR])

Roland Sawatsky (Curator of History, Manitoba Museum [Winnipeg MB])

Elizabeth Scarlett (Volunteer Archivist, Kootenay Lake Archives [Kaslo BC])

Jackie Schmidt (President, Heritage Regina [Regina SK])

Erin Sekulich (Provincial Archives of Alberta [Edmonton AB])

Christopher Smith (Registrar, Center for Sacramento History [Sacramento CA])

Megan Squires (Planner, Planning Department [District of Saanich BC])

Zoe Ann Stoltz (Reference Historian, Montana Historical Society Research Center [Helena MT])

Judy Thompson (Librarian, Maritime Museum of British Columbia [Victoria BC])

Brittany Vis (Director, Maritime Museum of British Columbia [Victoria BC])

Jan Westendorp (Kato Design & Photo [Burnaby BC])

Alyssa Wowchuk (Brandon General Museum & Archives [Brandon MB])

THE AUTHOR

JOHN MACFARLANE is a fifth generation Vancouver Islander whose family came there from California in 1859 for the Fraser River Goldrush. He has worked to protect and interpret Canada's natural and historical heritage since 1969 when he joined the Canadian National Parks Service. He has been the Curator Emeritus of the Maritime Museum of British Columbia in Victoria BC for more than 30 years. The author of 14 books, he was the co-recipient of the prestigious 2020 John Lyman Book Prize of the North American Society of Oceanic History for his best-selling book 'Around the World in a Dugout Canoe'. He is a Fellow of the Royal Geographical Society (London) and a recipient of the Sovereign's Medal for Volunteers. He lives on the central east coast of Vancouver Island. His almost full-time avocation is The Nauticapedia, an online nautical history resource, which is accessed on the internet more than 4 million times yearly.

THE NAUTICAPEDIA

THE NAUTICAPEDIA project was established in 1973, originally to record data about British Columbia vessels. It maintains a website containing two big databases that can be searched by anyone and accessed at **www.nauticapedia.ca**. One database contains biographies of over 59,000 individuals, companies and organizations that relate in some way to nautical history. The second database contains the detailed histories of more than 71,000 vessels, mainly from western North America, but also including Canadian naval vessels and vessels with strong links to the Arctic.

Detailed information on all the vessels mentioned in this book can be accessed through the searchable databases. Readers with more information to add to these histories can reach the author through the web page.

ENDNOTES

1. Roster of Yukon / Alaska Sternwheelers (explorenorth.com) (website viewed 03/04/2021)
2. McMullin, Jerry (1944) Paddlewheel Days In California. Stanford: Stanford University Press
3. Newell, Gordon (1966)
4. McMullin, Jerry (1944) Paddlewheel Days In California. Stanford: Stanford University Press
5. Ibid.
6. Ibid
7. Affleck, Edward L (2000)
8. Newell, Gordon (1966) page 4
9. The San Francisco Examiner (San Francisco CA) Monday, August 25, 1919, page 21
10. Hacking, Norman R. Steamboating on the Fraser in the Sixties (in British Columbia Historical Quarterly Vol. X No.1 January 1946)
11. https://arctos.database.museum/guid/UAM:EH:0656–0001 (website viewed 28/03/2021)
12. McMullin, Jerry (1944) Paddlewheel Days In California. Stanford: Stanford University Press
13. Nathan Kramer (Email to Nauticapedia 03/12/2020)
14. Affleck, Edward L (2000)
15. Ibid.
16. https://en.wikipedia.org/wiki/List_of_steamboats_on_the_Columbia_River (website viewed 21/022021)
17. McMullin, Jerry (1944) Paddlewheel Days In California. Stanford: Stanford University Press
18. Kootenai Herald 24/10/1891; Kootenai Herald 14/11/1891; Kootenai Herald 26/02/1892; Kootenai Herald 18/03/1892
19. The Evening Mail (Stockton CA) Wednesday May 25, 1904, page 5
20. https://en.wikipedia.org/wiki/List_of_steamboats_on_the_Columbia_River (website viewed 21/022021)
21. McMullin, Jerry (1944) Paddlewheel Days In California. Stanford: Stanford University Press
22. Ibid.
23. http://www.snugharbor.net/images2010/Steamboat_Slough-Sacramento_shipwrecks.pdf (website viewed 08/02/2021) Land Location & Boundary Section, California State Lands Commission (1988) A Map and Record Investigation of Historical Sites and Shipwrecks Along the Sacramento River Between Sacramento City and Sherman Island
24. Daily Alta California Vol. 23, No 7692, April 14, 1871
25. McMullin, Jerry (1944) Paddlewheel Days In California. Stanford: Stanford University Press
26. http://www.snugharbor.net/images2010/Steamboat_Slough-Sacramento_shipwrecks.pdf (website viewed 08/02/2021) Land Location & Boundary Section, California State Lands Commission (1988) A Map and Record Investigation of Historical Sites and Shipwrecks Along the Sacramento River Between Sacramento City and Sherman Island
27. https://en.wikipedia.org/wiki/List_of_steamboats_on_the_Columbia_River (website viewed 21/022021)
28. McMullin, Jerry (1944) Paddlewheel Days In California. Stanford: Stanford University Press
29. Ibid.
30. Ibid
31. https://www.americancruiselines.com/usa-riverboat-cruise-ships/authentic-paddlewheelers-cruise-ships/american-pride (website viewed 02/04/2021)

32. https://en.wikipedia.org/wiki/List_of_steamboats_on_the_Columbia_River (website viewed 21/02/2021)
33. McMullin, Jerry (1944) Paddlewheel Days In California. Stanford: Stanford University Press
34. Newell, Gordon (1966) page 4
35. Affleck, Edward L (2000)
36. Ibid.
37. Ibid.
38. Ibid.
39. The Klamath News (Klamath Falls OR) Wednesday, June 29, 1932, page 4
40. https://en.wikipedia.org/wiki/List_of_steamboats_on_the_Columbia_River (website viewed 21/022021)
41. Nathan Kramer http://www.mhs.mb.ca/docs/steamboats/antelope.shtml
42. Daily Alta California Vol. 23, No 7692, April 14, 1871
43. McMullin, Jerry (1944) Paddlewheel Days In California. Stanford: Stanford University Press
44. http://www.snugharbor.net/images2010/Steamboat_Slough-Sacramento_shipwrecks.pdf (website viewed 08/02/2021) Land Location & Boundary Section, California State Lands Commission (1988) A Map and Record Investigation of Historical Sites and Shipwrecks Along the Sacramento River Between Sacramento City and Sherman Island
45. Log Chips: John Lyman (1949)
46. McMullin, Jerry (1944) Paddlewheel Days In California. Stanford: Stanford University Press
47. Newell, G. (1966)
48. Affleck, Edward L (2000)
49. Ibid.
50. Sessional Papers (Vol. 14) (3rd Session of the 11th Parliament of the Dominion of Canada (1911)
51. Newell, G. (1966)
52. https://lakearrowheadqueen.com/
53. Affleck, Edward L (2000)
54. https://en.wikipedia.org/wiki/List_of_steamboats_on_the_Columbia_River (website viewed 21/022021)
55. Affleck, Edward L (2000)
56. Ibid.
57. McMullin, Jerry (1944) Paddlewheel Days In California. Stanford: Stanford University Press
58. Roster of Yukon / Alaska Sternwheelers (explorenorth.com) (website viewed 03/04/2021)
59. Ibid.
60. https://en.wikipedia.org/wiki/List_of_steamboats_on_the_Yukon_River (website viewed 12/02/2021)
61. Affleck, Edward L (2000)
62. https://en.wikipedia.org/wiki/List_of_steamboats_on_the_Columbia_River (website viewed 21/022021)
63. https://www.bahiahotel.com/bahia-belle (website viewed 24/01/2021)
64. Affleck, Edward L (2000)
65. https:// www.airbnb.ie/rooms/35062238?source_impression_id=p3_1611524152_6u2FozVnJkd4cHfp&guests=1&adults=1 (website viewed 24/01/2021)
66. Daily Alta California Vol. 23, No 7692, April 14, 1871
67. McMullin, Jerry (1944) Paddlewheel Days In California. Stanford: Stanford University Press
68. Affleck, Edward L (2000)
69. Roster of Yukon / Alaska Sternwheelers (explorenorth.com) (website viewed 03/04/2021)
70. McMullin, Jerry (1944) Paddlewheel Days In California. Stanford: Stanford University Press
71. Affleck, Edward L (2000)
72. Ibid.
73. Ibid.
74. http://www.twrps.com/history/the-steamer-beaver-2/ (website viewed 21/02/2021)
75. Affleck, Edward L (2000)

76. McMullin, Jerry (1944) Paddlewheel Days In California. Stanford: Stanford University Press
77. Land Location & Boundary Section, California State Lands Commission (1988)
78. McMullin, Jerry (1944) Paddlewheel Days In California. Stanford: Stanford University Press
79. Ibid.
80. https://www.nps.gov/parkhistory/online_books/noca/hbd/chap7.htm (website viewed 12/02/2021)
81. Harrison, Rebecca (2016) Aboard the Portland: A History of the Northwest Steamers.
82. Affleck, Edward L (2000)
83. McMullin, Jerry (1944) Paddlewheel Days In California. Stanford: Stanford University Press
84. Land Location & Boundary Section, California State Lands Commission (1988)
85. Affleck, Edward L (2000)
86. https://steamboats.com/museum/davet-photosnorthwest.html (webpage viewed 14/03/2021)
87. Wright, E.W. (ed.) (1967) Lewis & Dryden's Marine History of the Pacific Northwest
88. Affleck, Edward L (2000)
89. List of Shipping Casualties Resulting in Total Loss in British Columbia and Coastal Waters Since 1897 (undated manuscript document)
90. Statesman Journal (Salem OR) Tuesday November 13, 1888, page 3
91. Affleck, Edward L (2000)
92. https://en.wikipedia.org/wiki/Steamboats_on_Lake_Coeur_d%27Alene (website viewed 13/02/2021)
93. The Dalles Daily Chronicle (The Dalles OR) Friday December 16, 1892, page 1
94. Affleck, Edward L (2000)
95. Ibid.
96. Nathan Kramer in http://www.mhs.mb.ca/docs/steamboats/bonnitoba.shtml (website viewed 18/05/2020)
97. McMullin, Jerry (1944) Paddlewheel Days In California. Stanford: Stanford University Press
98. The Spokesman-Review (Spokane WA) Friday November 24, 1933, page 12
99. Affleck, Edward L (2000)
100. McMullin, Jerry (1944) Paddlewheel Days In California. Stanford: Stanford University Press
101. Ibid.
102. Ibid.
103. Ibid.
104. Affleck, Edward L (2000)
105. McMullin, Jerry (1944) Paddlewheel Days In California. Stanford: Stanford University Press
106. Ibid.
107. Newell, Gordon (1966) page 140
108. Affleck, Edward L (2000)
109. McMullin, Jerry (1944) Paddlewheel Days In California. Stanford: Stanford University Press
110. https://en.wikipedia.org/wiki/SS_California_%281848%29 (website viewed 02/04/2021)
111. Roster of Yukon / Alaska Sternwheelers (explorenorth.com) (website viewed 03/04/2021)
112. Affleck, Edward L (2000)
113. McMullin, Jerry (1944) Paddlewheel Days In California. Stanford: Stanford University Press
114. https://www.foundsf.org/index.php?title=Steamboat_Point,_1851–1864 (website viewed 08/02/2021)
115. Land Location & Boundary Section, California State Lands Commission (1988)
116. Affleck, Edward L (2000)
117. http://thewandererschuckandkate.blogspot.com/2012/10/the-ship-of-desert.html (website viewed 22/02/2021)
118. McMullin, Jerry (1944) Paddlewheel Days In California. Stanford: Stanford University Press
119. Daily Alta California Vol. 23, No 7692, April 14, 1871

120 McMullin, Jerry (1944) Paddlewheel Days In California. Stanford: Stanford University Press

121 Ibid.

122 Land Location & Boundary Section, California State Lands Commission (1988)

123 Ibid.

124 McMullin, Jerry (1944) Paddlewheel Days In California. Stanford: Stanford University Press

125 Newell, Gordon (1966)

126 Ibid.

127 McMullin, Jerry (1944) Paddlewheel Days In California. Stanford: Stanford University Press

128 Wright, E.W. (ed.) (1967) Lewis & Dryden's Marine History of the Pacific Northwest

129 Affleck, Edward L (2000)

130 Ibid.

131 Ibid.

132 Newell, Gordon & Joe Williamson (1957) Pacific Tugboats Bonanza Books: New York NY

133 Affleck, Edward L (2000)

134 Ibid.

135 Ibid.

136 Ibid.

137 McMullin, Jerry (1944) Paddlewheel Days In California. Stanford: Stanford University Press

138 Ibid.

139 Hacking, Norman R. Steamboating on the Fraser in the Sixties (in British Columbia Historical Quarterly Vol. X No.1 January 1946)

140 Affleck, Edward L (2000)

141 Ibid.

142 Ibid.

143 Ibid.

144 Ibid.

145 Newell, Gordon (1966)

146 Affleck, Edward L (2000)

147 McMullin, Jerry (1944) Paddlewheel Days In California. Stanford: Stanford University Press

148 Affleck, Edward L (2000)

149 Manitoba Archives Winnipeg MB Cheyenne March 1988

150 Nathan Kramer https://www.gov.mb.ca/chc/archives/hbca/ships_histories/pdf/cheyenne.pdf

151 Daily Alta California Vol. 23, No 7692, April 14, 1871

152 McMullin, Jerry (1944) Paddlewheel Days In California. Stanford: Stanford University Press

153 Land Location & Boundary Section, California State Lands Commission (1988)

154 Affleck, Edward L (2000)

155 McMullin, Jerry (1944) Paddlewheel Days In California. Stanford: Stanford University Press

156 http://www.sternwheelercharters.com/ (website viewed 08/02/2021)

157 Daily Alta California Vol. 23, No 7692, April 14, 1871

158 https://www.foundsf.org/index.php?title=Steamboat_Point,_1851–1864 (website viewed 08/02/20121)

159 Land Location & Boundary Section, California State Lands Commission (1988)

160 Affleck, Edward L (2000)

161 Newell, G. (1966)

162 Roster of Yukon / Alaska Sternwheelers (explorenorth.com) (website viewed 03/04/2021)

163 Van Alfen, Pater G. Sail and Steam: Great Salt Lake's Boats and Boatbuilders, 1847–1901 in Utah Historical Quarterly, Volume 63, No. 3, 1995 (Utah State Historical Society) Pages 6–33 (website viewed February 5, 2021, https://issuu.com/utah10/docs/uhq_volume63_1995_number3)

164 The Recorder (San Francisco CA) Friday April 1, 1904, page 1

165 McMullin, Jerry (1944) Paddlewheel Days In California. Stanford: Stanford University Press

166 Affleck, Edward L (2000)

167 Byrd, Robert (1992 rev.) Lake Chelan in the 1890s: Steamboats, Prospectors & Sightseers.Wenatchee WA: Byrd-Song Publishing

168 Affleck, Edward L (2000)

169 Ibid.

170 Ibid.

171 https://en.wikipedia.org/wiki/List_of_steamboats_on_the_Columbia_River (website viewed 21/022021)

172 Affleck, Edward L (2000)

173 Roster of Yukon / Alaska Sternwheelers (explorenorth.com) (website viewed 03/04/2021)

174 Affleck, Edward L (2000)

175 Ibid.

176 McMullin, Jerry (1944) Paddlewheel Days In California. Stanford: Stanford University Press

177 Ibid.

178 Affleck, Edward L (2000)

179 McMullin, Jerry (1944) Paddlewheel Days In California. Stanford: Stanford University Press

180 The San Francisco Call (San Francisco CA) Thursday December 5, 1901, page 3

181 McMullin, Jerry (1944) Paddlewheel Days In California. Stanford: Stanford University Press

182 Affleck, Edward L (2000)

183 Roster of Yukon / Alaska Sternwheelers (explorenorth.com) (website viewed 03/04/2021)

184 The Daily Astorian (Astoria OR) Wednesday March 2, 1881, page 3

185 Affleck, Edward L (2000)

186 Ibid.

187 https://cgmix.uscg.mil/psix/psixSearch.aspx (website viewed 10/05/2021)

188 https://en.wikipedia.org/wiki/List_of_steamboats_on_the_Columbia_River (website viewed 21/022021)

189 McMullin, Jerry (1944) Paddlewheel Days In California. Stanford: Stanford University Press

190 Affleck, Edward L (2000)

191 Lytle, William M and Forrest R Holdcamper (revised and edited by C Bradford Mitchell with the assistance of Kenneth R Hall) (1975) Merchant Vessels of the United States 1790–1868. Staten Island NY: The Steamship Historical Society of America Inc.

192 Newell, Gordon (1966) page 4

193 McMullin, Jerry (1944) Paddlewheel Days In California. Stanford: Stanford University Press

194 Ibid.

195 https://en.wikipedia.org/wiki/Steamboats_on_Lake_Coeur_d%27Alene (website viewed 13/02/2021)

196 Affleck, Edward L (2000)

197 Roster of Yukon / Alaska Sternwheelers (explorenorth.com) (website viewed 03/04/2021)

198 Harrison, Rebecca (2016) Aboard the Portland: A History of the Northwest Steamers.

199 McMullin, Jerry (1944) Paddlewheel Days In California. Stanford: Stanford University Press

200 Ibid.

201 Wright, E.W. (ed.) (1967) Lewis & Dryden's Marine History of the Pacific Northwest

202 Affleck, Edward L (2000)

203 https://intelligence.marinelink.com/vessels/vessel/columbia-gorge-312722 (website viewed 27/03/2021)

204 https://portofcascadelocks.org/sternwheeler-columbia-gorge/ (website viewed 15/02/2021)

205 Affleck, Edward L (2000)

206 Land Location & Boundary Section, California State Lands Commission (1988)

207 Lytle, William M and Forrest R Holdcamper

208 Land Location & Boundary Section, California State Lands Commission (1988)

209 Lytle, William M and Forrest R Holdcamper

210 Affleck, Edward L (2000)
211 McMullin, Jerry (1944) Paddlewheel Days In California. Stanford: Stanford University Press
212 Land Location & Boundary Section, California State Lands Commission (1988)
213 Lytle, William M and Forrest R Holdcamper
214 Daily Alta California Vol. 23, No 7692, April 14, 1871
215 McMullin, Jerry (1944) Paddlewheel Days In California. Stanford: Stanford University Press
216 Roster of Yukon / Alaska Sternwheelers (explorenorth.com) (website viewed 03/04/2021)
217 https://www.pdavis.nl/ShowShip.php?id=1277 (website viewed)
218 Daily Alta California Vol. 23, No 7692, April 14, 1871
219 McMullin, Jerry (1944) Paddlewheel Days In California. Stanford: Stanford University Press
220 Affleck, Edward L (2000)
221 https://en.wikipedia.org/wiki/Steamboats_on_Lake_Coeur_d%27Alene (website viewed 13/02/2021)
222 Affleck, Edward L (2000)
223 Ibid.
224 Roster of Yukon / Alaska Sternwheelers (explorenorth.com) (website viewed 03/04/2021)
225 McMullin, Jerry (1944) Paddlewheel Days In California. Stanford: Stanford University Press
226 Affleck, Edward L (2000)
227 McMullin, Jerry (1944) Paddlewheel Days In California. Stanford: Stanford University Press
228 Land Location & Boundary Section, California State Lands Commission (1988)
229 Affleck, Edward L (2000)
230 Ibid.
231 Kramer, Nathan at http://www.mhs.mb.ca/docs/steamboats/index.shtml (website viewed 05/02/2021)
232 Ibid.
233 Affleck, Edward L (2000)
234 San Francisco Call (San Francisco CA) Wednesday October 29, 1902, page 8
235 Los Angeles Times (Los Angeles CA) Monday April 15, 1901, page 3
236 Affleck, Edward L (2000)
237 McMullin, Jerry (1944) Paddlewheel Days In California. Stanford: Stanford University Press
238 The Evening Mail (Stockton CA) Tuesday August 27, 1901, page 2
239 McMullin, Jerry (1944) Paddlewheel Days In California. Stanford: Stanford University Press
240 Ibid.
241 Affleck, Edward L (2000)
242 Daily Alta California Vol. 23, No 7692, April 14, 1871
243 Lytle, William M and Forrest R Holdcamper
244 McMullin, Jerry (1944) Paddlewheel Days In California. Stanford: Stanford University Press
245 Land Location & Boundary Section, California State Lands Commission (1988)
246 https://steamboats.com/museum/deltaqueentimeline.html (website viewed 07/03/2021)
247 McMullin, Jerry (1944) Paddlewheel Days In California. Stanford: Stanford University Press
248 Land Location & Boundary Section, California State Lands Commission (1988)
249 https://www.lakemeadcruises.com/ (website viewed 25/01/2021)
250 Affleck, Edward L (2000)
251 Ibid.
252 Lytle, William M and Forrest R Holdcamper
253 Hunt, William R. North of 53 Degrees page 146
254 Roster of Yukon / Alaska Sternwheelers (explorenorth.com) (website viewed 03/04/2021)

255 https://en.wikipedia.org/wiki/Discovery_I (website viewed 23/03/2021)

256 https://en.wikipedia.org/wiki/Discovery_II (website viewed 23/03/2021)

257 https://en.wikipedia.org/wiki/Discovery_III (website viewed 23/03/2021)

258 https://www.zephyrcove.com/cruises/our-fleet/ (website viewed 19/03/2021)

259 https://www.golakehavasu.com/dixie_belle_rides_again (website viewed 19/03/2021)

260 Affleck, Edward L (2000)

261 McMullin, Jerry (1944) Paddlewheel Days In California. Stanford: Stanford University Press

262 Newell, Gordon (1966) page 190

263 McMullin, Jerry (1944) Paddlewheel Days In California. Stanford: Stanford University Press

264 Affleck, Edward L (2000)

265 Freeman, Lewis R. Down the Columbia (1921 reprinted 2001)

266 McMullin, Jerry (1944) Paddlewheel Days In California. Stanford: Stanford University Press

267 Land Location & Boundary Section, California State Lands Commission (1988)

268 Daily Alta California Vol. 23, No 7692, April 14, 1871

269 McMullin, Jerry (1944) Paddlewheel Days In California. Stanford: Stanford University Press

270 https://arctos.database.museum/guid/UAM:EH:0657-0001 (website viewed 28/03/2021)

271 Newell, Gordon (1966) page 4

272 The Evening Mail (Stockton CA) Tuesday July 9, 1901, page 5

273 Harrison, Rebecca (2016) Aboard the Portland: A History of the Northwest Steamers.

274 Morning Oregonian (Portland OR) Friday March 07, 1890, page 8

275 Affleck, Edward L (2000)

276 https://en.wikipedia.org/wiki/List_of_steamboats_on_the_Columbia_River (website viewed 14/03/2021)

277 Harrison, Rebecca (2016) Aboard the Portland: A History of the Northwest Steamers.

278 McMullin, Jerry (1944) Paddlewheel Days In California. Stanford: Stanford University Press

279 Affleck, Edward L (2000)

280 https://en.wikipedia.org/wiki/Triumph_(sternwheeler) (website viewed 23/01/2021)

281 FAQ - The Edmonton Riverboat (website viewed 04/03/2021)

282 https://edmontonjournal.com/news/local-news/may-4-1995-edmonton-queen-finally-launched (website viewed 16/02/2021)

283 McMullin, Jerry (1944) Paddlewheel Days In California. Stanford: Stanford University Press

284 Ibid.

285 Land Location & Boundary Section, California State Lands Commission (1988)

286 Affleck, Edward L (2000)

287 McMullin, Jerry (1944) Paddlewheel Days In California. Stanford: Stanford University Press

288 Affleck, Edward L (2000)

289 Ibid.

290 A Ibid.ffleck, Edward L (2000)

291 https://en.wikipedia.org/wiki/List_of_steamboats_on_the_Columbia_River (website viewed 14/03/2021)

292 Hacking, Norman, and W. Kaye Lamb (1974) The Princess Story: A Century and a Half of West Coast Shipping Page 90

293 http://www.riverboatdaves.com/riverboats/e.html (website viewed 08/02/2021)

294 Affleck, Edward L (2000)

295 https://en.wikipedia.org/wiki/Steamboats_on_Lake_Coeur_d%27Alene (website viewed 13/02/2021)

296 McMullin, Jerry (1944) Paddlewheel Days In California. Stanford: Stanford University Press

297 Ibid.
298 Ibid.
299 Ibid.
300 The Seattle Post-Intelligencer (Seattle WA) Tuesday December 12, 1893, page 8
301 https://www.wikiwand.com/en/Elwood_(sternwheeler) (website viewed 14/03/2021)
302 Roster of Yukon / Alaska Sternwheelers (explorenorth.com) (website viewed 03/04/2021)
303 Affleck, Edward L (2000)
304 McMullin, Jerry (1944) Paddlewheel Days In California. Stanford: Stanford University Press
305 Roster of Yukon / Alaska Sternwheelers (explorenorth.com) (website viewed 03/04/2021)
306 Affleck, Edward L (2000)
307 McMullin, Jerry (1944) Paddlewheel Days In California. Stanford: Stanford University Press
308 Daily Alta California Vol. 23, No 7692, April 14, 1871
309 McMullin, Jerry (1944) Paddlewheel Days In California. Stanford: Stanford University Press
310 https://i5bridgecam.wordpress.com/sternwheelers/ (website viewed 15/02/2021)
311 Affleck, Edward L (2000)
312 Ibid.
313 HBC Archives Winnipeg MB Enterprise February 1988
314 Victoria Colonist (Victoria BC) May 2, 1884
315 https://www.gov.mb.ca/chc/archives/hbca/ships_histories/pdf/enterprise.pdf (website viewed 21/03/2021)
316 McMullin, Jerry (1944) Paddlewheel Days In California. Stanford: Stanford University Press
317 Lytle, William M and Forrest R Holdcamper
318 Affleck, Edward L (2000)
319 McMullin, Jerry (1944) Paddlewheel Days In California. Stanford: Stanford University Press
320 Ibid.
321 Lytle, William M and Forrest R Holdcamper
322 Affleck, Edward L (2000)
323 Ibid.
324 Roster of Yukon / Alaska Sternwheelers (explorenorth.com) (website viewed 03/04/2021)
325 Land Location & Boundary Section, California State Lands Commission (1988)
326 Roster of Yukon / Alaska Sternwheelers (explorenorth.com) (website viewed 03/04/2021)
327 Grand Forks Herald (Grand Forks ND) Monday, March 14, 1910, page 1
328 McMullin, Jerry (1944) Paddlewheel Days In California. Stanford: Stanford University Press
329 Ibid.
330 Affleck, Edward L (2000)
331 Lytle, William M and Forrest R Holdcamper
332 McMullin, Jerry (1944) Paddlewheel Days In California. Stanford: Stanford University Press
333 The San Francisco Call (San Francisco CA) Tuesday November 26, 1907, page 11
334 Bismarck Tribune (Bismarck ND) Thursday, October 31, 1907, page 2
335 https://www.nwnewsnetwork.org/post/history-teacher-obsession-sunken-ship-and-crew-searching-its-wreck (website viewed)
336 McMullin, Jerry (1944) Paddlewheel Days In California. Stanford: Stanford University Press
337 Affleck, Edward L (2000)
338 McMullin, Jerry (1944) Paddlewheel Days In California. Stanford: Stanford University Press
339 Land Location & Boundary Section, California State Lands Commission (1988)
340 McMullin, Jerry (1944) Paddlewheel Days In California. Stanford: Stanford University Press
341 Affleck, Edward L (2000)

342 Ibid.

343 https://en.wikipedia.org/wiki/Steamboats_on_Lake_Coeur_d%27Alene (website viewed 13/02/2021)

344 Victoria Daily Colonist (Victoria BC) Saturday May 25, 1912, page 15

345 McMullin, Jerry (1944) Paddlewheel Days In California. Stanford: Stanford University Press

346 Ibid.

347 Land Location & Boundary Section, California State Lands Commission (1988)

348 Los Angeles Times (Los Angeles CA) Sunday April 15, 1928, page 15

349 Affleck, Edward L (2000)

350 Ibid.

351 Ibid.

352 Roster of Yukon / Alaska Sternwheelers (explorenorth.com) (website viewed 03/04/2021)

353 Wright, E.W. (ed.) (1967)

354 Hacking, Norman R. Steamboating on the Fraser in the Sixties (in British Columbia Historical Quarterly Vol. X No.1 January 1946)

355 San Francisco Examiner (San Francisco CA) Monday, August 19, 1907, page 4

356 McMullin, Jerry (1944) Paddlewheel Days In California. Stanford: Stanford University Press

357 San Francisco Examiner (San Francisco CA) Thursday October 17, 1955, page 32

358 McMullin, Jerry (1944) Paddlewheel Days In California. Stanford: Stanford University Press

359 Affleck, Edward L (2000)

360 McMullin, Jerry (1944) Paddlewheel Days In California. Stanford: Stanford University Press

361 Ibid.

362 Nathan Kramer http://www.mhs.mb.ca/docs/steamboats/international.shtml (website viewed 07/03/2021)

363 Lytle, William M and Forrest R Holdcamper

364 Affleck, Edward L (2000)

365 Roster of Yukon / Alaska Sternwheelers (explorenorth.com) (website viewed 03/04/2021)

366 McMullin, Jerry (1944) Paddlewheel Days In California. Stanford: Stanford University Press

367 Mills, R.V. (1947)

368 McMullin, Jerry (1944) Paddlewheel Days In California. Stanford: Stanford University Press

369 Ibid.

370 Ibid.

371 Affleck, Edward L (2000)

372 https://thereaderwiki.com/en/Wallamet_(sidewheeler_1853) (website viewed 19/02/2021);

373 Ibid.

374 Daily Alta California Vol. 23, No 7692, April 14, 1871

375 McMullin, Jerry (1944) Paddlewheel Days In California. Stanford: Stanford University Press

376 LAC RG 12, A1A, Vol 414 Shipping Registers Victoria BC; http://heritage.canadiana.ca/view/oocihm.lac_reel_c3185/171?r=0&s=5

377 McMullin, Jerry (1944) Paddlewheel Days In California. Stanford: Stanford University Press

378 Land Location & Boundary Section, California State Lands Commission (1988)

379 https://www.steamboats.org/traveller/sacramento-river.html (website viewed 08/02/2021)

380 McMullin, Jerry (1944) Paddlewheel Days In California. Stanford: Stanford University Press

381 Harrison, Rebecca (2016) Aboard the Portland: A History of the Northwest Steamers.

382 https://en.wikipedia.org/wiki/Steamboats_on_Lake_Coeur_d%27Alene (website viewed 13/02/2021)

383 Affleck, Edward L (2000)

384 Ibid.

385 Newell, Gordon (1966)

386 Affleck, Edward L (2000)

387 Los Angeles Times (Los Angeles CA) Tuesday April 8, 1902, page 3

388 https://www.nps.gov/parkhistory/online_books/noca/hbd/chap7.htm (website viewed 12/02/2021)

389 The San Francisco Examiner (San Francisco CA) Friday February 12, 1915, page 19

390 McMullin, Jerry (1944)

391 Affleck, Edward L (2000)

392 https://en.wikipedia.org/wiki/USCS_Active (website viewed 26/01/2021)

393 Wright, E.W. (ed.) (1967) Lewis & Dryden's Marine History of the Pacific Northwest

394 Roster of Yukon / Alaska Sternwheelers (explorenorth.com) (website viewed 03/04/2021)

395 The Vancouver Daily World (Vancouver BC) June 20, 1902

396 Roster of Yukon / Alaska Sternwheelers (explorenorth.com) (website viewed 03/04/2021)

397 Daily Alta California Vol. 23, No 7692, April 14, 1871

398 McMullin, Jerry (1944) Paddlewheel Days In California. Stanford: Stanford University Press

399 Ibid.

400 Land Location & Boundary Section, California State Lands Commission (1988)

401 Affleck, Edward L (2000)

402 McMullin, Jerry (1944) Paddlewheel Days In California. Stanford: Stanford University Press

403 Land Location & Boundary Section, California State Lands Commission (1988)

404 HBC Archives Winnipeg MB Grahame 1 March 1988

405 Affleck, Edward L (2000)

406 Roster of Yukon / Alaska Sternwheelers (explorenorth.com) (website viewed 03/04/2021)

407 https://www.gazettes.com/sports/on_the_water/on-the-water-next-chapter-for-grand-romance/article_d8e0e0a8–c4c0–11ea-8980–cfc273713e9e.html (website viewed 14/03/2021)

408 Affleck, Edward L (2000)

409 Ibid.

410 Affleck, Edward L (2000)

411 McMullin, Jerry (1944) Paddlewheel Days In California. Stanford: Stanford University Press

412 Affleck, Edward L (2000)

413 Roster of Yukon / Alaska Sternwheelers (explorenorth.com) (website viewed 03/04/2021)

414 Affleck, Edward L (2000)

415 Ibid.

416 Roster of Yukon / Alaska Sternwheelers (explorenorth.com) (website viewed 03/04/2021)

417 McMullin, Jerry (1944) Paddlewheel Days In California. Stanford: Stanford University Press

418 Affleck, Edward L (2000)

419 McMullin, Jerry (1944) Paddlewheel Days In California. Stanford: Stanford University Press

420 Ibid.

421 Ibid.

422 http://www.mhs.mb.ca/docs/transactions/3/steamboating.shtml (website viewed 12/02/2021)

423 McMullin, Jerry (1944) Paddlewheel Days In California. Stanford: Stanford University Press

424 https://en.wikipedia.org/wiki/Steamboats_on_Lake_Coeur_d%27Alene (website viewed 13/02/2021)

425 https://en.wikipedia.org/wiki/List_of_steamboats_on_the_Columbia_River (website viewed 21/022021)

426 Affleck, Edward L (2000)

427 Ibid.

428 Ibid.

429 Ibid.

430 McMullin, Jerry (1944) Paddlewheel Days In California. Stanford: Stanford University Press

431 Roster of Yukon / Alaska Sternwheelers (explorenorth.com) (website viewed 03/04/2021)
432 The San Francisco Examiner (San Francisco CA) Saturday May 24, 1924, page 17
433 Ships of the Royal Navy (2010) page180
434 http://cprr.org/Museum/Southern_Pacific_Bulletin/From_Trail_to_Rail_15.html (website viewed 20/02/2021)
435 Affleck, Edward L (2000)
436 Daily Alta California Vol. 23, No 7692, April 14, 1871
437 Land Location & Boundary Section, California State Lands Commission (1988)
438 Hacking, Norman R. Steamboating on the Fraser in the Sixties (in British Columbia Historical Quarterly Vol. X No.1 January 1946)
439 Affleck, Edward L (2000)
440 Newell, G. (1966); Newell, Gordon & Joe Williamson (1957)
441 McMullin, Jerry (1944) Paddlewheel Days In California. Stanford: Stanford University Press
442 Ibid.
443 Wright, E.W. (ed.) (1967) Lewis & Dryden's Marine History of the Pacific Northwest
444 Land Location & Boundary Section, California State Lands Commission (1988)
445 Hacking, Norman R. Steamboating on the Fraser in the Sixties (in British Columbia Historical Quarterly Vol. X No.1 January 1946)
446 Lytle, William M and Forrest R Holdcamper
447 McMullin, Jerry (1944) Paddlewheel Days In California. Stanford: Stanford University Press
448 Affleck, Edward L (2000)
449 Ibid.
450 Roster of Yukon / Alaska Sternwheelers (explorenorth.com) (website viewed 03/04/2021)
451 Affleck, Edward L (2000)

452 https://en.wikipedia.org/wiki/Steamboats_on_Lake_Coeur_d%27Alene (website viewed 13/02/2021)
453 Marshall, Don (1984). Oregon Shipwrecks. Portland, OR: Binford and Mort Publishing. page 207
454 Roster of Yukon / Alaska Sternwheelers (explorenorth.com) (website viewed 03/04/2021)
455 Ibid.
456 Newell, G. (1966)
457 Affleck, Edward L (2000)
458 Roster of Yukon / Alaska Sternwheelers (explorenorth.com) (website viewed 03/04/2021)
459 Ibid.
460 HBC Arcives Winnipeg MB International March 1988 (Revised Sep 2014)
461 http://www.mhs.mb.ca/docs/steamboats/international.shtml; http://heritage.canadiana.ca/view/oocihm.lac_reel_t11873/181?r=0&s=3
462 Needles Desert Star (Needles CA) Friday February 2, 1917, page 10
463 McMullin, Jerry (1944) Paddlewheel Days In California. Stanford: Stanford University Press
464 Affleck, Edward L (2000)
465 Ibid.
466 Ibid.
467 Hacking, Norman R. Steamboat Days 1870–1883. In British Columbia Historical Quarterly April 1947; Wilson, Hill (2005) The Marine Pilots of Canada's West Coast; LAC RG12, A1, Vol 414 Shipping Registers Victoria BC
468 McMullin, Jerry (1944) Paddlewheel Days In California. Stanford: Stanford University Press
469 Land Location & Boundary Section, California State Lands Commission (1988)
470 Ibid.
471 British Columbia Nautical History Facebook Group 25/02/2021
472 Daily National Democrat (Marysville CA) August 27, 1861, Chronicling America: Historic American Newspapers. Lib. of

Congress. <https://chroniclingamerica.loc.gov/lccn/sn84038814/1861-08-27/ed-1/seq-3/>

473 Land Location & Boundary Section, California State Lands Commission (1988)

474 Roster of Yukon / Alaska Sternwheelers (explorenorth.com) (website viewed 03/04/2021)

475 http://www.riverboatdaves.com/riverboats/j.html (website viewed 28/04/2021)

476 McMullin, Jerry (1944) Paddlewheel Days In California. Stanford: Stanford University Press

477 Newell, Gordon (ed.) The H.W. McCurdy Marine history of the Pacific Northwest 1966 Seattle WA: Superior Publishing Co.

478 Kramer, Nathan in http://www.mhs.mb.ca/docs/steamboats/index.shtml (website viewed 05/02/2021)

479 Newell, Gordon (1966) page 140

480 Affleck, Edward L (2000)

481 McMullin, Jerry (1944) Paddlewheel Days In California. Stanford: Stanford University Press

482 Ibid.

483 Land Location & Boundary Section, California State Lands Commission (1988)

484 McMullin, Jerry (1944) Paddlewheel Days In California. Stanford: Stanford University Press

485 Land Location & Boundary Section, California State Lands Commission (1988)

486 Wright, E.W. (ed.) (1967) Lewis & Dryden's Marine History of the Pacific Northwest

487 Roster of Yukon / Alaska Sternwheelers (explorenorth.com) (website viewed 03/04/2021)

488 McMullin, Jerry (1944) Paddlewheel Days In California. Stanford: Stanford University Press

489 Roster of Yukon / Alaska Sternwheelers (explorenorth.com) (website viewed 03/04/2021)

490 McMullin, Jerry (1944) Paddlewheel Days In California. Stanford: Stanford University Press

491 Ibid.

492 https://www.nps.gov/parkhistory/online_books/joda/hrs/hrs5a.htm

493 https://saltwaterpeoplehistoricalsociety.blogspot.com/search?q=sternwheeler (website viewed 10/02/2021)

494 Roster of Yukon / Alaska Sternwheelers (explorenorth.com) (website viewed 03/04/2021)

495 Affleck, Edward L (2000)

496 Roster of Yukon / Alaska Sternwheelers (explorenorth.com) (website viewed 03/04/2021)

497 The Chilliwack Progress (Chilliwack BC) Wednesday, January 6, 1909, page 1

498 Lytle, William M and Forrest R Holdcamper

499 Roster of Yukon / Alaska Sternwheelers (explorenorth.com) (website viewed 03/04/2021)

500 https://en.wikipedia.org/wiki/Joseph_Kellogg_(sternwheeler) (website reviewed February 11, 2021)

501 https://www.nps.gov/parkhistory/online_books/noca/hbd/chap7.htm (website viewed 12/02/2021)

502 McMullin, Jerry (1944) Paddlewheel Days In California. Stanford: Stanford University Press

503 Daily Alta California Vol. 23, No 7692, April 14, 1871

504 McMullin, Jerry (1944) Paddlewheel Days In California. Stanford: Stanford University Press

505 Land Location & Boundary Section, California State Lands Commission (1988)

506 The Sacramento Bee (Sacramento CA) Thursday June 29, 1911, page 10

507 Los Angeles Herald (Los Angeles CA) Saturday February 7, 1874

508 McMullin, Jerry (1944) Paddlewheel Days In California. Stanford: Stanford University Press

509 Van Alfen, Pater G. Sail and Steam: Great Salt Lake's Boats and Boatbuilders, 1847–1901 in Utah Historical Quarterly, Volume 63, No. 3, 1995 (Utah State Historical Society) Pages 6–33 (website viewed February 5, 2021, https://issuu.com/utah10/docs/uhq_volume63_1995_number3)

510 McMullin, Jerry (1944) Paddlewheel Days In California. Stanford: Stanford University Press

511 Roster of Yukon / Alaska Sternwheelers (explorenorth.com) (website viewed 03/04/2021)

512 McMullin, Jerry (1944) Paddlewheel Days In California. Stanford: Stanford University Press

513 https://www.seattlepi.com/local/article/Seattle-cracks-down-on-houseboat-like-boats-2400872.php (website viewed 21/01/2021); https://steamboats.com/research/50states.html (website viewed 23/01/2021)

514 Roster of Yukon / Alaska Sternwheelers (explorenorth.com) (website viewed 03/04/2021)

515 Ibid.

516 Newell, Gordon (1966) page 174

517 Roster of Yukon / Alaska Sternwheelers (explorenorth.com) (website viewed 03/04/2021)

518 Affleck, Edward L (2000)

519 Ibid.

520 Ibid.

521 https://www.klondikespirit.com/ (website viewed 24/03/2021)

522 McMullin, Jerry (1944) Paddlewheel Days In California. Stanford: Stanford University Press

523 https://en.wikipedia.org/wiki/Steamboats_on_Lake_Coeur_d%27Alene (website viewed 13/02/2021)

524 Roster of Yukon / Alaska Sternwheelers (explorenorth.com) (website viewed 03/04/2021)

525 http://www.thelacentermuseum.org/Sternwheeler_Gallery.html (website viewed 15/02/2021)

526 Wright, E.W. (ed.) 1967; Walbran, Captain John T. (1909)

527 HBC Archives Winnipeg MB Labouchere January 1988

528 McMullin, Jerry (1944) Paddlewheel Days In California. Stanford: Stanford University Press

529 The San Francisco Examiner (San Francisco CA) Saturday January 31, 1903, page 14

530 Daily Alta California Vol. 23, No 7692, April 14, 1871

531 McMullin, Jerry (1944) Paddlewheel Days In California. Stanford: Stanford University Press

532 The Shasta Courier (Shasta CA) July 9, 1859

533 Land Location & Boundary Section, California State Lands Commission (1988)

534 McMullin, Jerry (1944) Paddlewheel Days In California. Stanford: Stanford University Press

535 Ibid.

536 Affleck, Edward L (2000)

537 Ibid.

538 https://www.lewisandclarkriverboat.com/ (website viewed 21/01/2021)

539 Affleck, Edward L (2000)

540 https://www.gov.mb.ca/chc/archives/hbca/ships_histories/pdf/liard-river-i.pdf (website viewed 25/06/2021)

541 HBC Archives Winnipeg MB Lily February 1988/JHB

542 http://www.explorenorth.com/library/ships/sternwheelers-etc.html (website viewed 14/02/2021)

543 McMullin, Jerry (1944) Paddlewheel Days In California. Stanford: Stanford University Press

544 Wikipedia (Steamboats of the Oregon Coast) (Website viewed 18/02/2021)

545 Roster of Yukon / Alaska Sternwheelers (explorenorth.com) (website viewed 03/04/2021)

546 The Little Jim may have been propeller driven. (Listed by Murray Lundberg in his Roster of Yukon/Alaska Shipping but no other sources found.)

547 https://edmontonjournal.com/news/local-news/may-4-1995–edmonton-

queen-finally-launched (website viewed 16/02/2021)

548 Land Location & Boundary Section, California State Lands Commission (1988)

549 Roster of Yukon / Alaska Sternwheelers (explorenorth.com) (website viewed 03/04/2021)

550 Ibid.

551 The San Francisco Call (San Francisco CA) Monday March 14, 1892, page 6

552 http://www.riverboatdaves.com/riverboats/lizzie.html (website viewed 04/03/2021)

553 http://www.explorenorth.com/library/ships/sternwheelers.html (website viewed 03/03/2021)

554 Roster of Yukon / Alaska Sternwheelers (explorenorth.com) (website viewed 03/04/2021)

555 Ibid.

556 Wright, E.W. (ed.) (1967) Lewis & Dryden's Marine History of the Pacific Northwest

557 Lytle, William M and Forrest R Holdcamper

558 Roster of Yukon / Alaska Sternwheelers (explorenorth.com) (website viewed 03/04/2021)

559 Affleck, Edward L (2000)

560 Ibid.

561 Merchant Vessels of the United States (1922)

562 https://en.wikipedia.org/wiki/Tourist_sternwheelers_of_Oregon (website viewed 24/03/2021)

563 Roster of Yukon / Alaska Sternwheelers (explorenorth.com) (website viewed 03/04/2021)

564 Affleck, Edward L (2000)

565 Ibid.

566 Ibid.

567 Lytle, William M and Forrest R Holdcamper

568 HBC Archives Winnipeg MB Mackenzie River (Rev. March 1988/JHB)

569 https://en.wikipedia.org/wiki/Joseph_Kellogg_(sternwheeler) (website viewed February 11, 2021)

570 Bakersfield Californian (Bakersfield CA) Friday November 26, 1915, page 12

571 HBC Archive Winnipeg MB Manitoba April 1988 JHB

572 Kramer, Nathan in http://www.mhs.mb.ca/docs/steamboats/index.shtml (website viewed 05/02/2021)

573 Roster of Yukon / Alaska Sternwheelers (explorenorth.com) (website viewed 03/04/2021)

574 Ibid.

575 San Francisco Examiner (San Francisco CA) Saturday, October 23, 1897, page 6

576 Roster of Yukon / Alaska Sternwheelers (explorenorth.com) (website viewed 03/04/2021)

577 Land Location & Boundary Section, California State Lands Commission (1988)

578 McMullin, Jerry (1944) Paddlewheel Days In California. Stanford: Stanford University Press

579 http://www.explorenorth.com/library/ships/sternwheelers-etc.html (website viewed 14/02/2021)

580 https://www.gazettes.com/sports/on_the_water/on-the-water-next-chapter-for-grand-romance/article_d8e0e0a8-c4c0-11ea-8980-cfc273713e9e.html (website viewed 14/03/2021)

581 HBC Archives Winnipeg MB Marquette April 1988 JHB

582 HBC Archives Winnipeg MB Marquis April 1988/JHB

583 McMullin, Jerry (1944) Paddlewheel Days In California. Stanford: Stanford University Press

584 Ibid.

585 Affleck, Edward L (2000)

586 McMullin, Jerry (1944) Paddlewheel Days In California. Stanford: Stanford University Press

587 Affleck, Edward L (2000)

588 McMullin, Jerry (1944) Paddlewheel Days In California. Stanford: Stanford University Press

589 http://www.npshistory.com/publications/yuch/grauman/chap9.htm (website visited 14/02/2021)

590 Lytle, William M and Forrest R Holdcamper

591 McMullin, Jerry (1944) Paddlewheel Days In California. Stanford: Stanford University Press

592 The Dalles Mountaineer (The Dalles OR) June 6, 1866, page 2

593 Lytle, William M and Forrest R Holdcamper

594 McMullin, Jerry (1944) Paddlewheel Days In California. Stanford: Stanford University Press

595 Hacking, Norman R. Steamboating on the Fraser in the Sixties (in British Columbia Historical Quarterly Vol. x No.1 January 1946)

596 Affleck, Edward L (2000)

597 Ibid.

598 https://www.dailyrepublic.com/all-dr-news/solano-news/suisun-city/excursion-boat-matthew-mckinley-gets-new-owner/

599 McMullin, Jerry (1944) Paddlewheel Days In California. Stanford: Stanford University Press

600 Affleck, Edward L (2000)

601 Ibid.

602 Ibid.

603 McMullin, Jerry (1944) Paddlewheel Days In California. Stanford: Stanford University Press

604 Land Location & Boundary Section, California State Lands Commission (1988)

605 Affleck, Edward L (2000)

606 https://commons.wikimedia.org/wiki/Category:Steamboats_of_the_Pend_Oreille_River#/media/File:Metaline_(sternwheeler)_lining_Box_Canyon_02.jpg (website viewed 13/02/2021)

607 Roster of Yukon / Alaska Sternwheelers (explorenorth.com) (website viewed 03/04/2021)

608 Newell, Gordon (1966) page 190

609 McMullin, Jerry (1944) Paddlewheel Days In California. Stanford: Stanford University Press

610 Land Location & Boundary Section, California State Lands Commission (1988)

611 Affleck, Edward L (2000)

612 Roster of Yukon / Alaska Sternwheelers (explorenorth.com) (website viewed 03/04/2021)

613 Affleck, Edward L (2000)

614 Charlebois, Peter (1978)

615 McMullin, Jerry (1944) Paddlewheel Days In California. Stanford: Stanford University Press

616 http://pineknotmarina.com/activities/lake-tours/ (website viewed 03/03/2021)

617 Affleck, Edward L (2000)

618 McMullin, Jerry (1944) Paddlewheel Days In California. Stanford: Stanford University Press

619 Ibid.

620 Affleck, Edward L (2000)

621 Ibid.

622 McMullin, Jerry (1944) Paddlewheel Days In California. Stanford: Stanford University Press

623 Los Angeles Times (Los Angeles CA) Tuesday April 8, 1902, page 3

624 Affleck, Edward L (2000)

625 Ibid.

626 McMullin, Jerry (1944) Paddlewheel Days In California. Stanford: Stanford University Press

627 Lytle, William M and Forrest R Holdcamper

628 McMullin, Jerry (1944) Paddlewheel Days In California. Stanford: Stanford University Press

629 HBC Archives Winnipeg MB Mount Royal AM/ek March 1989

630 The San Francisco Examiner (San Francisco CA) Saturday May 24, 1924, page 17
631 Affleck, Edward L (2000)
632 Ibid.
633 https://en.wikipedia.org/wiki/Steamboats_of_the_Oregon_Coast (website viewed 18/02/2021)
634 Wright, E.W. (ed.) (1967) Lewis & Dryden's Marine History of the Pacific Northwest
635 https://en.wikipedia.org/wiki/List_of_steamboats_on_the_Columbia_River (website viewed 21/022021)
636 Ibid.
637 Oakland Tribune (Oakland CA) Wednesday February 19, 1930, page 37
638 Affleck, Edward L (2000)
639 LAC RG 12, Vol. 679 Register of Wrecks Atlantic & Pacific Coasts; Vancouver Daily World (Vancouver BC) Tuesday December 28, 1897, page 4
640 Roster of Yukon / Alaska Sternwheelers (explorenorth.com) (website viewed 03/04/2021)
641 McMullin, Jerry (1944) Paddlewheel Days In California. Stanford: Stanford University Press
642 https://www.nelsonstar.com/news/the-nasookin-ashore/ (website viewed 16/02/2021)
643 Affleck, Edward L (2000)
644 https://vancouverpaddlewheeler.com/about/our-vessels/ (website viewed 28/03/2021)
645 McMullin, Jerry (1944) Paddlewheel Days In California. Stanford: Stanford University Press
646 Land Location & Boundary Section, California State Lands Commission (1988)
647 Affleck, Edward L (2000)
648 Ibid.
649 https://en.wikipedia.org/wiki/Nenana_(steamer) (website viewed 08/02/2021); https://web.archive.org/web/20110606085650//http://tps.cr.nps.gov/nhl/detail.cfm?ResourceId=1302&ResourceType=Structure (website viewed 08/02/2021)

650 Personal Communication (Jodi Balon – John MacFarlane letter dated 29/04/2021)
651 McMullin, Jerry (1944)
652 Land Location & Boundary Section, California State Lands Commission (1988)
653 Affleck, Edward L (2000)
654 McMullin, Jerry (1944) Paddlewheel Days In California. Stanford: Stanford University Press
655 Land Location & Boundary Section, California State Lands Commission (1988)
656 McMullin, Jerry (1944) Paddlewheel Days In California. Stanford: Stanford University Press
657 Affleck, Edward L (2000)
658 Ibid.
659 McMullin, Jerry (1944) Paddlewheel Days In California. Stanford: Stanford University Press
660 Land Location & Boundary Section, California State Lands Commission (1988)
661 https://www.newportbelle.com/ (website viewed 08/02/2021)
662 http://www.sternwheelercharters.com/ (website viewed 08/02/2021)
663 McMullin, Jerry (1944) Paddlewheel Days In California. Stanford: Stanford University Press
664 Affleck, Edward L (2000)
665 McMullin, Jerry (1944) Paddlewheel Days In California. Stanford: Stanford University Press
666 http://www.riverboatdaves.com/riverboats/alaskanriverboats.html#COPP (website viewed 21/02/2021)
667 Affleck, Edward L (2000)
668 Newell, Gordon (1966)
669 Affleck, Edward L (2000)
670 Newell, Gordon (1966)
671 HBC Archives Winnipeg MB Northcote February 1988/JHB
672 Nathan Kramer https://www.gov.mb.ca/chc/archives/hbca/ships_histories/pdf/northcote.pdf

673 Roster of Yukon / Alaska Sternwheelers (explorenorth.com) (website viewed 03/04/2021)
674 Affleck, Edward L (2000)
675 Affleck, Edward L in BC Historical News Winter 1999/2000
676 HBC Archive Winnipeg MB Northland Echo Dec/1986/AM
677 HBC Archives North West 1988/04 JHB
678 Nathan Kramer http://www.mhs.mb.ca/docs/steamboats/index.shtml
679 http://heritage.canadiana.ca/view/oocihm.lac_reel_t111873/400?r=0&s=4 (website viewed 15/01/2021)
680 Roster of Yukon / Alaska Sternwheelers (explorenorth.com) (website viewed 03/04/2021)
681 McMullin, Jerry (1944)
682 Affleck, Edward L (2000)
683 Ibid.
684 The Oregon Daily Journal (Portland OR) Saturday September 13, 1913, page 2
685 Affleck, Edward L (2000)
686 Roster of Yukon / Alaska Sternwheelers (explorenorth.com) (website viewed 03/04/2021)
687 Affleck, Edward L (2000)
688 Newell, Gordon (1966)
689 Ibid.
690 HBC Archives Winnipeg MB Princess Louise 1988 JHB
691 Affleck, Edward L (2000)
692 Ibid.
693 Fresno Morning Republican (Fresno CA) Sunday, June 21, 1903, page 2
694 McMullin, Jerry (1944)
695 Affleck, Edward L (2000)
696 Ibid.
697 McMullin, Jerry (1944)
698 Affleck, Edward L (2000)
699 Ibid.
700 Ibid.
701 Lytle, William M and Forrest R Holdcamper
702 McMullin, Jerry (1944)
703 Ibid.
704 Newell, Gordon (1966) page 4
705 https://en.wikipedia.org/wiki/List_of_steamboats_on_the_Columbia_River
706 Lytle, William M and Forrest R Holdcamper
707 Affleck, Edward L (2000)
708 Ibid.
709 McMullin, Jerry (1944)
710 Wikipedia (Steamboats of the Oregon Coast) (Website viewed 18/02/2021)
711 Daily Alta California Vol. 23, No 7692, April 14, 1871
712 McMullin, Jerry (1944)
713 Roster of Yukon / Alaska Sternwheelers (explorenorth.com) (website viewed 03/04/2021)
714 Canada List of Shipping; List of Shipping Casualties Resulting in Total Loss in British Columbia and Coastal Waters Since 1897 (undated manuscript document)
715 McMullin, Jerry (1944)
716 Land Location & Boundary Section, California State Lands Commission (1988)
717 Land Location & Boundary Section, California State Lands Commission (1988)
718 Wikipedia (Steamboats of the Oregon Coast) (website viewed 18/02/2021)
719 Roster of Yukon / Alaska Sternwheelers (explorenorth.com) (website viewed 03/04/2021)
720 Ibid.
721 Affleck, Edward L (2000)
722 https://en.wikipedia.org/wiki/List_of_steamboats_on_the_Columbia_River
723 Ibid.
724 Lytle, William M and Forrest R Holdcamper
725 Land Location & Boundary Section, California State Lands Commission (1988)

726 McMullin, Jerry (1944) Paddlewheel Days In California. Stanford: Stanford University Press

727 Ibid.

728 Canada List of Shipping; List of Shipping Casualties Resulting in Total Loss in British Columbia and Coastal Waters Since 1897 (undated manuscript document)

729 https://www.eaglevalleynews.com/news/new-life-wanted-for-mv-phoebe-ann/ (website viewed 27/03/2021)

730 McMullin, Jerry (1944) Paddlewheel Days In California. Stanford: Stanford University Press

731 Roster of Yukon / Alaska Sternwheelers (explorenorth.com) (website viewed 03/04/2021)

732 Affleck, Edward L (2000)

733 Land Location & Boundary Section, California State Lands Commission (1988)

734 McMullin, Jerry (1944) Paddlewheel Days In California. Stanford: Stanford University Press

735 Land Location & Boundary Section, California State Lands Commission (1988)

736 Lytle, William M and Forrest R Holdcamper

737 Roster of Yukon / Alaska Sternwheelers (explorenorth.com) (website viewed 03/04/2021)

738 The Legacy of the Politkofsky (fdlp.gov) (website viewed 10/03/2021)

739 Affleck, Edward L (2000)

740 HBC Archives Winnipeg MB Port Simpson Jan/1986/JHB

741 Wright, E.W. (ed.) (1967) Lewis & Dryden's Marine History of the Pacific Northwest

742 Ibid.

743 https://en.wikipedia.org/wiki/List_of_steamboats_on_the_Columbia_River

744 https://en.wikipedia.org/wiki/List_of_steamboats_on_the_Columbia_River

745 McMullin, Jerry (1944) Paddlewheel Days In California. Stanford: Stanford University Press

746 Roster of Yukon / Alaska Sternwheelers (explorenorth.com) (website viewed 03/04/2021)

747 Affleck, Edward L (2000)

748 https://cgmix.uscg.mil/psix/psixSearch.aspx (website Viewed 16/02/2021)

749 McMullin, Jerry (1944) Paddlewheel Days In California. Stanford: Stanford University Press

750 Van Alfen, Pater G. Sail and Steam: Great Salt Lake's Boats and Boatbuilders, 1847–1901 in Utah Historical Quarterly, Volume 63, No. 3, 1995 (Utah State Historical Society) Pages 6–33 (website viewed February 5, 2021, https://issuu.com/utah10/docs/uhq_volume63_1995_number3)

751 Newell, Gordon (1966) page 4

752 Affleck, Edward L (2000)

753 Roster of Yukon / Alaska Sternwheelers (explorenorth.com) (website viewed 03/04/2021)

754 https://www.calexplornia.com/spirit-sacramento-abandoned-riverboat-fascinating-tale/ (website viewed 21/02/2021)

755 https://i5bridgecam.wordpress.com/sternwheelers/ (website viewed 15/02/2021)

756 Oakland Tribune (Oakland CA) Thursday March 28, 1901, page 3

757 Provincial Archives of Saskatchewan R-A24158 (1)-(6) - Paddlewheeler S.S. Queen Mary, sailboats, and boathouse on Wascana Lake

758 The Leader Post (Regina SK) Saturday September 25, 1963

759 Statesman Journal (Salem OR) Saturday July 23, 1892, page 4

760 McMullin, Jerry (1944) Paddlewheel Days In California. Stanford: Stanford University Press

761 Land Location & Boundary Section, California State Lands Commission (1988)

762 Victoria Daily Times (Victoria BC) Saturday August 8, 1885, page 4

763 Affleck, Edward L (2000)

764 Ibid.

765 McMullin, Jerry (1944) Paddlewheel Days In California. Stanford: Stanford University Press

766 Affleck, Edward L (2000)

767 The Province (Vancouver BC) Thursday April 18, 1901 page 1

768 McMullin, Jerry (1944) Paddlewheel Days In California. Stanford: Stanford University Press

769 Affleck, Edward L (2000)

770 Daily Alta California Vol. 23, No 7692, April 14, 1871

771 McMullin, Jerry (1944) Paddlewheel Days In California. Stanford: Stanford University Press

772 Ibid.

773 Ibid.

774 Land Location & Boundary Section, California State Lands Commission (1988)

775 Petaluma Argus-Courier (Petaluma CA) Wednesday August 17, 1955, page 74

776 McMullin, Jerry (1944) Paddlewheel Days In California. Stanford: Stanford University Press

777 http://www.explorenorth.com/library/ships/sternwheelers.html (website viewed 12/02/2021)

778 http://heritage.canadiana.ca/view/oocihm.lac_reel_t11871/314?r=0&s=3 http://heritage.canadiana.ca/view/oocihm.lac_reel_c3185/56?r=0&s=5 (website viewed 2020);

779 McMullin, Jerry (1944) Paddlewheel Days In California. Stanford: Stanford University Press

780 Lytle, William M and Forrest R Holdcamper

781 McMullin, Jerry (1944) Paddlewheel Days In California. Stanford: Stanford University Press

782 Ibid.

783 Affleck, Edward L (2000)

784 Ibid.

785 Hacking, Norman R. Steamboating on the Fraser in the Sixties (in British Columbia Historical Quarterly Vol. X No.1 January 1946)

786 Wright, E.W. (ed.) (1967)

787 Affleck, Edward L (2000)

788 McMullin, Jerry (1944) Paddlewheel Days In California. Stanford: Stanford University Press

789 Affleck, Edward L (2000)

790 Ibid.

791 McMullin, Jerry (1944) Paddlewheel Days In California. Stanford: Stanford University Press

792 https://www.gazettes.com/sports/on_the_water/on-the-water-next-chapter-for-grand-romance/article_d8e0e0a8-c4c0-11ea-8980-cfc273713e9e.html (website viewed 14/03/2021)

793 https://www.facebook.com/BIMHS/posts/reuben-e-leesome-might-have-once-called-the-mississippi-river-style-steamer-that/2857960324220452/ (website viewed 04/03/2021)

794 McMullin, Jerry (1944) Paddlewheel Days In California. Stanford: Stanford University Press

795 Affleck, Edward L (2000)

796 Newell, G. (1966)

797 Ibid.

798 Affleck, Edward L (2000)

799 Wikipedia (Steamboats of the Oregon Coast) (Website viewed 18/02/2021)

800 https://en.wikipedia.org/wiki/List_of_steamboats_on_the_Columbia_River

801 Newell, Gordon (1966) page 140

802 Affleck, Edward L (2000)

803 https://en.wikipedia.org/wiki/List_of_steamboats_on_the_Columbia_River

804 Affleck, Edward L (2000)

805 Ibid.

806 Ibid.

807 Ibid.

808 Ibid.

809 McMullin, Jerry (1944) Paddlewheel Days In California. Stanford: Stanford University Press

810 Affleck, Edward L (2000)

811 Newell, Gordon R., ed.

812 Lytle, William M and Forrest R Holdcamper

813 Affleck, Edward L (2000)

814 Land Location & Boundary Section, California State Lands Commission (1988)

815 McMullin, Jerry (1944) Paddlewheel Days In California. Stanford: Stanford University Press

816 Ibid.

817 Land Location & Boundary Section, California State Lands Commission (1988)

818 McMullin, Jerry (1944) Paddlewheel Days In California. Stanford: Stanford University Press

819 Ibid.

820 Ibid.

821 http://www.navsource.org/archives/09/86/86476.htm (website viewed 09/03/2021)

822 https://www.boem.gov/sites/default/files/uploadedFiles/BOEM/About_BOEM/BOEM_Regions/Alaska_Region/Ships/2011_Shipwreck.pdf (website viewed 21/01/2021)

823 Affleck, Edward L (2000)

824 The San Francisco Examiner (San Francisco CA) Saturday September 7, 1918, page 15

825 https://en.wikipedia.org/wiki/Steamboats_on_Lake_Coeur_d%27Alene (website viewed 13/02/2021)

826 Affleck, Edward L (2000)

827 Ibid.

828 https://en.wikipedia.org/wiki/Steamboats_on_Lake_Coeur_d%27Alene (website viewed 13/02/2021)

829 Newell, Gordon (1966)

830 McMullin, Jerry (1944) Paddlewheel Days In California. Stanford: Stanford University Press

831 https://en.wikipedia.org/wiki/List_of_steamboats_on_the_Columbia_River

832 Affleck, Edward L (2000)

833 https://en.wikipedia.org/wiki/List_of_steamboats_on_the_Columbia_River

834 Eric Anderson (British Columbia Nautical History Facebook Group 01/03/2017)

835 Wilson, Hill (2005)

836 McMullin, Jerry (1944) Paddlewheel Days In California. Stanford: Stanford University Press

837 Land Location & Boundary Section, California State Lands Commission (1988)

838 Lytle, William M and Forrest R Holdcamper

839 McMullin, Jerry (1944) Paddlewheel Days In California. Stanford: Stanford University Press

840 Land Location & Boundary Section, California State Lands Commission (1988)

841 McMullin, Jerry (1944) Paddlewheel Days In California. Stanford: Stanford University Press

842 Land Location & Boundary Section, California State Lands Commission (1988)

843 McMullin, Jerry (1944) Paddlewheel Days In California. Stanford: Stanford University Press

844 Land Location & Boundary Section, California State Lands Commission (1988)

845 McMullin, Jerry (1944) Paddlewheel Days In California. Stanford: Stanford University Press

846 Land Location & Boundary Section, California State Lands Commission (1988)

847 Ibid.

848 McMullin, Jerry (1944) Paddlewheel Days In California. Stanford: Stanford University Press

849 Santa Barbara Daily News and The Independent (Santa Barbara CA) Wednesday November 5th, 1913, page 8

850 McMullin, Jerry (1944) Paddlewheel Days In California. Stanford: Stanford University Press

851 Ibid.

852 Newell, Gordon (1966) page 4

853 Affleck, Edward L (2000)
854 https://en.wikipedia.org/wiki/Steamboats_on_Lake_Coeur_d%27Alene (website Viewed 13/02/2021); (website viewed 13/02/2021)
855 HBC Archives Winnipeg MB Saskatchewan 1905–1909 April 1988
856 McMullin, Jerry (1944) Paddlewheel Days In California. Stanford: Stanford University Press
857 Ibid.
858 Ibid.
859 Ibid.
860 Ibid.
861 Ibid.
862 Affleck, Edward L (2000)
863 McMullin, Jerry (1944) Paddlewheel Days In California. Stanford: Stanford University Press
864 Land Location & Boundary Section, California State Lands Commission (1988)
865 The Journal of San Diego History San Diego Historical Society Quarterly July 1957, Volume 3, Number 3
866 McMullin, Jerry (1944) Paddlewheel Days In California. Stanford: Stanford University Press
867 Land Location & Boundary Section, California State Lands Commission (1988)
868 Affleck, Edward L (2000)
869 Roster of Yukon / Alaska Sternwheelers (explorenorth.com) (website viewed 03/04/2021)
870 McMullin, Jerry (1944) Paddlewheel Days In California. Stanford: Stanford University Press
871 Ibid.
872 Land Location & Boundary Section, California State Lands Commission (1988)
873 Affleck, Edward L (2000)
874 https://en.wikipedia.org/wiki/List_of_steamboats_on_the_Columbia_River
875 Freeman, Lewis R. Down the Columbia (1921 reprinted 2001)
876 https://en.wikipedia.org/wiki/Steamboats_on_Lake_Coeur_d%27Alene (website viewed 13/02/2021)
877 http://forum.woodenboat.com/showthread.php?163680-what-about-sternwheelers (website viewed 15/02/2021)
878 http://www.militarymuseum.org/CWDefensesofSF.pdf (website viewed 21/02/2021)
879 Roster of Yukon / Alaska Sternwheelers (explorenorth.com) (website viewed 03/04/2021)
880 Affleck, E.L. (2000)
881 Petaluma Argus-Courier (Petaluma CA) Wednesday August 17, 1955, page 74
882 McMullin, Jerry (1944) Paddlewheel Days In California. Stanford: Stanford University Press
883 The Province (Vancouver BC) Wednesday October 31, 1956, page 7
884 Affleck, Edward L (2000)
885 The Daily Colonist (Victoria BC) (May 20, 1882, Page 3)
886 Bawlf, M. (1973)
887 Affleck, Edward L (2000)
888 Daily Alta California Vol. 23, No 7692, April 14, 1871
889 McMullin, Jerry (1944) Paddlewheel Days In California. Stanford: Stanford University Press
890 Ibid.
891 Ibid.
892 Land Location & Boundary Section, California State Lands Commission (1988)
893 Affleck, Edward L (2000)
894 McMullin, Jerry (1944) Paddlewheel Days In California. Stanford: Stanford University Press
895 Roster of Yukon / Alaska Sternwheelers (explorenorth.com) (website viewed 03/04/2021)
896 Affleck, Edward L (2000)
897 Ibid.

898 Land Location & Boundary Section, California State Lands Commission (1988)

899 Canada List of Shipping; List of Shipping Casualties Resulting in Total Loss in British Columbia and Coastal Waters Since 1897 (undated manuscript document)

900 McMullin, Jerry (1944) Paddlewheel Days In California. Stanford: Stanford University Press

901 Newell, Gordon (1966)

902 HBC Archives Winnipeg MB Strathcona JHB/April 1988

903 San Francisco Examiner (San Francisco ca) Saturday September 16, 1916, page 7

904 https://en.wikipedia.org/wiki/Steamboats_of_the_Oregon_Coast (website viewed 18/02/2021)

905 McMullin, Jerry (1944) Paddlewheel Days In California. Stanford: Stanford University Press

906 Roster of Yukon / Alaska Sternwheelers (explorenorth.com) (website viewed 03/04/2021)

907 Marc, Jacques. (1999) Historic Shipwrecks of Northeastern Vancouver Island UASBC

908 https://en.wikipedia.org/wiki/USS_Suwanee_(1864) (website viewed 04/03/2021)

909 Affleck, Edward L (2000)

910 Lytle, William M and Forrest R Holdcamper

911 McMullin, Jerry (1944) Paddlewheel Days In California. Stanford: Stanford University Press

912 Ibid.

913 Dawson Daily News, Mining Edition (Dawson YT)

914 Affleck, Edward L (2000)

915 Ibid.

916 McMullin, Jerry (1944) Paddlewheel Days In California. Stanford: Stanford University Press

917 Affleck, Edward L (2000)

918 Lytle, William M and Forrest R Holdcamper

919 http://www.sfgenealogy.com/californiabound/cb135.htm (website viewed November 2020)

920 Roster of Yukon / Alaska Sternwheelers (explorenorth.com) (website viewed 03/04/2021)

921 Ibid.

922 McMullin, Jerry (1944) Paddlewheel Days In California. Stanford: Stanford University Press

923 Ibid.

924 Van Alfen, Pater G. Sail and Steam: Great Salt Lake's Boats and Boatbuilders, 1847–1901 in Utah Historical Quarterly, Volume 63, No. 3, 1995 (Utah State Historical Society) Pages 6–33 (website viewed February 5, 2021, https://issuu.com/utah10/docs/uhq_volume63_1995_number3)

925 Affleck, Edward L (2000)

926 Roster of Yukon / Alaska Sternwheelers (explorenorth.com) (website viewed 03/04/2021)

927 Affleck, Edward L (2000)

928 The Evening Mail (Stockton CA) Tuesday August 27, 1901, page 2

929 Daily Alta California Vol. 23, No 7692, April 14, 1871

930 McMullin, Jerry (1944) Paddlewheel Days In California. Stanford: Stanford University Press

931 Daily Alta California Vol. 23, No 7692, April 14, 1871

932 McMullin, Jerry (1944) Paddlewheel Days In California. Stanford: Stanford University Press

933 http://heritage.canadiana.ca/view/oocihm.lac_reel_t11930/1306?r=0&s=4 (website viewed 04/03/20121

934 https://yukon.ca/sites/yukon.ca/files/tc/tc-ss-tutshi.pdf (website viewed 15/02/2021)

935 Affleck, Edward L (2000)

936 Merchant Vessels of the United States (1929)

937 Lingenfelter, Richard E (1978) Steamboats on the Colorado River. Tucson AZ: University of Arizona Press.

938 McMullin, Jerry (1944) Paddlewheel Days In California. Stanford: Stanford University Press

939 Ibid.

940 Ibid.

941 Land Location & Boundary Section, California State Lands Commission (1988)

942 McMullin, Jerry (1944) Paddlewheel Days In California. Stanford: Stanford University Press

943 Ibid.

944 Ibid.

945 Lytle, William M and Forrest R Holdcamper

946 https://en.wikipedia.org/wiki/List_of_steamboats_on_the_Columbia_River (website viewed 21/03/2021)

947 Ibid.

948 Ibid.

949 Land Location & Boundary Section, California State Lands Commission (1988)

950 Weekly Trinity Journal (Weaverville CA) Saturday, August 13, 1859, page 1

951 Lytle, William M and Forrest R Holdcamper

952 Ibid.

953 McMullin, Jerry (1944) Paddlewheel Days In California. Stanford: Stanford University Press

954 Hacking, Norman R. Steamboating on the Fraser in the Sixties (in British Columbia Historical Quarterly Vol. X No.1 January 1946)

955 Newell, G. (1966); McDonald, Lucile (1984)

956 https://en.wikipedia.org/wiki/List_of_steamboats_on_the_Columbia_River

957 Affleck, Edward L (2000)

958 Walbran, Captain John T. (1909)

959 McMullin, Jerry (1944) Paddlewheel Days In California. Stanford: Stanford University Press

960 Land Location & Boundary Section, California State Lands Commission (1988)

961 https://en.wikipedia.org/wiki/List_of_steamboats_on_the_Columbia_River

962 Roster of Yukon / Alaska Sternwheelers (explorenorth.com) (website viewed 03/04/2021)

963 Ibid.

964 Newell, G. (1966); List of Shipping Casualties Resulting in Total Loss in British Columbia and Coastal Waters Since 1897 (undated manuscript document)

965 https://www.anacorteswa.gov/422/Maritime-Heritage-Center-and-the-WT-Pres (website viewed 28/03/2021)

966 https://thereaderwiki.com/en/Wallamet_(sidewheeler_1853) (website viewed 19/02/2021);

967 Affleck, Edward L (2000)

968 Ibid.

969 Wright, E.W. (ed.) (1967) Lewis & Dryden's Marine History of the Pacific Northwest

970 McMullin, Jerry (1944) Paddlewheel Days In California. Stanford: Stanford University Press

971 https://www.nps.gov/parkhistory/online_books/noca/hbd/chap7.htm (website viewed 12/02/2021)

972 McMullin, Jerry (1944) Paddlewheel Days In California. Stanford: Stanford University Press

973 Lytle, William M and Forrest R Holdcamper

974 Land Location & Boundary Section, California State Lands Commission (1988)

975 https://www.nps.gov/parkhistory/online_books/noca/hbd/chap7.htm (website viewed 12/02/2021)

976 Roster of Yukon / Alaska Sternwheelers (explorenorth.com) (website viewed 03/04/2021)

977 Clapp, Frank A. (1991) Lake and River Ferries. Victoria BC: Province of British Columbia

978 Ibid.

979 McMullin, Jerry (1944) Paddlewheel Days In California. Stanford: Stanford University Press

980 Land Location & Boundary Section, California State Lands Commission (1988)

981 Roster of Yukon / Alaska Sternwheelers (explorenorth.com) (website viewed 03/04/2021)

982 McMullin, Jerry (1944) Paddlewheel Days In California. Stanford: Stanford University Press

983 https://www.willamettequeen.net/ (website viewed 18/03/2021

984 US Coast Guard Port State Information Exchange https://cgmix.uscg.mil/psix/psixSearch.aspx (website viewed 10/02/2021)

985 https://i5bridgecam.wordpress.com/sternwheelers/ (website viewed 15/02/2021)

986 https://www.bahiahotel.com/blog/article/wedding-venue-william-d-evans-sternwheeler (website viewed 15/03/2021)

987 McMullin, Jerry (1944) Paddlewheel Days In California. Stanford: Stanford University Press

988 Land Location & Boundary Section, California State Lands Commission (1988)

989 Mills, R.V. (1947)

990 Affleck, Edward L (2000)

991 Mills, R.V. (1947)

992 Nathan Kramer (Email to John MacFarlane 05/03/2021)

993 Nathan Kramer http://www.mhs.mb.ca/docs/steamboats/winnitoba.shtml (website viewed 22/03/2021)

994 Affleck, Edward L (2000)

995 Mills, R.V. (1947)

996 Affleck, Edward L (2000)

997 Mills, R.V. (1947)

998 Ibid.

999 https://library.alaska.gov/hist/hist_docs/docs/ms010/ms10_general_marine_files_W.pdf (website viewed 11/01/2021)

1000 Mills, R.V. (1947)

1001 Ibid.

1002 Affleck, Edward L (2000)

1003 https://en.wikipedia.org/wiki/People%27s_Transportation_Company (website viewed 17/05/2021)

1004 Mills, R.V. (1947)

1005 Roster of Yukon / Alaska Sternwheelers (explorenorth.com) (website viewed 03/04/2021)

1006 Land Location & Boundary Section, California State Lands Commission (1988)

1007 Daily Alta California Vol. 23, No 7692, April 14, 1871

1008 McMullin, Jerry (1944) Paddlewheel Days In California. Stanford: Stanford University Press

1009 Ibid.

1010 Land Location & Boundary Section, California State Lands Commission (1988)

1011 McMullin, Jerry (1944) Paddlewheel Days In California. Stanford: Stanford University Press

1012 Ibid.

1013 Mills, R.V. (1947)

1014 Affleck, Edward L (2000)

1015 List of Merchant Vessels of the United States

1016 Napa Valley Register (Napa CA) Monday, May 27, 1929, page 6

1017 McMullin, Jerry (1944) Paddlewheel Days In California. Stanford: Stanford University Press

1018 Land Location & Boundary Section, California State Lands Commission (1988)

1019 Roster of Yukon / Alaska Sternwheelers (explorenorth.com) (website viewed 03/04/2021)

1020 Sheret, R. (1997) Smoke Ash and Steam. Victoria: Western Isles Cruise & Dive Co. Ltd.

1021 Ibid.

1022 Ibid.

1023 Ibid.

1024 William Falconer (1784) An Universal Dictionary of the Marine. London

1025 https://en.wikipedia.org/wiki/Discovery_II (website viewed 23/03/2021)

1026 https://en.wikipedia.org/wiki/Discovery_III (website viewed 23/03/2021)

1027 FAQ - The Edmonton Riverboat (website viewed 04/03/2021)

1028 Tim McShane, Museum Assistant, Esplanade Museum, Medicine Hat AB (Email 09/03/2021)

1029 https://www.golakehavasu.com/dixie_belle_rides_again (website viewed 19/03/2021)

1030 https://www.azbw.com/yumarivertours.php (website viewed 14/03/2021)

1031 https://www.newwestcity.ca/services/arts-and-heritage/museums-and-archives/sb_expander_articles/656.php (website viewed 27/03/2021)

1032 https://vancouverpaddlewheeler.com/about/our-vessels/ (website viewed 28/03/2021)

1033 http://sssicamous.ca/ (website viewed 28/03/2021)

1034 Elizabeth Hunter, Museum & Heritage Manager, Quesnel & District Museum & Archives (Email 11/03/2021)

1035 https://www.sicamousmuseum.ca/lake-vessels (website viewed 27/03/2021)

1036 http://fairweathercruises.com/constitution/ (website viewed 28/03/2021)

1037 https://lakearrowheadqueen.com/ (website viewed 27/03/2021)

1038 https://www.grandromanceriverboatca.com/ (website viewed 27/03/2021)

1039 https://www.bahiahotel.com/bahia-belle (website viewed 27/03/2021)

1040 https://www.scarlettbelle.com/ (website viewed 27/03/2021)

1041 https://museumni.org/exhibits-tours-events/permanent-exhibits/ (website viewed 02/04/2021)

1042 http://www.mhs.mb.ca/docs/sites/cheyenneboiler.shtml

1043 Roland Sawatzky, Curator of History, The Manitoba Museum (Email 11/03/2021)

1044 Jennifer Bottomly-O'looney (Email 09/03/2021) Montana Historical Society

1045 https://www.lakemeadcruises.com/ (website viewed 25/01/2021)

1046 https://www.lewisandclarkriverboat.com/ (website viewed 27/03/2021)

1047 https://www.americanqueensteamboatcompany.com/vessels/american-empress/ (website viewed 23/03/2021)

1048 https://www.portlandspirit.com/sternwheeler.php (website viewed 27/03/2021)

1049 https://www.willamettequeen.net/about-us (website viewed 24/03/2021)

1050 http://www.oregonmaritimemuseum.org/ (website viewed 23/03/2021)

1051 The Prairie Lily – Saskatoon's Riverboat! (website viewed 23/03/2021)

1052 Julie Jackson (Email 09/03/2021)

1053 https://www.anacorteswa.gov/422/Maritime-Heritage-Center-and-the-WT-Pres (website viewed 28/03/2021)

1054 http://www.sternwheelercharters.com/ (website viewed 28/03/2021)

1055 https://blog.seattlepi.com/lakeunionliving/2020/09/25/dual-stern-paddlewheel-seattle-houseboat/ (website viewed 28/03/2021)

1056 https://www.klondikespirit.com/ (website viewed 24/03/2021)

1057 https://www.pc.gc.ca/en/lhn-nhs/yt/klondike/culture/lhn-nhs_sskeno (website viewed 28/03/2021)

1058 https://www.pc.gc.ca/en/lhn-nhs/yt/ssklondike (website viewed 28/03/2021)

www.ingramcontent.com/pod-product-compliance
Lightning Source LLC
Chambersburg PA
CBHW070522010526
44118CB00012B/1051